Life of

Napoleon Bonaparte

By Sir Walter Scott

Volume IV

OmniaVeritas

SIR WALTER SCOTT

LIFE OF
NAPOLEON BONAPARTE
VOLUME IV
1827

PUBLISHED BY
OMNIA VERITAS LTD

www.omnia-veritas.com

Mayence

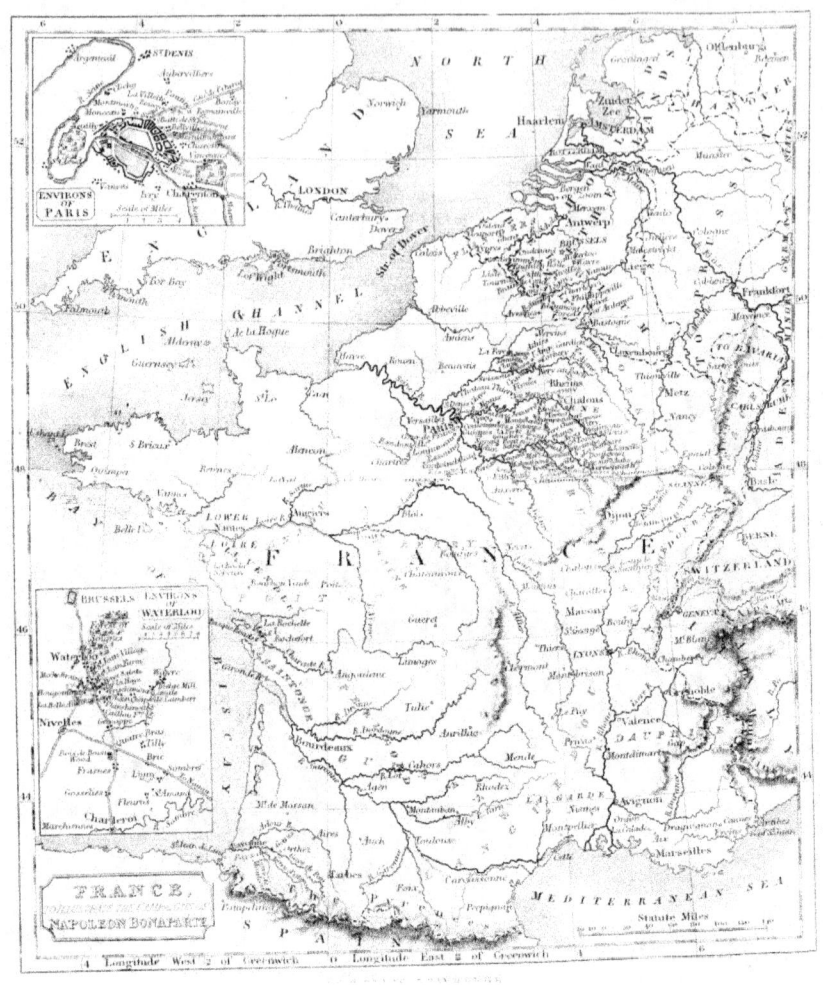

France,

to illustrate the campaigns of napoleon bonaparte.

CHAPTER XLIX **21**

Conduct of Russia and England during the War with Austria—Meditated Expedition of British Troops to the Continent—Sent to Walcheren—Its Calamitous Details and Result—Proceedings of Napoleon with regard to the Pope—General Miollis enters Rome—Napoleon publishes a Decree, uniting the States of the Church to the French Empire—Is Excommunicated—Pius VII. is banished from Rome, and sent to Grenoble—afterwards brought back to Savona—Buonaparte is attacked by an Assassin—Definitive Treaty of Peace signed at Schoenbrun—Napoleon returns to France on the 14th November, 1809. 21

BRITISH EXPEDITION *23*
WALCHEREN *25*
PIUS THE SEVENTH *28*
ROME... *31*
PIUS VII. BANISHED... *33*
PIUS THE SEVENTH *36*
THE ARCHDUKE CHARLES *39*

CHAPTER L... **43**

Change in Napoleon's Domestic Life—Causes which led to it—His anxiety for an Heir—A Son of his brother Louis is fixed upon, but dies in Childhood—Character and influence of Josephine—Strong mutual attachment betwixt her and Napoleon—Fouché opens to Josephine the Plan of a Divorce—her extreme Distress—On 5th December, Napoleon announces her Fate to Josephine—On 15th they are formally separated before the Imperial Council—Josephine retaining the rank of Empress for life—Espousals of Buonaparte and Maria Louisa of Austria take place at Vienna, 11th March, 1810. 43

CHANGE IN NAPOLEON'S DOMESTIC LIFE *43*
JOSEPHINE *44*
DIVORCE OF JOSEPHINE... *47*
MARIA LOUISA *53*

CHAPTER LI **59**

Almost all the foreign French Settlements fall into the hands of the British—French Squadron destroyed at the Isle of Aix, by Lord Cochrane—and at the Isle of Rosas, by Lord Collingwood—Return to the Proceedings in Spain—Soult takes Oporto—Attacked and Defeated by Sir Arthur Wellesley—Ferrol and Corunna retaken by the Patriots—Battle of Talavera, gained by Sir Arthur Wellesley—Created Lord Wellington—The French Armies take many towns and strong Places—Supreme Junta retreat to Cadiz—The Guerilla System—Growing disappointment of Buonaparte—His immense exertions—Battle of Busaco—Lord Wellington's famous Retreat on Torres Vedras. 59

SOULT OCCUPIES OPORTO *60*
BATTLE OF TALAVERA.. *62*
CATALONIA—THE GUERILLAS.. *65*
THE GUERILLAS *68*
SITUATION OF KING JOSEPH... *70*
TORRES VEDRAS *74*

CHAPTER LII **77**

Change in Napoleon's Principles of Government—Becomes suspicious of Talleyrand and Fouché—Fouché endeavours, without the knowledge of Napoleon, to ascertain the Views of England with respect to Peace—His Plan is defeated by a singular collision with a similar one of Napoleon—and Fouché is sent away as Governor-General of Rome—His Moral and Political Character—Murmurings of the People against the Austrian Alliance—Continental System—Ignorance of Napoleon of the Actual Political Feelings of Great Britain—The License System—Louis Buonaparte—Endeavours in vain to defend Holland from the Effects of the Continental System—He abdicates the Throne, and retires to Gratz in Styria—Holland is annexed to the French Empire. 77

CHANGES IN NAPOLEON'S GOVERNMENT *77*
TALLEYRAND—FOUCHÉ... *79*
FOUCHÉ *81*
M. OUVRARD—FOUCHÉ *84*
AUSTRIAN ALLIANCE UNPOPULAR *87*
THE CONTINENTAL SYSTEM.. *90*
LOUIS BUONAPARTE.. *92*
HOLLAND—ABDICATION OF LOUIS BUONAPARTE...................................... *94*
HOLLAND ANNEXED TO FRANCE *98*

CHAPTER LIII **101**

Gustavus IV. of Sweden is Dethroned and succeeded by his Uncle—The Crown Prince killed by a fall from his horse—Candidates proposed for the Succession—The Swedes, thinking to conciliate Napoleon, fix on Bernadotte—Buonaparte reluctantly acquiesces in the choice—Parting Interview between Bernadotte and Napoleon—Subsequent attempts of the latter to bind Sweden to the policy of France—The Crown Prince unwillingly accedes to the Continental System—Napoleon makes a Tour through Flanders and Holland—returns to Paris, and takes measures for extending the Continental System—Seizure of the Valois—Coast along the German Ocean annexed to France—Protest by the Czar against the appropriation of Oldenburg—Russia allows the importation, at certain

Seaports, of various articles of British Commerce—Negotiations for Exchange of Prisoners between France and England; and for a general Peace, broken off by Buonaparte's unreasonable Demands. 101

GUSTAVUS IV. OF SWEDEN DETHRONED 101
BERNADOTTE 104
SWEDEN 107
TOUR THROUGH BELGIUM 111
RUSSIAN PROTEST 115
EXCHANGE OF PRISONERS 116

CHAPTER LIV **119**

View of Napoleon's gigantic Power—The Empress Maria Louisa delivered of a Son—Criticism on the Title given him, of King of Rome—Speculations in regard to the advantages or disadvantages arising from this Event—Retrospect—Ex-Queen of Etruria—Her severe and unjustifiable Treatment by Napoleon—Lucien Buonaparte is invited to England, where he writes Epic Poetry—Attempt to deliver Ferdinand, defeated—Operations in Portugal—Retreat of Massena—Battles of Fuentes d'Onoro fought by Lord Wellington—On the South Frontier of Portugal, by Lord Beresford—Of Barossa, by General Graham—Enterprise of Arroyo-Molinos—Spaniards defeated under Blake—Valencia captured by the French, and he and his Army made Prisoners of War—Disunion among the French Generals—Joseph wishes to abdicate the Throne of Spain. 119

ACTUAL DOMINIONS 119
BIRTH OF THE KING OF ROME 123
THE EX-QUEEN OF ETRURIA 126
LUCIEN BUONAPARTE 127
MASSENA AND WELLINGTON 131
BATTLE OF FUENTES D'ONORO 133
JOSEPH WISHES TO ABDICATE 136

CHAPTER LV **137**

Retrospect of the causes leading to the Rupture with Russia—originate in the Treaty of Tilsit—Russia's alleged Reasons of Complaint—Arguments of Napoleon's Counsellors against War with Russia—Fouché is against the War—Presents a Memorial to Napoleon upon the Subject—His Answer—Napoleon's Views in favour of the War, as urged to his various Advisers. 137

RUPTURE WITH RUSSIA 137
COMPLAINTS OF THE CZAR 141
WAR WITH RUSSIA 143
FOUCHÉ'S MEMORIAL 145

RUPTURE WITH RUSSIA 148

CHAPTER LVI **151**

Allies on whose assistance Buonaparte might count—Causes which alienated from him the Prince-Royal of Sweden—who signs a Treaty with Russia—Delicate situation of the King of Prussia, whose alliance the Emperor Alexander on that account declines—A Treaty with France dictated to Prussia—Relations between Austria and France—in order to preserve them Buonaparte is obliged to come under an engagement not to revolutionize Poland—His error of policy in neglecting to cultivate the alliance of the Porte—Amount of Buonaparte's Army—Levies for the protection of France in the Emperor's absence—Storming of Ciudad Rodrigo by Lord Wellington—Buonaparte makes overtures of Peace to Lord Castlereagh—The Correspondence broken off—Ultimatum of Russia rejected—Napoleon sets out from Paris, 9th May, 1812—and meets the Sovereigns his allies at Dresden—A last attempt of Napoleon to negotiate with Alexander proves unsuccessful. 151

PRINCE-ROYAL OF SWEDEN 152
PRUSSIA 156
RELATIONS WITH AUSTRIA 159
TURKEY 161
STATE OF THE ARMY 163
CIUDAD RODRIGO—BADAJOS 166
HOSTILE PREPARATIONS 169
ROYAL FESTIVITIES 171
WAR WITH RUSSIA 174

CHAPTER LVII **177**

Napoleon's Plan of the Campaign against Russia—Understood and provided against by Barclay de Tolly, the Russian Generalissimo—Statement of the Grand French Army—Of the Grand Russian Army—Disaster on the river Wilia—Difficulties of the Campaign, on the part of the French—Their defective Commissariat and Hospital Department—Cause of Buonaparte's determination to advance—His forced marches occasion actual delay—Napoleon remains for some days at Wilna—Abbé de Pradt—His intrigues to excite the Poles—Neutralized by Napoleon's engagements with Austria—An attempt to excite Insurrection in Lithuania also fails. 177

BARCLAY DE TOLLY 179
MARCH UPON THE NIEMEN 182
DEFECTIVE COMMISSARIAT 185
IMMENSE LOSSES OF THE ARMY 187
WILNA 190

DIET OF WARSAW 192
LITHUANIA 194

CHAPTER LVIII 197

Proceedings of the Army under Prince Bagration—Napoleon's manœuvres against him—King Jerome of Westphalia is disgraced for alleged inactivity—Bagration is defeated by Davoust, but succeeds in gaining the interior of Russia, and re-establishing his communication with the Grand Army—which retreats to Drissa—Barclay and Bagration meet at Smolensk on the 20th July—The French Generals become anxious that Napoleon should close the campaign at Witepsk for the season—He persists in proceeding—Smolensk evacuated by De Tolly, after setting fire to the place—Reduced condition of the French, and growing strength of the Russian Armies—Peace effected between Russia, and England, Sweden, and Turkey—Napoleon resolves to advance upon Moscow. 197

PROTRACTED STAY AT WILNA 197
GENERAL WITGENSTEIN 202
WITEPSK 204
SMOLENSK 208
BATTLE OF SMOLENSK 210
SMOLENSK 211
ADVANCE UPON MOSCOW 215

CHAPTER LIX 217

Napoleon detaches Murat and other Generals in pursuit of the Russians—Bloody, but indecisive Action, at Valoutina—Barclay de Tolly's defensive system relinquished, and Koutousoff appointed to the chief command of the Russian Army—Napoleon advances from Smolensk—Battle of Borodino fought, on 5th September—Prince Bagration slain—Koutousoff retreats upon Mojaisk, and thence upon Moscow—Napoleon continues his advance on the 12th—Count Rostopchin, Governor of Moscow—His Character—The Russians abandon Moscow, which is evacuated by the Inhabitants—The Grand Russian Army marches through Moscow—Last public Court of Justice held there by Rostopchin, after which he follows the march of the Army. 217

ACTION AT VALOUTINA 218
BATTLE OF BORODINO 221
MOJAISK 226
THE RUSSIANS ABANDON MOSCOW 228

CHAPTER LX 231

On 14th September, Napoleon reaches Moscow, which he finds deserted by the Inhabitants—The City is discovered to be on fire—Napoleon takes up his quarters in the Kremlin—The fire is stopt next day, but arises again at night—Believed to be wilful, and several Russians apprehended and shot—On the third night, the Kremlin is discovered to be on Fire—Buonaparte leaves it, and takes his abode at Petrowsky—The Fire rages till the 19th, when four-fifths of the City are burnt down—On the 20th, Buonaparte returns to the Kremlin—Discussion as to the Origin of this great Conflagration—Disorganisation and Indiscipline of the French Army—Difficulty as to the Route on leaving Moscow—Lauriston sent with a Letter to the Emperor Alexander—Retrospect of the March of the Russian Army, after leaving Moscow—Lauriston has an Interview with Koutousoff on 5th October—The Result—Armistice made by Murat—Preparations for Retreat—The Emperor Alexander refuses to treat. 231

ENTRY INTO MOSCOW *233*
MISSION TO EMPEROR ALEXANDER *241*
GENERAL DAVIDOFF *244*
ARMISTICE MADE BY MURAT *246*
MOSCOW *248*

CHAPTER LXI 251

Murat's Armistice broken off—Napoleon leaves Moscow on 19th October—Bloody Skirmish at Malo-Yarowslavetz—Napoleon in great danger while reconnoitring—He retreats to Vereia, where he meets Mortier and the Young Guard—Winzengerode made Prisoner, and insulted by Buonaparte—The Kremlin is blown up by the French—Napoleon continues his Retreat towards Poland—Its Horrors—Conflict near Wiazma, on 3d November, where the French lose 4000 Men—Cross the River Wiazma during the Night—The Viceroy of Italy reaches Smolensk, in great distress—Buonaparte arrives at Smolensk, with the headmost division of the Grand Army—Calamitous Retreat of Ney's Division—The whole French Army now collected at Smolensk—Cautious conduct of Prince Schwartzenberg—Winzengerode freed on his road to Paris, by a body of Cossacks—Tchitchagoff occupies Minsk—Perilous situation of Napoleon. 251

MURAT ATTACKED AND DEFEATED..*251*
BATTLE OF MALO-YAROWSLAVETZ *254*
RETREAT ON VEREIA..*257*
WINZENGERODE MADE PRISONER...*259*
WINZENGERODE...*262*
GJATZ—WIAZMA *265*
OPERATIONS OF PRINCE EUGENE...*268*
SMOLENSK...*270*
OPERATIONS OF THE RUSSIANS *273*
ACTION NEAR WOLKOWITZ..*278*

CHAPTER LXII **281**

Napoleon divides his Army into four Corps, which leave Smolensk on their retreat towards Poland—Cautious proceedings of Koutousoff—The Viceroy's division is attacked by Miloradowitch, and effects a junction with Napoleon at Krasnoi, after severe loss—Koutousoff attacks the French at Krasnoi, but only by a distant cannonade—The division under Davoust is reunited to Napoleon, but in a miserable state—Napoleon marches to Liady; and Mortier and Davoust are attacked, and suffer heavy loss—Details of the retreat of Ney—He crosses the Losmina, with great loss of men and baggage, and joins Napoleon at Orcsa, with his division reduced to 1500 men—The whole Grand Army is now reduced to 12,000 effective men, besides 30,000 stragglers—Dreadful distress and difficulties of Buonaparte and his Army—Singular scene betwixt Napoleon and Duroc and Daru—Napoleon moves towards Borizoff, and falls in with the corps of Victor and Oudinot—Koutousoff halts at Kopyn, without attacking Buonaparte—Napoleon crosses the Beresina at Studzianka—Partouneaux's division cut off by Witgenstein—Severe fighting on both sides of the river—Dreadful losses of the French in crossing it—According to the Russian official account, 36,000 bodies were found in the Beresina after the thaw 281

NAPOLEON LEAVES SMOLENSK *281*
KRASNOI *284*
MARCHES ON LIADY—NEY'S RETREAT *287*
JUNCTION OF THE GRAND ARMY—BORIZOFF *290*
SUCCESS OF VICTOR AND OUDINOT *292*
STUDZIANKA *295*
PASSAGE OF THE BERESINA *298*
DREADFUL LOSSES OF THE FRENCH *300*

CHAPTER LXIII **303**

Napoleon determines to return to Paris—He leaves Smorgoni on 5th December—reaches Warsaw on the 10th—Curious Interview with the Abbé de Pradt—Arrives at Dresden on the 14th—and at Paris on the 18th, at midnight—Dreadful State of the Grand Army, when left by Napoleon—Arrive at Wilna, whence they are driven by the Cossacks, directing their flight upon Kowno—Dissensions among the French Generals—Cautious Policy of the Austrians under Schwartzenberg—Precarious state of Macdonald—He retreats upon Tilsit—D'Yorck separates his Troops from the French—Macdonald effects his retreat to Königsberg—Close of the Russian expedition, with a loss on the part of the French of 450,000 Men in Killed and Prisoners—Discussion of the Causes which led to this ruinous Catastrophe. 303

SMORGONI—SETS OUT FOR PARIS *304*
INTERVIEW WITH DE PRADT *307*
NAPOLEON LEAVES WARSAW *311*

DREADFUL STATE OF GRAND ARMY	312
WILNA—KOWNO	315
PRECARIOUS STATE OF MACDONALD	317
CLOSE OF THE RUSSIAN EXPEDITION	321
CAUSES OF THE CATASTROPHE	322

CHAPTER LXIV ... 331

Effects of Napoleon's return upon the Parisians—Congratulations and addresses by all the public Functionaries—Conspiracy of Mallet—very nearly successful—How at last defeated—The impression made by this event upon Buonaparte—Discussions with the Pope, who is brought to France, but remains inflexible—State of Affairs in Spain—Napoleon's great and successful exertions to recruit his Army—Guards of Honour—In the month of April, the army is raised to 350,000 men, independently of the troops left in garrison in Germany, and in Spain and Italy. ... 331

CONSPIRACY OF MALLET	333
PARIS	336
INTERVIEW WITH PIUS VII	340
EXERTIONS TO RECRUIT THE ARMY	342

CHAPTER LXV ... 345

Murat leaves the Grand Army abruptly—Eugene appointed in his place—Measures taken by the King of Prussia for his disenthraldom—He leaves Berlin for Breslau—Treaty signed between Russia and Prussia early in March—Alexander arrives at Breslau on 15th; on the 16th Prussia declares War against France—Warlike preparations of Prussia—Universal enthusiasm—Blucher appointed Generalissimo—Vindication of the Crown Prince of Sweden for joining the Confederacy against France—Proceedings of Austria—Unabated spirit and pretensions of Napoleon—A Regency is appointed in France during his absence, and Maria Louisa appointed Regent, with nominal powers. ... 345

EXERTIONS OF PRUSSIA	346
PRUSSIA DECLARES WAR	349
BLUCHER	351
PROCEEDINGS OF AUSTRIA	355
MARIA LOUISA APPOINTED REGENT	358

CHAPTER LXVI ... 359

State of the French Grand Army—The Russians advance, and show themselves on the Elbe—The French evacuate Berlin, and retreat on the Elbe—The Crown Prince of Sweden joins the Allies, with 35,000 Men—Dresden is occupied by the

Sovereigns of Russia and Prussia—Marshal Bessières killed on 1st May—Battle of Lutzen fought on the 2d.—The Allies retire to Bautzen—Hamburgh taken possession of by the Danes and French—Battle of Bautzen fought on the 20th and 21st May—The Allies retire in good order—The French Generals, Bruyères and Duroc, killed on the 22d.—Grief of Napoleon for the Death of the latter—An Armistice signed on 4th June. 359

CROWN PRINCE JOINS THE ALLIES 361
LUTZEN 363
BATTLE OF LUTZEN 364
HAMBURGH—DRESDEN 367
THE BATTLE OF BAUTZEN 370
ARMISTICE 374

CHAPTER LXVII 377

Change in the results formerly produced by the French Victories—Despondency of the Generals—Decay in the discipline of the Troops—Views of Austria—Arguments in favour of Peace stated and discussed—Pertinacity of Napoleon—State of the French Interior—hid from him by the slavery of the Press—Interview betwixt Napoleon and the Austrian Minister Metternich—Delays in the Negotiations—Plan of Pacification proposed by Austria, on 7th August—The Armistice broken off on the 10th, when Austria joins the Allies—Sudden placability of Napoleon at this period—Ascribed to the news of the Battle of Vittoria. 377

DISCIPLINE OF THE ARMY 378
THE QUESTION OF PEACE 379
TALLEYRAND AND FOUCHÉ 384
INTERVIEW WITH METTERNICH 387
AUSTRIA JOINS THE ALLIES 391

CHAPTER LXVIII 393

Amount and distribution of the French Army at the resumption of Hostilities—of the Armies of the Allies—Plan of the Campaign on both sides—Return of Moreau from America, to join the Allies—Attack on Dresden by the Allies on 26th August—Napoleon arrives to its succour—Battle continued on the 27th—Death of General Moreau—Defeat and Retreat of the Allies, with great loss—Napoleon returns from the pursuit to Dresden, indisposed—Vandamme attacks the Allies at Culm—is driven back towards Peterswald—Conflict on the heights of Peterswald—Vandamme is Defeated and made prisoner—Effects of the victory of Culm, on the Allies—and on Napoleon. 393

DISTRIBUTION OF THE ARMY 394

DRESDEN	*397*
DEATH OF MOREAU	*400*
VANDAMME	*403*
SURRENDER OF VANDAMME	*405*

CHAPTER LXIX **409**

Military Proceedings in the north of Germany—Luckau submits to the Crown Prince of Sweden—Battles of Gross-Beeren and Katzbach—Operations of Ney upon Berlin—He is defeated at Dennewitz on the 6th September—Difficult and embarrassing situation of Napoleon—He abandons all the right side of the Elbe to the Allies—Operations of the Allies in order to effect a junction—Counter-exertions of Napoleon—The French Generals averse to continuing the War in Germany—Dissensions betwixt them and the Emperor—Napoleon at length resolves to retreat upon Leipsic. 409

BERLIN	*409*
KATZBACH—SUCCESSES OF THE ALLIES	*411*
DENNEWITZ	*414*
RETREATS TOWARDS DRESDEN	*417*
OPERATIONS OF THE ALLIES	*419*
DISSENSIONS AMONG THE GENERALS	*422*

CHAPTER LXX **425**

Napoleon reaches Leipsic on 15th of October—Statement of the French and Allied Forces—Battle of Leipsic, commenced on 16th, and terminates with disadvantage to the French at nightfall—Napoleon despatches General Mehrfeldt (his prisoner) to the Emperor of Austria, with proposals for an armistice—No answer is returned—The battle is renewed on the morning of the 18th, and lasts till night, when the French are compelled to retreat, after immense loss on both sides—They evacuate Leipsic on the 19th, the Allies in full pursuit—Blowing up of one of the bridges—Prince Poniatowski drowned in the Elster—25,000 French are made prisoners—The Allied Sovereigns meet in triumph, at noon, in the Great Square at Leipsic—King of Saxony sent under a Guard to Berlin—Reflections. 425

FRENCH AND ALLIED FORCES	*427*
BATTLE OF LEIPSIC	*429*
PREPARATIONS FOR RETREAT	*433*
LEIPSIC	*437*
BRIDGE OF LEIPSIC	*439*

CHAPTER LXXI **445**

Retreat of the French from Germany—General Defection of Napoleon's Partisans—Battle of Hannau fought on 30th and 31st October—Napoleon arrives at Paris on 9th November—State in which he finds the public mind in the capital—Fate of the French Garrisons left in Germany—Arrival of the Allied Armies on the banks of the Rhine—General view of Napoleon's political relations—Italy—Spain—Restoration of Ferdinand—Liberation of the Pope, who returns to Rome—Emancipation of Holland..445

RETREAT FROM GERMANY 445
ERFURT—HANAU.. 447
LOSSES OF THE FRENCH 450
FRENCH GARRISONS IN GERMANY 452
ITALY—SPAIN... 455
RESTORATION OF FERDINAND 456
EMANCIPATION OF HOLLAND 461

CHAPTER LXXII **465**

Preparations of Napoleon against the Invasion of France—Terms of Peace offered by the Allies—Congress held at Manheim—Lord Castlereagh—Manifesto of the Allies—Buonaparte's Reply—State of Parties in France—The population of France, in general, wearied of the War, and desirous of the Deposition of Buonaparte—His unsuccessful attempts to arouse the national spirit—Council of State Extraordinary held Nov. 11th, when new taxes are imposed, and a new Conscription of 300,000 men decreed—Gloom of the Council, and violence of Buonaparte—Report of the State of the Nation presented to Napoleon by the Legislative Body—The Legislative Body is prorogued—Unceasing activity of the Emperor—National Guard called out—Napoleon, presenting to them his Empress and Child, takes leave of the People—He leaves Paris for the Armies. 465

CONGRESS AT PRAGUE 467
LORD CASTLEREAGH 470
REPLY TO THE MANIFESTO 471
STATE OF PARTIES—THE ROYALISTS... 476
GENERAL DISCONTENT—NEW TAXES IMPOSED 477
REPORT—STATE OF THE NATION 479
LEGISLATIVE BODY PROROGUED 483
HIS UNCEASING EXERTIONS.. 484

CHAPTER LXXIII **487**

Declaration of the Allies on entering France—Switzerland—Schwartzenberg crosses the Rhine—Apathy of the French—Junction of Blucher with the Grand Army—Crown Prince of Sweden—Inferiority of Napoleon's numerical Force—

Battles of Brienne—and La Rothière—Difficulties of Buonaparte, during which he meditates to resign the Crown—He makes a successful Attack on the Silesian Army at Champ-Aubert—Blucher is compelled to retreat—The Grand Army carries Nogent and Montereau—Buonaparte's violence to his Generals—The Austrians resolve on a general Retreat, as far as Nancy and Langres—Prince Wenceslaus sent to Buonaparte's headquarters—The French enter Troyes—Execution of Gouault, a Royalist—A Decree of Death against all wearing the Bourbon emblems, and all Emigrants who should join the Allies. 487

    THE ALLIES IN SWITZERLAND 489
    BERNADOTTE—HOLLAND 491
    PROGRESS OF THE ALLIES 493
    STATE OF THE ARMIES—BRIENNE 496
    BATTLE OF LA ROTHIÈRE—TROYES 499
    ATTACK ON BLUCHER 502
    MONTEREAU 505
    RETREAT OF THE AUSTRIANS 507
    EXECUTION OF GOUAULT 509

CHAPTER LXXIV 513

Retrospect of Events on the Frontiers—Defection of Murat—Its consequences—Augereau abandons Franche Comté—Carnot intrusted with the command of Antwerp—Attack on Bergen-op-Zoom, by Sir Thomas Graham—The Allies take, and evacuate Soissons—Bulow and Winzengerode unite with Blucher—Wellington forces his way through the Pays des Gaves—Royalists in the West—Discontent of the old Republicans—Views of the different Members of the Alliance as to the Dynasties of Bourbon, and Napoleon—Proceedings of the Dukes of Berri and Angoulême, and Monsieur—Battle of Orthez—Bordeaux surrendered to Marshal Beresford—Negotiations of Chatillon—Treaty of Chaumont—Napoleon's contre-projet—Congress at Chatillon broken up. 513

    DEFECTION OF MURAT 513
    AUGEREAU 515
    ROYALISTS OF THE WEST 518
    THE BOURBONS 522
    THE BATTLE OF ORTHEZ 524
    SURRENDER OF BORDEAUX 526
    NEGOTIATIONS AT CHATILLON 529
    CONGRESS AT CHATILLON 531
    TREATY OF CHAUMONT 534
    CONGRESS DISSOLVED 536

APPENDIX 539

No. I 539

REFLECTIONS ON THE CONDUCT OF NAPOLEON TOWARDS THE PRINCE-ROYAL OF SWEDEN 539

No. II 550

EXTRACT FROM MANUSCRIPT OBSERVATIONS ON NAPOLEON'S RUSSIAN CAMPAIGN, BY AN ENGLISH OFFICER OF RANK 550

Chapter XLIX

Conduct of Russia and England during the War with Austria—Meditated Expedition of British Troops to the Continent—Sent to Walcheren—Its Calamitous Details and Result—Proceedings of Napoleon with regard to the Pope—General Miollis enters Rome—Napoleon publishes a Decree, uniting the States of the Church to the French Empire—Is Excommunicated—Pius VII. is banished from Rome, and sent to Grenoble—afterwards brought back to Savona—Buonaparte is attacked by an Assassin—Definitive Treaty of Peace signed at Schoenbrun—Napoleon returns to France on the 14th November, 1809.

The particular conditions of the peace with Austria were not adjusted until the 14th October, 1809, although the armistice was signed nearly three months before. We avail ourselves of the interval to notice other remarkable events, which happened during this eventful summer; and first, we must briefly revert to the conduct of Russia and England during the war.

Notwithstanding the personal friendship betwixt the Emperors Alexander and Napoleon—notwithstanding their engagements entered into at Tilsit, and so lately revived at Erfurt, it seems to have been impossible to engage Russia heartily as an ally of Napoleon, in a war which had the destruction or absolute humiliation of Austria. The Court of St. Petersburgh had, it is true, lost no time in securing the advantages which had been stipulated for Russia in the conferences alluded to. Finland had been conquered, torn from Sweden, to which the province had so long belonged, and united with Russia, to whom it furnished a most important frontier and barrier.[1] Russia was also, with connivance of

---

[1] See Russian proclamation to the inhabitants of Finland, Feb. 18, 1808 Annual Register, vol. l., p. 301.

France, making war on the Porte, in order to enlarge her dominions by the addition of Moldavia and Wallachia. But though the Court of St. Petersburgh had gained one of these advantages, and was in a way of obtaining the other, the Russian Ministers saw with anxiety the impending fate of Austria, the rather that they themselves were bound by treaty to lend their aid for her destruction. We have seen that Russia had interposed to prevent the war. She was now unwillingly compelled to take part in it; yet when Prince Galatzin marched into Galicia at the head of 30,000 Russians, the manifesto which he published could be hardly termed that of a hostile nation. The Emperor, it stated, had done all in his power to prevent things from coming to this extremity; but now, the war having actually broken out, he was bound by the faith of treaties to send the stipulated number of auxiliaries.[2] The motions of this body of Russians were slow, and their conduct in the Austrian dominions rather that of allies than enemies. Some of the Russian officers of rank avowed their politics to be in direct opposition to those of the Emperor, and declared that three-fourths of the generals commanding territorial divisions in Russia were of their opinion. These expressions, with the unusual slowness and lenity just alluded to, were for the present passed over without remark, but were recorded and remembered as matter of high offence, when Napoleon thought that the time was come to exact from Russia a severe account for every thing in which she had disappointed his expectations.

The exertions of England, at the same period, were of a nature and upon a scale to surprise the world. It seemed as if her flag literally overshadowed the whole seas on the coasts of Italy, Spain, the Ionian Islands, the Baltic Sea. Wherever there was the least show of resistance to the yoke of Buonaparte, the assistance of the English was appealed to, and was readily afforded. In Spain, particularly, the British troops, led by a general whose name began soon to be weighed against those of the best French commanders, displayed their usual gallantry under auspices which no longer permitted it to evaporate in actions of mere eclat.

---

[2] Annual Register, vol. l., p. 759.

Yet the British administration, while they had thus embraced a broader and more adventurous, but at the same time a far wiser system of conducting the war, showed in one most important instance, that they, or a part of them, were not entirely free from the ancient prejudices, which had so long rendered vain the efforts of Britain in favour of the liberties of the world. The general principle was indeed adopted, that the expeditions of Britain should be directed where they could do the cause of Europe the most benefit, and the interests of Napoleon the greatest harm; but still there remained a lurking wish that they could be so directed, as, at the same time, to acquire some peculiar and separate advantage to England, and to secure the accomplishment of what was called a British object. Some of the English ministers might thus be said to resemble the ancient converts from Judaism, who, in embracing the Christian faith, still held themselves bound by the ritual, and fettered by the prejudices of the Jewish people, separated as they were from the rest of mankind.

It is no wonder that the voice of what is in reality selfishness, is listened to in national councils with more respect than it deserves, since in that case it wears the mask and speaks the language of a species of patriotism, against which it can only be urged, that it is too exclusive in its zeal. Its effects, however, are not the less to be regretted, as disabling strong minds, and misleading wise men; of which the history of Britain affords but too many instances.

BRITISH EXPEDITION

Besides the forces already in the Peninsula, Britain had the means of disposing of, and the will to send to the continent, 40,000 men, with a fleet of thirty-five ships of the line, and twenty frigates, to assist on any point where their services could have been useful. Such an armament on the coast of Spain might have brought to a speedy decision the long and bloody contest in that country, saved much British blood, which the protracted war wasted, and struck a blow, the effects of which, as that of Trafalgar, Buonaparte might have felt on the banks of the Danube. Such an armament, if sent to the north of Germany, ere the destruction of Schill and the defeat of the Duke of Brunswick's enterprise, might have been the means of placing all the northern provinces in active opposition to France, by an effort for which the state of the public mind was already prepared. A successful action would even have given spirits to Prussia, and induced that depressed kingdom to resume the struggle for her independence. In a word, Britain might have had the honour of kindling the same flame, which, being excited by Russia in 1813, was the means of destroying the French influence in Germany, and breaking up the Confederation of the Rhine.

Unhappily, neither of these important objects seemed to the planners of this enterprise to be connected in a manner sufficiently direct, with objects exclusively interesting to Britain. It was therefore agreed, that the expedition should be sent against the strong fortresses, swampy isles, and dangerous coasts of the Netherlands, in order to seek for dock-yards to be destroyed, and ships to be carried off. Antwerp was particularly aimed at. But, although Napoleon attached great importance to the immense naval yards and docks which he had formed in the Scheldt, yet, weighed with the danger and difficulty of an attack upon them, the object of destroying them seems to have been very inadequate. Admitting that Buonaparte might succeed in building ships in the Scheldt, or elsewhere, there was no possibility, in the existing state of the world, that he could have been able to get sailors to man them; unless, at least, modern seamen could have been bred on dry land, like the crews of the Roman galleys during the war with Carthage. If even the ships could have been manned, it would have been long ere Napoleon, with his utmost exertions, could have brought out of the Scheldt such a fleet as would not have been defeated by half their own numbers of British ships. The dangers arising to Britain from the naval establishments in the Scheldt were remote, nor was the advantage of destroying them, should such destruction be found possible, commensurate with the expense and hazard of the enterprise which was directed against them. Besides, before Antwerp could be attacked, the islands of Beveland and Walcheren were to be taken possession of, and a long amphibious course of hostilities was to be maintained, to enable the expedition to reach the point where alone great results were expected.

The commander-in-chief was the Earl of Chatham, who, inheriting the family talents of his father, the great minister, was remarkable for a spirit of inactivity and procrastination, the consequences of which had been felt in all the public offices which he held, and which, therefore, were likely to be peculiarly fatal in an expedition requiring the utmost celerity and promptitude of action. It is remarkable, that though these points in Lord Chatham's character were generally known, the public voice at the time, in deference to the talents which distinguished his house, did not censure the nomination.

WALCHEREN

Upon the 30th of July, the English disembarked on the islands of South Beveland and Walcheren; on the 1st of August they attacked Flushing, the principal place in the neighbourhood, by land and sea. On the 15th of August, the place surrendered, and its garrison, four or five thousand men strong, were sent prisoners of war to England. But here the success of the British ended. The French, who had at first been very much alarmed, had time to recover from their consternation. Fouché, then at the head of the police, and it may be said of the government, (for he exercised for the time the power of minister of the interior,) showed the utmost readiness in getting under arms about 40,000 national guards, to replace the regular soldiers, of which the Low Countries had been drained. In awakening the military ardour of the citizens of France, in which he succeeded to an unusual degree, Fouché made use of these expressions:—"Let Europe see, that if the genius of Napoleon gives glory to France, still his presence is not necessary to enable her to repel her enemies from her soil." This phrase expressed more independence than was agreeable to Napoleon, and was set down as intimating a self-sufficiency, which counterbalanced the services of the minister.[3]

Neither did Fouché's selection of a military chief to command the new levies, prove more acceptable. Bernadotte, whom we have noticed as a general of republican fame, had been, at the time of

---

[3] Mémoires de Fouché, tom. i., p. 337.

Buonaparte's elevation, opposed to his interests, and attached to those of the Directory. Any species of rivalry, or pretence of dispute between them, was long since ended; yet still Bernadotte was scarce accounted an attached friend of the Emperor, though he was in some sort connected with the house of Napoleon, having married a sister-in-law of Joseph, the intrusive King of Spain.[4] In the campaign of Vienna, which we have detailed, Bernadotte, (created Prince of Ponte Corvo,) commanded a division of Saxons, and had incurred Buonaparte's censure more than once, and particularly at the battle of Wagram, for the slowness of his movements. The Prince of Ponte Corvo came, therefore, to Paris in a sort of disgrace, where Fouché, in conjunction with Clarke, the minister at war, invited him to take on himself the defence of Antwerp. Bernadotte hesitated to accept the charge; but having at length done so, he availed himself of the time afforded by the English to put the place in a complete state of defence, and assembled within, and under its walls, above thirty thousand men. The country was inundated by opening the sluices; strong batteries were erected on both sides of the Scheldt, and the ascending that river became almost impossible.[5]

The British naval and military officers also disagreed among themselves, as often happens where difficulties multiply, and there appears no presiding spirit to combat and control them. The final objects of the expedition were therefore abandoned; the navy returned to the English ports, and the British forces were concentrated—for what reason, or with what expectation, it is difficult to see—in that fatal conquest, the isle of Walcheren. Among the marshes, stagnant canals, and unwholesome trenches of this island, there broods continually, a fever of a kind deeply pestilential and malignant, and which, like most maladies of the same description, is more destructive to strangers than to the natives, whose constitutions become by habit proof against its

---

[4] In 1798, Bernadotte married Eugénie Cléry, the daughter of a considerable merchant at Marseilles, and sister to Julia, the wife of Joseph Buonaparte.
[5] "It was not Bernadotte whom Cambêcérès and the Duke of Feltre requested to undertake the defence of Antwerp; but it was I who received several couriers on this subject, and who in fact took the command of the combined army, sufficiently in time to prevent the English surprising Antwerp, as they already had done Walcheren. It was I who flooded the borders of the Scheldt, and erected batteries there. Bernadotte arrived a fortnight afterwards; and, in pursuance of the orders of Napoleon and Clarke, which were officially communicated to me, I resigned the command to him."—Louis Buonaparte, p. 60.

ravages. This dreadful disease broke out among our troops with the force of a pestilence, and besides the numerous victims who died on the spot, shattered, in many cases for ever, the constitution of the survivors. The joy with which Napoleon saw the army of his enemy thus consigned to an obscure and disgraceful death, broke out even in his bulletins, as if the pestilence under which they fell had been caused by his own policy, and was not the consequence of the climate, and of the ill-advised delay which prevented our soldiers being withdrawn from it. "We are rejoiced," he said, in a letter to the minister at war, "to see that the English have packed themselves in the morasses of Zealand. Let them be only kept in check, and the bad air and fevers peculiar to the country will soon destroy their army." At length, after the loss of more lives than would have been wasted in three general battles, the fortifications of Flushing were blown up, and the British forces returned to their own country.[6]

The evil consequences of this expedition did not end even here. The mode in which it had been directed and conducted, introduced dissensions into the British Cabinet, which occasioned the temporary secession of one of the most able and most eloquent of its members, Mr. George Canning, who was thus withdrawn from public affairs when his talents could be least spared by the country. On the other hand, the appointment of Marquis Wellesley to the situation of secretary at war, gave, in the estimation of the public, a strong pledge that the efficient measures suggested by the talents of that noble statesman, would be supported and carried through by his brother Sir Arthur, to whom alone, as a general, the army and the people began to look with hope and confidence.

While England was thus exerting herself, Buonaparte, from the castle of Schoenbrun, under the walls of Vienna, was deciding the fate of the continent on every point where British influence had no means of thwarting him. One of the revolutions which cost him little effort to accomplish, yet which struck Europe with surprise, by the numerous recollections which it excited, was his seizure of the city of Rome, and the territories of the Church, and depriving the Pope of his character of a temporal prince.

---

[6] See Papers relating to the expedition to the Scheldt, Parliamentary Debates, vol. xv., Appendix; and Annual Register, vol. l., pp. 543, 546, 559.

PIUS THE SEVENTH

It must be allowed, by the greatest admirers of Napoleon, that his policy, depending less upon principle than upon existing circumstances, was too apt to be suddenly changed, as opportunity or emergency seemed to give occasion. There could, for example, be scarce a measure of his reign adopted on more deep and profound consideration than that of the Concordat, by which he re-established the national religion of France, and once more united that country to the Catholic Church. In reward for this great service, Pope Pius VII., as we have seen, had the unusual complaisance to cross the Alps, and visit Paris, for the sake of adding religious solemnity, and the blessing of St. Peter's successor, to the ceremony of Napoleon's coronation. It might have been thought that a friendship thus cemented, and which, altogether essential to the safety of the Pope, was far from indifferent to the interests of Buonaparte, ought to have subsisted undisturbed, at least for some years. But the Emperor and Pontiff stood in a suspicious attitude with respect to each other. Pius VII. felt that he had made, in his character of chief of the Church, very great concessions to Napoleon, and such as he could hardly reconcile to the tenderness of his own conscience. He, therefore, expected gratitude in proportion to the scruples which he had surmounted, while Buonaparte was far from rating the services of his Holiness so high, or sympathizing with his conscientious scruples.

Besides, the Pope, in surrendering the rights of the Church in so many instances, must have felt that he was acting under motives of constraint, and in the character of a prisoner; for he had sacrificed more than had been yielded by any prelate who had held the see of Rome, since the days of Constantine. He may therefore have considered himself, not only as doubly bound to secure what remained of the authority of his predecessors, but even at liberty, should opportunity offer, to reclaim some part of that which he had unwillingly yielded up. Thus circumstanced in respect to each other, Pius VII. felt that he had done more in complaisance to Buonaparte than he could justify to his conscience; while Napoleon, who considered the reunion of France to Rome, in its spiritual relations, as entirely his own work, thought it of such consequence as to deserve greater concessions than his Holiness had yet granted.

The Pope, on his first return to Italy, showed favourable prepossessions for Napoleon, whom he commemorated in his address to the College of Cardinals, as that mighty Emperor of France, whose name extended to the most remote regions of the earth; whom Heaven had used as the means of reviving religion in France, when it was at the lowest ebb; and whose courtesies towards his own person, and compliance with his requests, merited his highest regard and requital. Yet Napoleon complained, that subsequent to this period, Pius VII. began by degrees to receive counsel from the enemies of France, and that he listened to advisers, who encouraged him to hold the rights of the Church higher than the desire to gratify the Emperor. Thus a suppressed and unavowed, but perpetual struggle took place, and was carried on betwixt the Emperor and the Pope; the former desirous to extend and consolidate his recent authority, the latter to defend what remained of the ancient privileges of the Church.

It is probable, however, that, had there been only spiritual matters in discussion between them, Napoleon would have avoided an open rupture with the Holy Father, to which he was conscious much scandal would attach. But in the present situation of Italy, the temporal states of the Pope furnished a strong temptation for his ambition. These extend, as is well known, betwixt the kingdom of Naples, then governed by Joachim Murat, and the northern Italian provinces, all of which, by the late appropriation of Tuscany, were now amalgamated into one state, and had become, under the name of the kingdom of Italy, a part of the dominions of Buonaparte. Thus the patrimony of the Church was the only portion of the Italian peninsula which was not either directly, or indirectly, under the empire of France; and, as it divided the Neapolitan dominions from those of Napoleon, it afforded facilities for descents of British troops, either from Sicily or Sardinia, and, what Buonaparte was not less anxious to prevent, great opportunities for the importation of English commodities. The war with Austria in 1809, and the large army which the Archduke John then led into Italy, and with which, but for the defeat at Eckmühl, he might have accomplished great changes, rendered the independence of the Roman States the subject of still greater dislike and suspicion to Buonaparte.

His ambassador, therefore, had instructions to press on the Pope the necessity of shutting his ports against British commerce, and adhering to the continental system; together with the further decisive measure, of acceding to the confederacy formed between the kingdom of Italy and that of Naples, or, in other words, becoming a party to the war against Austria and England. Pius VII. reluctantly submitted to shut his ports, but he positively refused to become a party to the war. He was, he said, the father of all Christian nations; he could not, consistently with that character, become the enemy of any.[7]

Upon receiving this refusal, Buonaparte would no longer keep terms with him; and, in order, as he said, to protect himself against the inconveniences which he apprehended from the pertinacity of the Holy Father, he caused the towns of Ancona and Civita Vecchia to be occupied by French troops, which were necessarily admitted when there were no means of resistance.

This act of aggression, to which the Pope might have seen it prudent to submit without remonstrance, as to what he could not avoid, would probably have sufficiently answered all the immediate purposes of Buonaparte; nor would he, it may be supposed, have incurred the further scandal of a direct and irreconcilable breach with Pius VII., but for recollections, that Rome had been the seat of empire over the Christian world, and that the universal sovereignty to which he aspired, would hardly be thought to exist in the full extent of majesty which he desired to attach to it, unless the ancient capital of the world made a part of his dominions. Napoleon was himself an Italian,[8] and showed his sense of his origin by the

---

[7] See Declaration of the Pope against the usurpations of Napoleon, dated May 19, 1808; Annual Register, vol. l., p. 314.
[8] "Napoleon was of Italian origin, but he was born a Frenchman. It is difficult to comprehend for what purpose are those continual repetitions of his Italian origin. His partiality for Italy was natural enough, since he had conquered it, and this beautiful peninsula was a trophy of the national glory, of which Sir Walter Scott allows Napoleon to have been very jealous. I nevertheless doubt whether he had the intention of uniting Italy, and making Rome its capital. Many of my brother's actions contradict the supposition. I was near him one day when he received the report of some victories in Spain, and amongst

particular care which he always took of that nation, where whatever benefits his administrations conferred on the people, reached them both more profusely and more directly than in any other part of his empire. That swelling spirit entertained the proud, and, could it have been accomplished consistently with justice, the noble idea, of uniting the beautiful peninsula of Italy into one kingdom, of which Rome should once more be the capital. He also nourished the hope of clearing out the Eternal City from the ruins in which she was buried, of preserving her ancient monuments, and of restoring what was possible of her ancient splendour.[9] Such ideas as these, dearer to Napoleon, because involving a sort of fame which no conquest elsewhere could be attended with, must have had charms for a mind which constant success had palled to the ordinary enjoyment of victory; and no doubt the recollection that the existence of the Pope as a temporal prince was totally inconsistent with this fair dream of the restoration of Rome and Italy, determined his resolution to put an end to his power.

ROME

On the 2d February, 1809, General Miollis, with a body of French troops, took possession of Rome itself, disarmed and disbanded the Pope's guard of gentlemen, and sent his other soldiers to the north of Italy, promising them as a boon that they should be no longer under the command of a priest. The French cardinals, or those born in countries occupied by, or subjected to the French, were ordered to retire to the various lands of their birth, in order to prevent the Holy Father from finding support in the councils of the conclave. The proposal of his joining the Italian League, offensive

---

others, of one in which the Italian troops had greatly distinguished themselves. One of the persons who were with him exclaimed, at this news—that the Italians would show themselves worthy of obtaining their independence, and it was to be desired that the whole of Italy should be united into one national body. 'Heaven forbid it!' exclaimed Napoleon, with involuntary emotion, 'they would soon be masters of the Gauls.' Amongst all the calumnies heaped against him, there are none more unjust than those which attack his patriotism: he was essentially French, indeed, too exclusively so; for all excess is bad."—Louis Buonaparte, p. 62.

[9] "With regard to the removal of the monuments of antiquity, and to the works undertaken by my brother for their preservation, they were not merely projected; they were not only begun, but even far advanced, and many of them finished."—Louis Buonaparte, p. 63.

and defensive, was then again pressed on the Pope as the only means of reconciliation. He was also urged to cede some portion of the estates of the Church, as the price of securing the rest. On both points, Pius VII. was resolute; he would neither enter into an alliance which he conceived injurious to his conscience, nor consent to spoil the See of any part of its territories. This excellent man knew, that though the temporal strength of the Popedom appeared to be gone, every thing depended on the courage to be manifested by the Pope personally.

At length, on the 17th May, Napoleon published a decree,[10] in which, assuming the character of successor of Charlemagne, he set forth, 1st, That his august predecessor had granted Rome and certain other territories in feoff to the bishops of that city, but without parting with the sovereignty thereof. 2d, That the union of the religious and civil authority had proved the source of constant discord, of which many of the Pontiffs had availed themselves to extend their secular dominion, under pretext of maintaining their religious authority. 3d, That the temporal pretensions of the Pope were irreconcilable with the tranquillity and well-being of the nations whom Napoleon governed; and that all proposals which he had made on the subject had been rejected. Therefore it was declared by the decree, that the estates of the Church were reunited to the French empire. A few articles followed for the preservation of the classical monuments, for assigning to the Pope a free income of two millions of francs, and for declaring that the property and palace belonging to the See were free of all burdens or right of inspection. Lastly, The decree provided for the interior government of Rome by a Consultum, or Committee of Administrators, to whom was delegated the power of bringing the city under the Italian constitution. A proclamation of the Consultum, issued upon the 10th June, in consequence of the Imperial rescript, declared that the temporal dominion of Rome had passed to Napoleon, but she would still continue to be the residence of the visible Head of the Catholic Church.

---

[10] Published, May 17, at Vienna, and proclaimed in all the public squares, markets, &c., of that capital.

It had doubtless been thought possible to persuade the Pope to acquiesce in the annihilation of his secular power, as the Spanish Bourbons were compelled to ratify the usurpation of the Spanish crown, their inheritance. But Pius VII. had a mind of a firmer tenor. In the very night when the proclamation of the new functionaries finally divested him of his temporal principality, the Head of the Church assumed his spiritual weapons, and in the name of God, from whom he claimed authority, by missives drawn up by himself, and sealed with the seal of the Fisherman, declared Napoleon, Emperor of the French, with his adherents, favourers, and counsellors, to have incurred the solemn doom of excommunication, which he proceeded to launch against them accordingly.[11] To the honour of Pius VII. it must be added, that, different from the bulls which his predecessors used to send forth on similar occasions, the present sentence of excommunication was pronounced exclusively as a spiritual punishment, and contained a clause prohibiting all and any one from so construing its import, as to hold it authority for any attack on the person either of Napoleon or any of his adherents.

PIUS VII. BANISHED

The Emperor was highly incensed at the pertinacity and courage of the Pontiff in adopting so bold a measure, and determined on punishing him. In the night betwixt the 5th and 6th of July, the Quirinal palace, in which his Holiness resided, was forcibly entered by soldiers, and General Radet, presenting himself before the Holy Father, demanded that he should instantly execute a renunciation of the temporal estates belonging to the See of Rome. "I ought not—I will not—I cannot make such a cession," said Pius VII. "I have sworn to God to preserve inviolate the possessions of the Holy Church—I will not violate my oath." The general then informed his Holiness he must prepare to quit Rome. "This, then, is the gratitude of your Emperor," exclaimed the aged Pontiff, "for my great condescension towards the Gallican Church, and towards himself? Perhaps in that particular my conduct has been

---

[11] Annual Register, vol. li., p. 513; Botta, tom. iv., p. 394.

blameworthy in the eyes of God, and he is now desirous to punish me. I humbly stoop to his divine pleasure."

At three o'clock in the morning, the Pope was placed in a carriage, which one cardinal alone was permitted to share with him, and thus forcibly carried from his capital. As they arrived at the gate del Popolo, the general observed it was yet time for his Holiness to acquiesce in the transference of his secular estates. The Pontiff returned a strong negative, and the carriage proceeded.[12]

At Florence, Pius was separated from Cardinal Pacca, the only person of his court who had been hitherto permitted to attend him; and the attendance of General Radet was replaced by that of an officer of gendarmes. After a toilsome journey, partly performed in a litter, and sometimes by torch-light, the aged Pontiff was embarked for Alexandria, and transferred from thence to Mondovi, and then across the Alps to Grenoble.

But the strange sight of the Head of the Catholic Church travelling under a guard of gendarmes, with the secrecy and the vigilance used in transporting a state criminal, began to interest the people in the south of France. Crowds assembled to beseech the Holy Father's benediction, perhaps with more sincerity than when, as the guest of Buonaparte, he was received there with all the splendour the Imperial orders could command.

At the end of ten days, Grenoble no longer seemed a fitting place for his Holiness's residence, probably because he excited too much interest, and he was again transported to the Italian side of the Alps, and quartered at Savona. Here, it is said, he was treated with considerable harshness, and for a time at least confined to his apartment. The prefect of Savoy, M. de Chabrol, presented his Holiness with a letter from Napoleon, upbraiding him in strong terms for his wilful obstinacy, and threatening to convoke at Paris a Council of Bishops, with a view to his deposition. "I will lay his threats," said Pius VII., with the firmness which sustained him through his sufferings, "at the foot of the crucifix, and I leave with God the care of avenging my cause, since it has become his own."

---

[12] Botta, tom. iv., p. 395; Jomini, tom. iii., p. 242; Savary, tom. ii., part ii., p. 140.

The feelings of the Catholics were doubtless enhanced on this extraordinary occasion, by their belief in the sacred, and, it may be said, divine character, indissolubly united with the Head of the Church. But the world, Papist and Protestant, were alike sensible to the outrageous indecency with which an old man, a priest and a sovereign, so lately the friend and guest of Buonaparte, was treated, for no other reason that could be alleged, than to compel him to despoil himself of the territories of the Church, which he had sworn to transmit inviolate to his successors. Upon reflection, Napoleon seems to have become ashamed of the transaction, which he endeavoured to shift from his own shoulders, while in the same breath he apologized for it, as the act of the politician, not the individual.[13]

Regarded politically, never was any measure devised to which the interest of France and the Emperor was more diametrically opposed. Napoleon nominally gained the city of Rome, which, without this step, it was in his power to occupy at any time; but he lost the support, and incurred the mortal hatred of the Catholic clergy, and of all whom they could influence. He unravelled his own

---

[13] See Las Cases, vol. ii., pp. 12 and 13. He avowed that he himself would have refused, as a man and an officer, to mount guard on the Pope, "whose transportation into France," he added, "was done without my authority." Observing the surprise of Las Cases, he added, "that what he said was very true, together with other things which he would learn by and by. Besides," he proceeded, "you are to distinguish the deeds of a sovereign, who acts collectively, as different from those of an individual, who is restrained by no consideration that prevents him from following his own sentiments. Policy often permits, nay orders, a prince to do that which would be unpardonable in an individual." Of this denial and this apology, we shall only say, that the first seems very apocryphal, and the second would justify any crime which Machiavel or Achitophel could invent or recommend. Murat is the person whom the favourers of Napoleon are desirous to load with the violence committed on the Pope. But if Murat had dared to take so much upon himself, would it not have been as king of Naples? and by what warrant could he have transferred the Pontiff from place to place in the north of Italy, and even in France itself, the Emperor's dominions, and not his own? Besides, if Napoleon was, as has been stated, surprised, shocked, and incensed at the captivity of the Pope, why did he not instantly restore him to his liberty, with suitable apologies, and indemnification? His not doing so plainly shows, that if Murat and Radet had not express orders for what they did, they at least knew well it would be agreeable to the Emperor when done, and his acquiescence in their violence is a sufficient proof that they argued justly.—S.
"The Emperor knew nothing of the event until it had occurred; and then it was too late to disown it. He approved of what had been done, established the Pope at Savona, and afterwards united Rome to the French empire, thereby annulling the donation made of it by Charlemagne. This annexation was regretted by all, because every one desired peace."—Savary, tom. ii., part ii., p. 142

web, and destroyed, by this unjust and rash usurpation, all the merit which he had obtained by the re-establishment of the Gallican Church. Before this period he had said of the French clergy, and certainly had some right to use the language, "I have re-established them, I maintain them—they will surely continue attached to me." But in innovating upon their religious creed, in despoiling the Church, and maltreating its visible Head, he had cut the sinews of the league which he had formed betwixt the Church and his own government. It is easy to see the mistaken grounds on which he reckoned. Himself an egotist, Napoleon supposed, that when he had ascertained and secured to any man, or body of men, their own direct advantage in the system which he desired should be adopted, the parties interested were debarred from objecting to any innovations which he might afterwards introduce into that system, providing their own interest was not affected. The priests and sincere Catholics of France, on the other hand, thought, and in conscience could not think otherwise, that the Concordat engaged the Emperor to the preservation of the Catholic Church, as, on the other hand, it engaged them to fealty towards Napoleon. When, therefore, by his unprovoked aggression against the Head of the Church, he had incurred the spiritual censure of excommunication, they held, by consequence, that all their engagements to him were dissolved by his own act.

PIUS THE SEVENTH

The natural feelings of mankind acted also against the Emperor. The Pope, residing at Rome in the possession of temporal power and worldly splendour, was a far less interesting object to a devout imagination, than an old man hurried a prisoner from his capital, transported from place to place like a criminal, and at length detained in an obscure Italian town, under the control of the French police, and their instruments.[14]

---

[14] "In the eyes of Europe, Pius VII. was considered as an illustrious and affecting victim of greedy ambition. A prisoner at Savona, he was despoiled of all his external honours, and shut out from all communication with the cardinals, as well as deprived of all means of issuing bulls and assembling a council. What food for the *petite église*, for the turbulence of some priests, and for the hatred of some devotees! I immediately saw all these leavens

The consequences of this false step were almost as injurious as those which resulted from the unprincipled invasion of Spain. To place that kingdom under his more immediate control, Napoleon converted a whole nation of docile allies into irreconcilable enemies; and, for the vanity of adding to the empire of France the ancient capital of the world, he created a revolt in the opinion of the Catholics, which was in the long-run of the utmost prejudice to his authority. The bulls of the Pope, in spite of the attention of the police, and of the numerous arrests and severe punishments inflicted on those who dispersed them, obtained a general circulation; and, by affording a religious motive, enhanced and extended the disaffection to Napoleon, which, unavowed and obscure, began generally to arise against his person and government even in France, from the repeated draughts upon the conscription, the annihilation of commerce, and the other distressing consequences arising out of the measures of a government, which seemed only to exist in war.

While Buonaparte, at Schoenbrun, was thus disposing of Rome and its territories, and weighing in his bosom the alternative of dismembering Austria, or converting her into a friend, his life was exposed to one of those chances, to which despotic princes are peculiarly liable. It had often been predicted, that the dagger of some political or religious enthusiast, who might be willing to deposit his own life in gage for the success of his undertaking, was likely to put a period to Napoleon's extended plans of ambition. Fortunately, men like Felton[15] or Sandt[16] are rarely met with, for the powerful instinct of self-preservation is, in the common case, possessed of influence even over positive lunatics, as well as men of that melancholy and atrabilious temperament, whose dark determination partakes of insanity. Individuals, however, occur from time to time, who are willing to sacrifice their own existence, to accomplish the death of a private or public enemy.

---

would reproduce the secret associations we had with so much difficulty suppressed. In fact, Napoleon, by undoing all that he had hitherto done to calm and conciliate the minds of the people, disposed them in the end to withdraw themselves from his power, and even to ally themselves to his enemies, as soon as they had the courage to show themselves in force."—Fouché, tom. i., p. 335.

[15] The assassin of Villiers, Duke of Buckingham, in 1628.
[16] The political fanatic of Jena, who assassinated Kotzebue at Manheim, in 1819.

The life of Buonaparte at Schoenbrun was retired and obscure. He scarcely ever visited the city of Vienna;[17] and spent his time as if in the Tuileries, amid his generals, and a part of his ministers, who were obliged to attend him during his military expeditions. His most frequent appearance in public was when reviewing his troops. On one of these occasions [23d Sept.] while a body of the French guard was passing in review, a young man, well dressed, and of the middle rank, rushed suddenly forward, and attempted to plunge a long sharp knife, or poniard, in Napoleon's bosom. Berthier threw himself betwixt his master and the assassin, and Rapp made the latter prisoner. On his examination, the youth evinced the coolness of a fanatic. He was a native of Erfurt, son of a Lutheran clergyman, well educated, and of a decent condition in life. He avowed his purpose to have killed Napoleon, as called to the task by God, for the liberation of his country. No intrigue or correspondence with any party appeared to have prompted his unjustifiable purpose, nor did his behaviour or pulse testify any sign of insanity or mental alienation. He told Buonaparte, that he had so much respect for his talents, that if he could have obtained an audience of him, he would have commenced the conference by an exhortation to him to make peace; but if he could not succeed, he was determined to take his life. "What evil have I done you?" asked Napoleon. "To me personally, none; but you are the oppressor of my country, the oppressor of the world, and to have put you to death would have been the most glorious act a man of honour could do."

Stapps, for that was his name, was justly condemned to die; for no cause can justify assassination.[18] His death was marked by the same fanatical firmness which had accompanied his crime; and the adventure remained a warning, though a fruitless one, to Buonaparte, that any man who is indifferent to his own life, may

---

[17] "In the midst of the Emperor's occupations at Vienna, he was not unmindful of the memory of the Chevalier Bayard. The chapel of the village of Martinière, in which that hero had been christened, was repaired at great expense by his orders. He also directed that the heart of the chevalier should be removed to the said chapel with due ceremony; and an inscription, dictated by the Emperor himself, recording the praises of the knight 'without fear and without reproach,' was placed on the leaden box containing his heart."—Savary, tom. ii., part ii., p. 97.
[18] Las Cases, tom. ii., p. 12; Savary, tom. ii., part ii., p. 151; Rapp, p. 141.

endanger that of the most absolute sovereign upon earth, even when at the head of his military force.[19]

The negotiations for peace with Austria continued, notwithstanding the feeble state of the latter power, to be unusually protracted. The reason, at that time secret, became soon after publicly known.

THE ARCHDUKE CHARLES

Buonaparte's first intentions had been to dismember the empire, which he had found so obstinate and irreconcilable in its enmity, and, separating from the dominions of Austria either the kingdom of Hungary, or that of Bohemia, or both, to reduce the House of Hapsburg to the rank of a second-rate power in Europe. Napoleon himself affirmed, when in Saint Helena, that he was encouraged by one of the royal family (the Archduke Charles is indicated) to persist in his purpose, as the only means of avoiding future wars with Austria; and that the same prince was willing to have worn one of the crowns, thus to be torn from the brows of his brother Francis.[20] We can only say, that the avowals of Napoleon when in exile, like his bulletins when in power, seem so generally dictated by that which he wished to be believed, rather than by a frank adherence to truth, that we cannot hold his unsupported and inexplicit testimony as sufficient to impose the least stain on the noble, devoted, and patriotic character of the archduke, whose sword and talents had so often served his brother's cause, and whose life exhibits no indication of that meanness which would be implied in a wish to share the spoils of his country, or accept at the hands of the conqueror a tributary kingdom, reft from the dominions of his king and brother. Buonaparte himself paid the courage and devotion of the Austrian prince a flattering

---

[19] "The wretched young man was taken to Vienna, brought before a council of war, and executed on the 27th. He had taken no sustenance since the 24th, because, as he said, he had sufficient strength to walk to the place of execution. His last words were—'Liberty forever! Germany for ever! Death to the tyrant!' I delivered the report to Napoleon, who desired me to keep the knife that had been found upon the criminal. It is still in my possession."—Rapp, p. 147.
[20] Las Cases, tom. ii., p. 104.

compliment, when, in sending to him a decoration of the Legion of Honour, he chose that which was worn by the common soldier, as better suited to the determination and frankness of his character, than one of those richly ornamented, which were assigned to men of rank, who had perhaps never known, or only seen at some distance, the toils and dangers of battle.

The crisis, however, approached, which was to determine the fate of Austria. Buonaparte's favourite minister, Champagny, Duke of Cadore, had been for some time at Presburg, arranging with Metternich the extent of cession of territory by which Austria was to pay for her unfortunate assumption of hostilities. The definitive treaty of peace, when at length published, was found to contain the following articles:—I. Austria ceded, in favour of the Princes of the Confederation of the Rhine, Saltsburg, Berchtolsgaden, and a part of Upper Austria. II. To France directly, she ceded her only seaport of Trieste, the districts of Carniola, Friuli, the circle of Villach, and some part of Croatia and Dalmatia. These dominions tended to strengthen and enlarge the French province of Illyria, and to exclude Austria from the Adriatic, and the possibility of communication with Great Britain. A small lordship, called Razons, lying within the territories of the Grison League, was also relinquished. III. To the King of Saxony, in that character, Austria ceded some small part of Bohemia, and in the capacity of Duke of Warsaw, she gave up to him the city of Cracow, and the whole of Western Galicia. IV. Russia had a share, though a moderate one, in the spoils of Austria. She was to receive, in reward of her aid, though tardily and unwillingly tendered, a portion of Eastern Galicia, containing a population of four hundred thousand souls. But from this cession the town of Brody, a commercial place of consequence, was specially excepted; and it has been said that this exception made an unfavourable impression on the Emperor Alexander, which was not overbalanced by the satisfaction he received from the portion of spoil transferred to him.[21]

In his correspondence with the Russian Court, Napoleon expressed himself as having, from deference to Alexander's wishes, given Austria a more favourable peace than she had any reason to

---

[21] For a copy of the treaty, see Annual Register, vol. li., p. 791.

expect.[22] Indeed, Europe in general was surprised at the moderation of the terms; for though Austria, by her cessions at different points, yielded up a surface of 45,000 square miles, and a population of between three and four millions, yet the extremity in which she was placed seemed to render this a cheap ransom, as she still retained 180,000 square miles, and upwards, of territory, which, with a population of twenty-one millions, rendered her, after France and Russia, even yet the most formidable power on the continent. But her good angel had not slept. The House of Rodolph of Hapsburg had arisen, from small beginnings, to its immense power and magnitude, chiefly by matrimonial alliances,[23] and it was determined that, by another intermarriage of that Imperial House, with the most successful conqueror whom the world had ever seen, she should escape with comparative ease from the greatest extremity in which she had ever been placed. There is no doubt, also, that by secret articles of treaty, Napoleon, according to his maxim of making the conquered party sustain the expense of the war, exacted for that purpose heavy contributions from the Austrian Government.

He left Schoenbrun on the 16th October, the day after the definitive treaty of peace, which takes its name from that palace, had been signed there; and it is remarkable that no military caution was relaxed in the evacuation of the Austrian dominions by the French troops. They retreated by echelon, so as to be always in a position of mutual support, as if they had still been manœuvring in an enemy's country.

On the 14th November, Napoleon received at Paris the gratulations of the Senate, who too fondly complimented him on having acquired, by his triumphs, the palm of peace. That emblem, they said, should be placed high above his other laurels, upon a monument which should be dedicated by the gratitude of the French people. "To the Greatest of Heroes who never achieved victory but for the happiness of the world."

---

[22] Annual Register, vol. li., p. 790.
[23] The verses are well known,— "Bella gerant alii, tu, felix Austria, nube," &c.—S.

Chapter L

Change in Napoleon's Domestic Life—Causes which led to it—His anxiety for an Heir—A Son of his brother Louis is fixed upon, but dies in Childhood—Character and influence of Josephine—Strong mutual attachment betwixt her and Napoleon—Fouché opens to Josephine the Plan of a Divorce—her extreme Distress—On 5th December, Napoleon announces her Fate to Josephine—On 15th they are formally separated before the Imperial Council—Josephine retaining the rank of Empress for life—Espousals of Buonaparte and Maria Louisa of Austria take place at Vienna, 11th March, 1810.

CHANGE IN NAPOLEON'S DOMESTIC LIFE

There is perhaps no part of the varied life of the wonderful person of whom we treat, more deeply interesting, than the change which took place in his domestic establishment, shortly after the peace of Vienna. The main causes of that change are strongly rooted in human nature, but there were others which arose out of Napoleon's peculiar situation. The desire of posterity—of being represented long after our own earthly career is over, by those who derive their life and condition in society from us, is deeply rooted in our species. In all ages and countries, children are accounted a blessing, barrenness a misfortune at least, if not a curse. This desire of maintaining a posthumous connexion with the world, through the medium of our descendants, is increased, when there is property or rank to be inherited; and, however vain the thought, there are few to which men cling with such sincere fondness, as the prospect of bequeathing to their children's children the fortunes they have inherited from their fathers, or acquired by their own industry. There is kindness as well as some vanity in the feeling; for the attachment which we bear to the children whom we see and love, naturally flows downward to their lineage, whom we may never see. The love of distant posterity is in some degree the metaphysics of natural affection.

It was impossible that the founder of so vast an empire as that of Napoleon, could be insensible to a feeling which is so deeply grafted in our nature, as to influence the most petty proprietor of a house and a few acres—it is of a character to be felt in proportion to the extent of the inheritance; and so viewed, there never existed in the world before, and, it is devoutly to be hoped, will never be again permitted by Providence to arise, a power so extensive, so formidable as Napoleon's. Immense as it was, it had been, moreover, the work of his own talents; and, therefore, he must have anticipated, with the greater pain, that the system, perfected by so much labour and blood, should fall to pieces on the death of him by whom it had been erected, or that the reins of empire should be grasped after that event "by some unlineal hand,"

"No son of his succeeding."

The drop of gall, which the poet describes so naturally as embittering the cup of the Usurper of Scotland, infused, there is no doubt, its full bitterness into that of Napoleon.

JOSEPHINE

The sterility of the Empress Josephine was now rendered, by the course of nature, an irremediable evil, over which she mourned in hopeless distress; and conscious on what precarious circumstances the continuance of their union seemed now to depend, she gave way occasionally to fits of jealousy, less excited, according to Napoleon,[24] by personal attachment, than by suspicion

---

[24] "'A son by Josephine would have completed my happiness. It would have put an end to her jealousy, by which I was continually harassed. She despaired of having a child, and she in consequence looked forward with dread to the future.'"—Napoleon, *Las Cases*, tom. ii., p. 298.

that her influence over her husband's mind might be diminished, in case of his having offspring by some paramour.

She turned her thoughts to seek a remedy, and exerted her influence over her husband, to induce him to declare some one his successor, according to the unlimited powers vested in him by the Imperial constitution. In the selection, she naturally endeavoured to direct his choice towards his step-son, Eugene Beauharnois, her own son by her first marriage; but this did not meet Buonaparte's approbation. A child, the son of his brother Louis, by Hortense Beauharnois, appeared, during its brief existence, more likely to become the destined heir of this immense inheritance. Napoleon seemed attached to the boy; and when he manifested any spark of childish spirit, rejoiced in the sound of the drum, or showed pleasure in looking upon arms and the image of war, he is said to have exclaimed—"*There* is a child fit to succeed, perhaps to surpass me."[25]

The fixing his choice on an heir so intimately connected with herself, would have secured the influence of Josephine, as much as it could receive assurance from any thing save bearing her husband issue herself; but she was not long permitted to enjoy this prospect. The son of Louis and Hortense died of a disorder incident to childhood; and thus was broken, while yet a twig, the shoot, that, growing to maturity, might have been reckoned on as the stay of an empire. Napoleon showed the deepest grief, but Josephine sorrowed as one who had no hope.[26]

Yet, setting aside her having the misfortune to bear him no issue, the claims of Josephine on her husband's affections were as numerous as could be possessed by a wife. She had shared his more lowly fortunes, and, by her management and address during his absence in Egypt, had paved the way for the splendid success which he had attained on his return. She had also done much to render his government popular, by softening the sudden and fierce bursts of

---

[25] Fouché, tom. i., p. 324.
[26] "Never did I see Napoleon a prey to deeper and more concentrated grief; never did I see Josephine in more agonizing affliction. They appeared to find in it a mournful presentiment of a futurity without happiness and without hope."—Fouché, tom. i., p. 324.

passion to which his temperament induced him to give way. No one could understand, like Josephine, the peculiarities of her husband's temper—no one dared, like her, to encounter his displeasure, rather than not advise him for his better interest—no one could possess such opportunities of watching the fit season for intercession—and no one, it is allowed on all hands, made a more prudent, or a more beneficent use of the opportunities she enjoyed. The character of Buonaparte, vehement by temper, a soldier by education, and invested by Fortune with the most despotic power, required peculiarly the moderating influence of such a mind, which could interfere without intrusion, and remonstrate without offence.

To maintain this influence over her husband, Josephine made not only unreluctantly, but eagerly, the greatest personal sacrifices. In many of the rapid journeys which he performed, she was his companion. No obstacle of road or weather was permitted to interfere with her departure. However sudden the call, the Empress was ever ready; however untimely the hour, her carriage was in instant attendance. The influence which she maintained by the sacrifice of her personal comforts, was used for the advancement of her husband's best interests—the relief of those who were in distress, and the averting the consequences of hasty resolutions, formed in a moment of violence or irritation.

Besides her considerable talents, and her real beneficence of disposition, Josephine was possessed of other ties over the mind of her husband. The mutual passion which had subsisted between them for many years, if its warmth had subsided, seems to have left behind affectionate remembrances and mutual esteem. The grace and dignity with which Josephine played her part in the Imperial pageant, was calculated to gratify the pride of Napoleon, which might have been shocked at seeing the character of Empress discharged with less ease and adroitness; for her temper and manners enabled her, as one early accustomed to the society of persons of political influence, to conduct herself with singular dexterity in the intrigues of the splendid and busy court, where she filled so important a character. Lastly, it is certain that Buonaparte, who, like many of those that affect to despise superstition, had a reserve of it in his own bosom, believed that his fortunes were indissolubly connected with those of Josephine; and loving her as she deserved to be beloved, he held his union with her the more intimate, that there was attached to it, he thought, a spell affecting his own destinies, which had ever seemed most predominant when they had received the recent influence of Josephine's presence.

Notwithstanding all these mutual ties, it was evident to the politicians of the Tuileries, that whatever attachment and veneration for the Empress Napoleon might profess and feel, it was likely, in the long-run, to give way to the eager desire of a lineal succession, to which he might bequeath his splendid inheritance. As age advanced, every year weakened, though in an imperceptible degree, the influence of the Empress, and must have rendered more eager the desire of her husband to form a new alliance, while he was yet at a period of life enabling him to hope he might live to train to maturity the expected heir.

DIVORCE OF JOSEPHINE

Fouché, the minister of police, the boldest political intriguer of his time, discovered speedily to what point the Emperor must ultimately arrive, and seems to have meditated the ensuring his own power and continuance in favour, by taking the initiative in a measure in which, perhaps, Napoleon might be ashamed to break the ice in person.[27] Sounding artfully his master's disposition, Fouché was able to discover that the Emperor was struggling betwixt the supposed political advantages to be derived from a new matrimonial union on the one hand, and, on the other, love for his present consort, habits of society which particularly attached him to Josephine, and the species of superstition which we have already noticed. Having been able to conjecture the state of the Emperor's inclinations, the crafty counsellor determined to make Josephine

---

[27] "It would ill have become me to have kept within my own breast the suggestions of my foresight. In a confidential memoir, which I read to Napoleon himself, I represented to him the necessity of dissolving his marriage; of immediately forming, as Emperor, a new alliance more suitable and more happy; and of giving an heir to the throne on which Providence had placed him. Without declaring any thing positive, Napoleon let me perceive, that, in a political point of view, the dissolution of his marriage was already determined in his mind."—Fouché, tom. i., p. 326.

herself the medium of suggesting to Buonaparte the measure of her own divorce, and his second marriage, as a sacrifice necessary to consolidate the empire, and complete the happiness of the Emperor.

One evening at Fontainbleau, as the Empress was returning from mass, Fouché detained her in the embrasure of a window in the gallery, while, with an audacity almost incomprehensible, he explained, with all the alleviating qualifications his ingenuity could suggest, the necessity of a sacrifice, which he represented as equally sublime and inevitable. The tears gathered in Josephine's eyes—her colour came and went—her lips swelled—and the least which the counsellor had to fear, was his advice having brought on a severe nervous affection. She commanded her emotions, however, sufficiently to ask Fouché, with a faltering voice, whether he had any commission to hold such language to her. He replied in the negative, and said that he had only ventured on such an insinuation from his having predicted with certainty what must necessarily come to pass; and from his desire to turn her attention to what so nearly concerned her glory and happiness.[28]

In consequence of this interview, an impassioned and interesting scene is said to have taken place betwixt Buonaparte and his consort, in which he naturally and truly disavowed the communication of Fouché, and attempted, by every means in his power, to dispel her apprehensions. But he refused to dismiss Fouché, when she demanded it as the punishment due to that minister's audacity, in tampering with her feelings; and this refusal alone might have convinced Josephine, that though ancient habitual affection might for a time maintain its influence in the nuptial chamber, it must at length give way before the suggestions of political interest, which were sure to predominate in the cabinet. In fact, when the idea had once been started, the chief objection was removed, and Buonaparte, being spared the pain of directly communicating the unkind and ungrateful proposal to Josephine, had now only to afford her time to familiarise herself with the idea of a divorce, as that which political combinations rendered inevitable.

---

[28] Fouché, tom. i., p. 328.

The communication of Fouché was made before Napoleon undertook his operations in Spain; and by the time of the meeting at Erfurt, the divorce seems to have been a matter determined, since the subject of a match betwixt Buonaparte and one of the archduchesses, the possibility of which had been anticipated as far back as the treaty of Tilsit, was resumed, seriously treated of, and if not received with cordiality by the Imperial family of Russia, was equally far from being finally rejected. The reigning Empress, and the Empress Mother, were, however, opposed to it. The ostensible motive was, as we have elsewhere said, the difference of religion; but these high-minded princesses rejected the alliance chiefly on account of the personal character of the suitor. And although it must have been managed with the greatest secrecy imaginable, it seems probable that the idea of substituting an Archduchess of Austria for her whose hand was refused him, was started in the course of the treaty of Schoenbrun, and had its effects in providing lenient terms for the weaker party. Napoleon himself says, that he renounced his purpose of dismembering Austria when his marriage was fixed upon. But the conditions of peace were signed on the 15th of October, and therefore the motive which influenced Napoleon in granting them must have had existence previous to that period.

Yet the contrary is boldly asserted. The idea of the match is said to have been suggested by the Austrian government at a later period, upon understanding that difficulties had occurred in Napoleon's negotiation for a matrimonial alliance in the family of Alexander. Fouché ascribes the whole to the address of his own agent, the Comte de Narbonne, a Frenchman of the old school, witty, pliant, gay, well-mannered, and insinuating, who was ambassador at Vienna in the month of January 1810.[29]

But, whether the successor of Josephine were or were not already determined upon, the measures for separating this amiable and interesting woman from him whose fortunes she had assisted to raise, and to whose person she was so much attached, were in full and public operation soon after her husband's return from the campaign of Wagram. Upon the 3d of December, Buonaparte attended the solemn service of Te Deum for his victories. He was

---

[29] Mémoires de Fouché, tom. i., p. 348.

clad with unusual magnificence, wearing the Spanish costume, and displaying in his hat an enormous plume of feathers. The Kings of Saxony and Wirtemberg, who attended as his satellites on this occasion, were placed beside him in full uniform, and remained uncovered during the ceremony.

From the cathedral, Napoleon passed to the opening of the Legislative Body, and boasted, in the oration he addressed to them, of the victories which he had achieved, and the trophies which he had acquired; nay, he vaunted of his having reunited Tuscany to the empire—as if the spoiling the inoffensive and unresisting widow and orphan could ever be a legitimate subject of triumph. From the existing affairs of Spain, no direct reason for gratulation could be derived; but when Napoleon could no longer claim praise from things as they presently stood, he was profuse in his promises of a rapid change to the better, and spoke as a prophet when he ceased to be the reporter of agreeable facts. "When I," he said, "show myself on the other side of the Pyrenees, the terrified Leopard shall plunge into the ocean, to avoid shame, defeat, and destruction. The triumph of my arms shall be that of the Genius of Good over the Genius of Evil, of moderation, order, and morals, over civil war, anarchy, and the malevolent passions." With such fair colouring will ambition and injustice attempt to screen their purposes. A poetical reply from M. de Fontanes assured the Emperor, that whatever was connected with him must arise to grandeur, whatever was subjected to any other influence was threatened with a speedy fall. "It was therefore necessary," he continued, "to submit to your ascendency, whose counsels are at once recommended by heroism and by policy." To this speech Buonaparte made a rejoinder, in which, resuming the well-worn themes of his own praises, he alluded to the obstacles which he had surmounted, and concluded, "I and my family will always know how to sacrifice our most tender affections to the interests and welfare of the Great Nation." These concluding words, the meaning of which was already guessed by all who belonged to the Court, were soon no riddle to the public in general.

Two days afterwards, Napoleon made Josephine acquainted with the cruel certainty, that the separation was ultimately determined upon. But not the many months which had passed since the subject was first touched upon by Fouché—not the conviction which she must have long since received from various quarters, that the measure was unalterably resolved upon, could strengthen her to hear the tongue of her beloved husband announce what was in fact, though not in name, a sentence of repudiation. She fell into a long and profound swoon. Napoleon was much affected, but his resolution was taken, and could not be altered. The preparations for the separation went on without delay.

On the 15th December, just ten days after the official communication of her fate had been given to the Empress, Napoleon and Josephine appeared in presence of the Arch-Chancellor, the family of Napoleon, the principal officers of state—in a word, the full Imperial Council. In this assembly, Napoleon stated the deep national interest which required that he should have successors of his own body, the heirs of his love for his people, to occupy the throne on which Providence had placed him. He informed them, that he had for several years renounced the hope of having children by his well-beloved Empress Josephine; and that therefore he had resolved to subject the feelings of his heart to the good of the state, and desire the dissolution of their marriage. He was, he said, but forty years old, and might well hope to live to train up such children as Providence might send him, in his own sentiments and arts of government. Again he dwelt on the truth and tenderness of his beloved spouse, his partner during fifteen years of happy union. Crowned as she had been by his own hand, he desired she should retain the rank of Empress during her life.

Josephine arose, and with a faltering voice, and eyes suffused with tears, expressed in a few words[30] sentiments similar to those of

---

[30] "By the permission of our dear and august consort, I ought to declare, that not perceiving any hope of having children, which may fulfil the wants of his policy and the interests of France, I am pleased to give him the greatest proof of attachment and devotion which has ever been given on earth. I possess all from his bounty; it was his hand which crowned me; and from the height of this throne I have received nothing but proofs of affection and love from the French people. I think I prove myself grateful in consenting to the dissolution of a marriage which heretofore was an obstacle to the welfare of France, which deprived it of the happiness of being one day governed by the descendant of a great man, evidently raised up by Providence, to efface the evils of a terrible revolution, and to re-establish the altar, the throne, and social order. But the dissolution of my marriage will in no degree change the sentiments of my heart; the Emperor will ever have in me his best

her husband. The Imperial pair then demanded from the Arch-Chancellor a written instrument in evidence of their mutual desire of separation; and it was granted accordingly, in all due form, with the authority of the Council.

The Senate were next assembled; and on the 16th December, pronounced a consultum, or decree, authorising the separation of the Emperor and Empress, and assuring to Josephine a dowry of two millions of francs, and the rank of Empress during her life. Addresses were voted to both the Imperial parties, in which all possible changes were rung on the duty of subjecting our dearest affections to the public good; and the conduct of Buonaparte in exchanging his old consort for a young one, was proclaimed a sacrifice, for which the eternal love of the French people could alone console his heart.

The union of Napoleon and Josephine being thus abrogated by the supreme civil power, it only remained to procure the intervention of the spiritual authorities. The Arch-Chancellor, duly authorised by the Imperial pair, presented a request for this purpose to the Diocesan of the Officiality, or ecclesiastical court of Paris, who did not hesitate to declare the marriage dissolved, assigning, however, no reason for such their doom. They announced it, indeed, as conforming to the decrees of councils, and the usages of the Gallican Church—a proposition which would have cost the learned and reverend officials much trouble, if they had been required to make it good either by argument or authority.

When this sentence had finally dissolved their union, the Emperor retired to St. Cloud, where he lived in seclusion for some days. Josephine, on her part, took up her residence in the beautiful villa of Malmaison, near St. Germains. Here she principally dwelt for the remaining years of her life, which were just prolonged to see the first fall of her husband; an event which might have been averted had he been content to listen more frequently to her lessons of moderation. Her life was chiefly spent in cultivating the fine arts, of

---

friend. I know how much this act, demanded by policy, and by interest so great, has chilled his heart; but both of us exult in the sacrifice which we make for the good of the country."—*Moniteur*, Dec. 17, 1809; *Annual Register*, vol. li., p. 808.

which she collected some beautiful specimens, and in pursuing the science of botany; but especially in the almost daily practice of acts of benevolence and charity, of which the English *détenus*, of whom there were several at St. Germains, frequently shared the benefit.[31] Napoleon visited her very frequently, and always treated her with the respect to which she was entitled. He added also to her dowry a third million of francs, that she might feel no inconvenience from the habits of expense to which it was her foible to be addicted.

MARIA LOUISA

This important state measure was no sooner completed, than the Great Council was summoned, on the 1st February, to assist the Emperor in the selection of a new spouse. They were given to understand, that a match with a Grand Duchess of Russia had been proposed, but was likely to be embarrassed by disputes concerning religion. A daughter of the King of Saxony was also mentioned, but it was easily indicated to the Council that their choice ought to fall upon a Princess of the House of Austria. At the conclusion of the meeting, Eugene, the son of the repudiated Josephine, was commissioned by the Council to propose to the Austrian ambassador a match between Napoleon and the Archduchess Maria Louisa.[32] Prince Schwartzenberg had his instructions on the subject; so that the match was proposed, discussed, and decided in the Council, and afterwards adjusted between plenipotentiaries on either side, in the space of twenty-four hours.[33] The espousals of Napoleon and Maria Louisa were celebrated at Vienna, 11th March, 1810. The person of Buonaparte was represented by his favourite Berthier,

---

[31] "In quitting the court, Josephine drew the hearts of all its votaries after her: she was endeared to all by a kindness of disposition which was without a parallel. She never did the smallest injury to any one in the days of her power: her very enemies found in her a protectress: not a day of her life but what she asked a favour for some person, oftentimes unknown to her, but whom she found to be deserving of her protection. Regardless of self, her whole time was engaged in attending to the wants of others."—Savary, tom. ii., part ii., p. 177.
[32] Maria Louisa, the eldest daughter of the Emperor of Austria and Maria Theresa of Naples, was born the 12th December, 1791. Her stature was sufficiently majestic, her complexion fresh and blooming, her eyes blue and animated, her hair light, and her hand and foot so beautiful, that they might have served as models for the sculptor.
[33] Fouché, tom. i., p. 350.

while the Archduke Charles assisted at the ceremony, in the name of the Emperor Francis. A few days afterwards, the youthful bride, accompanied by the Queen of Naples, proceeded towards France.

With good taste, Napoleon dispensed with the ceremonies used in the reception of Marie Antoinette, whose marriage with Louis XVI., though never named or alluded to, was in other respects the model of the present solemnity. Near Soissons, a single horseman, no way distinguished by dress, rode past the carriage in which the young Empress was seated, and had the boldness to return, as if to reconnoitre more closely. The carriage stopped, the door was opened, and Napoleon, breaking through all the tediousness of ceremony, introduced himself to his bride, and came with her to Soissons.[34] The marriage ceremony was performed at St. Cloud by Buonaparte's uncle, the Cardinal Fesch. The most splendid rejoicings, illuminations, concerts, festivals, took place upon this important occasion. But a great calamity occurred, which threw a shade over these demonstrations of joy. Prince Schwartzenberg had given a distinguished ball on the occasion, when unhappily the dancing-room, which was temporary, and erected in the garden, caught fire. No efforts could stop the progress of the flames, in which several persons perished, and amongst them even the sister of Prince Schwartzenberg. This tragic circumstance struck a damp on the public mind, and was considered as a bad omen, especially when it was remembered that the marriage of Louis XVI. with a former Princess of Austria had been signalized by a similar disaster.[35]

As a domestic occurrence, nothing could more contribute to Buonaparte's happiness than his union with Maria Louisa. He was wont to compare her with Josephine, by giving the latter all the advantages of art and grace; the former the charms of simple modesty and innocence. His former Empress used every art to support or enhance her personal charms; but with so much prudence and mystery, that the secret cares of her toilette could never be traced—her successor trusted for the power of pleasing, to

---

[34] "She had always been given to understand that Berthier, who had married her by proxy at Vienna, in person and age exactly resembled the Emperor: she, however, signified that she observed a very pleasing difference between them."—Las Cases, tom. i., p. 312.

[35] "The most unfortunate presages were drawn from it; Napoleon himself was struck with it."—Fouché, tom. i., p. 355.

youth and nature. Josephine mismanaged her revenue, and incurred debt without scruple. Maria Louisa lived within her income, or if she desired any indulgence beyond it, which was rarely the case, she asked it as a favour of Napoleon. Josephine, accustomed to political intrigue, loved to manage, to influence, and to guide her husband; Maria Louisa desired only to please and to obey him. Both were excellent women, of great sweetness of temper, and fondly attached to Napoleon.[36] In the difference between these distinguished persons, we can easily discriminate the leading features of the Parisian, and of the simple German beauty; but it is certainly singular that the artificial character should have belonged to the daughter of the West Indian planter; that marked by nature and simplicity, to a princess of the proudest court in Europe.

Buonaparte, whose domestic conduct was generally praiseworthy, behaved with the utmost kindness to his princely bride. He observed, however, the strictest etiquette, and required it from the Empress. If it happened, for example, as was often the case, that he was prevented from attending at the hour when dinner was placed on the table, he was displeased if, in the interim of his absence, which was often prolonged, she either took a book or had recourse to any female occupation—if, in short, he did not find her in the attitude of waiting for the signal to take her place at table. Perhaps a sense of his inferior birth made Napoleon more tenacious of this species of form, as what he could not afford to relinquish. On the other hand, Maria Louisa is said to have expressed her surprise at her husband's dispensing with the use of arms and attendance of guards, and at his moving about with the freedom of an individual;[37] although this could be no great novelty to a member of the Imperial Family of Austria, most of whom, and especially the Emperor Francis, are in the habit of mixing familiarly with the people of Vienna, at public places, and in the public walks.

As it influenced his political fate, Buonaparte has registered his complaint, that the Austrian match was a precipice covered with flowers, which he was rashly induced to approach by the hopes of

---

[36] Las Cases, tom. i., p. 310.
[37] Voice from St. Helena, vol. ii., p. 225.

domestic happiness.[38] But if this proved so, it was the fault of Napoleon himself; his subjects and his allies augured very differently of its consequences, and to himself alone it was owing that these auguries were disappointed. It was to have been expected, that a connexion formed with the most ancient Imperial Family in Christendom, might have induced Buonaparte to adopt some of those sentiments of moderation which regard rather the stability than the increase of power. It constituted a point at which he might pause. It might have been thought that, satiated with success, and wearied with enterprise, he would have busied himself more in consolidating the power which he desired to transmit to his expected posterity, than in aiming at rendering his grandeur more invidious and more precarious, by further schemes of ambition. Even the charms which this union added to his domestic life, might, it was hoped, bring on a taste for repose, which, could it have influenced that fiery imagination and frame of iron, might have been of such essential advantage to Europe.

Napoleon knew what was expected, and endeavoured to vindicate himself beforehand for the disappointment which he foresaw was about to ensue. "The good citizens rejoice sincerely at my marriage, monsieur?" he said to Decrés, his minister.—"Very much, Sire."—"I understand they think the Lion will go to slumber, ha?"—"To speak the truth, Sire, they entertain some hopes of that nature." Napoleon paused an instant, and then replied, "They are mistaken; yet it is not the fault of the Lion; slumber would be as agreeable to him as to others. But see you not that while I have the air of being constantly the attacking party, I am, in fact, acting only on the defensive?" This sophism, by which Napoleon endeavoured to persuade all men, that his constant wars arose, not from choice, but out of the necessity of his situation, will be best discussed hereafter.

In the meantime, we may only notice, that the Emperor Alexander judged most accurately of the consequences of the

---

[38] "Austria had become a portion of my family; and yet my marriage ruined me. If I had not thought myself safe, and protected by this alliance, I should have delayed the insurrection of Poland: I should have waited until Spain was subdued and tranquil. I set foot on an abyss, concealed by a bed of flowers!"—Napoleon, *Las Cases*, tom. ii., p. 105.

Austrian match, when he said, on receiving the news, "Then the next task will be, to drive me back to my forests;" so certain he was that Napoleon would make his intimate alliance with the Emperor Francis, the means of an attack upon Russia; and so acute was he in seeing the germs of future and more desperate wars, in a union from which more shortsighted politicians were looking for the blessings of peace.

Chapter LI

Almost all the foreign French Settlements fall into the hands of the British—French Squadron destroyed at the Isle of Aix, by Lord Cochrane—and at the Isle of Rosas, by Lord Collingwood—Return to the Proceedings in Spain—Soult takes Oporto—Attacked and Defeated by Sir Arthur Wellesley—Ferrol and Corunna retaken by the Patriots—Battle of Talavera, gained by Sir Arthur Wellesley—Created Lord Wellington—The French Armies take many towns and strong Places—Supreme Junta retreat to Cadiz—The Guerilla System—Growing disappointment of Buonaparte—His immense exertions—Battle of Busaco—Lord Wellington's famous Retreat on Torres Vedras.

Notwithstanding the credit which Napoleon had acquired, by dictating to the House of Austria the triumphant treaty of Schoenbrun, and also by allying himself with that ancient Imperial House, which had, on different occasions, showed towards him the signs of persevering enmity, this period of his history did not pass without his experiencing several reverses of fortune. The few foreign settlements which hitherto remained united to France, were now successively taken by the British. Cayenne, Martinico, Senegal, and Saint Domingo, were conquered and occupied in the West Indies; while Lord Collingwood, with troops furnished from Sicily, occupied the islands of Cephalonia, Zante, Ithaca, and Cerigo.

A French squadron of men-of-war being blockaded in the roadstead of the isle of Aix, the determined valour of Lord Cochrane was employed for their destruction. Fire-ships were sent against the French vessels, and though the execution was less complete than had been expected, owing to some misunderstanding between Lord Cochrane and Admiral Gambier, who commanded in chief, yet the greater part of the French ships were burnt, or driven ashore and destroyed. Lord Collingwood also destroyed an important French convoy, with the armed vessels who protected it, in the isle of Rosas. Every thing announced that England retained the full command of what has been termed her native element; while the transactions in Spain showed, that, under a general who understood at once how to gain victories, and profit by them when obtained, the land forces of Britain were no less formidable than her navy. This subject draws our attention to the affairs of the Peninsula, where it might be truly said "the land was burning."

The evacuation of Corunna by the army of the late Sir John Moore, and their return to England, which their disastrous condition rendered indispensable, left Soult in seeming possession of Galicia, Ferrol and Corunna having both surrendered to him. But the strength of the Spanish cause did not lie in walls and ramparts, but in the indomitable courage of the gallant patriots. The Galicians continued to distinguish themselves by a war of posts, in which the invaders could claim small advantages; and when Soult determined to enter Portugal, he was obliged to leave Ney, with considerable forces, to secure his communication with Spain.

SOULT OCCUPIES OPORTO

Soult's expedition began prosperously, though it was doomed to terminate very differently. He defeated General Romana, and compelled him to retreat to Senabria. The frontier town of Chaves was taken by Soult, after some resistance, and he forced his way towards Oporto. But no sooner had the main body of Soult's army left Chaves, than, in spite of the efforts of the garrison, the place was relieved by an insurrectionary army of Portuguese, under General Silviera. The invader, neglecting these operations in his rear, continued to advance upon Oporto, carried that fine city by storm, after a desultory defence of three days, and suffered his troops to commit the greatest cruelties, both on the soldiers and unarmed citizens.[39]

---

[39] "It was in vain that Soult strove with all his power to stop the slaughter. The frightful scene of rape, pillage, and murder, closed not for many hours, and what with those who fell

But when Marshal Soult had succeeded thus far, his situation became embarrassing. The Galicians, recovering their full energy, had retaken Vigo and other places; and Silviera, advancing from Chaves to the bridge of Amarante, interposed betwixt the French general and Galicia, and placed himself in communication with the Spaniards.

While Soult was thus cooped up in Oporto, the English Ministry, undaunted by the failure of their late expedition, resolved to continue the defence of the Portuguese, and to enter into still closer alliance with the Supreme Junta of Spain. Consulting their own opinion and the public voice, all consideration of rank and long service was laid aside, in order to confer the command of the troops which were to be sent to the continent, on Sir Arthur Wellesley, whose conduct in the battle of Vimeiro, and the subsequent explanations which he afforded at the Court of Inquiry, had taught all Britain to believe, that if Portugal could be defended at all, it must be by the victor of that day. He was scarce landed at Lisbon [April 22] ere he fully justified the good opinion of his countrymen. He crossed the Douro at different points with a celerity for which the French were unprepared, and, after a brilliant action under the walls of Oporto, compelled Soult to evacuate that city, and commence a retreat, so disastrous as to resemble that of Sir John Moore. In this retrograde movement, the French left behind them cannon, equipments, baggage—all that can strengthen an army, and enable it to act as such; and, after all these sacrifices, their leader could hardly make his escape into Galicia, with scarce three-fourths of his army remaining, where he found great difficulty in remodelling his forces. Ney, whom he had left as governor of that province, was hard pressed by the patriots, who defeated the French in several battles, and eventually retook the towns of Ferrol and Corunna.

Sir Arthur Wellesley was prevented from completing Soult's defeat by pursuing him into Galicia, because, after the Spaniards had sustained the severe defeat of Tudela, the French had penetrated

---

in battle, those who were drowned, and those sacrificed to revenge, it is said that 10,000 Portuguese died on that unhappy day! The loss of the French did not exceed 500 men."—Napier, vol. ii., p. 207. See also Southey, vol. iii., p. 249.

into Andalusia in great strength, where they were only opposed by an ill-equipped and dispirited army of 40,000 men, under the rash and ill-starred General Cuesta. It was evident, that Marshal Victor, who commanded in Andalusia, had it in his power to have detached a considerable part of his force on Lisbon, supposing that city had been uncovered, by Sir Arthur Wellesley's carrying his forces in pursuit of Soult. This was to be prevented, if possible. The English general formed the magnificent plan, for which Napoleon's departure to the Austrian campaign afforded a favourable opportunity, of marching into Andalusia, uniting the British forces with those of Cuesta, and acting against the invaders with such vigour, as might at once check their progress in the South, and endanger their occupation of Madrid. Unhappily an ill-timed jealousy seems to have taken possession of Cuesta, which manifested itself in every possible shape, in which frowardness, and a petty obstinacy of spirit, could be exhibited. To no one of the combined plans, submitted to him by the English general, would he give assent or effectual concurrence; and when a favourable opportunity arrived of attacking Victor, before he was united with the forces which Joseph Buonaparte and Sebastiani were bringing from Madrid to his support, Cuesta alleged he would not give battle on a Sunday.[40]

BATTLE OF TALAVERA

The golden opportunity was thus lost; and when the allies were obliged to receive battle instead of giving it, on the 28th July, 1809, it was without the advantages which the former occasion held out. Yet the famous battle of Talavera de la Reina, in which the French were completely defeated, was, under these unfavourable circumstances, achieved by Sir Arthur Wellesley. The event of this action, in which the British forces had been able to defend themselves against double their own number, with but little assistance from the Spanish army, became, owing to the continued wilfulness of Cuesta, very different from what such a victory ought

---

[40] Southey, vol. iv., p. 10. The reader is requested to compare this account with that given by Lord Burghersh, in his "Memoir on the Early Campaigns of Wellington," p. 77—where the details are somewhat differently represented—Ed. (1842.)

to have produced. The French troops, assembling from every point, left Sir Arthur no other mode of assuring the safety of his army, than by a retreat on Portugal; and for want of means of transport, which the Spanish general ought to have furnished, more than fifteen hundred of the wounded were left to the mercy of the French.[41] They were treated as became a courteous enemy, yet the incident afforded a fine pretext to contest the victory, which the French had resigned by flying from the field.

The assertions of the bulletins in the *Moniteur* could not deceive men on the true state of affairs. The Spanish Junta were sensible of the services rendered by the English general, and, somewhat of the latest, removed Cuesta from the command, to manifest their disapprobation of his unaccountable conduct. At home, Sir Arthur Wellesley was promoted to the peerage, by the title of Lord Wellington, who was destined to ascend, with the universal applause of the nation, as high as our constitution will permit. But Buonaparte paid the greatest compliment to the victor of Talavera, by the splenetic resentment with which he was filled by the news. He had received the tidings by his private intelligence, before the officer arrived with the regular despatches. He was extremely ill received by the Emperor; and, as if the messengers had been responsible for the tidings they brought, a second officer, with a duplicate of the same intelligence, was treated still more harshly, and for a time put under arrest. This explosion of passion could not be occasioned by the consequences of the action, for the experienced eye of Napoleon must have discriminated the circumstances by which the effects of victory were in a great measure lost to the allied armies; but he saw in the battle of Talavera, an assurance given to both English and Spanish soldiers, that, duly resisted, the French would fly from them. He foresaw, also, that the British Government would be tempted to maintain the contest on the continent, and that the Spaniards would be encouraged to persevere in resistance. He foresaw, in short, that war of six desperate and bloody campaigns, which did not terminate till the battle of Tholouse, in 1814.

---

[41] "Victor sent soldiers to every house, with orders to the inhabitants immediately to receive and accommodate the wounded of the two nations, who were lodged together, one English and one Frenchman; and he expressly directed that the Englishman should always be served first."—Southey, vol. iv., p. 49.

But it needed no anticipation to fill Napoleon's mind with anxiety on the subject of Spain. It is true, fortune seemed every where to smile on his arms. Zaragossa, once more besieged, maintained its former name, but without the former brilliant result. After a defence as distinguished as in the first siege, the brave garrison and citizens, deprived of means of defence, and desperate of all hope of relief, had been compelled to surrender some months before.[42]

Gerona, Tarragona, Tortosa, though still vigorously defended, were so powerfully invested, that it seemed as if Catalonia, the most warlike of the Spanish departments, was effectually subdued; and, accordingly, these fortresses also were afterwards obliged to capitulate.

Andalusia, the richest province which sustained the patriot cause, certainly was conquered, in consequence of a total defeat encountered by the Spanish grand army, under Areizaga, at Ocana, November 1809, after the English troops had retreated to the Portuguese frontier.[43] Joseph Buonaparte, whose road was cleared by this last success, entered Cordoba in triumph upon the 17th of January, 1810, and proud Seville itself upon the 1st of February following. Yet the chief prize of victory had not yet been gained. The Supreme Junta had effected their retreat to Cadiz, which city, situated in an island, and cut off from the mainland, on one side by a canal, and on the other three by the ocean, was capable of the most strenuous defence.

Cadiz contained a garrison of 20,000 men, English, Spanish, and Portuguese, under the command of General Graham, a distinguished officer, whose merits, like those of Buonaparte, had been first distinguished at the siege of Toulon. Marshal Soult, as first in command in Spain, disposed himself to form the siege of this city, the capture of which would have been almost the death-knell to the cause of the patriots.

---

[42] Southey, vol. iii., p. 168.
[43] Southey, vol. iv., p. 159.

But although these important successes read well in the *Moniteur*, yet such was the indomitable character of the Spaniards, which Napoleon had contrived fully to awaken, that misfortunes, which would have crushed all hope in any other people, seemed to them only an incentive to further and more desperate resistance. When they talked of the state of their country, they expressed no dismay at their present adverse circumstances. It had cost their ancestors, they said, two centuries to rid themselves of the Moors; they had no doubt that in a shorter time they should free themselves of the yoke of France; but they must reckon on time and opportunity, as well as valour. The events of the war in many respects gave credit to their hopes. The Spaniards, often found weak where they thought themselves strongest, proved sometimes most powerful, where, to all human appearance, they seemed weakest. While they lost Andalusia, believed to be so defensible, the mountainous province of Galicia, through which the French had so lately marched triumphantly in pursuit of the British, taking in their progress the important maritime towns of Corunna and Ferrol, was wrenched from the conquerors by the exertions of Romana, assisted by the warlike natives of the country, and at the head of an undisciplined and ill-equipped army.

CATALONIA—THE GUERILLAS

In Catalonia, too, the French had hardly time to accomplish the conquest of towns and fortresses to which we have alluded, when they found themselves checked, baffled, and sometimes defeated, by the Catalans, under Lacy, O'Donnell, and D'Eroles, who maintained the patriotic cause at the head of those energetic marksmen, the Somatenes, or Miquelets. Nay, while the French were extending their seeming conquests to the Mediterranean Sea, and thundering at the gates of Cadiz, so little were they in peaceful possession of Navarre, and the other provinces adjoining to France, that not an officer with despatches could pass from Burgos to Bayonne without a powerful escort, and bands of Spaniards even showed themselves on the French frontier, and passed it for the purpose of skirmishing and raising contributions. Such being the case on the frontiers nearest to France, it may be well supposed, that the midland provinces were not more subordinate. In fact, through the whole Peninsula the French held no influence whatever that was not inspired by the force of the bayonet and sabre; and where these could not operate, the country was in universal insurrection.

The basis of this extensive and persevering resistance was laid in the general system of Guerilla, or partisan warfare, to which the genius of the Spanish people, and the character of their country, are peculiarly fitted, and which offered a resistance to the invaders more formidable by far than that of regular armies, because less tangible, and less susceptible of being crushed in general actions. It was with the defenders of Spain, as with the guardian of the enchanted castle in the Italian romance. An armed warrior first encountered the champion who attempted the adventure, and when he had fallen under the sword of the assailant, the post which he had occupied appeared manned by a body of pigmies, small in size, but so numerous and so enterprising as to annoy the knight-errant far more than the gigantic force of his first adversary. The qualities of a partisan, or irregular soldier, are inherent in the national character of the Spaniard. Calm, temperate, capable of much fatigue, and veiling under a cold demeanour an ardent and fiery character, they are qualified to wait for opportunities of advantage, and are not easily discouraged by difficulty or defeat. Good marksmen in general, and handling the lance, sword, and dagger with address, they are formidable in an ambush, and not less so in a close mêlée, where men fight hand to hand, more as nature dictates than according to the rules of war. The obstinacy of the Castilian character also, had its advantages in this peculiar state of warfare. Neither promises nor threats made any impression on them; and the severities executed in fulfilment of menaces, only inflamed the spirit of hostility by that of private revenge, to which the Spaniard is far more accessible than either to the voice of caution or persuasion.

Neither were the officers less qualified for the task than the men. The command of a guerilla was of a character not to be desired by any who did not find himself equal to, and in some measure called upon to accept, the dangerous pre-eminence. There were few Spanish officers possessed of the scientific knowledge of war, and of course few adequate to lead armies into the field; but the properties necessary for a guerilla leader are imprinted in the human mind, and ready for exercise whenever they are required. These leaders were, as it chanced: some of them men of high birth and military education; some had been smugglers or peasants, or had practised other professions; as was discovered from their noms-de-guerre, as the Curate, the Doctor, the Shepherd, and so forth.[44] Many of their names will be long associated with the recollection of their gallant actions; and those of others, as of Mina and the Empecinado,[45] will, at the same time, remind us of the gross ingratitude with which their heroic efforts have been rewarded.

These daring men possessed the most perfect knowledge of the passes, strengths, woods, mountains, and wildernesses, of the provinces in which they warred; and the exact intelligence which they obtained from the peasantry, made them intimately acquainted with the motions of the enemy. Was too weak a French detachment moved, it ran the risk of being cut off; was the garrison too feeble at the place which it left, the fort was taken. The slightest as well as the most important objects, met the attention of the guerillas; a courier could not move without a large escort, nor could the intrusive King take the amusement of hunting, however near to his capital, unless, like Earl Percy in the ballad, attended by a guard of fifteen hundred men. The Juramentados, those Spaniards that is, who had sworn allegiance to King Joseph, were of course closely watched by the guerillas, and if they rendered themselves inconveniently or obnoxiously active in the cause they had espoused, were often kidnapped and punished as traitors; examples which rendered submission to, or active co-operation with the French, at least as imprudent as boldly opposing the invaders.

---

[44] Napier, vol. ii., p. 349; Southey, vol. iii., p. 511.
[45] "Various explanations have been offered of this name. One account says, that upon finding his family murdered by the French, Juan Martin Diaz smeared his face with pitch and made a solemn vow of vengeance. Another, that he was so called because of his swarthy complexion. But in the account of his life it is said, that all the inhabitants of Castrillo de Duero, where he was born, have this nickname indiscriminately given them by their neighbours, in consequence of a black mud, called *pecina*, deposited by a little stream which runs through the place; and the appellation became peculiar to him from his celebrity."—Southey, vol. iii., p. 511.

THE GUERILLAS

The numbers of the guerillas varied at different times, as the chiefs rose or declined in reputation, and as they possessed the means of maintaining their followers. Some led small flying armies of two thousand and upwards. Others, or the same chiefs under a reverse of fortune, had only ten or twenty followers. The French often attempted to surprise and destroy the parties by which they suffered most, and for that purpose detached moveable columns from different points, to assemble on the rendezvous of the guerilla. But, notwithstanding all their activity and dexterity on such expeditions, they rarely succeeded in catching their enemy at unawares; or if it so happened, the individuals composing the band broke up, and dispersed by ways only known to themselves; and when the French officers accounted them totally annihilated, they were again assembled on another point, exercising a partisan war on the rear, and upon the communications, of those who lately expected to have them at their mercy. Thus invisible when they were sought for, the guerillas seemed every where present when damage could be done to the invaders. To chase them was to pursue the wind, and to circumvent them was to detain water with a sieve.

Soult had recourse to severity to intimidate these desultory but most annoying enemies, by publishing a proclamation [May 9] threatening to treat the members of the guerillas, not as regular soldiers, but as banditti taken in the fact, and thus execute such of them as chanced to be made prisoners. The chiefs, in reply to this proclamation, published a royal decree, as they termed it, declaring that each Spaniard was, by the necessity of the times, a soldier, and that he was entitled to all military privileges when taken with arms in his hands. They therefore announced, that having ample means of retaliation in their power, they would not scruple to make use of them, by executing three Frenchmen for every one of their followers who should suffer in consequence of Soult's unjust and inhuman proclamation.[46] These threats were fulfilled on both sides. It is said, a horrid example of cruelty was given by a French general, who in a manner crucified, by nailing to trees, eight prisoners, whom he had

---

[46] Southey, vol. iv., p. 405.

taken from the guerillas of the Empecinado. The daring Spaniard's passions were wound up too high to listen either to pity or fear; he retaliated the cruelty by nailing the same number of Frenchmen to the same trees, and leaving them to fill the forest of Guadarama with their groans. But these excesses became rare on either side; for the mutual interest of both parties soon led them to recur to the ordinary rules of war.

We have given a slight sketch of the peculiar character of this singular warfare, which constitutes a curious and interesting chapter in the history of mankind, and serves to show how difficult it is to subject, by the most formidable military means, a people who are determined not to submit to the yoke. The probability of the case had not escaped the acute eye of Buonaparte himself, who, though prescient of the consequences, had not been able to resist the temptation of seizing upon this splendid sovereignty, and who was still determined, as he is said to have expressed himself, to reign at least over Spain, if he could not reign over the Spanish people. But even this stern wish, adopted in vengeance rather than in soberness of mind, could not, if gratified, have removed the perplexity which was annexed to the affairs of the Peninsula.

Buonaparte, in the spirit of calculation which was one of his great attributes, had reckoned that Spain, when in his hands, would retain the same channels of wealth which she had possessed from her South American provinces. Had he been able to carry into execution his whole plan—had the old king really embarked for Peru or Mexico, it might have happened, that Napoleon's influence over Charles, his Queen, and her favourite Godoy, could have been used to realize these expectations. But, in consequence of the rupture which had taken place, the Spanish colonies, at first taking part with the patriots of the mother country, made large remittances to Cadiz for the support of the war against the French; and when afterwards, adopting another view of the subject, the opportunity appeared to them favourable for effecting their own independence, the golden tide which annually carried tribute to Old Spain was entirely dried up.

This Buonaparte had not reckoned upon, and he had now to regret an improvident avidity, similar to that of Esop's boy, who killed the bird which laid eggs of gold. The disappointment was as great as unexpected. Napoleon had, from his private treasure, and the means he possessed in France, discharged the whole expense of the two large armies, by whom the territory of Spain was first occupied; and it was natural for him to suppose, that in this, as in so many other cases, the French troops should, after this first expedition, be paid and maintained at the expense of the provinces in which they were quartered. This was the rather to be expected, when Andalusia, Grenada, Valencia, fertile and rich provinces, were added to the districts overrun by the invading army. But, so general was the disinclination to the French, so universal the disappearance of specie, so unintermitting the disturbances excited by the guerillas, that both King Joseph, his court, and the French army, were obliged to have constant recourse to Napoleon for the means of supporting themselves; and such large remittances were made for these purposes, that in all the countries occupied by the French, the Spanish coin gradually disappeared from the circulation, and was replaced by that of France. The being obliged, therefore, to send supplies to the kingdom from which he had expected to receive them, was a subject of great mortification to Napoleon, which was not, however, the only one connected with the government he had established there.

SITUATION OF KING JOSEPH

In accepting the crown of Spain at the hands of Napoleon, Joseph, who was a man of sense and penetration, must have been sufficiently aware that it was an emblem of borrowed and dependent sovereignty, gleaming but with such reflected light as his brother's Imperial diadem might shed upon it. He could not but know, that in making him King of Spain, Napoleon retained over him all his rights as a subject of France, to whose Emperor, in his regal as well as personal capacity, he still, though a nominal monarch, was accounted to owe all vassalage. For this he must have been fully prepared. But Joseph, who had a share of the family pride, expected to possess with all others, save Buonaparte, the external appearance at least of sovereignty, and was much dissatisfied with the proceedings of the marshals and generals sent by his brother to his assistance. Each of these, accustomed to command his own separate corps d'armée, with no subordination save that to the Emperor only, proceeded to act on his own authority, and his own responsibility, levied contributions at pleasure, and regarded the authority of King Joseph as that of a useless and ineffective civilian, who followed the march along with the impediments and baggage of the camp, and to whom little honour was reckoned due, and no obedience. In a word, so complicated became the state of the war and of the government, so embarrassing the rival pretensions set up by the several French generals, against Joseph and against each other, that when Joseph came to Paris to assist at the marriage of Napoleon and Maria Louisa, he made an express demand, that all the French troops in Spain should be placed under his own command, or rather that of his Major-General; and in case this was declined, he proposed to abdicate the crown, or, what was equivalent, that the French auxiliaries should be withdrawn from Spain. Buonaparte had on a former occasion, named his brother generalissimo of the troops within his pretended dominions; he now agreed that the French generals serving in Spain should be subjected, without exception, to the control of Marshal Jourdan, as Major-General of King Joseph. But as these commanders were removed from Buonaparte's immediate eye, and were obliged to render an account of their proceedings both to the intrusive king and to Napoleon, it was not difficult for them to contrive to play off the one against the other, and in fact to conduct themselves as if independent of both.

These very embarrassing circumstances were increased by the presence of the English army, which, having twice driven the French from Portugal, showed no intention of returning to their ships, but lay on the frontiers of the latter kingdom, ready to encourage and assist the continued resistance of Spain. It was not the fault of the commander-in-chief that their duties were, for the present, in a great measure limited to those of an army of observation. If the troops which assisted in the ill-advised Walcheren expedition had been united to those under the command of Lord Wellington, they would, at a loss infinitely less, and yet greatly more honourably incurred, have driven the French beyond the Ebro, or, more probably, have compelled them to evacuate Spain. But the British Cabinet, though adopting new and more bold, as well as more just ideas of the force of the country, could not be expected perhaps all at once, and amid the clamour of an Opposition who saw nothing but reckless desperation in whatever measures were calculated to resist France, to hazard so much of the national force upon one single adventure, although bearing in their own eyes a promising aspect. Statesmen, and even those of no mean character, are apt to forget, that where a large supply of men and money is necessary to ensure the object aimed at, it is miserable policy to attempt to economize either; and that such ill-timed thrift must render the difficulties attending the expedition either altogether insurmountable, or greatly add to the loss which must be encountered to overcome them.

In the meantime, Buonaparte, with respect to the Peninsula, convulsed as it was by civil war in every province—half-subdued and half-emancipated—causing him an immense expense, as well as endless contradiction and mortification—stood much in the condition, to use a popular simile, of one, who, having hold of a wolf, feels it equally difficult to overpower the furious animal, and dangerous to let him go. His power over the general mind, however, rested a great deal on the opinion commonly received, that he was destined to succeed in whatever enterprise he undertook. He himself entertained some such ideas concerning the force of his own destiny; and as it was no part either of his temper or his policy to abandon what he had once undertaken, he determined to make a gigantic effort to drive the Leopards and their Sepoy general, as the French papers called the British and Lord Wellington, out of Portugal; to possess himself of Lisbon; and to shut that avenue against foreign forces again attempting to enter the Peninsula.

In obedience to the Emperor's commands, an army, to be termed that of Portugal, was assembled, on a scale which the Peninsula had scarcely yet seen. It was called by the French themselves 110,000 men, but certainly rather exceeded than fell short of the number of 80,000. This large force was put under the command of Massena, Prince of Essling, the greatest name in the

French army, after that of Napoleon, and so favoured by fortune, that his master was wont to call him the Spoilt Child of Victory.[47]

Lord Wellington's British troops did not exceed 25,000 in number, and there were among them so many invalids, that his motions were necessarily entirely limited to the defensive. He had, however, a subsidiary force under his command, consisting of 30,000 Portuguese, in whom other generals might have rested little confidence; but they were receiving British pay and British allowances, were disciplined in the British manner, and commanded by British officers; and Lord Wellington, who had seen the unwarlike Hindu behave himself in similar circumstances, like a companion not unworthy of the English soldier, had little doubt of being able to awaken the dormant and suppressed, but natural ardour of the natives of Portugal. This force had been, in a great measure, trained under the auspices of Marshal Beresford, an officer who has eternal claims on the gratitude of his country, for the generous manner in which he devoted himself to a labour, which had at first little that was flattering or promising; and for the very great perfection to which, by dint of skill, good temper, and knowledge of human nature, he was able to bring his task to completion at such an important crisis.

It was, however, of the utmost importance to avoid trusting too much to the Portuguese troops, which were so recently levied and trained, until they had acquired something of the practice, as well as the theory, of the military profession.

Thus, between the weak state of the British, and the imperfect discipline of the Portuguese, Lord Wellington was reduced to temporary inactivity, and had the mortification to see the frontier places of Ciudad Rodrigo and Almeida taken almost in the presence of his army. The fears of the British nation were as usual excited in an unreasonable degree by these two sinister events; but they had both come within the calculations of Lord Wellington, whose advance to the frontier was without the intention of incurring any risk for the preservation of those places, but merely, by inducing the garrisons to hold out, to protract as long as possible a defence, the

---

[47] Southey, vol. iv., p. 415.

duration of which must be equally advantageous to the allies, and wasteful to the French.

TORRES VEDRAS

The position on which he meant to maintain the defence of Portugal, had been long since fixed upon, and the fortifications had been as long in progress. It was that of Torres Vedras, where, as appears from his own evidence before the Cintra Court of Inquiry, he had expected Junot to make a defence, after the battle of Vimeiro. All Lord Wellington's previous movements were adjusted carefully, for the purpose of drawing the enemy from his supplies and communications to that point, beyond which he proposed the invader should pass no farther.

Admirably as Lord Wellington's premises were connected with the conclusion he aimed at, chance, or rather the presumption of the French general, favoured him with an unexpected opportunity of adding glory to a retreat, which was dictated by prudence. Massena, if he did justice to British courage, thought himself entitled to set the military skill of their general at utter defiance. He saw, indeed, their retrograde movements, from the banks of the Coa towards Lisbon, conducted with all the deliberate and guarded caution of a game at chess; but still these movements were retrograde, nor could he resist the temptation, by a bold and sudden attack, to attempt to precipitate the retreat of the British, and drive them, if not into the sea, at least into their ships, to which he doubted not they were ultimately bound.

This led to the battle of Busaco, which was fought on the 27th of September 1810. Upon that memorable day the British army was assembled on the Sierra, or ridge of the hills called Busaco. Massena, by turning the extremity of the ridge, might have compelled the English general to recommence his retreat; but he meditated a direct attack on the position. It was made by five strong divisions of the French. Two attacked on the right, one of which, forcing its way to the top of the ridge, was bayoneted and driven headlong down; the other, suffering great loss from the fire, gave way before reaching the top. Three divisions attacked on the left, with nearly the same fate. Defeated upon such unfavourable ground, the enemy lost, it was computed, at least 2000 men slain, besides very many wounded. The moral effect of the battle of Busaco was immense. It assured both the English themselves, and the people of Portugal, that the retreat of Lord Wellington's army was not the effect of fear, but of a deliberate choice. It evinced, also, what degree of trust might be securely reposed in the Portuguese levies. "They had shown themselves worthy of contending," said Lord Wellington, in his official despatch, "in the same ranks with British troops;" and they felt their own confidence rise as their merits became acknowledged.[48]

The French army, declining any farther attack on the Sierra, proceeded to turn its extremity, and move upon Lisbon by the way of Coimbra. Here Massena established a strong rear-guard with his hospitals and wounded, but the inspiration occasioned by the victory of Busaco had not yet subsided among the Portuguese. Colonel Trant, a British officer, who commanded a body of Portuguese militia, rushed gallantly into Coimbra, and carried the place by a sudden attack. About 5000 men, many of course wounded, with all the French hospital stores, fell into the hands of the Portuguese; and Massena who could not recover the place, suffered all the loss of stores and provisions which that city afforded as a depôt, and which the fertile district in the neighbourhood might have enabled him to collect.

Great was the surprise of both armies when the retreat of the British, and advance of the French, suddenly terminated. The former entered a regular position, which, by the utmost exertion of skill and labour, had been rendered almost impregnable, being most formidably protected by field-works and heavy guns. They found that the Tagus and port of Lisbon afforded them assurance of subsistence, even in plenty, and that their inferiority in numbers was completely made-up to them by the strength of their position.

The French, on the contrary, who had fondly expected to enter Lisbon as conquerors, found themselves in a country wasted

---

[48] Southey, vol. iv., p. 482.

by the hands of its cultivators; without hospitals or magazines in their rear; in front a foe, of whom they had lately felt the strength; and around, a hostile population, for the greater part in arms. If, in such a situation, Massena could be said to besiege Lisbon, he was, nevertheless, in the utmost danger of suffering those extremities of famine which usually fall to the lot of the beleaguered party. He seemed, by some strange transmutation, to have changed lots with the natives of Lisbon, and to suffer all the evils which he expected to inflict.

The war now paused on both sides. Lord Wellington had reached the point of his defence. Massena seemed at a loss where to commence his attack. The deer was turned to bay, but the dog sprung not. The eyes of all Europe were rested upon the Tagus, on whose banks were to be decided the pretensions to superiority asserted by two great generals in the name of two mighty nations. But that event was suspended for several months, during which it is fitting that we should resume the narrative of other matters.

Chapter LII

Change in Napoleon's Principles of Government—Becomes suspicious of Talleyrand and Fouché—Fouché endeavours, without the knowledge of Napoleon, to ascertain the Views of England with respect to Peace—His Plan is defeated by a singular collision with a similar one of Napoleon—and Fouché is sent away as Governor-General of Rome—His Moral and Political Character—Murmurings of the People against the Austrian Alliance—Continental System—Ignorance of Napoleon of the Actual Political Feelings of Great Britain—The License System—Louis Buonaparte—Endeavours in vain to defend Holland from the Effects of the Continental System—He abdicates the Throne, and retires to Gratz in Styria—Holland is annexed to the French Empire.

CHANGES IN NAPOLEON'S GOVERNMENT

Since Buonaparte obtained, in 1804, the absolute rule of the French Republic, a change had been gradually taking place in his principles of government, and in the character of the statesmen whom he employed as his ministers and advisers. For the first two years, and more, he had governed on the principle of a limited monarch, who avails himself of the best talents he can find among his subjects, and shows a deference to those who are distinguished, either for the political part which they have performed, or the share they possess in the good opinion of the public. Among his advisers at this period, we find many of the leading men of the Revolution; persons who, though they had been induced, from various motives, to see the rise of Napoleon with equanimity, and even to aid him, then their equal, in his attempt to climb to supreme power, yet still remembered in what relation he and they had originally stood to each other. In counselling an Emperor, these statesmen did it with the more freedom, that they remembered a period when they were on a level with him, nay, perhaps, when they stood a good deal higher.

This period of his reign, during which Napoleon suffered the wild and powerful flights of his own ambition to be, in some degree, restrained and directed by the judgment of others, formed the most laudable and useful certainly, if not the most brilliant part of his career. But, gradually as his power became augmented and consolidated, the Emperor began to prefer that class of complaisant ministers, who would rather reflect his own opinions, prefaced with additional recommendations and arguments, than less courteously attempt to criticise and refute them.

The history of Napoleon justifies, or at least excuses him, for falling into this natural error. He felt, and justly, that he was the sole projector of his gigantic plans, and also, in a great measure, the agent who carried them through; and he was led to believe, that, because he did so much, he might as well do the whole. The schemes which he had himself originally formed, were executed by his own military genius; and thus it seemed as if the advice of counsellors, so indispensable to other princes, might be unnecessary to a sovereign who had shown himself all-sufficient alike in the cabinet and in the field. Yet this, though a plausible, was a delusive argument, even though it appeared to be borne out by the actual fact. It may be true, that in Buonaparte's councils, few measures of consequence were suggested by his ministers, and that he himself generally took the lead in affairs of importance. But still it was of great consequence that such plans, having been proposed, should be critically weighed, and canvassed by men of too much experience to be deceived by appearances, and too much courage to be prevented from speaking their mind. The advice of such men as Talleyrand and Fouché, operated as a restraint upon schemes hastily adopted, or opinionatively maintained; and their influence, though unseen and unheard, save in the Imperial cabinet, might yet be compared to the keel of a vessel, which, though invisible, serves to steady her among the waves, and regulate the force by which she is propelled by her swelling canvass; or to the pendulum of a time-piece, which checks and controls the mainspring of the machinery. Yet, though Buonaparte must have been sensible of these advantages, he was still more accessible to the feelings of jealousy, which made him suspect that these statesmen were disposed rather to establish separate interests for themselves in the government and nation, than to hold themselves completely dependent on the Imperial authority.

TALLEYRAND—FOUCHÉ

The character of both Talleyrand and Fouché, indeed, authorised some such suspicion. They had been distinguished in the French Revolution before Napoleon's name had been heard of, were intimately acquainted with all the springs which had moved it, and retained, as Buonaparte might suspect, the inclination, and even the power, to interfere at some possible state-crisis more effectually than accorded with his views of policy. He had gorged them indeed with wealth; but, if he consulted his own bosom, he might learn that wealth is but an indifferent compensation for the loss of political power. In a word, he suspected that the great services which Talleyrand rendered him with regard to foreign relations, and Fouché as minister of police, were calculated to raise them into necessary and indispensable agents, who might thus become, to a certain degree, independent of his Authority. He doubted, moreover, that they still kept up relations with a political society called Philadelphes, consisting of old republicans and others, of different political creeds, but who were united in their views of obtaining some degree of freedom, either by availing themselves of such slender means of restraint as the constitution, so carefully purged of every means of opposing the Imperial will, might yet afford, or by waiting for some disaster befalling Napoleon which might render their voice potential.[49]

The suspicions with which Buonaparte regarded his ministers did not rest on vague conjecture. While he was in Spain, he received information, appearing to indicate that a party was forming itself in the Legislative Assembly, the bond connecting which was opposition to the Imperial will. That body voted, it must be

---

[49] Southey, vol. iii., p. 405; Fouché, tom. i., p. 339.

remembered, by ballot; and great was the surprise and alarm of the assembly, when black balls, disapproving a measure suggested to their consideration by government, were counted to the number of an hundred and twenty-five, being a full third of the members present.[50]

An official note, dated from Valladolid, 4th December, instantly recalled the presumptuous dissentients to a sense that the power of rejecting the laws laid before them in the Emperor's name, which they had attempted thus boldly to exercise, was only intrusted to them for show, but was meant to contain no really effectual power of control. The words of Napoleon, the friend, as has been pretended, of liberal institutions, are well worthy of remark. "Our evils," he said, "have arisen in part from an exaggeration of ideas, which has tempted the Legislative Body to consider itself as representing the nation; an idea which is chimerical and even criminal, since implying a claim of representation which is vested in the Emperor alone. The Legislative Body ought to be called the Legislative Council—it does not possess the right of making laws, since it has not the right of propounding them. In the constitutional hierarchy, the Emperor, and the ministers his organs, are the first representatives of the nation. If any other pretensions, pretending to be constitutional, should pervert the principles of our monarchical constitution, every thing is undone."[51]

This is all very intelligible, and shows that in principle, if not in practice, the monarchical constitution of France rested upon the same basis of despotism which supports the monarchical constitution of Constantinople, where the Ulemats, or men of law, have an ostensible title to resist the Grand Signior's edicts, and are only exposed to the penalty of being pounded to death in a mortar, should they presume to exercise it. Yet, a member of the French Legislative Body might have been pardoned for being inquisitive on two subjects. 1st, He might wish to know, if that body, chosen by the people, though indeed not directly, did not represent their electors, whom was it that they did represent? 2dly, What was their real authority in the state, since they were not to enjoy the power of

---

[50] Fouché, tom. i., p. 329.
[51] Fouché, tom. i., p. 329.

rejecting the overtures which the constitution contended should be laid before them, before they were passed into laws?

FOUCHÉ

Buonaparte entertained strong suspicion that this recalcitrating humour, so suddenly testified by so complaisant an assembly, must have had the countenance of Talleyrand and of Fouché. So soon as he returned to Paris, therefore, he sounded the latter minister on the revolt in the Legislative Body, and desired his opinion on the sort of measures by which he had repressed it. Fouché had been too long a spy upon the private thoughts of others, to be capable of the weakness of betraying his own. He expatiated, in a tone of panegyric, on the decisive tone of the official note, affirmed that this was the only way to govern a kingdom, and added, that if any constitutional body arrogated the right of national representation, the sovereign had no choice but instantly to dissolve it. "If Louis XVI. had acted thus," said the minister, "he might have been alive, and King of France at this day." Astonished at the zeal and promptitude of this reply, Buonaparte looked for an instant with wonder at his minister, who thus avouched sentiments so different from those which had governed the earlier part of his political life. "And yet, Duke of Otranto," said the Emperor to the ex-jacobin, "methinks you were yourself one of those whose voices sent Louis XVI. to the scaffold?"—"I was," answered the supple statesman, without confusion or hesitation; "and it was the first service which I had the honour to render to your Majesty."[52]—This courtly answer saved the minister for the moment; but Napoleon did not the less continue to see in Fouché an object of suspicion and apprehension, whose power, owing to his having been so long at the head of the police, was immense; whose duplicity was unfathomable, and who evinced many indications of desiring to secure some separate individual authority, either by being too necessary to be dismissed, or too formidable to be offended.

Fouché himself has, indeed, admitted, that he endeavoured to regulate the duties of his office, so as to secure as much power to

---

[52] Mémoires de Fouché, tom. i., p. 331.

himself as possible, and was anxious, out of a desire of popularity, as well as from respect for the virtue which he did not himself possess, to execute those duties with the least possible harm to individuals. His mode of transacting business with the Emperor was thus characteristically described by himself. A person of rank, one of the *détenus*, desirous of escaping from the durance in which he was confined, had been fortunate enough to engage the interest of Fouché in his behalf. He had received more than one intimation from this statesman, that his passport would certainly be granted, but still it never received the Imperial signature; and Fouché, who began to fear that his own sincerity might be called in question, commenced one morning, in the presence of our informer, and of one of the distinguished generals of the empire, the following oblique explanation of the cause of his failure. "You no doubt think yourself a brave man?" said he, addressing the general.—"Bah!" replied the other, entering in to the same vein of raillery—"Brave? brave as an hundred lions."—"But I," continued the statesman, "am much braver than you. Look you, I desire some favour, the liberation of a friend, or the like; I watch the happy moment of access, select the moment of persuasion, am insinuating—eloquent—at length, by argument or importunity, I am successful. Next day, the paper which should ratify the boon which I had requested, is rejected when offered, torn perhaps, or flung beneath a heap of petitions and supplications. Now, herein is displayed my courage, which consists in daring again and again to recommence the unacceptable suit, and, what is perhaps the last verge of audacity, to claim it as a promise, which, being once pledged, can only be redeemed by specific performance." In this confession we read the account of a minister, still possessing influence, but declining in favour, and already become the object of his sovereign's jealousy; to whose personal request a favour cannot be decently refused, although a promise, reluctantly conceded to importunity, is willingly forgotten, or at length tardily and disobligingly granted.

Standing on these terms with a master at once watchful and jealous, we cannot be surprised at the audacity of Fouché, who feared not to affect a sort of independence, by anticipating the desires of Napoleon in the public service, and even in the Imperial family. A striking instance of the last occurred in his intrigue with

Josephine on the subject of the divorce;[53] and perhaps it was his escape out of that former involvement,[54] without loss of power or credit, which urged him to a second interference of a more public and national character, by which he endeavoured to sound the possibility of accomplishing a peace with England.

We may discover more than one motive for Fouché's proceeding in this most important business without either the knowledge or consent of Napoleon. He was aware that his master might have rendered it, in his way of treating, impossible even at starting, to discover on what terms Great Britain would conclude peace, by stating as preliminaries certain concessions which it was probable would not be granted, but from which, once stated, Napoleon could not himself recede. If, therefore, Fouché could find some secret mode of ascertaining upon what terms a treaty with England might really be obtained, he was doing a service to France, to Britain, to Napoleon himself, and to the world. It is not the Duke of Otranto, however, in particular, whom we would expect to incur disgrace, and even personal hazard, on mere public grounds. But, besides the pleasure which those who have long engaged in political intrigues find in carrying them on, until the habit becomes as inveterate as that of the gambler, we can see that Fouché might reasonably propose to himself an important accession of influence by the success of such a negotiation. If he could once acquire a knowledge of the price at which Napoleon might obtain that peace for which the world sighed in vain, he would become possessed of an influence over public opinion, both at home and abroad, which could not but render him a person of extreme importance; and if he was able to become the agent in turning such knowledge to advantage, and negotiating such an important treaty, he might fix himself even on Napoleon, as one of those ministers frequently met with in history, whom their sovereign may have disliked, but could not find means to dismiss.

---

[53] Fouché, tom. i., p. 32.
[54] "It is well known that Josephine never spoke to the Emperor otherwise than in favourable terms of all those who were about his person; she was even of service to M. Fouché, though he had attempted to become the instrument for bringing about her divorce."—Savary, tom. ii., p. 178.

M. OUVRARD—FOUCHÉ

Acting upon such motives, or on others which we can less easily penetrate, Fouché anxiously looked around, to consider what concessions France might afford to make, to soothe the jealousy of England; trusting it would be possible to come to some understanding with the British Ministry, weakened by the loss of Mr. Canning, and disheartened by the defeats sustained by the Spanish patriots, and the sinister event of the Walcheren expedition. The terms which he would have been willing to have granted, comprehended an assurance of the independence of the two kingdoms of Holland and Spain (as if such a guarantee could have availed any thing while these kingdoms had for sovereigns the brothers of Napoleon, men reigning as his prefects, and, we shall presently see, subject to removal at his pleasure,) together with the acknowledgment of the Sicilian monarchy in the present King, and that of Portugal in the House of Braganza. M. Ouvrard, a gentleman who had been permitted to go to London on commercial business, was employed by Fouché to open this delicate and furtive negotiation with the Marquis of Wellesley. But the negotiation was disconcerted by a singular circumstance.[55]

---

[55] "Although Sir Walter Scott does not mention me, I am able to speak pertinently to this affair: the following is the truth. I went to Paris in 1809, against my inclination, to comply with the wish of the principal Dutch, who imagined that I could prevent, or at least adjourn by my presence in Paris, and my immediate efforts, the evident intention of seizing upon Holland. During my stay at Paris, I was persuaded that all the tricks, the attacks, and ill-treatment, of which I was the object, had not for their real end the union of Holland, since it was the interest of France to aggrandise that kingdom, but that it was a political stratagem, to induce the English government to repeal its decrees of council, and to conclude the peace; and I was therefore prevailed upon while at Paris to send M. Labouchère from Amsterdam to London with instructions to make known to the Marquis Wellesley, that if England did not withdraw its decrees of council, the union of Holland with France was inevitable. The reply of the marquis proved at once how favourable my government in Holland had been to France, since the English Government declared, 'that the fate of Holland could not fail to occasion much interest in England; but that, in the present state of that country, the influence of France was so entire there, that the political change spoken of, must have some weight in the determination of the British Cabinet.' This attempt having proved useless, I could only succeed in delaying the union of Holland, the decree for which being prepared beforehand, and always in readiness, was often placed before me—by sacrificing Brabant and Zealand. After my return to Amsterdam, I was requested to allow M. Ouvrard a passage to England. I consented to this the more willingly, as I imagined that it was in consequence of the step I had already taken in sending M.

The idea of endeavouring to know on what terms peace could be obtained, had occurred to Napoleon as well as to Fouché; and the sovereign, on his part, unsuccessful as he had been on two occasions in his attempt to open a personal correspondence with the King of England, had followed the steps of his minister, in making M. Labouchère, a commercial person, agent of a great Dutch mercantile establishment, the medium of communication with the British Government. The consequence was, that Ouvrard, and the agent of the Emperor, neither of whom knew of the other's mission, entered about the same time into correspondence with the Marquis Wellesley, who, returned from his Spanish mission, was now secretary at war. The British statesman, surprised at this double application, became naturally suspicious of some intended deception, and broke off all correspondence both with Ouvrard and his competitor for the office of negotiator.[56]

Napoleon must naturally have been so highly incensed with Fouché for tampering without his consent[57] in a matter of such vital consequence, that one is almost surprised to find him limiting the effects of his resentment to disgracing the minister. He sent for Fouché [June 2,] and having extorted from him an avowal of his secret negotiation, he remarked, "So, then, you make peace or war without my leave?"[58] The consequence was, that the Duke of Otranto was deprived of his office of minister of police, in which he was succeeded by Savary; and he was shortly after sent into a species of honourable exile, in the character of Governor-general of Rome.[59] It cost Buonaparte no little trouble to redeem from the

---

Labouchère to London. A short time after, the Emperor visited Antwerp. Whilst conversing with him there, I assured him that there had been no communication with England except that which had taken place through M. Ouvrard, according to his request. My astonishment was extreme on learning, that not only it was without his request, but that he was ignorant of it, and from that moment he determined on the discharge of M. Fouché, who had allowed so singular a proceeding."—Louis Buonaparte, p. 65.
[56] Fouché, tom. i., p. 354; Savary, tom. ii., part ii., p. 208.
[57] "Ah, Fouché! how well the Emperor knew you, when he said, that your ugly foot was sure to be thrust in every body's shoes."—Las Cases, tom. ii., p. 18.
[58] "Napoleon left the council, and gave orders to Savary to arrest M. Ouvrard; at the same time, I was forbidden to have any communication with the prisoner. The next day the portfolio of the police was given to Savary. This time it was a real disgrace."—Fouché, tom. i., p. 358.
[59] "The decree constituting Fouché Governor-general of Rome, bears date June 3, 1810. 'This nomination,' says Fouché, 'was nothing but an honourable veil woven by Napoleon's

clutches of his late minister the confidential notes which he had himself written to him upon affairs of police. For a long time Fouché pretended that he had consigned these important documents to the flames; and it was not until he had before his eyes the alternative of submission or a dungeon, that he at length delivered up the Imperial warrants, containing, no doubt, much that would have been precious to history. Dismissed at present from the stage, we shall again meet with this bold statesman at other periods of our history, when, as is observed of some kinds of sea-fowl, his appearance seldom failed to announce danger and tempest.

The character of Fouché, in point of principle or morality, could scarcely be accounted even tolerable; but he had high talents, and in many points the soundness of his judgment led him to pursue and recommend moderate and beneficent measures, out of policy, if not from a higher motive. On other accounts, also, many of the French had some partiality to him; especially those who cast their eyes backward upon their national history, and regretted the total loss of that freedom, so eagerly longed for, so briefly possessed, and which they could never be properly said to have enjoyed; and to the recovery of which, in part at least, Fouché was understood to be favourable as far as he could or dared. The remnant of the sterner Republicans might despise him as a time server, yet they respected him, at the same time, as a relic of the Revolution, and on different occasions experienced his protection. To the Royalists also he had been courteous, and so decidedly so, as encouraged one of the boldest agents of the Bourbons to penetrate to his presence, and endeavour to bring him over to the cause of the exiled family. Fouché dismissed him, indeed, with a peremptory refusal to listen to his proposal; but he did not deliver him to the police, and he allowed him twenty-four hours to leave the kingdom. These various feelings occasioned to many, alarm and regret at the dismissal of the Duke of Otranto.

The discharge of this able minister seemed the more portentous, that shortly before it occurred, the terrible charge of which he was about to be deprived, had received an alarming

---

policy, in order to conceal and mitigate, in the eyes of the public, my disgrace, of which his intimates alone had the secret."—*Mémoires*, tom. ii., p. 7.

extension of jurisdiction. The number of state prisons was extended from one, being the old tower of Vincennes, to no less than six, situated in different parts of France.[60] These Bastiles, chiefly old Gothic castles, were destined to be the abode of captives, whom the Government described as persons who could not be convicted of any crime perpetrated, but whom, as entertaining dangerous thoughts, and principles, it was not safe to permit to remain at large. The *lettre de cachet*, by authority of which these victims of political suspicion were to be secluded from liberty, was to consist in a decree of the Privy Council, which might have been as well termed the pleasure of the Emperor. This measure was adopted on the 3d of March, 1810, upon a report made to the Council of State in the name of Fouché, and agreed to by them; but it was well understood, that, in this and similar instances, the individual at the head of any department was obliged to father the obloquy of such measures as Napoleon desired to introduce into it. The minister of police was therefore held guiltless of recommending an extension of the Government's encroachments upon public liberty; which, in fact, were the exclusive device of Napoleon and his Privy Council.[61]

AUSTRIAN ALLIANCE UNPOPULAR

It was another unfortunate circumstance for Napoleon, that the observers of the times ascribed the dismissal of the old Republican counsellors, and the more rigorous measures adopted against political malecontents, to the influence of the Austrian alliance. With many persons in France, Buonaparte, as the Heir of the Revolution, might, like Danton, Robespierre, and others, have exercised the most despotic authority, providing he claimed his right to do so by and through the Revolution. But they could not endure to see the Emperor Napoleon, while exercising the same authority with a thousand times more lenity, attempt to improve his right to the submission of his subjects by an alliance with one of the ancient houses of Europe, against whom the principles of the Revolution had declared eternal war. Every class of politicians has its fanatics, and in that of the ancient Jacobins were many who would rather

---

[60] Saumar, Ham, Landskaone, Pierre-Châtel, and Fennestrelles.
[61] Fouché, tom. i., p. 352.

have perished by the short, sharp terrors of the Republican guillotine, than survived to linger in a dungeon during the pleasure of a son-in-law of the Emperor of Germany. Such ideas, inconsistent as they were in themselves, and utterly irreconcilable with the quiet, gentle, and irreproachable character of Maria Louisa, who could never be justly accused of even attempting to influence her husband upon any political subject, circulated, nevertheless, and were even accredited in political society. There was indeed this argument in their favour, that no other motive could be assigned for Buonaparte's sparing Austria when she was lying at his mercy, and choosing a partner out of her royal family, than the desire of allying himself with the House of Hapsburg, and of gaining such access as could be attained by such an alliance to a share in the rights and privileges of the most ancient hereditary dynasty of Europe. But in approaching to that fraternal alliance with legitimate royalty, Napoleon proportionally abandoned those revolutionary principles and associates, by whose means he had first climbed to power; and by this change, rather of the basis of his authority than of the authority itself, he offended many of the Republicans, without effectually gaining the aristocrats, to whom his new connexion might have seemed a recommendation. Indeed, when his right to sovereignty was considered without reference to his possession, and his power to maintain it, Napoleon was in some measure censured like the bat in the fable. The democrats urged against him his matrimonial alliance with a house of the ancient régime; while the aristocrats held him disqualified on account of the origin of his power under the revolutionary system.

But although such objections existed among the zealots of both political factions, the great body of the French people would have cared little on what principle Napoleon had ascribed his title to the Imperial crown, providing he had but been contented to allow the subject and himself the advantage of a short repose from wars and conquests. This tranquillity, however, was becoming every day less probable, for new incidents seemed to dictate new acquisitions to the empire; and, unhappily for his own and other countries, the opportunity of aggrandisement was with Buonaparte all that it wanted to recommend it, and the pressure of the occasion was always a complete justification of any measure which the time rendered expedient.

That which now chiefly occupied him, since the overtures for peace with England had been rendered abortive by the collision of his own confidential emissary with that of Fouché, was the destruction of the strength, and the sapping of the resources of that country, by dint of enforcing and extending what he called the European Continental System; which consisted of the abolition of all commerce, and the reducing each nation, as in the days of primitive barbarism, to remain satisfied with its own productions, however inadequate to the real or artificial wants to which its progress in society had gradually given rise.

Like most foreigners, Napoleon understood little or nothing of the constitutional opinions, or influential principles belonging to England. He was well acquainted with human character, as modified by the governments and customs of France and Italy; but this experience no more qualified him to judge of the English character, than the most perfect acquaintance with the rise and fall of the Mediterranean, amounting to five or six inches in height, would prepare a navigator to buffet with the powerful tides which burst and foam on the shores of the British islands. The information which he received from that hostile country, Buonaparte construed according to his wishes; and when it was supplied by private intelligencers, they were of course desirous of enhancing the value of what they told, by exaggerating its importance. It was, indeed, no difficult task to impose on a statesman, ignorant enough of the present state of North Britain, to believe that he could, even at this time of day, have disturbed the security of the reigning family, by landing in Scotland some candidate, having pretensions to the crown through the House of Stuart. With the same inaccuracy, he concluded every warm speech in Parliament a summons to revolt—every temporary riot or testimony of popular displeasure, from whatever cause, a commencement of open rebellion. He could not be convinced, that from the peculiarity of the English constitution, and the temper of her people, such disturbances and such violent debates must frequently exist; and although, like eruptions on the human body, they are both unpleasant and unseemly, they are yet the price at which sound internal health is preserved.

THE CONTINENTAL SYSTEM

Actuated by such erroneous views as we have stated, Napoleon conceived that in 1810 he saw in England the important results of his Continental System, or interdiction of British commerce with the continent.

The associations of the Luddites, as they were called, were at this time giving great disturbance in the manufacturing districts of England. These, it is well known, were framed to prevent the introduction of looms wrought by machinery, or power-looms, to the superseding the ordinary looms wrought by hand. The cause would have equally existed, and the discontent also, if the Continental System had never been heard of; for such discontent must and will exist in every trade where a number of men are suddenly thrown out of employment by the introduction of abbreviated means of labour. Yet Napoleon never doubted that these heart-burnings, and the violence of the Parliamentary debates, arose entirely from the new mode he had found of striking at Great Britain by the destruction of her commerce. He, therefore, as we shall presently see, examined all Europe, with the intention of shutting every creek and fishing-port, through which cargoes of muslins or cotton goods could by possibility penetrate; and the absolute authority which he could exercise over the whole continent, with the exception of Russia, and of the "still vexed" Peninsula, entitles us to compare him to the heedful governor of a jail, who traverses his gloomy dominions at stated hours, striking with his hammer every bar to ascertain that it rings sound, and proving every lock, to see that no secret means of communication exists with the free part of humanity. Thus commerce, the silken tie which binds nations to each other, whose influence is so salutary to all states, so essential to the very existence of many, was in danger of being totally abrogated, unless in as far as it was carried on by a system of licenses.

The adoption of this system, which went in a great measure to counteract the effects of that very Continental System which he made it such an especial point to press and enforce upon all neutral powers, was a singular sacrifice made by Napoleon, partly to necessity, partly to the desire of accumulating treasure.

The license system was a relaxation of the continental blockade, of which England had set the example by giving protections to such neutral vessels, as, clearing out from a British port, had a certain proportion of their cargo made up of British goods or colonial produce. This was what, in mercantile language, is termed a real transaction—the British merchandise was purchased by such as designed to make a profit, by selling it again upon any part of the continent to which they might be able to introduce it. Buonaparte, in like manner, granted Imperial licenses, purchased for large sums of money, by which trading vessels were permitted to import a certain quantity of colonial produce, on condition of exporting an equal proportion of French manufactures. This system differed from that of England, in this important respect, that the demand for articles of the French manufactures was entirely simulated. The goods were not wanted in Britain, could not be re-sold there without payment of heavy duties, and were often thrown into the sea in preference to discharging the English duties upon them. Editions of books, a commodity thus exported, and thus disposed of, were wittily said to be *ad usum Delphini*. The prime cost at which these French goods had been purchased, in compliance with Buonaparte's regulations, was of course laid upon the colonial goods, which were the only actual subject of trade. Thus, if the French manufacturers derived any profit from the transaction, it was raised, not by their goods being exported and sold in foreign countries, in the usual course of trade, but by the prime cost being imposed as a tax upon the colonial produce imported; and the price was paid, of course, not by the foreign market, which the goods seldom reached, but by the French consumers of sugar, rum, and coffee.

The real temptation for continuing this attempt to force a trade, was, as we have seen, the impossibility of dispensing with colonial produce entirely, and the large revenue accruing to the

French government from these licenses, who, in this manner, exercising a complete monopoly in a trade which they interdicted to all others, made immense additions to the treasure which almost choked the vaults of the pavilion Marsan, in the Tuileries. The language held by the minister of Napoleon to the powers thus affected, amounted therefore to the following proposition:—"You shall shut your ports against British commodities; for without your doing so, it will be impossible for the Emperor Napoleon to humble the Mistress of the Seas. But while you are thus deprived of all commerce, whether passive or active, Napoleon reserves to himself, by the system of license, the privilege of purchasing and dealing in the commodities of Britain and her colonies, which, reaching your country by any other mode than through his permission, will be subject to confiscation, nay, to destruction."

At a later period, Buonaparte greatly regretted that he had suffered the emolument derived from the license-trade, to seduce him into relaxing his Continental System.[62] He seems to lament having relinquished his supposed advantage, as a vindictive freebooter might regret his having been reduced to let go his hold on his enemy's throat, by the tempting opportunity of plunging his hand into the pocket of a bystander. The injustice which thus imposed on neutrals the necessity of abstaining from a lucrative commerce, which France, the belligerent power, reserved to herself the privilege of carrying on, in such degree as she might find convenient, was of so crying a description, that, at any other time than during the irresistible ascendency of Napoleon, the very mention of it would have revolted all Europe. And even as times stood, the non-compliance with terms so harsh and unjust, cost the fall of two European thrones, ere it became the means of undermining that of Napoleon himself.

LOUIS BUONAPARTE

The first of the royal sufferers was the brother of Napoleon, Louis Buonaparte, who had been created King of Holland. By every account which we have been able to collect, Louis was an amiable,

---

[62] Las Cases, tom. ii., p. 283.

well-intentioned, and upright man, of a romantic disposition, and a melancholic complexion, which he had increased by studying the sentimental philosophy of Rousseau.[63] But he was, in his brother's language, an ideologist; that is, one who is disposed to do that which is right according to principle, rather than that which circumstances render expedient. He was embarrassed by some family disputes, and lived on indifferent terms with his wife,[64] who was a greater favourite with Napoleon than was Louis himself. Since he had been under the necessity of accepting the crown of Holland, he had endeavoured to afford that country all the protection which could be derived from his near relationship to Napoleon; and if he could not save his subjects entirely from the evils of a conquered and dependent state, he endeavoured to diminish these as much as his means permitted. The Dutch, a calm and deliberate people, gave Louis full credit for his efforts, and, in general, regarded him as their friend and protector. But at the period we treat of, the evils which approached their state were far beyond Louis' power to avert or even to modify. Other countries may have more or less of a commercial character, but Holland exists by commerce entirely. It was the influence of commerce which gained her amphibious territory from the waves, and, were that influence withdrawn, her fair towns must again become fishing villages; her rich pastures must return to their original state of salt-water marshes, shallows, and sand-banks. The French exactions already paid, to the amount of one hundred millions of francs, had purchased, as the natives of Holland fondly imagined, some right to exert the small means of commerce which remained to them, and which, under King Louis' sanction, were almost entirely engaged in traffic with England, now declared contraband.

Napoleon used threats and commands to induce Louis to bring his subjects to a more rigorous observance of the Continental

---

[63] See *ante*, vol. ii., *note*. "Louis had been spoiled by reading the works of Rousseau."—Napoleon, *Las Cases*, tom. ii., p. 306.
[64] "As Louis and Hortensia had lived almost always separate since their marriage, except three short periods of a few months, they each demanded of the family council a separation, presently after Louis arrived at Paris in 1809. But after a meeting of the said council was granted, the separation was refused, though it had long existed in point of fact. He was informed of the refusal verbally: no document whatever was transmitted to him on a result, on which however depended the ease, condition, and fame of a man of honour."—Louis Buonaparte, *La Hollande*, tom. iii., p. 199.

System, while Louis employed expostulation and entreaty in behalf of the nation over whom he had been called to rule. Each brother grew more obstinate in his opinion, and at length, as the Emperor began to see that neither fear nor favour could induce Louis to become the agent of oppression in Holland, his removal from that country was distinctly pointed at as the consequence of his obstinacy. It was intimated, in a report by Champagny, the Duke de Cadore, that the situation of Louis on the throne of Holland was rendered critical, by his feelings being divided betwixt the imprescriptible duties which he owed to France and to his family, and the interest which it was natural he should take in the welfare of Dutch commerce. To terminate this strife in his brother's mind, the report informed the public that Napoleon meant to recall the prince of his blood whom he had placed on the Dutch throne, since the first duty of a French prince having a place in the succession to that monarchy, was to France exclusively; and it was intimated, that Holland, divested of her King, and her nominal independence, would be reduced to the condition of a province of France, occupied by French troops, and French officers of the revenue; and thus deprived of the means of thwarting the Continental System, so necessary for the subjugation of Britain, by the obstinate continuance of commercial intercourse with a nation under the ban of the empire.[65]

HOLLAND—ABDICATION OF LOUIS BUONAPARTE

This report is peculiarly interesting, as explanatory of Buonaparte's views respecting the rights and regal authority of the sovereigns whom he created and displaced at pleasure, as the interests of France, or rather as his own, required, or seemed to require. Either, however, Napoleon became, for the moment, ashamed to acknowledge this fact so broadly; or he thought that such a contradiction of his repeated declarations might have a bad effect upon the Westphalian subjects of Jerome, and upon the Spaniards, whom he desired to become those of Joseph; or, perhaps, the remonstrances of Louis produced some temporary effect upon his mind; for he stopped short in his full purpose, and on the 16th

---

[65] Documens Historiques sur la Hollande, tom. iii., p. 238.

March concluded a treaty with Louis, the terms of which were calculated, it was said, to arrange disputed points betwixt the sovereigns, and render the independence of Holland consistent with the necessary conformity to the Continental System.

July 1.

By this treaty, Zealand, Dutch Brabant, and the whole course of the Rhine, as well the right as the left bank, were transferred from Holland to France. French officers of the customs were to be placed in all the Dutch harbours; 18,000 troops were to be maintained by the kingdom of Holland, of whom 6000 were to be French; a fleet was to be fitted out by the same kingdom for the service of France; English manufactures were to be prohibited by the Dutch government; and other restrictions were subscribed to by Louis,[66] in hopes his brother's stern resolution might be so far softened as to leave the remaining portions of the territories of Holland in a state of nominal independence. But he was soon made sensible that this was no part of Napoleon's intentions. Instead of 6000 French troops, 20,000 were assembled at Utrecht, with the purpose of being poured into Holland. Instead of this foreign soldiery being stationed on the coasts, where alone their presence could be requisite to prevent the contraband trade, which was the sole pretext of introducing them at all, Louis was informed, that they were to take military possession of the whole country; and that the headquarters of this army, which was totally independent of his authority, were to be established at Amsterdam, his capital.

Seeing himself thus deprived by his brother of all power in the kingdom which was still called his, Louis generously refused to play the pageant part of a monarch, who could neither exert his rights nor protect his subjects. On the 1st of July he executed a deed of abdication in favour of his son, then a minor, expressing an affectionate hope, that though he himself had been so unhappy as to offend his brother the Emperor, he would not, nevertheless, visit with his displeasure his innocent and unoffending family. In a letter

---

[66] "This treaty, which was rather a capitulation, was imposed by the Emperor, signed by Verhueil, and ratified conditionally by the King, who added the words, '*as far as possible.*'"— Louis Buonaparte, *Documens Hist.*, tom. iii., p. 248.

from Haarlem, dated the 1st July, Louis enlarged on the causes of his abdication, in a manner honourable to his head and his heart, and with a moderation, when he spoke of his brother, which gave weight to his just complaints. "He could not," he said, "consent to retain the mere title of King, separated from all real authority in his kingdom, his capital, or even his palace. He should be, in such a case, the witness of all that passed, without the power of influencing the current of events for the good of his people, yet remaining responsible for evils which he could neither remedy nor prevent. He had long foreseen the extremity to which he was now reduced, but could not avoid it without sacrificing his most sacred duties, without ceasing to bear at heart the happiness of his people, and to connect his own fate with that of the country. This," he said, "was impossible. Perhaps," he continued, "I am the only obstacle to the reconciliation of Holland with France. Should that prove the case, I may find some consolation in dragging out the remainder of a wandering and languishing life, at a distance from my family, my country, and the good people of Holland, so lately my subjects."[67]

Having finished his vindication, and adjusted means for making it public, which he could only do by transmitting it to England, the Ex-King of Holland entertained a chosen party of friends at his palace at Haarlem until near midnight, and then, throwing himself into a plain carriage which was in attendance, left behind him the kingly name and the kingly revenue, rather than hold them without the power of discharging the corresponding duties of a sovereign. Louis retired to Gratz, in Styria, where he lived in a private manner, upon a moderate pension,[68] amusing his leisure with literature.[69] His more ambitious consort, with a much more ample

---

[67] Documens Historiques, tom. iii., p. 310.
[68] "This is not correct. I did not, nor could not, receive a pension from any one: my revenue was derived principally from the sale of my decorations and jewels, and the interest of the obligations I had taken upon me, in order to encourage the loan from Holland to Prussia at the time of the greatest misfortunes of the virtuous sovereign of that country, who, in spite of all opposition and every political consideration, was anxious to acquit himself towards me with scrupulous exactitude."—Louis Buonaparte, p. 69.
[69] In 1808, Louis gave to the world a sentimental romance, called "Marie, ou les Peines de l'Amour," of which a second edition appeared in 1814, under the title of "Marie, ou les Hollandaises." A distinguished critic describes the royal production as "a farrago of dulness, folly, and bad taste."—(*Quart. Rev.*, vol. xii., p. 391.) His treatise, entitled "Documens Historiques, et Réflexions sur le Gouvernement de la Hollande," is an unpresuming account of his administration in Holland.

revenue, settled herself at Paris, where her wit and talents, independent of her connexion with Napoleon, attracted around her the world of fashion, of which she was a distinguished ornament.

Buonaparte, as was to have been expected, paid no regard to the claim of Louis's son, in whose favour his father had abdicated. He created that young person Grand Duke of Berg, and, although he was yet a child, he took an opportunity to make him a speech, which we have elsewhere adverted to, in which, after inculpating the conduct of his brother, the tenor of which he stated could be accounted for by *malady* alone,[70] he explained in few words the duties incurred by his satellite sovereigns. "Never forget, that whatever position you may be required to occupy, in order to conform to my line of politics, and the interest of my empire, your first duty must always regard ME, your second must have reference to France. All your other duties, even those towards the countries which I commit to your charge, are secondary to these primary obligations."

Thus was the leading principle clearly announced, upon which the nominal independence of kingdoms allied to France was in future to be understood as resting. The monarchs, to whom crowns were assigned, were but to be regarded as the lieutenants of the kingdoms in which they ruled; and whatever part the interest of their dominions might call upon them to act, they were still subject, in the first instance, to the summons and control of their liege lord the Emperor, and compelled to prefer what his pleasure should term the weal of France, to every other call of duty whatever.

---

[70] "The conduct of your father grieves me to the heart: his disorder alone can account for it. When you are grown up you will pay his debt and your own."—*Documens Hist.*, tom. iii., p. 326; and *Moniteur*, July 23, 1810. "When Napoleon received the news of his brother's abdication, he was struck with astonishment: he remained silent for a few moments, and after a kind of momentary stupor, suddenly appeared to be greatly agitated. His heart was ready to burst, when he exclaimed, 'Was it possible to suspect so mischievous a conduct in the brother most indebted to me.' When I was a mere lieutenant of artillery, I brought him up with the scanty means which my pay afforded me I divided my bread with him; and this is the return he makes for my kindness!' The Emperor was so overpowered by his emotion, that his grief was said to have vented itself in sobs."—Savary, tom. ii., part ii., p. 239.

HOLLAND ANNEXED TO FRANCE

The fate of Holland was not long undecided. Indeed, it had probably been determined on as far back as Champagny's first report, in which it had been intimated, that Holland, with all its provinces, was to become an integral part of France. This was contrary to the pledge given by Napoleon to the Senate, that the Rhine should be considered as the natural boundary of France; nor was it less inconsistent with his pretended determination, that the independence of Holland should be respected and maintained. But both these engagements yielded to the force of the reasoning used by his mouth-piece Champagny, in recommending the union of Holland with the French empire, and with France itself. They are worth quoting, were it only to show how little men of sense are ashamed to produce the weakest and most inconsistent arguments, when they speak as having both the power and the settled purpose to do wrong. "Holland," said the minister, whose very effrontery renders his arguments interesting; "is in a manner an emanation from the territory of France, and is necessary to the full complement of the empire. To possess the entire Rhine," (which had been proposed as the natural boundary of France,) "your majesty must extend the frontier to the Zuyder-Zee. Thus the course of all the rivers which arise in France, or which bathe her frontier, will belong to her as far as the sea. To leave in the hands of strangers the mouths of our rivers, would be, Sire, to confine your power to an ill-bounded monarchy, instead of extending its dominions to the natural limits befitting an imperial throne." On such precious reasoning (much on a par with the claim which Napoleon set up to Great Britain as the natural appendage of France, along with the isle of Oleron,) Holland was, 9th July, 1810, declared an integral part of the French empire.

But the usurpation was not unavenged. It cost Buonaparte a greater declension in public opinion than had arisen even from his unprincipled attempts on Spain. It is true, none of the bloody and extensively miserable consequences had occurred in Holland, which had been occasioned by the transactions at Bayonne. But the seizure of Holland brought Buonaparte's worst fault, his ambition, before the public, in a more broad and decided point of view.[71]

There were people who could endure his robbing strangers, who were yet shocked that he, so fond of his kindred, and in general so liberal to them, should not have hesitated to dethrone his own brother, merely for entertaining sentiments becoming the rank to which he had been raised by himself; to disinherit his nephew; to go nigh taxing so near a relation with mental imbecility; and all on so slight a provocation;—for the only real point of difference, that, viz. respecting the English commerce, had been yielded by Louis in the treaty which Napoleon had signed, but only, it seemed, for the purpose of breaking it. It was observed, too, that in the manly, but respectful opposition made by Louis to his brother's wishes, there appeared nothing to provoke the displeasure of Napoleon, though one of the most irritable of men on subjects with which his ambition was implicated. It seemed a species of gratuitous violence, acted as if to show that no circumstance of relationship, family feeling, or compassion (to make no mention of justice or moderation,) could interfere with or check the progress of Napoleon's ambition; and whilst the more sanguine prophesied, that he who ran so rashly, might one day run himself to a close, all agreed that his empire, composed of such heterogeneous parts, could not, in all probability, survive the mortal date of the founder, supposing it to last so long. In the meantime, it was evident, that the condition of no state, however solemnly guaranteed by Buonaparte himself, could be considered as secure or free from change while it was subject to his influence. To conclude the whole, the Dutch were informed by the Emperor with bitter composure, that "he had hoped to unite them to France as allies, by giving them a prince of his own blood as a ruler; that his hopes, however, had been deceived; and that he had shown more forbearance than consisted with his character, or than his rights required;"—thus intimating some farther and unexpressed severity, which he might have felt himself justified in adding to the virtual exile of his brother, and the confiscation of his late dominions; and insinuating, that the Dutch

---

[71] Napoleon acknowledged at St. Helena, that the "annexation of Louis' kingdom to his own was a measure which contributed to ruin his credit in Europe."—Las Cases, tom. ii., p. 307.

had escaped cheaply with the loss of their separate national existence.

CHAPTER LIII

Gustavus IV. of Sweden is Dethroned and succeeded by his Uncle—The Crown Prince killed by a fall from his horse—Candidates proposed for the Succession—The Swedes, thinking to conciliate Napoleon, fix on Bernadotte—Buonaparte reluctantly acquiesces in the choice—Parting Interview between Bernadotte and Napoleon—Subsequent attempts of the latter to bind Sweden to the policy of France—The Crown Prince unwillingly accedes to the Continental System—Napoleon makes a Tour through Flanders and Holland—returns to Paris, and takes measures for extending the Continental System—Seizure of the Valois—Coast along the German Ocean annexed to France—Protest by the Czar against the appropriation of Oldenburg—Russia allows the importation, at certain Seaports, of various articles of British Commerce—Negotiations for Exchange of Prisoners between France and England; and for a general Peace, broken off by Buonaparte's unreasonable Demands.

GUSTAVUS IV. OF SWEDEN DETHRONED

In the destruction of the kingdom of Holland, a new sceptre, and that of Napoleon's own forming, was broken, as he wrenched it out of the hands of his brother. In the case of Sweden, and in hopes of ensuring the patronage of the French Emperor, or averting his enmity, a diadem was placed on the brows of one, who, like Napoleon himself, had commenced his career as a soldier of fortune.

We have repeatedly observed, that the high spirit and intrepid enterprise of Gustavus IV., unsupported as they were either by distinguished military abilities, or by effectual power, seemed as if he aped the parts of Gustavus Adolphus or Charles XII., without considering the declined condition of the country he governed, or the inferiority of his own talents. Sweden had suffered great losses by the daring manner in which this prince maintained the ancient principles of aristocracy against the overwhelming power of France.

Pomerania, being the only dominion belonging to Sweden on the south side of the Baltic, had been taken possession of by France in the war of 1806-7; and Russia, who had been a party to that war, and who had encouraged Gustavus to maintain it, had, since changing her politics at the treaty of Tilsit, herself declared war against Sweden, for the sole and undisguised purpose of possessing herself of Finland, which she had succeeded in appropriating. Sweden had, therefore, lost, under this ill-fated monarch, above one-third of her territories, and the inhabitants became anxious to secure, even were it by desperate measures, the independence of that which remained. There were fears lest Russia should aspire to the conquest of the rest of the ancient kingdom—fears that France might reward the adhesion and the sufferings of Denmark, by uniting the crown of Sweden with that of Denmark and Norway, and aiding the subjugation of the country with an auxiliary army. While these calamities impended over their ancient state, the Swedes felt confident that Gustavus was too rash to avert the storm by submission, too weak, and perhaps too unlucky, to resist its violence. This conviction led to a conspiracy, perhaps one of the most universally known in history.

The unfortunate king was seized upon and made prisoner in March, 1809, without any other resistance than his own unassisted sword could maintain; and so little were the conspirators afraid of his being able to find a party in the state desirous of replacing him in the government, that they were content he should have his liberty and a suitable pension on his agreeing to consider himself as an exile from Sweden;[72] in which sentence of banishment, with little

---

[72] Annual Register, vol. li., p. 475.

pretence to justice, his wife, sister of the Empress of Russia, and his children, comprehending the heir of his crown, were also included.[73]

The Duke of Sudermania, uncle of the dethroned prince, was called to the throne, and the succession of the kingdom was destined to Christian of Augustenberg, a prince of the house of Holstein. Peace was made by the new King with Russia, at the expense of ceding Finland and the isle of Aland to that power. Soon afterwards a treaty was signed at Paris, by which Charles XIII. promised to adhere to the Continental System, and to shut his ports against all British commerce, with certain indulgences on the articles of salt and colonial produce. In requital, Napoleon restored to Sweden her continental province of Pomerania, with the isle of Rugen, reserving, however, such dotations or pensions as he had assigned to his soldiers or followers, upon those territories. But though the politics of Sweden were thus entirely changed, its revolution was destined to proceed.

The King being aged, the eyes of the people were much fixed on the successor, or Crown Prince, who took upon himself the chief labour of the government, and appears to have given satisfaction to the nation. But his government was of short duration. On the 28th of May, 1810, while reviewing some troops, he suddenly fell from his horse, and expired on the spot, leaving Sweden again without any head excepting the old King. This event agitated the whole nation, and various candidates were proposed for the succession of the kingdom.

Among these was the King of Denmark, who, after the sacrifices he had made for Buonaparte, had some right to expect his support. The son of the late unfortunate monarch, rightful heir of the crown, and named like him Gustavus, was also proposed as a candidate. The Duke of Oldenburg, brother-in-law of the Emperor

---

[73] "A conspiracy of no common kind tore him from the throne, and transported him out of his states. The unanimity evinced against him is, no doubt, a proof of the wrongs he had committed. I am ready to admit, that he was inexcusable and even mad; but it is, notwithstanding, extraordinary and unexampled, that, in that crisis a single sword was not drawn in his defence, whether from affection, from gratitude, from virtuous feeling, or even from mere simplicity, if it must be so; and truly, it is a circumstance which does little honour to the atmosphere of kings."—Napoleon, *Las Cases*, tom. iii., p. 169.

of Russia, had partisans. To each of these candidates there lay practical objections. To have followed the line of lawful succession, and called Gustavus to the throne (which could not be forfeited by his father's infirmity, so far as he was concerned,) would have been to place a child at the head of the state, and must have inferred, amid this most arduous crisis, all the doubts and difficulties of choosing a regent. Such choice might, too, be the means, at a future time, of reviving his father's claim to the crown. The countries of Denmark and Sweden had been too long rivals for the Swedes to subject themselves to the yoke of the King of Denmark; and to choose the Duke of Oldenburg would have been, in effect, to submit themselves to Russia, of whose last behaviour towards her Sweden had considerable reason to complain.

BERNADOTTE

In this embarrassment they were thought to start a happy idea, who proposed to conciliate Napoleon by bestowing the ancient crown of the Goths upon one of his own field-marshals, and a high noble of his empire, namely, John Baptiste Julian Bernadotte, Prince of Ponte Corvo. This distinguished officer was married to a sister of Joseph Buonaparte's wife (daughter of a wealthy and respectable individual, named Cléry,) through whom he had the advantage of an alliance with the Imperial family of Napoleon, and he had acquired a high reputation in the north of Europe, both when governor of Hanover, and administrator of Swedish Pomerania. On the latter occasion, Bernadotte was said to have shown himself in a particular manner the friend and protector of the Swedish nation; and it was even insinuated, that he would not be averse to exchange the errors of Popery for the reformed tenets of Luther. The Swedish nation fell very generally into the line of policy which prompted this choice. Humiliating as it might, at another period, have been to a people proud of their ancient renown, to choose for their master a foreign soldier, differing from them in birth and religious faith, such an election yet promised to place at the head of the nation a person admirably qualified to comprehend and encounter the difficulties of the time; and it was a choice, sure, as they thought, to be agreeable to him upon whose nod the world seemed to depend.

Yet, there is the best reason to doubt, whether, in preferring Bernadotte to their vacant throne, the Swedes did a thing which was gratifying to Napoleon. The name of the Crown Prince of Sweden elect, had been known in the wars of the Revolution, before that of Buonaparte had been heard of. Bernadotte had been the older, though certainly not therefore the better soldier. On the 18th Brumaire, he was so far from joining Buonaparte in his enterprise against the Council of Five Hundred, notwithstanding all advances made to him, that he was on the spot at St. Cloud armed and prepared, had circumstances permitted, to place himself at the head of any part of the military, who might be brought to declare for the Directory. And although, like every one else, Bernadotte submitted to the Consular system, and held the government of Holland under Buonaparte, yet then, as well as under the empire, he was always understood to belong to a class of officers, whom Napoleon employed indeed, and rewarded, but without loving them, or perhaps relying on them, more than he was compelled to do, although their character was in most instances a warrant for their fidelity.

These officers formed a comparatively small class yet comprehending some of the most distinguished names in the French army, who, in seeing the visionary Republic glide from their grasp, had been, nevertheless, unable to forget the promises held out to them by the earlier dawn of the Revolution. Reconciled by necessity to a state of servitude which they could not avoid, this party considered themselves as the soldiers of France, not of Napoleon, and followed the banner of their country rather than the fortunes of the Emperor. Without being personally Napoleon's enemies, they were not the friends of his despotic power; and it was to be expected, should any opportunity occur, that men so thinking would make a stand, for the purpose of introducing some modifications into the arbitrary system which the Emperor had established.

Napoleon, always deeply politic, unless when carried off by sudden bursts of temperament, took, as already mentioned, great care, in his distribution of duties and honours, at once to conceal from the public the existence of a difference in opinion among his general officers, and also to arm the interests of those patriots themselves against their own speculative opinions, by rendering the present state of things too beneficial to them for their being easily induced to attempt any change. Still it may nevertheless be conceived, that it was not out of this class of lukewarm adherents he would have voluntarily selected a candidate for a kingdom, which, being removed at some distance from the influence of France, he would more willingly have seen conferred on some one, whose devotion to the will of his Emperor was not likely to be disturbed by any intrusion of conscientious patriotism.

But, besides the suspicion entertained by Napoleon of Bernadotte's political opinions, subjects of positive discord had recently arisen between them. Bernadotte had been blamed by the Emperor for permitting the escape of Romana and the Spaniards, as already mentioned. At a later period, he was commander of the Saxon troops in the campaign of Wagram; and, notwithstanding a set of very scientific manœuvres, by which he detained General Bellegarde on the frontiers of Bohemia, when his presence might have been essentially useful to the Archduke Charles, he was censured by Napoleon as tardy in his movements.

The landing of the English at Walcheren induced Fouché, as has been already said, with the concurrence of Clarke, then minister at war, to intrust Bernadotte with the charge of the defence of Flanders and Holland. But neither in this service had he the good fortune to please the Emperor. Fouché, at whose instance he had accepted the situation, was already tottering in office; and the ill-selected expression, "that however necessary Napoleon was to the glory of France, yet his presence was not indispensable to repel invasion,"[74] was interpreted into a magnifying of themselves at the expense of the Emperor. Napoleon made his displeasure manifest by depriving Bernadotte of the command in Belgium, and sending him back to the north of Germany; and it is said that the general, on his part, was so little inclined to make a secret of his resentment, that he was remarked as a fiery Gascon, who, if he should ever have an opportunity, would be likely to do mischief.

---

[74] Fouché, tom. i., p. 337.

SWEDEN

But while such were the bad terms betwixt the Emperor and his general, the Swedes, unsuspicious of the true state of the case, imagined, that in choosing Bernadotte for successor to their throne, they were paying to Buonaparte the most acceptable tribute. And notwithstanding that Napoleon was actually at variance with Bernadotte, and although, in a political view, he would much rather have given his aid to the pretensions of the King of Denmark,[75] he was under the necessity of reflecting, that Sweden retained a certain degree of independence; that the sea separated her shores from his armies; and that, however willing to conciliate him, the Swedes were not in a condition absolutely to be compelled to receive laws at his hand. It was necessary to acquiesce in their choice, since he could not dictate to them; and by doing so he might at the same time exhibit another splendid example of the height to which his service conducted his generals, of his own desire to assist their promotion, and of that which might be much more doubtful than the two first propositions—of his willingness to pay deference to the claims of a people in electing their chief magistrate. When, therefore, Bernadotte, protesting that he would be exclusively guided by Napoleon's wishes in pursuing or relinquishing this important object, besought him for his countenance with the States of Sweden, who were to elect the Crown Prince, Buonaparte answered, that he would not interfere in the election by any solicitations or arguments, but that he gave the Prince of Ponte Corvo his permission to be a candidate, and should be well pleased if he proved a successful one. Such is Napoleon's account of the transaction.[76] We have, however, been favoured with some manuscript observations, in which a very

---

[75] "The real king," he said, "according to my political system and the true interests of France, was the king of Denmark; because I should then have governed Sweden by the influence of my simple contact with the Danish provinces."

[76] "I, the elected monarch of the people, had to answer, that I could not set myself against the elections of other people. It was what I told Bernadotte, whose whole attitude betrayed the anxiety excited by the expectation of my answer. I added, that he had only to take advantage of the good-will of which he had been the object; that I wished to be considered as having had no weight in his election, but that it had my approbation and my best wishes. I felt, however, shall I say it, a secret instinct, which made the thing disagreeable and painful. Bernadotte was, in fact, the serpent which I nourished in my bosom."—Napoleon, *Las Cases*, tom. iii., p. 171.

different colour is given to Napoleon's proceedings, and which prove distinctly, that while Napoleon treated the Crown Prince Elect of Sweden with fair language, he endeavoured by underhand intrigues to prevent the accomplishment of his hopes.[77]

The Swedes, however, remained fixed in their choice, notwithstanding the insinuations of Desaugier, the French envoy, whom Napoleon afterwards affected to disown and recall, for supporting in the diet of Orebro, the interest of the King of Denmark, instead of that of Bernadotte.

Napoleon's cold assent, or rather an assurance that he would not dissent, being thus wrung reluctantly from him, Bernadotte, owing to his excellent character among the Swedes, and their opinion of his interest with Napoleon, was chosen Crown Prince of Sweden, by the States of that kingdom, 21st August, 1810. Napoleon, as he himself acknowledges, was enabled to resist, though with difficulty, a strong temptation to retract his consent, and defeat the intended election. Perhaps this unfriendly disposition might be in some degree overcome by the expectation, that by their present choice the Emperor of France would secure the accession of Sweden to the anti-commercial system; whereas, by attempting a game which he was not equally sure of winning, he might, indeed, have disappointed a man whom he loved not, but by doing so must run the risk of throwing the States of Sweden, who were not likely to be equally unanimous in behalf of any other French candidate, into the arms of England, his avowed foe; or of Russia, who, since the treaty of Schoenbrun, and Napoleon's union with the House of Austria, could only be termed a doubtful and cloudy friend.

But he endeavoured to obtain from Bernadotte some guarantee of his dependence upon France and its Emperor. He took the opportunity of making the attempt when Bernadotte applied to him for letters of emancipation from his allegiance to France, which could not decently be withheld from the Prince Royal of another country. "The expediting of the letters patent," said Napoleon, "has been retarded by a proposal made by the Council, that Bernadotte

---

[77] See Reflections on the Conduct of Napoleon towards the Crown Prince of Sweden, in the Appendix to this Volume, No. I.

should previously bind himself never to bear arms against Napoleon." Bernadotte exclaimed against a proposal which must have left him in the rank of a French general. The Emperor was ashamed to persist in a demand so unreasonable, and dismissed him with the almost prophetic words—"Go—our destinies must be accomplished." He promised the Prince Royal two millions of francs as an indemnity for the principality of Ponte Corvo, and other possessions which had been assigned to him in Holland, and which he restored on ceasing to be a subject of France. It is singular enough that Napoleon, while at St. Helena, permitted himself to assert that he had made a present of this money (of which only one million was ever paid,) to enable Bernadotte to take possession of his new dignity with becoming splendour.

To bring the affairs of Sweden to a close for the present, we may here add, that, though that nation were desirous to escape the renewal of the desperate and hopeless struggle with France, they were most unwilling, nevertheless, to lose the advantages of their commerce with England. The conduct of the national business soon devolved entirely upon the Crown Prince, the age and infirmities of the King not permitting him to conduct them any longer. It became Bernadotte's, or, as he was now named, Charles John's difficult and delicate task, to endeavour at once to propitiate France, and to find excuses which might dispose Buonaparte to grant some relaxation on the subject of the Continental System. But as it was impossible for the Prince of Sweden to disguise his motive for evading a cordial co-operation in Napoleon's favourite measure, so the latter, about three months after the accession of his former companion in arms to supreme power, grew impatient enough to overwhelm the Swedish minister, Baron Lagerbjelke, with a tirade similar to his celebrated attack on Lord Whitworth. He discoursed with the utmost volubility for an hour and a quarter, leaving the astonished ambassador scarce an opening to thrust in a word by way of observation, defence, or answer. "Do they believe in Sweden that I am to be so easily duped? Do they think I will be satisfied with this half state of things? Give me no sentiments! it is from facts we form our opinions. You signed the peace with me in the beginning of the year, and engaged yourself then to break off all communication with Britain; yet you retained an English agent till late in the summer, and kept the communication open by way of Gottenburg. Your small islands are so many smuggling magazines; your vessels meet the English and exchange freights. I have not slept an hour to-night on account of your affairs; yet you ought to suffer me to take repose, I have need of it. You have vessels in every port in England. You talk of the necessity of buying salt, forsooth. Is it for salt you go into the Thames?—You talk of suffering, by superseding the trade. Do you not believe that I suffer? That Germany, Bourdeaux, Holland, and France suffer? But it must all be ended. You must fire on the English, and you must confiscate their merchandise, or you must have war with France. Open war, or constant friendship—this is my last word, my ultimate determination. Could they think in Sweden that I would modify my system, because I love and esteem the Prince Royal? Did I not love and esteem the King of Holland? He is my brother, yet I have broken with him: I have silenced the voice of nature to give ear to that of the general interest." These, and many violent expressions to the same purpose, Buonaparte poured out in an elevation of voice that might be heard in the adjoining apartments.

The Emperor's remonstrances, transmitted by the ambassador, were seconded at the Court of Stockholm by the arguments of Denmark and Russia; and the Crown Prince was at last obliged to give the national adherence of Sweden to the Continental System, and to declare war against England.[78] The British Government were fully sensible of the constraint under which Sweden acted, and, so far from acting hostilely towards that kingdom, did not seem to make any perceptible change in the relations which had before subsisted between the countries.

In the meantime, Bernadotte and Napoleon, for a time, veiled under the usual forms of courtesy their mutual dislike and resentment. But the Crown Prince could not forgive the Emperor for an attempt to lord it over him like a superior over a vassal, and compelling him, notwithstanding his entreaties, to distress his subjects, and to render his government unpopular, by sacrificing a lucrative trade. Napoleon, on the other hand, was incensed that Bernadotte, whose greatness he considered as existing only by his

---

[78] Annual Register, vol. lii., p. 518.

own permission, should affect to differ in opinion from him, or hesitate betwixt obliging France and injuring Sweden.

On other occasional differences betwixt the sovereigns, it appeared that there was no eager desire on the part of the Crown Prince of Sweden to oblige the Emperor of France. Repeated demands for sailors and soldiers to be engaged in the French service, were made by Napoleon. These Bernadotte always contrived to evade, by referring to the laws of Sweden, as a limited monarchy, which did not permit him, like the absolute Majesty of Denmark, to dispose of her sailors at pleasure; and by enlarging on the nature of the Swedes, who, bold and willing soldiers at home, were too much attached to their own climate and manners, to endure those of any other country. In these, and such like excuses, no one could read more readily than Napoleon, a fixed resolution on the part of his old companion in arms, not to yield to the influence of France in any point in which he could avoid it. And though an outward show of friendship was maintained between the countries, and even between the sovereigns, yet it was of that insincere kind which was sure to be broken off on the slightest collision of their mutual interests. It remained, however, undisturbed till the eventful year of 1812.—We return to the affairs of France.

TOUR THROUGH BELGIUM

The Emperor undertook a tour through the provinces of Flanders and Holland with his young Empress, with the view of enforcing his views and purposes in church and state. In the course of this journey, one or two remarkable circumstances took place. The first was his furious reproaches to the clergy of Brabant, who, more rigorous Papists than in some other Catholic countries, had circulated among their congregations the bull of excommunication fulminated by the Pope against Napoleon. The provocation was certainly considerable, but the mode of resenting it was indecently violent. He was especially angry that they appeared without their canonical dresses. "You call yourselves priests," he said; "where are your vestments? Are you attorneys, notaries, or peasants? You begin by forgetting the respect due to me; whereas, the principle of the

Christian Church, as these gentlemen" (turning to the Protestant deputies) "can teach you, is, as they have just professed, to render unto Cæsar the things which are Cæsar's. But you—you will not pray for your sovereign, because a Romish priest excommunicated me. But who gave him such a right? Perhaps it is your wish to bring back tortures and scaffolds, but I will take care to baffle you. I bear the temporal sword, and know how to use it. I am a monarch of God's creation, and you reptiles of the earth dare not oppose me. I render an account of my government to none save God and Jesus Christ. Do you think I am one formed to kiss the Pope's slipper? Had you the power, you would shave my head, clap a cowl on me, and plunge me in a cloister. But if you preach not the Gospel as the Apostles did, I will banish you from the empire, and disperse you like so many Jews.—And, Monsieur le Préfet, see that these men swear to the Concordat; and take care that the orthodox Gospel be taught in the ecclesiastical seminaries, that they may send out men of sense, and not idiots like these." Thus closed this edifying admonition.

The Dutch were under the necessity of assuming the appearance of great rejoicing; yet even the danger of indulging their blunt humour, could not altogether restrain these downright merchants. When the Emperor made a stir about establishing a Chamber of Commerce at Amsterdam, one of the burgomasters gravely observed, there was no need of a chamber, since a closet would hold all the commerce left them. In like manner, when Napoleon was vaunting, that he would soon have a fleet of two hundred sail; "And when you have got them," said a plain-spoken citizen, "the English will have double the number."

But, more formidable than blunt truths and indifferent jests, there appeared, while Buonaparte was in Holland, one of those stern invocations exciting the people against foreign tyranny, which have often occasioned the downfall of unjust power, and always rendered those who possess it unhappy and insecure. "People of Holland," said this singular paper (which may be compared to the tract called Killing no Murder, which drove sleep from Cromwell's pillow,) "why do you fear your oppressor?—he is one, you are many. Appeal to his very soldiers; their desertions in Spain show how they hate him; and even his generals would abandon him, could they secure their own rank and grandeur independent of his. But above all, arise to the task of your own redemption; rise in the fulness of national strength. A general revolt of the Continent will ensue; the oppressor will fall, and your triumph will be a warning to tyrants, and an example to the world." This address produced no perceptible effect at the time, but, with other papers of the kind, it made a profound impression on the public mind.

On his return to Paris, Napoleon set himself still farther to impose the extension of the Continental System, which he was induced to attempt by the appropriation of Holland, and the revolution in Sweden. Holding his plan as much more decisive than it could have been, even if his power and his spleen had been adequate to effect his purpose, he cast his eyes in every direction, to close every aperture, however small, through which British commerce, the victim he hoped entirely to smother, might draw ever so slight a gasp of breath.

It was a feature of Buonaparte's ambition—as indeed it is of inordinate ambition in general—that whatever additions were made to his Empire extended his wish of acquisition. Holland, whose traders were princes, and she herself the Queen of Commerce, had been already devoured, with her ample sea-coast and far-famed harbours. But other cities, less wealthy and famed, yet still venerable from their ancient importance, must become a part of France, ere Buonaparte thought his blockade against British commerce complete and impervious.

The seizure of the poor regions called the Valais, which had hitherto been suffered to exist as a free republic, gave France the absolute command of the road over the Simplon; the property, and perhaps the command of which passage, it being the great means of communication betwixt France and Italy, Napoleon did not incline should remain with a petty republic. It was a sufficient reason, at this unhappy period, for depriving any country of its independence, that France was to be benefited by the change. It was not in this case a bloodless one. The poor mountaineers drew to arms, and it required some fighting before they were compelled to submission, and their barren mountains were annexed to France.

But it was of much greater importance, in Napoleon's eye, to prevent the commerce which he had expelled from Holland from shifting its residence to the trading towns of the north of Germany, composing what was called the Hanseatic League. A new appropriation of territory, therefore, united to France the whole sea-coast along the German Ocean, comprehending the mouths of the Scheldt, the Meuse, and the Rhine; the Ems, the Weser, and the Elbe. And it was the Emperor's proposal to unite these maritime territories to France by a canal, which was to join the Baltic ocean to the Seine. A considerable proportion of the kingdom of Westphalia, and of the Grand Duchy of Berg, both principalities of Napoleon's own creation, fell under this appropriation, and formed another example, had not that of Holland been sufficient, to show how little respect Napoleon was disposed to pay even to those rights which emanated from himself, when they interfered with fresher plans and wider prospects of ambition.

Had Prussia retained her ancient influence as protector of the North, Hamburgh, Bremen, and Lubeck, would not have been thus unceremoniously melted down and confounded with the French Empire. But while these venerable and well-known free cities sunk without protection or resistance under a despotism which threatened to become universal, a petty state of far less consequence, scarce known as having an independent existence by any who was not intimate with the divisions of the north of Germany, found a patron, and a powerful one. This was Oldenburg, a dukedom, the present prince of which was related to the Emperor of Russia, as both were descended of the House of Holstein Gottorp, and was, moreover, Alexander's brother-in-law. This state of Oldenburg had been studiously excepted from the changes made in the North of Germany, after the treaty of Tilsit, which made the present confiscation of its territory an act of more marked slight towards the court of Russia. A formal expostulation being transmitted to Napoleon, he proposed to repair the injury of the Duke of Oldenburg, by assigning to him the town and territory of Erfurt, with the lordship of Blankenheim. But the duke felt himself too strongly supported to be under the necessity of surrendering his dominions, and receiving others in exchange. The offer of indemnity was haughtily rejected; France persevered in her purpose of usurping Oldenburg; and the Emperor Alexander, in a protest, gravely but temperately worded, a copy of which was delivered to every member of the diplomatic body, intimated that he did not acquiesce in the injury done to a prince of his family, although he continued to adhere to that great line of political interest which had occasioned the alliance between France and Russia.

The real truth was, that Napoleon, secure of the friendship of Austria by the late alliance, had not, it would seem, regarded Russia as any longer worthy of the same observance which he had originally found it politic to pay to the Emperor Alexander. The Czar himself felt this; and the very large proportion of his subjects, composing the party of Old Russians, as they termed themselves, who were favourable to the English alliance, and detested the connexion with France, improved the opportunity by pointing out the evils which all classes in the country endured, from the Czar's having, in complaisance to the plans of Napoleon, decreed the abolition of English commerce. They showed that this compliance with the views of France had been attended with great detriment to his own subjects, who could neither sell their commodities, and the produce of their estates, for which Britain always offered a market, nor acquire the colonial produce and British manufactured goods, which the consumption of Russia almost peremptorily demanded.

RUSSIAN PROTEST

An ukase was issued on the 31st of December, 1810, which was drawn up with considerable art; for while in words it seemed to affirm the exclusion of British manufactures from the empire in general, it permitted importations to be made at Archangel, Petersburgh, Riga, Revel, and five or six other seaports, where various articles of merchandise, and, in particular, colonial produce, unless proved to belong to Britain, might be freely imported. So that, while appearing to quote and respect the Continental System, Napoleon could not but be sensible that Russia virtually renounced it. But as Alexander had not ventured to avail himself of the seizure of Oldenburg as a reason for breaking off his alliance with France, so Napoleon, on his part, though the changed tone of Russian policy could not escape him, paused, nevertheless, in coming to a final rupture with an enemy so powerful, upon the subject of the ukase of December 1810.

EXCHANGE OF PRISONERS

Meantime, the French Emperor became probably sensible that peace with England was the surest ground upon which he could secure his throne. In the month of April, 1810, some attempt at obtaining terms of pacification had been made during the mission of Mr. Mackenzie, who was sent to Morlaix as agent on the part of the British Government. It had been not the least cruel peculiarity of this inveterate war, that no cartel for exchange of prisoners had been effected on either side, and, of course, that those unhappy persons whom chance had thrown into the power of the enemy, had no visible alternative but to linger out their lives in a distant and hostile country, or at least remain captives till the conclusion of hostilities, to which no one could presume to assign a date. The original impediment to such an exchange, which has in all civilized countries been considered as a debt indispensably due to soften the rigours of war and lessen the sufferings of its victims, was a demand of Napoleon that the persons possessing no military character, whom he had made prisoners contrary to the law of nations at the commencement of hostilities, should be exchanged against French sailors and soldiers. The British ministers for a long time resisted so unusual an application, to which policy, indeed, forbade them to accede. At length, however, the sufferings of individuals, and of their families, induced the British government to allow the French Emperor the advantage of his oppressive act in detaining these unfortunate persons, and agree that they should be included in the proposed cartel. But when the commissioners met at Morlaix, Mr. Mackenzie found himself as far from approaching an agreement as ever. The number of French prisoners in Britain was more by many thousands than that of the British in France; and Buonaparte, who seldom made a bargain in which he did not secure the advantage to himself, insisted that the surplus of French prisoners should be exchanged for Germans, Spaniards, Portuguese, or others who should be captive in France.

This was readily agreed to, so far as regarded foreign troops in British pay; but it was equally unreasonable and contrary to usage to require that we should restore to France her native subjects, whose services she might use to augment her military force, while we received in exchange foreigners, unconnected with us by service or allegiance, and who, perhaps, when set at liberty, might be as apt to join the French ranks, as those of the nation in whose name they had obtained freedom.

After much wrangling and dispute, Mr. Mackenzie, to show the sincere desire which the British government entertained of releasing the prisoners on both sides, made a proposal that the exchange should commence by liberating as many French prisoners as could be balanced by British captives in the French prisons; that after this, captives of every nation should be exchanged indifferently on both sides; and whatever number of prisoners might remain on either side, after the general balance had been struck, should also be set at liberty, upon an engagement not to serve till regularly exchanged. To this proposal—a more liberal one could hardly be made—the French only answered by starting new demands, and making new objections. Among these, perhaps, it will scarcely be believed, that Moustier, the French commissioner, had the modesty to propose that Lord Wellington and his army, lying in the lines at Torres Vedras, should be reckoned as French prisoners in the proposed cartel! Mr. Mackenzie answered with becoming spirit, that he would neither be the medium through which his Government should be insulted by such a proposal, nor would he proceed in the negotiation until this impertinence were atoned for.

It is needless to proceed farther in the elusory detail of a treaty, which Napoleon had previously determined should be brought to no useful issue. He had calculated which country could best support the absence of their prisoners, or rather to whom their services were of most consequence. He felt that he himself, by the conscription, as well as by the auxiliary troops which he could summon at pleasure from his neighbours or dependents, could always command a sufficiency of men even for his gigantic undertakings; while to Britain, whose soldiers could only be obtained by a high bounty, the deliverance of her prisoners was proportionally more valuable. Whatever was his view in establishing the negotiation, which was probably only to satisfy the French army, by evincing a seeming interest in the unfortunate portion of their brethren in arms who were immured in English prisons, they gave way to the consideration, that while things remained as they were, Britain suffered more in proportion than France.

Some proposals for a general peace had been made during the conferences at Morlaix; and the British Government had stated three different principles, any of which they expressed themselves willing to admit as a basis. These were, first, the state of possession before the war; or, secondly, the present state of possession; or, thirdly, a plan of reciprocal compensations. But none of these principles suited the French Government to act upon; so that the treaty for a general peace, and that for restoring, taking into calculation the prisoners on both sides, upwards of a hundred thousand human beings to liberty, their country, and their home, proved both of them altogether nugatory.

The note of defiance was therefore resumed, so soon as it had been ascertained that Britain would reject any terms of peace which were not founded on equal and liberal principles. An oration of Count Semonville demonstrated, that it was all owing to the persevering ambition of England that Buonaparte had been obliged to possess himself of the sea-coast of Europe—that all his encroachments on the land were the necessary consequences of her empire of the seas. He then demanded, in prophetic fury, to know what in future would be the bounds of possibility. "It is the part of England," he said, "to reply. Let her turn her eyes on the past, and learn to judge from thence the events of the future. France and Napoleon will never change."

Chapter LIV

View of Napoleon's gigantic Power—The Empress Maria Louisa delivered of a Son—Criticism on the Title given him, of King of Rome—Speculations in regard to the advantages or disadvantages arising from this Event—Retrospect—Ex-Queen of Etruria—Her severe and unjustifiable Treatment by Napoleon—Lucien Buonaparte is invited to England, where he writes Epic Poetry—Attempt to deliver Ferdinand, defeated—Operations in Portugal—Retreat of Massena—Battles of Fuentes d'Onoro fought by Lord Wellington—On the South Frontier of Portugal, by Lord Beresford—Of Barossa, by General Graham—Enterprise of Arroyo-Molinas—Spaniards defeated under Blake—Valencia captured by the French, and he and his Army made Prisoners of War—Disunion among the French Generals—Joseph wishes to abdicate the Throne of Spain.

ACTUAL DOMINIONS

The natural consequences of an overgrown empire were already sapping that of Napoleon; for extent of territory does not constitute power, any more than corpulence in the human frame constitutes strength or health; and Napoleon's real authority was in truth greater some years before, than now when his dominion was so much enlarged. The war in Spain, maintained at such an expense of blood and treasure, was a wasting and consuming sore. The kingdom of Holland had afforded him supplies more readily, and had more the means of doing so, when under the dominion of his brother Louis, than the Dutch now either showed or possessed, when ranked as a constituent part of the French empire. The same might be said of the states and free towns in the north of Germany; where, in many instances, strong bands of smugglers, dressed and armed as guerilla parties, maintained a desultory war with the officers of the French customs; and, moved equally by national hatred and the love of gain won by desperate risks, made in some districts a kind of petty civil war. Yet, though such cankerworms gnawed the root of the tree, the branches and foliage, to all outward appearance, extended a broader shade than ever. It was especially when a formal annunciation, both in France and Austria, called the good subjects of both realms to rejoice in the prospect that Maria Louisa would soon give an heir to Napoleon, that men who opened the map of Europe saw with fear and wonder the tremendous inheritance to which the expected infant was likely to succeed.

The actual dominions of France, governed by Napoleon in his own proper right as Emperor of the French, had gradually attained the following extravagant dimensions. They extended, from north-east to south-west, from Travemunde, on the Baltic ocean, to the foot of the Pyrenees; and, from north-west to south-east, from the port of Brest to Terracina, on the confines of the Neapolitan territories. A population of forty-two millions of people, fitted in various ways to secure the prosperity of a state, and inhabiting, for wealth, richness of soil, and felicity of climate, by far the finest portion of the civilized earth, formed the immediate liege subjects of this magnificent empire.

Yet, to stop here were greatly to undervalue the extent of Napoleon's power. We have to add to his personal empire Carniola and the Illyrian provinces, and also the fine kingdom of Italy. Then, in his character of Mediator of the Helvetian Republic, the Emperor exercised an almost absolute authority in Switzerland, which furnished him, though unwillingly, with several fine regiments of auxiliaries. The German confederation of the Rhine, though numbering kings among their league, were at the slightest hint bound to supply him each with his prescribed quota of forces, with a readiness and an affectation of zeal very different from the slack and reluctant manner in which they formerly supplied their paltry contingents to the Emperor of Germany.

Murat, with his kingdom of Naples, was at his brother-in-law's disposal; and if, as Buonaparte's hopes whispered, the Peninsula should ultimately prove unable to resist the war he waged, then Spain and Portugal would be added to his immense empire, being now in the state of sturdy and contumacious rebels, whose resistance seemed in the speedy prospect of being finally subdued. Thus, an empire of 800,000 square miles, and containing a population of 85 millions, in territory one-fifth part, and in the number of inhabitants one-half, of united Europe, was either in quiet subjection to Napoleon's sceptre, or on the point, as was supposed, of becoming so.

Of those who shared amongst them the residue of Europe, and still maintained some claim to independence, Britain might make the proud boast, that she was diametrically in opposition to the Ruler of the world; that, in the long-continued strife, she had dealt him injuries as deep as she had ever received, and had disdained, under any circumstances, to treat with him on less terms than those of equality. Not to that fair land be the praise, though she supported many burdens and endured great losses; but to Providence, who favoured her efforts and strengthened her resolutions; who gave her power to uphold her own good cause, which, in truth, was that of European independence, and courage to trust in the justice of Heaven, when the odds mustered against her seemed, in earthly calculation, so dreadful as to deprive, the wise of the head to counsel; the brave, of the heart to resist!

Denmark, so powerful was the voice which France had in her councils, might almost be accounted humbled to one of the federative principalities.

Sweden had but a moderate and second-rate degree of power. She felt, as other German nations, the withering blight of the Continental, or Anti-social System; but, circumstanced as she was, with the possession of Swedish Pomerania dependent on French pleasure, she had no other remedy than to wait her opportunity.

Still more was this the case with Prussia, through all her provinces the mortal enemy of the French name, but whom the large garrisons which France had planted in her dominions, and the numerous forces which she maintained there, compelled for the time to be as submissive as a handmaiden. It was true that the court were as noiselessly as possible, endeavouring to revive their military establishment; that they were dismissing the villains who had sold and betrayed their country, and replacing them by age which had been tried, or youth which had witnessed the agony of their country, and been trained up in thinking, that to avenge her was their dearest duty. True it was, also, that the people in Prussia, and many other parts of Germany, waited as for the day dawning, for the hope of winning back their freedom; but outward appearances indicated nothing of these smothered hopes, wishes, and preparations; and the general eye saw in Prussia only a nation resigned to her bondage, without, apparently, any hope of redemption.

Austria, besides the terrible losses which the last war had brought upon her, was now fettered to Napoleon by a link which gave the proud House of Hapsburg an apology for the submission, or at least the observance, which she paid to the son-in-law of her Emperor.

Turkey, though she would have had her turn, had the tide of fortune continued to keep the course in which it had so long flowed, was not yet in the way of being comprehended in Napoleon's plan of politics.

Russia was waging with the Porte an impolitic war of acquisition, to realise some of the selfish plans of aggrandisement which Napoleon had assented to, or perhaps suggested, at Tilsit and Erfurt. But he now witnessed them without wishing them success, and listened to the complaints of Austria, who unwillingly saw the ambitious views of Russia in these provinces. Of all the continental states, therefore, assuming even the semblance of independence, Russia seemed alone to possess it in reality; and from late acts of estrangement—such as the protest on the subject of the Duchy of Oldenburg, and the reception of British ships and merchandise into her ports—it certainly appeared that a different spirit was in the councils of this great empire than had ruled them during the meetings at Tilsit and Erfurt. Yet there were but few who thought that Russia, in opposition to the whole continent of Europe, would dare confront Napoleon; and still fewer, even of the most sanguine politicians, had any deep-grounded hope that her opposition would be effectual. Out of such a Cimmerian midnight, to all human views, was the day-spring of European liberty destined to arise.

America, happy in the Atlantic which severed her from Europe, now an almost universal scene of war or slavery, looked on in conscious security, and by reviving at this crisis disputed claims upon Britain, seemed to listen more to the recollection of recent enmity, than of mutual language, manners, and descent.

BIRTH OF THE KING OF ROME

Within a year after her marriage with Napoleon, the young Empress was announced to have been taken with the pains of labour. The case was a difficult and distressing one; and the professional person employed lost courage, and was afraid to do what was necessary. Napoleon appeared in the apartment, and commanded him to proceed as if the patient were the wife of an ordinary burgess. She was at length successfully and safely delivered of a fine boy, which Buonaparte, with feelings, doubtless, as highly strung as after a battle gained, carried into the next apartment, and exhibited in triumph to the great officers and courtiers, by whom he was unanimously hailed King of Rome, the dignity which had been destined to the heir of the French Republic.

The title did not, indeed, pass uncriticised. Some said, that taking the regal designation from a city where the very name of king had been accounted unlucky, had an ominous presage. Catholics objected to it, as it necessarily carried with it the recollection of the sacrilegious violence which had stripped the Pope of his temporal possessions. And lastly, it was asked, what chance there ever was of the execution of that part of the Italian constitution, which, after Napoleon's death, guaranteed the succession in the kingdom of Italy to some one different from the Emperor of France, when the title of King of Rome was assumed as that of the heir of the French empire?[79]

Such ominous remarks, however, only circulated among the disaffected, or passed with anti-imperial jests, satires, and calembourgs, through such saloons of the Faubourg St. Germain, as were still tenanted by the ancient and faithful adherents of the House of Bourbon. The city of Paris made as general a show of rejoicing as they ever testified when an heir was born to one of their most beloved sovereigns; deputations with addresses came from public bodies of every description; and, that flattery might sound the very base string of humility, the fashionable colour of dress for the season bore a name alluding to the young King of Rome, which delicacy, if not pride, ought to have rejected. But, perhaps, the strangest circumstance of the whole was, that the old dethroned King of Spain, and his consort, undertook a journey, for the purpose of carrying their personal congratulations on the birth of an heir, to one who had deposed, and was detaining in prison their own lineage, and had laid Spain, their native dominions, in blood, from the Pyrenees to the Pillars of Hercules.

Napoleon, and his more devoted admirers, rejoiced in this happy incident, as that which was most likely, in their eyes, to sustain the Empire of France, when fate should remove him by whom it was founded. The protection of the House of Austria, and the charm flung around the child by the high fame of the father, could not, it was thought, but ensure a peaceful accession to the throne, and an undisturbed security in possessing it. His life, too, was ensured in future against such fanatics as that of Schoenbrun; for what purpose would it serve to cut off the Emperor, when the empire was to survive, and descend in all its strength upon his son and heir?

---

[79] Jests, as well as serious observations, were made on this occasion. "Have you any commands for France?" said a Frenchman at Naples to an English friend; "I shall be there in two days."—"In France?" answered his friend, "I thought you were setting off for Rome."—"True; but Rome, by a decree of the Emperor, is now indissolubly united to France."—"I have no news to burden you with," said his friend; "but can I do any thing for you in England? I shall be there in half an hour."—"In England?" said the Frenchman, "and in half an hour!"—"Yes," said his friend, "within that time I shall be at sea, and the sea has been indissolubly united to the British empire."—S.

Others there were, who pretended that the advantages arising from the birth of the King of Rome, were balanced by corresponding inconveniences. These asserted, that several of the French great generals had followed the fortunes of Napoleon, in hopes that, upon his death in battle, or upon his natural decease, they, or some of them, might, like the successors of Alexander the Great, share amongst them the ample succession of kingdoms and principalities which were likely to become the property of the strongest and bravest, in the lottery which might be expected to take place on the death of the great favourite of Fortune. These great soldiers, it was surmised, being cut short of this fair prospect, would no longer have the same motives for serving the living Napoleon, whose inheritance at his death was now to descend, like the patrimony of a peasant or burgess, in the regular and lawful line of inheritance. But the politicians who argued thus, did not sufficiently regard the pitch of superiority which Napoleon had attained over those around him; his habit of absolute command, theirs of implicit obedience; and the small likelihood there was of any one who served under him venturing to incur his displeasure, and the risk of losing the rank and fortune which most had actually obtained, by showing any marks of coldness or dissatisfaction, on account of the disappointment of distant and visionary hopes.

There were others who augured different consequences, from the effect of the same event on the feelings of Buonaparte's enemies, both open and unavowed. It had been a general belief, and certainly was founded on probability, that the immense but ill-constructed empire which Napoleon had erected would fall to pieces, so soon as it was not kept steady and compact by the fear and admiration of his personal talents. Hence the damp cast by persons affecting a wise caution, upon the general desire to shake off the yoke of France. They enlarged upon the invincible talent, upon the inevitable destinies of Napoleon personally; but they consoled the more impatient patriots, by counselling them to await his death, before making a daring attempt to vindicate their freedom. Such counsels were favourably listened to, because men are, in spite of themselves, always willing to listen to prudent arguments, when they tend to postpone desperate risks. But this species of argument was ended, when the inheritance of despotism seemed ready to be transmitted from father to son in direct descent. There was no termination seen to the melancholy prospect, nor was it easy for the most lukewarm of patriots to assign any longer a reason for putting off till Napoleon's death the resistance which to-day demanded. Under these various lights was the birth of the King of Rome considered; and it may after all remain a matter of doubt, whether the blessing of a son and heir, acceptable as it must necessarily have been to his domestic feelings, was politically of that advantage to him which the Emperor of France unquestionably expected.

And now, before we begin to trace the growing differences betwixt France and Russia, which speedily led to such important consequences, we may briefly notice some circumstances connected with Spain and with Spanish affairs, though the two incidents which we are to mention first, are rather of a detached and insulated nature.

THE EX-QUEEN OF ETRURIA

The first of these refers to the Ex-Queen of Etruria, a daughter, it will be remembered, of Charles, King of Spain, and a sister of Ferdinand. Upon this princess and her son, Buonaparte had settled the kingdom of Etruria, or Tuscany. Preparatory to the Bayonne intrigue, he had forcibly deprived her of this dignity, in order to offer it as an indemnification to Ferdinand for the cession, which he proposed to that unhappy prince, of the inheritance of Spain. Having contrived to obtain that cession without any compensation, Buonaparte reserved Etruria to himself, and retained the late Queen as a hostage. For some time she was permitted to reside with her parents at Compeigne; but afterwards, under pretext of conducting her to Parma, she was escorted to Nice, and there subjected to the severe vigilance of the police. The princess appears to have been quicker in her feelings than the greater part of her family, which does not, indeed, argue any violent degree of sensibility. Terrified, however, and alarmed at the situation in which she found herself, she endeavoured to effect an escape into England. Two gentlemen of her retinue were sent to Holland, for the purpose of arranging her flight, but her project was discovered. On the 16th April, 1811, officers of police and gendarmes broke into the residence of the Queen at Nice, seized her person and papers, and, after detaining her in custody for two months, and threatening to try her by a military tribunal, they at length intimated to her a sentence, condemning her, with her daughter (her son had been left very much indisposed at Compeigne,) to be detained close prisoners in a monastery at Rome, to which she was compelled to repair within twenty-four hours after the notice of her doom. Her two agents, who had been previously made prisoners, were sent to Paris. They were condemned to death by a military commission, and were brought out for that purpose to the plain of Gresnelle. One was shot on the spot, and pardon was extended to his companion when he was about to suffer the same punishment. The mental agony of the poor man had, however, affected the sources of life, and he died within a few days after the reprieve. The severity of this conduct towards a princess—a Queen indeed—who had placed her person in Napoleon's hands, under the expectation that her liberty at least should not be abridged, was equally a breach of justice, humanity, and gentlemanlike courtesy.[80]

LUCIEN BUONAPARTE

It is curious, that about the same time when Napoleon treated with so much cruelty a foreign and independent princess, merely because she expressed a desire to exchange her residence from France to England, his own brother, Lucien, was received with hospitality in that island, so heartily detested, so frequently devoted to the fate of a second Carthage. Napoleon, who was always resolute in considering the princes of his own blood as the first slaves in the state, had become of late very urgent with Lucien to dismiss his wife, and unite himself with some of the royal families on the continent, or at least to agree to bestow the hand of his daughter upon young Ferdinand of Spain, who had risen in favour by his behaviour on an occasion immediately to be mentioned. But Lucien, determined at this time not to connect himself or his family with the career of his relative's ambition, resolved to settle in America, and

---

[80] See Mémoires de Savary, tom. iii., part i., p. 37.

place the Atlantic betwixt himself and the importunities of his Imperial brother. He applied to the British minister at Sardinia for a pass, who was under the necessity of referring him to his Government. On this second application he was invited to England, where he was permitted to live in freedom upon his parole, one officer only having a superintendence of his movements and correspondence.[81] These were in every respect blameless; and the ex-statesman, who had played so distinguished a part in the great revolutionary game, was found able to amuse himself with the composition of an epic poem on the subject of Charlemagne;[82]— somewhat more harmlessly than did his brother Napoleon, in endeavouring again to rebuild and consolidate the vast empire of the son of Pepin.

---

[81] Lucien landed at Portsmouth in December, 1810, and was conveyed to Ludlow, which he soon after quitted for an estate called Thorngrove, fifteen miles from that town. Restored to personal liberty by the peace of Paris in 1814, he reached Rome in May; and was received by the sovereign pontiff on the very night of his arrival. The holy father immediately conferred on him the dignity of a Roman prince; and on the next day all the nobles came to salute him, by the title of Prince of Canino.

[82] Lucien's poem of "Charlemagne, ou l'Eglise Delivrée," an epic in twenty-four books, commenced at Tusculum, continued at Malta, and completed in England, appeared in 1814. It was translated into English by Dr. Butler and Mr. Hodgson. From the eighteenth canto, which was written at Malta, and which opens with a digression personal to the poet, we shall make a short extract:— "Je n'oublirai jamais ta bonté paternelle Favori du très-haut, Clermont, Pontife-roi! Au nouvel hémisphère entrainé loin de toi, Je t'y conserverai le cœur le plus fidèle: Confiant à la mer et ma femme et mes fils Sur des bords ennemis, J'espérai vainement un asile éphémère, Par un triste refus rejetté sur les flots, Après avoir long temps erré loin de la terre, Mélite dans son port enferma nos vaisseaux.

"De la captivité je sens ici le poids! Rien ne plait en ces lieux à mon ame abbattue; Rien ne parle à mon cœur; rien ne s'offre à ma vue Accourez, mes enfants: viens, épouse chérie. Doux charme de ma vie, D'un seul de tes regards viens me rendre la paix. Il n'est plus de désert, ou brille ton sourire, Fuyez, sombres chagrins, souvenirs inquiets, Sur ce roc Africain, je resaissis ma lyre."

"Prince Pontiff! loved of heaven—O, Clermont, say, What filial duties shall thy cares repay? E'en on the shores that skirt the western main, Still shall this heart its loyal faith maintain. My precious freight confiding to the deep, Children and wife, I left Frescati's steep, And ask'd a short retreat—I sought no more— But vainly sought it on a hostile shore. Thence by refusal stern and harsh repell'd, O'er the wide wat'ry waste my course I held, In sufferings oft, and oft in perils cast, Till Malta's port received our ships at last.

"Here sad captivity's dull weight I find; Nought pleases here, nought soothes my listless mind: Nought here can bid my sickening heart rejoice, Speak to my soul, or animate my voice. Run to my knees, my children! cherish'd wife, Come, softest charm and solace of my life, One look from thee shall all my peace restore: Where beams thy smile, the desert is no more. Hence, restless memory—hence, repinings vain!— On Afric's rock I seize my lyre again."

Another intrigue of a singular character, and which terminated in an unexpected manner, originated in an attempt of the English Ministry to achieve the liberty of Ferdinand, the lawful King of Spain. A royal and a popular party had begun to show themselves in that distracted country, and to divert the attention of the patriots from uniting their efforts to accomplish the object of most engrossing importance, the recovery, namely, of their country, from the intruding monarch and the French armies. The English Government were naturally persuaded that Ferdinand, to whose name his subjects were so strongly attached, would be desirous and capable of placing himself, were he at liberty, at their head, putting an end to their disputes by his authority, and giving their efforts an impulse, which could be communicated by no one but the King of Spain to the Spanish nation. It is no doubt true, that, had the Government of England known the real character of this prince, a wish for his deliverance from France, or his presence in Spain, would have been the last which they would have formed. This misapprehension, however, was natural, and was acted upon.

A Piedmontese, of Irish extraction, called the Baron Kolli (or Kelly,) the selected agent of the British government, was furnished with some diamonds and valuable articles, under pretext of disposing of which he was to obtain admission to the Prince, then a prisoner at Valençay, where his chief amusement, it is believed, was embroidering a gown and petticoat, to be presented to the Virgin Mary. Kolli was then to have informed the Prince of his errand, effected Ferdinand's escape by means of confederates among the royalist party, and conveyed him to the coast, where a small squadron awaited the event of the enterprise, designed to carry the King of Spain to Gibraltar, or whither else he chose. In March 1810, Kolli was put ashore in Quiberon bay, whence he went to Paris, to prepare for his enterprise. He was discovered, however, by the police,[83] and arrested at the moment when he was setting out for Valençay. Some attempts were made to induce him to proceed with the scheme, of which his papers enabled the police to comprehend

---

[83] "He was discovered by his always drinking a bottle of the best wine, which so ill corresponded with his dress and apparent poverty, that it excited a suspicion amongst some of the spies, and he was arrested, searched, and his papers taken from him."—Napoleon, *Voice, &c.*, vol. ii., p. 119.

the general plan, keeping communication at the same time with the French minister. As he disdained to undertake this treacherous character, Kolli was committed close prisoner to the castle of Vincennes, while a person—the same who betrayed his principal, and whose exterior in some degree answered the description of the British emissary—was sent to represent him at the castle of Valençay.

But Ferdinand, either suspicious of the snare which was laid for him, or poor-spirited enough to prefer a safe bondage to a brave risk incurred for liberty, would not listen to the supposed agent of Britain, and indeed denounced the pretended Kolli to Barthemy, the governor of the castle. The false Kolli, therefore, returned to Paris, while the real one remained in the castle of Vincennes till the capture of Paris by the allies. Ferdinand took credit, in a letter to Buonaparte, for having resisted the temptation held out to him by the British Government, who had, as he pathetically observed, abused his name, and occasioned, by doing so, the shedding of much blood in Spain. He again manifested his ardent wish to become the adopted son of the Emperor; his hope that the author and abettors of the scheme to deliver him might be brought to condign punishment; and concluded with a hint, that he was extremely desirous to leave Valençay, a residence which had nothing about it but what was unpleasant, and was not in any respect fitted for him. The hint of Ferdinand about a union with Buonaparte's family, probably led to the fresh importunity on the Emperor's part, which induced Lucien to leave Italy. Ferdinand did not obtain the change of residence he desired, nor does he seem to have profited in any way by his candour towards his keeper, excepting that he evaded the strict confinement, or yet worse fate, to which he might have been condemned, had he imprudently confided in the false Baron Kolli.[84]

---

[84] See "Report concerning Kolli's Plan for liberating Ferdinand, King of Spain," Annual Register, vol. lii., p. 497.

MASSENA AND WELLINGTON

In Portugal, the great struggle betwixt Massena and Wellington, upon which, as we formerly observed, the eyes of the world were fixed, had been finally decided in favour of the English general. This advantage was attained by no assistance of the elements—by none of those casual occurrences which are called chances of war—by no dubious, or even venturous risks—by the decision of no single battle lost or won; but solely by the superiority of one great general over another, at the awful game in which neither had yet met a rival.

For more than four months, Massena, with as fine an army as had ever left France, lay looking at the impregnable lines with which the British forces, so greatly inferior in numerical strength, were covering Lisbon, the object of his expedition. To assail in such a position troops, whose valour he had felt at Busaco, would have been throwing away the lives of his soldiers; and to retreat, was to abandon the enterprise which his master had intrusted to him, with a confidence in his skill and his good fortune, which must, in that case, have been thereafter sorely abated. Massena tried every effort which military skill could supply, to draw his foe out of his place of advantage. He threatened to carry the war across the Tagus—he threatened to extend his army towards Oporto; but each demonstration he made had been calculated upon and anticipated by his antagonist, and was foiled almost without an effort. At length, exhausted by the want of supplies, and the interruption of his communications, after lying one month at Alenquer, Massena retreated to Santarem, as preferable winter-quarters; but, in the beginning of March, he found that these were equally untenable, and became fully sensible, that if he desired to save the remnant of a sickly and diminished army, it must necessarily be by a speedy retreat.

This celebrated movement, decisive of the fate of the campaign, commenced about the 4th of March. There are two different points in which Massena's conduct may be regarded, and they differ as light and darkness. If it be considered in the capacity of that of a human being, the indignant reader, were we to detail the horrors which he permitted his soldiers to perpetrate, would almost deny his title to the name. It is a vulgar superstition, that when the Enemy of mankind is invoked, and appears, he destroys in his retreat the building which has witnessed the apparition. It seemed as if the French, in leaving Portugal, were determined that ruins alone should remain to show they had once been there. Military license was let loose in its most odious and frightful shape, and the crimes which were committed embraced all that is horrible to humanity. But if a curtain is dropped on these horrors, and Massena is regarded merely as a military leader, his retreat, perhaps, did him as much honour as any of the great achievements which formerly had made his name famous. If he had been rightly called Fortune's favourite, he now showed that his reputation did not depend on her smile, but could be maintained by his own talents, while she shone on other banners. In retreating through the north of Portugal, a rugged and mountainous country, he was followed by Lord Wellington, who allowed him not a moment's respite. The movements of the troops, to those who understood, and had the calmness to consider them, were as regular consequences of each other, as occur in the game of chess.[85]

The French were repeatedly seen drawn up on ground where it seemed impossible to dislodge them; and as often the bayonets of a British column, which had marched by some distant route, were observed twinkling in the direction of their flank, intimating that their line was about to be turned. But this was only the signal for Massena to recommence his retreat, which he did before the English troops could come up; nor did he fail again to halt where opportunity offered, until again dislodged by his sagacious and persevering pursuer. At length the French were fairly driven out of the Portuguese territory, excepting the garrison in the frontier town of Almeida, of which Lord Wellington formed first the blockade, and afterwards the siege.

---

[85] Savary, tom. iii., part i., p. 53.

BATTLE OF FUENTES D'ONORO

So soon as he escaped from the limits of Portugal, Massena hastened to draw together such reinforcements as he could obtain in Castile, collected once more a large force, and within about a fortnight after he had effected his retreat, resumed the offensive, with the view of relieving Almeida, which was the sole trophy remaining to show his triumphant advance in the preceding season. Lord Wellington did not refuse the battle, which took place on the 5th of May, near Fuentes d'Onoro. The conflict was well disputed, but the French general sustained a defeat, notwithstanding his superiority of numbers, and particularly of cavalry. He then retreated from the Portuguese frontier, having previously sent orders for the evacuation of Almeida by the garrison, which the French commandant executed with much dexterity.[86]

On the more southern frontier of Portugal, Lord Beresford fought also a dreadful and sanguinary battle. The action was in some measure indecisive, but Soult, who commanded the French, failed in obtaining such a success as enabled him to accomplish his object, which was the raising of the siege of Badajos. In Portugal, therefore, and along its frontiers, the British had been uniformly successful, and their countrymen at home began once more to open their ears to the suggestions of hope and courage.

Cadiz, also, the remaining bulwark of the patriots, had been witness to a splendid action. General Graham, with a body of British troops, had sallied out from the garrison in March 1811, and obtained a victory upon the heights of Barossa, which, had he been properly seconded by the Spanish General Lapena, would have been productive of a serious influence upon the events of the siege; and which, even though it remained imperfect, gave heart and confidence to the besieged, and struck a perpetual damp into the besiegers, who found themselves bearded in their own position. There had been much fighting through Spain with various results.

---

[86] "The Emperor recalled Massena, who was quite exhausted by fatigue, and unable to bestow that attention to his troops which was necessary for restoring them to their former state of efficiency; and he selected for his successor in the command Marshal Marmont, the Governor of Illyria."—Savary, tom. iii., part i., p. 54.

But if we dare venture to use such an emblem, the bush, though burning, was not consumed, and Spain continued that sort of general resistance which seemed to begin after all usual means of regular opposition had failed, as Nature often musters her strength to combat a disease which the medical assistants have pronounced mortal.

Catalonia, though her strongholds were lost, continued, under the command of De Lacy and D'Eroles, to gain occasional advantages over the enemy; and Spain saw Figueras, one of her strongest fortresses, recovered by the bold stratagem of Rovira, a doctor of divinity, and commander of a guerilla party. Being instantly besieged by the French, and ill supplied with provisions, the place was indeed speedily regained; but the possibility of its being taken, was, to the peculiarly tenacious spirit of the Spaniards, more encouraging than its recapture was matter of dismay.

But chiefly the auxiliary British, with the Portuguese, who, trained by the care of Lord Beresford, were fit to sustain their part in line by the side of their allies, showed that they were conducted in a different spirit from that which made their leaders in former expeditions stand with one foot on sea and one on land, never venturing from the sight of the ocean, as if they led amphibious creatures, who required the use of both elements to secure their existence; and the scheme of whose campaign was to rout and repel, as they best could, the attacks of the enemy, but seldom to venture upon anticipating or disconcerting his plans. To protect Galicia, for example, when invaded by the French, Lord Wellington, though with a much inferior army than he was well aware could be brought against him, formed the blockade of Ciudad Rodrigo; thus compelling the enemy to desist from their proposed attempt on that province, and to concentrate their forces for the relief of that important place. Such a concentration could not, in the condition of the French armies, be effected without much disadvantage. It afforded breathing space for all the guerillas, and an opportunity, which they never neglected, of acting with their usual courage and sagacity against small parties and convoys of the French, as well as that of seizing upon any posts which the enemy might have been obliged to leave imperfectly defended. And when the French had collected their whole force to overwhelm the British general and his forces, Marmont had the mortification to see the former withdraw from the presence of a superior enemy, with as much calmness and security as if marching through a peaceful country.

Nothing remained for the French general, save to detail in the pages of the *Moniteur*, what must have been the fate of the English but for their hasty and precipitate flight, when the well-concerted and boldly-executed enterprise of Arroyo-Molinos, convinced him to his cost that a retreat was no rout. In this village upwards of 1400 French were taken prisoners, at a moment when they least expected to be attacked. This little action showed a spirit of hazard, a disposition to assume the offensive, which the French did not expect from the British forces; and they were, for the first time, foiled in their own military qualities of vigilance, enterprise, and activity. In Britain, also, the nation perceived that their army showed the same courage and the same superiority, which had been considered as the exclusive property of their gallant sailors. The French were defeated under the rock of Gibraltar by the Spanish General Ballasteros, and their general, Godinet, blew out his own brains, rather than face the account, to which Soult, his commander-in-chief, was about to summon him. Tarifa, in the same quarter, was defended successfully by a garrison of mingled Spaniards and British, and the French were computed to have lost before it about two thousand five hundred men.

On the other hand, the French discipline continued to render them superior over the patriots, wherever the latter could be brought to face them in any thing resembling a pitched battle. Thus Blake, after a gallant action, was totally defeated near Murviedro, and that town itself fell into possession of the enemy. A more severe consequence of the battle of Ocana, as that disastrous action was termed, was the capture of Valencia, where Blake and the remainder of his army were made prisoners.

But amid those vicissitudes of good or bad fortune, Spain continued to Buonaparte the same harassing and exhausting undertaking, which it had been almost from the commencement. Sickness and want made more ravages amongst the French troops than the sword of the enemy, though that did not lie idle. Many of the districts are unhealthy to strangers; but of these, as well as others, it was necessary for the invaders to retain possession. There, while numerous deaths happened among the troops, the guerillas watched the remnant, until sickness and fatigue had reduced the garrisons to a number insufficient for defence, and then pounced upon them like birds of prey on a fallen animal, upon whom they have been long in attendance.

JOSEPH WISHES TO ABDICATE

Besides, disunion continued to reign among the French generals. Joseph, although in point of power the very shadow of what a king ought to be, had spirit enough to resent the condition in which he was placed amid the haughty military chiefs who acknowledged no superior beside the Emperor, and listened to no commands save those emanating from Paris. He wrote to his brother a letter, accompanying a formal abdication of the throne of Spain, unless he was to be placed in more complete authority than even the orders of Napoleon himself had hitherto enabled him to attain. But the prospect of a northern war approaching nearer and nearer, Napoleon was induced to postpone his brother's request, although so pressingly urged, and Spain was in some measure left to its fate during the still more urgent events of the Russian campaign.[87]

---

[87] Fouché, tom. ii., p. 71.

CHAPTER LV

Retrospect of the causes leading to the Rupture with Russia—originate in the Treaty of Tilsit—Russia's alleged Reasons of Complaint—Arguments of Napoleon's Counsellors against War with Russia—Fouché is against the War—Presents a Memorial to Napoleon upon the Subject—His Answer—Napoleon's Views in favour of the War, as urged to his various Advisers.

RUPTURE WITH RUSSIA

We are now approaching the verge of that fated year, when Fortune, hitherto unwearied in her partiality towards Napoleon, turned first upon himself, personally, a clouded and stormy aspect. Losses he had sustained both by land and sea, but he could still remark, as when he first heard of the defeat at Trafalgar—"I was not there—I could not be every where at once." But he was soon to experience misfortunes, to the narrative of which he could not apply this proud commentary. The reader must be first put in remembrance of the causes of the incipient quarrel betwixt the empire of France and that of Russia.

Notwithstanding the subsequent personal intimacy which took place betwixt the two sovereigns, and which for five years prevented the springing up of any enmity betwixt Alexander and Napoleon, the seeds of that quarrel were, nevertheless, to be found in the treaty of pacification of Tilsit itself.[88] Russia, lying remote from aggression in every other part of her immense territory, is open to injury on that important western frontier by which she is united with Europe, and in those possessions by virtue of which she claims to be a member of the European republic. The partition of Poland, unjust as it was in every point of view, was a measure of far

---
[88] Fouché, tom. ii., p. 71.

greater importance to Russia than either to Austria or Prussia; for, while that state possessed its former semi-barbarous and stormy independence, it lay interposed in a great measure betwixt Russia and the rest of Europe, or, in other words, betwixt her and the civilized world. Any revolution which might restore Poland to the independence, for which the inhabitants had not ceased to sigh, would have effectually thrust the Czar back upon his forests, destroyed his interest and influence in European affairs, and reduced him comparatively to the rank of an Asiatic sovereign. This liberation of their country, and the reunion of its dismembered provinces under a national constitution, was what the Poles expected from Buonaparte. For this they crowded to his standard after the battle of Jena; and although he was too cautious to promise any thing explicitly concerning the restoration of Poland to its rank among nations, yet most of his measures indicated a future purpose of accomplishing that work. Thus, when those Polish provinces which had fallen to the portion of Prussia, were formed into the Grand Duchy of Warsaw, as an independent principality, and the sovereignty was conferred, not without a secret meaning, on the King of Saxony, a descendant of the ancient monarchs of Poland, what could this be supposed to indicate, save the commencement of an independent state, to which might be added, as opportunity occurred, the remaining districts of Poland which had been seized upon by Austria and Russia? "To what purpose," asked those statesmen, who belonged to the old Russian or anti-Gallican party in the empire, "are those stipulations for a free military road and passage of troops from Saxony to Warsaw and its territory, through Silesia, if it is not that France may preserve the means of throwing an overpowering force into the duchy, so soon as it shall be her pleasure to undo the work of the sage Catherine, by depriving Russia of those rich Polish provinces, which her policy had added to the empire? Wherefore," asked the same persons, "should there have been a special article in the same treaty of Tilsit, that France should retain Dantzic until a maritime peace, unless it was to serve as a place of arms in the event of a new war with Russia, the probability of which Napoleon, therefore, must certainly have calculated upon, even at the very moment when he cultivated such close personal intimacy with the Emperor Alexander?"

These suspicions were considerably increased by the articles of peace concluded with Austria at Schoenbrun. By that treaty all Western Galicia, together with the city of Cracow, and other territories, were disjoined from Austria, and added to the dukedom of Warsaw, marking, it was supposed, still farther, the intention of Napoleon, at one time or another, to restore in its integrity the ancient kingdom of Poland, of which Russia alone now held the full share allotted to her by the partition treaties.

Other causes led to the same conclusion. The old Russians, a numerous and strong party in the empire, which comprehended the greater part of the large landholders, felt, as they had done under the Emperor Paul, much distress, national and personal, from the interruption of the British trade by Buonaparte's Continental System. Their timber, their pitch, their potash, their hemp, and other bulky and weighty commodities, the chief produce of their estates, for which the British had been ready customers, remained on their hands, while they were deprived of the colonial produce and manufactures of Britain, which they were wont to receive in exchange for those articles, with mutual profit and convenience to both parties. It was in vain that, to reconcile them to this state of interdiction, they saw in the speeches and decrees of Buonaparte, tirades about the freedom of the seas, and the maritime tyranny of England. It seemed an ill-omened species of liberation, which began by the destruction of their commerce and impoverishment of their estates; and the Russian Boyards could no more comprehend the declamation of Buonaparte against the English, than the millers of the Ebro could be made to understand the denunciation of Don Quixote against their customers. These magnates only saw that the Ruler of France wished them to submit to great commercial distress and inconvenience, in order to accelerate his plan of ruining Great Britain, after which achievement he might find it a more easy undertaking to destroy their own natural importance as a European power, by re-establishing Poland, and resuming the fertile provinces on the western boundary; thus leading the Russian Cabinet, if the French interest should remain paramount there, by a very disadvantageous road to a still more disastrous conclusion.

There was, besides, spread through the Russian nation generally, a sense that France was treating their Emperor rather on the footing of an inferior. It is a thing entirely unknown in diplomacy, that one government should pretend a right to dictate to another who is upon terms of equality, the conditions on which she should conduct her commerce; and the assuming such a right, seconded by threatening language in case of non-compliance, has been always held a legitimate cause of war. Indeed, the opinion that the French league disgraced the Russian nation, plunged their country into embarrassments, and was likely to occasion still farther misfortunes to them, became so general, that the Emperor must have paid some attention to the wishes of his people, even if his own friendship with Buonaparte had not been cooled by late occurrences.

The alliance with Austria was of a character calculated to alarm Alexander. Russia and Austria, though they had a common interest to withstand the overpowering strength of Buonaparte, had been in ordinary times always rivals, and sometimes enemies. It was the interference of Austria, which, upon several occasions, checked the progress of the Russians in Turkey, and it was Austria also which formed a barrier against the increase of their power in the south of Europe. The family connexion, therefore, formed by Buonaparte with the House of Hapsburg, made him still more formidable to Russia, as likely to embrace the quarrels and forward the pretensions of that power against the Czar, even if France herself should have none to discuss with him.

But there was no need to have recourse to remote causes of suspicion. Russia had, and must always have had, direct and immediate cause of jealousy, while France or her Emperor claimed the permanent right of thinking and deciding for her, as well as other nations, in the relations of commerce and others, in which every independent state is most desirous of exercising the right of deliberating for herself. This was the true state of the case. To remain the ally of Buonaparte, Alexander must have become his vassal; to attempt to be independent of him, was to make him his enemy; and it can be no wonder that a sovereign so proud and powerful as the Czar, chose rather to stand the hazard of battle, than diminish the lustre, or compromise the independence, of his ancient crown.

The time, too, for resistance, seemed as favourable as Russia could ever expect. The war of Spain, though chequered in its fortune, was in no respect near a sudden end. It occupied 250,000 of the best and oldest French troops; demanded also an immense expenditure, and diminished, of course, the power of the French Emperor to carry on the war on the frontiers of Russia. A conclusion of these wasting hostilities would have rendered him far more formidable with respect to the quality, as well as the number, of his disposable forces, and it seemed the interest of Russia not to wait till that period should arrive.

The same arguments which recommended to Russia to choose the immediate moment for resisting the extravagant pretensions of France, ought, in point of prudence, to have induced Napoleon to desist from urging such pretensions, and to avoid the voluntarily engaging in two wars at the same time, both of a character decidedly national, and to only one of which he could give the influence of his own talents and his own presence. His best and wisest generals, whom he consulted, or, to speak more properly, to whom he opened his purpose, used various arguments to induce him to alter, or at least defer his resolution. He himself hesitated for more than a year, and was repeatedly upon the point of settling with Russia the grounds of disagreement betwixt them upon amicable terms.

COMPLAINTS OF THE CZAR

The reasons of complaint, on the part of the Czar, were four in number.

I. The alarm given to Russia by the extension of the grand duchy of Warsaw by the treaty of Schoenbrun, as if it were destined to be the central part of an independent state, or kingdom, in Poland, to which those provinces of that dismembered country, which had become part of Russia, were at some convenient time to be united. On this point the Czar demanded an explicit engagement, on the part of the French Emperor, that the kingdom of Poland should not be again established. Napoleon declined this form of guarantee, as it seemed to engage him to warrant Russia against an event which might happen without his co-operation; but he offered to pledge himself that he would not favour any enterprise which should, directly or indirectly, lead to the re-establishment of Poland as an independent state. This modified acquiescence in what was required by Russia fell considerably short of what the Czar wished; for the stipulation, as at first worded, would have amounted to an engagement on the part of France to join in opposing any step towards Polish independence; whereas, according to the modification which it received at Paris, it only implied that France should remain neuter if such an attempt should take place.

II. The wrong done by including the duchy of Oldenburg, though guaranteed by the treaty of Tilsit to its prince, the Czar's near relative and ally, in the territory annexed to France, admitted of being compensated by an indemnification. But Russia desired that this indemnification should be either the city of Dantzic, or some equally important territory, on the frontiers of the grand duchy of Warsaw, which might offer an additional guarantee against the apprehended enlargement of that state. France would not listen to this, though she did not object to compensation elsewhere.

III. The third point in question, was the degree to which the Russian commerce with England was to be restricted. Napoleon proposed to grant some relaxation on the occasions where the produce of Russia was exported in exchange for that of England, to be effected by the way of mutual licenses.

IV. It was proposed to revise the Russian tariff of 1810, so as, without injuring the interests of Russia, it might relax the heavy duties imposed on the objects of French commerce.

From this statement, which comprehends the last basis on which Napoleon expressed himself willing to treat, it is quite evident, that had there not been a deeper feeling of jealousy and animosity betwixt the two Emperors, than those expressed in the subjects of actual debate betwixt them, these might have been accommodated in an amicable way. But as it was impossible for Napoleon to endure being called to account, like a sovereign of the second rate, or at least in the tone of an equal, by the Emperor of Russia; so the latter, more and more alarmed by the motions of the French armies, which were advancing into Pomerania, could not persuade himself, that, in agreeing to admit the present grounds of complaint, Napoleon meant more than to postpone the fatal struggle for superiority, until he should find a convenient time to commence it with a more absolute prospect of success.

In the meantime, and ere the negotiations were finally broken off, Buonaparte's counsellors urged him with as much argument as they dared, to desist from running the hazard of an enterprise so remote, so hazardous, and so little called for. They contended, that no French interest, and no national point of honour, were involved in the disagreement which had arisen. The principles upon which the points of dispute might be settled, being in a manner agreed upon, they argued that their master should stop in their military preparations. To march an army into Prussia, and to call forth the Prussians as auxiliaries, would, they contended, be using measures towards Russia, which could not but bring on the war which they anxiously deprecated. To submit to menaces supported by demonstrations of open force, would be destructive of the influence of Russia, both at home and abroad. She could not be expected to give way without a struggle.

WAR WITH RUSSIA

These advisers allowed, that a case might be conceived for justifying an exertion to destroy the power of Russia, a case arising out of the transactions between France and the other states of Europe, and out of the apprehension that these states, aggrieved and irritated by the conduct of France, might be tempted to seek a leader, patron, and protector, in the Emperor Alexander. But this extremity, they alleged, could not exist so long as France had the means of avoiding a perilous war, by a mitigation of her policy towards her vassals and auxiliaries; for if the states whose revolt (so to call it) was apprehended, could be reconciled to France by a more lenient course of measures to be adopted towards them, they would lose all temptation to fly to Russia as a protector. In such case the power of Russia would no longer give jealousy to France, or compel her to rush to a dubious conflict, for the purpose of diminishing an influence which could not then become dangerous to the southern empire, by depriving France of her clientage.

It might have been added, though it could not be so broadly spoken out, that in this point of view nothing would have been more easy for France, than to modify or soften her line of policy in favour of the inferior states, in whose favour the Russian interference was expected or apprehended. That policy had uniformly been a system of insult and menace. The influence which France had gained in Europe grew less out of treaty than fear, founded on the recollection of former wars. All the states of Germany felt the melancholy consequences of the existence of despotic power vested in men, who, like Napoleon himself, and the military governors whom he employed, were new to the exercise and enjoyment of their authority; and, on the other hand, the French Emperor and his satellites felt, towards the people of the conquered, or subjected states, the constant apprehension which a conscious sense of injustice produces in the minds of oppressors, namely, that the oppressed only watch for a safe opportunity to turn against them. There was, therefore, no French interest, or even point of honour, which called on Napoleon to make war on Alexander; and the temptation seems to have amounted solely to the desire on Napoleon's part to fight a great battle—to gain a great victory—to occupy, with his victorious army, another great capital—and, in fine, to subject to his arms the power of Russia, which, of all the states on the continent, remained the only one that could be properly termed independent of France.

It was in this light that the question of peace and war was viewed by the French politicians of the day; and it is curious to observe, in the reports we have of their arguments, the total absence of principle which they display in the examination of it. They dwell on the difficulty of Napoleon's undertaking, upon its dangers, upon its expense, upon the slender prospect of any remuneration by the usual modes of confiscation, plunder, or levy of contributions. They enlarge, too, upon the little probability there was that success in the intended war would bring to a conclusion the disastrous contest in Spain; and all these various arguments are insinuated or urged with more or less vehemence, according to the character, the station, or the degree of intimacy with Napoleon, of the counsellor who ventured to use the topics. But among his advisers, none that we read or hear of, had the open and manly courage to ask, Where was the justice of this attack upon Russia? What had she done to merit it? The Emperors were friends by the treaty of Tilsit, confirmed by personal intimacy and the closest intercourse at Erfurt. How had they ceased to be such? What had happened since that period to place Russia, then the friend and confessed equal of France, in the situation of a subordinate and tributary state? On what pretence did Napoleon confiscate to his own use the duchy of Oldenburg, acknowledged as the property of Alexander's brother-in-law, by an express article in the treaty of Tilsit? By what just right could he condemn the Russian nation to all the distresses of his Anti-commercial System, while he allowed them to be a free and independent state?—Above all, while he considered them as a sovereign and a people entitled to be treated with the usual respect due between powers that are connected by friendly treaties, with what pretence of justice, or even decency, could he proceed to enforce claims so unfounded in themselves, by introducing his own forces on their frontier, and arming their neighbours against them for the same purpose? Of these pleas, in moral justice, there was not a word urged; nor was silence wonderful on this fruitful topic, since to insist upon it would have been to strike at the fundamental principle of Buonaparte's policy, which was, never to neglect a present advantage for the sake of observing a general principle. "Let us hear of no general principles," said Buonaparte's favourite minister of the period. "Ours is a government not regulated by theory, but by emerging circumstances."

FOUCHÉ'S MEMORIAL

We ought not to omit to mention that Fouché, among others, took up a testimony against the Russian war. He had been permitted to return to his chateau of Ferrières, near Paris, under the apology that the air of Italy did not agree with his constitution. But Napoleon distrusted him, and the police were commissioned to watch with the utmost accuracy the proceedings of their late master. Fouché was well aware of this; and, desirous that his remonstrance with the Emperor should have all the force of an unexpected argument, he shut himself up in the strictest seclusion while engaged in composing a production, which perhaps he hoped might be a means of recalling him to recollection, if not to favour.[89]

In an able and eloquent memorial, Fouché reminded Buonaparte, that he was already the absolute master of the finest empire the world had ever seen; and that all the lessons of history went to demonstrate the impossibility of attaining universal monarchy. The French empire had arrived, according to the reasoning of this able statesman, at that point when its ruler should rather think of securing and consolidating his present acquisitions, than of achieving farther conquests, since, whatever his empire might acquire in extent, it was sure to lose in solidity. Fouché stated the extent of the country which Napoleon was about to invade, the poverty of the soil, the rigour of the climate, and the distance which each fresh victory must remove him from his resources, annoyed as his communications were sure to be by nations of Cossacks and Tartars. He implored the Emperor to remember the fate of Charles XII. of Sweden. "If that warlike monarch," he said, "had not, like Napoleon, half Europe in arms at his back, neither had his opponent, the Czar Peter, four hundred thousand soldiers, and fifty thousand Cossacks. The invader, it was stated, would have against him the dislike of the higher ranks, the fanaticism of the peasantry, the exertions of soldiers accustomed to the severity of the climate. There were, besides, to be dreaded, in case of the slightest reverse, the intrigues of the English, the fickleness of his continental allies, and even the awakening of discontent and conspiracy in France itself, should an idea generally arise, that he was sacrificing the welfare of the state to the insatiable desire of fresh enterprises and distant conquests."

---

[89] Fouché, tom. ii., p. 80.

Fouché presented himself at the Tuileries, and requested an audience of the Emperor, hoping, doubtless, that the unexpected circumstance of his appearing there, and the reasoning in his memorial, would excite Napoleon's attention. To his great surprise, Napoleon, with an air of easy indifference, began the audience. "I am no stranger, Monsieur le Duc, to your errand here. You have a memorial to present me—give it me; I will read it, though I know already its contents. The war with Russia is not more agreeable to you than that of Spain."—"Your Imperial Majesty will pardon my having ventured to offer some observations on this important crisis?" said the statesman, astonished to find himself anticipated, when he believed he had laboured in the most absolute secrecy.

"It is no crisis," resumed Napoleon; "merely a war of a character entirely political. Spain will fall when I have annihilated the English influence at St. Petersburgh. I have 800,000 men; and to one who has such an army, Europe is but an old prostitute, who must obey his pleasure. Was it not yourself who told me that the word *impossible* was not good French? I regulate my conduct more on the opinion of my army than the sentiments of you grandees, who are become too rich; and while you pretend anxiety for me, only are apprehensive of the general confusion which would follow my death. Don't disquiet yourself, but consider the Russian war as a wise measure, demanded by the true interests of France, and the general security. Am I to blame, because the great degree of power I have already attained forces me to assume the dictatorship of the world? My destiny is not yet accomplished—my present situation is but a sketch of a picture which I must finish. There must be one universal European code, one court of appeal. The same money, the same weights and measures, the same laws, must have currency through Europe. I must make one nation out of all the European states, and Paris must be the capital of the world. At present you no longer serve me well, because you think my affairs are in danger; but before a year is over you will assist me with the same zeal and ardour as at the periods of Marengo and Austerlitz. You will see more than all this—it is I who assure you of it. Adieu, Monsieur le Duc. Do not play the disgraced courtier, or the captious critic of public affairs; and be so good as to put a little confidence in your Emperor."[90]

He then turned his back on Fouché, and left him to reflect by what means he, who so well knew all the machinations of the police, could himself have become exposed to their universal vigilance, with some cause, perhaps, to rejoice, that his secret employment, though unpleasing to Buonaparte, was not of a character to attract punishment as well as animadversion.[91]

RUPTURE WITH RUSSIA

As Napoleon discountenanced and bore down the remonstrances of the subtle Fouché, so he represented to his various advisers the war upon which he was unalterably determined, in the light most proper to bring them over to his own opinion. To the army in general the mere name of war was in itself a sufficient recommendation. It comprehended preferment, employment, plunder, distinction, and pensions. To the generals, it afforded mareschals' batons; to the mareschals, crowns and sceptres; to the civilians he urged, as to Fouché, that it was a war of policy—of necessity—the last act in the drama, but indispensably requisite to conclude the whole; to his most intimate friends he expressed his conviction that his fortune could not stand still—that it was founded on public opinion—and that, if he did not continue to advance, he must necessarily retrograde. To his uncle, Cardinal Fesch, he used a still more extraordinary argument. This prelate, a devout Catholic, had begun to have compunction about his nephew's behaviour towards the Pope; and these sentiments mingled like an ominous feeling with the alarms excited by the risks of this tremendous undertaking. With more than usual freedom, he

---

[90] Mémoires de Fouché, tom. ii., p. 90.
[91] Fouché afterwards remembered, that an individual in his neighbourhood, mayor of a municipality, and whom he himself had employed in matters of police, had one morning intruded rather hastily on him in his study, under pretext of pleading the cause of a distressed tenant; and concluded, that while he was searching for the papers concerning his visitor's ostensible business, Mr. Mayor had an opportunity to glance at the sheets on his scrutoire, where the repetition of V. M. I. and R. M. (intimating your Imperial and Royal Majesty,) betrayed that he was drawing up a memorial to Napoleon, and a word or two of the context explained its purport.

conjured his kinsman to abstain from tempting Providence. He entreated him not to defy heaven and earth, the wrath of man, and the fury of the elements, at the same time; and expressed his apprehension that he must at length sink under the weight of the enmity which he incurred daily.[92] The only answer which Buonaparte vouchsafed, was to lead the cardinal to the window, and, opening the casement, and pointing upwards, to ask him, "If he saw yonder star?"—"No, Sire," answered the astonished cardinal. "But I see it," answered Buonaparte; and turned from his relation as if he had fully confuted his arguments.

This speech might admit of two meanings; either that Napoleon wished in this manner to express that his own powers of penetration were superior to those of the cardinal, or it might have reference to a certain superstitious confidence in his predestined good fortune, which, we have already observed, he was known to entertain. But as it was not Napoleon's fashion, whatever reliance he might place on such auguries, to neglect any means of ensuring success within his power, we are next to inquire what political measures he had taken to carry on the proposed Russian war to advantage.

---

[92] It is not unworthy of notice, that the Emperor's mother (Madame Mère, as she was termed) always expressed a presentiment, that the fortunes of her family, splendid as they were, would be altered before her death; and when ridiculed by her children for her frugal disposition, she used to allege she was saving money for them in their distress; and in fact she lived to apply her boards to that purpose.—S.

Chapter LVI

Allies on whose assistance Buonaparte might count—Causes which alienated from him the Prince-Royal of Sweden—who signs a Treaty with Russia—Delicate situation of the King of Prussia, whose alliance the Emperor Alexander on that account declines—A Treaty with France dictated to Prussia—Relations between Austria and France—in order to preserve them Buonaparte is obliged to come under an engagement not to revolutionize Poland—His error of policy in neglecting to cultivate the alliance of the Porte—Amount of Buonaparte's Army—Levies for the protection of France in the Emperor's absence—Storming of Ciudad Rodrigo by Lord Wellington—Buonaparte makes overtures of Peace to Lord Castlereagh—The Correspondence broken off—Ultimatum of Russia rejected—Napoleon sets out from Paris, 9th May, 1812—and meets the Sovereigns his allies at Dresden—A last attempt of Napoleon to negotiate with Alexander proves unsuccessful.

The several powers, who might in their different degrees of strength aid or impede the last and most daring of Buonaparte's undertakings, were—Denmark, Saxony, Sweden, and Prussia, in the north of Europe; in the south, Austria, and the Turkish empire.

Denmark and Saxony were both devoted to the cause of France; but the former power, who had made over to Napoleon her seamen, had no land troops to spare for his assistance. The few that she had on foot were scarce sufficient to protect her against any enterprise of Sweden or England.

Saxony was also the firm friend of Napoleon, who had enlarged her dominions, and changed her ruler's electoral bonnet into a royal crown. It is true, if Poland was to be regenerated, as seemed to be the natural consequence of a war with Russia, the King of Saxony must have reckoned upon losing his ducal interest in the grand duchy of Warsaw. But from this he derived little present advantage; and as he was secure of indemnification, the apprehension of that loss did not prevent him from following the banner of Napoleon, with the same good-will as ever.

PRINCE-ROYAL OF SWEDEN

Very different was the condition of Sweden. That kingdom, since the reign of Francis I., had been the ancient and natural ally of France against Russia; in acting against which last power her local advantages afforded great facility. Sweden was also governed at the moment by a Frenchman. But the Prince-Royal had received more injuries and affronts than favours at the hands of the Emperor Napoleon; and the violent policy which the latter was in the habit of using towards those of his allies and neighbours, who did not submit unresistingly to all his demands, had alienated from France the hearts of the Swedes, and from his own person the friendship of his old companion in arms. We have mentioned the mode of argument, or rather declamation, which he had used to compel the Swedes into a total exclusion of English manufactures, contrary to a reservation made in a recent treaty, by which the Swedes had retained the right of importing colonial goods and salt, while consenting to exclude British commodities generally. With the same urgency and menaces, he had compelled the Crown Prince to declare war against Britain.

But although Napoleon succeeded in both points, he could not oblige Britain to treat Sweden as a belligerent power. On the contrary, England seemed not in the slightest degree to alter the relations of amity to a state whom she considered as having adopted the attitude of an enemy towards her, merely from compulsion too powerful to be resisted. This moderation on the part of Great Britain did not prevent Sweden from feeling all the evils of the anti-social system of Buonaparte. Her commerce was reduced to a mere coasting trade, and her vessels skulked from port to port, exposed to the depredations of Danish and French privateers, who seized upon and confiscated upwards of fifty Swedish ships, under pretence of enforcing the non-intercourse system. The Prince-Royal applied for redress at the court of Paris; but although vague promises were given, yet neither were the acts of piracy discontinued, nor any amends made for those daily committed. The Baron Alquier, who was the French envoy at Stockholm, used, according to Bernadotte's expression, the language of a Roman proconsul, without remembering that he did not speak to slaves.[93]

When asked, for example, to state categorically what Napoleon expected from Sweden, and what he proposed to grant her in return, Alquier answered, that "the Emperor expected from Sweden compliance in every point conformable to his system; after which it would be time enough to inquire into what his Imperial Majesty might be disposed to do in favour of Sweden."

On another occasion, the French envoy had the assurance to decline farther intercourse with the Crown Prince on the subject of his mission, and to desire that some other person might be appointed to communicate with him. There can be no doubt, that, in this singular course of diplomacy, Baron Alquier obeyed his master's instructions, who was determined to treat the Prince-Royal of Sweden, emancipated as he was from his allegiance to France by letters-patent from the Imperial Chancery, as if he had still been his subject, and serving in his armies. Napoleon went so far as to say, before his courtiers, that he had a mind to make Bernadotte finish his lessons in the Swedish language in the Castle of Vincennes. It is even said, that the Emperor thought seriously of putting this threat into execution, and that a plot was actually formed to seize the person of the Prince-Royal, putting him on board a vessel, and bringing him prisoner to France. But he escaped this danger by the information of an officer named Salazar, formerly an aide-de-camp

---

[93] Meredith's Memorials of Charles John, King of Sweden and Norway, p. 25.

of Marmont, who conveyed to the Prince timely information of the outrage which was intended.[94]

With so many causes of mutual animosity between France and Sweden, all arising out of the impolitic vehemence by which Buonaparte endeavoured to drive, rather than lead, the Prince-Royal into the measures he desired, it can hardly be supposed that the last would neglect any opportunity to assert his independence, and his resolution not to submit to a superiority so degrading in itself, and so ungraciously and even unmercifully exercised.

Such was the state of matters betwixt the two countries, when, from the approaching war with Russia, the assistance of Sweden became essential to France. But what bait could Napoleon hold out to bring back an alienated friend? He might, indeed, offer to assist Bernadotte in regaining the province of Finland, which, by the connivance of Napoleon, had been conquered by Russia. But the Crown Prince concluded, that, to enter into a war with the view of recovering Finland, would occasion expenses which the country could not afford, and which the acquisition of Finland could not compensate, even supposing it sure to be accomplished. Besides, the repossession of Finland would engage Sweden in perpetual disputes with Russia, whereas the two nations, separated by the Gulf of Bothnia, had at present no cause of difference. On the other hand, by siding with Russia in the great contest which was impending, Sweden might expect the assistance of that empire, as well as of Britain, to achieve from Denmark, the ally of France, the conquest of her kingdom of Norway, which, in its geographical situation, lay so conveniently for Sweden, and afforded her the whole range of sea-coast along the western shores of Scandinavia. It is said that the Prince-Royal offered to Napoleon to enter into a league, offensive and defensive, with France, providing Norway as well as Finland were added to his dominions; but the Emperor rejected the terms with disdain. The whole alleged negotiation, however, has been disputed and denied.[95]

---

[94] See Appendix to this Volume, No. I.
[95] See Meredith's Memorials, p. 38.

So soon as Bonaparte found there was no hope of conciliating the Prince-Royal, which indeed he scarce seems seriously to have attempted, he proceeded, without waiting for the ceremony of declaring war, to strike against Sweden the most severe, or rather the only blow, in his power. In January 1812, General Davoust marched into Swedish Pomerania, the only possession of Sweden south of the Baltic sea, seized upon the country and its capital, and proceeded to menace the military occupation of Prussia, so far as that country was not already in the hands of France.

Receiving no satisfaction for this aggression, Sweden, 24th March, 1812, signed a treaty with Russia, declaring war against France, and proposing a diversion, with a joint force of 25 or 30,000 Swedes, together with 15 or 20,000 Russians, upon some point of Germany. And the Emperor of Russia became bound, either by negotiation or military co-operation, to unite the kingdom of Norway to that of Sweden, and to hold the Russian army, which was at present in Finland, as disposable for that purpose. Thus was the force of Sweden, rendered yet more considerable by the high military character of its present chief, thrown into the scale against France, to whom, but for the passionate and impolitic character of Napoleon's proceedings towards her, she might, in all probability, have remained the same useful and faithful ally which she had been since the alliance of Francis I. with Gustavus Vasa.

No reason can be discovered for insulting Sweden at the precise moment when her co-operation would have been so useful, excepting the animosity of Napoleon against a prince, whom he regarded as an ancient rival before the 18th Brumaire, and now as a contumacious and rebellious vassal. A due regard to the honour and interest of France would have induced him to lay aside such personal considerations. But this does not appear to have been in Buonaparte's nature, who, if he remembered benefits, had also a tenacious recollection of enmities, said to be peculiar to the natives of Corsica. When this feeling obtained the ascendency, he was too apt to sacrifice his policy to his spleen.

PRUSSIA

The situation of the King of Prussia, at the breaking out of the dispute between the empires of France and Russia, was truly embarrassing. His position lying betwixt the contending parties, rendered neutrality almost impossible; and if he took up arms, it was a matter of distracting doubt on which side he ought to employ them. Oppressed by French exactions and French garrisons; instigated, besides, by the secret influence of the Tugendbund, the people of Prussia were almost unanimous in their eager wish to seize the sword against France, nor was the King less desirous to redeem the independence, and revenge the sufferings, of his kingdom. The recollections of an amiable and beloved Queen, who had died in the prime of life, heart-broken with the distresses of her country, with her hands locked in those of her husband, called also for revenge on France, which had insulted her when living, and slandered her when dead.[96]

Accordingly it is now well understood, that the first impulse of the King of Prussia's mind was to throw himself into the arms of Russia, and offer, should it cost him his life and crown, to take share in the war as his faithful ally. But the Emperor Alexander was sensible that, in accepting this offered devotion, he would come under an obligation to protect Prussia in case of those reverses, which might be almost reckoned on as likely to occur in the early part of the campaign. The strongest fortresses in Prussia were in the hands of the French, the army of the King did not amount to more than 40,000 men, and there was no time to arm or organise the national forces. In order to form a junction with these 40,000 men, or as many of them as could be collected, it would be necessary that Alexander should precipitate the war, and march a strong army into Silesia, upon which the Prussians might rally. But such an army,

---

[96] In the *Moniteur*, a scandalous intrigue was repeatedly alluded to as existing between this princess and the Emperor Alexander, and both to M. Las Cases, and to others; Buonaparte affirmed the same personally; telling, at the same time, as a good jest, that he himself had kept the King of Prussia out of the way, to provide the lovers a stolen meeting [vol. ii.] These averments are so inconsistent with the character universally assigned to this high-spirited and unhappy princess, that we have no hesitation to assign them directly to calumny; a weapon which Napoleon never disdained to wield, whether in private or national controversy.—S.

when it had attained its object, must have had in front the whole forces of France, Saxony, and the Confederacy of the Rhine, while the hostile troops of the grand duchy of Warsaw, with probably a body of Austrian auxiliaries, would have been in their rear. This premature movement in advance, would have resembled the conduct of Austria in the unhappy campaigns of 1805 and 1809; in both of which she precipitated her armies into Bavaria, in hopes of acquiring allies, but only exposed them to the decisive defeats of Ulm and Eckmühl. It would also have been like the equally ill-omened advance of the Prussian army in 1806, when hurrying forward to compel Saxony to join him, the Duke of Brunswick gave occasion to the unhappy battle of Jena.

Experience and reflection, therefore, had led the Russian Emperor and cabinet to be of opinion, that they ought to avoid encountering the French in the early part of the campaign; and, in consequence, that far from advancing to meet them, they should rather suffer the invaders to involve themselves in the immense wastes and forests of the territories of Russia itself, where supplies and provisions were not to be found by the invader, and where every peasant would prove an armed enemy. The support which could be derived from an auxiliary army of Prussians, amounting only to 40,000 men, of whom perhaps the half could not be drawn together, was not, it appeared, an adequate motive for altering the plan of the campaign, which had been founded on the most mature consideration. The Emperor Alexander, therefore, declined accepting of the King of Prussia's alliance, as only tending to bring upon that Prince misfortunes, which Russia had not even the chance of averting, without entirely altering those plans of the campaign which had been deliberately adopted. Foreseeing at the same time that this refusal on his part must have made it necessary for Frederick, whose situation rendered neutrality impossible, to take part with France, the Emperor Alexander generously left him at liberty to take the measures, and form the connexions, which his circumstances rendered inevitable, assuring him, nevertheless, that if Russia gained the ascendant, Prussia should derive the same advantage from the victory, whatever part she might be compelled to adopt during the struggle.

While the King of Prussia saw his alliance declined by Russia, as rather burdensome than beneficial, he did not find France at all eager to receive him on her part as a brother of the war. He offered his alliance to Buonaparte repeatedly, and especially in the months of March, May, and August, 1811; but receiving no satisfaction, he began to be apprehensive that his destruction was intended. There was some reason for this fear, for Napoleon seems to have entertained a personal dislike towards Frederick, and is said to have exclaimed, when he was looking over a map of the Prussian territories, "Is it possible I can have been simple enough to leave that man in possession of so large a kingdom?" There is great reason, besides, to suppose, that Napoleon may have either become acquainted with the secret negotiations betwixt Prussia and Russia, or may have been induced to assume from probability the fact that such had existed. He hesitated, certainly, whether or not he would permit Prussia to remain an independent power.

At length, however, on the 24th of February, 1812, a treaty was dictated to Frederick, under condition of subscribing which, the name and title of King of Prussia were to be yet left him; failing his compliance, Davoust, who had occupied Swedish Pomerania, was to march into Prussia, and treat it as a hostile country. In thus sparing for the time a monarch, of whom he had every reason to be jealous, Napoleon seems to have considered it more advisable to use Frederick's assistance, than to throw him into the arms of Russia. The conditions of this lenity were severe; Prussia was to place at the disposal of France about 20,000 men, with sixty pieces of artillery, the disposable part of the poor remnant of the standing army of the great Frederick. She was also to supply the French army with every thing necessary for their sustenance as they passed through her dominions; but the expense of these supplies was to be imputed as part of the contributions imposed on Prussia by France, and not yet paid. Various other measures were taken to render it easy for the French, in case of necessity, to seize such fortresses belonging to Prussia as were not already in their hands, and to keep the Prussian people as much as possible disarmed, a rising amongst them being considered inevitable if the French arms should sustain any reverse. Thus, while Russia fortified herself with the assistance of France's old ally Sweden, France advanced against Russia, supported by the remaining army of Frederick of Prussia, who was at heart Alexander's best well-wisher.

RELATIONS WITH AUSTRIA

Napoleon had, of course, a weighty voice in the councils of his father-in-law of Austria. But the Austrian cabinet were far from regarding his plans of ambitious aggrandisement with a partial eye. The acute Metternich had been able to discover and report to his master, on his return to Vienna in the spring of 1811, that the marriage which had just been celebrated, would not have the effect of inducing Napoleon to sheathe his sword, or of giving to Europe permanent tranquillity. And now, although on the approach of the hostilities into which they were to be involved by their formidable ally, Austria agreed to supply an auxiliary army of 30,000 men, under Prince Schwartzenberg, it seems probable that she remembered, at the same time, the moderate and lenient mode of carrying on the war practised by Russia, when the ally of Napoleon during the campaign of Wagram, and gave her general secret instructions to be no further active in the campaign than the decent supporting of the part of an auxiliary peremptorily required.

In one most material particular, the necessity of consulting the interests of Austria interfered with Napoleon's readiest and most formidable means of annoying Russia. We have repeatedly alluded to the re-establishment of Poland as an independent kingdom, as a measure which would have rent from Russia some of the finest provinces which connect her with Europe, and would have gone a certain length in thrusting her back into the character of an Asiatic sovereignty, unconnected with the politics of the civilized world. Such re-construction of Poland was however impossible, so long as Austria continued to hold Galicia; and that state, in her treaty of alliance with France against Russia, made it an express condition that no attempt should be made for the restoration of Polish independence by Napoleon, without the consent of Austria, or without making compensation to her for being, in the event supposed, deprived of her share of Poland. This compensation, it was stipulated, was to consist in the retrocession, on the part of

France, of the Illyrian provinces, yielded up by his Imperial Majesty of Austria at the treaty of Schoenbrun.

By submitting to this embargo on his proceedings in Poland, Napoleon lost all opportunity of revolutionizing that military country, from which he drew therefore little advantage, unless from the duchy of Warsaw. Nothing but the tenacity with which Buonaparte retained every territory that fell into his power, would have prevented him from at once simplifying this complicated engagement, by assigning to Austria those Illyrian provinces, which were entirely useless to France, but on which her ally set great value, and stipulating in return—what Austria would then have willingly granted—the power of disposing, according to his own pleasure, as well of Galicia, as of such parts of the Polish provinces as should be conquered from Russia; or in case, as De Pradt insinuates,[97] the Court of Austria were averse to the exchange, it was in the power of Napoleon to have certainly removed their objections, by throwing Venice itself into the scale. But we have good reason to believe that Illyria would have been a sufficient inducement to the transaction.

We cannot suppose Buonaparte blind to the importance of putting, as he expressed it, all Poland on horseback; but whether it was, that in reality he did not desire to establish an independent state upon any terms, or whether he thought it hard to give up the Illyrian provinces, ceded to France in property, in order to reconstruct a kingdom, which, nominally at least, was to be independent; or whether, in fine, he had an idea, that, by vague promises and hopes, he could obtain from the Poles all the assistance he desired—it is certain that he embarrassed himself with this condition in favour of Austria, in a manner which tended to render complex and difficult all that he afterwards attempted in Polish affairs; and lost the zealous co-operation and assistance of the Lithuanians, at a time when it would have been invaluable to him.

---

[97] Histoire de l'Ambassade dans le Grand Duché de Varsovie en 1812.

TURKEY

Turkey remains to be noticed as the sole remaining power whom Buonaparte ought in prudence to have propitiated, previous to attacking Russia, of which empire she is the natural enemy, as she was also held the natural and ancient ally of France. Were it not that the talents of Napoleon were much better fitted to crush enemies than to gain or maintain friends, it would be difficult to account for his losing influence over the Porte at this important period. The Turkish Government had been rendered hostile to France by the memorable invasion of Egypt; but Sultan Selim, an admirer of Napoleon's valour and genius, had become the friend of the Emperor of France. Selim was cut off by a conspiracy, and his successor was more partial to the English interests. In the treaty of Tilsit, the partition of Turkey was actually agreed upon, though the term was adjourned;[98] as, at the negotiations of Erfurt, Napoleon agreed to abandon the Turkish dominions as far as the Danube, to become the property of Russia, if it should be in her power to conquer them.

The Court of St. Petersburgh were ill-advised enough to make the attempt, although they ought to have foreseen, even then, that the increasing power of France should have withheld them from engaging in any scheme of conquest at that period. Indeed, their undertaking this war with the Ottoman empire, a proceeding so impolitic in case of a rupture with France, may be quoted to show the Emperor Alexander's confidence that no such event was likely to take place, and consequently to prove his own determination to observe good faith towards Napoleon.

The Turks made a far better defence than had been anticipated; and though the events of war were at first unfavourable

---

[98] The fact is now pretty generally admitted to have been as stated in the text. But in the public treaty, it appeared that France negotiated an armistice, called that of Slobodsea, by which it was stipulated, that the two disputed provinces of Moldavia and Wallachia were to be restored to the Turks. But the armistice, as had previously been settled between Napoleon and Alexander, broke up without any such restoration; and a congress, which was held at Jassy for the arrangement of the quarrel between the Porte and Court of St. Petersburgh, having been also dissolved without coming to an agreement, the war between the Turks and Russians recommenced upon the Danube.—S.

to them, yet at length the Grand Vizier obtained a victory before Routschouk, or at least gave the Russian general such a serious check as obliged him to raise the siege of that place. But the gleam of victory on the Turkish banners was of brief duration. They were attacked by the Russians in their intrenched camp, and defeated in a battle so sanguinary, that the vanquished army was almost annihilated.[99] The Turks, however, continued to maintain the war, forgotten and neglected as they were by the Emperor of France, whose interest it chiefly was, considering his views against Russia, to have sustained them in their unequal struggle against that formidable power. In the meanwhile, hostilities languished, and negotiations were commenced; for the Russians were of course desirous, so soon as a war against France became a probable event, to close that with Turkey, which must keep engaged a very considerable army, at a time when all their forces were necessary to oppose the expected attack of Napoleon.

At this period, and so late as the 21st March, 1812, it seemed to occur all at once to Buonaparte's recollection, that it would be highly politic to maintain, or rather to renew, his league with a nation, of whom it was at the time most important to secure the confidence. His ambassador was directed to urge the Grand Signior in person to move towards the Danube, at the head of 100,000 men; in consideration of which, the French Emperor proposed not only to obtain possession for them of the two disputed provinces of Moldavia and Wallachia, but also to procure the restoration to the Porte of the Crimea.

This war-breathing message arrived too late, the Porte having adopted a specific line of policy. The splendid promises of France succeeded too abruptly to so many years of neglect, to obtain credit for sincerity. The envoys of England, with a dexterity which it has not been always their fortune to display, obtained a complete victory in diplomacy over those of France, and were able to impress on the Sublime Porte the belief, that though Russia was their natural enemy among European nations, yet a peace of some permanence might be secured with her, under the guarantee of England and Sweden; whereas, if Napoleon should altogether destroy Russia, the Turkish

---

[99] Jomini, tom. iii., p. 541.

empire, of which he had already meditated the division, would be a measure no state could have influence to prevent, as, in subduing Russia, he would overcome the last terrestrial barrier to his absolute power. It gives no slight idea of the general terror and suspicion impressed by the very name of Napoleon, that a barbarous people like the Turks, who generally only comprehend so much of politics as lies straight before them, should have been able to understand that there was wisdom in giving peace on reasonable terms to an old and inveterate enemy, rather than, by assisting in his destruction, to contribute to the elevation of a power still more formidable, more ambitious, and less easily opposed. The peace of Bucharest was accordingly negotiated betwixt Russia and Turkey; of which we shall hereafter have occasion to speak.

Thus was France, on the approaching struggle, deprived of her two ancient allies, Sweden and Turkey. Prussia she brought to the field like a slave at her chariot-wheels; Denmark and Saxony in the character of allies, who were favoured so long as they were sufficiently subservient; and Austria, as a more equal confederate, but who had contrived to stipulate, that, in requital of an aid coldly and unwillingly granted, the French Emperor should tie himself down by engagements respecting Poland, which interfered with his using his influence over that country in the manner which would best have served his purposes. The result must lead to one of two conclusions. Either that Napoleon, confident in the immense preparations of his military force, disdained to enter into negotiations to obtain that assistance which he could not directly command, or else that his talents in politics were inferior to those which he displayed in military affairs.

STATE OF THE ARMY

It is true, that if the numbers, and we may add the quality, of the army which France brought into the field on this momentous occasion, were alone to be considered, Napoleon might be excused for holding cheap the assistance which he might have derived from Sweden or the Porte. He had anticipated the conscription of 1811, and he now called out that of 1812; so that it became plain, that so long as Napoleon lived and warred, the conscription of the first class would be—not a conditional regulation, to be acted or not acted upon according to occasion—but a regular and never-to-be-remitted tax of eighty thousand men, annually levied, without distinction, on the youth of France. To the amount of these conscriptions for two years, were to be added the contingents of household kings, vassal princes, subjected republics—of two-thirds of Europe, in short, which were placed under Buonaparte's command. No such army had taken the field since the reign of Xerxes, supposing the exaggerated accounts of the Persian invasion to be admitted as historical. The head almost turns dizzy as we read the amount of their numbers.

The gross amount of the whole forces of the empire of France, and its dependencies and allies, is thus given by Boutourlin:—[100]

Total amount of the French army,	850,000	men.
The army of Italy, under the Viceroy Eugene,	50,000	
of the Grand Duchy of Warsaw, with other Poles,	60,000	
of Bavaria,	40,000	
of Saxony,	30,000	
of Westphalia,	30,000	
of Wurtemberg,	15,000	
of Baden,	9,000	
of the Princes of the Confederacy of the Rhine,	23,000	
The corps of Prussian auxiliaries,	20,000	
of Austrian auxiliaries,	30,000	
The army of Naples,	30,000	
1,187,000		men.

But to approximate the actual force, we must deduce from this total of 1,187,000, about 387,000 men, for those in the hospital, absent upon furlough, and for incomplete regiments. Still there remains the appalling balance of 800,000 men, ready to maintain the

---

[100] Histoire Militaire de la Campagne de Russie en 1812.

war; so that Buonaparte was enabled to detach an army to Russia greatly superior to what the Emperor Alexander could, without immense exertions, get under arms, and this without withdrawing any part of his forces from Spain.

Still, however, in calculating all the chances attending the eventful game on which so much was to be staked, and to encounter such attempts upon France as England might, by his absence, be tempted to make, Napoleon judged it prudent to have recourse to additional means of national defence, which might extend the duty of military service still more widely among his subjects than was effected even by the conscription. As the measure was never but in one particular brought into general activity, it may be treated of the more slightly. The system consisted in a levy of national guards, divided into three general classes—the Ban, the Second Ban, and Arriere-Ban; for Buonaparte loved to retain the phrases of the old feudal institutions. The First Ban was to contain all men, from twenty to twenty-six years, who had not been called to serve in the army. The Second Ban included all capable of bearing arms, from the age of twenty-six to that of forty. The Arriere-Ban comprehended all able-bodied men from forty to sixty. The levies from these classes were not to be sent beyond the frontiers of France, and were to be called out in succession, as the danger pressed. They were divided into cohorts of 1120 men each. But it was the essential part of this project, that it placed one hundred cohorts of the First Ban—(that is, upwards of 100,000 men, between twenty and twenty-six years)—at the immediate disposal of the minister of war. In short, it was a new form of conscription, with the advantage, to the recruits, of limited service.

The celebrated philosopher Count La Cepède, who, from his researches into natural history, as well as from the ready eloquence with which he could express the acquiescence of the Senate in whatever scheme was proposed by the Emperor, had acquired the title of King of Reptiles, had upon this occasion his usual task of justifying the Imperial measures. In this allotment of another mighty draught of the youth of France to the purposes of military service, at a time when only the unbounded ambition of Napoleon rendered such a measure necessary, he could discover nothing save a new and affecting proof of the Emperor's paternal regard for his subjects. The youths, he said, would be relieved by one-sixth part of a cohort at a time; and, being at an age when ardour of mind is united to strength of body, they would find in the exercise of arms rather salutary sport, and agreeable recreation, than painful labour or severe duty. Then the express prohibition to quit the frontiers would be, their parents might rest assured, an absolute check on the fiery and impetuous character of the French soldier, and prevent the young men from listening to their headlong courage, and rushing forward into distant fields of combat, which no doubt there might be otherwise reason to apprehend. All this sounded very well, but the time was not long ere the Senate removed their writ *ne exeat regno*, in the case of these hundred cohorts; and, whether hurried on by their own impetuous valour, or forced forward by command of their leaders, they were all engaged in foreign service, and marched off to distant and bloody fields, from which few of them had the good fortune to return.

CIUDAD RODRIGO—BADAJOS

While the question of peace or war was yet trembling in the scales, news arrived from Spain that Lord Wellington had opened the campaign by an enterprise equally successfully conceived and daringly executed. Ciudad Rodrigo, which the French had greatly strengthened, was one of the keys of the frontier between Spain and Portugal. Lord Wellington had blockaded it, as we have seen, on the preceding year, but more with the purpose of compelling General Marmont to concentrate his forces for its relief, than with any hope of taking the place. But, in the beginning of January 1812, the French heard with surprise and alarm that the English army, suddenly put in motion, had opened trenches before Ciudad Rodrigo, and were battering in breach.

Marmont once more put his whole forces in motion, to prevent the fall of a place which was of the greatest consequence to both parties; and he had every reason to hope for success, since Ciudad Rodrigo, before its fortifications had been improved by the French, had held out against Massena for more than a month, though his army consisted of 100,000 men. But, in the present instance, within ten days from the opening of the siege, the place was carried by storm, almost under the very eyes of the experienced general who was advancing to its relief, and who had no alternative but to retire again to cantonments, and ponder upon the skill and activity which seemed of a sudden to have inspired the British forces.

Lord Wellington was none of those generals who think that an advantage, or a victory gained, is sufficient work for one campaign. The French were hardly reconciled to the loss of Ciudad Rodrigo, so extraordinary did it appear to them, when Badajos was invested, a much stronger place, which had stood a siege of thirty-six days against the French in the year 1811, although the defences were then much weaker, and the place commanded by an officer of no talent, and dubious fidelity. It was now, with incomprehensible celerity, battered, breached, stormed, and taken, within twelve days after the opening of the trenches. Two French Marshals had in vain interfered to prevent this catastrophe. Marmont made an unsuccessful attempt upon Ciudad Rodrigo, and assumed the air of pushing into Portugal; but no sooner did he learn the fall of the place, than he commenced his retreat from Castel-Branco. Soult, who had advanced rapidly to relieve Badajos, was in the act, it is said, of informing a circle of his officers that it was the commands of the Emperor—commands never under any circumstances to be disobeyed—that Badajos should be relieved, when an officer, who had been sent forward to reconnoitre, interrupted the shouts of "*Vive l'Empereur!*" with the equally dispiriting and incredible information, that the English colours were flying on the walls.

These two brilliant achievements were not only of great importance by their influence on the events of the campaign, but still more so as they indicated that our military operations had assumed an entirely new character, and that the British soldiers, as now conducted, had not only the advantage of their own strength of body and natural courage, not only the benefit of the resources copiously supplied by the wealthy nation to whom they belonged, but also, as began to be generally allowed, an undoubted superiority in military art and science. The objects of the campaign were admirably chosen, for the exertion to be made was calculated with a degree of accuracy which dazzled and bewildered the enemy; and though the loss incurred in their attainment was very considerable, yet it was not in proportion to the much greater advantages attained by success.

Badajos fell on the 7th April; and on the 18th of that month, an overture of pacific tendency was made by the French Government to that of Britain. It is not unlikely that Buonaparte, on beholding his best commanders completely out-generalled before Ciudad Rodrigo and Badajos, might foresee in this inauspicious commencement the long train of defeat and disaster which befell the French in the campaign of 1812, the events of which could not have failed to give liberty to Spain, had Spain, or rather had her Government, been united among themselves, and cordial in supporting their allies.

It might be Lord Wellington's successes, or the lingering anxiety to avoid a war involving so many contingencies as that of Russia; or it might be a desire to impress the French public that he was always disposed towards peace, that induced Napoleon to direct the Duke of Bassano[101] to write a letter to Lord Castlereagh, proposing that the integrity and independence of Spain should be guaranteed under the *present reigning dynasty*; that Portugal should remain under the rule of the Princes of Braganza; Sicily under that of Ferdinand; and Naples under Murat; each nation, in this manner, retaining possession of that which the other had not been able to wrench from them by force of war. Lord Castlereagh immediately replied, that if the reign of King Joseph were meant by the phrase,

---

[101] "When Napoleon had determined that all the springs of his diplomacy should be put in motion towards the north, he changed his minister of foreign affairs, the complication of so many intrigues and manœuvres becoming too much, not indeed for the zeal, but for the energy of Champagny-Cadore. Napoleon did not think himself secure in confiding the weight of affairs so important to any other person than Maret, the chief of his *secrétariat*—that is to say, all foreign affairs were, from that moment, concentrated in his cabinet, and received no other impulse than from him. Under this point of view, Maret, who was a true official machine, was the very man whom the Emperor wanted. He really admired his master, with whose thoughts, secrets, and inclinations he was acquainted. It was also he who kept the secret-book, in which the Emperor made his notes of such individuals of all countries and parties who might be useful to him, as well as of men who were pointed out to his notice, and whose intentions he suspected."—Fouché.

"the dynasty actually reigning," he must answer explicitly, that England's engagements to Ferdinand VII. and the Cortes presently governing Spain, rendered her acknowledging him impossible.[102]

The correspondence went no farther.[103] The nature of the overture served to show the tenacity of Buonaparte's character, who, in treating for peace, would yield nothing save that which the fate of war had actually placed beyond his reach; and expected the British to yield up to him the very kingdom of Spain, whose fate depended upon the bloody arbitrement of the sword. It also manifested the insincerity with which he could use words to mislead those who treated with him. He had in many instances, some of which we have quoted, laid it down as a sacred principle, that princes of his blood, called to reign over foreign states, should remain still the subjects of France and vassals of its Emperor, whose interest they were bound to prefer on all occasions to that of the countries they were called to govern. Upon these grounds he had compelled the abdication of King Louis of Holland; and how was it possible for him to expect to receive credit, when he proposed to render Spain independent under Joseph, whose authority was unable to control even the French marshals who acted in his name?

HOSTILE PREPARATIONS

This feeble effort towards a general peace having altogether miscarried, it became subject of consideration, whether the approaching breach betwixt the two great empires could yet be prevented. The most active preparations for war were taking place on both sides. Those of Russia were defensive; but she mustered great armies on the Niemen, as if in expectation of an assault; while France was rapidly pouring troops into Prussia, and into the grand duchy of Warsaw, and assuming those positions most favourable for invading the Russian frontier. Yet amid preparations for war, made

---

[102] "Here the matter dropped. Ashamed of its overtures, our cabinet, whose only object was to have drawn Russia into some act of weakness, perceived too late that it had impressed upon our diplomacy a character of fickleness, bad faith, and ignorance."—Fouché.

[103] For copies of the Correspondence with the French Government relative to Peace, see Parliamentary Debates, vol. xxiii., p. 10, 56.

on such an immense scale as Europe had never before witnessed, there seemed to be a lingering wish on the part of both Sovereigns, even at this late hour, to avoid the conflict. This indeed might have been easily done, had there been on the part of Napoleon a hearty desire to make peace, instead of what could only be termed a degree of hesitation to commence hostilities. In fact, the original causes of quarrel were already settled, or, what is the same thing, principles had been fixed, on which their arrangement might be easily adjusted. Yet still the preparations for invading Russia became more and more evident—the purpose was distinctly expressed in the treaty between France and Prussia; and the war did not appear the less certain that the causes of it seemed to be in a great measure abandoned. The anxiety of Alexander was therefore diverted from the source of the dispute to its important consequences; and he became most naturally more solicitous about having the French troops withdrawn from the frontiers of Poland, than about the cause that originally brought them there.

Accordingly, Prince Kourakin, the Russian plenipotentiary, had orders to communicate to the Duke of Bassano his master's ultimatum. The grounds of arrangement proposed by the Czar were, the evacuation of Prussia and Pomerania by the French troops; a diminution of the garrison of Dantzic; and an amicable arrangement of the dispute between Napoleon and Alexander. On these conditions, which, in fact, were no more than necessary to assure Russia of France's peaceable intentions, the Czar agreed to place his commerce upon a system of licenses as conducted in France; to introduce the clauses necessary to protect the French trade; and farther, to use his influence with the Duke of Oldenburg, to obtain his consent to accept some reasonable indemnification for the territory which had been so summarily annexed to France.

In looking back at this document, it appears to possess as much the character of moderation, and even of deference, as could be expected from the chief of a great empire. His demand that France, unless it were her determined purpose to make war, should withdraw the armies which threatened the Russian frontier, seems no more than common sense or prudence would commend. Yet this condition was made by Napoleon, however unreasonably, the direct cause of hostilities.

The person, in a private brawl, who should say to an angry and violent opponent, "Sheathe your sword, or at least lower its point, and I will accommodate with you, on your own terms, the original cause of quarrel," would surely not be considered as having given him any affront, or other cause for instant violence. Yet Buonaparte, in nearly the same situation, resented as an unatonable offence, the demand that he should withdraw his armies from a position, where they could have no other purpose save to overawe Russia. The demand, he said, was insolent; he was not accustomed to be addressed in that style, nor to regulate his movements by the commands of a foreign sovereign. The Russian ambassador received his passports; and the unreasonable caprice of Napoleon, which considered an overture towards an amicable treaty as a gross offence, because it summoned him to desist from his menacing attitude, led to the death of millions, and the irretrievable downfall of the most extraordinary empire which the world had ever seen. On the 9th May, 1812, Buonaparte left Paris; the Russian ambassador had his passports for departure two days later.

ROYAL FESTIVITIES

Upon his former military expeditions, it had been usual for Napoleon to join his army suddenly, and with a slender attendance; but on the present occasion he assumed a style of splendour and dignity becoming one, who might, if any earthly sovereign ever could, have assumed the title of King of Kings. Dresden was appointed as a mutual rendezvous for all the Kings, Dominations, Princes, Dukes, and dependent royalties of every description, who were subordinate to Napoleon, or hoped for good or evil at his hands. The Emperor of Austria, with his Empress, met his mighty son-in-law upon this occasion, and the city was crowded with princes of the most ancient birth, as well as with others who claimed still higher rank, as belonging to the family of Napoleon. The King of Prussia also was present, neither a willing nor a welcome guest, unless so far as his attendance was necessary to swell the victor's triumph. Melancholy in heart and in looks, he wandered through the gay and splendid scenes, a mourner rather than a reveller. But fate had amends in store, for a prince whose course, in times of unparalleled distress, had been marked by courage and patriotism.[104]

Amidst all these dignitaries, no one interested the public so much as he, for whom, and by whom the assembly was collected; the wonderful being who could have governed the world, but could not rule his own restless mind. When visible, Napoleon was the principal figure of the group; when absent, every eye was on the door, expecting his entrance.[105] He was chiefly employed in business in his cabinet, while the other crowned personages (to whom, indeed, he left but little to do) were wandering abroad in quest of amusement. The feasts and banquets, as well as the assemblies of the royal personages and their suites, after the theatrical representations, were almost all at Napoleon's expense, and were conducted in a style of splendour, which made those attempted by any of the other potentates seem mean and paltry.

The youthful Empress had her share of these days of grandeur. "The reign of Maria Louisa," said her husband, when at St. Helena, "has been very short, but she had much to make her enjoy it. She had the world at her feet." Her superior magnificence in dress and ornaments, gave her a great pre-eminence over her mother-in-law, the Empress of Austria, betwixt whom and Maria Louisa there seems to have existed something of that petty feud, which is apt to divide such relations in private life. To make the Austrian Empress some amends, Buonaparte informs us, that she often visited her daughter-in-law's toilette, and seldom went back

---

[104] "Napoleon had expressed a wish that the Emperor of Austria, several kings, and a crowd of princes, should meet him at Dresden: his desire was fulfilled; all thronged to meet him; some induced by hope, others prompted by fear; for himself, his motives were to feel his power, to exhibit it, and enjoy it."—Count Philip de Ségur, *Hist. de Napoleon, et de la Grande Armée, en 1812*, tom. i., p. 89.

[105] "Whole nations had quitted their homes to throng his path; rich and poor, nobles and plebeians, friends and enemies, all hurried to the scene. Their curious and anxious groups were seen collecting in the streets, the roads, and the public places. It was not his crown, his rank, the luxury of his court, but him—himself—on whom they desired to feast their eyes; a memento of his features which they were anxious to obtain: they wished to be able to say to their less fortunate countrymen and posterity that they had seen Napoleon."—Ségur, tom. i., p. 90.

without receiving some marks of her munificence.[106] Perhaps we may say of this information, as Napoleon says of something else, that an Emperor should not have known these circumstances, or at least should not have told them. The truth is, Buonaparte did not love the Empress of Austria; and though he represents that high personage as showing him much attention, the dislike was mutual. The daughter of the Duke of Modena had not forgot her father's sufferings by the campaigns of Italy.[107]

In a short time, however, the active spirit of Napoleon led him to tire of a scene, where his vanity might for a time be gratified, but which soon palled on his imagination as empty and frivolous. He sent for De Pradt, the Archbishop of Malines, whose talents he desired to employ as ambassador at Warsaw, and in a singular style of diplomacy, thus gave him his commission: "I am about to make a trial of you. You may believe I did not send for you here to say mass" (which ceremony the Archbishop had performed that morning.) "You must keep a great establishment; have an eye to the women, their influence is essential in that country. You know Poland; you have read Rulhières. For me, I go to beat the Russians; time is flying; we must have all over by the end of September; perhaps we are even already too late. I am tired to death here; I have been here eight days playing the courtier to the Empress of Austria." He then threw out indistinct hints of compelling Austria to quit her hold on Galicia, and accept an indemnification in Illyria, or otherwise remain without any. As to Prussia, he avowed his intention, when the war was over, to ruin her completely, and to strip her of Silesia. "I am on my way to Moscow," he added. "Two battles there will do the business. I will burn Thoula; the Emperor Alexander will come on his knees, and then is Russia disarmed. All is ready, and only waits my presence. Moscow is the heart of their empire; besides, I make war at the expense of the blood of the Poles. I will leave fifty thousand of my Frenchmen in Poland. I will convert Dantzic into another Gibraltar. I will give fifty millions a-

---

[106] Las Cases, tom. i., p. 299.
[107] "The Empress of Austria made herself remarked, by her aversion, which she vainly endeavoured to disguise; it escaped from her by an involuntary impulse, which Napoleon instantly detected, and subdued by a smile: but she employed her spirit and attraction in gently winning hearts to her opinion, in order to sow them afterwards with the seeds of hate."—Ségur, tom. i., p. 92.

year in subsidies to the Poles. I can afford the expense. Without Russia be included, the Continental System would be mere folly. Spain costs me very dear; without her I should be master of the world; but when I am so, my son will have nothing to do but to keep his place, and it does not require to be very clever to do that. Go, take your instructions from Maret."[108]

The complete confidence of success implied in these disjointed, yet striking expressions, was general through all who approached Napoleon's person, whether French or foreigners. The young military men looked on the expedition against Russia as on a hunting party which was to last for two months. The army rushed to the fatal country, all alive with the hopes of plunder, pensions, and promotion. All the soldiers who were not included railed against their own bad luck, or the partiality of Napoleon, for detaining them from so triumphant an enterprise.[109]

WAR WITH RUSSIA

Meantime, Buonaparte made a last attempt at negotiation, or rather to discover what was the state of the Emperor Alexander's mind, who, while he was himself surrounded by sovereigns, as the sun by planets, remained lonely in his own orbit, collecting around him means of defence, which, immense as they were, seemed scarcely adequate to the awful crisis in which he stood. General Lauriston had been despatched to Wilna, to communicate definitively with Alexander. Count de Narbonne, already noticed as the most adroit courtier of the Tuileries was sent to invite the Czar to meet Napoleon at Dresden, in hopes that, in a personal treaty, the two sovereigns might resume their habits of intimacy, and settle between themselves what they had been unable to arrange through their ambassadors. But Lauriston could obtain no audience of the Emperor, and the report of Narbonne was decidedly warlike. He found the Russians neither depressed nor elated, but arrived at the general conclusion, that war was become inevitable, and therefore

---

[108] De Pradt, Histoire de l'Ambassade en Pologne, p. 55.
[109] De Pradt, Histoire de l'Ambassade en Pologne, p. 58.

determined to submit to its evils, rather than avoid them by a dishonourable peace.[110]

---

[110] Ségur, tom. i., p. 97.

Chapter LVII

Napoleon's Plan of the Campaign against Russia—Understood and provided against by Barclay de Tolly, the Russian Generalissimo—Statement of the Grand French Army—Of the Grand Russian Army—Disaster on the river Wilia—Difficulties of the Campaign, on the part of the French—Their defective Commissariat and Hospital Department—Cause of Buonaparte's determination to advance—His forced marches occasion actual delay—Napoleon remains for some days at Wilna—Abbé de Pradt—His intrigues to excite the Poles—Neutralized by Napoleon's engagements with Austria—An attempt to excite Insurrection in Lithuania also fails.

In ancient history, we often read of the inhabitants of the northern regions, impelled by want, and by the desire of exchanging their frozen deserts for the bounties of a more genial climate, breaking forth from their own bleak regions, and, with all the terrors of an avalanche, bursting down upon those of the south. But it was reserved for our generation to behold the invasion reversed, and to see immense hosts of French, Germans, and Italians, leaving their own fruitful, rich, and delightful regions, to carry at once conquest and desolation through the dreary pine forests, swamps, and barren wildernesses of Scythia. The philosopher, Hume, dedicated an essay to consider, whether futurity might expect a new inundation of barbarian conquerors; a fresh "living cloud of war," from the northern hives; but neither to him nor any one else had it occurred to anticipate the opposite danger, of combined hundreds of thousands from the fairest and most fertile regions of Europe, moving at the command of a single man, for the purpose of bereaving the wildest country of Europe of its national independence. "Russia," said Buonaparte, in one of his Delphic proclamations, "is dragged on by her fate; her destiny must be accomplished. Let us march; let us cross the Niemen; let us carry war into her territories. The second war of Poland will be as glorious to the French arms as the first; but the peace we shall conclude shall carry with it its guarantee, and terminate that haughty influence which Russia has exercised for more than fifty years on the affairs of Europe."[111] Napoleon's final object was here spoken out; it was to thrust Russia back upon her Asiatic dominions, and deprive her of her influence in European politics.

The address of the Russian Emperor to his troops was in a different, more manly, rational, and intelligible strain, devoid of those blustering attempts at prophetic eloquence, which are in bad taste when uttered, and, if they may acquire some credit among the vulgar when followed by a successful campaign, become the most bitter of satires, if fortune does not smile on the vatication. Alexander enforced on his subjects the various efforts which he had made for the preservation of peace, but which had proved fruitless. "It now only remains," he said, "after invoking the Almighty Being who is the witness and defender of the true cause, to oppose our forces to those of the enemy. It is unnecessary to recall to generals, officers, and soldiers, what is expected from their loyalty and courage; the blood of the ancient Sclavonians circulates in their veins. Soldiers, you fight for your religion, your liberty, and your native land. Your Emperor is amongst you, and God is the enemy of the aggressor."[112]

The sovereigns who addressed their troops, each in his own peculiar mode of exhortation, had their different plans for the campaign. Buonaparte's was formed on his usual system of warfare. It was his primary object to accumulate a great force on the centre of the Russian line, to break it asunder, and cut off effectually as many divisions, as activity could surprise and overmaster in such a struggle. To secure the possession of large towns, if possible one of the two capitals, Petersburgh or Moscow; and to grant that which he doubted not would by that time be humbly craved, the terms of a

---

[111] Second Bulletin of the Grand Army, dated Wilkowiski, June 22, 1812.
[112] Dated Wilna, June 25. "The difference between the two nations, the two sovereigns, and their reciprocal position, were remarked in these proclamations. In fact, the one which was defensive was unadorned and moderate; the other, offensive, was replete with audacity and the confidence of victory. The first sought support in religion, the other in fatality; the one in love of country, the other in love of glory."—Ségur, tom. i., p. 117.

peace which should strip Russia of her European influence, and establish a Polish nation in her bosom, composed of provinces rent from her own dominions—would have crowned the undertaking.

BARCLAY DE TOLLY

The tactics of Napoleon had, by long practice, been pretty well understood, by those studious of military affairs. Barclay de Tolly, whom Alexander had made his generalissimo, a German by birth, a Scotchman by extraction, had laid down and recommended to the Czar, with whom he was in great favour, a plan of foiling Buonaparte upon his own system. He proposed that the Russians should first show only so much opposition on the frontier of their country, as should lay the invaders under the necessity of marching with precaution and leisure; that they should omit no means of annoying their communications, and disturbing the base on which they rested, but should carefully avoid every thing approaching to a general action.[113] On this principle it was proposed to fall back before the invaders, refusing to engage in any other action than skirmishes, and those upon advantage, until the French lines of communication, extended to an immeasurable length, should become liable to be cut off even by the insurgent peasantry. In the meanwhile, as the French became straitened in provisions, and deprived of recruits and supplies, the Russians were to be reinforcing their army, and at the same time refreshing it. Thus, it was the object of this plan of the campaign not to fight the French forces, until the bad roads, want of provisions, toilsome marches, diseases, and loss in skirmishes, should have deprived the invading army of all its original advantages of numbers, spirit, and discipline. This procrastinating system of tactics suited Russia the better, that her preparations for defensive war were very far from being completed, and that it was important to gain time to receive arms and other supplies from England, as well as, by making peace with

---

[113] The *base* of military operations is, in strategie, understood to mean that space of country which every army, marching through a hostile territory, must keep open and free in the rear, otherwise his main body must necessarily be deprived of its communications, and probably cut off. The base, therefore, contains the supplies and depôts of the army.—S.

the Turks, to obtain the disposal of the large army now engaged upon the Danube.

At the same time it was easy to foresee, that so long a retreat, together with the desolation occasioned to the Russian territory by the presence of an invading army, might wear out the patience of the Russian soldiery. Some advantageous position was therefore to be selected, and skilfully fortified before hand, in which a stand might be made, like that of Lord Wellington in the lines at Torres Vedras. For this purpose, a very large fortified camp was prepared at Drissa, on the river Düna, or Dwina, which, supposing the object of the French to have been St. Petersburgh, would have been well calculated to cover that capital. On the other hand, were the French to move on Moscow, which proved their final determination, the intrenchments at Drissa were of no importance.

We must speak of the immense hosts combined under Buonaparte, as if they were all constituent parts of one army, although the theatre of war which they occupied was not less than an hundred and twenty French leagues in extent of front.

Macdonald commanded the left wing of the whole French army, which consisted of above 30,000 men: his orders were to penetrate into Courland, and threaten the right flank of the Russians; and, if it were found advisable, to besiege Riga, or at least to threaten that important sea-port. The extreme right of Napoleon's army was placed towards Pinsk, in Volhynia, and consisted almost entirely of the Austrian auxiliaries, under Prince Schwartzenberg. They were opposed to the Russian army under General Tormazoff, which had been destined to protect Volhynia. This was a false step of Napoleon, adopted, doubtless, to allay the irritable jealousy of his ally Austria, on the subject of freeing and restoring the kingdom of Poland. The natives of Volhynia, it must be remembered, are Poles, subjected to the yoke of Russia. Had French troops, or those of the grand duchy of Warsaw, been sent amongst them, the Volhynians would probably have risen in arms to vindicate their liberty. But they had little temptation to do so when they only saw the Austrians, by whose arms Galicia was yet detained in subjection, and whose Emperor was as liable as Alexander himself to suffer from the resuscitation of Polish independence.

Betwixt the left wing, commanded by Macdonald, and the right under Schwartzenberg, lay the grand French army, divided into three masses. Buonaparte himself moved with his Guards, of which Bessières commanded the cavalry, the Maréschals Lefebvre and Mortier the infantry. The Emperor had also under his immediate command and corps d'armée, commanded by Davoust, Oudinot, and Ney; which, with the divisions of cavalry under Grouchy, Montbrun, and Nansouty, amounting, it was computed, to no fewer than 250,000 men, were ready to rush forward and overpower the opposite army of Russians, called the Army of the West. King Jerome of Westphalia, with the divisions of Junot, Poniatowski, and Regnier, and the cavalry of Latour Maubourg, forming a mass of about 80,000 men, were destined in the same manner to move forward on the Russian second, or supporting army. Lastly, a central army, under Eugene, the Viceroy of Italy, had it in charge to press between the first and second Russian army, increase their separation, render their junction impossible, and act against either, or both, as opportunity should arise. Such was the disposition of the invading force. Murat, King of Naples, well-known by his old name of *"Le Beau Sabreur,"* commanded the whole cavalry of this immense army.

On the other hand, the grand Russian army, commanded by the Emperor in person, and more immediately by Barclay de Tolly, advanced its headquarters as far as Wilna; not that it was their purpose to defend Lithuania, or its capital, but to oblige the French to manœuvre, and so show their intentions. It amounted to 120,000 men. On the north, towards Courland, this grand army communicated with a division of 10,000 men, under Count Essen; and on the south held communication, but on a line rather too much prolonged, with the second army under the gallant Prince Bagration, one of the best and bravest of the Russian generals. Platoff, the celebrated Hettman, or captain-general of the Cossacks, attended this second army, with 12,000 of his children of the desert. Independent of these, Bagration's army might amount to 80,000 men. On the extreme left, and watching the Austrians, from whom perhaps no very vigorous measures were apprehended, was

Tormazoff, with what was termed the army of Volhynia, amounting to 20,000 men. Two armies of reserve were in the course of being formed at Novogorod and Smolensk. They might amount to about 20,000 men each.[114]

Thus, on the whole, the Russians entered upon the campaign with a sum total of 260,000 men, opposed to 470,000, or with an odds of almost one half against them. But during the course of the war, Russia raised reinforcements of militia and volunteers to greatly more than the balance which was against her at the commencement.

MARCH UPON THE NIEMEN

The grand imperial army marched upon the river Niemen in its three overwhelming masses; the King of Westphalia upon Grodno, the Viceroy of Italy on Pilony, and the Emperor himself on a point called Nagaraiski, three leagues beyond Kowno. When the head of Napoleon's columns reached the river which rolled silently along under cover of immense forests on the Russian side, he advanced in person to reconnoitre the banks, when his horse stumbled and threw him. "A bad omen," said a voice, but whether that of the Emperor or one of his suite, could not be distinguished; "a Roman would return." On the Russian bank appeared only a single Cossack, who challenged the first party of French that crossed the river, and demanded their purpose in the territories of Russia. "To beat you, and to take Wilna," was the reply. The patrol withdrew, nor was another soldier seen.[115]

A dreadful thunder-storm was the welcome which they received in this wild land; and shortly after the Emperor received intelligence that the Russians were falling back on every side, and manifested an evident intention to evacuate Lithuania without a battle. The Emperor urged forward his columns with even more than his usual promptitude, eager to strike one of those formidable blows by which he was wont to annihilate his enemy at the very commencement of the campaign. This gave rise to an event more

---

[114] Ségur, tom. i., p. 117; Jomini, tom. iv., p. 50.
[115] Ségur, tom. i., p. 122.

ominous than the fall of his horse, or the tempest which received him on the banks of the Niemen. The river Wilia being swollen with rain, and the bridges destroyed, the Emperor, impatient of the obstacle, commanded a body of Polish cavalry to cross by swimming. They did not hesitate to dash into the river. But ere they reached the middle of the stream, the irresistible torrent broke their ranks, and they were swept down and lost almost to a man, before the eyes of Napoleon, to whom some of them in the last struggle turned their faces, exclaiming, "*Vive l'Empereur!*" The spectators were struck with horror.[116] But much greater would that feeling have been, could they have known that the fate of this handful of brave men was but an anticipation of that which impended over the hundreds of thousands, who, high in health and hope, were about to rush upon natural and artificial obstacles, no less formidable and no less insurmountable than the torrent which had swept away their unfortunate advanced guard.

While his immense masses were traversing Lithuania, Napoleon fixed his headquarters at Wilna,[117] the ancient capital of that province, where he began to experience the first pressure of those difficulties which attended his gigantic undertaking. We must pause to detail them; for they tend to show the great mistake of those who have followed Napoleon himself in supposing, that the Russian expedition was a hopeful and well-conceived plan, which would certainly have proved successful, if not unexpectedly disconcerted by the burning of Moscow, and the severity of the weather, by which the French armies were compelled to retreat into Poland.

We have elsewhere mentioned, that, according to Napoleon's usual style of tactics, the French troops set out upon their campaign

---

[116] Ségur, tom. i., p. 128.

[117] "Napoleon, at Wilna, had a new empire to organise; the politics of Europe, the war of Spain, and the government of France to direct. His political, military, and administrative correspondence, which he had suffered to accumulate for some days, imperiously demanded his attention. Such, indeed, was his custom, on the eve of a great event, as that would necessarily decide the character of many of his replies, and impart a colouring to all. He therefore established himself at his quarters, and in the first instance, threw himself on a bed, less for the sake of sleep than of quiet meditation; whence, abruptly starting up directly after, he rapidly dictated the orders which he had conceived."—Ségur, tom. i., p. 131.

with bread and biscuit for a few days, and when that was expended (which, betwixt waste and consumption, usually happened before the calculated period,) they lived on such supplies as they could collect in the country, by the means of marauding or pillage, which they had converted into a regular system. But Napoleon had far too much experience and prudence to trust, amid the wastes of Russia, to a system of supplies, which had sufficed for maintenance of the army in the rich fields of Austria. He knew well that he was plunging with half a million of men into inhospitable deserts, where Charles XII. could not find subsistence for twenty thousand Swedes. He was aware, besides, of the impolicy there would be in harassing the Lithuanians by marauding exactions. To conciliate them was a great branch of his plan, for Lithuania, in respect to Russia, was a conquered province, into which Napoleon hoped to inspire the same desire of independence which animated Poland, and thus to find friends and allies among the very subjects of his enemy. The utmost exertion of his splendid talents, putting into activity the full extent of his almost unlimited power, had been, therefore, turned towards collecting immense magazines of provisions, and for securing the means of transporting them along with the army. His strong and impassioned genius was, for months before the expedition, directed to this important object, which he pressed upon his generals with the utmost solicitude. "For masses like those we are about to move, if precautions be not taken, the grain of no country can suffice," he said, in one part of his correspondence.—In another, "All the provision-waggons must be loaded with flour, rice, bread, vegetables, and brandy, besides what is necessary for the hospital service. The result of my movements will assemble 400,000 men on a single point. There will be nothing to expect from the country, and it will be necessary to have every thing within ourselves."

These undeniable views were followed up by preparations, which, abstractedly considered, must be regarded as gigantic. The cars and waggons, which were almost innumerable, destined for the carriage of provisions, were divided into battalions and squadrons. Each battalion of cars was capable of transporting 6000 quintals of flour; each squadron of heavy waggons nearly 4800 quintals; besides the immense number dedicated to the service of the engineers and the hospitals, or engaged in transporting besieging materiel and pontoons.

DEFECTIVE COMMISSARIAT

This sketch must convince the reader that Napoleon had in his eye, from the outset, the prospect of deficiency in supplying his army with provisions, and that he had bent his mind to the task of overcoming it by timely preparation. But all his precautions proved totally inadequate. It was found a vain attempt to introduce military discipline amidst the carters and waggon-drivers; and when wretched roads were encumbered with fallen horses and broken carriages, when the soldiers and wain-drivers began to plunder the contents of the cars and waggons which they were appointed to protect and to manage, the confusion became totally inextricable. Very far from reaching Lithuania, where their presence was so essential, few of the heavy waggons ever attained the banks of the Vistula, and almost none proceeded to the Niemen. Weeks and months after the army had passed, some of the light cars and herds of cattle did arrive, but comparatively few in number, and in most miserable plight. The soldiers were, therefore, at the very commencement of the campaign, compelled to have recourse to their usual mode of supplying themselves, by laying contributions on the country; which, while they continued in Poland, the immense fertility of the soil enabled it to supply. But matters became greatly worse after entering Lithuania, which the Russians had previously endeavoured to strip of all that could benefit the French.

Thus, in the very first march from the Niemen and the Wilia, through a country which was regarded as friendly, and before they had seen an enemy, the immense army of Napoleon were incurring great loss themselves, and doing infinite damage to the country on which they lived at free cost, in spite of all the measures which Buonaparte had devised, and all the efforts he had made to maintain them from their own stores.

This uncertain mode of subsistence was common to the whole army, though its consequences were especially disastrous in particular corps. Ségur[118] informs us, that the armies under Eugene and Davoust were regular in their work of collecting contributions, and distributing them among the soldiers; so that their system of marauding was less burdensome to the country, and more advantageous to themselves. On the other hand, the Westphalian, and other German auxiliaries, under King Jerome, having learned the lesson of pillaging from the French, and wanting, according to Ségur, the elegant manner of their teachers, practised the arts they had acquired with a coarse rapacity, which made the French ashamed of their pupils and imitators. Thus the Lithuanians, terrified, alienated, and disgusted, with the injuries they sustained, were far from listening to the promises of Napoleon, or making common cause with him against Russia, who had governed them kindly, and with considerable respect to their own habits and customs.

---

[118] Here and elsewhere we quote, as a work of complete authority, Count Philip de Ségur's account of this memorable expedition. The author is, we have always understood, a man of honour, and his work evinces him to be a man of talent. We have had the opinion of several officers of high character, who have themselves served in the campaign, that although unquestionably there may be some errors among the details, and although in some places the author may have given way to the temptation of working up a description, or producing effect by a dialogue, yet his narrative on the whole is candid, fair, and liberal. The unfriendly criticism of General Gourgaud ["Examen Critique de l'Ouvrage de Ségur"] impeaches Count Ségur's opportunities of knowing the facts he relates, because his duty did not call him into the line of battle, where he might have seen the military events with his own eyes. We conceive with deference, that, as an historian, Count Ségur's situation was more favourable for collecting intelligence than if he had been actually engaged. We speak from high authority in saying, that a battle is in one respect like a ball—every one recollects the next morning, the partner with whom he danced, and what passed betwixt them, but none save a bystander can give a general account of the whole party. Now, Count Ségur eminently resembled the bystander in his opportunities of collecting exact information concerning the whole events of the campaign. His duty was to take up and distribute the lodgings at the general headquarters. It was, therefore, seldom that an officer could go to or return from headquarters without holding communication with Count Ségur; and, having his plan of a narrative in view, he could not be the man of ability he appears, if he did not obtain from those who arrived at or left headquarters such information as they had to communicate. As he had no pressing military duty to perform, he had nothing to prevent his arranging and recording the information he collected; and when General Gourgaud urges the impossibility of the historian's being present at some of the most secret councils, he forgets that many such secrets *percolate* from the cabinet into the better-informed circles around it, even before the seal of secrecy is removed, but especially when, as in the present case, a total change of circumstances renders secrecy no longer necessary. We have only to add, that though the idolatry of Count Ségur towards Napoleon is not sufficient to satisfy his critic, he must in other eyes be considered as an admirer of the late Emperor; and that those who knew the French army, will find no reason to suspect him of being a false brother.—S.

IMMENSE LOSSES OF THE ARMY

But this was not the only evil. The direct loss sustained by the French army was very great. In the course of the very first marches from the Niemen and the Wilia, not less than 10,000 horses, and numbers of men were left dead on the road. Of the young conscripts especially, many died of hunger and fatigue; and there were instances of some who committed suicide, rather than practise the cruel course of pillage by which only they could subsist; and of others, who took the same desperate step, from remorse at having participated in such cruelties. Thousands turned stragglers, and subsisted by robbery. The Duke of Treviso, who followed the march of the grand army, informed Napoleon, that, from the Niemen to the Wilia, he had seen nothing but ruined habitations abandoned, carriages overturned, broke open and pillaged, corpses of men and horses—all the horrible appearances, in short, which present themselves in the route of a defeated army.[119]

Those who desired to flatter Buonaparte, ascribed this loss to the storm of rain, which fell at the time they were entering Lithuania. But summer rain, whatever its violence, does not destroy the horses of an army by hundreds and thousands. That which does destroy them, and renders those that survive almost unfit for service during the campaign, and incapable of bearing the hardships of winter, is hard work, forced marches, want of corn or dry fodder, and the supporting them on the green crop which is growing in the fields. It was now the season when, of all others, a commander, who values the serviceable condition of his army, will avoid such enterprises as require from his cavalry hard work and forced marches. In like manner, storms of summer rain do not destroy the foot soldiers exposed to them, more than other men; but forced marches on bad roads, and through a country unprovided with shelter, and without provisions, must ruin infantry, since every man, who, from fatigue, or from having straggled too far in quest of food, chances to be left behind, is left exposed without shelter to the effects of the climate, and if he cannot follow and rejoin his corps, has no resource but to lie down and die.

---

[119] Ségur, tom. i., p. 147; Jomini, tom. iv., p. 58.

The provisions of the hospital department had been as precarious as those of the commissariat. Only 6000 patients could be accommodated in the hospitals at Wilna, which is too small a proportion for an army of 400,000 men, even if lying in quarters in a healthy and peaceful country, where one invalid in fifty is a most restricted allowance; but totally inadequate to the numbers which actually required assistance, as well from the maladies introduced by fatigue and bad diet, as by the casualties of war. Although no battle, and scarce a skirmish had been fought, 25,000 patients encumbered the hospitals of Wilna; and the villages were filled with soldiers who were dying for want of medical assistance. The King of Westphalia must be exempted from this general censure; his army was well provided with hospitals, and lost much fewer men than the others. This imperfection of the hospital department was an original defect in the conception of the expedition, and continued to influence it most unfavourably from beginning to end.

Napoleon sometimes repined under these losses and calamities, sometimes tried to remedy them by threats against marauders, and sometimes endeavoured to harden himself against the thought of the distress of his army, as an evil which must be endured, until victory should put an end to it. But repining and anger availed nothing; denunciations against marauders could not reasonably be executed upon men who had no other means of subsistence; and it was impossible to obtain a victory over an enemy who would not risk a battle.

The reader may here put the natural question, Why Buonaparte, when he found the stores, which he considered as essential to the maintenance of his army, had not reached the Vistula, should have passed on, instead of suspending his enterprise until he was provided with those means, which he had all along judged essential to its success? He might in this manner have lost time, but he would have saved his men and horses, and avoided distressing a country which he desired to conciliate. The truth is, that Napoleon had suffered his sound and cooler judgment to be led astray, by strong and ardent desire to finish the war by one brilliant battle and victory. The hope of surprising the Emperor Alexander at Wilna, of defeating his grand army, or at least cutting off some of its principal corps, resembled too much many of his former exploits, not to have captivation for him. For this purpose, and with this expectation, forced marches were to be undertaken, from the Vistula even to the Dwina and Dnieper; the carts, carriages, cattle, all the supplies brought from France, Italy, and Germany, were left behind, the difficulties of the enterprise forgotten, and nothing thought of but the expectation of finding the enemy at unawares, and totally destroying him at one blow. The fatal consequence of the forced marches we have stated; but what may appear most strange is, that Napoleon, who had recourse to this expeditious and reckless advance, solely to surprise his enemy by an unexpected attack, rather lost than gained that advantage of time, to procure which he had made such sacrifices. This will appear from the following detail:—

The army which had been quartered on the Vistula, broke up from thence about the 1st of June, and advanced in different columns, and by forced marches upon the Niemen, which it reached upon different points, but chiefly near Kowno, upon the 23d, and commenced the passage on the 24th of the same month. From the Vistula to the Niemen is about 250 wersts, equal to 235 or 240 English miles; from Kowno, on the banks of the Niemen, to Vitepsk, on the Dwina, is nearly the same distance. The whole space might be marched by an army, moving with its baggage, in the course of forty marches, at the rate of twelve miles a-day; yet the traversing this distance took, as we shall presently see, four days more, notwithstanding the acceleration of forced marches, than would have been occupied by an army moving at an ordinary and easy rate, and carrying its own supplies along with its columns. The cause why this overhaste should have been attended with actual delay, was partly owing to the great mass of troops which were to be supplied by the principle of the marauding system, partly to the condition of the country, which was doomed to afford them; and partly, it may be, to the political circumstances which detained Napoleon twenty precious days at Wilna. The first reason is too obvious to need illustration, as a flying army of 20,000 men bears comparatively light on the resources of a country, and may be pushed through it in haste; but those immense columns, whose demands were so unbounded, could neither move rapidly, nor have their wants hastily supplied. But, besides, in a country like Lithuania, the march could not be regular, and it was often necessary to suspend the advance; thus losing in some places the time which great exertion had gained in others. Wildernesses and pathless forests were necessarily to be traversed in the utmost haste, as they afforded nothing for the marauders, on whose success the army depended for support. To make amends for this, it was necessary to halt the troops for one day, or even more, in the richest districts, or in the neighbourhood of large towns, to give leisure and opportunity to recruit their supplies at the expense of the country. Thus the time gained by the forced marches was lost in inevitable delays; and the advance, though attended with such tragic consequences to the soldier, did not secure the advantage which the general proposed to attain.

WILNA

Upon arriving at Wilna, Napoleon had the mortification to find, that although the Emperor Alexander had not left the place until two days after he had himself crossed the Niemen, yet the Russian retreat had been made with the utmost regularity; all magazines and provisions, which could yield any advantage to the invaders, having been previously destroyed to a very large amount. While Buonaparte's generals had orders to press forward on their traces, the French Emperor himself remained at Wilna, to conduct some political measures, which seemed of the last importance to the events of the campaign.

The Abbé de Pradt had executed with ability the task intrusted to him, of exciting the Poles of the grand duchy of Warsaw, with the hope of a general restoration of Polish freedom. This brave but unhappy country, destined, it would seem, to spend its blood in every cause but its own, had, in that portion of it which formerly belonged to Prussia, and now formed the grand duchy of Warsaw, gained but little by its nominal independence. This state had only a population of about five millions of inhabitants, yet maintained for the service of France, rather than for its own, an armed force of 85,000 men. Eighteen regiments of these were embodied with the Emperor's army, and paid by France; but the formation and expense of the rest far exceeded the revenues of the duchy. The last amounted only to forty millions of francs, while the expenses more than doubled that sum. The grand duchy had also suffered its full share of distress from the Continental System of Napoleon. The revenue of Poland depends on the sale of the grain which her fertile soil produces; and that grain, in the years previous to the present, had lain rotting in the warehouses. The misery of the poor was extreme; the opulence of the rich classes had disappeared, and they could not relieve them. The year 1811 had been a year of scarcity here as well as elsewhere; and, as in former years the Poles had grain which they could not send to market, so at present they had neither corn nor means to purchase it. To all these disadvantages must be added, the plunder and misery sustained by the duchy during the march of Buonaparte's numerous forces from the Vistula to the Niemen.

Yet so highly toned is the national patriotism of the Poles, that it kindled at the name of independence, notwithstanding the various accumulated circumstances which tended to damp the flame. When, therefore, a diet of the duchy of Warsaw was convened, where the nobles assembled according to ancient form, all were anxious to meet Napoleon's wishes; but an unfortunate hint which the Emperor had thrown out concerning the length of the discourse with which the Diet was to be opened, induced the worthy Count Mathuchewitz, whose duty it was to draw up the peroration, to extend it to fifty pages of very close writing.

As all the assembly exclaimed against the prolixity of this mortal harangue, the French ambassador, the Abbé de Pradt, was required to substitute something more suitable for the occasion. Accordingly, he framed a discourse more brief, more in the taste of his own country, and, we doubt not, more spirited and able than that of Count Mathuchewitz. It was hailed by the warm and enthusiastic applause of the Diet. Notwithstanding which, when sent to Napoleon, then at Wilna, he disapproved of it, as too obviously written in the French style of composition, and intimated, in plain terms, that language, like that of an ancient Pole, speaking his national sentiments in the Oriental tropes of his national language, would better have suited the occasion.

The intimation of this dissatisfaction tore the veil from the Abbé de Pradt's eyes, as he himself assures us. He foresaw that the infatuated want of judgment which the Emperor displayed in disliking his discourse, was that of a doomed and falling man; he dated from that epoch the overthrow of Napoleon's power, and was so much moved with the spirit of prophecy, that he could not withhold his predictions even before the young persons connected with his embassy.

DIET OF WARSAW

But a more fatal sign of Napoleon's prospects than could be inferred by any except the author, from his disapprobation of the Abbé de Pradt's discourse, occurred in his answer to the address of the Diet of the grand duchy.

The Diet of Warsaw, anticipating, as they supposed, Napoleon's wishes, had declared the whole kingdom, in all its parts, free and independent, as if the partition treaties had never existed; and no just-thinking person will doubt their right to do so. They entered into a general confederation, declared the kingdom of Poland restored, summoned all Poles to quit the service of Russia, and finally, sent deputations to the Grand Duke and the King of Saxony, and another to Napoleon, announcing their desire to accelerate the political regeneration of Poland, and their hope to be recognised by the entire Polish nation as the centre of a general union. The expressions addressed to Napoleon were in a tone of idolatry. They applied for the countenance of the "Hero who dictated his history to the age, in whom resided the force of Providence," language which is usually reserved to the Deity alone. "Let the Great Napoleon," they said, "only pronounce his fiat that the kingdom of Poland should exist, and it will exist accordingly. The natives of Poland will unite themselves at once and unanimously to the service of Him to whom ages are as a moment, and space no more than a point." In another case, this exaggerated eloquence would have induced some suspicion of sincerity on the part of those who used it; but the Poles, like the Gascons, to whom they have been compared, are fond of superlatives, and of an exalted and enthusiastic tone of language, which, however, they have in all ages been observed to support by their actions in the field.

The answer of Buonaparte to this high-toned address was unexpectedly cold, doubtful, and indecisive. It was at this moment, probably, he felt the pressure of his previous engagements with Austria, which prevented his at once acquiescing in the wishes of the Polish mission. "He loved the Polish nation," he said, "and in the situation of the Diet at Warsaw, would act as they did. But he had many interests to reconcile, and many duties to fulfil. Had he reigned when Poland was subjected to those unjust partitions which had deprived her of independence, he would have armed in her behalf, and as matters stood, when he conquered Warsaw and its surrounding territories, he instantly restored them to a state of freedom.——He applauded what they had done—authorised their future efforts, and would do all he could to second their resolution. If their efforts were unanimous, they might compel their oppressors to recognise their rights; but these hopes must rest on the exertions of the population." These uncertain and cool assurances of his general interest in the Polish cause, were followed by the express declaration, "That he had guaranteed to the Emperor of Austria the integrity of his dominions, and he could not. sanction any manœuvre, or the least movement, tending to disturb the peaceable possession of what remained to *him* of the Polish provinces. As for the provinces of Poland attached to Russia, he was content with assuring them, that, providing they were animated by the spirit evinced in the grand duchy, Providence would crown their good cause with success."

This answer, so different from that which the Poles had expected, struck the mission with doubt and dismay. Instead of countenancing the reunion of Poland, Napoleon had given an assurance, that, in the case of Galicia, he neither could nor would interfere to detach that province from Austria; and in that of the Polish provinces attached to Russia, he exhorted the natives to be unanimous, in which case, instead of assuring them of his powerful assistance, he was content with recommending them to the care of that Providence, in whose place the terms of their bombastic address had appeared to install Napoleon himself. The Poles accordingly began from that period to distrust the intentions of Napoleon towards the re-establishment of their independence, the more so, as they observed that neither Polish nor French troops were employed in Volhynia or elsewhere, whose presence might have given countenance to their efforts, but Austrians only, who, for example's sake, were as unwilling to encourage the Russian provinces of Poland to declare for the cause of independence, as they would have been to preach the same doctrines in those which belonged to Austria.[120]

Napoleon afterwards often and bitterly regretted the sacrifice which he made on this occasion to the wishes of Austria; and he had the more occasion for this regret, as the error seemed to be gratuitous. It is true, that to have pressed Austria on the subject of emancipating Galicia, might have had the effect of throwing her into the arms of Russia; but this might probably have been avoided by the cession of the Illyrian provinces as an indemnity. And, if this exchange could not be rendered acceptable to Austria, by throwing in Trieste, or even Venice, Napoleon ought then to have admitted the impossibility of reinstating the independence of Poland, to have operated as a reason for entirely declining the fatal war with Russia.

LITHUANIA

The French ruler miscarried also in an effort to excite an insurrection in Lithuania, although he named a provisional government in the province, and declared the country was free of the Russian yoke. But the Lithuanians, a colder people than the Poles, were not in general much dissatisfied with the government of Russia, while the conduct of the French armies in their territories alienated their minds from Napoleon. They observed also the evasive answer which he returned to the Poles, and concluded, that if the French Emperor should have occasion to make peace with Alexander, he would not hesitate to do so at the expense of those whom he was now encouraging to rise in insurrection. Thus the moral effect which Napoleon expected to produce on the Russian frontier, was entirely checked and counteracted; insomuch that of a

---

[120] Ségur, tom. i., p. 122; De Pradt, p. 119.

guard of honour, which the Lithuanians had proposed to serve for the Emperor's person, only three troopers ever made their appearance on parade. Nor did the country at large take any steps, either generally or individually, to intimate a national interest in the events of the war, seeming to refer themselves entirely to the course of events.

Chapter LVIII

Proceedings of the Army under Prince Bagration—Napoleon's manœuvres against him—King Jerome of Westphalia is disgraced for alleged inactivity—Bagration is defeated by Davoust, but succeeds in gaining the interior of Russia, and re-establishing his communication with the Grand Army—which retreats to Drissa—Barclay and Bagration meet at Smolensk on the 20th July—The French Generals become anxious that Napoleon should close the campaign at Witepsk for the season—He persists in proceeding—Smolensk evacuated by De Tolly, after setting fire to the place—Reduced condition of the French, and growing strength of the Russian Armies—Peace effected between Russia, and England, Sweden, and Turkey—Napoleon resolves to advance upon Moscow.

PROTRACTED STAY AT WILNA

Napoleon continued to occupy his headquarters at Wilna, from 28th June to 16th July, the space of eighteen days. It was not usual with him to make such long halts; but Wilna was his last point of communication with Europe, and he had probably much to arrange ere he could plunge into the forests and deserts of Russia, whence all external intercourse must be partial and precarious. He named Maret Duke of Bassano, Governor of Lithuania, and placed under the management of that minister the whole charge of correspondence with Paris and with the armies; thus rendering him the centre of administrative, political, and even military communication between the Emperor and his dominions.

It must not be supposed, however, that these eighteen days passed without military movements of high importance. The reader must remember, that the grand army of Russia was divided into two unequal portions. That commanded under the Emperor by Barclay de Tolly, had occupied Wilna and the vicinity, until the French entered Lithuania, when, by a preconcerted and well-executed retreat, they fell back on their strong fortified camp at Drissa. The smaller army, under Prince Bagration, was much farther advanced to the south-westward, and continued to occupy a part of Poland. The Prince's headquarters were at Wolkowisk; Platoff, with 7000 Cossacks, lay at Grodno, and both he and Bagration maintained communication with the main army through its left wing, which, under Dorokhoff, extended as far as Lida. The army of Bagration had been posted thus far to the south-west, in order that when Napoleon crossed the Niemen, this army might be placed in his rear as he advanced to Wilna. To execute this plan became impossible, so much greater was the invading army than the Russians had anticipated. On the contrary, the French were able to protect the flank of their advance against Wilna by an army of 30,000 men, under the King of Westphalia, placed betwixt them and this secondary Russian army. And far from having it in his power to annoy the enemy, Bagration was placed so much in advance, as greatly to hazard being separated from the main body, and entirely cut off. The Russian prince accordingly had directions from Barclay de Tolly to get his army out of their perilous situation; and again, on the 13th of July, he had orders from Alexander to move on the camp of Drissa.

When Napoleon arrived at Wilna, the danger of Bagration became imminent; for the intrenched camp at Drissa was the rendezvous of all the Russian corps, and Napoleon being 150 wersts, or seven days' march, nearer to Drissa than Bagration, neither Napoleon nor any other general had ever so fair an opportunity for carrying into execution the French Emperor's favourite manœuvre, of dividing into two the line of his enemy, which was unquestionably too much extended.

It was the 30th of July ere Napoleon was certain of the advantage which he possessed, and he hastened to improve it. He had despatched the greater part of his cavalry under Murat, to press on the retreat of the grand Russian army; the second corps under

Oudinot, and the third under Ney, with three divisions of the first corps, were pushed towards the Dwina on the same service, and constituted a force too strong for the army of Barclay de Tolly to oppose. On the right of the army, the King of Westphalia had directions to press upon Bagration in front, and throw him upon the army of Davoust, which was to advance on his flank and towards his rear. It was concluded, that Bagration, cut off from the grand army, and attacked at once by Jerome and Davoust, must necessarily surrender or be destroyed.

Having thus detached very superior forces against the only two Russian armies which were opposed to him, Buonaparte himself, with the Guards, the army of Italy, the Bavarian army, and three divisions of Davoust's corps d'armée was at liberty to have marched forward upon Witepsk, occupying the interval between the corps of Murat, who pressed upon Alexander and De Tolly, and of Davoust, who was pursuing Bagration. By thus pressing on where there was no hostile force opposed to him, Napoleon might have penetrated between the two Russian armies, to each of whom a superior force was opposed, might have forced himself between them and occupied Witepsk, and threatened both St. Petersburgh and Moscow; or, if he decided for the latter capital, might have advanced as far as Smolensk. That Buonaparte, formed this plan of the campaign on the 10th of July at Wilna, we are assured by Ségur; but it was then too late for putting it in execution—yet another week was lost at Wilna.[121] All seem to have been sensible of an unusual slowness in Napoleon's motions on this important occasion; and Ségur attributes it to a premature decay of constitution,[122] of which, however, we see no traces in the campaigns of 1813 and 1814.[123] But the terrible disorder of an army,

---

[121] "The fortnight's halt at Wilna decided, in all probability, the fate of the war. This delay, on the part of the conqueror of Ratisbon and Ulm is so extraordinary, that it can alone be attributed to a cause which will for ever remain a secret."—Jomini, tom. iv., p. 58.

[122] "Those who were nearest to Napoleon's person said to each other, that a genius so vast as his, and always increasing in activity and audacity, was not now seconded as it had been formerly by a vigorous constitution. They were alarmed at no longer finding their chief insensible to the heat of a burning atmosphere; and they remarked to each other with melancholy forebodings, the tendency to corpulence by which his frame was now distinguished, the certain forerunner of premature decay."—Ségur, tom. i., p. 165.

[123] "How happens it that the English author is more just towards Napoleon than one of his generals? Sir Walter allows here, what I have already observed, namely, the inconceivable

the sick and stragglers of which absolutely filled Lithuania, and that army one of such immense size, required considerable time to remodel and new-organise it; and this of itself, a misfortune inherent in the enterprise, is sufficient to account for the halt at Wilna.

Meantime Bagration, in a precarious situation, defended himself with the greatest skill and gallantry. Being cut off from the direct road to Drissa, it was his object to retreat eastward to his rear, instead of moving northward by his right flank, and thus to make his way towards the Dwina, either through Ostrowno and Minsk, or by the town of Borizoff. When he gained the Dwina, Bagration trusted to form a junction with the grand army, from which he was now so fearfully separated. The actual strength of his army was, however, increased not only by the Hettman Platoff with his Cossacks, who, being advanced south-westward as far as Grodno, made in fact a part of Bagration's command, and assisted him materially in his retreat; but also by the division of General Dorokhoff, which, forming the extreme left of the grand Russian army, was cut off in the retreat upon Drissa by the advance of the French, and therefore had been placed also in communication with Bagration. So that, numerically, the prince might have under his command from 40 to 50,000 men.

The ground which Bagration had to traverse was the high plain of Lithuania, where arise the sources of the rivers which take different directions to the Black and Baltic Seas. The soil is unusually marshy, and traversed by long causeways, which the Russians made use of in defending themselves against the attacks of Jerome's advanced guard. But while Bagration struggled against the

---

accusation brought against the faculties of Napoleon at a time when he showed so much energy and perseverance, and when he not only resisted, and extricated himself from, the most frightful reverses imaginable, but even rose from them with surprising splendour. In an operation so gigantic as the attack upon Russia, in a plan for the boldest campaign, prudence and extreme slowness were imperative. How then, under such circumstances, can a general officer, a pupil, as it were, of Napoleon, criticise his stay at Wilna, and the extraordinary slowness of his movements? Would to heaven that this delay had been carried far enough to prevent the grand army from crossing the Dnieper during this campaign! But the great inconvenience of Napoleon, as general of the grand army, was the necessity of not prolonging his absence from Paris, and consequently of terminating the campaign as quickly as possible; and this is another powerful reason why he should not have hazarded so distant an expedition."—Louis Buonaparte, p. 82.

attempt on his front, Davoust, having occupied all the posts on the Russian's right flank, and succeeded in preventing him taking the shortest road to Drissa, began next to cut him off from his more circuitous route to the east, occupying the town of Minsk, and the defiles by which Bagration must issue from Lithuania towards Witepsk and the Dwina. The occupation of Minsk greatly embarrassed the retreat of Bagration; insomuch, that the French were of opinion that it was only the want of skill and enterprise on the part of King Jerome of Westphalia, who did not, it was said, press the Russians with sufficient vigour, that prevented the Russian prince being thrust back on Davoust, and totally destroyed. At any rate, Jerome, whether guilty or not of the alleged slowness of movement, was, according to the fashion in which the chief of the Napoleon dynasty treated the independent princes whom he called to sovereignty, sent back in disgrace to his Westphalian dominions, unaccompanied even by a soldier of his guards, for all of whom Napoleon had sufficient employment.

Several skirmishes were fought between the corps of Bagration, and those opposed to it, of which the event was dubious. Platoff and his Cossacks had more than one distinguished success over the Polish cavalry, who, with all their fiery courage, had not yet the intimate acquaintance with partisan war, which seems to be a natural attribute of the modern Scythians. In the meanwhile, Bagration, continuing his attempts at extricating his army, made another circuitous march towards the south, and avoiding his pursuers, he effected the passage of the Beresina at Bobruisk. The Dnieper (anciently the Borysthenes) was the next obstacle to be overcome, and with a view to regain the ground he had lost, Bagration ascended that stream as far as Mohiloff. Here he found himself again anticipated by Davoust, who was equally, though less unpleasantly surprised, by finding himself in front of Bagration, who prepared to clear his way by the sword. The combat was at first advantageous to the Russians, but they were at length repulsed roughly, and lost the battle; without, however, suffering much, except in the failure of their purpose. Disappointed in this attempt, Bagration, with unabated activity, once more altered his line of retreat, descended the Dnieper so far as to reach Nevoi-Bikoff, finally crossed at that point, and thus gained the interior of Russia, and an opportunity of again placing himself in communication with the grand Russian army, from which he had been so nearly cut off.[124]

It was certainly a new event in the history of Napoleon's wars, that two large armies of French should be baffled and out-manœuvred by a foreign general. And yet this was clearly the case; for, admitting that the Russians committed originally the great error of extending their line too far from Drissa, the intended point of union, and although, in consequence, the army of Bagration run great risk of being cut off, yet the manœuvres by which he effectually eluded the enemy, showed superior military talent on the part of the general, as well as excellent discipline on that of the soldiers, and were sufficient for the extrication of both.[125]

GENERAL WITGENSTEIN

We return to the grand army, commanded by the Emperor, or rather by Barclay de Tolly, which, though pressed by Murat, at the head of the greater part of the French cavalry, as well as by Oudinot and Ney, all burning for combat, made a regular and successful retreat to the intrenched camp at Drissa, where the Russian army had been appointed to concentrate itself. The French troops, on their part, approached the left bank of the Dwina, and that river now separated the hostile armies, and there took place only partial actions between detached corps with various success. But the Russian general Witgenstein, whose name began to be distinguished both for enterprise and conduct, observing that Sebastiani's vanguard of French cavalry had quartered themselves with little precaution in the town of Drissa, he passed the river unexpectedly on the night of the 2d July, beat up Sebastiani's quarters, and was

---

[124] "This was no doubt taking a great circuit; but the prince succeeded in his object, and restored to the hostile army a large body of troops, which would have been rendered completely useless if Napoleon's orders had been punctually executed. The success of this movement proved for the Russians fully equivalent to the gain of a battle. They were drawing nearer to their resources, whilst the French army was compelled to follow them through vast barren wastes, where it could not fail to be eventually annihilated."—Savary, tom. ii., p. 187.
[125] Jomini, tom. iv., p. 66; Ségur, tom. i., p. 160.

completely successful in the skirmish which ensued. Enterprises of this sort show a firm and energetic character, and Napoleon began already to be aware of the nature of the task he had before him, and of the necessity of employing his own talents in the campaign.

In the meantime, Barclay was led to change his plan, from learning the danger to which Prince Bagration was exposed. The camp at Drissa became too distant a point of junction, and there was every risk that the whole body of the French army, which was now getting itself into motion, would force a passage across the Dwina at Witepsk, a good deal higher up than Drissa, and thus at once turn Barclay's left flank, and entirely separate him from Bagration and his corps d'armée. Alarmed at this prospect, Barclay evacuated the camp, and began to ascend the right side of the Dwina, by Polotsk, towards Witepsk. This line of movement converged with that of Bagration's retreat, and served essentially to favour the desired junction of the two Russian armies. Witgenstein was left near Drissa to observe the enemy, and cover the road to St. Petersburgh. The army first arrived at Polotsk, when the Emperor Alexander left the troops and hastened to Moscow, to recommend and enforce energetic measures, and solicit the heavy sacrifices which the emergency demanded. Barclay continued his march upon Witepsk, hoping to get into communication with Bagration, to whom he had sent orders, directing him to descend the Dnieper as far as Orcsa (or Orcha,) which is about fifty-six wersts from Witepsk.

At this period Napoleon was directing his whole reserved forces upon the same point of Witepsk, with a purpose as anxious to prevent the junction of the two Russian armies, as that of Barclay to accomplish that important movement. Had Napoleon's march commenced earlier, there can be no doubt that he must have attained the disputed position sooner by marching from Wilna, than Barclay could have reached it by ascending the Dwina from Drissa. Hasting from Wilna upon the 4th, he might easily have reached Witepsk on the 20th, and would then have found himself, with a chosen army of 120,000 men, without an enemy on his front, posted between the two hostile armies, each of which was pressed by a force superior to their own, and having their flanks and communications at his mercy. Instead of this advantageous condition, the Emperor found himself in front of the grand army of Russia, in a situation where they could not easily be brought to action, although severe and bloody skirmishes took place between the cavalry on both sides.

On his part, Barclay was far from easy. He heard nothing of Bagration, whom he expected to approach from Orcsa; and rather than abandon him to his fate by a retreat, he formed, on the 14th July, the almost desperate resolution of risking a general action with very superior forces commanded by Napoleon. But just as he had made his dispositions for battle, the Russian general received news from one of the prince's aides-de-camp, which made him joyfully alter his determination. The repulse at Mohiloff had, as before noticed, obliged Bagration to change his line of retreat, which was now directed upon Smolensk. Barclay, renouncing instantly his purpose of battle, commenced a retreat upon the same point, and arriving at Smolensk on the 20th, was joined by Bagration within two days after. The result of these manœuvres had been on the whole disappointing to the Emperor of the French. The two armies of Russians had united without material loss, and placed themselves upon their own lines of communication. No battle had been fought and won; and although Napoleon obtained possession of the fortified camp at Drissa, and afterwards of Witepsk, it was only as positions which it no longer served the enemy's purpose to retain.[126]

WITEPSK

The marshals and generals who surrounded Napoleon began to wish and hope that he would close at Witepsk the campaign of the season, and, quartering his troops on the Dwina, await supplies, and the influence of the invasion upon the mind of the Russian nation, till next spring. But this suggestion Buonaparte treated with contempt, asking those who favoured such a sentiment, whether they thought he had come so far only to conquer a parcel of

---

[126] Ségur, tom. i., p. 171; Jomini, tom. iv., p. 84.

wretched huts.[127] If ever, therefore, he had seriously thought of settling his winter-quarters at Witepsk, which Ségur affirms, and Gourgaud positively denies, it had been but a passing purpose. Indeed, his pride must have revolted at the very idea of fortifying himself with intrenchments and redoubts in the middle of summer, and confessing his weakness to Europe, by stopping short in the midst of a campaign, in which he had lost one-third of the active part of his great army, without even having fought a general action, far less won a decisive victory.

Meanwhile the Russians, finding their two wings united, to the number of 120,000, were not inclined to remain inactive. The French army at Witepsk lay considerably more dispersed than their own, and their plan was, by moving suddenly upon Napoleon, to surprise him ere his army could be concentrated. With this view, General Barclay directed the march of a great part of the grand army upon Rudneia, a place about half-way between Witepsk and Smolensk, being nearly the centre of the French line of position. Their march commenced on the 26th July; but on the next day, Barclay received information from the out-posts, which induced him to conclude that Napoleon was strengthening his left flank for the purpose of turning the Russian right wing, and assaulting the town of Smolensk in their rear. To prevent this misfortune, Barclay suspended his march in front, and began by a flank movement to extend his right wing, for the purpose of covering Smolensk. This error, for such it was, led to his advanced guard, who had not been informed of the change of plan, being placed in some danger at Inkowo, a place about two wersts from Rudneia. Platoff, however, had the advantage in the cavalry skirmish which took place. The

---

[127] "Surrounded by disapproving countenances, and opinions contrary to his own, he felt himself uncomfortable. All the officers of his household opposed his plan, each in the way that marked his peculiar character; Berthier, by a melancholy countenance, by lamentations, and even tears; Lobau and Caulaincourt, by a frankness, which in the first was stamped by a cold and haughty roughness, excusable in so brave a warrior; and which, in the second, was persevering even to obstinacy, and impetuous even to violence. The Emperor exclaimed, 'that he had enriched his generals too much; that all they now aspired to was to follow the pleasures of the chase, and to display their brilliant equipages in Paris; and that doubtless they had become disgusted with war.' When their honour was thus attacked, there was no longer any reply to be made; they merely bowed and remained silent. During one of his impatient fits, he told one of the generals of his guard, 'you were born in a bivouac, in a bivouac you will die.'"—Ségur, tom. i., p. 200.

Russian general, in consequence of the extension of his flank, discovered that there was no French force on the left, and consequently, that he was in no danger on that point; and he resumed his original plan of pressing the French at Rudneia. But while Barclay lost four days in these fruitless marches and countermarches, he at length learned, that the most speedy retreat towards Smolensk would be necessary to save him from that disaster which he had truly apprehended, though he mistook the quarter from which the danger was to come.

While Barclay was in hopes of surprising Napoleon, the Emperor had laid a scheme of a singularly audacious character, for inflicting the surprise with which he had been himself threatened. Without allowing his purpose to be suspended by the skirmishing on his front, he resolved entirely to change his line of operations from Witepsk[128] upon the Dwina, to concentrate his army on the Dnieper, making Orcsa the central point of his operations, and thus, turning the left of the Russians instead of their right, as Barclay had apprehended, he hoped to gain the rear of their forces, occupy Smolensk, and act upon their lines of communication with Moscow. With this purpose Napoleon withdrew his forces from Witepsk and the line of the Dwina, with equal skill and rapidity, and, by throwing four bridges over the Dnieper, effected a passage for Ney, the Viceroy and Davoust. The King of Naples accompanied them, at the head of two large corps of cavalry. Poniatowski, with Junot, advanced by different routes to support the movement. Ney and Murat, who commanded the vanguard, drove every thing before them until they approached Krasnoi, upon 14th August, where a remarkable action took place.[129] This manœuvre, which transferred

---

[128] "This town contained 20,000 inhabitants, and presented, from the beauty of its situation, a most delightful aspect. Poland and Lithuania had, during more than two months, and through a space of more than 300 leagues, offered nothing to our view but deserted villages, and a ravaged country. Destruction seemed to precede our steps, and in every direction the whole population was seen flying at our approach, leaving their habitations to hordes of Cossacks, who destroyed every thing which they could not carry away. Having long experienced the most painful deprivations, we regarded, with envious eyes, those well-built and elegant houses, where peace and abundance seemed to dwell. But that repose, which we had so eagerly anticipated, was again denied us, and we were compelled to renew our pursuit of the Russians, leaving on our left this town, the object of our most ardent wishes, and our dearest hopes."—Labaume, *Relation de la Campagne de Russie en 1812*, p. 74.

[129] Jomini, tom. iv., p. 95; Thirteenth Bulletin of Grand Army; Ségur, tom. i., p. 221.

the Emperor's line of operations from the Dwina to the Dnieper, has been much admired by French and Russian tacticians, but it has not escaped military criticism.[130]

General Newerowskoi had been stationed at Krasnoi with above 6000 men, a part of the garrison of Smolensk, which had been sent out for the purpose of making a strong recognisance. But finding himself attacked by a body of infantry stronger than his own, and no less than 18,000 cavalry besides, the Russian general commenced his retreat upon the road to Smolensk. The ground through which the road lay was open, flat, and favourable for the action of cavalry. Murat, who led the pursuit, and, while he affected the dress and appearance of a cavalier of romance, had the fiery courage necessary to support the character, sent some of his light squadrons to menace the front of the Russian corps, while with his heavy horse he annoyed their flanks or thundered upon their rear. To add to the difficulties of the Russians, their columns consisted of raw troops, who had never been under fire, and who might have been expected to shrink from the furious onset of the cavalry. They behaved bravely, however, and availed themselves of a double row of trees which borders the high road to Smolensk on each side, to make their musketry effectual, and to screen themselves from the repeated charges. Protecting themselves as they retreated by a heavy fire, Newerowskoi made good a lion-like retreat into Smolensk, having lost 400 men, chiefly by the artillery, and five guns, but receiving from friend and foe the testimony due to a movement so bravely and ably conducted.[131]

Upon the 14th of August,[132] the same day with this skirmish, Napoleon arrived at Rassassina, upon the Dnieper, and continued

---

[130] See in the Appendix, No. II., an interesting extract from "Manuscript Observations on Napoleon's Russian Campaign, by an English Officer of Rank."
[131] Ségur, tom. i., p. 223; Thirteenth Bulletin of the Grand Army.
[132] "As chance would have it, the day of this success was the Emperor's birth-day. The army never thought of celebrating it. In the disposition of the men and of the place, there was nothing that harmonized with such a celebration; empty acclamations would have been lost amid those vast deserts. In our situation there was no other festival than the day of a complete victory. Murat and Ney, however, in reporting their success to the Emperor, paid homage to that anniversary. They caused a salute of a hundred guns to be fired. The Emperor remarked, with displeasure, that in Russia it was necessary to be more sparing of French powder; he was answered that it was Russian powder taken the preceding day. The

during the 15th to press forward towards Smolensk, in the rear of Ney and Murat. Prince Bagration, in the meantime, threw General Raefskoi into Smolensk, with a strong division, to reinforce Newerowskoi, and advanced himself to the Dnieper, along the left bank of which he pressed with all possible speed towards the endangered town. Barclay de Tolly was now made aware, as we have already stated, that while he was engaged in false manœuvres to the right, his left had been in fact turned, and that Smolensk was in the utmost danger. Thus the two Russian generals pressed forward from different points to the relief of the city, whilst Napoleon used every effort to carry the place before their arrival.

SMOLENSK

Smolensk, a town of consequence in the empire, and, like Moscow, honoured by the appellation of the Sacred, and of the Key of Russia, contains about 12,600 inhabitants. It is situated on the heights of the left bank of the Dnieper, and was then surrounded by fortifications of the ancient Gothic character. An old wall, in some places dilapidated, was defended by about thirty towers, which seemed to flank the battlements; and there was an ill-contrived work, called the Royal Bastion, which served as a species of citadel. The walls, however, being eighteen feet thick, and twenty-five high, and there being a ditch of some depth, the town, though not defensible if regularly approached, might be held out against a *coup-de-main*. The greatest inconvenience arose from the suburbs of the place, which, approaching near to the wall of the town, preserved the assailants from the fire of the besieged, as they approached it. Raefskoi prepared to defend Smolensk at the head of about sixteen thousand men. He was reinforced on the 16th of August by a division of grenadiers under Prince Charles of Mecklenberg, who were detached for that purpose by Bagration.

Ney arrived first under the walls of the city, and instantly rushed forward to attack the citadel. He failed entirely, being himself

---

idea of having his birth-day celebrated at the expense of the enemy drew a smile from Napoleon. It was admitted that this very rare species of flattery became such men."— Ségur, tom. i., p. 223.

wounded, and two-thirds of the storming party cut off. A second attempt was made to as little purpose, and at length he was forced to confine his efforts to a cannonade, which was returned from the place with equal spirit. Later in the day, the troops of Napoleon appeared advancing from the eastward on one side of the Dnieper, while almost at the same moment there were seen upon the opposite bank clouds of dust enveloping long columns of men, moving from different points with uncommon celerity. This was the grand army of Russia under Barclay, and the troops of Bagration, who, breathless with haste and anxiety, were pressing forward to the relief of Smolensk.

"At length," said Napoleon, as he gazed on the advance from the opposite side, "at length I have them!"[133] He had no doubt it was the purpose of the Russians to pass through the city, and, deploying from its gates, to offer him under the walls that general action for which he longed, and on which so much depended. He took all the necessary measures for preparing his line of battle.

But the cautious Barclay de Tolly was determined, that not even for the protection of the sacred city would he endanger the safety of his army, so indispensably necessary to the defence of the empire. He dismissed to Ellnia his more impatient coadjutor, Prince Bagration, who would willingly have fought a battle, incensed as he was at beholding the cities of Russia sacked, and her fields laid waste, without the satisfaction either of resistance or revenge. Barclay in the meanwhile occupied Smolensk, but only for the purpose of covering the flight of the inhabitants, and emptying the magazines.

Buonaparte's last look that evening, was on the still empty fields betwixt his army and Smolensk. There was no sign of any advance from its gates, and Murat prophesied that the Russians had no purpose of fighting. Davoust entertained a different opinion; and Napoleon, continuing to believe what he most wished, expected with the peep of day to see the whole Russian army drawn up betwixt his own front and the walls of Smolensk. Morning came, however, and the space in which he expected to see the enemy was

---

[133] Ségur, tom. i., p. 230.

vacant as before. On the other hand, the high-road on the opposite side of the Dnieper was filled with troops and artillery, which showed that the grand army of the Russians was in full retreat. Disappointed and incensed, Napoleon appointed instant measures to be taken to storm the place, resolving as speedily as possible to possess himself of the town, that he might have the use of its bridge in crossing to the other side of the Dnieper, in order to pursue the fugitive Russians. There are moments when men of ordinary capacity may advise the wisest. Murat remarked to Buonaparte, that as the Russians had retired, Smolensk, left to its fate, would fall without the loss that must be sustained in an attack by storm, and he more than hinted the imprudence of penetrating farther into Russia at this late season of the year. The answer of Napoleon[134] must have been almost insulting; for Murat, having exclaimed that a march to Moscow would be the destruction of the army, spurred his horse like a desperate man to the banks of the river, where the Russian guns from the opposite side were cannonading a French battery, placed himself under a tremendous fire, as if he had been courting death, and was with difficulty forced from the dangerous spot.[135]

BATTLE OF SMOLENSK

Meantime, the attack commenced on Smolensk, but the place was defended with the same vigour as on the day before. The field-guns were found unable to penetrate the walls; and the French lost four or five thousand men in returning repeatedly to the attack. But this successful defence did not alter Barclay's resolution of

---

[134] "The Emperor replied; but the rest of their conversation was not overheard. As, however, the King afterwards declared that he 'had thrown himself at the knees of his brother, and conjured him to stop, but that Napoleon saw nothing but Moscow; that honour, glory, rest, every thing for him was there; that this Moscow would be our ruin!'—it was obvious what had been the cause of their disagreement. So much is certain that when Murat quitted his brother-in-law, his face wore the expression of deep chagrin; his motions were abrupt; a gloomy and concentrated vehemence agitated him; and the name of Moscow several times escaped his lips."—Ségur, tom. i., p. 234.

[135] "Belliard warned him that he was sacrificing his life to no purpose and without glory. Murat answered only by pushing on still farther. Belliard observed to him, that his temerity would be the destruction of those about him. 'Well then,' replied Murat, 'do you retire and leave me here by myself.' All refused to leave him; when the King angrily turning about, tore himself from the scene of carnage, like a man who is suffering violence."—Ségur, tom. i., p. 235.

evacuating the place. It might no doubt have been defended for several days more, but the Russian general feared that a protracted resistance on this advanced point might give Napoleon time to secure the road to Moscow, and drive the Russian armies back upon the barren and exhausted provinces of the northwest, besides getting betwixt them and the ancient capital of Russia. In the middle of the night, then, while the French were throwing some shells into the place, they saw fires beginning to kindle, far faster and more generally than their bombardment could have occasioned.[136] They were the work of the Russian troops, who, having completed their task of carrying off or destroying the magazines, and having covered the flight of the inhabitants, had now set the dreadful example of destroying their own town, rather than that its houses or walls should afford assistance to the enemy.

SMOLENSK

When the Frenchmen entered Smolensk, which they did the next morning, 18th August, most of the town, which consisted chiefly of wooden houses, was yet blazing—elsewhere they found nothing but blood and ashes.[137] The French troops were struck with horror at the inveterate animosity of the Russians, and the desperation of the resistance which they met with; and all began to wish a period to a war, where there was nothing to be gained from the retreating enemy, except a long vista of advance through an inhospitable wilderness of swamps, pine-forests, and deserts;

---

[136] "Napoleon, seated before his tent, contemplated in silence this awful spectacle. It was as yet impossible to ascertain either the cause or the result, and the night was passed under arms."—Ségur, tom. i., p. 236.

[137] "The bridges and public buildings were a prey to the flames. The churches, in particular, poured out torrents of fire and smoke. The domes, the spires, and the multitude of small towers which arose above the conflagration, added to the effect of the picture, and produced these ill-defined emotions which are only to be found on the field of battle. We entered the place. It was half-consumed, of a barbarous appearance, encumbered with the bodies of the dead and wounded, which the flames had already reached. The spectacle was frightful. What a train is that of glory!"—*Mémoires de Rapp*, p. 190.

"The army entered within the walls; it traversed the reeking and bloodstained ruins with its accustomed order, pomp, and martial music, and having no other witness of its glory but itself;—a show without spectators, an almost fruitless victory, a melancholy glory, of which the smoke that surrounded us and seemed to be our only conquest, was but too faithful an emblem."—Ségur, tom. i., p. 237.

without provisions, and without shelter; without hospitals for the sick, and dressings for the wounded; and without even a shed where the weary might repose, or the wounded might die.

Buonaparte himself hesitated,[138] and is reported to have then spoken of concluding the campaign at Smolensk, which would, he said, be an admirable head of cantonments.[139] "Here," he said, "the troops might rest and receive reinforcements. Enough was done for the campaign. Poland was conquered, which seemed a sufficient result for one year. The next year they would have peace, or they would seek it at Moscow." But in the interior of his councils, he held a different language, and endeavoured to cover, with the language of prudence, the pride and pertinacity of character which forbade him to stop short in an enterprise which had yet produced him no harvest of renown. He stated to his generals the exhausted state of the country, in which his soldiers were living from hand to mouth; and the risk and difficulty of drawing his supplies from Dantzic or Poland, through Russian roads, and in the winter season. He alleged the disorganised state of the army, which might move on, though it was incapable of stopping. "Motion," he said, "might keep it together; a halt or a retreat would be at once to dissolve it. It was an army of attack, not of defence; an army of operation, not of position. The result was, they must advance on Moscow, possess themselves of the capital, and there dictate a peace."[140]

The language which Ségur has placed in the mouth of the Emperor, by no means exaggerates the dreadful condition of the French army. When Napoleon entered the country, only six weeks before, the corps which formed his operating army amounted to 297,000 men; and by the 5th August, when preparing to break up from Witepsk, that number was diminished to 185,000, not two-thirds of their original number, and a great additional loss had been

---

[138] "Napoleon slowly proceeded towards his barren conquest. He inspected the field of battle. Melancholy review of the dead and dying! dismal account to make up and deliver! The pain felt by the Emperor might be inferred from the contraction of his features and his irritation; but in him policy was a second nature, which soon imposed silence on the first."—Ségur, tom. i., p. 238.

[139] "In the passage through its massive walls, Count Lobau exclaimed, 'What a fine head for cantonments!' This was the same thing as advising the Emperor to stop there; but he returned no other answer to this counsel than a stern look."—Ségur, tom. i., p. 244.

[140] Ségur, tom. i., p. 250.

sustained in the movements and encounters on the Dnieper. The wounded of the army were in the most miserable state, and it was in vain that the surgeons tore up their own linen for dressings; they were obliged to use parchment, and the down that grows on the birch-trees; it is no wonder that few recovered.

Thus it may be concluded, that this rash enterprise carried with it, from the beginning, the seeds of destruction, which, even without the conflagration of Moscow, or the Russian climate, though the latter must have been at all events included, made the expedition resemble that of Cambyses into Egypt; of Crassus, and after him Julian, into Parthia; and so many others of the same character, where the extent of preparation only rendered the subsequent fate of the invaders more signally calamitous.

While the French army was thus suffering a gradual or rather hasty decay, that of the Russians was now receiving rapid reinforcements. The Emperor Alexander, on leaving the army for Moscow, had convoked the nobles and the merchants of that capital in their several assemblies, had pledged to them his purpose never to make peace while a Frenchman remained in Russia, and had received the most enthusiastic assurances from both ranks of the state, of their being devoted to his cause with life and property. A large sum was voted by the merchants as a general tax, besides which, they opened a voluntary subscription, which produced great supplies. The nobility offered a levy of ten men in the hundred through all their estates; many were at the sole expense of fitting out and arming their recruits, and some of these wealthy boyards furnished companies, nay battalions, entirely at their own expense. The word peace was not mentioned, or only thought of as that which could not be concluded with an invader, without an indelible disgrace to Russia.

Other external circumstances occurred, which greatly added to the effect of these patriotic exertions.

A peace with England, and the restoration of commerce, was the instant consequence of war with France. Russia had all the support which British diplomacy could afford her, in operating a reconciliation with Sweden, and a peace with Turkey. The former being accomplished, under the mediation of England, and the Crown Prince being assured in possession of Norway, the Russian army under General Steigenteil, or Steingel, which was, while Bernadotte's amicable disposition might be doubted, necessarily detained in Finland, was now set at liberty, for the more pressing service of defending the empire.

A peace, even still more important, was made with the Turks, at Bucharest, on the 16th May. The Porte yielded up to Russia, Bessarabia, and that part of Moldavia situated on the left of the river Pruth, and Russia renounced all claim to the rest of the two provinces of Moldavia and Wallachia. But the great advantage which accrued to Russia by this treaty, was its setting at liberty a veteran army of 45,000 men, and rendering them a disposable force in the rear of the French troops.

If the able statesman who at that period conducted the foreign affairs of Great Britain [Lord Castlereagh] had never rendered to his own country and to the world any other service than the influence which he successfully exercised in these important diplomatic affairs, he must have gone down to posterity as the minister who had foreseen and provided, in the most critical moment, the mode of strengthening Russia to combat with her formidable invaders, and which, after all her exertions, was the means of turning the balance in her favour.

It was at Witepsk that Napoleon learned that the Turks had made peace; and as it had only instigated him to precipitate his measures against Smolensk, so now the same reason urged him to continue his march on Moscow. Hitherto his wings had had the advantage of the enemy. Macdonald, in blockading Riga, kept all Courland at his disposal, and alarmed St. Petersburgh. More to the south, Saint Cyr had some hard fighting with Witgenstein, and, after a severe battle at Polotsk, had reduced that enterprising officer to the defensive.

Equally favourable intelligence had reached from Volhynia, the extreme right of the terrible line of invasion. The Russian

General Tormasoff had made, when least expected, his appearance in the grand duchy, driven before him Regnier, who was covering that part of Poland, destroyed a Saxon brigade, and alarmed Warsaw. But Regnier united himself with the Austrian general Schwartzenberg, advanced on Tormasoff, and engaging him near a place called Gorodeczna, defeated him with loss, and compelled him to retreat. It was obvious, however, that the advantage of these two victories at Polotsk and Gorodeczna, would be entirely lost, if General Steingel, with the Finland army, should join Witgenstein, while Tormasoff fell back on the Moldavian army of Russia, commanded by Admiral Tchitchagoff.[141]

ADVANCE UPON MOSCOW

For Napoleon to await in cantonments at Smolensk, in a wasted country, the consequences of these junctions, which were likely to include the destruction of his two wings, would have been a desperate resolution. It seemed waiting for the fate which he had been wont to command. To move forward was a bold measure. But the French army, in its state of disorganisation, somewhat resembled an intoxicated person, who possesses the power to run, though he is unable to support himself if he stand still. If Napoleon could yet strike a gallant blow at the Russian grand army; if he could yet obtain possession of Moscow the Holy, he reckoned on sending dismay into the heart of Alexander, and dictating to the Czar, as he had done to many other princes, the conditions of peace from within the walls of his own palace. Buonaparte, therefore, resolved to advance upon Moscow. And perhaps, circumstanced as he was, he had no safer course, unless he had abandoned his whole undertaking, and fallen back upon Poland, which would have been an acknowledgment of defeat that we can hardly conceive his stooping to, while he was yet at the head of an army.

---

[141] Ségur, tom. i., p. 242; Jomini, tom. iv., p. 105.

Chapter LIX

Napoleon detaches Murat and other Generals in pursuit of the Russians—Bloody, but indecisive Action, at Valoutina—Barclay de Tolly's defensive system relinquished, and Koutousoff appointed to the chief command of the Russian Army—Napoleon advances from Smolensk—Battle of Borodino fought, on 5th September—Prince Bagration slain—Koutousoff retreats upon Mojaisk, and thence upon Moscow—Napoleon continues his advance on the 12th—Count Rostopchin, Governor of Moscow—His Character—The Russians abandon Moscow, which is evacuated by the Inhabitants—The Grand Russian Army marches through Moscow—Last public Court of Justice held there by Rostopchin, after which he follows the march of the Army.

Without communicating his purpose of advancing in person from Smolensk, and completing, without any interval of delay, his great undertaking, Napoleon failed not to detach Murat, Ney, Junot, and Davoust, in pursuit of the Russians, as they retired from Smolensk. Either, however, his own mind was not made up, or he did not wish his purpose of going onward to be known. He represented this demonstration as arising merely out of the desire of pressing the Russian retreat, though in fact it was preliminary to his own advance.

Barclay de Tolly having performed the stern duty of burning Smolensk, had retired for two or three miles along the road to St. Petersburgh, which route he chose in order to avoid a cannonade from the left side of the Dnieper. Having proceeded a little way in this direction, he turned southward to regain the road to Moscow, which he would have taken at first, but for its exposing him to loss from the enemy's artillery, where it bordered on the river. The French could not for some time determine on which route they were to pursue the Russians. At length, finding the track, they overtook the rear-guard at a place called Valoutina, encumbered as it was with guns and baggage. Here a desperate action took place, the Russians reinforcing their rear-guard as fast as the French brought new bodies to attack them. Both parties fought most obstinately, and the distinguished French general Gudin was mortally wounded. The French blamed Junot,[142] who having been despatched across the Dnieper, showed no alertness in advancing to charge the enemy. There was seen, indeed, in this affair of Valoutina, or Lombino, that the marshals and the great officers who had been accustomed each to command a separate corps d'armée, disdained to receive either orders, or even advice or hints, from a brother of the same rank. Wherever there were two or three of these dignitaries on the field, it was necessary Buonaparte should be within reach, to issue the necessary orders; for no voice save that of the Emperor was implicitly obeyed by all.[143]

ACTION AT VALOUTINA

In the meantime, the bloody action of Valoutina had an unsatisfactory result. The Russians, whose rear-guard had been attacked, had moved off without losing either guns, prisoners, or baggage. They had lost equal numbers with the French, but the time was fast approaching when they must possess a numerical superiority, and when, of course, an equal loss would tell in favour of the party which was nearest to its resources.[144]

---

[142] "Napoleon, on the following day, visited the places where the action had been fought, and gazing with an angry look on the position which Junot had occupied, he exclaimed, 'It was there that the Westphalians should have attacked! all the battle was there! what was Junot about?' His irritation became so violent, that nothing could at first allay it. He called Rapp, and told him to 'take the command from the Duke of Abrantes:—he had lost his marshal's staff without retrieve! this blunder would probably block the road to Moscow against them; that to him, Rapp, he should intrust the Westphalians.' But Rapp refused the place of his old companion in arms; he appeased the Emperor, whose anger always subsided quickly, as soon as it had vented itself in words."—Ségur, tom. i., p. 259; Rapp, p. 191.

[143] Jomini, tom. iv., p. 99; Ségur, tom. i., p. 255; Rapp, p. 192; Fourteenth Bulletin of the Grand Army.

[144] "When Napoleon learned that his men had proceeded eight leagues without overtaking the enemy, the spell was dissolved. In his return to Smolensk, the jolting of his carriage over the relics of the fight, the stoppages caused on the road by the long file of the

The plan of Barclay de Tolly had hitherto been scrupulously adhered to. All general actions had been cautiously avoided; and while no means were left unemployed to weaken the enemy in partial actions, and to draw him on from swamp to swamp, from conflagration to conflagration, from one wild and waste scene to another of equal sterility and disconsolation, the end had been in a great measure attained, of undermining the force and breaking the moral courage of the invading army, who wandered forward like men in a dream, feeling on all hands a sense of oppressive and stifling opposition, yet unable to encounter any thing substantial which the slumberer can struggle with and overcome. Barclay de Tolly, if he had made some faults by extending his line too much at the commencement of the campaign, and afterwards by his false movements upon Rudneia, had more than atoned for these errors by the dexterity with which he had manœuvred before Smolensk, and the advantages which he had gained over the enemy on various other occasions. But they were now approaching Moscow the Grand, the Sanctified—and the military councils of Russia were about to change their character.

The spirit of the Russians, especially of the new levies, was more and more exasperated at the retreat, which seemed to have no end; and at the style of defence, which seemed only to consist in inflicting on the country, by the hands of Cossacks or Tartars, the very desolation which was perhaps the worst evil they could experience from the French. The natural zeal of the new levies, their confidence and their desire to be led to fight in the cause for which they were enlisted, eagerly declared against further retreat; and they demanded a halt, and a battle under a Russian general, more interested, as they supposed such must be, in the defence of the country, than a German stranger. The Emperor almost alone continued to adhere to the opinion of Barclay de Tolly. But he could not bid defiance to the united voice of his people and his military council. The political causes which demanded a great battle in defence of Moscow, were strong and numerous, and overcame the

---

wounded, who were crawling or being carried back, and in Smolensk by the tumbrils of amputated limbs going to be thrown away at a distance, in a word, all that is horrible and odious out of fields of battle, completely disarmed him. Smolensk was but one vast hospital, and the loud groans which issued from it drowned the shout of glory which had just been raised on the fields of Valoutina."—Ségur, tom. i., p. 264.

military reasons which certainly recommended that a risk so tremendous should not be incurred.

In compliance, therefore, with the necessity of the case, the Emperor sacrificed his own opinion. General Koutousoff, an officer high in military esteem among the Russians, was sent for from the corps which had been employed on the Danube against the Turks, to take the chief command of the grand army; and it was to Barclay's great honour, that, thus superseded, he continued to serve with the utmost zeal and good faith in a subordinate situation.

The French were not long of learning that their enemy's system of war was to be changed, and that the new Russian general was to give them battle, the object which they had so long panted for. Buonaparte, who had halted six days at Smolensk, moved from thence on the 24th August, and now pressed forward to join the advanced guard of his army at Gjatz. In this place his followers found a Frenchman who had dwelt long in Russia. They learned from this man the promotion of Koutousoff to the chief command of the army opposed to them, and that he was placed there for the express purpose of giving battle to the French army. The news were confirmed by the manner of a Russian officer, who arrived under some pretext with a flag of truce, but probably to espy the state of the invader's army. There was defiance in the look of this man; and when he was asked by a French general what they would find between Wiazma and Moscow, he answered sternly, "Pultowa." There was, therefore, no doubt, that battle was approaching.[145]

But the confusion of Buonaparte's troops was still such, that he was obliged to halt two days at Gjatz,[146] in order to collect and repose his army. He arrived at the destined field of battle, an elevated plain, called Borodino, which the Russians had secured with lines and batteries.

---

[145] Ségur, tom. i., p. 304.
[146] "Napoleon quietly employed himself in exploring the environs of his headquarters. At the sight of the Gjatz, which pours its waters into the Wolga, he who had conquered so many rivers, felt anew the first emotions of his glory; he was heard to boast of being the master of those waves destined to visit Asia—as if they were going to announce his approach, and to open for him the way to that quarter of the globe."—Ségur, tom. i., p. 308.

BATTLE OF BORODINO

The French army were opposed to them on the 5th September, having consumed seventeen days in marching 280 wersts. Their first operation was a successful attack upon a redoubt in the Russian front, but which—a great error in war—was situated too distant from it to be effectually supported. The French gained it and kept it. The armies lay in presence of each other all the next day, preparing for the approaching contest. Upon a position naturally strong, the Russians had raised very formidable fieldworks. Their right flank rested on a wood, which was covered by some detached intrenchments. A brook, occupying in its course a deep ravine, covered the front of the right wing and the centre of the position as far as the river of Borodino; from that village the left extended down to another village, called Semoneskoie, which is more open, yet protected by ravines and thickets in front. This, as the most accessible point, was anxiously secured by redoubts and batteries; and in the centre of the position, upon a gentle elevation, arose a sort of double battery, like a citadel, for the protection of the whole line.

In this strong position was stationed the Russian army, equal now in numbers to the French, as each army might be about 120,000 men. They were commanded by a veteran, slow, cautious, tenacious of his purpose, wily, too, as Napoleon afterwards found to his cost, but perhaps not otherwise eminent as a military leader. The army he led were of one nation and language, all conscious that this battle had been granted to their own ardent wishes, and determined to make good the eagerness with which they had called for it.

The French army, again, consisted of various nations; but they were the *élite*, and seasoned soldiers who had survived the distresses of a most calamitous march; they were the veterans of the victors of Europe; they were headed by Napoleon in person, and under his immediate command by those marshals, whose names in arms were only inferior to his own. Besides a consciousness of their superiority in action, of which, from the manner in which they had covered themselves in intrenchments, the enemy seemed aware, the French had before them the prospect of utter destruction, if they should sustain a defeat in a country so difficult that they could hardly advance even as a successful army, and certainly could never hope to retreat as a routed one. Buonaparte's address to his troops[147] had less of the tinsel of oratory than he generally used on such occasions. "Soldiers," he said, "here is the battle you have longed for; it is necessary, for it brings us plenty, good winter-quarters, and a safe return to France. Behave yourselves so that posterity may say of each of you, 'He was in that great battle under the walls of Moscow.'"[148]

In the Russian camp was a scene of a different kind, calculated to awaken feelings to which France had long ceased to appeal. The Greek clergy showed themselves to the troops, arrayed in their rich vestments, and displaying for general worship the images of their holiest saints. They told their countrymen of the wrongs which had been offered by the invaders to earth as well as Heaven, and exhorted them to merit a place in paradise by their behaviour in that day's battle. The Russians answered with shouts.

Two deeply interesting circumstances occurred to Napoleon the day before the battle. An officer brought him a portrait of his boy, the King of Rome, which he displayed on the outside of the tent, not only to satisfy the officers, but the soldiers, who crowded to look upon the son of their Emperor. The other was the arrival of an officer from Spain with despatches, giving Napoleon news of the loss of the battle of Salamanca. He bore the evil tidings with temper and firmness, and soon turned his thoughts alike from domestic

---

[147] Eighteenth Bulletin of the Grand Army.
[148] "I slept in Napoleon's tent. At three in the morning he called a valet-de-chambre, and made him bring some punch; I had the honour of taking some with him. He said, 'we shall have an affair to-day with this famous Koutousoff. It was he who commanded at Braunau in the campaign of Austerlitz. He remained three weeks in that place without leaving his chamber once.' He took a glass of punch, read the reports, and added, 'Well, Rapp, do you think that we shall manage our concerns properly to-day?'—'There is not the least doubt of it, Sire; we have exhausted all our resources, we are obliged to conquer.' Napoleon continued his discourse, and replied, 'Fortune is a liberal mistress; I have often said so, and begin to experience it.' He sent for Prince Berthier, and transacted business till half-past five. We mounted on horseback; the trumpets sounded, the drums were beaten; and as soon as the troops knew it, there was nothing but acclamations. 'It is the enthusiasm of Austerlitz,' cried Napoleon, 'let the proclamation be read.'"—Rapp, p. 202.

enjoyments and foreign defeats, to forming the necessary plans for the action before him.[149]

Davoust proposed a plan for turning the left of the enemy's intrenched line, by following the old road from Smolensk to Moscow, and placing 35,000 men in the flank and rear of that part of the Russian position. This operation was partly to be accomplished by a night march, partly on the morning, while the rest of the army was engaging the enemy's attention in front. The ground to which this road would have conducted Davoust and his troops, forms the highest land in the neighbourhood, as appears from the rivulets taking their source there. Upon this commanding position the attacking corps might have been formed in the rear of the Russian line. Such a movement on that point must have cut off the Russians from their point of retreat on Mojaisk and Moscow, and Davoust might have come down their line, driving every thing before him, advancing from redoubt to redoubt, and dispersing reserve after reserve, till the Russians should no longer have the semblance of an army. Perhaps Napoleon considered this plan as too hazardous, as it implied a great weakening of his front line, which, in that case, might have been attacked and broken before the corps d'armée under Davoust had attained the desired position.[150]

The Emperor therefore determined that Poniatowski, with not more than 5000 men, should make a demonstration, that should commence upon their left, in the direction proposed by Davoust, and that then a general attack should commence on the Russian right and centre. Foreseeing an obstinate resistance, he had ordered as much artillery as possible to be brought into line, and the guns on each side are said to have amounted to a thousand.[151] The battle

---

[149] Ségur, tom. i., p. 328.
[150] "Davoust, from conviction, persisted in his point; he protested that in another hour the greatest part of its effects would be produced. Napoleon, impatient of contradiction, sharply replied, with this exclamation, 'Ah! you are always for turning the enemy; it is too dangerous a manœuvre!' The marshal, after this rebuff, said no more, but returned to his post, murmuring against a prudence to which he was not accustomed."—Ségur, tom. i., p. 321.
[151] "On General Caulaincourt's return from the conquered redoubt, as no prisoners had fallen into our hands, Napoleon, surprised, kept asking him repeatedly, 'Had not his cavalry then charged à propos? Were the Russians determined to conquer or die?' The answer was, that 'being fanaticised by their leaders, and accustomed to fight with the Turks, who gave

began about seven o'clock, by Ney's attacking the bastioned redoubt on the Russian centre, with the greatest violence, while Prince Eugene made equal efforts to dislodge the enemy from the village of Semoneskoie, and the adjoining fortifications. No action was ever more keenly debated, nor at such a wasteful expenditure of human life. The fury of the French onset at length carried the redoubts, but the Russians rallied under the very line of their enemy's fire, and advanced again to the combat, to recover their intrenchments. Regiments of peasants, who till that day had never seen war, and who still had no other uniform than their grey jackets, formed with the steadiness of veterans, crossed their brows, and having uttered their national exclamation—"*Gospodee pomiloui nas!*—God have mercy upon us!"—rushed into the thickest of the battle, where the survivors, without feeling fear or astonishment, closed their ranks over their comrades as they fell, while, supported at once by enthusiasm for their cause, and by a religious sense of predestination, life and death seemed alike indifferent to them.

The fate of the day seemed more than once so critical, that Napoleon was strongly urged on more than one occasion to bring up the Young Guard, whom he had in reserve, as the last means of deciding the contest. He was censured by some of those around him for not having done so; and it has been imputed to illness, as he had passed a bad night, and seemed unusually languid during the whole of the day. But the secret of his refusal seems to be contained in his reply to Berthier, when he urged him on the subject—"And if there is another battle to-morrow, where is my army?"[152] The fact is, that this body of 10,000 household troops were his last reserve. They had been spared as far as possible in the march, and had, of course, retained their discipline in a proportional degree; and had they sustained any considerable loss, which, from the obstinate resistance and repeated efforts of the Russians, was to be apprehended,

---

no quarter, they would be killed sooner than surrender!' The Emperor then fell into a deep meditation; and judging that a battle of artillery would be the most certain, he multiplied his orders to bring up with speed all the parks which had not yet joined him."—Ségur, tom. i., p. 314.

[152] "The Emperor said also to Bessières, 'that nothing was yet sufficiently unravelled: that to make him give his reserves, he wanted to see more clearly upon his chess-board.' This was his expression, which he repeated several times, at the same time pointing to the great redoubt, against which the efforts of Prince Eugene had been ineffectual."—Ségur, tom. i., p. 342.

Buonaparte, whom even victory must leave in a perilous condition, would in that case have lost the only corps upon whom, in the general disorganisation of his army, he could thoroughly depend. The compromising the last reserve is an expedient reluctantly resorted to by prudent generals; and perhaps, if Napoleon had been as circumspect on that subject at Waterloo as at Borodino, his retreat from that bloody field might have been less calamitous than it proved.

The Russians, whose desperate efforts to recover their line of redoubts had exposed them to so much loss, were at length commanded to retreat; and although the victory was certainly with the French, yet their enemies might be said rather to desist from fighting, than to have suffered a defeat. Indeed, it was the French who, after the battle, drew off to their original ground, and left the Russians in possession of the bloody field of battle, where they buried their dead, and carried off their wounded, at their leisure. Their cavalry even alarmed the French camp on the very night of their victory.

Both parties sustained a dreadful loss in this sanguinary battle. Among that of the Russians, the death of the gallant Prince Bagration, whose admirable retreat from Poland we have had occasion to commemorate, was generally lamented. General Touczkoff also died of his wounds; and many other Russian generals were wounded. Their loss amounted to the awful sum total of 15,000 men killed, and more than 30,000 wounded. The French were supposed to have at least 10,000 men killed, and double the number wounded. Of these last few recovered, for the great convent of Kolotskoi, which served them as an hospital, was very ill-provided with any thing for their relief; and the medical attendants could not procure a party to scour the neighbouring villages, to obtain lint and other necessaries—for it seems even the necessaries of an hospital could, in this ill-fated army, only be collected by marauding. Eight French generals were slain, of whom Monbrun and Caulaincourt, brother of the grand equerry, were men of distinguished reputation. About thirty other generals were wounded. Neither party could make any boast of military trophies, for the Russians made a thousand prisoners, and the French scarce twice the number; and Koutousoff carried away ten pieces of cannon belonging to the French, leaving in their hands thirteen guns of his own. So slight, except in the numbers of slain, had been the consequences of the battle, that it might have seemed to have been fought, as in the games of chivalry, merely to ascertain which party had the superior strength and courage.[153]

MOJAISK

According to the Russian accounts, Koutousoff entertained thoughts of giving battle again the next day; but the reports from various corps having made him acquainted with the very large loss they had sustained, he deemed the army too much exhausted to incur such a risk. He retreated the next day upon Mojaisk, without leaving behind him a single fragment to indicate that he had the day before sustained such an immense loss. Upon the 9th September, the French arrived at Mojaisk, and came again in sight of the Russian rear-guard, and made dispositions to attack them. But on the 11th, they found that the Russian army had again disappeared, by a retreat so well conducted, and so effectually masked and concealed, as to leave Napoleon altogether uncertain whether they had taken the road to Moscow, or to Kalouga. Owing to this uncertainty, Napoleon was obliged to remain at Mojaisk till the 12th, when he received positive intelligence that the Russian army had retreated upon their capital.

It is impossible to avoid observing, how often the Russian army, though large, and consisting of new levies, had, in the course of this campaign, escaped from the front of the French, and left Napoleon at a loss to conjecture whither they had gone. Besides the present occasion, the same circumstance took place at Witepsk, and again before the walls of Moscow. No doubt the Russians were in their own country, and possessed clouds of Cossacks, by means of whom they might cover the retreat of their main body; yet with all these advantages, we are led to admire the natural spirit of

---

[153] "The day ended; 50,000 men lay on the field of battle. A multitude of generals were killed and wounded: we had forty disabled. We made some prisoners; took some pieces of cannon. This result did not compensate for the losses which it had cost us."—Rapp, p. 208.

obedience, and instinct of discipline, by which they were brought to execute that movement with such steadiness, that not a single straggler remained to betray their secret.

On the 12th September, Buonaparte resumed his march, the army having no better guide than the direction of the high road, and the men no better food than horse flesh and bruised wheat. Upon the previous day, Murat and Mortier, who led the vanguard, found the Russians strongly posted near Krymskoie, where the inconsiderate valour of the King of Naples brought on an action, in which the French lost two thousand men. Still Buonaparte pursued the traces of the Russians, because he could not suppose it possible that they would resign their capital without a second struggle. He was the more anxious to meet it, as two divisions of the Italian army, under Laborde and Pino, had joined him from Smolensk, which again carried his numbers, sore thinned after the battle of Borodino, to upwards of one hundred thousand men.

A council of war, of the Russian generals, had been called to deliberate on the awful question, whether they should expose the only army which they had in the centre of Russia, to the consequences of a too probable defeat, or whether they should abandon without a struggle, and as a prey to the spoiler, the holy Moscow—the Jerusalem of Russia—the city beloved of God and dear to man, with the name and existence of which so many historical, patriotic, national, and individual feelings were now involved. Reason spoke one language, pride and affection held another.

To hazard a second battle, was in a great measure to place the fate of their grand army upon the issue; and this was too perilous an adventure, even for the protection of the capital. The consideration seems to have prevailed, that Napoleon being now in the centre of Russia, with an army daily diminishing, and the hard season coming on, every hour during which a decisive action could be delayed was a loss to France, and an advantage to Russia. This was the rather the case, that Witgenstein, on the northern frontier, being reinforced by Steingel with the army of Finland; and, on the south, that of Moldavia being united to Tormasoff—Lithuania, and Poland, which formed the base of Napoleon's operations, were in hazard of being occupied by the Russians from both flanks, an event which must endanger his supplies, magazines, reserves, and communications of every kind, and put in peril at once his person and his army. Besides, the Russian generals reflected, that by evacuating Moscow, a measure which the inhabitants could more easily accomplish than those of any other city in the civilized world, they would diminish the prize to the victor, and leave him nothing to triumph over save the senseless buildings. It was therefore determined, that the preservation of the army was more essential to Russia than the defence of Moscow, and it was agreed that the ancient capital of the Czars should be abandoned to its fate.

Count Rostopchin, the governor of Moscow, was a man of worth and talent, of wit also, as we have been informed, joined to a certain eccentricity. He had, since the commencement of the war, kept up the spirits of the citizens with favourable reports and loyal declarations, qualified to infuse security into the public mind. After the fate of Smolensk, however, and especially after the recommencement of Buonaparte's march eastward, many of the wealthy inhabitants of Moscow removed or concealed their most valuable effects, and left the city themselves. Rostopchin continued, however, his assurances, and took various means to convince the people that there was no danger. Among other contrivances, he engaged a great number of females in the task of constructing a very large balloon, from which he was to shower down fire, as the people believed, upon the French army. Under this pretext, he is stated to have collected a large quantity of fire-work and combustibles, actually destined for a very different purpose.

THE RUSSIANS ABANDON MOSCOW

As time passed on, however, the inhabitants became more and more alarmed, and forming a dreadful idea of the French, and of the horrors which would attend their entrance into the city, not only the nobility, gentry, and those of the learned professions, but tradesmen, mechanics, and the lower orders in general, left Moscow by thousands, while the governor, though keeping up the language of defiance, did all he could to superintend and encourage the emigration. The archives and the public treasures were removed; the magazines, particularly those of provisions, were emptied, as far as time permitted; and the roads, especially to the south, were crowded with files of carriages, and long columns of men, women, and children on foot, singing the hymns of their church, and often turning their eyes back to the magnificent city, which was so soon destined to be a pile of ruins.

The grand army of Moscow arrived in the position of Fili, near the capital; not, it was now acknowledged, to defend the sacred city, but to traverse its devoted streets, associating with their march the garrison, and such of the citizens as were fit to bear arms, and so leave the capital to its fate. On the 14th of September, the troops marched with downcast looks, furled banners, and silent drums, through the streets of the metropolis, and went out at the Kolomna gate. Their long columns of retreat were followed by the greater part of the remaining population. Meanwhile Rostopchin, ere departing, held a public court of justice. Two men were brought before him, one a Russian, an enthusiast, who had learned in Germany, and been foolish enough to express at Moscow, some of the old French republican doctrines. The other was a Frenchman, whom the near approach of his countrymen had emboldened to hold some indiscreet political language. The father of the Russian delinquent was present. He was expected to interfere. He did so; but it was to demand his son's death. "I grant you," said the governor, "some moments to take leave and to bless him."—"Shall I bless a rebel?" said this Scythian Brutus. "Be my curse upon him that has betrayed his country!" The criminal was hewed down on the spot. "Stranger," said Rostopchin to the Frenchman, "thou hast been imprudent; yet it is but natural thou shouldst desire the coming of thy countrymen. Be free, then, and go to meet them. Tell them there was one traitor in Russia, and thou hast seen him punished."

The governor then caused the jails to be opened, and the criminals to be set at liberty; and, abandoning the desolate city to these banditti, and a few of the lowest rabble, he mounted his horse, and putting himself at the head of his retainers, followed the march of the army.

Chapter LX

On 14th September, Napoleon reaches Moscow, which he finds deserted by the Inhabitants—The City is discovered to be on fire—Napoleon takes up his quarters in the Kremlin—The fire is stopt next day, but arises again at night—Believed to be wilful, and several Russians apprehended and shot—On the third night, the Kremlin is discovered to be on Fire—Buonaparte leaves it, and takes his abode at Petrowsky—The Fire rages till the 19th, when four-fifths of the City are burnt down—On the 20th, Buonaparte returns to the Kremlin—Discussion as to the Origin of this great Conflagration—Disorganisation and Indiscipline of the French Army—Difficulty as to the Route on leaving Moscow—Lauriston sent with a Letter to the Emperor Alexander—Retrospect of the March of the Russian Army, after leaving Moscow—Lauriston has an Interview with Koutousoff on 5th October—The Result—Armistice made by Murat—Preparations for Retreat—The Emperor Alexander refuses to treat.

On the 14th September, 1812, while the rearguard of the Russians were in the act of evacuating Moscow, Napoleon reached the hill called the Mount of Salvation, because it is there where the natives kneel and cross themselves at first sight of the Holy City.

Moscow seemed lordly and striking as ever, with the steeples of its thirty churches, and its copper domes glittering in the sun; its palaces of Eastern architecture mingled with trees, and surrounded with gardens; and its Kremlin, a huge triangular mass of towers, something between a palace and a castle, which rose like a citadel out of the general mass of groves and buildings. But not a chimney sent up smoke, not a man appeared on the battlements, or at the gates. Napoleon gazed every moment, expecting to see a train of bearded boyards arriving to fling themselves at his feet, and place their wealth at his disposal. His first exclamation was, "Behold at last that celebrated city!"—His next, "It was full time." His army, less regardful of the past or the future, fixed their eyes on the goal of their wishes, and a shout of "Moscow!—Moscow!"—passed from rank to rank.[154]

Meantime no one interrupted his meditations, until a message came from Murat. He had pushed in among the Cossacks, who covered the rear of the Russians, and readily admitted to a parley the chivalrous champion, whom they at once recognised, having so often seen him blazing in the van of the French cavalry.[155] The message which he sent to Buonaparte intimated, that Miloradovitch threatened to burn the town, if his rear was not allowed time to march through it. This was a tone of defiance. Napoleon, however, granted the armistice, for which no inhabitants were left to be grateful.

After waiting two hours, he received from some French inhabitants, who had hidden themselves during the evacuation, the strange intelligence that Moscow was deserted by its population. The tidings that a population of 250,000 persons had left their native city was incredible, and Napoleon still commanded the boyards, the public functionaries, to be brought before him; nor could he be convinced of what had actually happened, till they led to his presence some of that refuse of humanity, the only live creatures they could find in the city, but they were wretches of the lowest

---

[154] "Every one quickened his pace; the troops hurried on in disorder; and the whole army clapping their hands, repeated with transport, 'Moscow! Moscow!' just as sailors shout 'land! land!' at the conclusion of a long and tedious voyage."—Ségur, tom. ii., p. 28. "At the sound of this wished for name, the soldiers ran up the hill in crowds, and each discovered new wonders every instant. One admired a noble chateau on our left, the elegant architecture of which displayed more than Eastern magnificence; another directed his attention towards a palace or a temple; but all were struck with the superb picture which this immense town afforded."—Labaume, p. 179.

[155] "Murat was recognised by the Cossacks, who thronged around him, and by their gestures and exclamations extolled his valour, and intoxicated him with their admiration. The king took the watches of his officers, and distributed them among these yet barbarous warriors. One of them called him his *hettman*. Murat was for a moment tempted to believe that in these officers he should find a new Mazeppa, or that he himself should become one; he imagined that he had gained them over."—Ségur, tom. ii., p. 31.

rank. When he was at last convinced that the desertion of the capital was universal, he smiled bitterly, and said, "The Russians will soon learn better the value of their capital."[156]

The signal was now given for the troops to advance; and the columns, still in a state of wonder at the solitude and silence which received them every where, penetrated through that assemblage of huts, mingled with palaces, where it seemed that Penury, which had scarce means to obtain the ordinary necessaries of life, had for her next door neighbour all the wealth and profuse expenditure of the East. At once the silence was broken by a volley of musketry, which some miserable fanatics poured from the battlements of the Kremlin on the first French troops that approached the palace of the Czars. These wretches were most of them intoxicated; yet the determined obstinacy with which they threw away their lives, was another feature of that rugged patriotism of which the French had seen, and were yet to see, so many instances.

ENTRY INTO MOSCOW

When he entered the gates of Moscow, Buonaparte, as if unwilling to encounter the sight of the empty streets, stopt immediately on entering the first suburb.[157] His troops were quartered in the desolate city. During the first few hours after their arrival, an obscure rumour, which could not be traced, but one of those which are sometimes found to get abroad before the approach of some awful certainty, announced that the city would be endangered by fire in the course of the night. The report seemed to arise from those evident circumstances which rendered the event probable, but no one took any notice of it, until at midnight, when the soldiers were startled from their quarters by the report that the town was in flames. The memorable conflagration began amongst the coachmakers' warehouses and workshops in the Bazaar, or general market, which was the most rich district of the city. It was

---

[156] Ségur, tom. ii., p. 33.
[157] "Napoleon appointed Marshal Mortier governor of the capital. 'Above all,' said he to him, 'no pillage! For this you shall be answerable to me with your life. Defend Moscow against all, whether friend or foe.'"—Ségur, tom. ii., p. 38.

imputed to accident, and the progress of the flames was subdued by the exertions of the French soldiers. Napoleon, who had been roused by the tumult, hurried to the spot, and when the alarm seemed at an end, he retired, not to his former quarters in the suburbs, but to the Kremlin,[158] the hereditary palace of the only sovereign whom he had ever treated as an equal, and over whom his successful arms had now attained such an apparently immense superiority. Yet he did not suffer himself to be dazzled by the advantage he had obtained, but availed himself of the light of the blazing Bazaar, to write to the Emperor proposals of peace with his own hand. They were despatched by a Russian officer of rank, who had been disabled by indisposition from following the army. But no answer was ever returned.

Next day the flames had disappeared, and the French officers luxuriously employed themselves in selecting out of the deserted palaces of Moscow, that which best pleased the fancy of each for his residence. At night the flames again arose in the north and west quarters of the city. As far the greater part of the houses were built of wood, the conflagration spread with the most dreadful rapidity. This was at first imputed to the blazing brands and sparkles which were carried by the wind; but at length it was observed, that, as often as the wind changed, and it changed three times in that terrible night, new flames broke always forth in that direction, where the existing gale was calculated to direct them on the Kremlin. These horrors were increased by the chance of explosion. There was, though as yet unknown to the French, a magazine of powder in the Kremlin; besides that a park of artillery, with its ammunition, was drawn up under the Emperor's window. Morning came, and with it a dreadful scene. During the whole night, the metropolis had glared with an untimely and unnatural light. It was now covered with a thick and suffocating atmosphere, of almost palpable smoke. The flames defied the efforts of the French soldiery, and it is said that the fountains of the city had been rendered inaccessible, the water-pipes cut, and the fire-engines destroyed or carried off.

---

[158] "Napoleon pensively entered the Kremlin. 'At length,' he exclaimed, 'I am in Moscow, in the ancient palace of the Czars, in the Kremlin.' He examined every part of it with pride, curiosity, and gratification."—Ségur, tom. ii., p. 39.

Then came the reports of fire-balls having been found burning in deserted houses; of men and women, that, like demons, had been seen openly spreading the flames, and who were said to be furnished with combustibles for rendering their dreadful work more secure. Several wretches against whom such acts had been charged, were seized upon, and, probably without much inquiry, were shot on the spot.[159] While it was almost impossible to keep the roof of the Kremlin clear of the burning brands which showered down the wind, Napoleon watched from the windows the course of the fire which devoured his fair conquest, and the exclamation burst from him, "These are indeed Scythians!"[160]

The equinoctial gales rose higher and higher upon the third night, and extended the flames, with which there was no longer any human power of contending. At the dead hour of midnight, the Kremlin itself was found to be on fire. A soldier of the Russian police, charged with being the incendiary, was turned over to the summary vengeance of the Imperial Guard.[161] Buonaparte was then, at length, persuaded, by the entreaties of all around him, to relinquish his quarters in the Kremlin, to which, as the visible mark of his conquest, he had seemed to cling with the tenacity of a lion holding a fragment of his prey. He encountered both difficulty and danger in retiring from the palace, and before he could gain the citygate, he had to traverse with his suite streets arched with fire,[162] and in which the very air they breathed was suffocating. At length, he gained the open country, and took up his abode in a palace of the

---

[159] "Three hundred incendiaries have been arrested and shot; they were provided with fuses, six inches long; they had also squibs, which they threw upon the roofs of the houses. The wretch Rostopchin had these prepared on the pretence that he wished to send up a balloon, full of combustible matter, amidst the French army."—*Twenty-first Bulletin.*

[160] "Napoleon was seized with extreme agitation; he seemed to be consumed by the fires which surrounded him. He traversed his apartments with quick steps. Short and incoherent exclamations burst from his labouring bosom."—Ségur, tom. ii., p. 45.

[161] "Napoleon caused the man to be interrogated in his presence. He had executed his commission at the signal given by his chief. The gestures of the Emperor betokened disdain and vexation. The wretch was hurried into the first court, where the enraged grenadiers despatched him with their bayonets."—Ségur, tom. ii., p. 46.

[162] "I saw Napoleon pass by, and could not, without abhorrence, behold the chief of a barbarous expedition evidently endeavouring to escape the decided testimony of public indignation, by seeking the darkest road. He sought it, however, in vain. On every side the flames seemed to pursue him; and their horrible and mournful glare, flashing on his guilty head, reminded me of the torches of the Eumenides pursuing the destined victims of the Furies."—Labaume, p. 206.

Czar's called Petrowsky, about a French league from the city. As he looked back on the fire, which, under the influence of the autumnal wind, swelled and surged around the Kremlin, like an infernal ocean around a sable Pandemonium, he could not suppress the ominous expression, "This bodes us great misfortune."[163]

The fire continued to triumph unopposed, and consumed in a few days what it had cost centuries to raise. "Palaces and temples," says a Russian author, "monuments of art, and miracles of luxury, the remains of ages which had past away, and those which had been the creation of yesterday; the tombs of ancestors, and the nursery-cradles of the present generation, were indiscriminately destroyed. Nothing was left of Moscow save the remembrance of the city, and the deep resolution to avenge its fall."[164]

The fire raged till the 19th with unabated violence, and then began to slacken for want of fuel. It is said, four-fifths of this great city were laid in ruins. On the 20th, Buonaparte returned to the Kremlin;[165] and, as if in defiance of the terrible scene which he had witnessed, took measures as if he were disposed to make Moscow his residence for some time. He even caused a theatre to be fitted up, and plays to be acted by performers sent from Paris, to show, perhaps, that it was not in the most terrible of elements to overawe his spirit, or interrupt his usual habits of life. In the same style of indifference or affectation, a set of very precise regulations respecting the Théâtre Français was drawn up by the Emperor amid the ruins of Moscow. He was not superior to the affectation of choosing distant places and foreign capitals for the date of domestic and trifling ordinances. It gave the Emperor an air of ubiquity, to issue rules for a Parisian theatre from the Kremlin. It had already

---

[163] Ségur, tom. ii., p. 49.
[164] Karamzin, a Russian historian of eminence, whose works were expressly excepted from the censorship by the late Emperor Alexander.—See *Histoire de l'Empire de Russie*, traduit par St. Thomas, Jauffret, et de Divoff.
[165] "On his re-entering the Kremlin, a few houses scattered among the ruins were all that was left of the mighty Moscow. The suburbs were sprinkled with Russians of both sexes, covered with garments nearly burned. They flitted like spectres among the ruins; squatted in the gardens, some of them were scratching up the earth in quest of vegetables; while others were disputing with the crows for the relics of the dead animals which the army had left behind."—Ségur, tom. ii., p. 54.

been prophesied that he would sacrifice his army to have the pleasure of dating a decree from Moscow.[166]

The conflagration of Moscow was so complete in its devastation; so important in its consequences; so critical in the moment of its commencement, that almost all the eye-witnesses have imputed it to a sublime, yet almost horrible exertion of patriotic decision on the part of the Russians, their government, and, in particular, of the governor, Rostopchin. Nor has the positive denial of Count Rostopchin himself diminished the general conviction, that the fire was directed by him. All the French officers continue to this day to ascribe the conflagration to persons whom he had employed.

On the other hand, there are many, and those good judges of the probabilities in such an event, who have shown strong reasons for believing, that Moscow shared but the fate of a deserted city, which is almost always burnt as well as pillaged. We shall only observe, that should the scale of evidence incline to the side of accident, History will lose one of the grandest, as well as most terrible incidents which she has on record. Considered as a voluntary Russian act, the burning of their capital is an incident of gigantic character, which we consider with awe and terror; our faculties so confused by the immensity of the object, considered in its different bearings, that we hardly know whether to term it vice or virtue, patriotism or vengeance.

Whether the conflagration of Moscow was, or was not, the work of Russian will, and Russian hands, the effects which it was to produce on the campaign were likely to be of the most important character. Buonaparte's object in pressing on to the capital at every

---

[166] "Amidst the dreadful storm of men and elements which was gathering around him, his ministers and his aides-de-camp saw him pass whole days in discussing the merits of some new verses which he had received, or the regulations for the Comédie Française at Paris, which he took three evenings to finish. As they were acquainted with his deep anxiety, they admired the strength of his genius, and the facility with which he could take off or fix the whole force of his attention on whatever he pleased. It was remarked, too, that he prolonged his meals, which had hitherto been so simple and so short. He seemed desirous of stifling thought by repletion. He would pass whole hours, half reclined, as if torpid, and awaiting, with a novel in his hand, the catastrophe of his terrible history."—Ségur, tom. ii., p. 67-87.

risk, was to grasp a pledge, for the redemption of which he had no doubt Alexander would be glad to make peace on his own terms. But the prize of his victory, however fair to the sight, had, like that fabled fruit, said to grow on the banks of the Dead Sea, proved in the end but soot and ashes. Moscow, indeed, he had seized, but it had perished in his grasp; and far from being able to work upon Alexander's fears for its safety, it was reasonable to think that its total destruction had produced the most vehement resentment on the part of the Russian monarch, since Napoleon received not even the civility of an answer to his conciliatory letter. And thus the acquisition so much desired as the means of procuring peace, had become, by this catastrophe, the cause of the most irreconcilable enmity.

Neither was it a trifling consideration, that Napoleon had lost by this dreadful fire a great part of the supplies, which he expected the capture of the metropolis would have contributed for the support of his famished army. Had there existed in Moscow the usual population of a capital, he would have found the usual modes of furnishing its markets in full activity. These, doubtless, are not of the common kind, for provisions are sent to this capital, not, as is usual, from fertile districts around the city, but from distant regions, whence they are brought by water-carriage in the summer, and by sledges, which travel on the ice and frozen snow, in the winter time. To Moscow, with its usual inhabitants, these supplies must have been remitted as usual, lest the numerous population of 250,000 and upwards, should be famished, as well as the enemy's army. But Moscow deserted—Moscow burnt, and reduced to mountains of cinders and ashes—had no occasion for such supplies; nor was it to be supposed that the provinces from which they were usually remitted, would send them to a heap of ruins, where there remained none to be fed, save the soldiers of the invading army. This conviction came with heavy anticipation on the Emperor of France and his principal officers.

Meanwhile, the ruins of Moscow, and the remnant which was left standing, afforded the common soldiers an abundance of booty during their short day of rest; and, as is their nature, they enjoyed the present moment without thinking of futurity. The army was dispersed over the city, plundering at pleasure whatever they could find; sometimes discovering quantities of melted gold and silver, sometimes rich merchandize and precious articles, of which they knew not the value; sometimes articles of luxury, which contrasted strangely with their general want of comforts, and even necessaries. It was not uncommon to see the most tattered, shoeless wretches, sitting among bales of rich merchandize, or displaying costly shawls, precious furs, and vestments rich with barbaric pearl and gold.[167] In another place, there were to be seen soldiers possessed of tea, sugar, coffee, and similar luxuries, while the same individuals could scarce procure carrion to eat, or muddy water to drink. Of sugar, in particular, they had such quantities, that they mixed it with their horse-flesh soup. The whole was a contrast of the wildest and most lavish excess, with the last degree of necessity, disgusting to witness, and most ominous in its presage. *They* esteemed themselves happiest of all, who could procure intoxicating liquors, and escape by some hours of insensibility from the scene of confusion around them.[168]

Napoleon and his officers toiled hard to restore some degree of organisation to the army. The plundering, which could not be discontinued, was latterly set about more regularly; and detachments were sent to pillage the ruins of Moscow, as in turn of duty. The rest of the troops were withdrawn from the city, or confined to their quarters in the buildings which remained entire. Everything was done to protect the few peasants, who brought provisions to the camp for sale. Nevertheless, few appeared, and at length not one was to be seen. The utmost exertion, therefore, could not, it was obvious, render Moscow a place of rest for many days; and the difficulty of choosing the route by which to leave it, became now an embarrassing consideration.

There were three modes of proceeding on evacuating Moscow, all of which had in their turn Napoleon's anxious consideration. First, he might march on St. Petersburgh, and deal

---

[167] "It was common to see walking in our camp soldiers dressed *à la Tartare, à la Cosaque, à la Chinoise*; one wore the Polish cap, another the high bonnet of the Persians, the Baskirs, or the Kalmouks. In short, our army presented the image of a carnival; and from what followed, it was justly said, that our retreat commenced with a masquerade, and ended with a funeral."—Labaume, p. 222.
[168] Labaume, p. 222; Ségur, tom. ii., p. 56.

with the modern, as he had with the ancient capital of Russia. This counsel best suited the daring genius of Buonaparte, ever bent upon the game by which all is to be lost, or all won. He even spoke of that measure as a thing resolved; but Berthier and Bessières prevailed in convincing him, that the lateness of the season, the state of the roads, the want of provisions, and the condition of the army, rendered such an attempt totally desperate. The second proposed measure, was to move southwards upon the fertile province of Kalouga, and thence to proceed westward towards Smolensk, which was their first depôt. In this route Napoleon must have fought a general action with Koutousoff, who, as we shall presently see, had taken a position to the south of Moscow. This, indeed, would have been, in many respects, a motive with Napoleon to take the route to Kalouga; but a second battle of Borodino, as obstinately fought, and as doubtful in its termination, would have been a bad commencement for a retreat, the flanks of which would certainly be annoyed, even if the Moldavian army did not intercept the front. The third plan was, to return by the route on which he had advanced, and on which, by a few places hastily fortified, he still preserved a precarious communication with Smolensk, Witepsk, and so on to Wilna. This line, however, lay through the countries which had been totally destroyed and wasted by the advance of the army, and where all the villages and hamlets had been burned and abandoned, either by the French or the Russians themselves. To take this direction was to confront famine.[169]

    Napoleon's hesitation on this important point, was increased by the eagerness with which he still adhered to his own plan for the conclusion of the war, by a triumphant peace with Alexander, concluded on the ruins of his capital. His mind, which ever clung with tenacity to the opinions he had once formed, revolved the repeated instances in which his voice had in such circumstances commanded peace, and dictated the articles. The idea which he had formed of Alexander's disposition during the interviews of Tilsit and Erfurt, had made him regard the Czar as docile, and disposed to submit to the rebuke of his own predominant genius. But he mistook the character of the sovereign, and of the nation he commanded. The one, although he had hitherto encountered

---

[169] Jomini, tom. iv., p. 154.

nothing but defeat and disaster, was determined not to submit, while his immense resources furnished the means of resistance. The other, in all probability, would not have permitted the sovereign to act otherwise, for the popular indignation was now at spring-tide; and from the palace of the Czar to the hut of the slave, there was nothing breathed save resistance and revenge.

MISSION TO EMPEROR ALEXANDER

It was in vain, therefore, that Napoleon expected that Alexander would open some communication on the subject of, or would answer, the letter which he had sent, during the first night he possessed Moscow, by a Russian officer. He grew impatient at length, and resolved himself to make further advances. But not even to his confidential advisers would he own that he sought peace on his own score; he affected to be anxious only on account of Alexander. "He is my friend," he said; "a prince of excellent qualities; and should he yield to his inclinations, and propose peace, the barbarians in their rage will dethrone and put him to death, and fill the throne with some one less tractable. We will send Caulaincourt to break the way for negotiation, and prevent the odium which Alexander might incur, by being the first to propose a treaty." The Emperor abode by this resolution, excepting in so far as he was persuaded with some difficulty to despatch General Count Lauriston, his aide-de-camp, upon this embassy; lest Caulaincourt's superior rank of Master of the Horse, might indicate that his master sought a treaty, less for Alexander's security than his own, and that of his army. Lauriston, who was well acquainted with the Russian character, urged several doubts against the policy of the mission intrusted to him, as betraying their necessity to the enemy; and recommended that the army should, without losing a day, commence its retreat by Kalouga, and the more southern route. Buonaparte, however, retained his determination, and Lauriston was dismissed with a letter to the Emperor Alexander, and the parting instruction,—"I must have peace, and will sacrifice, to obtain it, all except my honour."[170]

---

[170] Ségur, tom. ii., p. 70.

Before we give the result of Lauriston's mission, it is proper to trace the movements of the Russian grand army, since their melancholy march through the city of Moscow. They left the city by the route of Kolomna, and marched for two days in that direction; and having thus imposed on the enemy a belief, that they were bent in securing a retreat to the south-east, leaving at once the eastern and southern provinces undefended, Koutousoff executed one of the most dexterous movements of the Russian army during the campaign. The observation of the Petersburgh road was intrusted to Winzengerode, with a small flying army. Koutousoff himself, turning to the southward, performed a circular march, of which Moscow was the centre, so as to transfer the grand army to the route towards Kalouga. They marched in stern dejection; for the wind, great as the distance was, showered among their ranks the ashes of their burning capital, and in the darkness, the flames were seen to rage like a huge ocean of fire. The movement was a bold one also, for, although performed at a respectful distance from the French army, yet the march was for three days a flank march, and consequently of a very delicate character. The Russians manœuvred, however, with such precision, that they performed their movements in perfect safety; and while the French troops, who had been sent in their pursuit, were amusing themselves with pursuing two regiments of horse, which had been left on the Kolomna road, they were astonished to find that the grand Russian army had assumed a position on the south-eastern side of Moscow, from which they could operate upon and harass, nay, intercept at pleasure, Napoleon's line of communication with Smolensk and with Poland, and at the same time cover the town of Kalouga, where great magazines had been assembled, and that of Toula, famed for the fabrication of arms and artillery.[171]

The ardent King of Naples, with the advanced guard of his brother-in-law's army, at length moved against their enemies on the Kalouga road; but little took place save skirmishes, by which the Russians protected their rear, until they took up a stationary posture

---

[171] "This movement of the Russians, though censured by Wilson, Vaudoncourt, and Fain, is one of the most skilful operations of the war. By what fatality is it, that we ever condemn that in the enemy, which we applaud vehemently, when it happens to be effected by ourselves."—Jomini, tom. iv., p. 152.

in the strong position of Taroutino. They were here admirably placed for the purpose of covering the important town of Kalouga. There are three routes which lead from Moscow to that city; and Taroutino being situated in the middle road, an army placed there can with little trouble, by moving to the right or the left, occupy either of the other two. The front of the Russian position was covered by the river Nara. The camp was amply supplied with provisions from the wealthy and plentiful districts in the rear; and as the spirit of the country more and more developed itself, recruits and new-raised regiments arrived faster than the exertions of the veteran soldiers could train them to arms, although the Russian, from his docility and habits of obedience, receives military discipline with unusual readiness. The Ukraine and Don sent twenty regiments of Cossacks, most of them men who, having already served their stipulated time, were excused from military duty, but who universally assumed the lance and sabre at a crisis of such emergency.

Murat at the same time pressed forward to establish himself in front of the Russian camp, for the purpose of watching their motions. In his progress, he passed what had been a splendid domain, belonging to Count Rostopchin, the governor of Moscow. It was in ashes; and a letter from the proprietor informed the French he had destroyed it, lest it should give an invader comfort or shelter.[172] The same spirit possessed the peasantry. They set fire to their hamlets, wherever they could be of use to the invaders; proclaimed the punishment of death to all of their own order, who, from avarice or fear, should be tempted to supply the enemy with provisions; and they inflicted it without mercy on such as incurred the penalty. It is an admitted fact, that when the French, in order to induce their refractory prisoners to labour in their service, branded some of them on the hand with the letter N, as a sign that they were the serfs of Napoleon, one peasant laid his branded hand on a log of wood, and struck it off with the axe which he held in the other, in order to free himself from the supposed thraldom. The French who

---

[172] "Frenchmen," this was the tenor of this remarkable intimation, "for eight years it has been my pleasure to embellish this my family residence. The inhabitants, 1720 in number, will leave it as you approach; and it will be reduced to ashes that not one of you may pollute it by your presence. I have left you two palaces in Moscow, with their furniture, worth half a million of rubles. Here you will only find ashes."—*Twenty-third Bulletin.*—S.

looked on shuddered, and cursed the hour which brought them into collision with enemies of such a rugged and inexorable disposition. The patriotism of the peasants in general had been turned to still better account by the partisan or guerilla warfare, for which Spain had given an example.

GENERAL DAVIDOFF

Lieutenant-Colonel Dennis Davidoff, who became well known to the French by the name of *le Capitaine Noir*, had suggested this species of war to Prince Bagration, a little before the battle of Borodino; and had obtained distinguished success at the head of a small party of Cossacks and hussars, by his operations on the route betwixt Gjatz and Wiazma, in cutting off supplies, and defeating small detached parties of the enemy. He was speedily put at the head of a much larger force; and other free corps of the same kind were raised, with brave and active spirits at their head. They scoured the country, infested the French lines of communication, drove in their outposts, and distressed them on every point.

The peasants also took arms, and formed themselves into bodies of partisans, rendered formidable by their perfect knowledge of the woods, by-paths, and passes. They have a natural contempt for foreigners, for whom they have no other name than "the deaf and dumb," to denote their ignorance of the Russian language. The events of the campaign, especially the conflagration of Moscow, had converted their scorn into deadly hatred; and whatever soldier of Napoleon fell into their hands, was put to death without scruple or pity.

Meantime the cavalry of Murat, which afforded the best means of chastising and repressing these bands, gradually declined under hard work and want of subsistence; and, although little used to droop or distress himself about the future, the King of Naples wrote repeatedly from his advanced post, to press Napoleon no longer to delay a retreat which was become absolutely necessary. It was while matters were in this state that General Lauriston arrived at the Russian outposts, and after a good deal of difficulty, real or affected, was at length admitted to an interview with Koutousoff, at midnight on the 5th October. His reception was such as to make him consider himself a welcome envoy.

Lauriston opened his business with a proposal for exchange of prisoners, which was of course declined on the part of Koutousoff, aware, that while soldiers were plenty among the Russians, the ranks of Napoleon must become every day thinner. Lauriston next introduced the subject of the independent bands, and proposed that an end should be put to this species of unusual war, in which so many cruelties were committed. Koutousoff replied, that this kind of partisan war did not depend on his orders, but arose from the native spirit of the country, which led the Russians to regard the French invasion as an incursion of Tartars. General Lauriston then entered on the real business of his mission, by asking whether "this war, which had assumed such an unheard-of character, was to last for ever?" declaring, at the same time, his master the Emperor of France's sincere desire, to terminate hostilities between two great and generous nations.

The astucious old Russian saw Buonaparte's evident necessity in his affected wish for peace, and immediately adopted the course most likely to gain time, which must at once increase the difficulties of the French, and his own power of availing himself of them. He affected a sincere desire to promote a pacification, but declared he was absolutely prohibited either to receive any proposal to that effect himself, or to transmit such to the Emperor. He therefore declined to grant General Lauriston the desired passport to the presence of Alexander, but he offered to send General Wolkonsky, an aide-de-camp of the Czar, to learn his imperial pleasure.

The express charge which Lauriston had received from his master, that peace was to be obtained on any terms not inferring dishonour, did not permit him to object to this arrangement. He was even encouraged to hope it might prove effectual, so much satisfaction was expressed by General Koutousoff and the officers of his military family, all of whom seemed to deplore the continuance of the war, and went so far as to say, that this annunciation of a treaty would be received at Petersburgh with public rejoicings. These accounts being transmitted to Napoleon, lulled him into a false security. He returned to his original opinion, which had been shaken, but not subverted; and announced to his generals, with much satisfaction, that they had but to wait a fortnight for a triumphant pacification. He boasted his own superior knowledge of the Russian character, and declared, that on the arrival of his overture for peace, Petersburgh would be full of bonfires.[173]

ARMISTICE MADE BY MURAT

Napoleon, however, was not so confident of peace as to approve a singular sort of armistice which Murat had entered into with the Russians. It was to be broken off, on an intimation of three hours' space, by either party to the other; and, while in existence, it only subsisted along the fronts of the two armies, leaving the Russians at liberty to carry on their partisan war on the flanks as much as ever. The French could not obtain a load of furze, or a cart of provisions, without fighting for it, and often to disadvantage. A large party of the dragoons of the Imperial Guard were surprised and piked by the Cossacks. Two considerable convoys were surprised and cut off on the road to Mojaisk, the only communication which the French army had with its magazines and reinforcements. The French were surprised, and lost a detachment in the town of Vereia, on Murat's left flank. Thus the war continued everywhere except on the front of the armies, where it had the greatest chance to be favourable to the French.

This bad policy is not to be imputed to Napoleon, who had refused to authorise the armistice, but to the vanity of Murat, under whose authority it was still observed. It gave him an opportunity of amusing himself, by caracoling on the neutral ground betwixt the camps, displaying his handsome form, gallant horsemanship, and splendid dresses, to the soldiers on both sides; receiving the respectful salutes of the Russian patrols, and the applause of the Cossacks. These last used to crowd around him, partly in real admiration of his chivalrous appearance and character, which was of a kind to captivate these primitive warriors, and partly, doubtless,

---

[173] Ségur, tom. ii., p. 71; Jomini, tom. iv., p. 153.

from their natural shrewdness which saw the utility of maintaining his delusion. They called him their Hettman; and he was so intoxicated with their applause, as to have been said to nourish the wild idea of becoming in earnest King of the Cossacks.[174]

Such delusions could not for ever lull Murat's vigilance to sleep. The war was all around him, and his forces were sinking under a succession of petty hostilities; while the continual rolling of drums, and the frequent platoon firing, heard from behind the Russian encampment, intimated how busily they were engaged in drilling numerous bodies of fresh recruits. The Russian officers at the outposts began to hold ominous language, and ask the French if they had made a composition with the Northern Winter, Russia's most fearful ally. "Stay another fortnight," they said, "and your nails will drop off, and your fingers fall from your hands, like boughs from a blighted tree." The numbers of the Cossacks increased so much, as to resemble one of the ancient Scythian emigrations; and wild and fantastic figures, on unbroken horses, whose manes swept the ground, seemed to announce that the inmost recesses of the desert had sent forth their inhabitants. Their grey-bearded chiefs sometimes held expostulations with the French officers, in a tone very different from that which soothed the ears of Murat. "Had you not," they said, "in France, food enough, water enough, air enough, to subsist you while you lived—earth enough to cover you when you died; and why come you to enrich our soil with your remains, which by right belong to the land where you were born?" Such evil bodements affected the van of the army, from whence Murat transmitted them to the Emperor.[175]

Immured in the recesses of the Kremlin, Napoleon persisted in awaiting the answer to the letter despatched by Lauriston. It had been sent to Petersburgh on the 6th, and an answer could not be expected before the 26th. To have moved before that period, might be thought prudent in a military point of view; but, politically considered, it would greatly injure his reputation for sagacity, and destroy the impression of his infallibility. Thus sensible, and almost admitting that he was wrong, he determined, nevertheless, to

---

[174] Ségur, tom. ii., p. 74.
[175] Ségur, tom. ii., p. 77.

persevere in the course he had chosen, in hopes that Fortune, which never before failed him, might yet stand his friend in extremity.

MOSCOW

A bold scheme is said to have been suggested by Daru, to turn Moscow into an intrenched camp, and occupy it as winter-quarters. They might kill the remainder of the horses, he said, and salt them down; foraging must do the rest. Napoleon approved of what he termed a Lion's counsel. But the fear of what might happen in France, from which this plan would have secluded them for six months, induced him finally to reject it. It might be added, that the obtaining supplies by marauding was likely to become more and more difficult, as winter and the scarcity increased, especially now that the country around Moscow was completely ruined. Besides, if Napoleon fixed himself at Moscow for the winter, not only his line of communications, but Lithuania, and the grand duchy, which formed the base of his operations, ran every risk of being invaded. On the south-west, the dubious faith of Austria was all he had to trust to, for the purpose of resisting the united armies of Tchitchagoff and Tormasoff, which might be augmented to 100,000 men, and make themselves masters of Warsaw and Wilna. On the northern extremity of his general line of operations, Macdonald and St. Cyr might prove unable to resist Witgenstein and Steingel; and he had in his rear Prussia, the population of which Napoleon justly considered as ready to take arms against him at the first favourable opportunity. The scheme, therefore, for occupying winter-quarters at Moscow was rejected as fraught with dangers.[176]

Even when appearances of a fall of snow reminded the Emperor of the climate which he was braving, his preparations for retreat were slowly and reluctantly made; and some of them were dictated by his vanity, rather than his judgment. All the pictures, images, and ornaments of the churches, which were left unburnt, were collected, and loaded upon wains, to follow the line of march, already too much encumbered with baggage. A gigantic cross, which stood on the tower of Ivan the Great, the tallest steeple of Moscow,

---

[176] Ségur, tom. ii., p. 86.

was dismounted with much labour,[177] that it might add to the trophies, which were already sufficiently cumbrous. On the same principle, Napoleon was angry when it was proposed to leave some of his immense train of artillery, which was greatly too numerous for the reduced size of his army. "He would leave no trophy for the Russians to triumph over." That all the artillery and baggage might be transported, he surprised his officers by an order to buy twenty thousand horses, where, perhaps, there were not an hundred to be sold, and when those which they had already were daily dying for want of forage. The latter article, he ordered, should be provided for two months, in depôts on his route. This mandate might make known his wants; but as it certainly could contribute little to supply them, it must only have been issued for the purpose of keeping up appearances. Perhaps the desire to have some excuse to himself and others for indulging in his lingering wish to remain a day or two longer, to await the answer from St Petersburgh, might be a secret cause of issuing orders, which must occasion some inquiry ere it could be reported in what extent they could be obeyed.

If this were the case, it was the rash indulgence of a groundless hope. The Emperor Alexander refused to hear of any negotiation for peace, and took no other notice of that which had been transmitted to him by Walkonsky, than to pass a censure on the Russian officers concerned, and Prince Koutousoff himself, for having had the least intercourse with the French generals. He reminded the generalissimo how positive his instructions had been on this subject, and that he had enjoined him on no account to enter into negotiations or correspondence with the invaders; and he revived and enforced his injunctions to that effect.

The sagacious general was not, it is to be supposed, greatly affected by a rebuke which was only given for form's sake. He made

---

[177] "During the work, it was remarked that great numbers of ravens surrounded this cross, and that Napoleon, weary of their hoarse croaking, exclaimed, that 'it seemed as if these flocks of ill-omened birds meant to defend it.' We cannot pretend to tell all that he thought in this critical situation, but it is well known that he was accessible to every kind of presentiment. His daily excursions, always illumined by a brilliant sun, in which he strove himself to perceive and to make others recognise his star, did not amuse him. To the sullen silence of inanimate Moscow was superadded that of the surrounding deserts, and the still more menacing silence of Alexander."—Ségur.

his soldiers acquainted with the Emperor's unalterable resolution to give no terms to the invaders; and spreading through the camp, at the same time, the news of the victory at Salamanca, and the evacuation of Madrid, pointed out to them, that Frenchmen, like others, were liable to defeat; and called on his soldiers to emulate the courage of the British and patriotism of the Spaniards. While the minds of the soldiery were thus excited and encouraged, Koutousoff took measures for anticipating Napoleon, by putting an end to the armistice and assuming an offensive posture.[178]

---

[178] "Koutousoff made his camp ring with the news of the victory of Salamanca. 'The French,' said he, 'are expelled from Madrid: the hand of the Most High presses heavily upon Napoleon. Moscow will be his prison, his grave, and that of all his grand army. We shall soon take France in Russia.'"—Ségur, tom. ii., p. 88.

Chapter LXI

Murat's Armistice broken off—Napoleon leaves Moscow on 19th October—Bloody Skirmish at Malo-Yarowslavetz—Napoleon in great danger while reconnoitring—He retreats to Vereia, where he meets Mortier and the Young Guard—Winzengerode made Prisoner, and insulted by Buonaparte—The Kremlin is blown up by the French—Napoleon continues his Retreat towards Poland—Its Horrors—Conflict near Wiazma, on 3d November, where the French lose 4000 Men—Cross the River Wiazma during the Night—The Viceroy of Italy reaches Smolensk, in great distress—Buonaparte arrives at Smolensk, with the headmost division of the Grand Army—Calamitous Retreat of Ney's Division—The whole French Army now collected at Smolensk—Cautious conduct of Prince Schwartzenberg—Winzengerode freed on his road to Paris, by a body of Cossacks—Tchitchagoff occupies Minsk—Perilous situation of Napoleon.

MURAT ATTACKED AND DEFEATED

It was easy to make Murat himself the active person in breaking off the armistice, a step which the Russian general preferred, lest a formal intimation of rupture on his own side, might lead the King of Naples to suspect his further purpose. Accordingly, a Cossack having fired his carabine when Murat was examining the advanced guards, irritated, as it was designed to do, that fiery soldier, and induced him to announce to the Russian generals that the armistice was ended. The Russians were the first to commence hostilities.

The camp, or position, which Murat occupied, Worodonow, was covered on the right, and on the centre, by a rivulet or brook, running in a deep ravine; but the stream taking another direction, left a good part of the left wing uncovered, which was at the same time exposed to surprise from a wood covering a little plain where his left rested. The sum of Murat's force, which consisted of the cavalry, and Poniatowski's division, was computed to be upwards of 30,000. It is singular that since the King of Naples expected an attack, as was intimated by his letter to his brother-in-law, he did not take the precaution of placing videttes and advanced guards in the woody plain. But the French, from their long train of success, were accustomed to despise their enemies, and to consider a surprise as a species of affront which they were never to be exposed to.

The Russians had laid a plan, which, had it been dexterously executed, must have destroyed the whole French advanced guard. An attack upon the left of Murat's position, by two Russian columns, under Count Orloff Dennizoff, was completely successful; but other two columns, by whom he should have been supported, did not arrive in time upon the point of action; the Poles, under Poniatowski, made a glorious defence upon the right, and the vanguard was saved from utter destruction. But there was a complete defeat; the King of Naples lost his cannon, his position, and his baggage, had 2000 men killed, and lost 1500 prisoners. The French cavalry, except a few of those belonging to the guard, might be said to be utterly destroyed. Every thing which the Russians saw in the enemy's camp, convinced them of the distress to which the French were reduced. Flayed cats and horse-flesh were the dainties found in the King of Naples' kitchen.

It was the 18th of October when first the noise of the cannon, and soon after, the arrival of an officer, brought intelligence of this mishap to Buonaparte. His energy of character, which had appeared to slumber during the days he had spent in a species of irresolution at Moscow, seemed at once restored. He poured forth, without hesitation, a torrent of orders suited for the occasion, directing the march of the troops to support Murat at Worodonow. Notwithstanding the miscellaneous variety of directions, each was distinct in itself, yet critically connected with the others, so as to form, on the whole, a perfect and well-connected plan of movements. Part of the army marched that night; the rest had their route for the next morning. A garrison, under Maréchal Mortier, was left as a rear-guard in the Kremlin; from which it may be inferred that Napoleon did not as yet intend a final retreat.

On the 19th October, before day-break, the Emperor in person left Moscow, after an abode of thirty-four days. "Let us march," he said, "on Kalouga, and woe to those who shall oppose us."[179] In this brief sentence he announced the whole plan of his retreat which was to defeat the army of Koutousoff, or compel him to retire, and then himself to return to the frontiers of Poland, by the unwasted route of Kalouga, Medyn, Ynkowo, Elnia, and Smolensk.

The French army, which now filed from the gates of Moscow, and which continued to move on in a living mass for many hours, comprehended about 120,000 men, indifferently well appointed, and marching in good order. They were followed by no less than 550 pieces of cannon, a train beyond proportion to their numbers, and 2000 artillery waggons.[180] So far the march had a martial and imposing aspect. But in the rear of these came a confused crowd of many thousands, consisting of followers of the camp, stragglers who had rejoined it, and prisoners, many of them employed in carrying, or driving forward in wheelbarrows, the spoil of the conquerors.[181]

Among these were French families formerly inhabitants of Moscow, and composing what was called the French colony there, who could no longer reckon upon it as a safe place of abode, and who took the opportunity of retiring with their countrymen. There

---

[179] Ségur, tom. ii., p. 92; Twenty-fifth Bulletin of the Grand French Army.
[180] "When we were about three leagues from Moscow, the Emperor stopped to wait for news from Mortier, who had orders to destroy the Kremlin on leaving the place. He was walking in a field with M. Daru; this gentleman left him; I was called—'Well, Rapp, we are going to retreat to the frontiers of Poland by the road to Kalouga; I shall take up good winter-quarters. I hope that Alexander will make peace.'—'You have waited a long time, Sire; the inhabitants foretell that it will be a severe winter.'—'Poh! poh! with your inhabitants. It is the 19th of October to-day; you see how fine it is. Do you not recognise my star.' But all that he said to me in the way of encouragement did not deceive even himself: his countenance bore the marks of uneasiness."—Rapp, p. 222.
[181] Jomini, tom. iv., p. 163.

was, besides, a mixture and confusion of all imaginable kind of carriages, charged with the baggage of the army, and with the spoils of Moscow, to swell those trophies which Napoleon had seized upon to amuse the Parisians, as well as what had been seized by individuals. This miscellaneous crowd resembled, according to Ségur, a horde of Tartars returning from a successful invasion.[182]

BATTLE OF MALO-YAROWSLAVETZ

There were, as has been said, three routes from Moscow to Kalouga. The central, or old road, was that upon which the Russians lay encamped at their grand position of Taroutino, and in front of it was that of Worodonow, or Ynkowo, where they had so lately defeated Murat. Napoleon advanced a day's march on this route, in order to induce Koutousoff to believe that he proposed to attack his army in front; but this was only a feint, for, on the next day, he turned off by cross-roads into the western, or new road to Kalouga, with the view of advancing by that route until he should be past the Russian camp at Taroutino, on the right flank, and then of again crossing from the new road to the old one, and thus getting possession of Borowsk and Malo-Yarowslavetz, towns on the same road to the southward of Taroutino. Thus the Russian position would be turned and avoided, while the main body of the French Emperor would be interposed betwixt Koutousoff and Kalouga, and the fertile southern provinces laid open to supply his army.

On the 23d, the Emperor with his main body, attained Borowsk, and learned that the division of Delzons, which formed his vanguard, had occupied Malo-Yarowslavetz without opposition. Thus far all seemed to have succeeded according to Napoleon's wish.

But Koutousoff, so soon as he was aware of the danger in which he stood of being cut off from Kalouga, retaliated upon Napoleon his own manœuvre, and detached Generals Doktoroff and Raefskoi to the southward with a strong division, to outmarch

---

[182] Ségur, tom. ii., p. 95.

the French, and occupy the position of Malo-Yarowslavetz, or to regain it if it was taken. He himself breaking up his camp at Taroutino, followed with his whole army by the road of Lectazowo, and marched so rapidly as to outstrip the French army, and reach the southward of Malo-Yarowslavetz, and consequently again interpose himself between Napoleon and Kalouga.

Malo-Yarowslavetz offers a strong position. The town is built on a rapid declivity, broken with cliffs, the bottom of which is washed by the river Louja. On the northern side of the Louja, and connected with the town by a bridge, is a small plain with some huts, where Delzon's army bivouacked, having stationed two battalions to defend the town, and to watch the motions of the enemy. About four in the morning, when all were asleep, save the few sentinels who kept a careless watch, the Russians rushed into the place with dreadful outcries, drove the two battalions out of the town, and pushed them down the declivity and across the Louja to their main body. The noise of the artillery drew the attention of Eugene the viceroy, who being only about three leagues from the scene of action, arrived there about the dawn. The soldiers of Delzons' division were then discovered struggling to regain the southern bank on which the town was situated. Encouraged by the approach of Eugene, Delzons pushed forward across the bridge, repelled the Russians, gained the middle of the village, and was shot dead. His brother, who endeavoured to drag the general's body from the spot, incurred the same fate. General Guilleminot succeeded to the command, and threw a strong party of French into the church, which served as a citadel during the continuance of the action. The Russians rushed in once more, and drove Guilleminot back to the bridge. He was, however, succoured by Prince Eugene, who, after various less serious attempts, directed a whole division on the town.[183]

Malo-Yarowslavetz was then recovered by the French; but, on reconnoitring a little farther, the whole of Koutousoff's army appeared on the plain beyond it, upwards of 100,000 men in number, and already possessed of a good position, which they were

---

[183] Jomini, tom. iv., p. 166; Ségur, tom. ii., p. 101; Labaume, p. 247; Twenty-seventh Bulletin.

improving by intrenchments. Reinforcements from the Russian ranks immediately attacked the French, who were driven back on the town, which, being composed of wooden huts, was now in flames, and the French were again dispossessed of Malo-Yarowslavetz. The miserable ruins of this place were five times won and lost. At length, as the main body of the grand army came up under Napoleon himself, he found the French still in possession of the disputed village and its steep bank. But beyond them lay the numerous Russian army, stationed and intrenched, supported by a very large train of artillery, and seeming to render a battle absolutely indispensable to dislodge them from the position they had taken, and the fortifications with which they had secured themselves.

A council of war was held in the headquarters of the Emperor, the hut of a poor weaver, divided by a screen, which served as the only partition.[184] Here he received and meditated upon the reports of his generals, together with their opinions, and learned, to his distress, that Bessières, and other good officers, reported that the position occupied by Koutousoff was unassailable.[185] He resolved to judge with his own eyes on the next day, and in the meantime turned a negligent ear to the reports which informed him that the Cossacks were stealing through the woods, and insinuating themselves betwixt him and his advanced guard.

At dawning, Napoleon mounted his horse, in order to reconnoitre, and incurred in the attempt a great risk of his life or freedom. It was about daybreak, when, as attended by his staff and orderly soldiers, he crossed the little plain on the northern side of the Louja in order to gain the bridge, the level ground was suddenly filled with fugitives, in the rear of whom appeared some black masses. At first, the cries they made seemed to be those of *Vive l'Empereur*; but the wild hourra of the Cossacks, and the swiftness of

---

[184] "In the habitation of a weaver—an old, crazy, filthy, wooden hut, and in a dirty, dark room—was the fate of the army and of Europe about to be decided."—Ségur, tom. ii., p. 107.

[185] "'O heavens!' exclaimed Napoleon, clasping his hands, 'Are you sure you are right? Are you not mistaken? Will you answer for that?' Bessières repeated his assertion. He affirmed that '300 grenadiers would suffice to keep in check a whole army.' Napoleon then crossed his arms with a look of consternation, hung his head, and remained as if overwhelmed with the deepest dejection."—Ségur, tom. ii., p. 108.

their advance, soon announced the children of the desert. "It is the Cossacks," said Rapp, seizing the reins of the Emperor's bridle. "You must turn back." Napoleon refused to retreat, drew his sword, as did his attendants, and placed themselves on the side of the highway. Rapp's horse was wounded, and borne down by one of these lancers; but the Emperor and suite preserved their liberty by standing their ground, while the cloud of Cossacks, more intent on plunder than prisoners, passed them within lance's length, without observing the inestimable prey which was within their grasp, and threw themselves upon some carriages which were more attractive. The arrival of the cavalry of the guard cleared the plain of this desultory but venturous and pertinacious enemy; and Napoleon proceeded to cross the river and ascend the further bank, for the purpose of reconnoitring. In the meantime, the audacity of the Cossacks in their retreat, was equal to the wild character of their advance. They halted between the intervals of the French cavalry to load their pistols and carabines, perfectly secure that if pressed, their horses, at a touch of the whip which is attached to their bridle, would outstrip the exhausted chargers of the French Imperial Guard.[186]

When the plain was attained, Napoleon saw on the front, and barring the road to Kalouga, Koutousoff, strongly posted with upwards of 100,000 men, and on the right, Platoff and 6000 Cossacks, with artillery. To this belonged the pulk which he had just encountered, and who were returning from the flanks of his line, loaded with booty, while others seemed to meditate a similar attack. He returned to his miserable headquarters, after having finished his reconnoitring party.

RETREAT ON VEREIA

A second council of war was held, in which Buonaparte, having heard the conflicting opinions of Murat, who gave his advice for attacking Koutousoff, and of Davoust, who considered the position of the Russian general as one which, covering a long succession of defiles, might be defended inch by inch, at length

---

[186] Mémoires de Rapp, p. 227; Ségur, tom. ii., p. 110.

found himself obliged to decide between the angry chiefs, and with a grief which seemed to deprive him of his senses for a little while, gave the unusual orders—to retreat.[187] Buonaparte's own personal experience had convinced him how much, in advancing, his flanks would be exposed to the Hettman and his Cossacks, who had mustered in great force in the neighbourhood of Medyn. Other intelligence informed him that his rear had been attacked by another body of Cossacks coming from Twer, and who belonged not to Koutousoff's army, but to another Russian division under the command of Winzengerode, which was advancing from the northward to re-occupy Moscow. This showed that the communications of the French were at the enemy's mercy on the west and the north, on flank and in rear, and seems to have determined the Emperor to give at length, and most reluctantly, the orders to retreat, for the purpose of returning to the frontiers by Vereia and Wiazma, the same road by which they had advanced.

It was very seldom that Napoleon resigned the settled purpose of his own mind, either to the advice of those around him, or to any combination of opposing circumstances. He usually received any objection founded on the difficulty of executing his orders, with an evasive answer, "*Ah, on ne peut pas!*" which, from the sarcastic mode in which he uttered the words, plainly showed that he imputed the alleged impossibility to the imbecility of the officer who used the apology. It might have been better for Napoleon, in many instances, had he somewhat abated this pertinacity of disposition; and yet it happened, that by yielding with unwonted docility to the advice of his generals upon the present occasion, he actually retreated at the very moment when the grand Russian army were withdrawing from the position in which Davoust had pronounced them unassailable. The reason of this retrograde movement, which involved the most serious risk, and which, had Napoleon been aware of it, might have yielded him access to the most fertile and unharassed provinces of Russia, was said to be Koutousoff's fears that the French, moving from their right flank, might have marched round the Russian army by the way of Medyn. The truth seems to be, that Koutousoff, though placed in command of the grand army, in order to indulge the soldiers with a general action, was slow and cautious by nature,

---

[187] Ségur, tom. ii., p. 117.

and rendered more so by his advanced age. He forgot, that in war, to gain brilliant results, or even to prevent great reverses, some risks must be run; and having received just praise for his practised and cautious movements from the battle of Borodino till that of Malo-Yarowslavetz, he now carried the qualities of prudence and circumspection to the extreme, and shunned a general action, or rather the hazard of a general attack from the French, when he might certainly have trusted, first, in the chance (which turned out the reality) of Buonaparte's retreat; secondly, in the courage of his troops, and the strength of his position. "But Fortune," says Tacitus, "has the chief influence on warlike events;" and she so ordered it, that both the hostile armies retired at once. So that while Buonaparte retreated towards Borowsk and Vereia, the route by which he had advanced, the Russians were leaving open before him the road to Kalouga, to gain which he had fought, and fought in vain, the bloody battle of Malo-Yarowslavetz. Favoured, however, by their immense clouds of light cavalry, the Russians learned the retrograde movement of Napoleon long before he could have any certain knowledge of theirs; and in consequence, manœuvred from their left so as to approach the points of Wiazma and Gjatz, by which the French must needs pass, if they meant to march on Smolensk.

WINZENGERODE MADE PRISONER

At Vereia, where Napoleon had his headquarters on the 27th October, he had the satisfaction to meet with Mortier, and that part of the Young Guard which had garrisoned the Kremlin. They brought with them an important prisoner, whom chance, or rather his own imprudence, had thrown into their hands. We have said incidentally, that upon the French army evacuating Moscow, Winzengerode, with a considerable body of forces, advanced upon the Twer to regain possession of the city. All was vacant and silent except where the French garrison lay, deserted and moody in the Kremlin, with a few detached outposts. Winzengerode, with a single aide-de-camp, rode imprudently forward, and both were seized by the French soldiers. The general waved a white handkerchief, and claimed the privilege of a flag of truce, alleging that he came to summon the French marshal to surrender. But Mortier refused him the privilege he claimed, observing, plausibly, that it was not the custom of general officers to summon garrisons in person.

Before leaving Moscow, the French, by the especial command of Napoleon, prepared to blow up the ancient palace of the Czars. As the Kremlin was totally useless as a fortification, even if Napoleon could have hoped ever to return to Moscow as a victor, this act of wanton mischief can only be imputed to a desire to do something personally displeasing to Alexander, because he had been found to possess a firmer character than his former friend had anticipated.[188] The mode of executing this mandate, which, however, should be probably ascribed to the engineers, was a piece of additional barbarity. Aware that some of the Russians who were left behind, men of the lowest rank and habits, would crowd in to plunder the palace when the French retreated, they attached long slow-matches to the gunpowder which was stored in the vaults of the palace, and lighted them when the rear of the French column marched out. The French were but at a short distance, when the explosion took place, which laid a considerable part of the Kremlin in ruins, and destroyed at the same time, in mere wantonness, a number of wretches, whom curiosity or love of plunder had, as was anticipated, induced to crowd within the palace.[189] The Russian troops poured in, destroyed the mines which had not yet exploded, and extinguished the fire which had already caught the building. The patriotic foresight of the Russian peasants was now made manifest. We have mentioned the extreme wants of the French in the desolate city. No sooner was the Russian flag hoisted, than these wants vanished, as if by magic. Eighteen hundred cars, loaded with bread, poured in from the neighbourhood, on the very day that saw

---

[188] Jomini, tom. iv., p. 165.
[189] "Barrels of powder had been placed in all the halls of the palace of the Czars, and 183,000 pounds under the vaults which supported them. While Mortier was rapidly retiring, some Cossacks and squalid Muscovites approached: they listened, and emboldened by the apparent quiet which pervaded the fortress, they ventured to penetrate into it; they ascended, and their hands eager after plunder, were already stretched forth, when in a moment they were all destroyed, crushed, hurled into the air, with the buildings which they had come to pillage, and 30,000 stand of arms that had been left behind there; and then their mangled limbs, mixed with fragments of walls and shattered weapons, blown to a great distance, descended in a horrible shower."—Ségur, tom. ii., p. 129.

Moscow re-occupied. The bread, and the mode of conveying it, had been in secret prepared by these rustic patriots.

We return to the movements of the French army.

The dreadful explosion of the Kremlin shook the ground like an earthquake, and announced to Napoleon, then on his march against Koutousoff, that his commands had been obeyed. On the next day, a bulletin announced in a triumphant tone that the Kremlin, coeval with the Russian monarchy, *had existed*; and that Moscow was now but an impure laystall, while "the 200,000 persons which once formed her population, wandered through the forests, subsisting on wild roots, or perishing for want of them." With yet more audacity, the same official annunciation represents the retreat of the French as an advance on the road to victory. "The army expects to be put in motion on the 24th, to gain the Dwina, and to assume a position which will place it eighty leagues nearer to St. Petersburgh, and to Wilna; a double advantage, since it will bring us nearer the mark we aim at, and the means by which it may be accomplished."[190] While such splendid figments were circulated for the satisfaction of the people of Paris, the real question was, not whether the French were to approach St. Petersburgh, but by what means they were to get out of Russia with the semblance of an army remaining together.

Napoleon's spirit was observed to be soured by the result of the affair at Malo-Yarowslavetz. It was indeed an operation of the last consequence, since it compelled a broken and suffering army to retreat through a country already wasted by their own advance, and by the acts of the Russians, where the houses were burnt, the inhabitants fled, and the roads broken up, instead of taking the road by Kalouga, through a region which offered both the means of subsistence and shelter. When the advanced season of the year was considered, it might be said that the retreat upon Vereia sounded the death-knell of the French army. These melancholy considerations did not escape Buonaparte himself, though he endeavoured to disguise them from others, by asserting, in a bulletin dated from Borowsk, that the country around was extremely rich, might be

---

[190] Twenty-sixth Bulletin of the Grand Army.

compared to the best parts of France and Germany, and that the weather reminded the troops of the sun and the delicious climate of Fontainbleau.[191] His temper was visibly altered. Among other modes of venting his displeasure, he bitterly upbraided his prisoner Winzengerode, who was then brought before him.—"Who are you?" he exclaimed[192]—"A man without a country!—You have ever been my enemy—You were in the Austrian ranks when I fought against them—I have become Austria's friend, and I find you in those of Russia—You have been a warm instigator of the war; nevertheless, you are a native of the Confederation of the Rhine—you are my subject—you are a rebel—Seize on him, gendarmes!—Let him be brought to trial!"[193]

WINZENGERODE

To this threat, which showed that Napoleon accounted the states of the Confederacy not as appertaining in sovereignty to the princes whose names they bore, but as the immediate subjects of France, from whom the French Emperor was entitled to expect direct fealty, Napoleon added other terms of abuse; and called Winzengerode an English hireling and incendiary, while he behaved with civility to his aide-de-camp Narishkin, a native Russian. This violence, however, had no other consequence than that of the dismissal of Winzengerode, a close prisoner, to Lithuania, to be from thence forwarded to Paris.[194] The presence of a captive of rank and reputation, an aide-de-camp of the Emperor of Russia, was designed of course to give countenance to the favourable accounts, which Napoleon might find it convenient to circulate on the events of the campaign. It was not, however, Winzengerode's fortune to

---

[191] "The inhabitants of Russia do not recollect such a season as we have had for the last twenty years. The army is in an extremely rich country: it may be compared to the best in France or Germany."—*Twenty-sixth Bulletin.*
[192] "Crossing his arms with violence, as if to grasp and to restrain himself."—Ségur, tom. ii., p. 131.
[193] "The gendarmes remained motionless, like men accustomed to see these violent scenes terminate without effect, and sure of obeying best by disobeying."—Ségur, tom. ii., p. 131.
[194] "Each of us endeavoured to appease the Emperor; the King of Naples, the Duke de Vicenza particularly, suggested to him how much, in the present situation of things, any violence towards a man who had his origin under the quality of a Russian general, would be to be lamented; there was no council of war, and the affair rested there."—Rapp, p. 229.

make this disagreeable journey. He was, as will be hereafter mentioned, released in Lithuania, when such an event was least to be hoped for.

Accounts had been received, tending to confirm the opinion that the Russian army were moving on Medyn, with the obvious purpose of intercepting the French army, or at least harassing their passage at Wiazma or at Gjatz. By the orders of Napoleon, therefore, the army pressed forward on the last named town. They marched on in three corps d'armée. Napoleon was with the first of these armies. The second was commanded by the Viceroy of Italy, Prince Eugene. The third, which was destined to act as a rear-guard, was led by Davoust, whose love of order and military discipline might be, it was hoped, some check upon the license and confusion of such a retreat. It was designed that one day's march should intervene between the movements of each of these bodies, to avoid confusion, and to facilitate the collecting subsistence; being a delay of two, or at most three days, betwixt the operations of the advanced guard and that of the rear.

It has been often asked, nor has the question ever been satisfactorily answered, why Napoleon preferred that his columns should thus creep over the same ground in succession, instead of the more combined and rapid mode of marching by three columns in front, by which he would have saved time, and increased, by the breadth of country which the march occupied, the means of collecting subsistence. The impracticability of the roads cannot be alleged, because the French army had come thither arranged in three columns, marching to the front abreast of each other, which was the reverse of their order in the retreat.

In the road, the army passed Borodino, the scene of the grand battle which exhibited so many vestiges of the French prowess, and of the loss they had sustained.[195] This, the most sanguinary conflict

---

[195] "The ground was covered all around with fragments of helmets and cuirasses, broken drums, gun-stocks, tatters of uniforms, and standards died with blood. On this desolate spot lay thirty thousand half-devoured corses. A number of skeletons, left on the summit of one of the hills, overlooked the whole. It seemed as if death had here fixed his empire: it was that terrible redoubt, the conquest and the grave of Caulaincourt. The cry, 'It is the field of the great battle!' formed a long and doleful murmur. Napoleon passed quickly—

of modern times, had been entirely without adequate advantages to the victors. The momentary possession of Moscow had annihilated every chance of an essential result by the catastrophe which followed; and the army which had been victorious at Borodino was now escaping from their conquests, surrounded by danger on every hand, and already disorganised on many points, by danger, pain, and privation. At the convent of Kolotskoi, which had been the grand hospital of the French after the battle, many of the wounded were found still alive, though thousands more had perished for want of materials necessary for surgical treatment, food of suitable quality, bandages, and the like. The survivors crawled to the door, and extended their supplicating hands to their countrymen as they passed onwards on their weary march. By Napoleon's orders, such of the patients as were able to bear being moved were placed on the suttlers' carts, while the rest were left in the convent, together with some wounded Russian prisoners, whose presence, it was hoped, might be a protection to the French.[196]

Several of those who had been placed in the carriages did not travel very far. The sordid wretches to whom the carts and wains, loaded with the plunder of Moscow, belonged, got rid in many cases of the additional burden imposed on them, by lagging behind the column of march in desolate places, and murdering the men intrusted to their charge. In other parts of the column, the Russian prisoners were seen lying on the road, their brains shot out by the soldiers appointed to guard them, but who took this mode of freeing themselves of the trouble. It is thus that a continued course of calamity renders men's minds selfish, ravenous, and fiendish, indifferent to what evil they inflict, because it can scarcely equal that which they endure; as divines say of the condemned spirits, that they are urged to malevolent actions against men, by a consciousness of their own state of reprobation.

---

nobody stopped. Cold, hunger, and the enemy urged us on; we merely turned our faces as we proceeded, to take a last melancholy look at the vast grave of our companions in arms."—Ségur, tom. ii., p. 137.—"On arriving at Borodino, my consternation was inexpressible at finding the 20,000 men, who had perished there, yet lying exposed. In one place were to be seen garments yet red with blood, and bones gnawed by dogs and birds of prey; in another were broken arms, drums, helmets, and swords."—Labaume, p. 265.
[196] Ségur, tom. ii., p. 138.

GJATZ—WIAZMA

Napoleon, with his first division of the grand army, reached Gjatz[197] without any other inconvenience than arose from the state of the roads, and the distresses of the soldiery. From Gjatz he advanced in two marches to Wiazma, and halted there to allow Prince Eugene and Marshal Davoust to come up, who had fallen five days' march to the rear, instead of three days only, as had been directed. On the 1st November, the Emperor again resumed his painful retreat, leaving, however, the corps of Ney at Wiazma to reinforce and relieve the rear-guard under Davoust, who, he concluded, must be worn out with the duty. He resumed with his Old Guard the road to Dorogobouje, on which town he thought it probable the Russians might be moving to cut him off, and it was most important to prevent them.

Another order of Napoleon's confirms his sense of the danger which had now begun to oppress him. He commanded the spoils of Moscow, ancient armour, cannon, and the great cross of Ivan, to be thrown into the lake of Semelin, as trophies which he was unwilling to restore, and unable to carry off.[198] Some of the artillery, which the unfed horses where unable to drag forward, were also now necessarily left behind, though the circumstance was not communicated in every instance to Napoleon, who, bred in the artillery department, cherished, like many officers of that branch of service, a sort of superstitious reverence for his guns.

The Emperor, and the vanguard of his army, had hitherto passed unopposed. It was not so with the centre and rear. They were attacked, during the whole course of that march, by clouds of Cossacks, bringing with them a species of light artillery mounted on sledges, which, keeping pace with their motions, threw showers of

---

[197] "On approaching Gjatz, we felt the sincerest regret when we perceived that the whole town had disappeared. Gjatz, constructed entirely of wood, was consumed in a day. It contained many excellent manufactories of cloth and leather, and furnished the Russian navy with considerable quantities of tar, cordage, and marine stores."—Labaume, p. 270.

[198] "In this vast wreck, the army, like a great ship tossed by the most tremendous of tempests, threw, without hesitation, into that sea of ice and snow, all that could slacken or impede its progress."—Ségur, tom. ii., p. 159.

balls among the columns of the French; while the menaced charge of these irregular cavalry frequently obliged the march to halt, that the men might form lines or squares to protect themselves. The passage of streams where the bridges were broken down, and the horses and waggons were overturned on the precipitous banks, or in the miry fords, and where drivers and horses dropped down exhausted, added to this confusion when such obstacles occurred. The two divisions, however, having as yet seen no regular forces, passed the night of the 2d November in deceitful tranquillity, within two leagues of Wiazma, where Ney was lying ready to join them.

In that fatal night, Miloradowitch, one of the boldest, most enterprising, and active of the Russian generals, and whom the French were wont to call the Russian Murat, arrived with the vanguard of the Russian regulars, supported by Platoff and many thousand Cossacks, and being the harbinger of Koutousoff, and the whole grand army of Russia.

The old Russian general, when he learned the French Emperor's plan of retiring by Gjatz and Wiazma, instantly turning his own retreat into a movement to the left, arrived by cross-roads from Malo-Yarowslavetz. The Russians now reached the point of action at daybreak, pushed through Prince Eugene's line of march, and insulated his vanguard, while the Cossacks rode like a whirlwind among the host of stragglers and followers of the army, and drove them along the plain at the lance's point. The viceroy was succoured by a regiment which Ney, though himself hardly pressed, despatched to his aid from Wiazma, and his rear-guard was disengaged by the exertions of Davoust, who marched hastily forward to extricate them. The Russian artillery, which is superior in calibre, and carries farther than the French, manœuvred with rapidity, and kept up a tremendous cannonade, to which the French had no adequate means of replying. Eugene and Davoust made a most gallant defence; yet they would not have been able to maintain their ground, had Koutousoff, as was to have been expected, either come up in person, or sent a strong detachment to support his vanguard.

The battle lasted from seven in the morning till towards evening, when Eugene and Davoust pushed through Wiazma with the remains of their divisions, pursued by and almost mingled with the Russians, whose army marched into the town at the charging step, with drums beating, and all the indications of victory. The French divisions, under cover of the night, and having passed the river (which, like the town, is called Wiazma,) established themselves in obscurity and comparative safety upon the left bank. The day had been disastrous to the French arms, though their honour remained unsullied. They had lost about 4000 men, their regiments were mouldered down to battalions, their battalions to companies, their companies to weak picquets.[199]

All tacticians agree, that, if Koutousoff had reinforced Miloradowitch as warmly urged by Sir Robert Wilson, or if he had forced the town of Wiazma, which his numbers might have enabled him to do, both the centre and rear divisions of Napoleon's force, and probably the troops under Ney also, must have been inevitably cut off. But the aged general confided in the approach of the Russian winter, and declined to purchase, by the blood of his countrymen, a victory of which he held himself secured by the climate. The French were so far from any place where they could procure either food or shelter; they were so hemmed in, and confined to the desolated high-roads, which every column as it passed rendered more impracticable to the rest, that he refused to gain, at the sword's point, advantages which he deemed himself sure of possessing without effort. Determined, therefore, to avoid a general battle, yet to maintain his advantages over the French by manœuvring, Koutousoff, turning a deaf ear to the remonstrances, and even threats, of those who differed in opinion from him, removed his headquarters to Krasnoi, leaving to Miloradowitch the duty of beating up the rear of the French on their retreat, by following the course of the high-road, while the Hettman Platoff, flanking the French march with his Cossacks, took advantage of every opportunity to distress them.

In the meanwhile, the viceroy received orders from Napoleon to abandon the straight road to Smolensk, which was the route of

---

[199] Jomini, tom. iv., p. 173; Ségur, tom. ii., p. 150; Twenty-eighth Bulletin.

the corps of Davoust and Ney, and to move northward on Dowkhowtchina and Poreczie, to afford countenance and support to Maréchal Oudinot, now understood to be hard pressed by Witgenstein, who, as we shall presently see, had regained the superiority in the north of Russia. The viceroy, in obedience to this order, began his march on the new route which was enjoined him, by marching himself upon Zasselie, closely pursued, watched, and harassed by his usual Scythian attendants. He was compelled to leave behind him sixty-four pieces of cannon; and these, with three thousand stragglers, fell into the prompt grasp of the pursuers.

OPERATIONS OF PRINCE EUGENE

A large cloud of Cossacks, with Platoff at their head, accompanied the movements of the viceroy and his Italian army. Whoever strayed from the column was inevitably their prey. Eugene passed a night at Zasselie, without having as yet encountered any great misfortune. But in advancing from thence to Dowkhowtchina, the French had to cross the Wop, a river swelled by rains, while the passage to the ford was steep and frozen. Here the viceroy passed over his infantry with great difficulty, but was obliged to abandon twenty-three pieces of cannon and all his baggage to the Cossacks. The unhappy Italians, wetted from head to foot, were compelled to pass a miserable night in bivouac upon the other side; and many expired there, whose thoughts, when perishing so miserably, must have been on their own mild climate and delicious country. Next day, the shivering, half-naked, and persecuted column reached Dowkhowtchina, where they expected some relief; but their first welcome was from a fresh swarm of Cossacks, which rushed out from the gates with cannon. These were the advanced corps of the troops which had occupied Moscow, and were now pressing westward where their services were more necessary.

Notwithstanding their opposition, Prince Eugene forced his way into the place with much gallantry, and took up quarters for the night. But having lost his baggage, the greater part of his artillery and ammunition, and with the utter destruction of his cavalry, he saw no prospect of being able to march forward to Witepsk to support Oudinot, nor was he in a condition to have afforded him assistance, even if he had been in communication. In this situation of distress, the viceroy determined to rejoin the grand army, and for that purpose marched upon Wlodimerowa, and from thence to Smolensk, where, harassed by the Cossacks, he arrived in a miserable condition upon the 13th of November, having fallen in with Maréchal Ney, upon his march, as we shall afterwards mention.

The Emperor, in the meantime, had halted at Stakawo, during the 3d and 4th November. On the 5th he slept at Dorogobuje.

On the 6th November commenced that terrible Russian winter of which the French had not yet experienced the horrors, although the weather had been cold, frosty, and threatening. No sun was visible, and the dense and murky fog which hung on the marching column, was changed into a heavy fall of snow in large broad flakes, which at once chilled and blinded the soldiers. The march, however, stumbled forward, the men struggling, and at last sinking, in the holes and ravines which were concealed from them by the new and disguised appearance of the face of nature. Those who yet retained discipline and their ranks, stood some chance of receiving assistance; but amid the mass of the stragglers, men's hearts, intent upon self-preservation, became hardened and closed against every feeling of sympathy and compassion, the sentiments of which are sometimes excluded by the selfishness of prosperity, but are almost always destroyed by the egotism of general and overwhelming misfortune. A stormy wind also began to arise, and whirl the snow from the earth, as well as that from the heavens, into dizzy eddies around the soldiers' heads. There were many hurled to the earth in this manner, where the same snows furnished them with an instant grave, under which they were concealed until the next summer came, and displayed their ghastly remains in the open air. A great number of slight hillocks on each side of the road, intimated, in the meanwhile, the fate of these unfortunate men.[200]

---

[200] Labaume, p. 287; Ségur, tom. ii., p. 160.

SMOLENSK

There was only the word Smolensk, which, echoed from man to man, served as a talisman to keep up the spirits of the soldiers. The troops had been taught to repeat that name, as indicating the place where they were once more to be welcomed to plenty and repose. It was counted upon as a depôt of stores for the army, especially of such supplies as they had outstripped by their forced marches, first on Wilna, and afterwards on Moscow. They were now falling back, as was hoped and trusted, upon these resources, and continued their march with tolerable spirit, which even the snow-storm could not entirely depress. They reckoned also upon a reinforcement of 30,000 men under Victor, who were waiting their arrival at Smolensk; but a concourse of evil tidings had made the services of that division necessary elsewhere.

On the same fatal 6th of November, Buonaparte received intelligence of two events, both of deep import, and which corresponded but too well with the storms around him. The one was the singular conspiracy of Mallet, so remarkable for its temporary success, and its equally sudden discomfiture. This carried his mind to Paris, with the conviction that all could not be well with an empire where such an explosion could so nearly attain success.[201] On the other hand, his thoughts were recalled to his present situation by the unpleasing intelligence that Witgenstein had assumed the offensive, beaten St. Cyr, taken Polotsk and Witepsk, and re-occupied the whole line of the Dwina. Here was an unexpected obstacle to his retreat, which he endeavoured to remove by ordering Victor to move from Smolensk with the division just mentioned, and instantly to drive Witgenstein behind the Dwina;

---

[201] "I delivered the despatches to the Emperor. He opened the packet with haste: a *Moniteur* was uppermost. He ran it over; the first article which caught his eye was the enterprise of Mallet: 'What is this! what! plots! conspiracies!' He tore open his letters: they contained the detail of the attempt: he was thunderstruck."—Rapp, p. 232.—"As soon as he was alone with the most devoted of his officers, all his emotions burst forth at once in exclamations of astonishment, humiliation, and anger. Presently after he sent for several others, to observe the effect which so extraordinary a piece of intelligence would produce upon them. He perceived a painful uneasiness, consternation, and confidence in the stability of his government completely shaken."—Ségur, tom. ii., p. 161.

not perhaps considering, with sufficient accuracy, whether the force which his marshal commanded was equal to the task.

Similar bad news came from other quarters. Four demi-brigades of recruits from France had arrived at Smolensk. Baraguay d'Hilliers, their general, had, by command from Buonaparte, sent forward these troops towards Ellnia, intimating at the time, that they should clear the road towards Kalouga, by which last town he then expected the Emperor to approach Smolensk. As Napoleon was excluded from the Kalouga road, these troops, as no longer useful at Ellnia, ought to have been drawn back on Smolensk; but Baraguay d'Hilliers had no certain information of this change of route. The consequence was, that the celebrated Russian partisans, Orloff-Denizoff, Davidoff, Seslavin, and others, surprised these raw troops in their cantonments, and made them all prisoners, to the number of better than two thousand men. Other detachments of the French about the same time fell into the hands of the Russians.

At length the longed-for Smolensk was visible. At the sight of its strong walls and lofty towers, the whole stragglers of the army, which now included treble the number of those who kept their ranks, rushed headlong to the place. But instead of giving them ready admission, their countrymen in the town shut the gates against them with horror; for their confused and irregular state, their wild, dirty, and unshaved appearance, their impatient cries for entrance—above all, their emaciated forms, and starved, yet ferocious aspects—made them to be regarded rather as banditti than soldiers. At length, the Imperial Guards arrived and were admitted; the miscellaneous crowd rushed in after them. To the guards, and some few others who had kept order, rations were regularly delivered; but the mass of stragglers, being unable to give any account of themselves or their regiments, or to bring with them a responsible officer, died, many of them, while they besieged in vain the doors of the magazines. Such was the promised distribution of food—the promised quarters were nowhere to be found. Smolensk, as is already recorded, had been burnt by the Russians, and no other covering was to be had than was afforded by miserable sheds, reared against such blackened walls as remained yet standing. But even this was shelter and repose, compared to the exposed bivouac on wreaths of snow; and as the straggling soldiers were compelled by hunger to unite themselves once more with their regiments, they at length obtained their share in the regular distribution of rations, and an approach towards order and discipline began to prevail in the headmost division of the Grand Army of France.

The central part of the army, under Davoust, who had relinquished the rear-guard to Ney, continued to advance from Wiazma to Dorogobuje; but at this point his distress became extreme, from the combined influence of the storm, the enemy, and the disheartened condition of men driven from their standards by want of food, searching for it in vain, and afterwards unable from weakness to resume their ranks. Many fell into the hands of the incensed peasants, by whom they were either killed, or stripped naked and driven back to the high-road.

The rear-guard, under Ney, suffered yet more than these. Every house had been burnt before their arrival, and their sufferings from the enemy were the severer, that they were the last French whom they had to work their revenge upon. Yet Ney continued to evince a degree of personal firmness and resolution which has been rarely witnessed. At the passage of the Dnieper, he was attacked by the enemy, and all was nearly lost in one general confusion, when the Maréchal, seizing a musket to encourage the few men who could be brought to act, succeeded, against all the hopes of the Russians, and equally against the despairing calculations of the French, in bringing over a part of his rear-guard. But he lost on this fatal spot a great part of his artillery, and a great number of his soldiers. We can give only one unvarying sketch of Ney's dreadful retreat. On every point he was attacked by the same wasting, wearying warfare, and every cessation from fighting was necessarily employed in pushing forward towards Smolensk, which he was approaching on the 13th of November, when suddenly the hills to his left were covered with a disorderly mob of fugitives, whom a band of Cossacks were pursuing and slaughtering at pleasure. Having succeeded in dispersing the Cossacks, the next apparition was that of the army of Italy, to which the flying stragglers belonged. This corps d'armée was on its return, as the reader is aware, from Dowkhowtchina towards Smolensk, and was, as usual, severely pushed at every step by the Cossacks. The passage of the Wop had stripped the soldiers of baggage, provisions such as they had, and artillery and cavalry. They kept their march, however, with sufficient regularity. It was only the stragglers whom the Cossacks chased before them, and wounded, took, and slew at pleasure.

These wretched fugitives no sooner saw Ney's army, than they flew to shelter themselves under its protection, and by doing so communicated their own terror to the Maréchal's ranks. All, both stragglers and soldiers, began to hurry towards the Dnieper, over which was a bridge, which their numbers soon choked up. Great loss was sustained, until Eugene and the indefatigable Ney again presented a defensive front, and repelled the assailants, who had again gathered around them. They were so near Smolensk, that Napoleon could send them refreshments and succour, during the action. The viceroy and Ney at length extricated themselves from their persecutors, and entered Smolensk, where Davoust had before found refuge. Napoleon allowed his army, which was now entirely collected, five days to consume such supplies as were to be found in the place, and to prepare for the terrors of a farther retreat. But though such a delay was indispensable, the evil news which continued to arrive from every quarter, positively prohibited his prolonging this period of repose.[202]

OPERATIONS OF THE RUSSIANS

It is now necessary to trace more particularly the incidents which had taken place on the extreme flanks of Napoleon's line of advance, on both of which, as we have already intimated, the Russians, powerfully reinforced, had assumed the offensive, with the apparent purpose of forming a communication with each other, and acting in conjunction, to intercept the retreat of the grand army.

Upon the 18th of August, St. Cyr having beaten Witgenstein, and taken Polotsk, the war had languished in that quarter. The French army lay in an intrenched camp, well secured with barracks

---

[202] Jomini, tom. iv., p. 186; Rapp, p. 239; Ségur, tom. ii., p. 165.

for shelter, and fortifications for defence. But in the partisan war which they carried on for two months, St. Cyr's army sustained great loss, while that of Witgenstein was more than doubled by the arrival of recruits. Finally, General Steingel, with two divisions of the Russian army from Finland, amounting to 15,000, landed at Riga, and after some inefficient movements against Macdonald, marched to the support of Witgenstein. The Russian general, thus reinforced, began to act on the offensive with great vigour. On the 17th of October, the French outposts were driven into their intrenched camp at Polotsk. On the 18th, the camp itself was furiously attacked, and the redoubts by which it was protected were taken and retaken several times. The French remained in possession of them, but St. Cyr was wounded, and his situation became very precarious. In fact, the next day, 19th October, the attack was renewed by Witgenstein on the right bank of the Dwina, while Steingel, advancing up the opposite bank, threatened to occupy Polotsk and its bridge, and thus to enclose St. Cyr in the intrenched camp.

Fortunately for the French general, night and a thick mist enabled him to cross the river to the left bank, and thus to effect a retreat, which Steingel was unable to prevent. But besides the disasters of the loss of the camp, and of the important place of Polotsk, which the Russians occupied on the 20th October, discord broke out between the Bavarian General Wrede and St. Cyr. When the latter was wounded, the command naturally devolved in course upon the Bavarian; but the other French generals refused to submit to this substitution, and St. Cyr was obliged, in spite of his wounds, to continue to act as commander-in-chief. Wrede, in the meanwhile, assumed an independence of movement quite unusual in an auxiliary general, who was acting with a French maréchal; and, separating altogether from St. Cyr, fell back upon Vileika, near Wilna, and withdrew himself from action entirely. The French division must have been cut off, had not Victor, who was then lying at Smolensk with a covering army of 25,000 men, received, as lately mentioned, Napoleon's orders, despatched on the 6th November, to advance and reinforce St. Cyr, who thus became once more superior to Witgenstein. Victor was under orders, however, to run no unnecessary risk, but to keep as far as possible on the defensive; because it was to this army, and that under Schwartzenberg, that

Napoleon in a great measure trusted to clear the way for his retreat, and prevent his being intercepted ere he gained the Polish frontiers. But when Witgenstein, even in the presence of Victor, took Witepsk, and began to establish himself on the Dwina, Napoleon caused Oudinot, as a more enterprising soldier, to replace the Duke of Belluno; and ordered Eugene to move from Wiazma to Dowkhowtchina, for the purpose of reinforcing that army. Eugene's march, as we have formerly shown, was rendered useless, by his misfortune at crossing the river Wop; and he was compelled to move towards Smolensk, where he arrived in a most dilapidated condition.

In the meantime, Witgenstein received reinforcements, and not only kept Oudinot in complete check, but gradually advanced towards Borizoff, and threatened at that town, which lay directly in the course of Napoleon's retreat, to form a junction with the army of the Danube, which was marching northward with the same purpose of co-operation, and to the movements of which we have now to direct the reader's attention.

It has been mentioned, that General Tormasoff had, on the 12th of August, been defeated at Gorodeczno by the Austrians under Schwartzenberg, and the French under Regnier, and that the Russians had fallen back beyond the Styr. Schwartzenberg, satisfied with this advantage, showed no vehement desire to complete the disaster of his enemy. The French go nigh to bring an accusation against him of treachery, which we do not believe. But his heart was not in the war. He was conscious, that the success of Alexander would improve the condition of Austria, as well as of Europe in general, and he fought no harder than was absolutely necessary to sustain the part of a general of an auxiliary army, who felt by no means disposed to assume the character of a principal combatant.

While Tormasoff and the Austrians watched each other upon the Styr, two smaller corps of Russians and Poles were making demonstrations in the same country. Prince Bagration, upon retreating from the banks of the Dwina, had not altogether deprived that neighbourhood of Russian troops. At Bobruisk he had left a considerable garrison, which had been blockaded first by the French cavalry under Latour Maubourg, and afterwards, when Maubourg was summoned to join Napoleon, by the Polish General Dombrowski. The garrison was supported by a Russian corps under General Ertell. It was an instance of Napoleon's extreme unwillingness to credit any thing that contradicted his wishes, that he persisted in believing, or desiring to have it believed, that the Russians on this point, which commanded still an access from Russia to Poland, were inferior to the Poles, whom he had opposed to them; and while Dombrowski was acting against Ertell, he overwhelmed the embarrassed general with repeated orders to attack and destroy the enemy, before whom he could scarce maintain his ground.

The armies were thus occupied, when Admiral Tchitchagoff, with 50,000 Russians, whom the peace with the Turks permitted to leave Moldavia, advanced upon Volhynia, with the purpose of co-operating with Tormasoff and Ertell; and, finally, of acting in combination with Witgenstein, for intercepting Buonaparte's retreat.

On the 14th September, this important junction betwixt the armies of Tormasoff and Tchitchagoff was effected; and the Russian army, increased to 60,000 men, became superior to all the force, whether of French, Austrians, or Poles, which could be opposed to them. They crossed the Styr, and moved forward on the duchy of Warsaw, while Schwartzenberg, not without loss, retreated to the banks of the Bug. His pursuers might have pressed on him still closer, but for the arrival of Prince Czernicheff, the aide-de-camp of the Emperor, who, escorted by a body of chosen Cossacks, had executed a perilous march in order to bring fresh orders to Tormasoff and Tchitchagoff. The former was directed to repair to the grand army, to occupy the situation formerly held by Prince Bagration, while the command of the united Volhynian army was devolved upon Admiral Tchitchagoff, who, to judge by subsequent events, does not seem to have been, on great emergencies, very well fitted for so important a trust.

Prince Czernicheff then set out with his band of Scythians, to carry to the army of Witgenstein tidings of the purposes and movements of that of Moldavia. The direct course between the

Russian armies was held by the Franco-Austrian army. To escape this obstacle, Czernicheff took his course westwards, and, penetrating deep into Poland, made so long a circuit, as completely to turn the whole army of Schwartzenberg. Marching with extraordinary despatch through the wildest and most secret paths, he traversed the interior of Poland, avoiding at once the unfriendly population and the numerous detachments of the enemy, and sustaining his cavalry, horses and men, in a way in which none but Cossacks, and Cossack horses, could have supported existence. We have good evidence, that this flying party, on one occasion travelled nearly 100 English miles in twenty-four hours.

This extraordinary expedition was marked by a peculiar and pleasing circumstance. The reader must recollect the capture of the German General Winzengerode before the Kremlin, and the ungenerous manner in which Buonaparte expressed himself to that officer. Winzengerode, with another Russian general, were despatched, under a suitable guard, from Moscow to Wilna, in order to their being sent from thence to Paris, where the presence of two captives of such distinction might somewhat gild the gloomy news which the Emperor was under the necessity of transmitting from Russia. When Winzengerode was prosecuting his melancholy and involuntary journey, far advanced into Poland, and out of all hope either of relief or escape, he saw by the side of a wood a figure, which retreated so suddenly as hardly gave even his experienced eye time to recognise a Cossack's cap and lance. A ray of hope was awakened, which was changed into certainty, as a band of Cossacks, bursting from the wood, overcame the guard, and delivered the prisoners. Czernicheff proceeded successfully on his expedition, embellished by this agreeable incident, and moving eastward with the same speed, sagacity, and successful enterprise, joined Witgenstein's army, then lying between Witepsk and Tchakniki, with communications from the Moldavian army, and directions how Witgenstein was to co-operate with them in the intended plan of cutting off Napoleon's return to Poland.

In virtue of the orders which he had received, Tchitchagoff advanced upon Schwartzenberg, from whom Napoleon might have first expected the service of a covering army, so soon as his broken and diminished troops should approach Poland. But when Tchitchagoff appeared in force, this Franco-Austrian, or rather Austro-Saxon army, was, after some skirmishing, compelled to retire behind the Bug. The admiral left General Sacken, a brave and active officer, to observe Schwartzenberg and Regnier, and keep them at least in check, whilst he himself retrograded towards the Beresina, where he expected to be able to intercept Buonaparte.

Tchitchagoff succeeded, on the 14th November, in occupying Minsk; a most essential conquest at the moment, for it contained a very large proportion of those stores which had been destined to relieve the grand army, or rather its remains, so soon as they should approach Poland. This success was followed by another equally important. Count Lambert, one of Tchitchagoff's generals, marched against Borizoff, situated on the Beresina, at the very point where it was probable that Napoleon would be desirous to effect a passage. The valiant Polish General Dombrowski hastened to defend a place, in the loss of which the Emperor's safety must stand completely compromised. The battle began about daybreak on the 21st November, and, after severe fighting, Lambert obtained possession of Borizoff, after a victory, in which Dombrowski lost eight cannon, and 2500 prisoners. The Admiral Tchitchagoff removed his headquarters thither, as directed by the combined plan for farther operations.

ACTION NEAR WOLKOWITZ

While Tchitchagoff marched eastward to his place of destination on the Beresina, Sacken, whom he had left in Volhynia, sensible of the importance of the service destined for the admiral, made every exertion to draw the whole attention of Schwartzenberg and Regnier upon himself. In this daring and generous scheme he completely succeeded. As the forces of the Austrian and the French generals were separated from each other, Sacken marched against Regnier, and not only surprised, but nearly made him prisoner. Nothing could have saved Regnier from destruction, except the alertness with which Schwartzenberg came to his assistance. The Austrian, with strong reinforcements, arrived nearly in the moment when his presence must have annihilated Sacken, who, not aware of the Austrians being so near, had, on the 15th November, engaged in a serious action with Regnier near Wolkowitz. The Russian suffered considerable loss, and effected a retreat with difficulty. He concentrated his army, however, and continued his retreat from point to point upon the position of Brzest, from which he had commenced his advance. In this manner, Sacken withdrew the attention of Schwartzenberg and the Austro-Saxon army to the banks of the Bug, at a moment when it ought to have been riveted on the decisive scenes which were about to take place on those of the Beresina.[203]

The French writers complain of the Austrian general on this occasion. They cannot deny that Schwartzenberg was active and victorious; but they complain that his activity exerted itself in a quarter which could not greatly affect the issue of the campaign. Some tacticians account for this, by supposing that his secret instructions, given when the Emperor of Austria could not foresee that the personal safety of his son-in-law would be implicated, prohibited Schwartzenberg to extend his military operations beyond Volhynia and Lithuania.

From these details, it appears that Fortune was bending her blackest and most ominous frowns on the favourite of so many years. Napoleon was quartered, with the wretched relics of his grand army, amid the ruins of the burnt town of Smolensk, in which he could not remain, although his means of escape appeared almost utterly desperate.[204] The grand army of the Russians waited on his flank to assault his columns the instant they were in motion; and should he escape a pursuing enemy, all the Polish towns in the front, where supplies had been provided for his relief, had been taken, and the two large armies of Tchitchagoff and Witgenstein lay in position on the Beresina to intercept him. Hemmed in betwixt pursuers, and those who, in sportsman's phrase, were stationed to head him back, destitute of cavalry to oppose the nations of Cossacks which

---

[203] Jomini, tom. iv., p. 193; Twenty-eighth Bulletin of the Grand Army; Ségur, tom. ii., p. 181-202.
[204] "Napoleon arrived at Smolensk on the 9th of November, amidst this scene of desolation. He shut himself up in one of the houses in the New Square, and never quitted it till the 14th, to continue his retreat."—Ségur, tom. ii., p. 178.

infested every motion, and having but little artillery to oppose to that of the Russians, all probability of escape seemed removed to an immeasurable distance.

CHAPTER LXII

Napoleon divides his Army into four Corps, which leave Smolensk on their retreat towards Poland—Cautious proceedings of Koutousoff—The Viceroy's division is attacked by Miloradowitch, and effects a junction with Napoleon at Krasnoi, after severe loss—Koutousoff attacks the French at Krasnoi, but only by a distant cannonade—The division under Davoust is reunited to Napoleon, but in a miserable state—Napoleon marches to Liady; and Mortier and Davoust are attacked, and suffer heavy loss—Details of the retreat of Ney—He crosses the Losmina, with great loss of men and baggage, and joins Napoleon at Orcsa, with his division reduced to 1500 men—The whole Grand Army is now reduced to 12,000 effective men, besides 30,000 stragglers—Dreadful distress and difficulties of Buonaparte and his Army—Singular scene betwixt Napoleon and Duroc and Daru—Napoleon moves towards Borizoff, and falls in with the corps of Victor and Oudinot—Koutousoff halts at Kopyn, without attacking Buonaparte—Napoleon crosses the Beresina at Studzianka—Partouneaux's division cut off by Witgenstein—Severe fighting on both sides of the river—Dreadful losses of the French in crossing it—According to the Russian official account, 36,000 bodies were found in the Beresina after the thaw.

NAPOLEON LEAVES SMOLENSK

Cooped up, as we have said, in the ruins of Smolensk, and the slender provision of food and supplies which that place offered to his army almost entirely exhausted, Napoleon had now seriously to consider in what direction he should make an effort to escape. As he had heard of the loss of Witepsk, by which town he had advanced, and understood that Witgenstein was in possession of the line of the Dwina, he naturally determined to take the road to Wilna, by Krasnoi, Borizoff, and Minsk. The two latter towns were stored with the provisions which he so much wanted; and, ignorant as yet of what had happened on the south of Lithuania, he might expect to find the banks of the Beresina in possession of the Austro-Saxon army under Schwartzenberg.

For this effort he proceeded, as well as circumstances would admit, to re-organise his army. It was reduced to about 40,000 men, with a disproportioned train of baggage and of artillery, although much of the former, and three hundred and fifty cannon, had already been left behind. This force the Emperor divided into four corps, which were to leave Smolensk, placing a day's interval betwixt the march of each. He himself led the van, with 6000 of his Guard, and about as many soldiers, the relics of different corps, amalgamated into battalions as well as circumstances would permit. The Emperor's division left Smolensk on the evening of the 13th and morning of the 14th November.

The division of the Viceroy Eugene, consisting of about the same number as that of Napoleon, but inferior in quality, as comprehending none of the Imperial Guard, could not be collected till late on the 15th November, when the wearied wretches were once more put into march, by promises of a safe arrival in that Lithuania, which so few of them were ever to see again.

On the 16th, Davoust, after some high words with Ney, who would have hurried his departure, set out with another fourth part of the grand army, approaching to, or exceeding 10,000 men in number.

Ney remained till the 17th of November. As he had once more the perilous task of covering the retreat, which duty he had performed so admirably betwixt Wiazma and Smolensk, his division was fortified with about 4000 of the Imperial Guard, to whom, as better fed than the other troops, besides their high character as veterans, more could be trusted even in the most desperate circumstances. Ere the French left the town, they obeyed the strict commands of the Emperor, in blowing up the towers with which Smolensk was surrounded, that it might not again, as Napoleon expressed himself, form an obstacle to a French army. Such was the language of this extraordinary man, as if affecting to provide for re-entering into Russia, at a time when it was the only question whether he himself, or any individual of his army, should ever be able to leave the fatal country.—We must next attend to the motions of the Russians.

The general voice of the Russian army had demanded Prince Golitcheff Koutousoff, as a chief who would put an end to Barclay de Tolly's system of retreat, and oppose the invaders in a pitched battle. He had done so at Borodino, but it was his last effort of the kind. His character was naturally the reverse of enterprising. Age had increased his disposition to extreme prudence, and the success which attended his procrastinating and cautious measures, while stationed at Taroutino, in the neighbourhood of Moscow, had riveted him to his own system, of risking as little as possible. It was in vain pointed out to him, that the Russian troops were in high condition, and that against an enemy so utterly broken and dispirited as the French then were, every thing might be trusted to those brave soldiers, who had not shrunk from an equal conflict with the same troops when in their vigour; and who, if then worsted, had left the enemy very little to boast of, having insulted his camp, and occupied the field of battle, even on the very night of his victory. Could Suwarrow have been recalled from the dead, or even the noble Bagration (the god of the army, as his name signifies in Russian;) or had Barclay de Tolly, Bennigsen, or Miloradowitch, been permitted to act when the moment of action approached, it seems probable that Napoleon would have revisited the Kremlin, not as a conqueror but as a prisoner. But Koutousoff, trusting to the climate of Russia, was contented to let the French army decay under its influence. He had determined not to encounter the slightest risk, but to glean up the wreck of the elements, rather than anticipate their work by the sword. His general plan was to maintain himself on the flank of Napoleon's army, and from time to time to attack them by his vanguard, but by no means to enter into a general action. He surrounded their corps with Cossacks, who brought with them light field-guns mounted on sledges, which did infinite damage on points where the heavy French guns could not be easily pointed, so as to reply to them. This system may be traced in the preceding pages, and still more in those which are about to follow. It has been applauded by many competent judges, as gaining every thing without putting any thing in hazard; but it is ridiculed by others, and especially by the French, who acknowledge themselves obliged to the tardiness of Koutousoff, and the blunders of the Admiral Tchitchagoff, for the escape of the poor remnant of the grand army which was preserved, and especially for the personal safety of the Emperor himself. With these explanations we resume our melancholy and momentous story.[205]

KRASNOI

Without any purpose of departing from his maxims of caution, Koutousoff commenced the attack on the retreating army by a movement which appeared to indicate a more vigorous plan of procedure. He put his army in motion towards Krasnoi, upon a parallel line with that of Buonaparte, moving on the left flank of the French, so as to place Napoleon's line of advance at his mercy, whenever he should think proper to assail it. At the same time, he detached several large bodies to operate on the march of the enemy's column.

Miloradowitch, with a large vanguard, pushed forward upon the high-road leading from Smolensk to Krasnoi. Buonaparte had already reached the latter point, at the head of his division, but Eugene, who brought up the rear of the column, was effectually cut off. They were summoned to lay down their arms, but the viceroy manfully rejected the proposal. Immediately each surrounding hill poured forth, like a volcano, a torrent of fire upon them. The French and Italians maintained their ground with unavailing bravery. Numbers were killed, others made prisoners, and the division almost entirely destroyed.

---

[205] Ségur, tom. ii., p. 220.

Still the viceroy made his defence good, till night, the friend of the overmatched, approached to protect him; when, at the head of his division, diminished to one half, he quitted the high-road, leaving his fires burning to mislead the enemy, and, gaining the open fields, accomplished, with great loss and ineffable fatigue, his junction with Napoleon at Krasnoi, which he reached by a circuitous route. The challenge of a sentinel during this delicate manœuvre might have been utter destruction—and in fact they did encounter such a challenge. They were saved from the consequences by a ready-witted Pole, who, answering the sentinel in Russian, imposed silence on him, pretending that they were the corps of Owaroff, employed upon a secret expedition.

At length, upon the next morning (17th November,) Eugene reached the headquarters of his father-in-law, who had been very anxious on his account. When the diminished division of Eugene was united to that of the Emperor, they did not exceed 15,000 men in total amount. Yet on being joined by Eugene, the active genius of Napoleon, in these most disadvantageous circumstances, displayed its ascendency. He had caused General Roguet, with a detachment of the Young Guard, in the night between the 15th and 16th, to beat up the quarters of a Russian detachment, which approached his own too closely; and having thus taught the hunters to respect the lair of the lion, he embraced the audacious resolution of remaining at Krasnoi in defiance of the Russian army, till the detachments of Davoust and Ney should again join him. Whatever had been his reasons for separating from these divisions, he now saw the necessity of once more uniting his forces.

Even the cold and cautious spirit of Koutousoff could not miss the opportunity occasioned by this halt of 15,000 men, in the face of perhaps three times their number. But neither the persuasions of his own officers, nor the reproaches of Sir Robert Wilson, the English commissioner, could prevail on the old general to attack with the vivacity which the occasion demanded. He would only consent to wage a distant engagement with artillery. At daybreak on the 17th, Eugene, whose forces the preceding battle had altogether disabled, was directed to take the advance towards Liady, the next miserable stage of the French army, while

Buonaparte drew his sword, and saying he had already played the Emperor, and must now once more be the general, led in person his 6000 guards, attended by Mortier at the head of 5000 soldiers more, to meet as great odds as it should please Koutousoff to despatch against him.[206] In the sort of battle which followed, the Russians acted with great caution. The name of Napoleon almost alone protected his army. The French suffered, indeed, from the fire of 100 pieces of artillery, and from charges of cavalry, which they had no means of answering or repelling; but though gaps were made in their line, and some of their squares were forced by the cavalry, yet neither success nor repulse could induce Koutousoff to hazard a serious attack upon Napoleon, for the purpose of altogether destroying the invader and his army. Even Boutourlin, a friendly critic, where the reputation of the old Russian general is concerned, regrets he had not taken the bold course of placing his army across the direct line of Buonaparte's retreat, when the French, overcome at once by physical suffering and moral depression, must, even supposing them equal in numbers, have been extremely inferior to their opponents. Upon the whole, Koutousoff seems to have acted towards Napoleon and the grand army, as the Greenland fishers do to the whale, whom they are careful not to approach in his dying agonies, when pain, fury, and a sense of revenge, render the last struggles of the leviathan peculiarly dangerous.

The battle, or cannonade of Krasnoi, was concluded by the appearance of Davoust and his column, surrounded and followed by a large body of Cossacks, from whom he endeavoured to extricate himself by a precipitate march. When they came in sight of Krasnoi, most of the soldiers, who had been horribly harassed since they left Smolensk, broke their ranks, and hurried across the fields to escape the Russians, and gain the cover of the town, in the streets of which their officers rallied them with difficulty. In this miserable condition

---

[206] Colonel Boutourlin praises the address of Koutousoff, who, he says, managed with such skill as always to present a superior force to that which the French had upon the field of battle, although his army was on the whole inferior to that of Napoleon. Without admitting the exactness of the last statement, which there is considerable cause to dispute, little merit can be assumed for the Russian general's dexterity in obtaining a numerical superiority at Wiazma, Krasnoi, and elsewhere, when it is considered that Napoleon himself had divided his army into four columns, and placed one day's march betwixt each. The Russians had, therefore, only one column of ten or twelve thousand men to deal with at once.—S.

was the third corps of the army, according to its latest division, when it was reunited to the main body. Upon inquiring after Ney and the rear-guard, Napoleon had the mortification to learn that Ney was probably still at Smolensk, or, if upon the road, that he must be surrounded with difficulties out of which it was impossible he could extricate himself.

MARCHES ON LIADY—NEY'S RETREAT

In the meantime, Napoleon learned that the Russians were acting with more vigour, and that Prince Galitzin was about to occupy Krasnoi; and further, that if he did not advance with all despatch on Liady,[207] he might probably find it in possession of the enemy. Gladly as Napoleon would have kept the field, in order to protect the approach of Ney, he now saw that such perseverance must necessarily expose himself and the remnant of his army to the greatest peril, without, in all human probability, being of use to his maréchal. Under this conviction, he put himself at the head of the Old Guard, to march on as fast as possible, and secure Liady, and with it the passage of the Dneiper, from which he might otherwise have been excluded.[208] Davoust and Mortier were left to defend Krasnoi, if practicable, till night-fall, and then to follow under cover of the darkness. The retreat of Napoleon seemed to remove the charm which had chilled the Russians and warmed the French. A very fierce assault was made on the second and third divisions, and Mortier and Ney, having both suffered greatly, made their escape to Liady with much difficulty. The French left on this fatal field forty-five pieces of cannon, upwards of 6000 prisoners, with a great number of slain, and as many wounded, who were necessarily left to

---

[207] "He called Mortier, and squeezing his hand sorrowfully, told him, that he had not a moment to lose; that the enemy were overwhelming him in all directions; that Koutousoff might have already reached Liady, perhaps Orcsa, and the last winding of the Boristhenes before him; that he would, therefore, proceed thither rapidly with his old guard, in order to occupy the passage. Then, with his heart full of Ney's misfortunes, and despair at being forced to abandon him, he withdrew slowly towards Liady."—Ségur, tom. ii., p. 227.

[208] "Napoleon marched on foot at the head of his guard, and often talked of Ney; he called to mind his *coup-d'œil* so accurate and true, his courage proof against every thing, in short all the qualities which made him so brilliant on the field of battle. 'He is lost. Well! I have three hundred millions in the Tuileries; I would give them all if he were restored to me.'"—Rapp, p. 242.

the mercy of the Russians. To complete their losses, Ney's division of the army was, by the direction of the other columns upon Liady, left with the whole Russian army betwixt himself and Napoleon. The retreat of that celebrated soldier must next be narrated.

On the 17th of November, Ney, last of the invading army, left Smolensk at the head of 7 or 8000 fighting men, leaving behind 5000 sick and wounded, and dragging along with them the remaining stragglers whom the cannon of Platoff, who entered the town immediately on Ney's departure, had compelled to resume their march. They advanced without much interruption till they reached the field of battle of Krasnoi, where they saw all the relics of a bloody action, and heaps of dead, from whose dress and appearance they could recognise the different corps in which they had served in Napoleon's army, though there was no one to tell the fate of the survivors. They had not proceeded much farther beyond this fatal spot, when they approached the banks of the Losmina, where all had been prepared at leisure for their reception. Miloradowitch lay here at the head of a great force; and a thick mist, which covered the ground, occasioned Ney's column to advance under the Russian batteries before being aware of the danger.

A single Russian officer appeared, and invited Ney to capitulate. "A Maréchal of France never surrenders," answered that intrepid general. The officer retired, and the Russian batteries opened a fire of grape-shot, at the distance of only 250 yards, while at the concussion the mist arose, and showed the devoted column of French, with a ravine in front manned by their enemies, subjected on every side to a fire of artillery, while the hills were black with the Russian troops placed to support their guns. Far from losing heart in so perilous a situation, the French Guards, with rare intrepidity, forced their way through the ravine of the Losmina, and rushed with the utmost fury on the Russian batteries. They were, however, charged in their turn with the bayonet, and such as had crossed the stream suffered dreadfully. In spite of this failure, Ney persevered in the attempt to cut his passage by main force through this superior body of Russians, who lay opposed to him in front. Again the French advanced upon the cannon, losing whole ranks, which were supplied by their comrades as fast as they fell. The assault was once more unsuccessful, and Ney, seeing that the general fate of his column was no longer doubtful, endeavoured at least to save a part from the wreck. Having selected about 4000 of the best men, he separated himself from the rest, and set forth under shelter of the night, moving to the rear, as if about to return to Smolensk. This, indeed, was the only road open to him, but he did not pursue it long; for as soon as he reached a rivulet, which had the appearance of being one of the feeders of the Dnieper, he adopted it for his guide to the banks of that river, which he reached in safety near the village of Syrokovenia. Here he found a single place in the river frozen over, though the ice was so thin that it bent beneath the steps of the soldiers.

Three hours were permitted, to allow stragglers from the column during the night-march to rally at this place, should their good fortune enable them to find it. These three hours Ney spent in profound sleep, lying on the banks of the river, and wrapped up in his cloak. When the stipulated time had elapsed, the passage to the other side began and continued, although the motion of the ice, and the awful sound of its splitting into large cracks, prevented more than one from crossing at once. The waggons, some loaded with sick and wounded, last attempted to pass; but the ice broke with them, and the heavy plunge and stifled moaning, apprised their companions of their fate. The Cossacks, as usual, speedily appeared in the rear, gleaned up some hundreds of prisoners, and took possession of the artillery and baggage.

Ney had thus put the Dnieper betwixt him and the regulars of the Russian army, by a retreat which has few parallels in military history. But he had not escaped the Cossacks, who were spread abroad over the face of the country, and soon assembled around the remains of his column, with their light artillery and long lances. By these enemies they were several times placed in the utmost jeopardy; nevertheless, at the head of a reduced band of 1500 men, the maréchal fought his way to Orcsa, to which town Napoleon had removed from Liady, having crossed the Dnieper. Ney arrived on the 20th November, and found Eugene, Mortier, and Davoust. The Emperor was two leagues in advance when they met. Napoleon hailed Ney with the undisputed title, the Bravest of the Brave, and declared he would have given all his treasures to be assured of his existence.[209] His comrades hastened to welcome and to relieve him, and being now in Poland, provisions and accommodation had become more plenty among them.[210]

JUNCTION OF THE GRAND ARMY—BORIZOFF

All Napoleon's grand army was now united. But the whole, which had at Smolensk amounted to 40,000, consisted now of scarcely 12,000 men who retained the name and discipline of soldiers, so much had want and the sword thinned the ranks of these invincible legions. There were besides, perhaps 30,000 stragglers of every description, but these added little or nothing to the strength of the army; and only served to encumber its numbers, as they were under no discipline, but plundered the country without mercy.

At this dreadful crisis, too, Napoleon had the mortification to learn the fall of Minsk, and the retreat of Schwartzenberg to cover Warsaw, which, of course, left him no hopes of receiving succour from the Austrians. He heard also that Victor and Oudinot had quarrelled in what manner Witgenstein should be attacked, and had on that account left him unattacked on any point. That general was therefore at freedom to threaten the left of the grand army, should it remain long on the Dnieper; while Koutousoff might resume, at his pleasure, his old station on Napoleon's left, and Tchitchagoff might occupy the Beresina in his front. In the bitterness of his heart the Emperor exclaimed, "Thus it befalls, when we commit faults upon faults."[211]

Minsk being out of the question, Napoleon's next point of direction was Borizoff. Here there was, over the Beresina, a bridge of 300 fathoms in length, the possession of which appeared essential

---

[209] "When Napoleon heard that Ney had just reappeared, he leaped and shouted for joy, and exclaimed, 'I have then saved my eagles! I would have given three hundred millions from my treasury sooner than have lost such a man.'"—Ségur, tom. ii., p. 268; Jomini, tom. iv., p. 190.
[210] Jomini, tom. iv., p. 189; Ségur, tom. ii., pp. 245-266.
[211] Ségur, tom. ii., p. 279.

to his final escape from Russia. But while Napoleon was considering what should be his next movement, after crossing the Beresina at Borizoff, he was once more surprised with the additional evil tidings, that this town also, with the bridge so necessary to him, was lost; that Borizoff was taken, as formerly mentioned, and Dombrowski defeated under its walls. "Is it then written," he said, looking upwards and striking the earth with his cane, "Is it written, that we shall commit nothing but errors!"

About the same gloomy period, Ségur relates the following anecdote:—Napoleon had stretched himself on a couch, and apparently slumbered, while his faithful servants, Duroc and Daru, sitting in his apartment, talked over their critical situation. In their whispered conversation, the words "prisoner of state," reached the sleepless ear of Napoleon. "How!" said he, raising himself, "do you think they would dare?"—In answer, Daru mentioned the phrase, well known to the Emperor, of state policy, as a thing independent of public law or of morality. "But France," said the Emperor, to whom state policy sounded at present less pleasantly than when it was appealed to for deciding some great movement of his own—"what will France say?"—"Who can answer that question, Sire?" continued Duroc; but added, "it was his warmest wish that the Emperor, at least, could reach France, were it through the air, if earth were stopped against his passage."—"Then I am in your way, I suppose?" said the Emperor. The reply was affirmative. "And you," continued the Emperor, with an affectation of treating the matter lightly, "have no wish to become a prisoner of state?"—"To be a prisoner of war is sufficient for me," said Daru. Napoleon was silent for a time; then asked if the reports of his ministers were burnt.—"Not yet," was the reply.—"Then let them be destroyed," he continued; "for it must be confessed we are in a most lamentable condition."[212]

---

[212] "Napoleon's confidence increased with his peril; in his eyes, and in the midst of these deserts of mud and ice, that handful of men was always the grand army! and himself the conqueror of Europe! and there was no infatuation in this firmness: we were certain of it, when, in this very town, we saw him burning with his own hands every thing belonging to him which might serve as trophies to the enemy, in the event of his fall. There also were unfortunately consumed all the papers which he had collected in order to write the history of his life; for such was his intention when he set out for that fatal war. He had then

This was the strongest sign he had yet given, of Napoleon's deep feeling of the situation to which he had reduced himself. In studying the map, to discover the fittest place to pass the Beresina, he approached his finger to the country of the Cossacks, and was heard to murmur, "Ah, Charles XII.; Pultawa." But these were only the momentary ejaculations dictated by a sense of his condition; all his resolutions were calmly and firmly taken, with a sense of what was due to himself and to his followers.[213]

It was finally determined, that, in despite of Tchitchagoff and his army, which occupied the left bank, the passage of the Beresina should be attempted, at a place above Borizoff called Studzianka, where the stream was only fifty-five fathoms across, and six feet deep. There were heights, it is true, on the opposite bank, surrounding a piece of meadow ground, and these the adventurers must look to find strongly occupied; so that those who adventured on the passage must expect to land in that marshy meadow, under a heavy fire from that position. Lastly, this perilous attempt must, in all probability, be made in the very teeth of the Moldavian army. With Napoleon's ten or twelve thousand fighting men, and twice or three times the number of disorderly stragglers, the attempt to force such a passage would have been utter insanity. But the star of Napoleon had not yet set.

SUCCESS OF VICTOR AND OUDINOT

The first dawn of reviving fortune was marked by the success of Victor and Oudinot. They were advancing with the hope of saving Borizoff, when they received intelligence that Dombrowski was routed by Witgenstein, and that the fragments of the Polish corps were close at hand, followed by the victorious Russians. Oudinot instantly gathered the scattered Poles under his protection, and moving on to meet the Russian advanced guard, they drove

---

determined to halt as a threatening conqueror on the borders of the Dwina and the Boristhenes, to which he now returned as a disarmed fugitive. At that time he regarded the ennui of six winter months, which he would have been detained on these rivers as his greatest enemy; and to overcome it, this second Cæsar intended there to have dictated his Commentaries."—Ségur, tom. ii., p. 235.
[213] Ségur, tom. ii., p. 278.

them back with considerable loss. Witgenstein, in consequence of this check, found himself obliged to abandon Borizoff, and once more to place the Beresina betwixt himself and the French. But in repassing that river, he took care to destroy the bridge at Borizoff, so that the town, though secured by the French, was no longer useful to them as a place of passage, and the Emperor, when he learned the news, was still compelled to abide by the plan of crossing, as he best could, at Studzianka. The task was rendered more easy, by the prospect of his scattered and broken army being reinforced by the troops of Victor and Oudinot, who were on the same side of the fatal river with himself, and might form an immediate junction with him.

Meantime, as a preparation for the march, the Emperor limited all the officers, even of the highest rank, to one carriage; and ordered one half of the waggons to be destroyed, that all the horses and draught-oxen might be applied to getting forward the ammunition and artillery. There is reason to think these commands were very imperfectly obeyed. Another order, marking strongly the exigencies of the time, respected such officers as still retained their horses. The cavalry, under Latour Maubourg, had, since leaving Smolensk, been reduced from 1800 to 150. To supply this deficiency, about 500 officers, all who remained mounted, were formed into a body called the Sacred Squadron, to attend upon the Emperor's person. Grouchy and Sebastiani had the command of this body, in which officers formed the privates, and generals of division served as captains. But it was not long ere fatigue and want of forage, no respecters of rank or condition, dismounted the greater part of the Sacred Squadron.[214]

The army thus in some small degree re-organised, and refreshed by the better quarters and nourishment which they had received since the battle of Krasnoi, now plunged into the immense pine forests which conceal the course of the Beresina, to disguise their adventurous march the more completely from the enemy. They were moving towards Borizoff, when loud shouts from the forest at first spread confusion among their ranks, under the idea of an unexpected attack; but this fear was soon changed into joy, when

---

[214] Ségur, tom. ii., p. 282.

they found themselves on the point of uniting with the army of Victor and Oudinot, amounting to 50,000 men, complete and provided with every thing. Yet whatever the joy on the part of the grand army, it was at least equalled by the astonishment of their comrades, when they recognised the remains of the innumerable host which had left them in such splendid equipment, and now returned in the guise, and with the gait and manner, of spectres raised from a churchyard. They filed past their happier comrades with squalid countenances, their uniform replaced by women's pelisses, or what various rags each could pick up; their feet bare and bleeding, or protected by bundles of filthy rags instead of shoes. All discipline seemed gone; the officer gave no command, the soldier obeyed none. A sense of common danger led them to keep together and to struggle forward, and mutual fatigue made them take repose by the same fires; but what else they had learned of discipline was practised rather by instinct than by duty, and in many cases was altogether forgotten.[215]

The army of the two Maréchals, however, though scarce recovered from their astonishment, joined the ranks of the grand army, and, as if disorder had been infectious, very soon showed a disposition to get rid of that military discipline, which their new associates had flung aside.—Leaving Napoleon on his advance to the river, it is now necessary to notice the motions of the Russians.

The glory and the trophies of the march of the grand army had been enough entirely to satisfy Koutousoff. They were indeed sufficient to gorge such a limited ambition as that general might be supposed to possess at his advanced age, when men are usually more bent on saving than on winning. From the 15th to the 19th November, the Russians had obtained possession of 228 guns, had made 26,000 prisoners, of whom 300 were officers, besides 10,000 men slain in battle, or destroyed by fatigue. Satisfied with such advantages, the cautious veteran proceeded by short journeys to Kopyn, on the Dnieper, without crossing that river, or attempting to second the defence of the Beresina by an attack on the rear of the enemy.

---

[215] Ségur, tom. ii., p. 283.

It is true, that the Russian army had sustained great losses; not less, it was said, than 30,000 sick and wounded, were for the present unable to serve, although the greater part of them afterwards recovered. It is no less true, that the Russian soldiers suffered greatly from want of hospitals, being unprovided for a struggle on such an extensive scale as Napoleon's invasion gave rise to. Nor can it be denied that Koutousoff's minute attention to the proper providing of his army with all necessaries was highly laudable. Yet we must still be of opinion, that an object so important as the capture of Buonaparte and the destruction of his army, would have vindicated, even if the soldier himself had been appealed to, two or three forced marches, with the hardships attending them. Such, however, was not Koutousoff's opinion; he halted at Kopyn, and contented himself with despatching his Cossacks and light troops to annoy Napoleon's rear.

STUDZIANKA

The danger not being pressing on the part of the grand army of Russia, Napoleon had only to apprehend the opposition of Tchitchagoff, whose army, about 35,000 men in all, was posted along the Beresina to oppose the passage of Buonaparte wherever it should be attempted. Unfortunately, the admiral was one of an ordinary description of people, who, having once determined in their own mind, that an adversary entertains a particular design, proceed to act upon that belief as an absolute certainty, and can rarely be brought to reason on the possibility of his having any other purpose. Thus, taking it for granted that Napoleon's attempt to cross the Beresina would take place *below* Borizoff, Tchitchagoff could not be persuaded that the passage might be as well essayed *above* that town. Napoleon, by various inquiries and reports transmitted through the Jews, who, for money, served as spies on both sides, contrived to strengthen Tchitchagoff in the belief that he was only designing a feint upon Studzianka, in order to withdraw the attention of the Russians from the Lower Beresina. Never was a stratagem more successful.[216]

On the very day when Napoleon prepared for the passage at Studzianka, Tchitchagoff, instead of noticing what was going forward above Borizoff, not only marched down the river with all the forces under his own immediate command, but issued orders to the division of Tschaplitz, which amounted to six thousand men, and at present watched the very spot where Napoleon meant to erect his bridges, to leave that position, and follow him in the same direction. These were the very orders which Buonaparte would have dictated to the Russian leader, if he had had his choice.

When the French arrived at Studzianka, their first business was to prepare two bridges, a work which was attended with much danger and difficulty. They laboured by night, expecting in the morning to be saluted with a cannonade from the Russian detachment under Tschaplitz, which occupied the heights already mentioned, on the opposite bank. The French generals, and particularly Murat, considered the peril as so eminent, that they wished Buonaparte to commit himself to the faith of some Poles who knew the country, and leave the army to their fate; but Napoleon rejected the proposal as unworthy of him.[217] All night the French laboured at the bridges, which were yet but little advanced, and might have been easily demolished by the artillery of the Russians. But what was the joy and surprise of the French to see,

---

[216] "The Emperor came out from his barrack, cast his eyes on the other side of the river. 'I have outwitted the admiral' (he could not pronounce the name Tchitchagoff;) 'he believes me to be at the point where I ordered the false attack; he is running to Borizoff.' His eyes sparkled with joy and impatience; he urged the erection of the bridges, and mounted twenty pieces of cannon in battery. These were commanded by a brave officer with a wooden leg, called Brechtel; a ball carried it off during the action, and knocked him down. 'Look,' he said, to one of his gunners, 'for another leg in waggon, No. 5.' He fitted it on, and continued his firing."—Rapp, p. 246.

[217] "Ney took me apart: he said to me in German, 'Our situation is unparalleled; if Napoleon extricates himself to-day, he must have the devil in him.' We were very uneasy, and there was sufficient cause. Murat came to us, and was not less solicitous. 'I have proposed to Napoleon,' he observed to us, 'to save himself, and cross the river at a few leagues distance from hence. I have some Poles who would answer for his safety, and would conduct him to Wilna, but he rejects the proposal, and will not even hear it mentioned. As for me, I do not think we can escape.' We were all three of the same opinion."—Rapp, p. 245.

with the earliest beams of the morning, that artillery, and those Russians in full march, retreating from their position! Availing himself of their disappearance, Buonaparte threw across a body of men who swam their horses over the river, with each a voltigeur behind him. Thus a footing was gained on the other bank of this perilous stream. Great part of Victor's army had moved up the river towards Studzianka, while the last division lay still at Borizoff, of which town that maréchal had possession. This constituted a rearguard to protect the army of Napoleon during the critical moment of its passage, from the interruption which might be expected from the corps of Witgenstein.

During the 26th and 27th, Napoleon pushed troops across the river, those of Oudinot forming the advance; and was soon so secure, that Tschaplitz, discovering his error, and moving back to regain his important position at Studzianka, found the French too strongly posted on the left bank of the Beresina, for his regaining the opportunity which he had lost. He halted, therefore, at Stakhowa, and waited for reinforcements and orders. Meanwhile, the passage of the Beresina continued, slowly indeed, for the number of stragglers and the quantity of baggage was immense; yet by noon Napoleon and his guards had crossed the river.[218] Victor, whose division constituted the rear-guard of the grand army, had relieved the Imperial Guards in their post on the left bank; and Partouneaux, who formed the rear of the whole army, was moving from Borizoff, where he had been stationed with the purpose of fixing the enemy's attention upon the spot. No sooner had he left the town than it was again in the hands of the Russians, being instantly occupied by Platoff.

But the indefatigable Witgenstein was in motion on the left bank, pressing forward as Victor closed up towards Napoleon; and, throwing himself betwixt Studzianka and Borizoff, on a plain called Staroi-Borizoff, he cut off Partouneaux's division from the rest of the French army. That general made a gallant resistance, and attempted to force his way at the sword's point through the troops

---

[218] "When Napoleon saw them fairly in possession of the opposite bank, he exclaimed, 'Behold my star again appear!' for he was a strong believer in fatality,"—Ségur, tom. ii., p. 295.

opposed to him. At length the Hettman Platoff, and the Russian partisan Seslawin, coming up, the French general found himself entirely overpowered, and after a brave resistance laid down his arms. Three generals, with artillery, and according to the Russian accounts, about 7000 men, fell into the hands of the Russians—a prize the more valuable, as the prisoners belonged chiefly to the unbroken and unexhausted division of Victor, and comprehended 800 fine cavalry in good order.[219]

PASSAGE OF THE BERESINA

To improve this advantage, the Russians threw a bridge of pontoons across the Beresina at Borizoff, and Tchitchagoff and Witgenstein having communicated, resolved on a joint attack upon both banks of the river at once. With this purpose, upon the 28th of November, Admiral Tchitchagoff moved to Stakhowa, upon the right bank, to reinforce Tschaplitz, and assault that part of the French army which had crossed the Beresina; and Witgenstein with Platoff marched towards Studzianka, to destroy the Emperor's rear-guard, which no exertion on the part of Napoleon or his generals had yet been able to get across the river. Thus, the extraordinary good fortune of finding a place of passage, and of being enabled by an uncommon chance to complete his bridges without opposition, was so far from placing Napoleon in safety, that his dangers seemed only to multiply around him. But yet upon his side of the river, now the right bank, his own presence of mind, and the bravery of his soldiers, gave him a decided superiority, and the tardiness, to say the least, of Tchitchagoff's motions, insured his safety.

Tschaplitz, who seems to have been a brave and active officer, commenced the battle by advancing from Stakhowa. But he was worsted by the French, who were superior in numbers, and he received no succours from the admiral, though repeatedly

---

[219] "Napoleon was deeply affected with so unexpected a misfortune—'Must this loss come to spoil all after having escaped as by a miracle, and having completely beaten the Russians.'"—Rapp, p. 246.

demanded.[220] In this manner were the French enabled to force their way towards a village called Brelowau, through deep morasses, and over long bridges or railways, formed of the trunks of pine-trees, where a bold attack might have rendered their advance impossible. The least exertion on the part of Tchitchagoff might have caused these bridges to be burnt; and as combustibles were laid ready for the purpose, it required but, according to Ségur's expression, a spark from the pipe of a Cossack, to have set them on fire. The destruction of this railway, enclosing the French between the morass and the river, must have rendered the passage of the Beresina entirely useless. But it was not so decreed; and the French, under Oudinot, were enabled to preserve the means of a movement so essential to their safety. Meanwhile, the scene on the left bank had become the wildest and most horrible which war can exhibit.

On the heights of Studzianka, Victor, who commanded the French rear-guard, amounting perhaps to 8000 or 10,000 men, was prepared to cover the retreat over the bridges. The right of this corps d'armée rested on the river; a ravine full of bushes covered their front, but the left wing had no point of support. It remained, according to the military phrase, *in the air*, and was covered by two regiments of cavalry. Behind this defensive line were many thousands of stragglers, mingled with the usual followers of a camp, and with all those individuals who, accompanying, for various reasons, the French from Moscow, had survived the horrors of the march. Women, children, domestics, the aged and the infants, were seen among the wretched mass, and wandered by the side of this fatal river, like the fabled spectres which throng the banks of the infernal Styx, and seek in vain for passage. The want of order, which it was impossible to preserve, the breaking of the bridges, and the time spent in the repair—the fears of the unhappy wretches to trust themselves to the dangerous and crowded passages, had all operated to detain them on the right bank. The baggage, which, in spite of the quantity already lost, of the difficulty of transportation, and of Napoleon's precise orders, amounted still to a very great number of carts, wains, and the like, and which was now augmented by all that

---

[220] The conduct of the admiral was so unaccountable on this occasion, that some attempted to explain it on his naval habits, and to suppose that he was prevented from sending the reinforcements by the wind being contrary.—S.

belonged to the troops of Oudinot and Victor, was seen, some filing towards the bridges, and the greater part standing in confusion upon the shore. The artillery itself, such as remained, was in no better state.

Such was the condition of matters at the bridge, when Witgenstein, warm from his victory over Partouneaux, marching down the left bank of the Beresina, engaged in a fierce combat with the rear-guard under Victor; and the balls of the Russians began to fall among the mingled and disordered mass which we have endeavoured to describe. It was then that the whole body of stragglers and fugitives rushed like distracted beings towards the bridges, every feeling of prudence or humanity swallowed up by the animal instinct of self-preservation. The horrible scene of disorder was augmented by the desperate violence of those who, determined to make their own way at all risks, threw down and trampled upon whatever came in their road. The weak and helpless either shrunk back from the fray, and sat down to wait their fate at a distance, or, mixing in it, were thrust over the bridges, crushed under carriages, cut down perhaps with sabres, or trampled to death under the feet of their countrymen. All this while the action continued with fury, and, as if the Heavens meant to match their wrath with that of man, a hurricane arose, and added terrors to a scene which was already of a character so dreadful.

DREADFUL LOSSES OF THE FRENCH

About mid-day the French, still bravely resisting, began to lose ground. The Russians, coming gradually up in strength, succeeded in forcing the ravine, and compelling them to assume a position nearer the bridges. About the same time, the larger bridge, that constructed for artillery and heavy carriages, broke down, and multitudes were forced into the water. The scream of mortal agony, which arose from the despairing multitude, became at this crisis for a moment so universal, that it rose shrilly audible over the noise of the elements and the thunders of war, above the wild whistling of the tempest, and the sustained and redoubled hourras of the Cossacks. The witness from whom we have this information, declares that the sound was in his ears for many weeks. This dreadful scene continued till dark, many being forced into the icy river, some throwing themselves in, betwixt absolute despair, and the faint hope of gaining the opposite bank by swimming, some getting across only to die of cold and exhaustion. As the obscurity came on, Victor, with the remainder of his troops, which was much reduced, quitted the station he had defended so bravely, and led them in their turn across. All night the miscellaneous multitude continued to throng along the bridge, under the fire of the Russian artillery, to whom, even in the darkness, the noise which accompanied their march made them a distinct mark. At daybreak, the French engineer, General Eblé, finally set fire to the bridge. All that remained on the other side, including many prisoners, and a great quantity of guns and baggage, became the prisoners and the prey of the Russians. The amount of the French loss was never exactly known; but the Russian report, concerning the bodies of the invaders which were collected and burnt as soon as the thaw permitted, states that upwards of 36,000 were found in the Beresina.[221]

---

[221] Ségur, tom. ii., p. 317; Jomini, tom. iv., p. 195.

Chapter LXIII

Napoleon determines to return to Paris—He leaves Smorgoni on 5th December—reaches Warsaw on the 10th—Curious Interview with the Abbé de Pradt—Arrives at Dresden on the 14th—and at Paris on the 18th, at midnight—Dreadful State of the Grand Army, when left by Napoleon—Arrive at Wilna, whence they are driven by the Cossacks, directing their flight upon Kowno—Dissensions among the French Generals—Cautious Policy of the Austrians under Schwartzenberg—Precarious state of Macdonald—He retreats upon Tilsit—D'Yorck separates his Troops from the French—Macdonald effects his retreat to Königsberg—Close of the Russian expedition, with a loss on the part of the French of 450,000 Men in Killed and Prisoners—Discussion of the Causes which led to this ruinous Catastrophe.

When the army of Buonaparte was assembled on the other side of the Beresina, they exhibited symptoms of total disorganisation. The village of Brilowau, where they halted on the night of their passage, was entirely pulled down, that the materials might supply camp-fires; and a considerable part of Buonaparte's headquarters was included in the same fate, his own apartment being with difficulty saved from the soldiery. They could scarcely be blamed for this want of discipline, for the night was deadly cold; and of the wet and shivering wretches who had been immersed in the icy river, many laid their heads down never to raise them more.

On the 29th November, the Emperor left the fatal banks of the Beresina, at the head of an army more disorganised than ever; for few of Oudinot's corps, and scarcely any belonging to Victor's, who were yet remaining, were able to resist the general contagion of disorder. They pushed on without any regular disposition, having no more vanguard, centre, or rear, than can be ascribed to a flock of sheep. To outstrip the Russians was their only desire, and yet numbers were daily surprised by the partisans and Cossacks. Most fortunately for Napoleon, the precaution of the Duke of Bassano had despatched to the banks of the Beresina a division of French, commanded by General Maison, who were sufficient to form a rear-guard, and to protect this disorderly and defenceless mass of fugitives. Thus they reached Malodeczno on the 3d December.[222]

Here Buonaparte opened to his chief confidants his resolution to leave the army, and push forward to Paris. The late conspiracy of Mallet had convinced him of the necessity of his presence there.[223] His remaining with an army, which scarce had existence in a military sense, could be of no use. He was near Prussia, where, from reluctant allies, the inhabitants were likely to be changed into bitter enemies. He was conscious of what he had meditated against the King of Prussia, had he returned victorious, and judged from his own purposes the part which Frederick was likely to adopt, in consequence of this great reverse in his fortunes.

This resolution being adopted, Napoleon announced that preparations for his departure should be made at Smorgoni, intending to remain at Malodeczno till he should be joined by General Maison with the rear-guard, which was left a day's march behind the main body. He now waited until it should close up with him. They came at last, but with Tschaplitz and the Russians at their heels. Intense cold (the thermometer being twenty degrees below zero) prevented any thing more than skirmishes between them.

SMORGONI—SETS OUT FOR PARIS

On the 5th December, Buonaparte was at Smorgoni, where he again received a welcome reinforcement, being joined by Loison,

---

[222] "For a long time we had had no news from France; we were ignorant of what was going on in the grand duchy; we were informed of it at Malodeczno. Napoleon received nineteen despatches at once."—Rapp, p. 249.
[223] The reader will find the details of this singular attempt in the succeeding chapter.

advancing at the head of the garrison of Wilna, to protect his retreat to that place, and whose opportune assistance gave a new rearguard, to supply that commanded by Maison, which the war and weather had already rendered as incapable of effectual service as those whom they had protected from the banks of the Beresina to Smorgoni. Loison had orders to take in his turn this destructive duty, for which purpose he was to remain a day's march, as usual, behind the mass of what had been the army.

The order of the march to Wilna thus arranged, Napoleon determined on his own departure. Three sledges were provided; one of which was prepared to carry him and Caulaincourt, whose title the Emperor proposed to assume while travelling incognito, although their figures were strikingly dissimilar, the Duke of Vicenza being a tall, raw-boned, stiff-looking man. In a general audience, at which were present the King of Naples, the viceroy, Berthier, and the maréchals, Napoleon announced to them that he had left Murat to command the army, as generalissimo. He talked to them in terms of hope and confidence. He promised to check the Austrians and Prussians in their disposition for war, by presenting himself at the head of the French nation, and 1,200,000 men;—he said he had ordered Ney to Wilna, to re-organise the army, and to strike such a blow as should discourage the advance of the Russians;—lastly, he assured them of winter-quarters beyond the Niemen. He then took an affectionate and individual farewell of each of his generals, and, stepping into his traineau, a lively emblem of the fishing-boat of Xerxes, he departed from Smorgoni at the late hour of ten at night.[224]

With what feelings this extraordinary man left the remains of the army, we have no means even of guessing. His outward bearing, during his extreme distresses, had been in general that of the utmost firmness; so that such expressions of grief or irritation, as at times broke from him, were picked up and registered by those who heard

---

[224] "Napoleon passed through the crowd of his officers, who were drawn up in an avenue as he passed, bidding them adieu merely by forced and melancholy smiles; their good wishes, equally silent, and expressed only by respectful gestures, he carried with him. He and Caulaincourt shut themselves up in a carriage; his Mameluke and Wakasowitch, captain of his guard, occupied the box; Duroc and Lobau followed in a sledge."—Ségur, tom. ii., p. 337.

them, as curious instances of departure from his usual state of composure. To preserve his tranquillity, he permitted no details to be given him of the want and misery with which he was surrounded. Thus, when Colonel d'Albignac brought news of Ney's distresses, after the battle of Wiazma, he stopped his mouth by saying sharply, "He desired to know no particulars." It was of a piece with this resolution, that he always gave out orders as if the whole Imperial army had existed in its various divisions, after two-thirds had been destroyed, and the remainder reduced to an undisciplined mob. "Would you deprive me of my tranquillity?" he said angrily to an officer, who thought it necessary to dwell on the actual circumstances of the army, when some orders, expressed in this manner, had been issued. And when the persevering functionary persisted to explain—thinking, perhaps, in his simplicity, that Napoleon did not know that which in fact he only was reluctant to dwell upon—he reiterated angrily, "I ask you, sir, why you would deprive me of my tranquillity?"[225]

It is evident, that Napoleon must have known the condition of his army as well as any one around him; but, to admit that he was acquainted with that which he could not remedy, would have been acknowledging a want of power inconsistent with the character of one, who would willingly be thought rather the controller than the subject of Fate. Napoleon was none of those princes mentioned by Horace, who, in poverty and exile, lay aside their titles of majesty, and language of authority. The headquarters of Smorgoni, and the residences of Porto Ferrajo and Saint Helena, can alike bear witness to the tenacity with which he clung not only to power, but to the forms and circumstance attendant upon sovereignty, at periods when the essence of that sovereignty was either endangered or lost. A deeper glance into his real feelings may be obtained from the report of the Abbé de Pradt, which is well worth transcribing.[226]

After narrowly escaping being taken by the Russian partisan Seslawin, at a hamlet called Youpranoui, Napoleon reached Warsaw upon the 10th December. Here the Abbé de Pradt, then minister of France to the Diet of Poland, was in the act of endeavouring to

---

[225] Ségur, tom. ii., p. 320.
[226] Histoire de l'Ambassade dans le Grand Duché de Varsovi, en 1812, p. 207.

reconcile the various rumours which poured in from every quarter, when a figure like a spectre, wrapped in furs, which were stiffened by hoar-frost, stalked into his apartments, supported by a domestic, and was with difficulty recognised by the ambassador as the Duke of Vicenza.

INTERVIEW WITH DE PRADT

"You here, Caulaincourt?" said the astonished prelate.—"And where is the Emperor?"—"At the hôtel d'Angleterre, waiting for you."—"Why not stop at the palace?"—"He travels incognito."—"Do you need any thing?"—"Some Burgundy or Malaga."—"All is at your service—but whither are you travelling?"—"To Paris."—"To Paris! But where is the army?"—"It exists no longer," said Caulaincourt, looking upwards.—"And the victory of the Beresina—and the 6000 prisoners?"[227]—"We got across, that is all—the prisoners were a few hundred men, who have escaped. We have had other business than to guard them."

His curiosity thus far satisfied, the Abbé de Pradt hastened to the hotel. In the yard stood three sledges in a dilapidated condition. One for the Emperor and Caulaincourt, the second for two officers of rank, the third for the Mameluke Rustan and another domestic. He was introduced with some mystery into a bad inn's bad room, where a servant wench was blowing a fire made of green wood. Here was the Emperor, whom the Abbé de Pradt had last seen when he played King of Kings among the assembled sovereigns of Dresden. He was dressed in a green pelisse, covered with lace and lined with furs, and, by walking briskly about the apartment, was endeavouring to obtain the warmth which the chimney refused. He saluted "Monsieur l'Ambassadeur," as he termed him, with gaiety. The abbé felt a movement of sensibility, to which he was disposed to give way, but, as he says, "The poor man did not understand me." He limited his expressions of devotion, therefore, to helping Napoleon off with his cloak. To us, it seems that Napoleon repelled the effusions of the Bishop of Maline's interest, because he did not

---

[227] This alludes to exaggerated reports circulated by Marat, Duke of Bassano, then residing at Wilna, of a pretended victory obtained by Napoleon, at the passage at Studzianka.—S.

choose to be the object either of his interest or his pity. He heard from his minister, that the minds of the inhabitants of the grand duchy had been much changed since they had been led to despair of the regeneration of their country; and that they were already, since they could not be free Polanders, studying how to reconcile themselves with their former governors of Prussia. The entrance of two Polish ministers checked the ambassador's communications. The conversation was maintained from that moment by Napoleon alone; or rather he indulged in a monologue, turning upon the sense he entertained that the failure of his Russian expedition would diminish his reputation, while he struggled against the painful conviction, by numbering up the plans by which he might repair his losses, and alleging the natural obstacles to which he had been obliged to succumb. "We must levy 10,000 Poles," he said, "and check the advance of these Russians. A lance and a horse are all that is necessary.—There is but a single step betwixt the sublime and the ridiculous."[228] The functionaries congratulated him on his escape from so many dangers. "Dangers!" he replied; "none in the world. I live in agitation. The more I bustle the better I am. It is for Kings of Cockaigne to fatten in their palaces—horseback and the fields are for me.—From the sublime to the ridiculous there is but a single step—Why do I find you so much alarmed here?"

"We are at a loss to gather the truth of the news about the army."

"Bah!" replied the Emperor; "the army is in a superb condition. I have 120,000 men—I have beat the Russians in every action—they are no longer the soldiers of Friedland and Eylau. The army will recruit at Wilna—I am going to bring up 300,000 men—Success will render the Russians fool-hardy—I will give them battle twice or thrice upon the Oder, and in a month I will be again on the Niemen—I have more weight when on my throne, than at the head of my army.—Certainly I quit my soldiers with regret; but I must watch Austria and Prussia, and I have more weight seated on my throne than at the head of my army. All that has happened goes for nothing—a mere misfortune, in which the enemy can claim no merit—I beat them every where—they wished to cut me off at the

---

[228] "Du sublime au ridicule il n'y a qu'un pas?"

Beresina—I made a fool of that ass of an admiral"—(He could never pronounce the name Tchitchagoff)—"I had good troops and cannon—the position was superb—500 toises of marsh—a river"——This he repeated twice, then run over the distinction in the 29th bulletin between men of strong and feeble minds, and proceeded. "I have seen worse affairs than this—At Marengo I was beaten till six o'clock in the evening—next day I was master of Italy—At Essling, that archduke tried to stop me—He published something or other—My army had already advanced a league and a half—I did not even condescend to make any disposition. All the world knows how such things are managed when I am in the field. I could not help the Danube rising sixteen feet in one night—Ah! without that, there would have been an end of the Austrian monarchy. But it was written in Heaven that I should marry an archduchess." (This was said with an air of much gaiety.) "In the same manner, in Russia, I could not prevent its freezing. They told me every morning that I had lost 10,000 horses during the night. Well, farewell to you!" He bade them adieu five or six times in the course of the harangue, but always returned to the subject. "Our Norman horses are less hardy than those of the Russians—they sink under ten degrees of cold (beneath zero.) It is the same with the men. Look at the Bavarians; there is not one left. Perhaps it may be said that I stopped too long at Moscow; that may be true, but the weather was fine—the winter came on prematurely—besides, I expected peace. On the 5th October, I sent Lauriston to treat. I thought of going to St. Petersburgh, and I had time enough to have done so, or to have gone to the south of Russia, or to Smolensk. Well, we will make head at Wilna; Murat is left there. Ha, ha, ha! It is a great political game. Nothing venture, nothing win—It is but one step from the sublime to the ludicrous. The Russians have shown they have character—their Emperor is beloved by his people—they have clouds of Cossacks—it is something to have such a kingdom—the peasants of the crown love their government—the nobility are all mounted on horseback. They proposed to me to set the slaves at liberty, but that I would not consent to—they would have massacred every one. I made regular war upon the Emperor Alexander, but who could have expected such a blow as the burning of Moscow? Now they would lay it on us, but it was in fact themselves who did it. That sacrifice would have done honour to ancient Rome."

He returned to his favourite purpose of checking the Russians, who had just annihilated his grand army, by raising a large body of Polish lancers, to whom, as things stood, it would have been difficult to have proposed any adequate motive for exertion. The fire went out, and the counsellors listened in frozen despair, while, keeping himself warm by walking up and down, and by his own energies, the Emperor went on with his monologue; now betraying, in spite of himself, feelings and sentiments which he would have concealed; now dwelling upon that which he wished others to believe; and often repeating, as the burden of his harangue, the aphorism which he has rendered immortal, concerning the vicinity of the sublime and the ludicrous.

His passage through Silesia being mentioned, he answered in a doubtful tone, "Ha, Prussia?" as if questioning the security of that route. At length he decided to depart in good earnest; cut short the respectful wishes for the preservation of his health with the brief assurance, that he "could not be in better health were the very devil in him;" and threw himself into the humble sledge which carried Cæsar and his fortunes. The horses sprung forward, nearly overturning the carriage as it crossed the courtyard gate, and disappeared in the darkness. Such is the lively account of the Abbé de Pradt, who declares solemnly, that on taxing his memory to the utmost, he accuses himself of neither want of accuracy nor forgetfulness. Napoleon does not deny that such a long conversation took place, but alleges that the abbé has caricatured it. In the meanwhile, he said he scratched an order for Monsieur l'Ambassadeur to return immediately to Paris;[229] which, considering what had happened in Russia, and was about to happen in Poland, could not but be a most welcome mandate, especially as it was likely to be soon enforced by the lances of the Cossacks.

---

[229] "He certainly had a long conversation with me, which he misrepresents, as might be expected; and it was at the very moment when he was delivering a long prosing speech, which appeared to me a mere string of absurdity and impertinence, that I scrawled on the corner of the chimney-piece the order to withdraw him from his embassy, and to send him as soon as possible to France; a circumstance which was the cause of a good deal of merriment at the time, and which the abbé seems very desirous of concealing."—Napoleon, *Las Cases*, tom. ii., p. 94.

NAPOLEON LEAVES WARSAW

Napoleon continued to pass on with as much speed as possible. He said, when at St. Helena, that he was nigh being arrested in Silesia.[230] "But the Prussians," he said, "passed the time in consulting which they ought to have employed in action. They acted like the Saxons, of whom Charles XII. said gaily, when he left Dresden, 'They will be deliberating to-day whether they should have arrested me yesterday.'" If such an idea was entertained by any one, it may have been by some of the Tugend-Bund, who might think it no crime to seize on one who made universal liberty his spoil. But we do not believe that Frederick ever harboured the thought, while he continued in alliance with France.

Meanwhile, Napoleon continued his journey in secrecy, and with rapidity. On the 14th December he was at Dresden, where he had a long private conference with the good old King, who did not feel his gratitude to the Emperor, as a benefactor, abated by his accumulated misfortunes. The interview—how different from their last—was held in the hotel where Buonaparte alighted, and where Augustus came to visit him incognito. On the 18th, in the evening, he arrived at Paris, where the city had been for two days agitated by the circulation of the Twenty-ninth Bulletin, in which the veil, though with a reluctant hand, was raised up to show the disasters of the Russian war.

It may not be thought minute to mention, that Napoleon and his attendant had difficulty in procuring admittance to the Tuileries at so late an hour. The Empress had retired to her private apartment. Two figures muffled in furs entered the anteroom, and one of them directed his course to the door of the Empress's sleeping chamber. The lady in waiting hastened to throw herself betwixt the intruder and the entrance, but, recognising the Emperor, she shrieked aloud, and alarmed Maria Louisa, who entered the anteroom. Their meeting was extremely affectionate, and showed,

---

[230] "In Silesia, Napoleon was very nearly taken prisoner by the Prussians; and at Dresden, he only escaped a plot for his seizure, because Lord Walpole, who was at Vienna, dared not give the signal."—Fouché, tom. ii., p. 117.

that, amidst all his late losses, Napoleon had still domestic happiness within his reach.

DREADFUL STATE OF GRAND ARMY

We return to the grand army, or rather to the assemblage of those who had once belonged to it, for of an army it had scarce the semblance left. The soldiers of the Imperial Guard, who had hitherto made it their pride to preserve some degree of discipline, would, after the departure of Napoleon, give obedience to no one else. Murat, to whom the chief command had been delegated, seemed scarcely to use it, nor when he did was he obeyed. If Ney, and some of the Maréchals, still retained authority, they were only attended to from habit, or because the instinct of discipline revived when the actual battle drew near. They could not, however, have offered any effectual defence, nor could they have escaped actual slaughter and dispersion, had it not been for Loison's troops, who continued to form the rear-guard, and who, never having been on the eastern side of the fatal Beresina, had, amid great suffering, still preserved sufficient discipline to keep their ranks, behave like soldiers, and make themselves be respected, not only by the Cossacks, but by Tschaplitz, Witgenstein, and the Russians detached from the main army, who followed them close, and annoyed them constantly. The division of Loison remained like a shield, to protect the disorderly retreat of the main body.

Still, some degree of order is so essential to human society, that, even in that disorganised mass, the stragglers, which now comprehended almost the whole army, divided into little bands, who assisted each other, and had sometimes the aid of a miserable horse, which, when it fell down under the burden of what they had piled on it, was torn to pieces and eaten, while life was yet palpitating in its veins. These bands had chiefs selected from among themselves. But this species of union, though advantageous on the whole, led to particular evils. Those associated into such a fraternity, would communicate to none save those of their own party, a mouthful of rye-dough, which, seasoned with gunpowder for want of salt, and eaten with a bouillé of horse-flesh, formed the best part of their food. Neither would they permit a stranger to warm himself at their fires, and when spoil was found, two of these companies often, especially if of different countries, fought for the possession of it; and a handful of meal was a sufficient temptation for putting to death the wretch who could not defend his booty. The prisoners, it is said (and we heartily wish the fact could be refuted,) were parked every night, without receiving any victuals whatever, and perished, like impounded cattle, from want of food, cold, and the delirious fury which such treatment inspired. Among these unfortunates some became cannibals, and the same horrible reproach has been cast on the French themselves.[231]

To enhance misfortunes so dreadful, the cold, which had been for some time endurable, increased on the 6th December to the most bitter degree of frost, being twenty-seven or twenty-eight degrees below zero. Many dropped down and expired in silence, the blood of others was determined to the head by the want of circulation; it gushed at length from eyes and mouth, and the wretches sunk down on the gory snow, and were relieved by death. At the night bivouacs, the soldiers approached their frozen limbs to the fire so closely, that, falling asleep in that posture, their feet were scorched to the bone, while their hair was frozen to the ground. In this condition they were often found by the Cossacks, and happy were those upon whom the pursuers bestowed a thrust with the lance to finish their misery. Other horrors there were, which are better left in silence. Enough has been said to show, that such a calamity, in such an extent, never before darkened the pages of history. In this horrible retreat, 20,000 recruits had joined the army since crossing the Beresina, where, including the corps of Oudinot and Victor, they amounted to 80,000 men. But of this sum of 80,000 men, one-half perished betwixt the Beresina and the walls of Wilna.[232]

In such a plight did the army arrive at Wilna, where great provision had been made for their reception. The magazines were groaning with plenty, but, as at Smolensk, the administrators and commissioners, terrified for their own responsibility, dared not issue

---

[231] Ségur, tom. ii., p. 341.
[232] Ségur, tom. ii., p. 351.

provisions to a disorderly mob, who could neither produce authority for drawing rations, nor give a regular receipt. The famished wretches fell down in the streets before the magazines, and died there, cursing with their latest breath the ill-timed punctiliousness of office, which refused to starving men the morsel that might have saved their lives. In other places of the town, stores both of provision and liquor were broken open by the desperate soldiery, plundered and wasted. Numbers became intoxicated, and to those, as they sunk down in the street, death came before sobriety. The sick who went to the hospitals found them crowded, not only with the dying, but with the dead, whose corpses were left to freeze or to putrefy on the stairs and in the corridors, and sometimes in the apartments of those who yet survived. Such were the comforts of Wilna, from which so much had been hoped.

Still, however, some of the citizens, moved by pity or terror, or from desire of gain (for many soldiers had still about their persons some remnants of the spoils of Moscow,) were willing to give lodging and food to these exhausted phantoms, who begged such relief sometimes with furious threats and imprecations, sometimes in the plaintive tone of men ready to perish. Distributions began also to be made at the public stores; and men who for long had not eat a morsel of bread, or reposed themselves upon any better lair than the frozen earth, or under any other canopy save that of the snow-fraught sky, deemed it Paradise to enjoy the most common household comforts, of which we think so little while we enjoy them, yet are miserable when they are abridged or withdrawn. Some wept for joy at receiving an ordinary loaf of bread, and finding themselves at liberty to eat it, seated, and under a roof.

On a sudden the repast, which seemed earnest of a return to safety and to social life, was disturbed by a distant cannonade, which came nigher and nigher—then by the fire of musketry—at length by their own drums beating to arms in the streets. Every alarm was in vain; even the Imperial Guard no longer attended to the summons. The soldiers were weary of their lives, and it seemed as if they would have been contented to perish like the Jews in the wilderness, with their food betwixt their teeth. At length the distant hourra, and the nearer cry of Cossacks! Cossacks! which for some time had been their most available signal for marching, compelled them to tear themselves from their refreshment, and rush into the street. There they found their rear-guard and Loison, although they had been reinforced by the body of Bavarians commanded by Wrede, who had been left on the verge of Volhynia, hurrying into the town in disorder like men defeated, and learned that they had been driven back by Witgenstein, with Platoff and other partisan leaders, who had followed them up to the gates.

WILNA—KOWNO

Wilna, besides the immense magazines belonging to the French army, contained a vast deposit of wealth and property, which had been left there in the advance upon Moscow, and, in particular, a quantity of treasure belonging to Napoleon. The town, though open, might have been made good till the magazines were destroyed and the baggage removed; but such was the confusion of the moment, that the Russians forced their way into the town by one access, whilst the French left it by another, directing their flight upon Kowno, with the most valuable part of their baggage, or such as could be most speedily harnessed. The inhabitants of the town, the lower orders that is, and particularly the Jews, now thought of propitiating the victors by butchering the wretches whom they had received into their houses; or, at best, stripping and thrusting them naked into the streets. For this inhumanity the Jews are said to have been afterwards punished by the Russians, who caused several of them to be hanged.

Meanwhile, the flying column had attained a hill and defile, called Ponari, when the carriages became entangled, and at length one of the treasure-waggons being overturned, burst, and discovered its contents. All shadow of discipline was then lost; and, as if to anticipate the Russians, the French soldiers themselves fell upon the baggage, broke open the wains, and appropriated their contents. The Cossacks rode up during the fray, and so rich was the booty, that even they were content to plunder in company, suspending for the instant their national animosity, where there seemed wealth enough for all, and no time to lose in fighting. Yet it is said that the privates of the Imperial Guard displayed a rare example of honour and discipline. The Count de Turenne, having beaten off the Cossacks who pressed in, distributed the private treasure of Napoleon among his guard, the individuals of which afterwards restored them. "Not a single piece of money," says Ségur, "was lost." This, however, must be partly imagination; for many of the guard fell after this, and the Cossacks, who became their executors, could have had little idea of making restitution.

It is not worth while to trace further the flight of this miserable body of wanderers. They arrived at length at Kowno, the last town of Russian Poland, Ney alone endeavouring to give them some military direction and assistance, while they were at every instant deserting him and themselves. At Kowno, it seems that about 1000 men were still under arms, about twenty times that number in total dispersion. The pursuit of the Russians appeared to cease after the fugitives had recrossed the Niemen on the ice; they did not choose to push the war into Prussia.

At Gumbinnen, the remaining maréchals and commanders held a council, in which Murat gave way to the stifled resentment he had long entertained against his brother-in-law. He had been displeased with Napoleon, for not severely repressing the insolence with which, as he conceived, he had been treated by Davoust, and at another time by Ney; and he openly inveighed against his relative as a madman, upon whose word no reliance was to be placed. In these moments of anger and mutiny, Murat blamed himself for rejecting the proposals of the English. Had he not done so, he said, he might still have been a great king, like the sovereigns of Austria and Russia. "These kings," answered Davoust, bitterly, "are monarchs by the grace of God, by the sanction of time, and the course of custom. But you—you are only a king by the grace of Napoleon, and through the blood of Frenchmen. You are grossly ungrateful, and as such I will denounce you to the Emperor."[233] Such was this strange scene, of which the maréchals were silent witnesses. It served to show how little unity there was in their councils when the Master Spirit ceased to preside among them.

---

[233] Ségur, tom. ii., p. 371.

From Gumbinnen the French went to show their miseries at Königsberg. Every where they were coldly, yet not coarsely, treated by the Prussians, who had before felt their oppression, but did not consider them in their present state as becoming objects of vengeance. At Königsberg they learnt the fate of their two extreme wings, which was of a nature to close all hopes.

On the right of the French original line of advance, Schwartzenberg had no sooner learned that the Emperor was totally defeated, and his army irretrievably dispersed, than, in the quality of a mere auxiliary, he thought himself no longer entitled to hazard a single Austrian life in the quarrel. There was an armistice concluded between the Austrians and Russians, by the terms of which they agreed to manœuvre as at a game of chess, but not to fight. Thus, when the Russians should gain such a position, as in actual war would have given them an advantage, the Austrians were under the engagement to retreat; and the campaign resembled nothing so much as a pacific field-day, in which two generals in the same service venture upon a trial of skill. Schwartzenberg, by his manœuvres, protected the French corps under Regnier as long as possible, obtained good terms for Warsaw, and gained for Regnier three days advantage, when at last he ceased to cover the place. Having thus protected his allies to the last, he retired into the Austrian territories; and although Regnier was finally overtaken and surprised at Khalish, it could not be imputed to Schwartzenberg's desertion of him, but to his own making too long a halt to protect some Polish depôts. The relics of Regnier's army, such at least as fled into the Austrian territories, were well received there, and afterwards restored to their own banners. Still the alliance with Austria, which in one sense had cost Napoleon so dear, was now dissolved, and his right wing totally dissipated by the defection of his allies. On the left wing matters had no better, or rather, they had a much worse appearance.

PRECARIOUS STATE OF MACDONALD

During the eventful six months of the Russian campaign, Macdonald, who commanded the left wing, had remained in

Courland, with an army of about 30,000 men, of whom 22,000 were Prussians, the rest Germans of different countries. It would seem that Napoleon had been averse from the beginning to employ these unwilling auxiliaries upon any service where their defection might influence the other parts of his army. Yet they behaved well upon several occasions, when Macdonald had occasion to repel the attacks and sallies of the numerous garrison of Riga, and their active exertions enabled him to save the park of heavy artillery destined for the siege of that place, which had almost fallen into the hands of the Russian general Lewis, at Mittau, on the 29th of September. But on this occasion, though having every reason to be pleased with the soldiers, Macdonald saw room to suspect their leader, D'Yorck, of coldness to the French cause. That officer was, indeed, engaged in a service which at heart he detested. He was one of the Tugend-Bund, so often mentioned, an ardent Prussian patriot, and eager to free his native country from a foreign yoke. He therefore eagerly watched for a plausible opportunity when he might, without dishonour, disunite his forces from those of the French maréchal.

About the beginning of December, the situation of Macdonald became precarious. Nothing was heard on every side, save of the rout and disasters of the French grand army, and the maréchal anxiously expected orders for a retreat while it was yet open to him. But such was the confusion at the headquarters after the Emperor's departure, that neither Murat nor Berthier thought of sending the necessary authority to Macdonald; and when they did, though the order to retreat might have reached him in five days, it was ten days on the road.

He commenced his retreat upon Tilsit, his vanguard consisting of Massenbach's Prussian division, chiefly cavalry, he himself following with the Bavarians, Saxons, &c., and D'Yorck bringing up the rear with 15,000 Prussians, the residue of that auxiliary army. In this order, with the Prussians divided into two corps, and his own posted between them, as if to secure against their combining, the maréchal marched on in sufficient anxiety, but without complaint on his side, or difficulties on that of the Prussian general. But when the maréchal, upon 28th January, arrived at Tilsit, which was in the line of their retreat, and had sent forward the cavalry of Massenbach as far as Regnitz, the troops of D'Yorck in the rear had detached themselves so far that Macdonald was obliged to halt for them. He sent letters to D'Yorck, pressing him to come up—he sent to the cavalry of Massenbach in the van, commanding them to return. From D'Yorck came no answer. At Regnitz, the French general, Bachelu, who had been sent to act as adjutant-general with Massenbach's corps, could find no obedience. The colonels of the Prussian cavalry objected to the weather, and the state of the roads; they would not give the order to sound to horse; and when the horses were at length reluctantly ordered out and produced, the soldiers were equally restive, they would not mount. While the Prussian troops were in this state of mutiny, a Russian emissary was heard to press them to deliver up the Frenchman; but the soldiers, though resolved to leave Bachelu, would not betray him. The proposal shocked their feelings of honour, and they mounted and marched back to Tilsit, to restore Bachelu to Macdonald's army. But their purpose was unchanged. As at Regnitz they had refused to mount their horses, so at Tilsit they refused to alight. At length they were prevailed upon to dismount and retire to their quarters, but it was only a feint; for, shortly after they were supposed asleep, the Prussians mounted in great silence, and, with Massenbach and their officers at their head, marched off to join their countrymen under D'Yorck.

That general had, now and for ever, separated his troops from the French. Upon 30th December, he had concluded an armistice with the Russian general, Dibbeitsch. By this agreement, the Prussian troops were to be cantoned in their own territories, and remain neutral for two months; at the end of that period, if their king so determined, they should be at liberty to rejoin the French troops. Both D'Yorck and Massenbach wrote to Macdonald, announcing their secession from his army. D'Yorck contented himself with stating, that he cared not what opinion the world might form on his conduct, it was dictated by the purest motives—his duty to his troops and to his country. Massenbach expressed his respect and esteem for General Macdonald, and declared, that his reason for leaving him without an interview, was the fear he felt that his personal regard for the Maréchal might have prevented his obeying the call of duty.

Thus did a Prussian general first set the example of deserting the cause in which he served so unwillingly—an example which soon spread fast and far. It was a choice of difficulties on D'Yorck's side, for his zeal as a patriot was in some degree placed in opposition to the usual ideas of soldierly honour. But he had not left Macdonald till the Maréchal's safety, and that of the remainder of his army, was in some measure provided for. He was out of the Russian territory, and free, or nearly so, from Russian pursuit. D'Yorck had become neutral, but not the enemy or his late commander.

Here the question arises, how long were the Prussians to be held bound to sacrifice their blood for the foreigners, by whom they had been conquered, pillaged, and oppressed; and to what extent were they bound to endure adversity for those who had uniformly trampled on them during their prosperity? One thing, we believe, we may affirm with certainty, namely, that D'Yorck acted entirely on his own responsibility, and without any encouragement, direct or indirect, from his sovereign. Nay, there is room to suppose, that though the armistice of Taurogen was afterwards declared good service by the King of Prussia, yet D'Yorck was not entirely forgiven by his prince for having entered into it. It was one of the numerous cases, in which a subject's departing from the letter of the sovereign's command, although for that sovereign's more effectual service, is still a line of conduct less grateful than implicit obedience. Upon receiving the news, Frederick disavowed the conduct of his general, and appointed Massenbach and him to be sent to Berlin for trial. But the officers retained their authority, for the Prussian army and people considered their sovereign as acting under the restraint of the French troops under Augereau, who then occupied his capital.

Macdonald, with the remains of his army, reduced to about 9000 men, accomplished his retreat to Königsberg after a sharp skirmish.

CLOSE OF THE RUSSIAN EXPEDITION

And thus ended the memorable Russian expedition, the first of Napoleon's undertakings in which he was utterly defeated, and of which we scarce know whether most to wonder at the daring audacity of the attempt, or the terrific catastrophe. The loss of the grand army was total, and the results are probably correctly stated by Boutourlin as follows:—

Slain in battle,	125,000
Died from fatigue, hunger, and the severity of the climate,	132,000
Prisoners, comprehending 48 generals, 3000 officers, and upwards of 190,000 men,	193,000
Total,	450,000

The relics of the troops which escaped from that overwhelming disaster, independent of the two auxiliary armies of Austrians and Prussians, who were never much engaged in its terrors, might be about 40,000 men, of whom scarcely 10,000 were Frenchmen.[234] The Russians, notwithstanding the care that was taken to destroy these trophies, took seventy-five eagles, colours, or standards, and upwards of 900 pieces of cannon.

Thus had the greatest military captain of the age, at the head of an innumerable array, rushed upon his gigantic adversary, defeated his army, and destroyed, or been the cause of the destruction of his capital, only to place himself in a situation where the ruin of nearly the whole of his own force, without even the intervention of a general action, became the indispensable price of his safe return.

---

[234] "Of 400,000 men in arms, who had crossed the Niemen, scarcely 30,000 repassed that river five months afterwards, and of those two-thirds had not seen the Kremlin."—Fouché, tom. ii., p. 118.

CAUSES OF THE CATASTROPHE

The causes of this total and calamitous failure lay in miscalculations, both moral and physical, which were involved in the first concoction of the enterprise, and began to operate from its very commencement. We are aware that this is, with the idolaters of Napoleon, an unpalatable view of the case. They believe, according to the doctrine which he himself promulgated, that he could be conquered by the elements alone. This was what he averred in the twenty-ninth bulletin. Till the 6th November he stated that he had been uniformly successful. The snow then fell, and in six days destroyed the character of the army, depressed their courage, elated that of the "despicable" Cossacks, deprived the French of artillery, baggage, and cavalry, and reduced them, with little aid from the Russians, to the melancholy state in which they returned to Poland. This opinion Napoleon wished to perpetuate in a medal, on which the retreat from Moscow is represented by the figure of Eolus blowing upon the soldiers, who are shown shrinking from the storm, or falling under it. The same statement he always supported; and it is one of those tenets which his extravagant admirers are least willing to relinquish.

Three questions, however, remain to be examined ere we can subscribe to this doctrine.—I. Does the mere fall of snow, nay, a march through a country covered with it, necessarily, and of itself, infer the extent of misfortune here attributed to its agency?—II. Was not the possibility of such a storm a contingency which ought in reason to have entered into Napoleon's calculations?—III. Was it the mere severity of the snow-storm, dreadful as it was, which occasioned the destruction of Buonaparte's army; or, did not the effects of climate rather come in to aid various causes of ruin, which were inherent in this extravagant expedition from the very beginning, and were operating actively, when the weather merely came to their assistance?

On the first question it is needless to say much. A snow, accompanied with hard frost, is not necessarily destructive to a retreating army. The weaker individuals must perish, but, to the army, it affords, if they are provided for the season, better opportunities of moving than rainy and open weather. In the snow, hard frozen upon the surface, as it is in Russia and Canada, the whole face of the country becomes a road; and an army, lightly equipped, and having sledges instead of wains, may move in as many parallel columns as they will, instead of being confined, as in moist weather, to one high-road, along which the divisions must follow each other in succession. Such an extension of the front, by multiplying the number of marching columns, must be particularly convenient to an army which, like that of Napoleon, is obliged to maintain itself as much as possible at the expense of the country. Where there are only prolonged columns, following each other over the same roads, the marauders from the first body must exhaust the country on each side; so that the corps which follow must send their purveyors beyond the ground which has been already pillaged, until at length the distance becomes so great, that the rearward must satisfy themselves with gleaning after the wasteful harvest of those who have preceded them. Supposing six, eight, or ten columns marching in parallel lines upon the same front, and leaving an interval betwixt each, they will cover six, eight, or ten times the breadth of country, and of course supply themselves more plentifully, as well as much more easily. Such columns, keeping a parallel front, can, if attacked, receive reciprocal aid by lateral movements more easily than when assistance must be sent from the van to the rear of one long moving line; and the march being lateral on such occasions, does not infer the loss of time, and other inconveniences inferred by a counter-march from the front to support the rear. Lastly, the frost often renders bridges unnecessary, fills ravines, and makes morasses passable; thus compensating, in some degree, to a marching army, for the rigorous temperature to which it subjects them.

But, 2dly, It may be asked, if frost and snow are so irresistible and destructive in Russia, as to infer the destruction of whole armies, why did not these casualties enter into the calculations of so great a general entering on such an immense undertaking? Does it never snow in Russia, or is frost a rare phenomenon there in the month of November? It is said that the cold weather began earlier than usual. This, we are assured, was not the case; but, at any rate, it was most unwise to suffer the safety of an army, and an army of such numbers and importance, to depend on the mere chance of a frost setting in a few days sooner or later.²³⁵

The fact is, that Napoleon, whose judgment was seldom misled save by the ardour of his wishes, had foreseen, in October, the coming of the frost, as he had been aware, in July, of the necessity of collecting sufficient supplies of food for his army, yet without making adequate provision against what he knew was to happen, in either case. In the 22d bulletin, it is intimated, that the Moskwa, and other rivers of Russia, might be expected to be frozen over about the middle of November, which ought to have prepared the Emperor for the snow and frost commencing five or six days sooner; which actually took place. In the 26th bulletin, the necessity of winter-quarters is admitted, and the Emperor is represented as looking luxuriously around him, to consider whether he should choose them in the south of Russia, or in the friendly country of Poland. The weather is then stated to be fine, "but on the first days of November cold was to be expected. Winter-quarters, therefore, must be thought upon; the cavalry, above all, stand in need of them."

It is impossible that he, under whose eye, or by whose hand, these bulletins were drawn up, could have been surprised by the arrival of snow on the 6th November. It was a probability foreseen, though left unprovided for.

Even the most ordinary precaution, that of rough-shoeing the horses of the cavalry and the draught-horses, was totally neglected; for the bulletins complain of the shoes being smooth. This is saying, in other words, that the animals had not been new-shod at all; for French horses may be termed always rough-shod, until the shoes are grown old and worn smooth through use. If, therefore, frost and

---

²³⁵ "Sir Walter takes great pains to prove that the extraordinary severity of the winter was not the principal cause of this frightful catastrophe. He is facetious about the snow, to which he believes, or pretends to believe, that the twenty-ninth bulletin attributes the disaster; whereas, it was not the snow alone, but a cold of thirty degrees below zero. And have we not often known, in the severe winters of the north of France, where the cold is slight in comparison with that of Russia—travellers to perish under the snow? How then can it be denied that the extreme severity of the winter was the cause of the disaster?"— Louis Buonaparte.

snow be so very dangerous to armies, Napoleon wilfully braved their rigour, and by his want of due preparations, brought upon himself the very disaster of which he complained so heavily.

Thirdly, Though unquestionably the severity of the frost did greatly increase the distress and loss of an army suffering under famine, nakedness, and privations of every kind, yet it was neither the first, nor, in any respect, the principal, cause of their disasters. The reader must keep in remembrance the march through Lithuania, in which, without a blow struck, Napoleon lost 10,000 horses at once, and nearly 100,000 men, when passing through a country which was friendly. Did this loss, which happened in June and July, arise from the premature snow, as it has been called, of the 6th of November? No, surely. It arose from what the bulletin itself describes as "the uncertainty, the distresses, the marches and counter-marches of the troops, their fatigues and sufferances;" to the system, in short, of forced marches, by which, after all, Napoleon was unable to gain any actual advance. This cost him one-fourth, or nearly so, of his army, before a blow was struck. If we suppose that he left on both his flanks, and in his rear, a force of 100,000 men, under Macdonald, Schwartzenberg, Oudinot, and others, he commenced the actual invasion of Russia Proper with 200,000 soldiers. A moiety of this large force perished before he reached Moscow, which he entered at the head of less than 100,000 men. The ranks had been thinned by fatigue, and the fields of battle and hospitals must answer for the remainder. Finally, Napoleon left Moscow on the 19th October, as a place where he could not remain, and yet from which he saw no safe mode of exit. He was then at the head of about 120,000 men; so much was his army recruited by convalescents, the collection of stragglers, and some reserves which had been brought up. He fought the unavailing though most honourably sustained battle of Malo-Yarowslavetz; failed in forcing his way to Kalouga and Toula; and, like a stag at bay, was forced back on the wasted and broken-up road to Smolensk by Borodino. On this road was fought the battle of Wiazma, in which the French loss was very considerable; and his columns were harassed by the Cossacks at every point of their march, and many thousands of prisoners were taken. Two battles so severely fought, besides the defeat of Murat and constant skirmishes, cost the French, in killed and wounded, (and every wounded man was lost to Napoleon,) not less than 25,000 men; and so far had the French army been diminished.

This brought him to the 6th November, until which day not a flake had fallen of that snow to which all his disasters are attributed, but which in fact did not commence until he had in a great measure experienced them. By this time also, his wings and reserves had undergone severe fighting and great loss, without any favourable results. Thus, wellnigh three-fourths of his original army were destroyed, and the remnant reduced to a most melancholy and disorderly condition, before commencement of the storm to which he found it afterwards convenient to impute his calamities. It is scarcely necessary to notice, that when the snow did begin to fall, it found Napoleon not a victor, but a fugitive, quitting ground before his antagonists, and indebted for his safety, not to the timidity of the Russians, but to the over-caution of their general. The Cossacks, long before the snow-tempest commenced, were muttering against Koutousoff for letting these skeletons, as they called the French army, walk back into a bloodless grave.

When the severe frost came, it aggravated greatly the misery, and increased the loss, of the French army. But Winter was only the ally of the Russians; not, as has been contended, their sole protectress. She rendered the retreat of the grand army more calamitous, but it had already been an indispensable measure; and was in the act of being executed at the lance-point of the Cossacks, before the storms of the north contributed to overwhelm the invaders.

What, then, occasioned this most calamitous catastrophe? We venture to reply, that a moral error, or rather a crime, converted Napoleon's wisdom into folly; and that he was misled, by the injustice of his views, into the great political, nay, military errors, which he acted upon in his attempt to realize them.[236]

---

[236] "Sir Walter Scott has not, in this outrage against Napoleon, the merit of novelty: and what is more painful, French writers have been guilty of repeating the ridiculous accusation. What! he who threw himself upon his gigantic adversary at the head of an

We are aware there are many who think that the justice of a quarrel is of little moment, providing the aggressor has strength and courage to make good what his adversary murmurs against as wrong. With such reasoners, the race is uniformly to the swift, and the battle to the strong; and they reply to others with the profane jest of the King of Prussia, that the Deity always espouses the cause of the most powerful. But the maxim is as false as it is impious. Without expecting miracles in this later age, we know that the world is subjected to moral as well as physical laws, and that the breach of the former frequently carries even a temporal punishment along with it. Let us try by this test the conduct of Napoleon in the Russian war.

The causes assigned for his breach with Russia, unjust in their essence, had been put upon a plan of settlement; yet his armies continued to bear down upon the frontiers of the Russian Empire; so that to have given up the questions in dispute, with the French bayonets at his breast, would have been on the part of Alexander a surrender of the national independence. The demands of Napoleon, unjust in themselves, and attempted to be enforced by means of intimidation, it was impossible for a proud people, and a high-spirited prince, to comply with. Thus the first act of Buonaparte went to excite a national feeling, from the banks of the Boristhenes to the wall of China, and to unite against him the wild and uncivilized inhabitants of an extended empire, possessed by a love to their religion, their government, and their country, and having a character of stern devotion, which he was incapable of estimating. It was a remarkable characteristic of Napoleon, that when he had once fixed his opinion, he saw every thing as he wished to see it, and was

---

innumerable army, and conducted it six hundred leagues from his country; who defeated all the armies of his enemy—burned his capital, or was the cause of its destruction—had such a man lost his senses? The expedition to Russia, according to common rules, was ill-judged and rash, and the more so when undertaken without the basis of Poland; and when we consider the formation of the grand army, composed of so many different nations, and that Napoleon persisted in the project in spite of all obstacles, and the disapprobation of the majority of his greatest generals, we are astonished how he succeeded in invading a great portion of the vast territory of Russia, and penetrated as far as the capital of that empire. Whatever his enemies may assert, had it not been for the extraordinary havoc of the winter, the grand army would have returned to the frontiers of Poland, established itself on that line, and menaced the Russian empire anew, and in a more definitive manner, during the following campaign."—Louis Buonaparte, p. 86.

apt to dispute even realities, if they did not coincide with his preconceived ideas. He had persuaded himself, that to beat an army and subdue a capital, was, with the influence of his personal ascendency, all that was necessary to obtain a triumphant peace. He had especially a confidence in his own command over the minds of such as he had been personally intimate with. Alexander's disposition, he believed, was perfectly known to him; and he entertained no doubt, that by beating his army, and taking his capital, he should resume the influence which he had once held over the Russian Emperor, by granting him a peace upon moderate terms, and in which the acknowledgment of the victor's superiority would have been the chief advantage stipulated. For this he hurried on by forced marches, losing so many thousands of men and horses in Lithuania, which an attention to ordinary rules would have saved from destruction. For this, when his own prudence, and that of his council, joined in recommending a halt at Witepsk or at Smolensk, he hurried forward to the fight, and to the capture of the metropolis, which he had flattered himself was to be the signal of peace. His wishes were apparently granted. Borodino, the bloodiest battle of our battling age, was gained—Moscow was taken—but he had totally failed to calculate the effect of these events upon the Russians and their emperor. When he expected their submission, and a ransom for their capital, the city was consumed in his presence; yet even the desertion and destruction of Moscow could not tear the veil from his eyes, or persuade him that the people and their prince would prefer death to disgrace. It was his reluctance to relinquish the visionary hopes which egotism still induced him to nourish, that prevented his quitting Moscow a month earlier than he did. He had no expectation that the mild climate of Fontainbleau would continue to gild the ruins of Moscow till the arrival of December; but he could not forego the flattering belief, that a letter and proposal of pacification must at last fulfil the anticipations which he so ardently entertained. It was only the attack upon Murat that finally dispelled this hope.

Thus a hallucination, for such it may be termed, led this great soldier into a train of conduct, which, as a military critic, he would have been the first to condemn, and which was the natural consequence of his deep moral error. He was hurried by this self-opinion, this ill-founded trust in the predominance of his own personal influence, into a gross neglect of the usual and prescribed rules of war. He put in motion an immense army, too vast in numbers to be supported either by the supplies of the country through which they marched, or by the provisions they could transport along with them. And when, plunging into Russia, he defeated her armies and took her metropolis, he neglected to calculate his line of advance on such an extent of base, as should enable him to consolidate his conquests, and turn to real advantage the victories which he attained. His army was but precariously connected with Lithuania when he was at Moscow, and all communication was soon afterwards entirely destroyed. Thus, one unjust purpose, strongly and passionately entertained, marred the councils of the wise, and rendered vain the exertions of the brave. We may read the moral in the words of Claudian,

"Jam non ad culmina rerum Injustos crevisse queror; tolluntur in altum, Ut lapsu graviore ruant."

Claudian, *in Rufinum*, Lib. i., v. 21.

Chapter LXIV

Effects of Napoleon's return upon the Parisians—Congratulations and addresses by all the public Functionaries—Conspiracy of Mallet—very nearly successful—How at last defeated—The impression made by this event upon Buonaparte—Discussions with the Pope, who is brought to France, but remains inflexible—State of Affairs in Spain—Napoleon's great and successful exertions to recruit his Army—Guards of Honour—In the month of April, the army is raised to 350,000 men, independently of the troops left in garrison in Germany, and in Spain and Italy.

Upon the morning succeeding his return, which was like the sudden appearance of one dropped from the heavens, Paris resounded with the news; which had, such was the force of Napoleon's character, and the habits of subjection to which the Parisians were inured, the effect of giving a new impulse to the whole capital. If the impressions made by the twenty-ninth bulletin could not be effaced, they were carefully concealed. The grumblers suppressed their murmurs, which had begun to be alarming. The mourners dried their tears, or shed them in solitude. The safe return of Napoleon was a sufficient cure for the loss of 500,000 men, and served to assuage the sorrows of as many widows and orphans.[237] The emperor convoked the Council of State. He spoke with apparent frankness of the misfortunes which had befallen his army, and imputed them all to the snow.—"All had gone well," he said; "Moscow was in our power—every obstacle was overcome—the conflagration of the city had produced no change on the flourishing condition of the French army; but winter has been productive of a

---

[237] "This was, on Napoleon's part, a new snare held out to the devotedness and credulity of a generous nation; who, struck with consternation, thought that their chief, chastened by misfortune, was ready to seize the first favourable opportunity of bringing back peace, and of at length consolidating the foundation of general happiness."—Fouché, tom. ii., p. 118.

general calamity, in consequence of which the army had sustained very great losses." One would have thought, from his mode of stating the matter, that the snow had surprised him in the midst of victory, and not in the course of a disastrous and inevitable retreat.

The *Moniteur* was at first silent on the news from Russia, and announced the advent of the Emperor as if he had returned from Fontainbleau; but after an interval of this apparent coldness, like the waters of a river in the thaw, accumulating behind, and at length precipitating themselves over, a barrier of ice, arose the general gratulation of the public functionaries, whose power and profit must stand or fall with the dominion of the Emperor, and whose voices alone were admitted to represent those of the people. The cities of Rome, Florence, Milan, Turin, Hamburgh, Amsterdam, Mayence, and whatever others there were of consequence in the empire, joined in the general asseveration, that the presence of the Emperor alone was all that was necessary to convert disquietude into happiness and tranquillity. The most exaggerated praise of Napoleon's great qualities, the most unlimited devotion to his service, the most implicit confidence in his wisdom, were the theme of these addresses. Their flattery was not only ill-timed, considering the great loss which the country had sustained; but it was so grossly exaggerated in some instances, as to throw ridicule even upon the high talents of the party to whom it was addressed, as daubers are often seen to make a ridiculous caricature of the finest original. In the few circles where criticism on these effusions of loyalty might be whispered, the authors of the addresses were compared to the duped devotee in Molière's comedy, who, instead of sympathizing in his wife's illness, and the general indisposition of his family, only rejoices to hear that Tartuffe is in admirable good health. Yet there were few even among these scoffers who would have dared to stay behind, had they been commanded to attend the Emperor to Notre Dame, that Te Deum might be celebrated for the safe return of Napoleon, though purchased by the total destruction of his great army.

CONSPIRACY OF MALLET

But it was amongst the public offices that the return of the Emperor so unexpectedly, produced the deepest sensation. They were accustomed to go on at a moderate rate with the ordinary routine of duty, while the Emperor was on any expedition; but his return had the sudden effect of the appearance of the master in the school, from which he had been a short time absent. All was bustle, alertness, exertion, and anticipation. On the present occasion, double diligence, or the show of it, was exerted; for all feared, and some with reason, that their conduct on a late event might have incurred the severe censure of the Emperor. We allude to the conspiracy of Mallet, a singular incident, the details of which we have omitted till now.

During Buonaparte's former periods of absence, the government of the interior of France, under the management of Cambacérès, went on in the ordinary course, as methodically, though not so actively, as when Napoleon was at the Tuileries; the system of administration was accurate, that of superintendence not less so. The obligations of the public functionaries were held as strict as those of military men. But during the length of Napoleon's absence on the Russian expedition, a plot was formed, which served to show how little firm was the hold which the system of the Imperial government had on the feelings of the nation, by what slight means its fall might be effected, and how small an interest a new revolution would have excited.[238] It seemed that the Emperor's power showed stately and stable to the eye, like a tall pine-tree, which, while it spreads its shade broad around, and raises its head to heaven, cannot send its roots, like those of the oak, deep into the

---

[238] "I shall make two observations on this passage: 1st, I am persuaded that this conspiracy was the work of the Jacobin faction, who always laid in wait to profit by every favourable occasion. This opinion is confirmed by many of the avowals which escaped Fouché in his memoirs. 2dly, The fallacy of the sentiment attributed by Sir Walter Scott to the notion with respect to Napoleon, is proved by the slight success of this conspiracy, when he was not only absent, but as well as his armies, at so considerable a distance from France; it is also proved by his return from the island of Elba, in the month of March, 1815. I think that all those who would after this deny the attachment of the nation to the Emperor, would also deny the light of day."—Louis Buonaparte, p. 86.

bowels of the earth, but, spreading them along the shallow surface, is liable to be overthrown by the first assault of the whirlwind.

The final purpose of Mallet is not known. He was of noble birth, and served in the Mousquetaires of the royal household before the Revolution, which inclined many to think that he had the interest of the Bourbons in view. As, however, he had risen to the head of chef de brigade in the Republican army, it is more probable that he belonged to the sect of Philadelphes.[239] In 1808, General Mallet was committed to prison, as concerned in an intrigue against the Emperor; and he was still under the restraint of the police, when he formed the audacious scheme which had so nearly succeeded. While under a confinement now lenient, in a Maison de Santé, he was able to execute, or procure to be executed, a forged paper, purporting to be a decree of the Senate, announcing officially the death of the Emperor, the abolition of the Imperial government, and the establishment of a provisional committee of administration. This document was to appearance attested by the official seal and signatures.

On the 22d of October, at midnight, he escaped from his place of confinement, dressed himself in his full uniform, and, accompanied by a corporal in the dress of an aide-de-camp, repaired to the prison of La Force, where he demanded and obtained the liberation of two generals, Lahorie and Guidal, who were confined under circumstances not dissimilar to his own. They went together to the barracks at the Minims, not then inhabited by any part of the truest and most attached followers of Napoleon, who, while his power was tottering at home, were strewing with their bones the snows of Russia and the deserts of Spain, but by battalions of raw conscripts and recruits. Here Mallet assumed an air of absolute

---

[239] "A secret society in the army, whose immediate object it was to overthrow the Imperial power, and whose ultimate purposes were not perhaps known to themselves. Their founder was Colonel Jacques Joseph Odet, a Swiss, at once a debauchee and an enthusiast, on the plan of his countryman Rousseau. He was shot the night before the battle of Wagram, not, as his followers alleged, by a party of Austrians, but by gendarmes, commissioned for that purpose. His sect continued to subsist, and Massena did not escape suspicions of being implicated in its intrigues. There was a communication in their name to Lord Wellington, in May 1809; but the negotiation was not of a character which the British general chose to encourage."—Southey's *Peninsular War*, vol. ii., p. 303.—S.

authority, commanded the drums to beat, ordered the troops on parade, and despatched parties upon different services.

No one disputed his right to be obeyed, and Soulier, commandant of the troops, placed them at his absolute disposal, being partly, as he himself alleged, confused in mind by a fever which afflicted him at the time, partly, perhaps, influenced by a check for 100,000 francs, which was laid down upon his bed, to cover, it was said, a gratuity to the soldiers, and an issue of double pay to the officers. One division seized Savary, the minister of police, and conducted him to prison. Another party found it as easy to arrest the person of the prefect of police. A battalion of soldiers, under the same authority, occupied the place de Grève, and took possession of the hôtel de Ville; while Compte Frochot, who had been for thirteen years the Prefect of the Seine, stupified by the suddenness of the intelligence, and flattered perhaps, by finding his own name in the list of the provisional committee of government, had the complaisance to put the conspirators in possession of the tower of St. Jacques, from which the tocsin was usually sounded, and get an apartment in the hôtel de Ville arranged for the reception of the new administration. But the principal conspirator, like Fiesco at Genoa, perished at the moment when his audacious enterprise seemed about to be crowned with success. Hitherto none had thought of disobeying the pretended decree of the Senate. Rumour had prepared all men for the death of the Emperor, and the subsequent revolution seemed a consequence so natural, that it was readily acquiesced in, and little interest shown on the subject.

But Mallet, who had himself gone to obtain possession of the headquarters in the place Vendôme, was unexpectedly resisted by General Hullin. Prepared for every circumstance, the desperado fired a pistol at the head of the general, and wounded him grievously; but in the meanwhile, he was himself recognised by Laborde, chief of the military police, who, incredulous that his late captive would have been selected by the Senate for the important duty which he was assuming, threw himself on Mallet, and made him prisoner. Thus ended the conspiracy.[240] The soldiers, who had been its blind instruments, were marched back to the barracks.

---

[240] Savary, tom. iii., pp. 13, 32; Fouché, tom. ii., pp. 109, 116.

Mallet, with twenty-four of his associates, most of them military men, were tried by a military tribunal, and twelve of them were shot in the plain of Grenelle, 30th of October. He met his death with the utmost firmness.[241] The sun was rising on the Hospital of Invalids, and the workmen were employed in gilding that splendid dome, for which Buonaparte had given express orders, in imitation, it was said, of those which he had seen in Moscow. The prisoner made some remarks upon the improvement which this would be to the capital. As he stepped towards the fatal ground, he said, mysteriously, but sternly, "You have got the tail, but you will not get the head." From this expression it has been gathered, that, as the conspiracy of the infernal machine, formed originally among the Jacobins, was executed by the Royalists, so this plot was the device of the Royalists, though committed to the execution of republican hands.[242] The truth, though it must be known to some now alive, has never been made public.

This was the news which reached Buonaparte on the fatal 6th of November, betwixt Wiazma and Smolensk, and which determined his retreat from the army at Smorgoni, and his rapid journey to Paris. It was not so much the conspiracy which alarmed him, as the supineness or levity with which the nation, at least Paris, its capital, seemed ready to abandon the dynasty which he had hoped to render perpetual. He was even startled by the number of executions, and exclaimed against the indiscriminate severity with which so many officers had been led to death, although rather dupes than accomplices of the principal conspirator. "It is a massacre," he said; "a fusillade! What impression will it make on France?"

PARIS

When Napoleon reached the metropolis, he found the Parisians as little interested in the execution of the criminals, as they had been in their ephemeral success. But the sting remained in his

---

[241] "Mallet died with great *sang froid*, carrying with him the secret of one of the boldest *coups-de-main* which the grand epocha of our Revolution bequeaths to history."—Fouché, tom. ii., p. 115.
[242] The Memoirs of Fouché contain a specific averment to this effect.—S.

own mind, and on the first audience of his ministers, he exclaimed against ideology, or, in other words, against any doctrine which, appealing to the general feelings of patriotism or of liberty, should resist the indefeasible and divine right of the sovereign. He sounded the praises of Harlai and Molé, ministers of justice, who had died in protecting the rights of the crown; and exclaimed, that the best death would be that of the soldier who falls on the field of battle, if the end of the magistrate, who dies in defence of the throne and laws, was not still more glorious.[243]

This key-note formed an admirable theme for the flourishes of the various counsellors of the sections, to whom the fate of Frochot, the peccant prefect, had been submitted with reference to the extent of his crime and his punishment. Not even the addresses to James II. of Britain (who had at least a hereditary right to the throne he occupied) poured forth such a torrent of professions, or were more indifferently backed with deeds, when the observant courtiers were brought to the proof, than did those of the French functionaries at this period. "What is life," said the Comte de Chabrol, who had been created Prefect of Paris in room of the timorous Frochot—"What is life, in comparison to the immense interests which rest on the sacred head of the heir of the empire? For me, whom an unexpected glance of your Imperial eye has called from a distance to a post so eminent, what I most value in the distinction, is the honour and right of setting the foremost example of loyal devotion."

It was the opinion of M. des Fontanges, senator, peer of France, and grand-master of the Imperial University, that "Reason pauses with respect before the mystery of power and obedience, and abandons all inquiry into its nature to that religion which made the persons of kings sacred, after the image of God himself. It is His voice which humbles anarchy and factions, in proclaiming the divine right of sovereigns; it is the Deity himself who has made it an unalterable maxim of France, an unchangeable article of the law of our fathers; it is Nature who appoints kings to succeed each other, while reason declares that the royalty itself is immutable. Permit, sire," he continued, "that the University of Paris turn their eyes for a

---

[243] Moniteur, Dec. 21, 1812; Fouché, tom. ii., p. 120.

moment from the throne which you fill with so much glory, to the august cradle of the heir of your grandeur. We unite him with your Majesty in the love and respect we owe to both; and swear to him beforehand the same boundless devotion which we owe to your Majesty."

In better taste, because with less affectation of eloquence, M. Seguier, the President of the Court of Paris, contented himself with declaring, that the magistrates of Paris were the surest supports of the Imperial authority—that their predecessors had encountered perils in defence of monarchy, and they in their turn were ready to sacrifice every thing for the sacred person of the Emperor, and for perpetuating his dynasty.

Under cover of these violent protestations, the unfortunate Frochot escaped, as a disabled vessel drops out of the line of battle under fire of her consorts. He was divested of his offices, but permitted to retire, either to prosecute his studies in ideology, or to indoctrinate himself into more deep acquaintance in the mysteries of hereditary right than he had hitherto shown himself possessed of.[244]

We have selected the above examples, not with the purpose of inquiring whether the orators (whom we believe, in their individual capacity, to have been men of honour and talents) did or did not redeem, by their after-exertions, the pledges of which they were so profuse; but to mark with deep reprobation the universal system of assentation and simulation, to which even such men did not disdain to lend countenance and example. By such overstrained flatteries and protestations, counsellors are degraded and princes are misled—truth and sincere advice become nauseous to the ear of the sovereign, falsehood grows familiar to the tongue of the subject, and public danger is not discovered until escape or rescue has become impossible.

Yet it cannot be denied that the universal tenor of these vows and protestations, supported by Buonaparte's sudden arrival and

---

[244] He obtained a pension on the restoration of Louis XVIII., with the title of honorary counsellor, which he had forfeited in July, 1815, in consequence of having accepted, during the Hundred Days, the situation of Prefect of the Bouches-du-Rhone. He died in 1828.

firm attitude, had the effect of suppressing for a time discontents, which were silently making way amongst the French people. The more unthinking were influenced by the tenor of sentiments which seemed to be universal through the empire; and, upon the whole, this universal tide of assentation operated upon the internal doubts, sorrows, discontents, and approaching disaffection of the empire, like an effusion of oil on the surface of a torrent, whose murmurs it may check, and whose bubbling ripples it may smooth to the eye, but the deep and dark energy of whose course the unction cannot in reality check or subdue.

To return to the current of our history. Buonaparte having tried the temper of his Senate, and not finding reason to apprehend any opposition among his subjects, proceeded, while straining every effort, as we shall presently see, for supporting foreign war, to take such means as were in his power for closing domestic wounds, which were the more dangerous that they bled inwardly, without any external effusion to indicate their existence.

The chief of these dissensions was the dispute with the Pope, which had occasioned, and continued to foster, so much scandal in the Gallican Church. We have mentioned already, that the Pope, refusing to consent to any alienation of his secular dominions, had been forcibly carried off from Rome, removed to Grenoble, then brought back over the Alps to Savona, in Italy. Napoleon, who denied that he had authorised this usage towards the father of the Church, yet continued to detain him at Savona. He was confined there until June, 1812. In the meantime, a deputation of the French bishops were sent with a decree by Napoleon, determining, that if his holiness should continue to refuse canonical institution to the French clergy, as he had done ever since the seizure of the city of Rome, and the patrimony of Saint Peter's, a council of prelates should be held for the purpose of pronouncing his deposition.

On 4th September, 1811, the holy father admitted the deputation, listened to their arguments with patience, then knelt down before them, and repeated the psalm, *Judica me, Domine.* When the prelates attempted to vindicate themselves, Pius VII., in an animated tone, threatened to fulminate an excommunication against any one who should attempt to justify his conduct. Then, instantly recovering his natural benignity of disposition, he offered his hand to the offended bishops, who kissed it with reverence. The French prelates took leave sorrowfully, and in tears. Several of them showed themselves afterwards opposed to the views of Napoleon, and sustained imprisonment in consequence of their adhesion to what appeared to them their duty.

The chemists of our time have discovered, that some substances can only be decomposed in particular varieties of gas; and apparently it was, in like manner, found that the air of Italy only confirmed the inflexibility of the Pope.

INTERVIEW WITH PIUS VII

His Holiness was hastily transported to Fontainbleau, where he arrived 19th June, 1812. The French historians boast, that the old man was not thrown into a dungeon, but, on the contrary, was well lodged in the palace, and was permitted to attend mass—a wonderful condescension towards the head of the Catholic religion. But still he was a captive. He abode at Fontainbleau till Napoleon's return from Russia; and it was on the 19th January, 1813, that the Emperor, having left Saint Cloud under pretext of a hunting-party, suddenly presented himself before his venerable prisoner. He exerted all the powers of influence which he possessed, and they were very great, to induce the Pontiff to close with his propositions; and we readily believe that the accounts, which charge him with having maltreated his person, are not only unauthenticated, but positively false.[245] He rendered the submission which he required more easy to the conscience of Pius VII., by not demanding from

---

[245] "I knew Pius the Seventh from the time of his journey to Paris in 1804, and from that period until his death I never ceased to receive from the venerable Pontiff marks, not of benevolence only, but even of confidence and affection. Since the year 1814 I have resided at Rome: I have often had occasion to see him, and I can affirm, that in many of my interviews with his holiness, he assured me that he was treated by Napoleon, in every personal respect, as he could have wished. These are his very words:—'Personalmente non ho avuto di che dolermi; non ho mai mancato di nulla; la mia persona fu sempre rispettata e trattata in modo da non potermi lagnare.' 'I had nothing to complain of personally; I wanted for nothing; my person was always respected, and treated in a way to afford me no ground of complaint.'"—Louis Buonaparte.

him any express cession of his temporal rights, and by granting a delay of six months on the subject of canonical instalment. Eleven articles were agreed on, and subscribed by the Emperor and the Pope.

But hardly was this done ere the feud broke out afresh. It was of importance to Napoleon to have the schism soldered up as soon as possible, since the Pope refused to acknowledge the validity of his second marriage, and, of course, to ratify the legitimacy of his son. He, therefore, published the articles of treaty in the *Moniteur*, as containing a new concordat.[246] The Pope complained of this, stating, that the articles published were not a concordat in themselves, but only the preliminaries, on which, after due consideration, such a treaty might have been formed. He was indignant at what he considered as circumvention on the part of the Emperor of France, and refused to abide by the alleged concordat. Thus failed Napoleon's attempt to close the schism of the Church, and the ecclesiastical feuds recommenced with more acrimony than ever.

Looking towards Spain, Napoleon saw his affairs there in a better posture than he could have expected, after the battle of Salamanca, and the capture of Madrid. Lord Wellington, indifferently supported by the Spanish army, among whom quarrels and jealousies soon rose high, had been unable, from want of a sufficient battering-train, to take the fortress of Burgos; and was placed in some danger of being intercepted by Soult's army, who had raised the siege of Cadiz, while engaged with that under D'Erlon, with whom was the intrusive King. The English general, therefore, with his usual prudence, retreated into the territories of Portugal, and Napoleon, seeing that his army in Spain amounted to 270,000 men, thought them more than sufficient to oppose what forces Spain could present, with the regular allied army of perhaps 70,000 at most, under Lord Wellington's command. He withdrew, accordingly, 150 skeletons of battalions, which he meant to make the means of disciplining his young conscripts.

---

[246] See Moniteur, Feb. 15, 1813.

EXERTIONS TO RECRUIT THE ARMY

It was now that the hundred cohorts, or 100,000 youths of the First Ban of National Guards, who had been placed in frontier garrisons, under the declaration that they were not, under any pretence, to go beyond the limits of France, were converted into ordinary soldiers of the line, and destined to fill up the skeleton corps which were brought from Spain. Four regiments of guards, one of Polish cavalry, and one of gendarmes, were at the same time withdrawn from the Peninsula. The sailors of the French fleet, whose services were now indeed perfectly nominal, were landed, or brought rather from the harbours and maritime towns in which they loitered away their time, and formed into corps of artillery. This reinforcement might comprehend 40,000 men. But while his credit continued with the nation, the conscription was Napoleon's best and never-failing resource, and with the assistance of a decree of the Senate, it once more placed in his hands the anticipation of the year 1814. This decree carried his levies of every kind to 350,000 men.

The remounting and recruiting of the cavalry was a matter of greater difficulty, and to that task was to be joined the restoration of the artillery and *materiel* of the army, all of which had been utterly destroyed in the late fatal retreat. But the vaults under the Tuileries were not yet exhausted, although they had contributed largely to the preparations for the campaign of the preceding year. A profusion of treasure was expended; every artisan, whose skill could be made use of, was set to work; horses were purchased or procured in every direction; and such was the active spirit of Napoleon, and the extent of his resources, that he was able to promise to the Legislative Representatives, that he would, without augmenting the national burdens, provide the sum of three hundred millions of francs, which were wanted to repair the losses of the Russian campaign.

We must not forget, that one of the ways and means of recruiting the cavalry, was a species of conscription of a new invention, and which was calculated to sweep into the ranks of the army the youth of the higher ranks, whom the former draughts had spared, or who had redeemed themselves from the service by finding a substitute. Out of this class, hitherto exempted from the conscription, Napoleon proposed to levy 10,000 youths of the higher ranks, to be formed into four regiments of Guards of Honour, who were to be regarded much as the troops of the royal household under the old system. This idea was encouraged among the courtiers and assentators, who represented the well-born and well-educated youths, as eager to exchange their fowling-pieces for muskets, their shooting-dresses for uniforms, and their rustic life for the toils of war. Politicians saw in it something of a deeper design than the mere adding ten thousand to the mass of recruits, and conceived that this corps of proprietors was proposed with the view of bringing into the Emperor's power a body of hostages, who should guarantee the fidelity of their fathers. The scheme, however, was interrupted, and for a time laid aside, owing to the jealousy of the Imperial Guard. These Prætorian Bands did not relish the introduction of such patrician corps as those proposed, whose privileges they conceived might interfere with their own; and accordingly the institution of the Guard of Honour was for some time suspended.

The wonderful energies of Napoleon's mind, and the influence which he could exert over the minds of others, were never so striking as at this period of his reign. He had returned to his seat of empire at a dreadful crisis, and in a most calamitous condition. His subjects had been ignorant, for six weeks, whether he was dead or alive, and a formidable conspiracy, which was all but successful, had at once shown that there was an awakening activity amongst his secret enemies, and an apathy and indifference amongst his apparent friends. When he arrived, it was to declare a dreadful catastrophe, of which his ambition had been the cause; the loss of 500,000 men, with all their arms, ammunition and artillery; the death of so many children of France as threw the whole country into mourning. He had left behind him cold and involuntary allies, changing fast into foes, and foes, encouraged by his losses and his flight, threatening to combine Europe in one great crusade, having for its object the demolition of his power. No sovereign ever presented himself before his people in a situation more precarious, or overclouded by such calamities, arrived or in prospect.

Yet Napoleon came, and seemed but to stamp on the earth, and armed legions arose at his call; the doubts and discontents of the public disappeared as mists at sun-rising, and the same confidence which had attended his prosperous fortunes revived in its full extent, despite of his late reverses. In the month of April his army was increased, as we have seen, by 350,000 men, in addition to the great garrisons maintained in Dantzic, Thorn, Modlin, Zamosk, Czenstochau, Custrin, &c., augmented as they now were by the remains of the grand army, which had found refuge in these places of strength. He had, besides, an active levy of forces in Italy, and a very large army in Spain, notwithstanding all the draughts which his present necessity had made him bring out of that slaughter-house. Whether, therefore, it was Napoleon's purpose to propose peace or carry on war, he was at the head of a force little inferior to that which he had heretofore commanded.

Having thus given some account of the internal state of France, it is now necessary to look abroad, and examine the consequences of the Russian campaign upon Europe in general.

Chapter LXV

Murat leaves the Grand Army abruptly—Eugene appointed in his place—Measures taken by the King of Prussia for his disenthraldom—He leaves Berlin for Breslau—Treaty signed between Russia and Prussia early in March—Alexander arrives at Breslau on 15th; on the 16th Prussia declares War against France—Warlike preparations of Prussia—Universal enthusiasm—Blucher appointed Generalissimo—Vindication of the Crown Prince of Sweden for joining the Confederacy against France—Proceedings of Austria—Unabated spirit and pretensions of Napoleon—A Regency is appointed in France during his absence, and Maria Louisa appointed Regent, with nominal powers.

The command of the relics of the grand army had been conferred upon Murat, when Napoleon left them at Smorgoni. It was of too painful and disagreeable a nature to afford any food to the ambition of the King of Naples; nor did he accept it as an adequate compensation for various mortifications which he had sustained during the campaign, and for which, as has already been noticed, he nourished considerable resentment against his brother-in-law. Having, besides, more of the soldier than of the general, war lost its charms for him when he was not displaying his bravery at the head of his cavalry; and to augment his impatience, he became jealous of the authority which his wife was exercising at Naples during his absence, and longed to return thither. He, therefore, hastily disposed of the troops in the various Prussian fortresses recently enumerated, where the French maintained garrisons, and suddenly left the army upon the 16th January. Napoleon, incensed at his conduct, announced his departure, and the substitution of Eugene, the Viceroy of Italy, in the general command of the army, with this note of censure:—"The viceroy is more accustomed to the management of military affairs on a large scale, and besides, enjoys the full confidence of the Emperor."[247] This oblique sarcasm greatly increased the coldness betwixt the two brothers-in-law.[248]

Meantime, the Russians continued to advance without opposition into Prussia, being desirous, by their presence, to bring that country to the decision which they had long expected. The manner in which Prussia had been treated by France; the extreme contributions which had been levied from her; the threats which had been held out of altogether annihilating her as a state; the occupation of her fortresses, and the depriving her of all the rights of independence, constituted an abuse of the rights of conquest, exercised in consequence of superior force, which was sure to be ended so soon as that force ceased to be predominant. Napoleon, it is true, had the affectation to express confidence in the friendship of Prussia in his adversity, which he had never cultivated in prosperity. It would have been as reasonable in the patron of a Turkish cruiser, to expect his galley-slaves to continue, out of a point of honour, to pull the oars, after the chain was broken which fettered them to their benches.

EXERTIONS OF PRUSSIA

Accordingly, King Frederick took his measures to shake himself free of the French yoke; but he did so with wisdom and moderation. Whatever wrongs the Prussians had sustained from the French, the King of Prussia had sought no means of avenging them, even when routed armies, falling back on his dominions in a defenceless condition, might have been destroyed, in their desolate state, by his peasantry alone. Popular violence, arising from the resentment of long-suffered injuries, did indeed practise cruelties on the French at Königsberg and elsewhere; but it was against the will

---

[247] Moniteur, 27th January, 1813. On the 24th, Napoleon wrote thus to his sister, the Queen of Naples:—"Your husband quitted the army on the 16th. He is a brave man in the field of battle; but he is more cowardly than a woman or a monk when not in presence of the enemy. He has no moral courage."—Baron Fain, *Manuscript de*, 1813, tom. i., p. 90.

[248] "The Emperor was very much dissatisfied with his conduct; and it is well for the King of Naples that he did not pass through France, where he would certainly have met with a very unfavourable reception."—Savary, tom. iii., p. 43.

of the government, which suppressed them as much as possible. The King did not take any measures to intercept the retreat even of Napoleon himself, although there was ground to expect he might have come to that resolution. He renewed the armistice concluded by D'Yorck; he suffered the distressed and frozen remains of the grand army to augment the hostile garrisons which had occupied his own strongest fortresses. He observed, in short, all the duties of an ally, though an unwilling one, until the war, in which he was engaged as an auxiliary, was totally ended, by the defeat and dispersion of the army of his principal. It is the more proper to enter at large into this topic, because the French historians usually mention the conduct of the King of Prussia on this occasion as defection, desertion, or some such word, indicating a breach of faith. Nothing can be more unjust.

It was not, surely, to be expected, that Frederick was to submit his own dominions to the devastation of the Russians, by continuing a war in which his share was only secondary; nor was it rational to believe, that a country so much oppressed would neglect the means of emancipation which now presented themselves. It is, therefore, no marvel that Prussia should have taken this favourable opportunity for throwing off a yoke which she had found so oppressive. Nay, it is believed, on good grounds, that the course adopted by the King of Prussia was not only that of wisdom and patriotism, but even of necessity; for it is very probable, that, if he had refused to lead his subjects against the French, they might, in that moment of excitation, have found some one else to have placed at the head of the government. He had, as we have already said, denounced the convention entered into by D'Yorck and Massenbach, and ordered them both to Berlin for the purpose of undergoing trial. But the generals had remained quietly in command of their troops, affording a strong example, that, had Frederick laboured ever so much for that purpose, it would have been vain, if not hazardous, to have opposed his royal authority to the impulse of the national spirit.

Before the King took his final resolution, he resolved, as a measure of prudence, to secure his own person, lest, like Ferdinand and the Spanish Bourbons, he should be seized upon as a hostage. He therefore suddenly left Berlin on 22d January, 1813, and betook himself to Breslau,[249] where there were no French soldiery. Immediately afterwards he published an address to his people, calling his armies together, and giving the signal to the patriotism of thousands who longed to arise in arms. The French ambassador was, nevertheless, invited to follow the King to Breslau, where a variety of discussions immediately took place betwixt him and the Prussian cabinet.

To the complaints of exactions and oppressions of every kind, the French negotiators could only reply by reminding the Prussians, that Napoleon had, after decisive victory, suffered the nation to retain the name of independence, and the King to wear a precarious crown. A robber would have the same defence against restoring the booty he had acquired from a traveller, if he stated, that though he had despoiled, he had not murdered him. It was by the right of the strongest that France had acquired that influence over Prussia which she exercised so severely; and, according to the dictates of common sense and human nature, when the advantage was on Prussia's side, she had a right to regain by strength what she had lost by weakness. Every obligation, according to the maxim of the civil law, is made void in the same manner in which it is rendered binding; as Arthegal, the emblematic champion of justice in Spenser's allegory, decrees as law, that what the sea has brought the sea may resume.

On the 1st of March, or about that period, Prussia, returning to a system which nothing but the extremity of her circumstances had ever interrupted, signed a treaty of alliance, offensive and defensive, with Russia. On the 15th March, the Emperor Alexander arrived at Breslau. The meeting was affecting betwixt the two sovereigns, who had been such intimate friends, and had always retained the same personal attachment for each other, although the circumstances of controlling necessity had made them enemies, at a period when it was of importance to Russia to have as few foes as possible thrown into the scale against her. The King of Prussia wept.

---

[249] "Upon receiving the news that the King of Prussia had escaped, Napoleon regretted he had not treated him as he had done Ferdinand VII. and the Pope. 'This is not the first instance,' said he, 'that in politics, generosity is a bad counsellor.' He generous towards Prussia!!"—Fouché, tom. ii., p. 127.

"Courage, my brother," said Alexander; "these are the last tears which Napoleon shall cause you to shed."

PRUSSIA DECLARES WAR

On the 16th March, Prussia declared war against France. There is, in the paper containing this denunciation, much reasoning respecting the extent of contributions due and received, which might have been summed up in the declaration, that "France had made Prussia her subject and her slave, but that now Prussia was enabled to act for herself, and shake off the fetters which violence had imposed on her." This real note was touched where the manifesto declares, that, "Abandoned to herself, and hopeless of receiving any effectual succour from an ally who had declined to render her even the demands of justice, Prussia must take counsel of herself, in order to raise anew and support her existence as a nation. It was in the love and courage of his people that the King sought means to extricate himself, and to restore to his monarchy the independence which is necessary to ensure the future prosperity of the kingdom."

The Emperor Napoleon received that declaration of war, with the calmness of one by whom it had been for some time expected. "It was better," he said, "to have a declared enemy than a doubtful ally."[250] By the Prussians at large it was heard with all the rapture of gratified hope, and the sacrifices which they made, not willingly only, but eagerly, show more completely than any thing else can, the general hatred against France, and the feelings which that nation had excited during her career of success.

From a country so trampled down and exhausted as Prussia, it might have been thought slender means of warfare could be provided. But vengeance is like the teeth of the dragon, a seed which, wherever sown, produces a crop of warriors. Freedom too, was at stake; and when a nation is warring for its own rights, who shall place a limit to its exertions? Some preparation had been made

---

[250] See Savary, tom. iii., p. 44.

by the monarch. The jealousy of France had limited the exercise of the Prussian militia to 25,000 men yearly. But the government had contrived to double this amount, by calling out the militia twice in the year, and training on the second occasion the same number, but different individuals from those who had been first summoned. Thus, a certain portion of discipline had become general among the Prussian youth, and, incited by the desire of their country's freedom, they rushed to battle against France as to a holy warfare. The means of providing artillery had also been sedulously augmented. This was not to be a war of posts or fortresses, but of fields of battle and of bayonets. Many, therefore, of the brass pieces of ordnance, which garnished the walls of such towns and fortresses as were yet unoccupied by the French, had been recast, and converted into field-pieces. Money was scarce, but England was liberal; and besides, the Prussian nobles and burgesses taxed themselves to the uttermost. Even the ladies gave up their diamonds and gold ornaments, for chains and bracelets beautifully wrought out of iron, the state enjoying the advantage of the exchange. In a future age, these relics, when found in the female casket, will be more valuable than the richest Indian jewels.

Meanwhile the resentment and desire of revenge, which had so long smouldered in the bosoms of the Prussians, broke forth with the force of a volcano. The youth of every description rushed to fill the ranks, the distinctions of birth were forgotten, nay, in a great measure abolished; no question was asked of the Prussian, but whether he was able and willing to assist in the liberation of his country. The students, the cultivation of whose minds generally adds to their feeling for national freedom and national honour, arrayed themselves into battalions and squadrons. Some formed the Black Bands, who at this time distinguished themselves; others assumed the arms and dress of the Cossacks, whose name had become so terrible to the French. In general, these volunteers were formed into mounted and dismounted squadrons of chasseurs, whose appearance differed from that of the line only in their uniform being dark green instead of blue. Their discipline, formed on a system devised by Scharnhorst, was admirably calculated to give fresh levies the degree of training and discipline necessary to render them serviceable, without pretending to give them the accuracy in details which experience alone can teach.

In a few weeks numerous armies were on foot, and Prussia, like a strong man rousing himself from slumber, stepped forward to assume her rank among independent nations. There could not be a greater contrast than between the same nation in her hour of presumption, her period of depression, and her present form of regeneration. To the battle of Jena the Prussians had marched as to an assured conquest, with a splendid army, well disposed, and admirably appointed, but conducted with that negligence which is inspired by a presumptuous degree of confidence, and that pride which goes before destruction. In the campaign of 1812, the Black Eagles stooping their dishonoured crests beneath those of France, they went a discouraged and reluctant band of auxiliaries, to assist in the destruction of that power, whose subjugation they were well aware must lead to their own irretrievable bondage. And now, such was the change of a few weeks, nay, not many days, that Prussia again entered the lists with an army, still deficient in its material provisions, but composed of soldiers whose hearts were in the trim, whom misfortunes had taught caution, and oppression had roused to resistance; who knew, by melancholy experience, the strength of their powerful adversary, but were not the less disposed to trust in their own good swords and good cause.

BLUCHER

A leader was selected, admirably formed by nature to command a national army at such a crisis. This was the celebrated Blucher, one of the few Prussian generals, who, even after the battle of Jena, continued to maintain the fame of the Great Frederick, under whom he had been trained, and to fight until every ray of hope had been entirely destroyed. This high-spirited and patriotic officer had remained in obscurity during the long period of the French domination. He was one of those ardent and inflexible characters that were dreaded by Napoleon, whose generosity, however it might display itself otherwise, was seldom observed to forgive those who had shown a steady and conscientious opposition to his power. Such men he held his enemies in every sense, personal as well as political; and, watched closely by the police, their safety could only be ensured by living strictly retired. But now the old warrior sprang eagerly from his obscure retreat, as in the ancient Roman shows a lion might have leaped from his dark den into the arena of the crowded amphitheatre, on which he was soon to act his terrible part. Blucher, was, indeed, by character and disposition, the very man whom the exigence and the Prussian nation required to support a national war. He was not possessed of war as a science, nor skilled in planning out the objects of a campaign. Scharnhorst, and after him Gneisnau, were intrusted with that part of the general's duty, as being completely acquainted with strategie; but in the field of battle no man possessed the confidence of his soldiers so completely as General Blucher. The first to advance, the last to retreat, he was seldom too much elated by victory, and never depressed by bad success. Defeated to-day, he was as ready to renew the battle to-morrow. In his army was no instance of whole divisions throwing down their arms, because they conceived their line broken or their flank turned. It was his system, that the greater part of fighting consists in taking and giving hard blows, and on all occasions he presented himself with a good grace to the bloody exercise. He was vigilant, too, as taught by the exercise of his youth in the light cavalry; and so enterprising and active, that Napoleon was heard to complain, with his accustomed sneer, that "he had more trouble from that old dissipated hussar, than from all the generals of the allies beside." Deeply resenting the injuries of his country, and his own exile, Blucher's whole soul was in the war against France and her Ruler; and utterly devoid of the milder feelings of modern military leaders, he entered into hostilities with the embittered and personal animosity which Hannibal entertained of old against the Roman name and nation.[251]

---

[251] "Sworn from his cradle Rome's relentless foe, Such generous hate the Punic champion bore; Thy lake, O Thrasymene, beheld it glow, And Cannæ's walls and Trebia's crimson'd shore." Shenstone.—S.

Such were the character and energies of the veteran to whom Prussia now confided the defence of her dearest rights, the leading of her youth, and the care of her freedom.[252]

Sweden, or, we ought rather to say, the Crown Prince, had joined the confederacy, as already mentioned, and the spleen of Buonaparte, personal as well as public, had been directed even more against him than against the King of Prussia. The latter was represented as a rebellious and ungrateful vassal, the first as a refugee Frenchman who had renounced his country.

The last accusation, so grossly urged, was, if possible, more unreasonably unjust than the first. The ties of our native country, strict and intimate as they are, may be dissolved in more ways than one. Its lawful government may be overthrown, and the faithful subjects of that government, exiled to foreign countries for their adherence to it, may lawfully bear arms, which, in that case, are not directed against the home of their fathers, but against the band of thieves and robbers by which it is temporarily occupied. If this is not the case, what are we to think of the Revolution of 1688, and the invasion of King William? In like manner, it is possible for a native of France or Britain so to link himself with another country, as to transfer to it the devotion which, in the general case, is only due to the land of his birth. In becoming the heir of the crown of Sweden, Bernadotte had become in fact a Swede; for no one, circumstanced as he was, is entitled, in interweaving his personal fortunes with the fate of the nation which adopts him, to make a reserve of any case in which he can be called to desert their interest for that of another country, though originally his own.

In assuming a French general for their Crown Prince, Sweden no doubt intended to give a pledge that she meant to remain on terms of amity with France; but it would be a wide step to argue from thence that it was her purpose to subject herself as a conquered province to that empire, and to hold the prince whom

---

[252] "Blucher," said Napoleon, at St. Helena, "is a very brave soldier, *un bon sabreur*. He is like a bull who shuts his eyes, and, seeing no danger, rushes on. He committed a thousand faults; and, had it not been for circumstances, I could repeatedly have made *him* prisoner. He is stubborn and indefatigable, afraid of nothing, and very much attached to his country."—*Napoleon in Exile*, vol. i., p. 200.

she had chosen to be no better than the lieutenant of Napoleon. This was indeed the construction which the French Emperor put upon the kingdoms of his own creation—Holland, Westphalia, Spain, and so forth. But in these countries the crowns were at least of his conferring. That of Sweden, on the other hand, was given by the Diet at Orebro, representing the Swedish people, to a person of their own election; nor had Buonaparte any thing to do in it farther, than by consenting that a French subject should become King of Sweden; which consent, if available for any thing, must be certainly held as releasing Bernadotte from every engagement to France, inconsistent with the duties of a sovereign to an independent kingdom.

When, therefore, at a period only a few months afterwards, Napoleon authorised piracies upon the Swedish commerce, and seized, with armed hand, upon the only portion of the Swedish territories which lay within his grasp, nothing could be more unreasonable than to require, that because the Crown Prince was born in Bearn, he should therefore submit to have war made upon him in his capacity of King of Sweden, without making all the resistance in his power. Supposing, what might easily have chanced, that Corsica had remained a constituent part of the British dominions, it would have been ridiculous to have considered Napoleon, when at the head of the French government, as bound by the duties of a liege subject of George III., simply because he was born at Ajaccio. Yet there is no difference betwixt the cases, excepting in the relative size and importance of France and Corsica; a circumstance which can have no influence upon the nature of the obligations incurred by those who are born in the two countries.

It may be readily granted, that a person in the situation of the Crown Prince must suffer as a man of feeling, when opposed to the ranks of his own countrymen. So must a judge, if unhappily called upon to sit in judgment and pronounce sentence upon a brother, or other near relation. In both cases, public duty must take place of private or personal sentiment.

PROCEEDINGS OF AUSTRIA

While the powers of the North formed this coalition, upon terms better concerted, and with forces of a different character from those which had existed upon former less fortunate occasions, Austria looked upon the approaching strife with a hesitating and doubtful eye. Her regard for a sovereign allied to her royal family by so close a tie as Napoleon, had not prevented her cabinet from feeling alarm at the overgrown power of France, and the ambition of her ruler. She had reluctantly contributed an auxiliary force to the assistance of France in the last campaign, and had taken the posture of a neutral so soon as circumstances permitted. The restoration of independence to the world must restore to Austria the provinces which she had lost, especially Illyria and the Tyrol, and at the same time her influence both in Italy and Germany. But this might be obtained from Napoleon disabled, and willing to purchase his ransom from the reprisals of allied Europe, by surrender of his pretensions to universal monarchy; and Austria therefore concluded it best to assume the office of mediator betwixt France and the allies, reserving to herself to throw her sword into the scales, in case the forces and ambition of Napoleon should again predominate; while, on the other hand, should peace be restored by a treaty formed under her auspices, she would at once protect the son-in-law of her Emperor, regain her lost provinces and decayed influence, and contribute, by destroying the arrogant pretensions of France, to the return of tranquillity to Europe.

Otto, the French minister at Vienna, could already see in the Austrian administration a disposition to revive the ancient claims which had been annulled by the victories of Napoleon, and wrote to his court, even in the beginning of January, that they were already making a merit of not instantly declaring war against France. A mission of General Bubna to Paris put a more favourable character upon the interference of the Austrian ministers. He informed the French Cabinet that the Emperor Francis was about to treat with

France as a good ally, providing Austria was permitted also to treat with others as an independent nation.[253]

It was in short the object of Austria, besides recovering her own losses (of which that cabinet, constantly tenacious of its objects, as it is well known to be, had never lost sight,) to restore, as far as possible, some equilibrium of power, by which the other states, of which the European republic was composed, might become, as formerly, guarantees for the freedom and independence of each other. Such was not the system of Napoleon. He would gladly gratify any state who assisted him in hostilities against and the destruction of another, with a handsome share of the spoil; but it was contrary to his policy to allow any one a protecting veto in behalf of a neutral power. It was according to his system, in the present case, to open to Austria his determination to destroy Prussia entirely, and to assure her of Silesia as her share of the booty, if she would be his ally in the war. But he found, to his surprise, that Austria had adopted a different idea of policy, and that she rather saw her interest in supporting the weak against the strong, than, while grasping at selfish objects, in winking at the engrossing ambition of the ruler of France. Neither did he leave the Austrian Cabinet long in the belief, that his losses had in any degree lowered his lofty pretensions, or induced him to descend from the high claims which he had formed of universal sovereignty. From his declarations to the Senate and Representative Body of France, one of two things was plain; either that no sense of past misfortunes, or fear of those which might arrive, would be of any avail to induce him to abandon the most unjustifiable of his usurpations, the most unreasonable of his pretensions; or else that he was determined to have his armed force re-established, and his sword once more in his hand; nay, that he had settled that a victory or two should wash out the memory of his retreat from Moscow, before he would enter into any treaty of pacification.

The notes in the *Moniteur*, during this winter of 1812-13, which were always written by himself, contained Buonaparte's bold defiance to Europe, and avowed his intention to maintain, abreast of each other, the two wars of Spain and Germany. He proposed at

---

[253] Fouché, tom. ii., p. 124.

once to open the campaign in Germany (though he had lost the alliance both of Prussia and Austria,) with an army of double the amount of that which marched against Russia, and to reinforce and keep up the armies of Spain at their complete establishment of 300,000 men. "If any one desired," he said, "the price at which he was willing to grant peace, it had been expressed in the Duke of Bassano's letter to Lord Castlereagh, before commencement of the campaign of 1812."[254]

When that document is referred to, it will be found to contain no cession whatever on the part of France, but a proposal that England should yield up Spain (now almost liberated,) to his brother Joseph, with the admission that Portugal and Sicily, none of which kingdoms Napoleon had the means of making a serious impression upon, might remain to their legitimate sovereigns. In other words, he would desist from pretensions which he had no means to make good, on condition that every point, which was yet doubtful, should be conceded in his favour.

It was extravagant to suppose that Britain, after the destruction occasioned by the Russian retreat, would accept terms which were refused when Napoleon was at the head of his fine army, and in the full hope of conquests. When, therefore, Austria offered herself as a mediator at the court of St. James's, the English ministers contented themselves with pointing out the extravagant pretensions expressed by France, in documents understood to be authentic, and demanding that these should be disavowed, and some concessions made or promised by Napoleon, ere they would hamper themselves by any approach to a treaty.

Upon the whole, it was clear, that the fate of the world was once more committed to the chance of war, and that probably much more human blood must be spilled, ere any principles could be settled, on which a general pacification might be grounded.

---

[254] Fouché, tom. ii., p. 125.

MARIA LOUISA APPOINTED REGENT

A step of state policy was adopted by Napoleon, obviously to conciliate his father-in-law, the Austrian Emperor. A regency was established during his absence, and the Empress, Maria Louisa, was named regent. But her authority was curtailed of all real or effectual power; for he reserved to himself exclusively the privilege of presenting all decrees to be passed by the Senate, and the Empress had only the right to preside in that body.[255]

---

[255] "As the Empress-Regent could not authorise, by her signature, the presentation of any *senatus consultum*, nor the promulgation of any law, the part she had to act was limited to her appearance at the council-board. Besides, she was herself under the tutorship of Cambacérès, who was himself directed by Savary. In fact, after the regency was set in motion, the soul of the government did not the less travel with Napoleon, who did not fail of issuing forth numerous decrees from all his moveable headquarters."—Fouché, tom. ii., p. 137.

Chapter LXVI

State of the French Grand Army—The Russians advance, and show themselves on the Elbe—The French evacuate Berlin, and retreat on the Elbe—The Crown Prince of Sweden joins the Allies, with 35,000 Men—Dresden is occupied by the Sovereigns of Russia and Prussia—Marshal Bessières killed on 1st May—Battle of Lutzen fought on the 2d.—The Allies retire to Bautzen—Hamburgh taken possession of by the Danes and French—Battle of Bautzen fought on the 20th and 21st May—The Allies retire in good order—The French Generals, Bruyères and Duroc, killed on the 22d.—Grief of Napoleon for the Death of the latter—An Armistice signed on 4th June.

We must once more look out upon Germany, to which country, so long the scene on which were fought the quarrels of Europe, the success of the Russians, and the total discomfiture of the army of Napoleon, had again removed the war. We left the wrecks of the grand army thronging in upon the fortresses held by their countrymen in Prussia, where they were deposited as follows:—

Into Thorn were thrown by Murat, before he left the grand army,	6,000	men.
Into Modlin,	8,000	
Into Zamosc,	4,000	
Into Graudentz, Prussians,	6,000	
Into Dantzic,	30,000	
54,000		

This total of 54,000 men comprehended the sole remaining part of what Napoleon continued to call the grand army of Russia;

in which country, however, not one-third of them had ever been, having been employed in Lithuania or Volhynia, and having thus escaped the horrors of the retreat. Almost all these troops were sickly, some distressingly so. The garrison towns, were, however, filled with them, and put in a state of defence judged sufficient to have checked the advance of the Russians.[256]

It would, in all probability, have done so upon any occasion of ordinary war; for Russia having not only gained back Lithuania, but taken possession of Warsaw, and that part of Poland which formerly belonged to Prussia, ought not, in a common case, to have endangered her success by advancing beyond the Vistula, or by plunging her armies into Silesia, leaving so many fortresses in the rear. But the condition of Prussia, waiting the arrival of the Russians as a signal for rising at once, and by her example encouraging the general insurrection of Germany, was a temptation too powerful to be resisted, although unquestionably there was a risk incurred in giving way to it. The various fortresses were therefore masked with a certain number of troops; and the Russian light corps, advancing beyond the line even of the Oder, began to show themselves on the Elbe, joined every where by the inhabitants of the country, who, influenced by the doctrines of the Tugend-Bund, and fired with detestation of the French, took arms wherever their deliverers appeared. The French every where retired, and Prince Eugene, evacuating Berlin, retreated upon the Elbe. It seemed as if the allies had come armed with lighted matches, and the ground had been strewed with gunpowder; so readily did the Germans rise in arms at the hourra of a body of Cossacks, or even at the distant gleam of their lances. The purpose of the war was not, however, to procure partial and desultory risings, from which no permanent benefit could be expected; but to prepare the means of occupying the north of Germany by an army conducted by one of the most celebrated generals of the age, and possessed of regular strength, sufficient to secure what advantages might be gained, and thus influence the final decision of the eventful campaign.

---

[256] See Jomini, tom. iv., p. 271.

CROWN PRINCE JOINS THE ALLIES

While the light troops of Russia and Prussia overran Germany, at least the eastern and northern provinces, the King of Sweden, in virtue of the convention into which he had entered at Abo, crossed over to Stralsund in the month of May, 1813, with a contingent amounting to 35,000 men, and anxiously awaited the junction which was to have placed under his command such corps of Russians and Germans as should increase his main body to 80,000 or 100,000. With such a force, the Crown Prince proposed to undertake the offensive, and thus to compel Napoleon, when he should take the field, to make head at once against his force upon his left flank, and defend himself in front against the advancing armies of Russia and Prussia. The proclamations of independence sent abroad by the allies, made them friends wherever they came; and three flying corps, under Czernicheff, Tettenborn, and Winzengerode, spread along both sides of the Elbe. The French retreated every where, to concentrate themselves under the walls of Madgeburg, and other fortified places, of which they still held possession. Meantime, Hamburgh, Lubeck, and other towns, declared for the allies, and received their troops with an alacrity, which, in the case of Hamburgh, was severely punished by subsequent events.

The French general, Morand, endeavoured to put a stop to the stream of what was termed defection, and occupied Luneburg, which had declared for the allies, with nearly 4000 men. His troops were already in the place, and about to proceed, it was said, to establish military tribunals, and punish the political crimes of the citizens, when the Russians, commanded by the active Czernicheff, suddenly appeared, forced their way sword in hand into the town, and on 2d April, 1813, killed or took prisoners the whole of Morand's corps. The Viceroy, Eugene, attempted to impose some bounds on the audacity now manifested by the allies, by striking a bold blow upon his side. He marched suddenly from the neighbourhood of Madgeburg, with a view of surprising Berlin; but was himself surprised at Mockern, driven back, defeated, and obliged to shut himself up in Madgeburg, where he was blockaded.

The predominance of the allies in the north of Germany seemed now so effectually ascertained, that the warmest adherents of France appeared disposed to desert her cause. Denmark began to treat with the allies, and even on one occasion, as will be hereafter noticed, made a demonstration to join them in arms.

The King of Saxony, who had been always Napoleon's most sincere friend, dared not now abide the storm. He retreated to a place of security in Franconia, while his army separated themselves from the French, and, throwing themselves into Torgau, began to stipulate for a neutrality, which would probably have terminated like that of D'Yorck, in their actually joining the allies.

Davoust retreated to the northward, after blowing up the fine bridge at Dresden, amid the tumultuary opposition and execration of the inhabitants. Dresden itself soon after became the headquarters of the Emperor of Russia and King of Prussia, who were received with joyful acclamations by all classes of the citizens.

In like manner, three of the fortresses held by the French in Prussia—Thorn, Spandau, and Czenstochau—surrendered to the allies, and afforded hope that the French might be dislodged from the rest in the course of the summer. But the farther results of the activity of the allied generals were in a great measure prevented, or postponed, by the arrival of the numerous forces which Napoleon had so speedily levied to restore his late losses.

It would be severe to give the name of rashness to the conduct of the allies, in this bold advance into the middle and north of Germany. A great part of their power was of a moral character, and consisted in acting upon the feelings of the Germans, who were enchanted with the prospect of freedom and independence. Still there was much audacity in the allied monarchs venturing across the Elbe, and subjecting themselves to the encounter of Napoleon and his numerous levies, before their own resources had been brought forward. It was now, however, no time to dispute which plan ought to have been preferred; the sovereigns of Russia and Prussia had no other alternative than to follow out boldly that from which they could not now retreat.

Eugene, at the approach of the new French levies through the passes of the Thuringian mountains, removed to Madgeburg, and formed a junction with them on the Saale. The force in total might amount to 115,000 present in the field; the greater part, however, were new levies, and many almost mere boys. The allied army was collected towards Leipsic, and lay full in Napoleon's road to that city, and from thence to Dresden, which was the point on which he advanced.

LUTZEN

It has been thought that the plains of Lutzen would have been the most advantageous field of battle for the allies, whose strength lay in their fine body of cavalry; to which it has been replied, that they expected to encounter Buonaparte on the other side of the Saale, and there to have obtained open ground for their cavalry, and a field fitting for their vengeance in the plains of Jena. But though the activity of the allies had of late been sufficient to distress Napoleon's lieutenants, it was not as yet adequate to match that of the Emperor himself.

An important change had lately taken place in their army, by the death of the veteran Koutousoff, in whose place Witgenstein had succeeded to the supreme command.

Skirmishes took place at Weissenfels and Poserna, upon 29th April and 1st May, on which last day an event occurred distressing to Buonaparte's feelings. A contest took place in the defile of Rippach, near Poserna, which was only remarkable for the death of an excellent officer. Marshal Bessières, whose name the reader must remember as the leader of Napoleon's household troops, from the time they bore the humble name of Guides, until now that they were the Imperial Guard, and he their Colonel-general, coming up to see how the action went, was killed by a cannon-shot. His body was covered with a white sheet, and the loss concealed as long as possible from the guards, who were much attached to him. Upon a former occasion, when his horse was killed, Buonaparte told him he was obliged to the bullet, for making it known to him how much he was beloved, since the whole guard had wept for him. His time was, however, now come. He was sincerely lamented by Napoleon, who was thus, when the world was going harder against him than formerly, deprived of an early and attached follower.[257]

But the war kept its pace. The French army continued to advance upon Leipsic on the south; the allies approached from the north to defend the place.

BATTLE OF LUTZEN

The centre of the French army was stationed at a village called Kaya. It was under the command of Ney. He was sustained by the Imperial Guard, with its fine artillery, drawn up before the well-known town of Lutzen, which, having seen the last conflict of Gustavus Adolphus, was now to witness a more bloody tragedy. Marmont, who commanded the right, extended as far as the defile of Poserna, and rested with his left upon the centre. The left wing of the French reached from Kaya to the Elster. As they did not expect to be brought to action in that place, or upon that day, (May 2d,) Napoleon was pressing forward from his right, Lauriston being at the head of the column, with the purpose of possessing himself of Leipsic, behind which he expected to see the army of the allies.

But these, encouraged by the presence of the Emperor Alexander and King of Prussia, had formed the daring resolution of marching southward along the left bank of the Elster during the night, transporting themselves to the right bank in the morning, and assaulting with the choicest of their troops, under Blucher, the centre of the French, led by Ney. The fury of the attack was irresistible, and, in despite of a most obstinate defence, the allies obtained possession of Kaya, the point on which the centre of the French army rested. This was a crisis worthy of Napoleon's genius,

---

[257] Napoleon caused the remains of Bessières to be conveyed to the Invalides at Paris, and intended extraordinary honours for them, of which subsequent events deprived them. "The death of this old and faithful servant produced," says Savary, "a void in the Emperor's heart: fate deprived him of his friends, as if to prepare him for the severe reverses which she had yet in store."

and he was not wanting to himself. Assailed on the flank when in the act of advancing in column, he yet contrived, by a masterly movement, to wheel up his two wings, so as in turn to outflank those of the enemy. He hurried in person to bring up his guard to support the centre, which was in fact nearly broken through. The combat was the more desperate and deplorable, that, on the one side, fought the flower of the Prussian youth, which had left their universities to support the cause of national honour and freedom; and on the other, the young men of Paris, many of them of the best rank, who bravely endeavoured to sustain their country's long pre-eminent claim to victory. Both combated under the eyes of their respective sovereigns, maintained the honour of their country, and paid an ample tribute to the carnage of the day.

The battle lasted for several hours, before it could be judged whether the allies would carry their point by breaking through the French centre, or whether the French, before sustaining that calamity, would be able to wheel their wings upon the flanks of the allies. At length the last event began to be anticipated as the most probable. The distant discharge of musketry was seen on right and left closing inwards on the central tumult, and recognised for the fire of Macdonald and Bertrand, who commanded the French wings. At the same time the Emperor made a successful struggle to recover the village of Kaya, and the allies, extricating themselves skilfully from the combat, led back their exhausted forces from between the forceps, as we may term it, formed by the closing wings of Napoleon, without further loss than the carnage sustained in the field of battle. But that was immense. The allies lost 20,000 men in killed and wounded. Among these was Scharnhorst, one of the best staff-officers in Europe, and who had organised with such ability the Prussian landwehr and volunteers. The Prince Leopold of Hesse Hombourg, and the Prince of Mecklenburg-Strelitz, nearly allied to the royal family of England, were also killed. The veteran Blucher was wounded, but, refusing to retire, had his wounds dressed upon the field of battle. Seven or eight French generals were also slain or wounded, and the loss of the French army was very severe.[258]

---

[258] Jomini, tom. iv., p. 274; Military Reports to the Empress; Savary, tom. iii., p. 66; Baron Fain, tom. i., p. 267; Lord Cathcart's Despatch, London Gazette, May 25.

Two circumstances greatly assisted to decide the fate of the action. General Bertrand, who was not come up when it began, arrived in time to act upon the left of the allies, and to permit Marmont, whose place he occupied, to unite himself in the hour of need, to the defence of the centre. On the part of the allies, on the contrary, the division of Miloradowitch, from some mistake or want of orders, never came into action. Few prisoners, and no artillery, were taken. The allies moved off in safety, protected by their fine cavalry, and the sole trophy of the victors was the possession of the bloody field.

But Napoleon had need of renown to animate his drooping partisans; and accordingly the battle was scarce ended ere the most exaggerated reports of the Emperor's success were despatched to every friendly court, and even so far as Constantinople. The very best of Napoleon's rhetorical ornaments were exhausted on this occasion. The battle of Lutzen was described as having, like a clap of thunder, pulverized all the schemes of the allies; and the cloudy train of intrigues, formed by the Cabinet of St. James's as having been destroyed, like the Gordian knot under the sword of Alexander. The eloquence of Cardinal Maury, who said *Te Deum* on the occasion at Paris,[259] was equally florid; until at length his wonder was raised so high, as scarce to admit that the hero who surmounted so many difficulties, performed so many duties, united so much activity to so much foresight, such brilliancy of conception to such accuracy of detail, was only, after all, a mortal like himself and the congregation.

The battle of Lutzen had indeed results of importance, though inferior by far to those on which such high colouring was bestowed by the court chaplain and the bulletins. The allied monarchs fell back upon the Mulda, and all hope of engaging Saxony in the general cause was necessarily adjourned. The French troops were again admitted into Torgau by the positive order of their Sovereign, notwithstanding the opposition of the Saxon general Thielman. The

---

[259] "The Empress expressed great joy at the event, because, she said, it would secure her countrymen, whom she suspected of wavering. She ordered *Te Deum* to be sung at Notre Dame, whither she herself repaired in state. She was attended by the whole court, and the troops of the guard, and the public, received her with expressions of the most ardent enthusiasm."—Savary, tom. iii., p. 67.

King of Saxony returned from Prague, his last place of refuge, and came to Dresden on the 12th. Napoleon made a military fête to receive the good old monarch, and conducted him in a kind of triumph through his beautiful capital. It could afford little pleasure at present to the paternal heart of Frederick Augustus; for while that part of Dresden which was on the left side of the Elbe was held by the French, the other was scarcely evacuated by the allies; and the bridge of boats, burnt to the water's edge, was still the subject of contest betwixt the parties—the French seeking to repair, the allies to destroy it.

Another consequence of the battle of Lutzen was, that the allies could no longer maintain themselves on the Elbe. The main army, however, only retired to Bautzen, a town near the sources of the Spree, about twelve French leagues from Dresden, where they selected a strong position. An army of observation, under Bulow, was destined to cover Berlin, should the enemy make any attempt in that direction; and they were thus in a situation equally convenient for receiving reinforcements, or retiring upon Silesia, in case of being attacked ere such succours came up. They also took measures for concentrating their army, by calling in their advanced corps in all directions.

HAMBURGH—DRESDEN

One of the most unpleasant consequences was their being obliged upon the whole line to withdraw to the right side of the Elbe. Czernicheff and Tettenborn, whose appearance had occasioned Hamburgh, and other towns in that direction, to declare themselves for the good cause, and levy men in behalf of the allies, were now under the necessity of abandoning them to the vengeance of the French, who were certain to treat them as revolted subjects. The fate of Hamburgh in particular, in itself a town so interesting, and which had distinguished itself by the number and spirit of the volunteers which were raised there in the cause of the allies, was peculiarly tantalizing.

No sooner were the main body of the allies withdrawn on the 9th May, than the place was fiercely attacked by Davoust at the head of 5000 or 6000 men, uttering denunciations of vengeance against the city for the part it had taken. When this force, which they possessed no adequate means of repelling, was in the act of approaching to storm the place, the alarmed citizens of Hamburgh, to their own wonder, were supported by Danish artillery and gun-boats, sent from Altona to protect the city. This kindness had not been expected at the hand of the Danes, who had as yet been understood to be the allies of France. But the reality was, that as the Danish treaty with the allies was still in dependence, it was thought that this voluntary espousal of the cause of their neighbour might have a good effect upon the negotiation. Something perhaps might arise from the personal zeal of Blucher, the commandant of Altona, who was a relation of the celebrated Prussian general. The Danes, however, after this show of friendship, evacuated Hamburgh on the evening of the 12th of May, to return shortly after in a very different character; for it being, in the interval, ascertained that the allies were determined to insist upon Denmark's ceding Norway to Sweden, and the news of the battle of Lutzen seeming to show that Napoleon's star was becoming again pre-eminent, the Danish Prince broke off his negotiation with the allies, and returned to his league, offensive and defensive, with France.

The hopes and fears of the citizens of Hamburgh were doomed to be yet further tantalized. The Crown Prince of Sweden was at Stralsund with a considerable army, and 3000 Swedes next appeared for the purpose of protecting Hamburgh. But as this Swedish army, as already mentioned, was intended to be augmented to the number of 90,000, by reinforcements of Russians and Prussians, which had not yet appeared, and which the Crown Prince was soliciting with the utmost anxiety, he could not divide his forces without risking the grand objects for which this large force was to be collected, and the additional chance of his Swedish army, of whose blood he was justly and wisely frugal, being destroyed in detail. We may add to this, that from a letter addressed by the Crown Prince to Alexander, at this very period, it appears he was agitated with the greatest doubt and anxiety concerning the arrival of these important reinforcements, and justly apprehensive for the probable consequences of their being delayed. At such a crisis, therefore, he was in no condition to throw any part of his forces into Hamburgh as a permanent garrison.

The reasons urged for withdrawing the Swedish troops seem sufficient, but the condition of the citizens of Hamburgh was not the less hard, alternately deserted by Russians, Danes, and Swedes. On the 30th of May, 5000 Danes, now the allies of France, and 1500 French troops, took possession of the town, in the name of Napoleon. They kept good discipline, and only plundered after the fashion of regular exactions; but this occupation was the prelude to a train of distresses, to which Hamburgh was subjected during the whole continuance of the war. Meanwhile, though this forlorn city was lost for the time, the war continued in its neighbourhood.

The gallant Czernicheff, as if to avenge himself for the compulsory retreat of his Cossacks from Hamburgh, contrived, near Halberstadt, to cut off a body of French infantry forming a hollow square of musketry, and having fourteen field-pieces. It was seen on this occasion, that these sons of the desert were something very different from miserable hordes, as they were termed in the language with which the French writers, and Napoleon himself, indulged their spleen. At one shrill whoop of their commander, they dispersed themselves much in the manner of a fan when thrown open; at another signal, each horseman, acting for himself, came on at full gallop. Thus they escaped in a considerable degree the fire of the enemy which could not be pointed against any mass, penetrated the square, took the cannon, made prisoners near 1000 men, and piked or sabred more than 700, not a Frenchman escaping from the field of battle. This skirmish was so successfully managed on Czernicheff's part, that a French force, much superior to his own, came up in time to see the execution done, but not to render assistance to their countrymen.

In the meanwhile, Dresden was the scene of political negotiations, and its neighbourhood resounded with the din of war. Count Bubna, on the part of the Austrian Emperor, made the strongest remonstrances to Buonaparte on the subject of a general peace, while it seems probable that Napoleon endeavoured to dazzle the Cabinet of Vienna with such views of individual advantage, as to make her declare without scruple for his side. The audiences of Count Bubna were prolonged till long past midnight, and matters of the last importance seemed to be under discussion.

The war was for a few days confined to skirmishes of doubtful and alternate success, maintained on the right bank of the Danube. On the 12th May, Ney crossed the river near Torgau, and menaced the Prussian territories, directing himself on Spremberg and Hoyerswerder, as if threatening Berlin, which was only protected by Bulow and his army of observation. The purpose was probably, by exciting an alarm for the Prussian capital, to induce the allies to leave their strong position at Bautzen. But they remained stationary there, so that Napoleon moved forward to dislodge them in person. On the 18th May he quitted Dresden. In his road towards Bautzen, he passed the ruins of the beautiful little town of Bischoffswerder, and expressed particular sympathy upon finding it had been burnt by the French soldiery, after a rencounter near the spot with a body of Russians. He declared that he would rebuild the place, and actually presented the inhabitants with 100,000 francs towards repairing their losses. On other occasions, riding where the recently wounded had not been yet removed, he expressed, as indeed was his custom, for he could never view bodily pain without sympathy, a very considerable degree of sensibility. "His wound is incurable, Sire," said a surgeon, upon whom he was laying his orders to attend to one of these miserable objects.—"Try, however," said Napoleon; and added in a suppressed voice—"There will always be one fewer of them,"—meaning, doubtless, of the victims of his wars.

Napoleon's is not the only instance in which men have trembled or wept at looking upon the details of misery which have followed in consequence of some abstract resolutions of their own.

THE BATTLE OF BAUTZEN

Arriving at Bautzen on the 21st, the Emperor in person reconnoitred the formidable position of the allies. They were formed to the rear of the town of Bautzen, which was too much advanced to make a part of their position, and had the Spree in their front. Their right wing rested on fortified eminences, their left upon wooded hills. On their right, towards Hoyerswerder, they were watched by Ney and Lauriston, who, of course, were prepared to act in communication with Napoleon. But the allies disconcerted this part of the Emperor's scheme with singular address and boldness. They surprised, by a movement from their right, a column of 7000 Italians, and so entirely routed them, that those who escaped dispersed and fled into Bohemia; after which exploit, De Tolly and D'Yorck, who had commanded the attacking division, again united themselves with the main force of the allies, and resumed their place in the line.

Ney moved to the support of the Italians, but too late either for rescue or revenge. He united himself with the Emperor about three in the afternoon, and the army accomplished the passage of the Spree at different points, in front of the allied army. Napoleon fixed his headquarters in the deserted town of Bautzen; and his army, advancing towards the enemy slowly and with caution, bivouacked, with their line extending north and south, and their front to the allies. The latter concentrated themselves with the same caution, abandoning whatever points they thought too distant to be effectually maintained; their position covering the principal road towards Zittau, and that to Goerlitz; their right wing (Prussians) resting upon the fortified heights of Klein, and Klein-Bautzen, which were the keys of the position, while the left wing (composed of Russians) was supported by wooded hills. The centre was rendered unapproachable by commanding batteries.

As it was vain to think of storming such a position in front, Napoleon had recourse to the manœuvre of modern war, which no general better understood—that of turning it, and thereby rendering it unserviceable. Ney was, therefore, directed to make a considerable circuit round the Russian extreme right, while their left was attacked more closely by Oudinot, who was to engage their attention by attempting to occupy the valleys, and debouching from the hills on which they rested. For this last attempt the Russians were prepared. Miloradowitch and the Prince of Wirtemberg made good the defence on this point with extreme gallantry, and the fortune of the day, notwithstanding the great exertions of Buonaparte, seemed to be with the allies. The next attempt was made on the fortified heights on the right of the allies, defended by the Prussians. Here also Napoleon encountered great difficulties, and sustained much loss. It was not till he brought up all his reserves, and combined them for one of those desperate exertions, which had so often turned the fate of battle, that he was able to succeed in his purpose. The attack was conducted by Soult, and it was maintained at the point of the bayonet. At the price of nearly four hours' struggle, in the course of which the heights were often gained, lost, and again retaken, the French remained masters of them.

At the very time when their right point of support was carried by the French, the corps of Ney, with that of Lauriston and that of Regnier, amounting to 60,000 men, had established themselves in the enemy's rear. It was then that Blucher was compelled to evacuate those heights which he had defended so long and so valiantly.

But although the allies were thus turned upon both flanks, and their wings in consequence forced in upon their centre, their retreat was as orderly as it had been after the battle of Lutzen. Not a gun was taken, scarce a prisoner made; the allies retired as if on the parade, placed their guns in position wherever the ground permitted, and repeatedly compelled the pursuers to deploy, for the purpose of turning them, in which operation the French suffered greatly.[260]

The night closed, and the only decided advantage which Napoleon had derived from this day of carnage, was the cutting off the allies from their retreat by the great roads on Silesia, and its capital, Breslau, and driving them on the more impracticable roads near to the Bohemian frontier. But they accomplished this unfavourable change of position without being thrown into disorder, or prevented from achieving the same skilful defence by which their retreat had hitherto been protected.

---

[260] Jomini, tom. iv., p. 304; Manuscript de 1813, tom. i., p. 415; Military Reports to the Empress.

The whole day of the 22d of May was spent in attacks upon the rear of the allies, which were always repelled by their coolness and military conduct. The Emperor Napoleon placed himself in the very front of the pursuing column, and exposed his person to the heavy and well-aimed fire by which Miloradowitch covered his retreat. He urged his generals to the pursuit, making use of such expressions as betokened his impetuosity. "You creep, scoundrel," was one which he applied to a general officer upon such an occasion. He lost patience, in fact, when he came to compare the cost of the battle with its consequences, and said, in a tone of bad humour, "What, no results after so much carnage—not a gun—not a prisoner?—these people will not leave me so much as a nail."

At the heights of Reichembach, the Russian rear-guard made a halt, and while the cuirassiers of the guards disputed the pass with the Russian lancers, the French general Bruyères was struck down by a bullet. He was a veteran of the army of Italy, and favoured by Buonaparte, as having been a companion of his early honours. But Fortune had reserved for that day a still more severe trial of Napoleon's feelings. As he surveyed the last point on which the Russians continued to make a stand, a ball killed a trooper of his escort close by his side. "Duroc," he said to his ancient and faithful follower and confidant, now the grand-master of his palace, "Fortune has a spite at us to-day." It was not yet exhausted.

Some time afterwards, as the Emperor with his suite rode along a hollow way, three cannon were fired. One ball shivered a tree close to Napoleon, and rebounding, killed General Kirchenner and mortally wounded Duroc, whom the Emperor had just spoken to. A halt was ordered, and for the rest of the day Napoleon remained in front of his tent, surrounded by his guard, who pitied their Emperor, as if he had lost one of his children. He visited the dying man, whose entrails were torn by the shot, and expressed his affection and regret. On no other but that single occasion was he ever observed so much exhausted, or absorbed by grief, as to decline listening to military details, or giving military orders. "Every thing to-morrow," was his answer to those who ventured to ask his commands. He made more than one decree in favour of Duroc's family, and impledged the sum of 200 Napoleons in the hands of the pastor in whose house Duroc had expired, to raise a monument to his memory, for which he dictated a modest and affecting epitaph.[261] In Bessières and Duroc, Napoleon lost two of his best officers and most attached friends, whose sentiments had more influence on him than others in whom he reposed less confidence. The double deprivation was omen of the worst kind for his fortunes.

In resuming the sum of the loss arising from the battle, we must observe that the French suffered most, because the strong position of the allies covered them from the fire. Nevertheless, the allies lost in slain and wounded about 10,000 men. It would take perhaps 5000 more to approximate the amount of the French loss.

ARMISTICE

On the day preceding that sanguinary battle, an armistice had been proposed by Count Nesselrode, in a letter to Caulaincourt, Duke of Vicenza, in compliance, it was stated, with the wishes of the Court of Vienna; it was seconded by a letter from Count Stadion to Talleyrand, whom, as well as Fouché, Napoleon had summoned to his presence, because, perhaps, he doubted the effect of their intrigues during his absence, and in his difficulties. This armistice was to be preliminary to a negotiation, in which Austria proposed to assume the character of mediator.

In the meanwhile Napoleon marched forward, occupied Breslau (from which the princesses of the Prussian royal family removed into Bohemia,) and relieved the blockade of Glogau, where the garrison had begun to suffer by famine. Some bloody skirmishes were fought without any general result, and where Victory seemed to distribute her favours equally. But the main body of the allies showed no inclination to a third general engagement, and retreating upon Upper Silesia, not even the demonstration of advance upon Berlin itself could bring them to action.

---

[261] Military Reports to the Empress; Savary, tom. iii., p. 72; Baron Fain, tom. i., p. 441.

The armistice was at length agreed upon, and signed on the 4th of June. Buonaparte showed either a sincere wish for peace, or a desire to be considered as entertaining such, by renouncing the possession of Breslau and Lower Silesia to the allies, which enabled them to regain their communications with Berlin. The interests of the world, which had been so long committed to the decision of the sword, seemed now about to be rested upon the arguments of a convention of politicians.

Chapter LXVII

Change in the results formerly produced by the French Victories—Despondency of the Generals—Decay in the discipline of the Troops—Views of Austria—Arguments in favour of Peace stated and discussed—Pertinacity of Napoleon—State of the French Interior—hid from him by the slavery of the Press—Interview betwixt Napoleon and the Austrian Minister Metternich—Delays in the Negotiations—Plan of Pacification proposed by Austria, on 7th August—The Armistice broken off on the 10th, when Austria joins the Allies—Sudden placability of Napoleon at this period—Ascribed to the news of the Battle of Vittoria.

The victories of Lutzen and Bautzen were so unexpected and so brilliant, that they completely dazzled all those who, reposing a superstitious confidence in Buonaparte's star, conceived that they again saw it reviving in all the splendour of its first rising. But the expressions of Augereau to Fouché, at Mentz,[262] as the latter passed to join Buonaparte at Dresden, show what was the sense of Napoleon's best officers. "Alas!" he said, "our sun has set. How little do the two actions of which they make so much at Paris, resemble our victories in Italy, when I taught Buonaparte the art of war, which he now abuses. How much labour has been thrown away only to win a few marches onward! At Lutzen our centre was broken, several regiments disbanded, and all was lost but for the Young Guard. We have taught the allies to beat us. After such a butchery as that of Bautzen, there were no results, no cannon taken, no prisoners made. The enemy every where opposed us with advantage, and we were roughly handled at Reichembach, the very day after the battle. Then one ball strikes off Bessières, another Duroc; Duroc, the only friend he had in the world. Bruyères and

---

[262] Mémoires de Fouché, tom. ii., p. 139.

Kirchenner are swept away by spent bullets. What a war! it will make an end of all of us. He will not make peace; you know him as well as I do; he will cause himself be surrounded by half a million of men, for, believe me, Austria will not be more faithful to him than Prussia. Yes, he will remain inflexible, and unless he be killed (as killed he will *not* be,) there is an end of all of us."[263]

It was, indeed, generally observed, that though the French troops had all their usual brilliancy of courage, and although their Emperor showed all his customary talent, the former effect of both upon the allies seemed in a great measure lost. The rapidity with which Buonaparte's soldiers made their attacks was now repelled with steadiness, or anticipated with yet superior alertness; so that the French, who, during their course of victory, had become so secure as to neglect the precautions of sentinels and patrols, now frequently suffered for their carelessness. On the other hand, the allies chose their days and hours of battle, continued the conflict as long as they found convenient, suspended it when it became unfavourable, and renewed it when they saw cause. There was an end to the times when a battle decided the fate of a campaign, and a campaign the course of the war.

DISCIPLINE OF THE ARMY

It was also seen, that though Buonaparte had been able to renew the numbers of his army, by an unparalleled effort of exertion, it was not even in *his* power to restore the discipline which the old soldiers had lost in the horrors of the Russian retreat, and which the young levies had never acquired. The Saxons and Silesians felt that the burdens which the presence of an armed force always must inflict, were no longer mitigated by the species of discipline

---

[263] "If Augereau did utter such nonsense, he would have bestowed upon himself the double charge of folly and absurdity. Augereau did not know Napoleon until the latter had become a general-in-chief; and certainly Napoleon has sufficiently proved, that he had completed his course of military study before he commenced his campaigns in Italy. The battles of Lutzen and Bautzen are at least as memorable in the eyes of soldiers as the first battles in Italy; perhaps more so, when we remember the French army was composed of conscripts, marines, deficient in cavalry; and when we call to mind the valour Napoleon displayed there. He supplied every thing by the force of his genius and enthusiasm."—Louis Buonaparte, p. 89.

which the French soldiers had formerly exercised amongst themselves, and which secured against wanton outrage, and waste of the plunder which they seized. But now, it was an ordinary thing to see one body of soldiers treading down and destroying the provisions, for want of which the next battalion was perhaps starving. The courage and energy of the French soldier were the same, but the recollection of former distresses had made him more selfish and more wasteful, as well as more ferocious.

Those who saw matters under this disadvantageous light, went so far, though friends both to France and Napoleon, as to wish that neither the battle of Lutzen or Bautzen had been fought, since they became, in their consequences, the greatest obstacles to a settled pacification. Even Eugene Beauharnois used this despairing language. It is true, they allowed that these memorable conflicts had sustained, or even elevated, the Emperor's military character, and that there was some truth in the courtly speech of Narbonne, who, when Napoleon desired to know what the people at Vienna thought of these actions, replied, "Some think you an angel, Sire; some a devil; but all agree you are more than man."[264] But according to the sentiments of such persons, these encomiums on a point of the Emperor's character, which had before rendered him sufficiently feared, and sufficiently hated, were only calculated to elevate his mind above prudential considerations, and to render his chance of effecting a permanent reconciliation with other nations more difficult, if not altogether impossible. The maxim of Europe at present seemed to be—

"Odi accipitrem qui semper vivit in armis."[265]

THE QUESTION OF PEACE

A point was now reached, when Buonaparte's talents as a soldier were rather likely to disturb a negotiation, which an opinion of his moderate views in future, could such have been entertained on plausible grounds, would certainly have influenced favourably.

---

[264] Fouché, tom. ii., p. 147.
[265] "I hate the hawk who always lives in war."

This was particularly felt by Austria, who, after having received so many humiliations from Napoleon, seemed now to be called upon to decide on his destiny. The views of that power could not be mistaken. She desired to regain her lost provinces, and her influence in Germany, and unquestionably would use this propitious hour to obtain both. But then she desired still farther, for the preservation of her dominions, and of her influence, that France should desist from her dream of absolute dominion, and Napoleon from those extravagant claims of universal royalty, which he had hitherto broadly acted upon. To what purpose, was asked by the friends of peace, could it avail Buonaparte to maintain large armies in Germany? To what purpose keep possession of the fortified towns, even on the eastern frontier of that empire, excepting to show, that, whatever temporary advantage Napoleon might look for in an alliance with Austria, it was no part of his plan to abandon his conquests, or to sink from his claims of supreme dominion, into a co-ordinate prince among the independent sovereigns of Europe.

If he meant to prosecute the war, they urged, that his lingering in Saxony and Prussia would certainly induce Austria to join the coalition against him; and that, supposing Dresden to be the pivot of his operations, he would be exposed to be taken in flank by the immense armies of Austria descending upon the valley of the Elbe, from the passes of the Bohemian mountains.

Another, and a very opposite course of measures, would, said the same counsellors, be at once a guarantee to Austria of the French Emperor's peaceable intentions, and tend to check and intimidate the other allies. Let Napoleon evacuate of free will the blockaded fortresses upon the Oder and Elbe, and thereby add to his army 50,000 veteran troops. Let him, with these and his present army, fall back on the Rhine, so often acknowledged as the natural boundary of France. Who would dare to attack him on his own strong frontier, with such an army in front, and all the resources of France in his rear? Not Austria; for, if assured that Napoleon had abandoned his scheme to make France victorious, and limited his views to making her happy, that power would surely desire to maintain a dynasty connected with her own, on a throne which might become a protection and ornament to Europe, instead of being her scourge and terror. The northern nations, Russia, Prussia, and Sweden, would have no motive to undertake so wild a crusade as a march to the Rhine; and Great Britain, her commerce restored, and the peace of the continent established, could not, if she were desirous, find any sound reason for protracting the war, which she had always carried on against the system, not the person, of Buonaparte, until events showed that they were indivisible. Thus France, by assuming an attitude which expressed moderation as well as firmness, might cause the swords of the allies to fall from their hands without another drop of blood being shed.

Indeed, although it may appear, that by the course recommended Napoleon must have made great sacrifices, yet, as circumstances stood, he resigned claims dependent on the chance of war, rather than advantages in possession, and yielded up little or nothing that was firmly and effectually part of his empire. This will appear from a glance at the terms of the supposed surrender.

Spain he must have relinquished all claim to. But Napoleon had just received accounts of the decisive battle of Vittoria, which sealed the emancipation of the Peninsula; and he must have been aware, that in this long-contested point he would lose nothing of which the fate of war had not previously deprived him, and would obtain for the south-western provinces of France protection against the army of the Duke of Wellington, which already threatened invasion.

Germany was indeed partly in Napoleon's possession, as far as the occupation of fortresses, and such treaties as he had imposed on his vassal-princes, could give him influence. But the whole nation, in every city and province, was alienated from France and her ruler, on account of the paramount sovereignty which he had assumed, and the distresses which he had brought upon them by the unceasing demand of troops for distant expeditions, and by his continental system. Besides, the enfranchisement of Germany was the very question of war and peace; and that not being granted, Napoleon must have been well aware that he must fight out the battle with Russia, Prussia, and Sweden, the insurgent Germans ready to arise on every hand, and all the weighty force of Austria to back them. If peace was to be established on any terms, the destruction of the unnatural influence of France on the right side of the Rhine must have been an indispensable article; and it was better for Napoleon to make the cession voluntarily, than to wait, till, through the insurrection of the people, and the discontent of the monarchs lately his dependents, the whole system should explode and go to pieces of itself.

England would, doubtless, insist on the liberation of Holland; yet even this could be no great sacrifice on the part of Napoleon, who would have retained Flanders, and the whole left side of the Rhine, from Huningen to Cleves, including the finest territories of the ancient Dukes of Burgundy, which had never belonged to the former Kings of France. The emancipation of Holland might have been also compensated, by the restoration of some of the French colonies. England has never made hard bargains on the occasion of a general peace.

There might have been difficulties on the subject of Italy; but the near connexion betwixt the Emperors of Austria and France offered various means of accommodating these. Italy might, for example, have made an appanage for Eugene, or, in the case of such existing, for Buonaparte's second son, so as to insure the kingdoms of France and Italy passing into distinct and independent sovereignties in the next reign; or, it is believed, that if Austria had been absolutely determined to break off the treaty for this sole object, she would have found the belligerent powers inclined in their turn to act as mediators, and been herself compelled to listen to moderate terms.

From what has been said, it would appear that such cessions as have been hinted at, would at once have put an end to the war, leaving Napoleon still in possession of the fairest kingdom of Europe, augmented to an extent of territory greatly beyond what her most powerful monarchs before him had ever possessed; while, on the other hand, the countries and claims which, in the case supposed, he was called upon to resign, resembled the wounded mast in the tempest, which the seaman cuts away purposely, as endangering the vessel which it has ceased to assist. But it unfortunately happened, that Buonaparte, generally tenacious of his own opinion, and particularly when his reputation was concerned, imagined to himself that he could not cut away the mast without striking the colours which were nailed to it; that he could not resign his high pretensions, however unreasonable, without dimming his personal glory, in the lustre of which he placed his happiness.[266]

He would not, therefore, listen to those, who, with such arguments as we have above stated, pressed him to make a virtue of necessity, and assume a merit from giving up what he could not attempt to hold, without its being in all probability wrested from him. He persisted in maintaining the contrary, referred back to the various instances in which he had come off in triumph, when every other person had despaired of his safety, and had previously protested against the hazardous means which he used to ascertain it. This pertinacity did not arise solely out of the natural confidence in his own superiority, which always attends minds so powerful and so determined; it was fostered by the whole course of his life. "At the age of thirty," he said of himself, "I had gained victories—I had influenced the world—I had appeased a national tempest—had melted parties into one—had rallied a nation. I have, it must be allowed, been spoiled by success—I have always been in supreme command. From my first entrance into life I have enjoyed high power, and circumstances and my own force of character have been such, that from the instant I gained a superiority, I have recognised neither masters nor laws."[267]

To a confession so ingenuous, the historian can add nothing. It is no wonder, that one to whom luck had been uniformly favourable, should love the excitation of the play, and, making cast after cast in confidence of his own fortune, press the winning game until it became a losing one, instead of withdrawing from the table, as prudence would have dictated, when the stakes deepened, and the

---

[266] "Sir Walter Scott must allow that the end has too clearly shown how well this opinion of Napoleon was founded. I confess having, at this period, urged a peace at whatever price it might be obtained, and having used every effort, however feeble, to influence my brother; but I also confess, I then believed peace really was desired; whereas subsequent events have proved, that the destruction of Napoleon and the abasement of France, were the object in view."—Louis Buonaparte.

[267] Journal, &c. par le Comte de Las Cases, tom. iv., partie 7tième, p. 26.—S.

luck began to change. Napoleon had established in his own mind, as well as that of others, an opinion, that he, in his proper person, enjoyed an amnesty from the ordinary chances of fortune.[268] This was a belief most useful to him, as it was received by others, but dangerous in his own adoption of it, since it hindered him from listening in his own case to calculations, which in that of others he would have allowed to be well founded.

TALLEYRAND AND FOUCHÉ

Both Talleyrand and Fouché gave their master the advantage of their experience on this occasion, and touched with less or more reserve upon the terror which his ambition had spread, and the determination of the allies, as well as Austria, not to make peace without such a guarantee as should protect them against future encroachments. Napoleon rejected their opinion and advice with disdain, imputing it to their doubts in the persevering exertions of his genius, or to an anxiety for their own private fortunes, which induced them to desire at all risks the end of the war.

His military counsellors endeavoured to enforce similar advice, with the same want of success. Berthier, with the assistance of the celebrated engineer, Rogniat, had drawn up a plan for removing the French army, reinforced with all the garrisons which they had in Germany, from the line of the Elbe to that of the Rhine.

"Good God!" exclaimed Buonaparte, as he glanced at the labours of his adjutant-general, "ten lost battles could not bring me so low as you would have me stoop, and that, too, when I command so many strong places on the Elbe and Oder. Dresden is the point on which I will manœuvre to receive all attacks, while my enemies develope themselves like a line of circumference round a centre. Do you suppose it possible for troops of various nations, and variously

---

[268] The following is a ludicrous instance. When the explosion of the infernal machine took place, a bystander rushed into a company, and exclaimed, "The First Consul is blown up." An Austrian veteran chancing to be of the party, who had witnessed Napoleon's wonderful escapes during the Italian campaigns, exclaimed, in ridicule of the facile credulity of the newsmonger, "*He* blown up!—Ah, you little know your man—I will wager at this moment he is as well as any of us. I know all his tricks many a day since."—S.

commanded, to act with regularity upon such an extensive line of operations? The enemy cannot force me back on the Rhine, till they have gained ten battles; but allow me only one victory, and I will march on their capitals of Berlin and Breslau, relieve my garrisons on the Vistula and Oder, and force the allies to such a peace as shall leave my glory untarnished. Your defensive retreat does not suit me; besides, I do not ask you for plans, but for assistance to carry into execution my own projects."[269]

Thus Napoleon silenced his military as well as his civil counsellors. But there was one adviser whose mouth he had stopt, whose advice, if it could have reached him, would probably have altered his fatal resolution. One of Buonaparte's most impolitic as well as unjustifiable measures had been, his total destruction of every mode by which the public opinion of the people of France could be manifested. His system of despotism, which had left no manner of expression whatever, either by public meetings, by means of the press, or through the representative bodies, by which the national sentiments on public affairs could be made known, became now a serious evil. The manifestation of public opinion was miserably supplied by the voices of hired functionaries, who, like artificial fountains, merely returned back with various flourishes the sentiments with which they had been supplied from the common reservoir at Paris. Had free agents of any kind been permitted to report upon the state of the public mind, Napoleon would have had before him a picture which would have quickly summoned him back to France. He would have heard that the nation, blind to the evils of war, while dazzled with victory and military glory, had become acutely sensible of them so soon as these evils became associated with defeats, and the occasion of new draughts on the population of France. He would have learned that the fatal retreat of Moscow, and this precarious campaign of Saxony, had awakened parties and interests which had long been dormant—that the name of the Bourbons was again mentioned in the west—that 50,000 recusant conscripts were wandering through France, forming themselves into bands, and ready to join any standard which was raised against the imperial authority; and that, in the Legislative Body, as well as the

---

[269] Fouché, tom. ii., p. 152.

Senate, there was already organised a tacit opposition to his government, that wanted but a moment of weakness to show itself.

All this, and more, he would have learned; and must have been taught the necessity of concentrating his forces, returning to the frontiers of France, recovering the allegiance of those who hesitated, by accepting the best terms of peace which he could extort from the allies, and assuming on the Rhine such a firm attitude of defence as should at once overawe domestic dissatisfaction, and repel foreign invasion. But the least spiracle, by which the voice of France could find its way to the ears of her sovereign, was effectually closed. The fate of Napoleon turned on this circumstance; for the sovereign who deprives himself of the means of collecting the general sense of the nation over which he rules, is like the householder who destroys his faithful mastiff. Both may, perhaps, alarm their master by baying without just cause, or at an inconvenient time; but when the hour of action comes, no other sentinel can supply the want of their vigilance.

The armistice now afforded an apt occasion for arranging a general peace, or rather (for that was the real purpose) for giving Austria an opportunity of declaring what were her real and definitive intentions in this unexpected crisis, which had rendered her to a great degree arbitress of the fate of Europe. Napoleon, from his first arrival in Saxony, had adopted a belief, that although Austria was likely to use the present crisis as an opportunity of compelling him to restore the Illyrian provinces, and perhaps other territories of which former wars had deprived her, yet that in the end, the family connexion, with the awe entertained for his talents, would prevail to hinder her cabinet from uniting their cause to that of the allies. An expression had dropt from the Austrian minister Metternich, which would have altered this belief, had it been reported to him.

Maret, Duke of Bassano, had pressed the Austrian hard on the ties arising from the marriage, when the Austrian answered emphatically, "The marriage—yes, the marriage—it was a match founded on political considerations; *but*"——

INTERVIEW WITH METTERNICH

This single brief word disclosed as much as does the least key when it opens the strongest cabinet—it made it clear that the connexion formed by the marriage would not prevent Austria from taking the line in the present dispute which general policy demanded. And this was soon seen when Count Metternich came to Dresden to have an audience of Napoleon.

This celebrated statesman and accomplished courtier had been very acceptable at the Tuileries, and Napoleon seems to have imagined him one of those persons whose gaiety and good-humour were combined with a flexible character, liable to be mastered and guided by one of power and energy like his own. This was a great mistake. Metternich, a man of liveliness and address when in society, was firm and decisive in business. He saw that the opportunity of controlling the absolute power of France and of Buonaparte had at length arrived, and was determined, so far as Austria was concerned, and under his administration, that no partial views or advantages should prevent its being effectually employed. His interview with Napoleon took place at Dresden on the 28th June, and the following particulars are accredited:—

Napoleon always piqued himself on a plain, down-right style of negotiation, or rather upon his system of at once announcing the only terms on which he would consent to negotiate. He would hear of no counter-project, and admit of no medium betwixt the resumption of hostilities, and acceptance of peace upon the terms which it suited him to dictate. This frank and unanswerable mode of treating greatly tended to abridge the formalities of diplomacy; it had but this single disadvantage, that it was only suitable for the lips of a victor, whose renewal of war was to be, in all human probability, the resuming a career of victory. Such a tone of negotiation became the Roman Prætor, when he environed with a circle the feeble Eastern monarch, and insisted on a categorical answer to the terms he had proposed, ere he should step beyond the line; and perhaps it became Napoleon, when, at Campo Formio, he threw down the piece of porcelain, declaring that the Austrian empire should be destroyed in the same manner, unless they instantly accepted his conditions. But the same abrupt dictatorial manner was less felicitously employed, when the question was to persuade Austria not to throw her force of 200,000 men into the scale of the allies, which already too equally balanced that of France; yet that ill-chosen tone may be observed in the following conference.

Napoleon upbraided Metternich with having favoured his adversaries, by being so tardy in opening the negotiation. He intimated that the Austrian minister perhaps staid away, in order that France might be reduced to a lower state than at the opening of the campaign; while now that he had gained two battles, Austria thrust in her mediation, that he might be prevented from following up his success. In claiming to be a negotiator, Austria, he said, was neither his friend nor his impartial judge—she was his enemy. "You were about to declare yourself," he said, "when the victory at Lutzen rendered it prudent in the first place to collect more forces. Now you have assembled behind the screen of the Bohemian mountains 200,000 men under Schwartzenberg's command. Ah, Metternich! I guess the purpose of your Cabinet. You wish to profit by my embarrassments, and seize on the favourable moment to regain as much as you can of what I have taken from you. The only question with you is, whether you will make most by allowing me to ransom myself, or by going to war with me?—You are uncertain on that point; and perhaps you only come here to ascertain which is your best course. Well, let us drive a bargain—how much is it you want?"

To this insulting commencement Metternich replied, that "the only advantage desired by his master, was to see that moderation and respect for the rights of nations which filled his own bosom, restored to the general councils of Europe, and such a well-balanced system introduced as should place the universal tranquillity under the guarantee of an association of independent states."

It was easy to see which way this pointed, and to anticipate the conclusion. Napoleon affected to treat it as a figure of speech, which was to cloak the private views of Austria. "I speak clearly," he said, "and come to the point. Will it suit you to accept of Illyria, and to remain neuter?—Your neutrality is all I require. I can deal with the Russians and Prussians with my own army."—"Ah, Sire," replied Metternich, "it depends solely on your Majesty to unite all our forces with yours. But the truth must be told. Matters are come to that extremity that Austria cannot remain neutral—We must be with you, or against you."[270]

After this explicit declaration, from which it was to be inferred that Austria would not lay aside her arms, unless Buonaparte would comply with the terms which she had fixed upon as the conditions of a general pacification, and that she was determined to refuse all that might be offered as a bribe for her neutrality, the Emperor of France and the Austrian statesman retired into a cabinet, apart from the secretaries, where it is to be presumed Metternich communicated more specifically the conditions which Austria had to propose. Napoleon's voice was presently heard exclaiming aloud, "What! not only Illyria, but half of Italy, the restoration of the Pope, and the abandoning of Poland, and the resignation of Spain, and Holland, and the confederation of the Rhine, and Switzerland! Is this your moderation? You hawk about your alliance from the one camp to the other, where the greatest partition of territory is to be obtained, and then you talk of the independence of nations! In plain truth, you would have Italy; Sweden demands Norway; Prussia requires Saxony; England would have Holland and Belgium—You would dismember the French empire; and all these changes to be operated by Austria's mere threat of going to war. Can you pretend to win, by a single stroke of the pen, so many of the strongest fortresses in Europe, the keys of which I have gained by battles and victories? And think you that I will be so docile as to march back my soldiers, with their arms reversed, over the Rhine, the Alps, and the Pyrenees, and by subscribing a treaty, which is one vast capitulation, deliver myself, like a fool, into the hands of my enemies, and trust for a doubtful permission to exist, to their generosity? Is it when my army is triumphing at the gates of Berlin and Breslau, that Austria hopes to extort such a cession from me, without striking a blow or drawing a sword? It is an affront to expect it. And is it my father-in-law who entertains such a project? Is it he who sends you to me? In what attitude would he place me before the eyes of the French people! He is in a strange mistake if he supposes that a mutilated throne can, in France, afford shelter to his daughter and his

---

[270] Fouché, tom. ii., p. 148. See also Savary, tom. iii., p. 78.

grandson——Ah, Metternich," he concluded, "what has England given you to induce you to make war on me?"

The Austrian minister, disdaining to defend himself against so coarse an accusation, only replied by a look of scorn and resentment. A profound silence followed, during which Napoleon and Metternich traversed the apartment with long steps, without looking at each other. Napoleon dropt his hat, perhaps to give a turn to this awkward situation. But Metternich was too deeply affronted for any office of courtesy, and the Emperor was obliged to lift it himself. Buonaparte then resumed the discourse, in a more temperate strain, and said he did not yet despair of peace. He insisted that the congress should be assembled, and that, even if hostilities should recommence, negotiations for peace should, nevertheless, not be discontinued. And, like a wary trader, when driving a bargain, he whispered Metternich, that his offer of Illyria was *not his last word*.[271]

His last word, however, had been in reality spoken, and both he and Metternich were fully acquainted with each other's views. Metternich had refused all private conditions which could be offered to detach Austria from the general cause, and Buonaparte had rejected as an insult any terms which went to lower him to a rank of equality with the other sovereigns of Europe. He would be Cæsar or nothing. It did not mend the prospect of negotiation, that he had formally insulted one of the persons most influential in the Austrian councils. The chance of peace seemed farther off than ever.

Accordingly, all the proceedings at the Congress of Prague were lingering and evasive. The meeting had been fixed for the 5th July, and the dissolution was postponed till the 10th August, in order to allow time for trying to adjust the disputed claims. England had declined being concerned with the armistice, alleging she was satisfied that Napoleon would come to no reasonable terms. Caulaincourt, to whom Buonaparte chiefly trusted the negotiation, did not appear till 25th July, detained, it was idly alleged, by his services as an officer of the palace. Austria spun out the time by proposing that the other commissioners should hold no direct

---

[271] Fouché, tom. ii., p. 150.

intercourse, but only negotiate through the medium of the mediator. Other disputes arose; and, in fact, it seems as if all parties manœuvred to gain time, with a view to forward military preparations, rather than to avail themselves of the brief space allowed for adjusting the articles of peace. At length, so late as the 7th August, Austria produced her plan of pacification, of which the bases were the following:—I. The dissolution of the grand duchy of Warsaw, which was to be divided between Russia, Prussia, and Austria. II. The re-establishment of the Hanseatic towns in their former independence. III. The reconstruction of Prussia, assigning to that kingdom a frontier on the Elbe. IV. The cession to Austria of the maritime town of Trieste, with the Illyrian provinces. The emancipation of Spain and Holland, as matters in which England, no party to the Congress, took chief interest, was not stirred for the present, but reserved for consideration at the general peace. A concluding article stipulated that the condition of the European powers, great and small, as might be settled at the peace, should be guaranteed to all and each of them, and not innovated upon except by general consent.

Buonaparte in return offered much, but most of his cessions were clogged with conditions, which at once showed how unwillingly they were made, and seemed in most cases, to provide the means of annulling them when times should be favourable.

I. The grand duchy of Warsaw Napoleon agreed to yield up, but stipulated that Dantzic, with its fortifications demolished, should remain a free town, and that Saxony should be indemnified for the cession of the duchy, at the expense of Prussia and Austria. II. The cession of the Illyrian provinces was agreed to, but the seaport of Trieste was reserved. III. Contained a stipulation that the German confederation should extend to the Oder. Lastly, the territory of Denmark was to be guaranteed.

AUSTRIA JOINS THE ALLIES

Before this tardy agreement to grant some of the terms which the allies had demanded, could arrive at Prague, the 10th of August, the day which concluded the armistice, had expired, and Austria had passed from the friendship of France into the federation of the allies. On the night betwixt the 10th and 11th, rockets of a new and brilliant kind flickered in the air from height to height, betwixt Prague and Trachenberg, the headquarters of the Emperor of Russia and King of Prussia, to announce to these sovereigns that the armistice was broken off.

Metternich and Caulaincourt still continued their negotiations; and Napoleon seemed on a sudden sincerely desirous of the peace about which he had hitherto trifled. Metternich persisted in his demand of Trieste and the Hanse towns. He rejected the extension of the Confederation of the Rhine, as a demand made at a time so ill-chosen as to be nearly ridiculous; and he required that the independence of Germany should be declared free, as well as that of Switzerland.

Buonaparte at length consented to all these demands, which, if they had been admitted during his interview with Metternich, on 28th June, or declared to the Congress before the 10th August, must have availed to secure peace. It is probable, either that Napoleon was unwilling to make his mind up to consent to terms which he thought humiliating, or that he made the concessions at a time when they would not, in all likelihood, be accepted, in order that he might obtain the chance of war, yet preserve with his subjects the credit of having been willing to make peace.

It has been said, with much plausibility, that the allies, on their part, were confirmed in their resolution to demand high terms, by the news of the decisive battle of Vittoria, and the probability, that, in consequence, the Duke of Wellington's army might be soon employed in the invasion of France. Napoleon entertained the same impression, and sent Soult, the ablest of his generals to make a stand, if possible, against the victorious English general and protect at least the territory of France itself.[272]

---

[272] The court of Napoleon were amused at this time by an incident connected with Soult's departure. As he had been designed to command in the German campaign, this new destination compelled him to sell his horses, and make various other inconvenient

Chapter LXVIII

Amount and distribution of the French Army at the resumption of Hostilities—of the Armies of the Allies—Plan of the Campaign on both sides—Return of Moreau from America, to join the Allies—Attack on Dresden by the Allies on 26th August—Napoleon arrives to its succour—Battle continued on the 27th—Death of General Moreau—Defeat and Retreat of the Allies, with great loss—Napoleon returns from the pursuit to Dresden, indisposed—Vandamme attacks the Allies at Culm—is driven back towards Peterswald—Conflict on the heights of Peterswald—Vandamme is Defeated and made prisoner—Effects of the victory of Culm, on the Allies—and on Napoleon.

At no period during the armistice had the hopes of peace been so probable, as to suspend for a moment the most active preparations for war.

Napoleon, determined, as we have already seen, to render Dresden the centre of his operations, had exerted the utmost industry in converting that beautiful capital into a species of citadel. All the trees in the neighbourhood, including those which so much adorned the public gardens and walks, had been cut down, and employed in the construction of a chain of redoubts and field-works, secured by fosses and palisades, which were calculated to

---

sacrifices to the hurry of the moment. His wife, the Duchess of Dalmatia, a lady of a spirit equal to that of the great soldier to whom she was wedded, went boldly into the Emperor's presence to state her grievances; to insist that her husband had been subjected to too much fatiguing service, and to remonstrate against his being employed in the Pyrenees. "Go, madam," said Napoleon sternly; "remember that I am not your husband, and if I were, you dared not use me thus. Go, and remember it is a wife's duty to assist her husband, not to tease him." Such was (with every respect to the lady, who might, notwithstanding, do well to be angry,) the Imperial "Taming of a Shrew."—S.—See *Mémoires de Fouché*, tom. ii., p. 144.

render the city very defensible. But, besides Dresden itself, with the neighbouring mountain-fortresses, the French Emperor possessed as strongly fortified places, Torgau, Wittenberg, Magdeburg, and others on the Elbe, which secured him the possession of the rich and beautiful valley of that river. He had established an intrenched camp at the celebrated position of Pirna, and thrown a bridge of boats over the Elbe, near Kœnigstein, for the purpose of maintaining a communication betwixt that mountain-fortress and the fort of Stolpen. This showed Napoleon's apprehension of an attack from the mountains of Bohemia, behind which the Austrians had been assembling their army. In this destined battle-ground, Napoleon assembled the young conscripts, who continued to pour from the French frontier; and who, by a singularly ingenious species of combination, were learning the duties of their new condition, even while, with arms in their hands for the first time, they were marching to the field of action.[273]

DISTRIBUTION OF THE ARMY

In the beginning of August, Napoleon had assembled about 250,000 men in Saxony and Silesia. This great force was stationed so as best to confront the enemy on the points where they had assembled their troops. At Leipsic, there were collected 60,000 men, under command of Oudinot. At Loewenberg, Goldberg, Bantzlau, and other towns on the borders of Silesia, were 100,000 men, commanded by Macdonald. Another army of 50,000 were quartered in Lusatia, near Zittau. St. Cyr, with 20,000, was stationed near Pirna, to observe the mountains of Bohemia, and the passes through which the Elbe discharges its waters upon Saxony. In Dresden the Emperor himself lay with his guard, amounting to 25,000 men, the flower of his army. Besides these hosts, Buonaparte had a

---

[273] According to orders accurately calculated, the little bands of recruits, setting off from different points, or depôts on the frontier, met together at places assigned, and, as their numbers increased by each successive junction, were formed first into companies, next into battalions, and last into regiments; learning, of course, to practise successively the duties belonging to these various bodies. When they joined the army, these combinations, which had but been adopted temporarily, were laid aside, the union of the marching battalion dissolved, and the conscripts distributed among old regiments, whose example might complete the discipline which they had thus learned in a general way.—S.

considerable army in Italy under the Viceroy Eugene; and 25,000 Bavarians were assembled as an army of reserve, under General Wrede. Almost all his old lieutenants, who had fought, and won so often in his cause, were summoned to attend this important war; and even Murat, who had been on indifferent terms with his relative, came anew from his beautiful capital of Naples, to enjoy the pleasure of wielding his sabre against his old friends the Cossacks.

The preparations of the allies were upon a scale equally ample. The accession of the Austrians had placed at disposal in Bohemia 120,000 men, to whom the allies joined 80,000 Russians and Prussians, which brought the whole force to 200,000 men. Schwartzenberg had been selected to command this, which was called the grand army of the allies—a judicious choice, not only as a fitting compliment to the Emperor of Austria, who had joined the confederacy at so critical a moment, but on account of Schwartzenberg's military talents, his excellent sound sense, penetration, good-humour, and placidity of temper; qualities essential in every general, but especially in him upon whom reposes the delicate duty of commanding an army composed of different nations. This large host lay in and about Prague, and, concealed by the chain of hills called the Erzgebirge, was ready to rush into Saxony as soon as an opportunity should offer of surprising Dresden.

The other moiety of the original invading army amounting to 80,000, consisting of Russians and Prussians, called the army of Silesia, and commanded by Blucher, defended the frontier of that country, and the road to Breslau. Nearer the gates of Berlin was the Crown Prince of Sweden, with an army consisting of 30,000 Swedes, and about 60,000 Prussians and Russians; the former being the corps of Bulow and Tauenzein, the latter those of Winzengerode and Woronzoff. Besides these armies, Walmoden, with a force consisting of 30,000 Russians, Prussians, and insurgent Germans, was at Schwerin, in the duchy of Mecklenberg; Hiller, with 40,000 Austrians, watched the Italian army of the Viceroy; and the Prince of Reuss confronted the Bavarian troops with an army equal in strength to Wrede's own.

The allies had agreed upon a plan of operations equally cautious and effective. It is believed to have been originally sketched by the Crown Prince of Sweden, and afterwards revised and approved by the celebrated Moreau. That renowned French general had been induced, by the complexion of matters in Europe, and the invitation of Russia, to leave America, join the camp of the allies, and bring all the knowledge of the art of war, for which he was so famous, to enlighten their military councils. His conduct in thus passing over to the camp of France's enemies, has been ably defended by some as the act of a patriot who desired to destroy the despotism which had been established in his country, while others have censured him for arming against his native land, in revenge for unworthy usage which he had received from its ruler. Much of the justice of the case must rest upon what we cannot know—the purpose, namely, of Moreau, in case of ultimate success. He certainly had not, as Bernadotte might plead, acquired such rights in, and such obligations to another country, as to supersede the natural claims of his birth-place. Yet he might be justified in the eye of patriotism, if his ultimate object really was to restore France to a rational degree of liberty, under a regulated government; and such it is stated to have been. Any purpose short of this must leave him guilty of the charge of having sacrificed his duty to his country to his private revenge. He was, however, highly honoured by the Emperor of Russia in particular; and his presence was justly considered as a great accession to the council of war of the allies.

So many men of talent, and two of them masters of the French tactics, had no difficulty in divining the mode in which Buonaparte meant to conduct the present campaign. They easily saw that he intended to join his strong and effective reserve of the Guard to any of the armies placed on the frontier of Saxony, where a point of attack presented itself; and thus advance upon, overpower, and destroy the enemy whom he should find in front, as the hunted tiger springs upon the victim which he has selected out of the circle of hunters, who surround him with protended spears. To meet this mode of attack, which might otherwise have been the means of the allied armies being defeated successively and in detail, it was resolved that the general against whom Buonaparte's first effort should be directed, should on no account accept of the proffered battle, but, withdrawing his troops before the Emperor, should decoy him as far as possible in pursuit, while at the same time the other armies of the allies should advance upon his rear, destroy his communications, and finally effect their purpose of closing round him in every direction.

DRESDEN

The grand army, commanded by Schwartzenberg, was particularly directed to this latter task, because, while it would have been dangerous in Napoleon on that point to have sought them out by storming the mountain-passes of Bohemia, nothing could be more easy for Schwartzenberg than to rush down upon Dresden when Buonaparte should leave that city uncovered, for however short an interval.

Blucher was the first who, advancing from Silesia, and menacing the armies of Macdonald and Ney, induced Buonaparte to march to join them with his Guard, and with a great body of cavalry commanded by Latour Maubourg. He left Dresden on the 15th August; he threw bridges over the Bober, and advanced with rapidity, bringing forward Macdonald's division in aid of his own force. But the Prussian general was faithful to the plan laid down. He made an admirable retreat across the Katzbach, admitting the French to nothing but skirmishes, in which the allies had some advantage. Finally, he established himself in a position on the river Niesse, near Jauer, so as to cover Silesia and its capital.

On the 21st August, Napoleon learned the interesting news, that while he was pressing forward on the retreating Prussians, Dresden was in the utmost danger of being taken. His guards had instant orders to return to Saxony. He himself set out early on the 23d. It was full time; for Schwartzenberg, with whom came the Sovereigns of Russia and Prussia, as well as General Moreau, had descended from Bohemia, and, concentrating their grand army on the left bank of the Elbe, were already approaching the walls of Dresden, Napoleon's point of support, and the pivot of his operations. Leaving, therefore, to Macdonald the task of controlling

Blucher, the Emperor set out with the élite of his army; yet, with all the speed he could exert, very nearly came too late to save the object of his solicitude.

General St. Cyr, who had been left with about 20,000 men to observe the Bohemian passes, was in no condition to make a stand, when they poured out upon him six or seven times his own number. He threw himself with his troops into Dresden, in hopes, by means of its recent fortifications, to defend it until the arrival of Napoleon. The allies having found little resistance on their march, displayed their huge army before the city, divided into four columns, about four o'clock on the 25th August, and instantly commenced the assault. If they should be able to take Dresden before it could be relieved by Buonaparte, the war might be considered as nearly ended, since they would in that case obtain complete command of his line of communication with France, and had at their mercy his recruits and supplies of every kind.

The scheme of attack was excellently laid, but the allied generals did not pursue it with the necessary activity. The signal for onset should have been given instantly, yet they paused for the arrival of Klenau, with an additional corps d'armée, and the assault was postponed until next morning.

On the 26th, at break of day, the allies advanced in six columns, under a tremendous fire. They carried a great redoubt near the city-gate of Dippoldiswalde, and soon after another; they closed on the French on every point; the bombs and balls began to fall thick on the streets and houses of the terrified city; and in engaging all his reserves, St. Cyr, whose conduct was heroical, felt he had yet too few men to defend works of such extent. It was at this crisis, while all thought a surrender was inevitable, that columns, rushing forward with the rapidity of a torrent, were seen advancing on Dresden from the right side of the Elbe, sweeping over its magnificent bridges, and pressing through the streets, to engage in the defence of the almost overpowered city. The Child of Destiny himself was beheld amidst his soldiers, who, far from exhibiting fatigue, notwithstanding a severe forced march from the frontiers of Silesia, demanded, with loud cries, to be led into immediate battle.

Napoleon halted to reassure the King of Saxony, who was apprehensive of the destruction of his capital, while his troops, marching through the city, halted on the western side, at those avenues, from which it was designed they should debouche upon the enemy.

Two sallies were then made under Napoleon's eye, by Ney and Mortier. The one column, pouring from the gate of Plauen, attacked the allies on the left flank; the others, issuing from that of Pirna, assailed their right. The Prussians were dislodged from an open space, called the Great Garden, which covered their advance upon the ramparts; and the war began already to change its face, the allies drawing off from the points they had attacked so fiercely, where they found them secured by these unexpected defenders. They remained, however, in front of each other, the sentinels on each side being in close vicinity, until next morning.

On the 27th of August, the battle was renewed under torrents of rain, and amid a tempest of wind. Napoleon, manœuvring with excellence altogether his own, caused his troops, now increased by concentration to nearly 200,000 men, to file out from the city upon different points, the several columns diverging from each other like the sticks of a fan when it is expanded; and thus directed them upon such points as seemed most assailable along the allies' whole position, which occupied the heights from Plauen to Strehlen. In this manner, his plan assisted by the stormy weather, which served to conceal his movements, he commenced an attack upon both flanks of the enemy. On the left he obtained an advantage, from a large interval left in the allied line, to receive the division of Klenau, who were in the act of coming up, but exhausted with fatigue and bad weather, and their muskets rendered almost unserviceable. In the meanwhile, as a heavy cannonade was continued on both sides, Napoleon observed one of the batteries of the Young Guard slacken its fire. General Gourgaud, sent to inquire the cause, brought information that the guns were placed too low to reply with advantage to the enemy's fire from the high ground, and that the balls from the French battery were most of them lost in the earth. "Fire on, nevertheless," was the Emperor's reply; "we must occupy the attention of the enemy on that point."

The fire was resumed, and from an extraordinary movement amongst the troops on the hill, the French became aware that some person of high rank had been struck down. Napoleon supposed that the sufferer must be Schwartzenberg. He paid him a tribute of regret, and added, with the sort of superstition peculiar to his mind, "*He*, then, was the victim whom the fatal fire at the ball indicated?[274] I always regarded it as a presage—it is now plain whom it concerned."

DEATH OF MOREAU

Next morning, however, a peasant brought to Napoleon more precise accounts. The officer of distinction had both legs shattered by the fatal bullet—he was transported from the field on a bier composed of lances—the Emperor of Russia and King of Prussia had expressed the greatest sorrow and solicitude. The man ended this account by bringing the fallen officer's dog, a greyhound, whose collar bore the name of Moreau. This great general died a few days afterwards, having suffered amputation of the wounded limbs, which he bore with great fortitude. His talents and personal worth were undisputed, and those who, more bold than we are, shall decide that his conduct in one instance too much resembled that of Coriolanus and the Constable of Bourbon, must yet allow that the fault, like that of those great men, was atoned for by an early and a violent death.

Moreau is said to have formed the plan on which the attack on Dresden was conducted. His death must therefore have disconcerted it. But besides this, the allies had calculated upon Buonaparte's absence, and upon the place being slightly defended. They were disappointed in both respects; and his sudden arrival at the head of a choice, if not a numerous army, had entirely changed the nature of the combat. They had become defenders at the very time when they reckoned on being assailants; and their troops, particularly the Austrians, who had in former wars received such dreadful cause to recollect the name of Napoleon, were discouraged. Even if they repelled the French into Dresden, they had provided

---

[274] Given on account of the marriage of Napoleon and Maria Louisa.—See *ante*.

no magazines of support in front of it, should the allied army be designed to remain there. Jomini, the celebrated Swiss engineer, who had exchanged, some short time before, the service of Napoleon for that of the Emperor Alexander, proposed the daring plan of changing the front of the army during the action, and attacking in force the left of the French, which might have turned the fortune of the day. But the experiment was thought, with some justice, too perilous to be attempted, with a discouraged and disordered army. A retreat was, therefore, resolved upon, and, owing to the weather, the state of the roads, and the close pursuit of the French, it was a disastrous one. The successful operations of the French had established the King of Naples on the western road to Bohemia, by Freyberg; and Vandamme, with a strong division, blocked up that which led directly southward up the Elbe, by Pirna.

The two principal roads being thus closed against Schwartzenberg and his army, nothing remained for them but to retreat through the interval between these highways by such country paths as they could find, which, bad in themselves, had been rendered almost impassable by the weather. They were pursued by the French in every direction, and lost, what had of late been unusual, a great number of prisoners. Seven or eight thousand of the French were killed and wounded; but the loss of the allies was as great, while their prisoners, almost all Austrians, amounted to from 13,000 to 15,000. This is admitted by Boutourlin. The French carry the loss to 50,000, which is an obvious exaggeration; but half the number does not probably exceed the real extent of the loss. It is singular, however, that in such roads as have been described, the allies, out of more than one hundred guns which they brought into position, should have lost only twenty-six. It was, notwithstanding, a battle with important consequences, such as had not of late resulted from any of Napoleon's great victories.[275] It proved, indeed, the last favour of an unmixed character which Fortune reserved for her ancient favourite, and it had all the dazzling rapidity and resistless strength of an unexpected thunderbolt.

---

[275] Jomini, tom. iv., p. 390; Savary, tom. iii., p. 106; Military Reports to the Empress; Baron Fain, tom. ii., p. 309.

Having seen this brilliant day to a close, Napoleon returned to Dresden on horseback, his grey capote and slouched hat streaming with water, while the indifferent appearance of his horse and furniture, his awkward seat and carriage, made a singular contrast with those of Murat, whose bearing as a horseman was inimitable, and whose battle-dress was always distinguished by its theatrical finery.[276]

The venerable King of Saxony received his deliverer with rapture, for to him, personally, Buonaparte certainly was such, though considered by many of his subjects in a very different light. Napoleon behaved generously after the action, distributing money among the citizens of Dresden, who had suffered from the cannonade, and causing the greatest care to be taken of the wounded and prisoners belonging to the allies.

The next morning this ever-vigilant spirit was again on horseback, directing his victorious troops in pursuit of the enemy. They were despatched in different columns, to pursue the allies on the broken roads by which they were compelled to retreat, and to allow them no rest nor refuge. No frame, even of iron, could have supported the fatigues of both mind and body to which Napoleon had subjected himself within the last three or four days. He was perpetually exposed to the storm, and had rarely taken rest or refreshment. He is also stated to have suffered from having eaten hastily some food of a coarse and indigestible quality.[277] Through one or other, or the whole of these causes combined, Napoleon became very much indisposed, and was prevailed upon to return in his carriage to Dresden, instead of remaining at Pirna, more close in the rear of his pursuing battalions, to direct their motions. The French officers, at least some of them, ascribe to this circumstance, as the primary cause, a great, critical, and most unexpected misfortune, which befell his arms at this time.

---

[276] Baron d'Odeleben, Relation Circonstanciée, tom. i., p. 198.
[277] To be precise—a shoulder of mutton, stuffed with garlic, was the only dinner which his attendants could procure for him on the 27th. Mahomet, who was a favourite of Napoleon, suffered by indulging in similar viands. But the shoulder of mutton, in the case of the Arabian prophet, had the condescension to give its consumer warning of its deleterious qualities, though not till he had eaten too much for his health.—S.

VANDAMME

On the 29th of August, the French still continued to push their advantages. The King of Naples, Marmont, and St. Cyr, were each pressing upon the pursuit of the columns of the allies, to which they had been severally attached. A corps d'armée, of about 30,000 men, had been intrusted to the conduct of Vandamme, whose character as a general, for skill, determined bravery, and activity, was respected, while he was detested by the Germans on account of his rudeness and rapacity, and disliked by his comrades because of the ferocious obstinacy of his disposition.[278] With this man, who, not without some of the good qualities which distinguished Buonaparte's officers, presented even a caricature of the vices ascribed to them, the misfortunes of his master in this campaign were destined to commence.

Vandamme had advanced as far as Peterswald, a small town in the Erzgebirge, or Bohemian mountains, forcing before him a column of Russians, feeble in number, but excellent in point of character and discipline, commanded by Count Ostermann, who were retreating upon Toplitz. This town was the point on which all the retiring, some of which might be almost termed the fugitive, divisions of the allies were directing their course. If Vandamme could have defeated Ostermann, and carried this place, he might have established himself, with his corps of 30,000 men, on the only road practicable for artillery, by which the allies could march to Prague; so that they must either have remained enclosed between his corps d'armée, and those of the other French generals who pressed on their rear, or else they must have abandoned their guns and baggage, and endeavoured to cross the mountains by such wild tracks as were used only by shepherds and peasants.

It was on the 29th, in the morning, that, acting under so strong a temptation as we have mentioned, Vandamme had the

---

[278] The Abbé de Pradt represents Vandamme at Warsaw, as beating with his own hand a priest, the secretary of a Polish bishop, for not having furnished him with a supply of Tokay, although the poor man had to plead in excuse that King Jerome had the day before carried off all that was in the cellar. A saying was ascribed to Buonaparte, "that if he had had two Vandammes in his service, he must have made the one hang the other."—S.

temerity to descend the hill from Peterswald to the village of Culm, which is situated in a very deep valley betwixt that town and Toplitz. As he advanced towards Toplitz, it appeared that his plan was about to be crowned with success. The persons of the Emperor of Russia and the King of Prussia, the members of their Cabinet, and the whole depôt of the headquarters of the allies, seemed now within his clutch, and, already alarmed, his expected prey were beginning to attempt their escape in different directions. Vandamme seemed within a hand's grasp of the prize, for his operation, if complete, must have totally disorganised the allied army, and the French might perhaps have pursued them to the very gates of Prague, nay, of Vienna. The French advanced-guard was within half a league of Toplitz, when of a sudden Count Ostermann, who had hitherto retreated slowly, halted, like a wild-boar brought to bay, and commenced the most obstinate and inflexible resistance. His troops were few, but, as already said, of excellent quality, being a part of the Imperial Russian Guard, whom their commander gave to understand, that the safety of their father (as the Russians affectionately term the Emperor) depended upon their maintaining their ground. Never was the saying of Frederick II., that the Russians might be slain but not routed, more completely verified. They stood firm as a grove of pines opposed to the tempest, while Vandamme led down corps after corps, to support his furious and repeated attacks, until at length he had brought his very last reserves from the commanding ground of Peterswald, and accumulated them in the deep valley between Culm and Toplitz. The brave Ostermann had lost an arm in the action, and his grenadiers had suffered severely; but they had gained the time necessary. Barclay de Tolly, who now approached the scene of action, brought up the first columns of the Russians to their support; Schwartzenberg sent other succours; and Vandamme, in his turn, overpowered by numbers, retreated to Culm as night closed.

Prudence would have recommended to the French to have continued their retreat during the night to the heights of Peterswald; but, expecting probably the appearance of some of the French columns of pursuit, morning found Vandamme in the valley of Culm, where night had set upon him. In the meantime, still greater numbers of the allied corps, which were wandering through these mountain regions, repaired to the banners of Schwartzenberg and Barclay, and the attack was renewed upon the French column at break of day on the 30th, with a superiority of force with which it was fruitless to contend. Vandamme therefore disposed himself to retreat towards the heights of Peterswald, from which he had descended. But at this moment took place one of the most singular accidents which distinguished this eventful war.

Among other corps d'armée of the allies, which were making their way through the mountains, to rally to the main body as they best could, was that of the Prussian General Kleist, who had evaded the pursuit of St. Cyr, by throwing himself into the wood of Schoenwald, out of which he debouched on the position of Peterswald, towards which Vandamme was making his retreat. While, therefore, Vandamme's retreating columns were ascending the heights, the ridge which they proposed to gain was seen suddenly occupied by the troops of Kleist, in such a state of disorder as announced they were escaped from some pressing scene of danger, or hurrying on to some hasty attack.

When the Prussians came in sight of the French, they conceived that the latter were there for the purpose of cutting them off; and, instead of taking a position on the heights to intercept Vandamme, they determined, it would seem, to precipitate themselves down, break their way through his troops, and force themselves on to Toplitz. On the other hand, the French, seeing their way interrupted, formed the same conclusion with regard to Kleist's corps, which the Prussians had done concerning them; and each army being bent on making its way through that opposed to them, the Prussians rushed down the hill, while the French ascended it with a bravery of despair, that supplied the advantage of ground.

SURRENDER OF VANDAMME

The two armies were thus hurled on each other like two conflicting mobs, enclosed in a deep and narrow road, forming the descent along the side of a mountain. The onset of the French horse, under Corbineau, was so desperate, that many or most of them broke through, although the acclivity against which they advanced would not, in other circumstances, have permitted them to ascend at a trot; and the guns of the Prussians were for a moment in the hands of the French, who slew many of the artillerymen. The Prussians, however, soon rallied, and the two struggling bodies again mixing together, fought less for the purpose of victory or slaughter, than to force their way through each other's ranks, and escape in opposite directions. All became for a time a mass of confusion, the Prussian generals finding themselves in the middle of the French—the French officers in the centre of the Prussians. But the army of the Russians, who were in pursuit of Vandamme, appearing in his rear, put an end to this singular conflict. Generals Vandamme, Haxo, and Guyot, were made prisoners, with two eagles and 7000 prisoners, besides a great loss in killed and wounded, and the total dispersion of the army, many of whom, however, afterwards rejoined their eagles.[279]

The victory of Culm, an event so unexpected and important in a military view, was beyond appreciation in the consequences which it produced upon the moral feelings of the allied troops. Before this most propitious event, they were retiring as a routed army, the officers and soldiers complaining of their generals, and their generals of each other. But now their note was entirely altered, and they could sing songs of triumph, and appeal to the train of guns and long columns of prisoners, in support of the victory which they claimed. The spirits of all were reconciled to the eager prosecution of the war, and the hopes of liberation spread wider and wider through Germany. The other French corps d'armée, on the contrary, fearful of committing themselves as Vandamme had done, paused on arriving at the verge of the Bohemian mountains, and followed no farther the advantages of the battle of Dresden. The King of Naples halted at Sayda, Marmont at Zinnwalde, and St. Cyr at Liebenau. The headquarters of the Emperor Alexander remained at Toplitz.

Napoleon received the news of this calamity, however unexpected, with the imperturbable calmness which was one of his distinguishing qualities. General Corbineau, who commanded in the

---

[279] Jomini, tom. iv., p. 339; Baron Fain, tom. ii., p. 321.

singular charge of the cavalry up the hill of Peterswald, presented himself before the Emperor in the condition in which he escaped from the field, covered with his own blood and that of the enemy, and holding in his hand a Prussian sabre, which, in the thick of the mêlée, he had exchanged for his own. Napoleon listened composedly to the details he had to give. "One should make a bridge of gold for a flying enemy," he said, "where it is impossible, as in Vandamme's case, to oppose to him a bulwark of steel." He then anxiously examined the instructions to Vandamme, to discover if any thing had inadvertently slipped in to them, to encourage the false step which that general had taken. But nothing was found which could justify or authorise his advancing beyond Peterswald, although the chance of possessing himself of Toplitz must have been acknowledged as a strong temptation.

"This is the fate of war," said Buonaparte, turning to Murat. "Exalted in the morning, low enough before night. There is but one step between triumph and ruin." He then fixed his eyes on the map which lay before him, took his compass, and repeated in a reverie, the following verses:—

"J'ai servi, commandé, vaincu quarante années; Du monde, entre mes mains, j'ai vu les destinées, Et j'ai toujours connu qu'en chaque événement Le destin des états dependait d'un moment."

Chapter LXIX

Military Proceedings in the north of Germany—Luckau submits to the Crown Prince of Sweden—Battles of Gross-Beeren and Katzbach—Operations of Ney upon Berlin—He is defeated at Dennewitz on the 6th September—Difficult and embarrassing situation of Napoleon—He abandons all the right side of the Elbe to the Allies—Operations of the Allies in order to effect a junction—Counter-exertions of Napoleon—The French Generals averse to continuing the War in Germany—Dissensions betwixt them and the Emperor—Napoleon at length resolves to retreat upon Leipsic.

The advices which arrived at Dresden from the north of Germany, were no balm to the bad tidings from Bohemia. We must necessarily treat with brevity the high deeds of arms performed at a considerable distance from Napoleon's person, great as was their influence upon his fortunes.

BERLIN

Maréchal Blucher, it will be remembered, retreated across the river Katzbach, to avoid the engagement which the Emperor of France endeavoured to press upon him. The Crown Prince of Sweden, on the other hand, had his headquarters at Potsdam. Napoleon, when departing to succour Dresden, on the 21st of August, left orders for Oudinot to advance on Berlin, and for Macdonald to march upon Breslau, trusting that the former had force enough to conquer the Crown Prince, the latter to defeat Blucher.

Oudinot began to move on Berlin by the road of Wittenberg, on the very day when he received the orders. On the other hand, the

Crown Prince of Sweden, concentrating his troops, opposed to the French general a total force of more than 80,000 men, drawn up for the protection of Berlin. The sight of that fair city, with its towers and steeples, determined Oudinot to try his fortune with his ancient comrade in arms. After a good deal of skirmishing, the two armies came to a more serious battle on the 23d August, in which General Regnier distinguished himself. He commanded a corps which formed the centre of Oudinot's army, at the head of which he made himself master of the village of Gross-Beeren, which was within a short distance of the centre of the allies. The Prussian general, Bulow, advanced to recover this important post, and with the assistance of Borstal, who attacked the flank of the enemy, he succeeded in pushing his columns into the village. A heavy rain having prevented the muskets from being serviceable, Gross-Beeren was disputed with the bayonet. Yet, towards nightfall, the two French divisions of Fournier and Guilleminot again attacked the village, took it, and remained in it till the morning. But this did not re-establish the battle, for Regnier having lost 1500 men and eight guns, Oudinot determined on a general retreat, which he conducted in the face of the enemy with great deliberation. The Crown Prince obtained other trophies; Luckau, with a garrison of a thousand French, submitted to his arms on 28th August.[280]

Besides these severe checks on the Prussian frontier, General Girard, in another quarter, had sustained a defeat of some consequence. He had sallied from the garrison of Magdeburg, after the battle of Gross-Beeren, with five or six thousand men. He was encouraged to this movement by the removal of the blockading brigade of Herschberg, who, in obedience to orders, had joined the Crown Prince to oppose the advance of Oudinot. But, after the battle of Gross-Beeren, as the Prussian brigade was returning to renew the blockade of Magdeburg, they encountered Girard and his division near Leitzkau, on 27th August. The French were at first successful, but Czernicheff having thrown himself on them with a large body of Cossacks, Girard's troops gave way, losing six cannons, fifteen hundred prisoners, and all their baggage.

---

[280] Baron Fain, tom. ii., p. 328; Jomini, tom. iv., p. 404.

During this active period, war had been no less busy on the frontiers of Silesia than on those of Bohemia and Brandenburg. Maréchal Macdonald, as already mentioned, had received orders from Napoleon to attack Blucher and his Prussians, who had retired beyond the Katzbach, and occupied a position near a town called Jauer. In obedience to this order, the maréchal had sent General Lauriston, who commanded his right wing, to occupy a position in front of Goldberg, with orders to despatch a part of his division under General Puthod, to march upon Jauer, by the circuitous route of Schonau. The eleventh corps, which formed the centre of Macdonald's force, crossed the Katzbach at break of day, under his own command, and advanced towards Jauer, up the side of a torrent called the Wuthende (*i. e.* raging) Niesse. The third corps, under Souham, destined to form the left wing, was to pass the Katzbach near Liegnitz, and then moving southward, were to come upon the maréchal's left. With this left wing marched the cavalry, under Sebastiani.[281]

KATZBACH—SUCCESSES OF THE ALLIES

It chanced that, on this very 26th of August, Blucher, aware that Buonaparte was engaged at Dresden by the descent of the allies from Bohemia, thought it a good time to seek out his opponent and fight him. For this purpose, he was in the act of descending the river in order to encounter Macdonald, when the maréchal, on his part, was ascending it, expecting to find him in his position near Jauer.

The stormy weather, so often referred to, with mist and heavy rain, concealed from each other the movements of the two armies, until they met in the fields. They encountered in the plains which extend between Wahlstadt and the Katzbach, but under circumstances highly unfavourable to the French maréchal. His right wing was divided from his centre; Lauriston being at Goldberg, and fiercely engaged with the Russian General Langeron, with whom he had come into contact in the front of that town; and Puthod at a much greater distance from the field of battle. Macdonald's left wing, with the cavalry, was also far in the rear. Blucher allowed no

---

[281] Jomini, tom. iv., p. 409; Baron Fain, tom. ii., p. 334.

leisure for the junction of these forces. His own cavalry being all in front, and ready for action, charged the French without permitting them leisure to get into position; and when they did, their right wing indeed rested on the Wuthende-Niesse, but the left, which should have been covered by Sebastiani's cavalry, was altogether unsupported.

Message on message was sent to hasten up the left wing; but a singular fatality prevented both the cavalry and infantry from arriving in time. Different lines of advance had been pointed out to Souham and Sebastiani; but Souham, hearing the firing, and impatient to place himself on the road which he thought likely to lead him most speedily into action, unluckily adopted that which was appointed for the cavalry. Thus 5000 horse, and five times the number of infantry, being thrown at once on the same line of march, soon confused and embarrassed each other's motions, especially in passing the streets of a village called Kroitsch, a long and narrow defile, which the troops presently crowded to such a degree with foot and horse, baggage and guns, that there was a total impossibility of effecting a passage.

Macdonald, in the meanwhile, supported his high reputation by the gallantry of his resistance, though charged on the left flank, which these mistakes had left uncovered, by four regiments of cavalry, and by General Karpoff, with a whole cloud of Cossacks. But at length the day was decidedly lost. The French line gave way, and falling back on the Wuthende-Niesse, now doubly raging from torrents of rain, and upon the Katzbach, they lost a great number of men. As a last resource, Macdonald put himself at the head of the troops, who were at length debouching from the defile of Kroitsch; but they were driven back with great slaughter, and the skirmish in that quarter concluded the battle, with much loss to the French.

The evil did not rest here. Lauriston being also under the necessity of retreating across the Katzbach, while Puthod, who had been detached towards Schonau, was left on the right-hand side of that river, this corps was speedily attacked by the enemy, and all who were not killed or taken remained prisoners. The army which Buonaparte destined to act in Silesia, and take Breslau, was, therefore, for the present, completely disabled. The French are admitted to have lost 15,000 men, and more than a hundred guns.

Though the battles of Gross-Beeren and Katzbach were severe blows to Buonaparte's plan of maintaining himself on the Elbe, he continued obstinate in his determination to keep his ground, with Dresden as his central point of support, and attempted to turn the bad fortune which seemed to haunt his lieutenants (but which in fact arose from their being obliged to attempt great achievements with inadequate means,) by appointing Ney to the command of the Northern army, with strict injunctions to plant his eagles on the walls of Berlin. Accordingly, on the 6th September, Ney took charge of the army which Oudinot had formerly commanded, and which was lying under the walls of Wittenberg, and, in obedience to the Emperor's orders, determined to advance on the Prussian capital. The enemy (being the army commanded by the Crown Prince) lay rather dispersed upon the grounds more to the east, occupying Juterbock, Belzig, and other villages. Ney was desirous to avoid approaching the quarters of any of them, or to give the least alarm. That maréchal's object was to leave them on the left, and, evading any encounter with the Crown Prince, to throw his force on the road from Torgua to Berlin, and enter into communication with any troops which Buonaparte might despatch from Dresden upon the same point.

On examining the plan more closely, it was found to comprehend the danger of rousing the Prince of Sweden and his army upon one point, and that was at Dennewitz, the most southern village held by the allies. It was occupied by Tauentzein with a large force, and could not be passed without the alarm being given. Dennewitz might, however, be masked by a sufficient body of troops, under screen of which the maréchal and his main body might push forward to Dahme, without risking an engagement. It was concluded, that the rapidity of their motions would be so great as to leave no time for the Crown Prince to concentrate his forces for interrupting them.

DENNEWITZ

On the 5th, Ney marched from Wittenberg. On the 6th, the division of Bertrand, destined to mask Dennewitz, formed the left flank of the army. When they approached the village, Tauentzein, who commanded there, took the alarm, and drew up between Dennewitz and the French division. If Bertrand had only had to maintain himself for a short interval in that dangerous position, it would have been well, and he might have made head against Tauentzein, till the last file of Ney's army had passed by; but by some miscalculation (which began to be more common now than formerly among the French officers of the staff,) the corps of Bertrand was appointed to march at seven in the morning, while the corps which were to be protected by him did not move till three hours later. Bertrand was thus detained so long in face of the enemy, that his demonstration was converted into an action, his false attack into a real skirmish. Presently after the battle became sharp and serious, and the corps on both sides advancing to sustain them were engaged. Bulow came to support Tauentzein—Regnier advanced to repel Bulow—Guilleminot hastened up on the French side—and Borstel came to support the Russians. However unpremeditated, the battle became general, as if by common consent.

The Prussians suffered heavily from the French artillery, but without giving way. The Swedes and Russians at length came up, and the line of Ney began to yield ground. That general, who had hardly, though all his forces were engaged, made his post good against the Russians alone, despaired of success when he saw these new enemies appear. He began to retreat; and his first movement in that direction was a signal of flight to the 7th corps, composed chiefly of Saxons not over well inclined to the cause of Napoleon, and who therefore made it no point of honour to fight to the death in his cause. A huge blank was created in the French line by their flight; and the cavalry of the allies rushing in at the gap, the army of Ney was cut into two parts; one of which pushed forwards to Dahme with the maréchal himself; the other, with Oudinot, retreated upon Scharnitz. Ney afterwards accomplished his retreat on Torgau. But the battle of Dennewitz had cost him 10,000 men, forty-three pieces of cannon, and abundance of warlike trophies, relinquished to the adversary, besides the total disappointment of his object in marching towards Berlin.[282]

These repeated defeats, of Gross-Beeren, Katzbach, and Dennewitz, seemed to intimate that the French were no longer the invincibles they had once been esteemed; or at least, that when they yet worked miracles, it was only when Buonaparte was at their head. Others saw the matter in a different point of view. They said that formerly, when means were plenty with Buonaparte, he took care that his lieutenants were supplied with forces adequate to the purposes on which they were to be employed. But it was surmised that now he kept the guard and the *élite* of his forces under his own immediate command, and expected his lieutenants to be as successful with few and raw troops as they had formerly been with numbers, and veterans. It cannot, however, be said that he saved his own exertions; for during the month of September, while he persisted in maintaining the war in Saxony, although no affair of consequence took place, yet a series of active measures showed how anxious he was to bring the war to a decision under his own eye.[283]

In perusing the brief abstract of movements which follows, the reader will remember, that it was the purpose of Buonaparte to bring the allies to a battle on some point, where, by superior numbers or superior skill, he might obtain a distinguished victory; while, on the other hand, it was the policy of the allies, dreading at once his talents and his despair, to avoid a general action; to lay waste the ground around the points he occupied; restrict his communications; raise Germany in arms around him; and finally, to encompass and hem him in when his ranks were grown thin, and the spirit of his soldiers diminished. Keeping these objects in his eye, the reader, with a single glance at the map, will conceive the meaning of the following movements on either side.

Having deputed to Ney, as we have just seen, the task of checking the progress of the Crown Prince, and taking Berlin if possible, Buonaparte started in person from Dresden on the 3d September, in hopes of fetching a blow at Blucher, whose Cossacks,

---

[282] Jomini, tom. iv., p. 416; Baron Fain, tom. ii., p. 334.
[283] Jomini, tom. iv., p. 423.

since the battle of the Katzbach, had advanced eastward, and intercepted a convoy even near Bautzen. But agreeably to the plan adopted at the general headquarters of the allies, the Prussian veteran fell back and avoided a battle. Meanwhile, Napoleon was recalled towards Dresden by the news of the defeat of Ney at Dennewitz, and the yet more pressing intelligence that the allies were on the point of descending into Saxony, and again arraying themselves under the walls of Dresden. The advanced guard of Witgenstein had shown itself, it was said, at Pirna, and the city was a prey to new alarms. The French Emperor posted back towards the Elbe, and on the 9th came in sight of Witgenstein. But the allied generals, afraid of one of those sudden strokes of inspiration, when Napoleon seemed almost to dictate terms to fate, had enjoined Witgenstein to retreat in his turn. The passes of the Erzgebirge received him, and Buonaparte, following him as far as Peterswald, gazed on the spot where Vandamme met his unaccountable defeat, and looked across the valley of Culm to Toplitz, where his rival Alexander still held his headquarters. With the glance of an eye, the most expert in military affairs, he saw the danger of involving himself in such impracticable defiles as the valley of Culm, and the roads which communicated with it, and resolved to proceed no farther.

Napoleon, therefore, returned towards Dresden, where he arrived on the 12th September. In his retreat, a trifling skirmish occurred, in which the son of Blucher was wounded, and made prisoner. A victory was claimed on account of this affair, in the bulletin. About the same period, Blucher advanced upon the French troops opposed to him, endangered their communications with Dresden, and compelled them to retreat from Bautzen, and Neustadt, towards Bischoffswerder and Stolpen. While Buonaparte thought of directing himself eastward towards this indefatigable enemy, his attention was of new summoned southward to the Bohemian mountains. Count Lobau, who was placed in observation near Gieshubel, was attacked by a detachment from Schwartzenberg's army. Napoleon hastened to his relief, and made a second attempt to penetrate into these mountain recesses, from which the eagles of the allies made such repeated descents. He penetrated, upon this second occasion, beyond Culm, and as far as

Nollendorf, and had a skirmish with the allies, which was rather unfavourable to him. The action was broken off by one of the tremendous storms which distinguished the season, and Buonaparte again retreated towards Gieshubel. On his return to Dresden, he met the unpleasant news, that the Prince-Royal was preparing to cross the Elbe, and that Bulow had opened trenches before Wittenberg; while Blucher, on his side, approached the right bank of the river, and neither Ney nor Macdonald had sufficient force to check their progress.

On the 21st September, Napoleon once again came in person against his veteran enemy, whom he met not far from Hartha; but it was once more in vain. The Prussian field-maréchal was like the phantom knight of the poet. Napoleon, when he advanced to attack him, found no substantial body against which to direct his blows.

The Emperor spent some hours at the miserable thrice-sacked village of Hartha, deliberating, probably, whether he should press on the Crown Prince or Blucher, and disable at least one of these adversaries by a single blow; but was deterred by reflecting, that the time necessary for bringing either of them to action would be employed by Schwartzenberg in accomplishing that purpose of seizing Dresden, which his movements had so frequently indicated.

RETREATS TOWARDS DRESDEN

Thus Napoleon could neither remain at Dresden, without suffering the Crown Prince and Blucher to enter Saxony, and make themselves masters of the valley of the Elbe, nor make any distant movement against those generals, without endangering the safety of Dresden, and, with it, of his lines of communication with France. The last, as the more irreparable evil, he resolved to guard against, by retreating to Dresden, which he reached on the 24th. His maréchals had orders to approach closer to the central point, where he himself had his headquarters; and all the right side of the Elbe was abandoned to the allies. It is said by Baron Odeleben,[284] that the

---

[284] Relation Circonstanciée de la Campagne de 1813 en Saxe, tom. i., p. 234.

severest orders were issued for destroying houses, driving off cattle, burning woods, and rooting up fruit-trees, reducing the country in short to a desert (an evil reward for the confidence and fidelity of the old King of Saxony,) but that they were left unexecuted, partly owing to the humanity of Napoleon's lieutenants, and partly to the rapid advance of the allies. There was little occasion for this additional cruelty; for so dreadfully had these provinces been harassed and pillaged by the repeated passing and repassing of troops on both sides, that grain, cattle, and forage of every kind, were exhausted, and they contained scarce any other sustenance for man or beast, except the potato crop, then in the ground.

After his return to Dresden, on the 24th September, Napoleon did not leave it till the period of his final departure; and the tenacity with which he held the place, has been compared by some critics to the wilful obstinacy which led to his tarrying so long at Moscow. But the cases were different. We have formerly endeavoured to show, that Napoleon's wisdom in the commencement of this campaign would have been to evacuate Germany, and, by consenting to its liberation, to have diminished the odium attached to his assumption of universal power. As, however, he had chosen to maintain his lofty pretensions at the expense of these bloody campaigns, it was surely prudent to hold Dresden to the last moment. His retreat from it, after so many losses and disappointments, would have decided the defection of the whole Confederation of the Rhine, which already was much to be dreaded. It would have given the allied armies, at present separated from each other, an opportunity to form a junction on the left side of the Elbe, the consequences of which could hardly fail to be decisive of his fate. On the other hand, while he remained at Dresden, Napoleon was in a condition to operate by short marches upon the communications of the allies, and might hope to the last that an opportunity would be afforded him of achieving some signal success against one or other of them, or perhaps of beating them successively, and in detail. The allied sovereigns and their generals were aware of this, and, therefore, as we have seen, acted upon a plan of extreme caution, for which they have been scoffed at by some French writers, as if it were the result of fear rather than of wisdom. But it was plain that the time for more decisive operations was approaching, and, with a view to such, each party drew towards them such reinforcements as they could command.

Buonaparte's soldiers had suffered much by fatigue and skirmishes, though no important battle had been fought; and he found himself obliged to order Augereau, who commanded about 16,000 men in the neighbourhood of Wurtzberg, to join him at Dresden. He might, however, be said to lose more than he gained by this supply; for the Bavarians, upon whose inclinations to desert the French cause Augereau's army had been a check, no sooner saw it depart, than an open and friendly intercourse took place betwixt their army and that of Austria, which lay opposed to them; negotiations were opened between their courts, without much affectation of concealment; and it was generally believed, that only some question about the Tyrol prevented their coming to an immediate agreement.

The allies received, on their side, the reinforcement of no less than 60,000 Russians, under the command of Bennigsen. The most of them came from the provinces eastward of Moscow; and there were to be seen attending them tribes of the wandering Baskirs and Tartars, figures unknown in European war, wearing sheep-skins, and armed with bows and arrows. But the main body consisted of regular troops, though some bore rather an Asiatic appearance. This was the last reinforcement which the allies were to expect; being the arriere-ban of the almost boundless empire of Russia. Some of the men had travelled from the wall of China to this universal military rendezvous.

OPERATIONS OF THE ALLIES

Their utmost force being now collected, in numbers greatly superior to that of their adversary, the allies proceeded to execute a joint movement by means of which they hoped to concentrate their forces on the left bank of the Elbe; so that if Napoleon should persist in remaining at Dresden, he might be cut off from communication with France. With this view Blucher, on the 3d October, crossed the Elbe near the junction of that river with the

Schwarze Elster, defeated Bertrand, who lay in an entrenched camp to dispute the passage, and fixed his headquarters at Duben. At the same time, the Crown Prince of Sweden in like manner transferred his army to the left bank of the Elbe, by crossing at Roslau, and entered into communication with the Silesian army. Thus these two great armies were both transferred to the left bank, excepting the division of Tauentzein, which was left to maintain the siege of Wittenberg. Ney, who was in front of these movements, having no means to resist such a preponderating force, retreated to Leipsic.

Simultaneously with the entrance of the Crown Prince and Blucher into the eastern division of Saxony from the north-west, the grand army of the allies was put in motion towards the same district, advancing from the south by Sebastians-Berg and Chemnitz. On the 5th October, the headquarters of Prince Schwartzenberg were at Marienberg.

These movements instantly showed Buonaparte the measures about to be taken by the allies, and the necessity of preventing their junction. This he proposed to accomplish by leaving Dresden with all his disposable force, attacking Blucher at Duben, and, if possible, annihilating that restless enemy, or, at least, driving him back across the Elbe. At the same time, far from thinking he was about to leave Dresden for ever, which he had been employed to the last in fortifying yet more strongly, he placed a garrison of upwards of 15,000 men in that city under St. Cyr. This force was to defend the city against any corps of the allies, which, left in the Bohemian mountains for that purpose, might otherwise have descended and occupied Dresden, so soon as Napoleon removed from it. The King of Saxony, his Queen and family, preferred accompanying Napoleon on his adventurous journey, to remaining in Dresden, where a siege was to be expected, and where subsistence was already become difficult.

The same alertness of movement, which secured Blucher on other occasions, saved him in the present case from the meditated attack on Duben. On the 9th of October, hearing of Napoleon's approach, he crossed the Mulda, and formed a junction with the army of the Crown Prince, near Zoerbig, on the left bank of that river. Napoleon, once more baffled, took up his headquarters at Duben on the 10th. Here he soon learned that the Crown Prince and Blucher, apprehensive that he might interpose betwixt them and the grand army of Schwartzenberg, had retreated upon the line of the Saale during the night preceding the 11th. They were thus still placed on his communications, but beyond his reach, and in a situation to communicate with their own grand army.

But this movement to the westward, on the part of the allies, had this great inconvenience, that it left Berlin exposed, or inadequately protected by the single division of Tauentzein at Dessau. This did not escape the falcon eye of Napoleon. He laid before his maréchals a more daring plan of tactics than even his own gigantic imagination had (excepting in the Moscow campaign) ever before conceived. He proposed to recross the Elbe to the right bank, and then resting his right wing on Dresden, and his left on Hamburgh, there to maintain himself, with the purpose of recrossing the Elbe on the first appearance of obtaining a success over the enemy, dashing down on Silesia, and raising the blockade of the fortresses upon the Oder. With this purpose he had already sent Regnier and Bertrand across the Elbe, though their ostensible mission had nothing more important than to raise the siege of Wittenberg.

The counsellors of the Emperor were to a man dissatisfied with this plan. It seemed to them that remaining in Germany was only clinging to the defence of what could no longer be defended. They appealed to the universal disaffection of all the Germans on the Rhine, and to the destruction of the kingdom of Westphalia, recently effected by no greater force than Czernicheff, with a pulk of Cossacks. They noticed the almost declared defection of all their former friends, alluded to their own diminished numbers, and remonstrated against a plan which was to detain the army in a wasted country inhabited by a population gradually becoming hostile, and surrounded with enemies whom they could not defeat, because they would never fight but at advantage, and who possessed the means of distressing them, while *they* had no means of retorting the injuries they received. This, they said, was the history of the last three months, only varied by the decisive defeats of Gross-Beeren, Katzbach, and Dennewitz.

Napoleon remained from the 11th to the 14th of October at Duben, concentrating his own forces, waiting for news of the allies' motions, and remaining in a state of uncertainty and inactivity, very different from his usual frame of mind and natural habits. "I have seen him at that time," says an eyewitness,[285] "seated on a sofa beside a table, on which lay his charts, totally unemployed, unless in scribbling mechanically large letters on a sheet of white paper." Consultations with his best generals, which ended without adopting any fixed determination, varied those unpleasing reveries. The councils were often seasons of dispute, almost of dissension. The want of success had made those dissatisfied with each other, whose friendship had been cemented by uniform and uninterrupted prosperity. Great misfortunes might have bound them together, and compelled them to regard each other as common sufferers. But a succession of failures exasperated their temper, as a constant drizzling shower is worse to endure than a thunder-storm.

DISSENSIONS AMONG THE GENERALS

Napoleon, while the maréchals were dissatisfied with each other and with him, complained, on his part, that fatigue and discouragement had overpowered most of his principal officers; that they had become indifferent, lukewarm, awkward, and therefore unfortunate. "The general officers," he said, "desired nothing but repose, and that at all rates."

On the other hand, the maréchals asserted that Napoleon no longer calculated his means to the ends which he proposed to attain—that he suffered himself to be deceived by phrases about the predominance of his star and his destiny—and ridiculed his declaration that the word Impossible was not good French. They said that such phrases were well enough to encourage soldiers; but that military councils ought to be founded on more logical

---

[285] Baron Odeleben, in his interesting Circumstantial Notice of the Campaigns in Saxony.—S.

arguments. They pleaded guilty of desiring repose; but asked which was to blame, the horse or the rider, when the over-ridden animal broke down with fatigue?

At length Napoleon either changed his own opinion, or deferred to that of his military advisers; the orders to Regnier and Bertrand to advance upon Berlin were annulled, and the retreat upon Leipsic was resolved upon. The loss of three days had rendered the utmost despatch necessary, and Buonaparte saw himself obliged to leave behind him in garrison, Davoust at Hamburgh, Lemarrois at Magdeburg, Lapoype at Wittenberg, and Count Narbonne at Torgau. Still he seems to have anticipated some favourable chance, which might again bring him back to the line of the Elbe. "A thunderbolt," as he himself expressed it, "alone could save him; but all was not lost while battle was in his power, and a single victory might restore Germany to his obedience."

Chapter LXX

Napoleon reaches Leipsic on 15th of October—Statement of the French and Allied Forces—Battle of Leipsic, commenced on 16th, and terminates with disadvantage to the French at nightfall—Napoleon despatches General Mehrfeldt (his prisoner) to the Emperor of Austria, with proposals for an armistice—No answer is returned—The battle is renewed on the morning of the 18th, and lasts till night, when the French are compelled to retreat, after immense loss on both sides—They evacuate Leipsic on the 19th, the Allies in full pursuit—Blowing up of one of the bridges—Prince Poniatowski drowned in the Elster—25,000 French are made prisoners—The Allied Sovereigns meet in triumph, at noon, in the Great Square at Leipsic—King of Saxony sent under a Guard to Berlin—Reflections.

The last act of the grand drama, so far as the scene lay in Germany, was now fast approaching.

During the two first weeks of October, the various movements of the troops had been of an indecisive character; but after the 14th, when the belligerent powers became aware of each other's plans, the corps of the allies, as well as those of the French, streamed towards Leipsic as to a common centre.

Leaving Duben, the Emperor reached Leipsic early on the 15th of October, and received the agreeable information that his whole force would be in twenty-four hours under the walls; that the grand army of Austria was fast approaching; but that his demonstration against Berlin had alarmed Blucher, and therefore that maréchal might be longer of advancing, from his anxiety to protect the Prussian capital. An opportunity of fighting the one army without the presence of the other, was what Napoleon most anxiously desired.

In the meantime, cannon were heard, and shortly after Murat brought an account of a desperate cavalry skirmish, in which each party claimed the victory. He himself, marked by the splendour of his dress, had with difficulty escaped from a young Prussian officer, who was killed by an orderly dragoon that waited upon the King of Naples. Another remarkable circumstance in this skirmish was, the distinguished behaviour of a Prussian regiment of cuirassiers. When complimented on their behaviour, they replied, "Could we do otherwise?—this is the anniversary of the battle of Jena." Such a spirit prevailed among the allies, nor is it to be supposed that that of the French was inferior. If the one had wrongs to avenge, the other had honours to preserve.

The venerable town of Leipsic forms an irregular square, surrounded by an ancient Gothic wall, with a terrace planted with trees. Four gates—on the north those of Halle and Ranstadt, on the east the gate of Grimma, and on the south that called Saint Peter's gate—lead from the town to the suburbs, which are of great extent, secured by walls and barriers. Upon the west side of the town, two rivers, the Pleisse and the Elster, wash its walls, and flowing through meadows, divide themselves into several branches, connected by marshy islands. Leipsic cannot, therefore, be esteemed capable of approach by an enemy in that direction, excepting by a succession of bridges which cross those rivers and their connecting streams. The first of these bridges leads to a village called Lindeneau, and thence to Mark-Ranstadt. It is close to the gate of the city which takes its name from that village. This road forms the sole communication betwixt Leipsic and the banks of the Rhine. On the east side, the river Partha makes a large semicircular bend around the city, enclosing extensive plains, with various heights and points of elevation, which make it well adapted for a military position; on the south the same species of ground continues, but more broken into eminences, one of which is called the Swedish Camp, from the wars, doubtless, of Gustavus Adolphus; another is called the Sheep-walk of Meusdorf; it is then bounded by the banks of the Pleisse. This line is marked by a variety of villages, which, in the fearful days which we are now to describe, gained a name in history. About the village of Connewitz begins the marshy ground, inundated by the Pleisse and Elster.

FRENCH AND ALLIED FORCES

It was on this last line that, on the 15th October, the columns of the grand army of the allies were seen hastily advancing. Napoleon immediately made his arrangements for defence. Lindenau, through which ran the Mark-Ranstadt road, by which the French must retreat, was occupied by Bertrand. Poniatowski, advancing to the right bank of the Pleisse, held all the villages along the side of the river—Connewitz, Lofsnig, Dooblitz, and so on to Markleberg. As the line of defence swept to the eastward, Augereau was established on the elevated plain of Wachau. He was supported by Victor and Lauriston at a considerable village called Leibertwolkowitz. Cavalry were posted on the wings of these divisions. The Imperial Guards were placed in the rear as a reserve, at a village named Probstheyda; and Macdonald occupied a gentle and sweeping rising-ground, extending from Stœtteriz to Holzhausen.

On the opposite, that is, the northern side of the city, Marmont occupied a line betwixt Moeckern and Euterizt. His troops were intended to make head against Blucher, whose approach from the north was momentarily to be apprehended. Almost all along the ground thus defended, but especially on the south front, the allies had prepared columns of attack; and the sentinels of both armies were, when evening fell, in some places within musket-shot of each other. Neither side, however, seemed willing to begin the battle, in which the great question was to be decided, whether France should leave other nations to be guided by their own princes, or retain the unnatural supremacy with which she had been invested by the talents of one great soldier.

The number of men who engaged the next morning, was said to be 136,000 French, omitting the corps of Souham, who was not engaged, and of Regnier, who was not yet come up. The allies are by the same accounts rated at 230,000, without counting the division of the Crown Prince, or that of Bennigsen, which had not as yet joined. Almost all the statements assign a predominating force to the allies of 80,000 or 100,000 men superior to their enemy. It thus appears that they had at last acted according to Napoleon's own idea of the art of war, which he defined as the art of assembling the greatest number upon a given point.

Napoleon himself visited all the posts, gave his last orders, and took the opportunity, as he frequently did on the eve of battle, to distribute eagles to those regiments of Augereau's division, which, being new levies, had not yet received these military emblems. The ceremony, performed with warlike pomp, may remind the reader of the ancient fashion of making knights on the eve of a battle. The soldiers were made to swear never to abandon their eagles; and the Emperor concluded by saying, in a loud voice, "Yonder lies the enemy. Swear that you will rather die than permit France to be dishonoured."—"We swear it!" exclaimed the battalions. "Long live the Emperor!" And unquestionably they kept their word in the tremendous series of actions which followed.

Napoleon's preparations were made chiefly upon the southern side of Leipsic. It has been supposed, though, we think, with small probability, that he scarce expected a serious attack upon the northern side at all. In the evening, however, of the 15th, three death-rockets (*feux de mort,*) displaying long brilliant trains of white light, were observed to rise high in the southerly quarter of the heavens, and they were presently answered by four of a red colour, which were seen in the distant north. It was concluded that these were signals of communication between the grand army of the allies, and those of the Crown Prince and Blucher. The latter, therefore, must be at no incalculable distance.

Napoleon remained in the rear of his own guards, behind the central position, almost opposite to a village called Gossa, which was occupied by the allies.

At break of day, on the 16th October, the battle began. The French position was attacked along all the southern front with the greatest fury. On the French right, the village of Markleberg was fiercely assaulted by Kleist, while the Austrian division of Mehrfeldt, making their way through the marshes to the left bank of the Pliesse, threatened to force themselves across that river. Poniatowski, to whom the defence was confided, was obliged to give ground, so that the Emperor was compelled to bring up the troops under Souham, which had joined during the night, and which had been designed to support Marmont on the north of Leipsic. Maréchal Victor defended the village of Wachau, in front of the position, against Prince Eugene of Wirtemberg. The town of Leibertwolkowitz was made good by Lauriston against Klenau. The allies made six desperate attempts on these points, but all were unsuccessful. They were now something in the condition of wrestlers who have exhausted themselves in vain and premature efforts; and Napoleon in turn assuming the offensive, began to show his skill and power.

BATTLE OF LEIPSIC

Macdonald was ordered to attack Klenau, and beat him back from Leibertwolkowitz, with the cavalry of Sebastiani; while two divisions descended to sustain General Lauriston. It was about noon when this general advance took place along the centre of the French. It was for some time fearfully successful. The village of Gossa, hitherto occupied by the allies, and in the very centre of their line, was carried by the bayonet. The eminence called the Sheepwalk was also in danger of being lost, and the exertions of Macdonald put him in possession of the redoubt called the Swedish Camp. The desperate impetuosity of the French had fairly broken through the centre of the allies; and Napoleon, as if desirous not to lose a moment in proclaiming his supposed victory, sent the tidings to the King of Saxony, who commanded all the church-bells in the city to be rung for rejoicing, even while the close continued roar of the cannon seemed to give the lie to the merry peal. The King of Naples, in the meantime, with Latour Maubourg, and Kellermann, poured through the gap in the enemy's centre, and at the head of the whole body of cavalry thundered forward as far as Magdeburg, a village in the rear of the allies, bearing down General Rayefskoi, with the grenadiers of the reserve, who threw themselves forward to oppose their passage.

But at this imminent moment of peril, while the French cavalry were disordered by their own success, Alexander ordered the Cossacks of his guard, who were in attendance on his person, to charge. They did so with the utmost fury, as fighting under the eye of their sovereign, disconcerted Buonaparte's manœuvre, and bore back with their long lances the dense mass of cavalry who had so nearly carried the day.

In the meantime, while the carnage was continuing on the southern side of Leipsic, a similar thunder of artillery commenced on the right, where Blucher had arrived before the city, and suddenly come into action with Marmont, with at least three men for one. Breathless aides-de-camp came galloping to reclaim the troops of Souham, which, for the purpose of supporting Poniatowski, had been withdrawn from their original destination of assisting Marmont. They could, not however, be replaced, and Blucher obtained, in consequence, great and decided results. He took the village of Mœckern, with twenty pieces of artillery, and two thousand prisoners; and when night separated the combat, had the advantage of having greatly narrowed the position of the enemy.

But the issue on the south side of Leipsic continued entirely indecisive, though furiously contested. Gossa was still disputed, taken and retaken repeatedly, but at length remained in possession of the allies. On the verge of the Pleisse, the combat was no less dreadful. The Austrians of Bianchi's division poured on Markleberg, close to the side of the river, with the most dreadful yells. Poniatowski, with Augereau's assistance, had the utmost difficulty in keeping his ground. From the left side of the Pleisse, Schwartzenberg manœuvred to push a body of horse across the swampy river, to take the French in the rear of the position. But such of the cavalry as got through a very bad ford, were instantly charged and driven back, and their leader, General Mehrfeldt, fell into the hands of the French. An Austrian division, that of Guilay, manœuvred on the left bank of the Pleisse, as far down as Lindenau, and the succession of bridges, which, we have said, forms on the western side the sole exit from Leipsic towards the Rhine. This was the only pass which remained for retreat to the French, should they fail in the dreadful action which was now fighting. Guilay might have destroyed these bridges; but it is believed he had orders to leave open that pass for retreat, lest the French should be rendered utterly desperate, when there was no anticipating what exertions they might be goaded to.

The battle, thus fiercely contested, continued to rage till nightfall, when the bloody work ceased as if by mutual consent. Three cannon-shot, fired as a signal to the more distant points, intimated that the conflict was ended for the time, and the armies on the southern line retired to rest, in each other's presence, in the very positions which they had occupied the night before. The French had lost the ground which at one period they had gained, but they had not relinquished one foot of their original position, though so fiercely attacked during the whole day by greatly superior numbers. On the north their defence had been less successful. Marmont had been forced back by Blucher, and the whole line of defence on that side was crowded nearer to the walls of Leipsic.[286]

Napoleon, in the meantime, had the melancholy task of arranging his soldiers for a defence, sure to be honourable, and yet at length to be unavailing. Retreat became inevitable; yet, how to accomplish it through the narrow streets of a crowded city; how to pass more than 100,000 men over a single bridge, while double that number were pressing on their rear, was a problem which even Buonaparte could not solve. In this perplexity, he thought of appealing to the sentiments of affection which the Emperor of Austria must necessarily be supposed to entertain for his daughter and grandchild. The capture of General Mehrfeldt served opportunely to afford the means of communication with the better grace, as, after the battle of Austerlitz, this was the individual, who, on the part of the Emperor of Germany, had solicited a personal interview, and favourable terms from Napoleon. In a private interview with this officer, Napoleon received the confirmation of what he had long apprehended, the defection of the King of

---

[286] Jomini, tom. iv., pp. 450, 462; Baron Fain, tom. ii., p. 384; Baron d'Odeleben, tom. ii., p. 32; Savary, tom. iii., p. 117.

Bavaria, the union of his army with that of Austria, and their determination to intercept him on his return to the Rhine. This fatal intelligence increased his desire of peace, and he requested, yet in terms of becoming dignity, the intercession of his father-in-law. He was now willing to adopt the terms proposed at Prague. He offered to renounce Poland and Illyria. He would consent to the independence of Holland, the Hanse towns, and Spain; but he wished this last to be delayed till a general peace. Italy, he proposed, should be considered as independent, and preserved in its integrity. Lastly, as the price of the armistice to be immediately concluded, he was willing to evacuate Germany and retreat towards the Rhine.

These terms contained what, at an early part of the campaign, and voluntarily tendered, would have been gladly accepted by the allies. But Buonaparte's own character for ability and pertinacity; the general impression, that, if he relinquished his views for a time, it was only to recur to them in a more favourable season; and his terrible power of making successful exertions for that purpose, hardened the hearts of the allied sovereigns against what, from another (could any other save Buonaparte be supposed in his situation) would, in the like circumstances, have been favourably received. "Adieu, General Mehrfeldt," said Napoleon, dismissing his prisoner; "when, on my part, you name the word armistice to the two Emperors, I doubt not that the voice which then strikes their ears will awaken many recollections." Words affecting by their simplicity, and which, coming from so proud a heart, and one who was reduced to ask the generosity which he had formerly extended, cannot be recorded without strong sympathy.

General Mehrfeldt went out, like the messenger from the ark, and long and anxiously did Buonaparte expect his return. But he was the raven envoy, and brought back no olive branch. Napoleon did not receive an answer until his troops had recrossed the Rhine. The allies had engaged themselves solemnly to each other, that they would enter into no treaty with him while an individual of the French army remained in Germany.

PREPARATIONS FOR RETREAT

Buonaparte was now engaged in preparations for retreat; yet he made them with less expedition than the necessities of the time required. Morning came, and the enemy did not renew the attack, waiting for Bennigsen and the Prince-Royal of Sweden. In the meanwhile, casks, and materials of all kinds being plenty, and labourers to be collected to any extent, it seems, that, by some of the various modes known to military engineers,[287] temporary bridges might have been thrown over the Elster and the Pleisse, which are tranquil still rivers, and the marshes betwixt them rendered sufficiently passable. Under far more disadvantageous circumstances Napoleon had bridged the Beresina within the space of twelve hours. This censure is confirmed by a most competent judge, the general of engineers, Rogniat, who affirms that there was time enough to have completed six bridges, had it been employed with activity. The answer, that he himself, as chief of the engineer department at the time, ought to have ordered and prepared these means of retreat, seems totally insufficient. Napoleon did not permit his generals to anticipate his commands on such important occasions. It is said, indeed, that the Emperor had given orders for three bridges, but that, in the confusion of this dreadful period, that was seldom completely accomplished which Napoleon could not look after with his own eyes. Nothing of the kind was actually attempted, except at a place called the Judges' Garden; and that, besides having its access, like the stone bridge, through the town of Leipsic, was constructed of too slight materials. Perhaps Napoleon trusted to the effect of Mehrfeldt's mission; perhaps he had still latent hopes that his retreat might be unnecessary; perhaps he abhorred the thought of that manœuvre so much, as to lead him entirely to confide the necessary preparations to another; but certain it is, the exertion was not made in a manner suitable to the occasion. The village of Lindenau, on the left side of the rivers, was nevertheless secured.

The 17th, as we have said, was spent in preparations on both sides, without any actual hostilities, excepting when a distant

---

[287] See Sir Howard Douglas's work on Military Bridges.—S.

cannonade, like the growling of some huge monster, showed that war was only slumbering, and that but lightly.

At eight o'clock on the 18th of October, the battle was renewed with tenfold fury. Napoleon had considerably contracted his circuit of defence; on the external range of heights and villages, which had been so desperately defended on the 16th, the allies now found no opposition but that of outposts. The French were posted in an interior line nearer to Leipsic, of which Probtshedya was the central point. Napoleon himself, stationed on an eminence called Thonberg, commanded a prospect of the whole field.

Masses were drawn up behind the villages, which relieved their defenders from time to time with fresh troops; cannon were placed in their front and on their flanks, and every patch of wooded ground which afforded the least shelter, was filled with tirailleurs. The battle then joined on all sides. The Poles, with their gallant general, Poniatowski, to whom this was to prove the last of his fields, defended the banks of the Pleisse, and the villages connected with it, against the Prince of Hesse Homberg, Bianchi, and Colleredo. In the centre, Barclay, Witgenstein, and Kleist, advanced on Probtsheyda, where they were opposed by the King of Naples, Victor, Augereau, and Lauriston, under the eye of Napoleon himself. On the left, Macdonald had drawn back his division from an advanced point called Holtzhausen, to a village called Stœtteritz, which was the post assigned to them on the new and restricted line of defence. Along all this extended southern line, the fire continued furious on both sides, nor could the terrified spectators, from the walls and steeples of Leipsic, perceive that it either advanced or recoiled. The French had the advantage of situation and cover, the allies that of greatly superior numbers; both were commanded by the first generals of their country and age.

About two o'clock afternoon, the allies, under General Pirch and Prince Augustus of Prussia, forced their way headlong into Probtsheyda; the camp followers began to fly; the noise of the tumult overcame almost the fire of the artillery. Napoleon in the rear, but yet on the verge of this tumult, preserved his entire tranquillity. He placed the reserve of the Old Guard in order, led them in person to recover the village, and saw them force their entrance, ere he retreated to the eminence from which he observed the action. During the whole of this eventful day, in which he might be said to fight less for victory than for safety, this wonderful man continued calm, decided, collected, and supported his diminished and broken squadrons in their valiant defence, with a presence of mind and courage, as determined as he had so often exhibited in directing the tide of onward victory. Perhaps his military talents were more to be admired, when thus contending at once against Fortune and the superiority of numbers, than in the most distinguished of his victories, when the fickle goddess fought upon his side.

The allies, notwithstanding their gallantry and their numbers, felt themselves obliged to desist from the murderous attacks upon the villages which cost them such immense loss; and drawing back their troops as they brought forward their guns and howitzers, contented themselves with maintaining a dreadful fire on the French masses as they showed themselves, and throwing shells into the villages. The French replied with great spirit; but they had fewer guns in position, and, besides, their ammunition was falling short. Still, however, Napoleon completely maintained the day on the south of Leipsic, where he was present in person.

On the north side of Leipsic, the superiority of numbers, still greater than that which existed on the south, placed Ney in a precarious situation. He was pressed at once by the army of Blucher, and by that of the Crown Prince, which was now come up in force. The latter general forced his way across the Partha, with three columns, and at three different points; and Ney saw himself obliged to retreat, in order to concentrate his forces nearer Leipsic, and communicate by his right with the army of Napoleon.

The Russians had orders to advance to force this new position, and particularly to drive back the advanced guard of Regnier, stationed on an eminence called Heiterblick, betwixt the villages of Taucha and Paunsdorf. On a sudden, the troops who occupied the French line on that point, came forward to meet the allies, with their swords sheathed, and colours of truce displayed.

This was a Saxon brigade, who, in the midst of the action, embraced the time and opportunity to desert the service of Napoleon, and declare for independence. These men had an unquestionable right to espouse the cause of their country, and shake off the yoke of a stranger, which Saxony had found so burdensome; but it is not while on the actual battle-ground that one side ought to be exchanged for the other; and those must be in every case accounted guilty of treachery, who, bringing their swords into the field for one party, shall suddenly, and without intimation given, turn them against the power in whose ranks they had stood.

The Russians, afraid of stratagem, sent the Saxon troops, about 10,000 in number, to the rear of the position. But their artillery were immediately brought into action; and having expended during that morning one half of their ammunition on the allies, they now bestowed the other half upon the French army. By this unexpected disaster, Ney was obliged to contract his line of defence once more. Even the valour and exertions of that distinguished general could not defend Schoenfeld. That fine village forms almost one of the northern suburbs of Leipsic. It was in vain that Buonaparte despatched his reserves of cavalry to check the advance of the Crown Prince. He defeated all opposition that presented itself, and pressed Ney into a position close under the walls of Leipsic. The battle once more ceased on all points; and after the solemn signal of three cannon-shot had been heard, the field was left to the slain and the wounded.[288]

Although the French army kept its ground most valiantly during the whole of this tremendous day, there was no prospect of their being able to sustain themselves any longer around or in Leipsic. The allies had approached so close to them, that their attacks might, on the third day, be expected to be more combined and simultaneous than before. The superiority of numbers became more efficient after the great carnage that had taken place, and that for the simple reason, that the army which had greatest numbers could best afford to lose lives. It is said also by Baron Fain,[289] that the enormous number of 250,000 cannon-bullets had been

---

[288] Jomini, tom. iv., pp. 465, 480; Baron Fain, tom. ii., p. 403.
[289] Manuscript de 1813, par le Baron Fain, tom. ii., p. 420.

expended by the French during the last four days, and that there only remained to serve their guns about 16,000 cartridges, which could scarce support a hot fire for two hours. This was owing to the great park of artillery having been directed on Torgau, another circumstance which serves to show how little Buonaparte dreamed of abandoning the Elbe when he moved from Dresden. To this the increasing scarcity of provisions is to be added; so that every thing combined to render Napoleon's longer stay at Dresden altogether impossible, especially when the Bavarian general, now his declared enemy, was master of his communications with France.

The retreat, however necessary, was doomed inevitably to be disastrous, as is evident from the situation of the French army, cooped up by superior forces under the walls of a large town, the narrow streets of which they must traverse to reach two bridges, one of recent and hasty construction, by which they must cross the Pleisse, the Elster, and the marshy ground, streams, and canals, which divide them from each other; and then, added to this was the necessity of the whole army debouching by one single road, that which leads to Lindenau, and on which it would be impossible to prevent dreadful confusion. But there was no remedy for these evils; they must necessarily be risked.

LEIPSIC

The retreat was commenced in the night time; and Buonaparte, retiring in person to Leipsic, spent a third exhausting night in dictating the necessary orders for drawing the corps of his army successively within the town, and transferring them to the western bank of the two rivers. The French troops accordingly came into Leipsic from all sides, and filling the town with the ineffable confusion which always must attend the retreat of so large a body in the presence of a victorious enemy, they proceeded to get out of it as they best could, by the way prescribed. Macdonald and Poniatowski, with their corps, were appointed to the perilous honour of protecting the rear. "Prince," said Napoleon, to the brave Polish prince, "you must defend the southern suburbs."—"Alas, sire," he answered, "I have but few soldiers left."—"Well, but you will defend them with what you have?"—"Doubt not, sire, but that we will make good our ground; we are all ready to die for your Majesty's service."—Napoleon parted with this brave and attached prince, upon whom he had recently bestowed a maréchal's baton. They never met again in this world.

The arrival of daylight had no sooner shown to the allies the commencement of the French retreat, than their columns began to advance in pursuit on every point, pushing forward, with all the animation of victory, to overtake the enemy in the suburbs and streets of Leipsic. The King of Saxony, the magistrates, and some of the French generals, endeavoured to secure the city from the dangers which were to be expected from a battle in the town, betwixt the rear-guard of the French and the advanced guard of the allies. They sent proposals, that the French army should be permitted to effect their retreat unmolested, in mercy to the unfortunate town. But when were victorious generals prevented from prosecuting military advantages, by the mere consideration of humanity? Napoleon, on his side, was urged to set fire to the suburbs, to check the pressure of the allies on his rear-guard. As this, however, must have occasioned a most extensive scene of misery, Buonaparte generously refused to give such a dreadful order, which, besides, could not have been executed without compromising the safety of a great part of his own rear, to whom the task of destruction must have been committed, and who would doubtless immediately have engaged in an extensive scene of plunder. Perhaps, also, Napoleon might be influenced by the feeling of what was due to the confidence and fidelity of Frederick Augustus of Saxony, who, having been so long the faithful follower of his fortunes, was now to be abandoned to his own. To have set fire to that unhappy monarch's city, when leaving him behind to make terms for himself as he could, would have been an evil requital for all he had done and suffered in the cause of France; nor would it have been much better had Napoleon removed the Saxon King from his dominions, and destroyed all chance of his making peace with the irritated sovereigns, by transporting him along with the French army in its calamitous retreat.

At nine o'clock Napoleon had a farewell interview with Frederick Augustus, releasing him formally from all the ties which had hitherto combined them, and leaving him at liberty to form such other alliances as the safety of his states might require. Their parting scene was hurried to a conclusion by the heavy discharge of musketry from several points, which intimated that the allies, forcing their way into the suburbs, were fighting hand to hand, and from house to house, with the French, who still continued to defend them. The King and Queen of Saxony conjured Buonaparte to mount his horse, and make his escape; but, before he did so, he discharged from their ties to France and to himself the King of Saxony's body guard, and left them for the protection of the royal family.

BRIDGE OF LEIPSIC

When Napoleon attempted to make his way to the single point of exit, by the gate of Ranstadt, which led to the bridge, or succession of bridges, so often mentioned, he found reason for thinking his personal safety in actual danger. It must be remembered, that the French army, still numbering nearly 100,000, were pouring into Leipsic, pursued by more than double that number, and that the streets were encumbered with the dead and wounded, with artillery and baggage, with columns so wedged up that it was impossible for them to get forward, and with others, who, almost desperate of their safety, would not be left behind. To fight his way through this confusion, was impossible even for Napoleon. He and his suite were obliged to give up all attempts to proceed in the direct road to the bridge, and turning in the other direction, he got out of the city through Saint Peter's Gate, moved on until he was in sight of the advancing columns of the allies, then turning along the eastern suburb, he found a circuitous by-way to the bridges, and was enabled to get across. But the temporary bridge which we have before mentioned had already given way, so that there remained only the old bridge on the road to Lindenau, to serve as an exit to the whole French army. The furious defence which was maintained in the suburbs, continued to check the advance of the allies, otherwise the greater part of the French army must inevitably have been destroyed. But the defenders themselves, with their brave commanders, were at length, after exhibiting prodigies of valour, compelled to retreat; and ere they could reach the banks of the river, a dreadful accident had taken place.

The bridge, so necessary to the escape of this distressed army, had been mined by Buonaparte's orders, and an officer of engineers was left to execute the necessary measure of destroying it, so soon as the allies should approach in force sufficient to occupy the pass. Whether the officer to whom this duty was intrusted had fled, or had fallen, or had been absent from his post by accident, no one seems to have known; but at this critical period a sergeant commanded the sappers in his stead. A body of Swedish sharp-shooters pushed up the side of the river about eleven o'clock, with loud cries and huzzas, firing upon the crowds who were winning their way slowly along the bridge, while Cossacks and Hulans were seen on the southern side, rushing towards the same spot; and the troops of Saxony and Baden, who had now entirely changed sides, were firing on the French from the wall of the suburbs, which they had been posted to defend against the allies, and annoying the retreat which they had been destined to cover. The non-commissioned officer of engineers imagined that the retreat of the French was cut off, and set fire to the mine, that the allies might not take possession of the bridge for pursuing Napoleon.[290] The bridge exploded with a horrible noise.

This catastrophe effectually intercepted the retreat of all who remained still on the Leipsic side of the river, excepting some

---

[290] This story was at first doubted, and it was supposed that Napoleon had commanded the bridge to be blown up, with the selfish purpose of securing his own retreat. But, from all concurring accounts, the explosion took place in the manner, and from the cause, mentioned in the text. There is, notwithstanding, an obscurity in the case. A French officer of engineers, by name Colonel Monfort, was publicly announced as the person through whose negligence or treachery the post was left to subordinate keeping. Nevertheless, it is said, that the only officer of that name, in the engineer service of Buonaparte's army, was actually at Mentz when the battle of Leipsic took place. This is alluded to by General Grouchy, who, in a note upon his interesting Observations on General Gourgaud's Account of the Campaign of 1815, has this remarkable passage.—"One would wish to forget the bulletin, which, after the battle of Leipsic, delivered to the bar of public opinion, as preliminary to bringing him before a military commission, Colonel Monfort of the engineer service, gratuitously accused of the breaking down the bridge at Leipsic." Neither the colonel nor the non-commissioned officer was ever brought to a court-martial.—S.

individuals who succeeded by swimming through the Pleisse and the Elster. Among these was the brave Maréchal Macdonald, who surmounted all the obstacles opposed to his escape. Poniatowski, the gallant nephew of Stanislaus, King of Poland, was less fortunate. He was the favourite of his countrymen, who saw in their imagination the crown of Poland glittering upon his brow. He himself, like most of the Poles of sense and reflection, regarded these hopes as delusive; but followed Napoleon with unflinching zeal, because he had always been his friend and benefactor. Besides a thousand other acts of valour, Poniatowski's recent defence of the extreme right of the French position was as brilliant as any part of the memorable resistance at Leipsic. He had been twice wounded in the previous battles. Seeing the bridge destroyed, and the enemy's forces thronging forward in all directions, he drew his sabre, and said to his suite, and a few Polish cuirassiers, who followed him, "Gentlemen, it is better to fall with honour than to surrender." He charged accordingly, and pushed through the troops of the allied army opposed to him, in the course of which desperate attempt he was wounded by a musket shot in the arm. Other enemies appeared; he threw himself upon them with the same success, making his way amongst them also, after receiving a wound through the cross of his decoration. He then plunged into the Pleisse, and with the assistance of his staff-officers, got across that river, in which his horse was lost. Though much exhausted, he mounted another horse, and seeing that the enemy were already occupying the banks of the Elster with riflemen, he plunged into that deep and marshy river, to rise no more. Thus bravely died a prince, who, in one sense, may be termed the last of the Poles.[291]

The remainder of the French army, after many had been killed and drowned in an attempt to cross these relentless rivers, received quarter from the enemy. About 25,000 men were made prisoners, and as Napoleon seems only to have had about 200 guns at the

---

[291] His body was found, and his obsequies performed with great military pomp; both the victors and vanquished attending him to the tomb, with every honour which could be rendered to his remains.—S.

battle of Hannau, many must have been abandoned in Leipsic and its neighbourhood.[292] The quantity of baggage taken was immense.

The triumph of the allied monarchs was complete. Advancing at the head of their victorious forces, each upon his own side, the Emperor of Russia, the King of Prussia, and the Crown Prince of Sweden, met and greeted each other in the great square of the city, where they were soon joined by the Emperor of Austria. General Bertrand, the French commandant of the city, surrendered his sword to these illustrious personages. No interview took place between the allied monarchs and the King of Saxony. He was sent under a guard of Cossacks to Berlin, nor was he afterwards restored to his throne, until he had paid a severe fine for his adherence to France.

When reflecting upon these scenes, the rank and dignity of the actors naturally attract our observation. It seems as if the example of Buonaparte, in placing himself at the head of his armies, had in some respects changed the condition of sovereigns, from the reserved and retired dignity in which most had remained, estranged from the actual toils of government and dangers of war, into the less abstracted condition of sharing the risk of battle, and the labours of negotiation. Such scenes as those which passed at Leipsic on this memorable day, whether we look at the parting of Napoleon from Frederick Augustus, amid the fire and shouting of hostile armies, or the triumphant meeting of the allied sovereigns in the great square of Leipsic, had been for centuries only to be paralleled in romance. But considering how important it is to the people that sovereigns should not be prompt to foster a love of war, there is great room for question whether the encouragement of this warlike propensity be upon the whole a subject for Europe to congratulate itself upon.

Policy and the science of war alike dictated a rapid and close pursuit after the routed French; but the allied army had been too much exhausted, by the efforts required to gain the battle, to admit of its deriving the full advantage from success. There was a great scarcity of provisions around Leipsic; and the stores of the city,

---

[292] "The French were computed to have lost 50,000 men, including the sick abandoned in the hospitals at Leipsic, and 250 guns."—Lord Burghersh, *Operations*, &c., p. 28.

exhausted by the French, afforded no relief. The bridge which had been destroyed was as necessary for the advance of the allies as the retreat of Napoleon. Besides, it must be admitted that an allied army is always less decided and rapid in its movements than one which receives all its impulses from a single commander of strong and vigorous talents. Of this we shall see more proofs. But, in the meantime, a great point was gained. The liberation of Germany was complete, even if Napoleon should escape the united armies of Austria and Bavaria, which still lay betwixt him and the banks of the Rhine. And indeed the battles which he fought for conquest terminated at Leipsic. Those which he afterwards waged were for his own life and the sceptre of France.

Chapter LXXI

Retreat of the French from Germany—General Defection of Napoleon's Partisans—Battle of Hannau fought on 30th and 31st October—Napoleon arrives at Paris on 9th November—State in which he finds the public mind in the capital—Fate of the French Garrisons left in Germany—Arrival of the Allied Armies on the banks of the Rhine—General view of Napoleon's political relations—Italy—Spain—Restoration of Ferdinand—Liberation of the Pope, who returns to Rome—Emancipation of Holland.

RETREAT FROM GERMANY

Napoleon was now on his retreat, and it proved a final one, from Germany towards France. It was performed with disorder enough, and great loss, though far less than that which had attended the famous departure from Moscow. The troops, according to Baron d'Odeleben, soured by misfortune, marched with a fierce and menacing air, and the guards in particular indulged in every excess. In this disordered condition, Napoleon passed through Lutzen, late the scene of his brilliant success, now witness to his disastrous losses. His own courage was unabated; he seemed indeed pensive, but was calm and composed, indulging in no vain regrets, still less in useless censures and recriminations. Harassed as he passed the defiles of Eckartsberg, by the light troops of the allies, he pushed on to Erfurt, where he hoped to be able to make some pause, and restore order to his disorganised followers.

On the 23d of October, he reached that city, which was rendered by its strong citadel a convenient rallying point; and upon collecting the report of his losses, had the misfortune to find them much greater than he had apprehended. Almost all the German troops of his army were now withdrawn from it. The Saxons and the troops of Baden he had dismissed with a good grace; other contingents, which saw their sovereigns on the point of being freed from Napoleon's supremacy, withdrew of themselves, and in most cases joined the allies. A great many of those Frenchmen who arrived at Erfurt were in a miserable condition, and without arms. Their wretched appearance extorted from Buonaparte the peevish observation, "They are a set of scoundrels, who are going to the devil!—In this way I shall lose 80,000 men before I can get to the Rhine."

The spirit of defection extended even to those who were nearest to the Emperor. Murat, discouraged and rendered impatient by the incessant misfortunes of his brother-in-law, took leave, under pretence, it was said, of bringing forces up from the French frontier, but in reality to return to his own dominions, without further allying his fortunes to those of Napoleon.[293] Buonaparte, as if influenced by some secret presentiment that they should never again meet, embraced his old companion-in-arms repeatedly ere they parted.

The Poles who remained in Napoleon's army showed a very generous spirit. He found himself obliged to appeal to their own honour, whether they chose to remain in his service, or to desert him at this crisis. A part had served so long under his banners, that they had become soldiers of fortune, to whom the French camp served for a native country. But many others were men who had assumed arms in the Russian campaign, with the intention of freeing Poland from the foreign yoke under which it had so long groaned. The manner in which Napoleon had disappointed their hopes could not be forgotten by them; but they had too much generosity to revenge, at this crisis, the injustice with which they had been treated, and agreed unanimously that they would not quit Napoleon's service until they had escorted him safely beyond the Rhine, reserving their right then to leave his standard, of which a great many accordingly availed themselves.

---

[293] "The hasty journey of the King of Naples through France created general surprise. The first idea excited by it was, that the Emperor had commissioned him to assemble the army and form a junction with the force under the viceroy, in order to protect Italy from an invasion, which appeared to be contemplated, and the execution of which was at that time rendered probable, by the movements of the English troops in Sicily. Nobody attributed his return to any other object."—Savary, tom. iii., p. 126.

ERFURT—HANAU

Napoleon passed nearly two days at Erfurt, during which the re-organisation of his troops advanced rapidly, as the magazines and stores of the place were sufficient to recruit them in every department. Their reassembled force amounted to about 80,000 men. This, together with the troops left to their fate in the garrison towns in Germany, was all that remained of 280,000, with which Napoleon had begun the campaign. The garrisons amounted to about 80,000, so that the loss of the French rose to 120,000 men. These garrisons, so imprudently left behind, were of course abandoned to their fate, or to the discretion of the enemy; Napoleon consoling himself with the boast, "that if they could form a junction in the valley of the Elbe, 80,000 Frenchmen might break through all obstacles." Instructions were sent to the various commanders, to evacuate the places they held, and form such a junction; but it is believed that none of them reached the generals to whom they were addressed.

It is probable that, but for the relief afforded by this halt, and the protection of the citadel and defences of Erfurt, Napoleon, in his retreat from Leipsic, must have lost all that remained to him of an army. He had received news, however, of a character to preclude his longer stay in this place of refuge. The Bavarian army, so lately his allies, with a strong auxiliary force of Austrians, amounting in all to 50,000, under Wrede, were hurrying from the banks of the Inn, and had reached Wurtzburg on the Mayne, with the purpose of throwing themselves in hostile fashion between the army of Napoleon and the frontier of France. In addition to this unpleasing intelligence, he learned that the Austrians and Prussians were pressing forward, as far as Weimar and Laugensalza, so that he was once more in danger of being completely surrounded. Urged by these circumstances, Napoleon left Erfurt on the 25th of October, amid weather as tempestuous as his fortunes.

An unfortunate determination of the allied councils directed Marshal Blucher to move in pursuit of Napoleon by Giessen and Wetzlar, and commanded him to leave the direct road to the banks of the Rhine, by Fulda and Gelnhaussen, open for the march of an

Austrian column, expected to advance from Schmalkald.[294] The most active and energetic of the pursuers was thus turned aside from Napoleon's direct path of retreat, and the Austrians, to whom it was yielded, did not come up in time to overtake the retreating enemy. The French were still followed, however, by the arrival of Cossacks under their adventurous leaders, Platoff, Czernicheff, Orloff-Denizoff, and Kowaiski, who continued their harassing and destructive operations on their flanks and their rear.

In the meanwhile, General Wrede, notwithstanding the inferiority of his forces to those of Buonaparte, persevered in his purpose of barring the return of Napoleon into France, and took up a position at Hanau for that purpose, where he was joined by the chiefs of the Cossacks already mentioned, who had pushed on before the advance of the French army, in hopes that they might afford Wrede their assistance. If Blucher and his troops had been now in the rear of Napoleon, his hour had in all probability arrived. But Wrede's force, of whom he had been unable to bring up above 45,000 men, was inferior to the attempt, almost always a dangerous one, of intercepting the retreat of a bold and desperate enemy upon the only road which can lead him to safety. It was upon a point, also, where the Bavarians had no particular advantage of position, which might have presented natural obstacles to the progress of the enemy.

Upon the 30th, the Bavarians had occupied the large wood of Lamboi, and were disposed in line on the right bank of a small river called the Kintzig, near a village named Neuhoff, where there is a bridge. The French threw a body of light troops into the wood, which was disputed from tree to tree, the close fire of the sharpshooters on both sides resembling that of a general *chasse*, such as is practised on the continent. The combat was sustained for several hours without decided success, until Buonaparte commanded an attack in force on the left of the Bavarians. Two battalions of the guards, under General Curial, were sent into the wood to support the French tirailleurs; and the Bavarians, at the sight of their grenadier-caps, imagined themselves attacked by the

---

[294] This account of Blucher's march is derived from Lord Burghersh's "Memoir of the Operations of the Allied Armies in 1813 and 1814," pp. 35, &c.—Ed. (1842.)

whole of that celebrated body, and gave way. A successful charge of cavalry was at the same time made on Wrede's left, which made it necessary for him to retreat behind the Kintzig. The Austro-Bavarian army continued to hold Hanau; but as the main road to Frankfort does not lead directly through that town, but passes on the south side of it, the desired line of retreat was left open to Napoleon, whose business it was to push forward to the Rhine, and avoid farther combat. But the rear-guard of the French army, consisting of 18,000 men, under command of Mortier, was still at Gelnhaussen; and Marmont was left with three corps of infantry to secure their retreat, while Buonaparte, with the advance, pushed on to Williamstadt, and from thence to Hockstadt, in the direction of Frankfort.

On the morning of the 31st, Marmont made a double attack upon the town of Hanau, and the position of Wrede. Of the first, he possessed himself by a bombardment. The other attack took place near the bridge of Neuhoff. The Bavarians had at first the advantage, and pushed a body of 1000 or 1200 men across the Kintzig; but the instant attack and destruction of these by the bayonet, impressed their general with greater caution. Wrede himself was at this moment dangerously wounded, and the Prince of Oettingen, his son-in-law, killed on the spot. General Fresnel, who succeeded Wrede in the command, acted with more reserve. He drew off from the combat; and the French, more intent on prosecuting their march to the Rhine than on improving their advantages over the Bavarians, followed the Emperor's line of retreat in the direction of Frankfort.

An instance of rustic loyalty and sagacity was displayed during the action, by a German miller, which may serve to vary the recurring detail of military movements. This man, observing the fate of the battle, and seeing a body of Bavarian infantry hard pressed by a large force of French cavalry, had the presence of mind to admit the water into his mill-stream when the Bavarians had passed its channel, and thus suddenly interposed an obstacle between them and the pursuers, which enabled the infantry to halt and resume their ranks. The sagacious peasant was rewarded with a pension by the King of Bavaria.

LOSSES OF THE FRENCH

The loss of the French in this sharp action was supposed to reach to about 6000 men; that of the Austro-Bavarians exceeded 10,000. Escaped from this additional danger, Napoleon arrived at Frankfort upon the 30th October, and left, upon the first November, a town which was soon destined to receive other guests. On the next day he arrived at Mayence, (Mentz,) which he left upon the 7th November, and arriving on the 9th at Paris, concluded his second unsuccessful campaign.

The Emperor had speedy information that the temper of the public was by no means tranquil. The victory of Hanau, though followed by no other effect than that of getting clear of the enemy, who had presumed to check the retreat of the Emperor, alone shed a lustre on the arms of Napoleon, which they greatly needed, for his late successive misfortunes had awakened both critics and murmurers. The rupture of the armistice seemed to be the date of his declension, as indeed the junction of the Austrians enabled the allies to bear him down by resistless numbers. Nine battles had been fought since that period, including the action at Culm, which, in its results, is well entitled to the name. Of these, Buonaparte only gained two—those of Dresden and Hanau; that at Wachau was indecisive; while at Gross-Beeren, at Jauer on the Katzbach, at Culm, at Dennewitz, at Mockern, and at Leipsic, the allies obtained decisive and important victories.

The French had been still more unfortunate in the number of bloody skirmishes which were fought almost every where through the scene of war. They were outnumbered in cavalry, and especially in light cavalry; they were outnumbered, too, in light corps of infantry and sharpshooters; for the Germans, who had entered into the war with general enthusiasm, furnished numerous reinforcements of this description to the regular armies of the allies. These disasters, however they might be glossed over, had not escaped the notice of the French; nor was it the sight of a few banners, and a column of 4000 Bavarian prisoners, ostentatiously paraded, that prevented their asking, what was become of upwards of 200,000 soldiers—what charm had dissolved the Confederation of the Rhine—and why they heard rumours of Russians, Austrians, Prussians, Germans, on the east, and of English, Spanish, and Portuguese on the south, approaching the inviolable frontiers of the great nation? During the bright sunshine of prosperity, a nation may be too much dazzled with victory; but the gloomy horizon, obscured by adversity, shows objects in their real colours.

The fate of the garrisons in Germany, which Buonaparte had so imprudently omitted to evacuate, was not such as to cure this incipient disaffection. The Emperor had never another opportunity during this war, to collect the veteran troops thus unhappily left behind, under his banner, though often missing them at his greatest need. The dates of their respective surrender, referring to a set of detached facts, which have no influence upon the general current of history, may be as well succinctly recited in this place.

St. Cyr, at Dresden, finding himself completely abandoned to his own slender resources, made on the 11th of November a capitulation to evacuate the place, with his garrison of 35,000 men, (of whom very many were, however, invalids,) who were to have a safe conduct to France, under engagement not to serve against the allies for six months. Schwartzenberg refused to ratify the capitulation, as being much too favourable to the besieged. He offered St. Cyr, who had already left Dresden, to replace him there in the same condition of defence which he enjoyed when the agreement was entered into. This was contrary to the rules of war; for how was it possible for the French commandant to be in the same situation as before the capitulation, when the enemy had become completely acquainted with his means of defence, and resources? But the French general conceived it more expedient to submit, with his army, to become prisoners of war, reserving his right to complain of breach of capitulation.

Stettin surrendered on the 21st of November, after an eight months' blockade. Eight thousand French remained prisoners of war. Here the Prussians regained no less than 350 pieces of artillery.

On the 29th of November, the important city of Dantzic surrendered, after trenches had been open before it for forty days.

As in the case of Dresden, the sovereigns refused to ratify the stipulation, which provided for the return of the garrison to France, but made the commandant, Rapp, the same proposal which had been offered to the Maréchal St. Cyr, which Rapp in like manner declined. About 9000 French were therefore sent prisoners into Russia. But the Bavarians, Westphalians, and Poles, belonging to the garrison, were permitted to return to their homes. Many of them took service with the allies. The detention of this garrison must also be recorded against the allies as a breach of faith, which the temptation of diminishing the enemy's forces cannot justify.

After the battle of Leipsic, Tauentzein had been detached to blockade Wittenberg, and besiege Torgau. The latter place was yielded on the 26th December, with a garrison of 10,000 wretches, amongst whom a pestilential fever was raging. Zamosc, in the duchy of Warsaw, capitulated on the 22d, and Modlin on the 25th of December.

At the conclusion of the year 1813, only the following places, situated in the rear of the allies, remained in the hands of the French; Hamburgh, Madgeburg, Wittenberg, Custrin, Glogau, with the citadels of Erfurt and of Wurtzburg, the French having in the last two instances evacuated the towns.

FRENCH GARRISONS IN GERMANY

Two circumstances are remarkable concerning the capture of the surrendered fortresses. The first is the dismal state of the garrisons. The men, who had survived the Russian campaign, and who had been distributed into these cities and fortresses by Murat, were almost all, from the hardships they had endured, and perhaps from their being too suddenly accommodated with more genial food, subject to diseases which speedily became infectious, and spread from the military to the inhabitants. When the severities of a blockade were added to this general tendency to illness, the deaths became numerous, and the case of the survivors made them envious of those who died. So virulent was the contagion at Torgau, that the Prussians, to whom the place was rendered on the 26th December, did not venture to take possession of it till a fortnight afterwards, when the ravage of the pestilence began to decline. Thus widely extended, and thus late prolonged, were the fatal effects of the Russian expedition.

The other point worth notice is, that the surrender of each fortress rendered disposable a blockading army of the allies, proportioned to the strength of the garrisons, which ought, according to the rules of war, to be at least two to one.[295] Thus, while thousands after thousands of the French were marched to distant prisons in Austria and Russia, an addition was regularly made to the armies of the allies, equal at least to double the number of those that were withdrawn from the French army.

While these successes were in the act of being obtained in their rear, the allied sovereigns of Russia and Prussia advanced upon the Rhine, the left bank of which was almost entirely liberated from the enemy. It is a river upon which all the Germans look with a national pride, that sometimes takes almost the appearance of filial devotion. When the advanced guard of the army of the allies first came in sight of its broad majesty of flood, they hailed the Father River with such reiterated shouts, that those who were behind stood to their arms, and pressed forward, supposing that an action was about to take place. The proud and exulting feeling of recovered independence was not confined to those brave men who had achieved the liberation of their country, but extended every where, and animated the whole mass of the population of Germany.

The retreat of the French armies, or their relics, across the land which they had so long overrun, and where they had levelled and confounded all national distinctions, might be compared to the abatement of the great deluge, when land-marks which had been long hid from the eye began to be once more visible and distinguished. The reconstruction of the ancient sovereignties was the instant occupation of the allies.

---

[295] Three to one, according to the general rule of war, is the proportion of a blockading army to the garrison which it masks. But where there is little apprehension of relief or of strong sorties, the number may be much reduced.—S.

From the very field of battle at Leipsic, the Electoral Prince of Hesse departed to assume, amid the acclamations of the inhabitants, the sovereignty of the territories of his fathers. The allies, on 2d November, took possession of Hanover and its dependencies in name of the King of England. The gallant Duke of Brunswick, whose courage, as well as his ardent animosity against Buonaparte, we have already had occasion to commemorate, returned at the same time into the possession of his hereditary estates; and the ephemeral kingdom of Westphalia, the appanage of Jerome Buonaparte, composed out of the spoils of these principalities, vanished into air, like the palace of Aladdin in the Arabian tale.

Those members of the Confederacy of the Rhine who had hitherto been contented to hold their crowns and coronets, under the condition of being liege vassals to Buonaparte, and who were as much tired of his constant exactions as ever a drudging fiend was of the authority of a necromancer, lost no time in renouncing his sway, after his talisman was broken. Bavaria and Wirtemberg had early joined the alliance—the latter power the more willingly, that the Crown Prince had, even during Napoleon's supremacy, refused to acknowledge his sway. The lesser princes, therefore, had no alternative but to declare, as fast as they could, their adherence to the same cause. Their ministers thronged to the headquarters of the allied sovereigns, where they were admitted to peace and fraternity on the same general terms; namely, that each state should contribute within a certain period, a year's income of their territories, with a contingent of soldiers double in numbers to that formerly exacted by Buonaparte, for maintaining the good cause of the alliance. They consented willingly; for though the demand might be heavy in the meantime, yet, with the downfall of the French Emperor, there was room to hope for that lasting peace which all men now believed to be inconsistent with a continuance of his power.

Waiting until their reinforcements should come from the interior of Germany, and until the subordinate princes should bring forward their respective contingents of troops, and desirous also to give Napoleon another opportunity of treating, the allied sovereigns halted on the banks of the Rhine, and cantoned their army along the banks of that river. This afforded a space to discover, whether the lofty mind of Napoleon could be yet induced to bend to such a peace as might consist with the material change in the circumstances of Europe, effected in the two last campaigns. Such a pacification was particularly the object of Austria; and the greater hope was entertained of its being practicable, that the same train of misfortunes which had driven Napoleon beyond the Rhine, had darkened his political horizon in other quarters.

ITALY—SPAIN

Italy, so long the scene of his triumphs, was now undergoing the same fate as his other conquests, and rapidly melting away from his grasp. At the beginning of the campaign, the Viceroy Eugene, with about 45,000 men, had defended the north of Italy, with great skill and valour, against the Austrian general, Hiller, who confronted him with superior forces. The frontiers of Illyria were the chief scene of their military operations. The French maintained themselves there until the defection of the Bavarians opened the passes of the Tyrol to the Austrian army, after which, Eugene was obliged to retire behind the Adige. The warlike Croatians declaring in favour of their ancient sovereigns of Austria, mutinied, and rose in arms on several points. The important seaport of Trieste was taken by the Austrians on the 21st of October. General Nugent had entered the mouth of the Po with an English squadron, with a force sufficient to occupy Ferrara and Ravenna, and organise a general insurrection against the French. It was known also, that Murat, who had begun to fear lest he should be involved in the approaching fall of Napoleon, and who remembered, with more feeling, the affronts which Napoleon had put upon him from time to time, than the greatness to which he had been elevated by him, was treating with the allies, and endeavouring to make a peace which should secure his own authority under their sanction. Thus, there was no point of view in which Italy could be regarded as a source of assistance to Buonaparte: on the contrary, that fair country, the subject of his pride and his favour, was in the greatest danger of being totally lost to him.

The Spanish Peninsula afforded a still more alarming prospect. The battle of Vittoria had entirely destroyed the usurped authority of Joseph Buonaparte, and Napoleon himself had become desirous to see the war ended, at the price of totally ceding the kingdom on which he had seized so unjustifiably, and which he had, in his fatal obstinacy, continued to grasp, like a furious madman holding a hot iron until it has scorched him to the bone.

After that decisive battle, there was no obstacle in front to prevent the Duke of Wellington from entering France, but he chose first to reduce the strong frontier fortresses of Saint Sebastian and Pampeluna. The first capitulated finally on the 9th September; and notwithstanding the skill and bravery of Soult, which were exerted to the uttermost, he could not relieve Pampeluna. The English army, at least its left wing, passed the Bidassoa upon the 7th October, and Pampeluna surrendered on the 31st of the same month. Thus was the most persevering and the most hated of Buonaparte's enemies placed in arms upon the French soil, under the command of a general who had been so uniformly successful, that he seemed to move hand in hand with victory. It was but a slender consolation, in this state of matters, that Suchet, the Duke of Albufera, still maintained himself in Catalonia, his headquarters being at Barcelona. In fact, it would have been of infinitely more importance to Buonaparte, had the maréchal and those troops, who had not yet been discouraged by defeat, been on the north side of the Pyrenees, and ready to co-operate in defence of the frontiers of France.

RESTORATION OF FERDINAND

To parry this pressing danger, Napoleon had recourse to a plan, which, had it been practised the year before, might have placed the affairs of Spain on a very different footing. He resolved, as we have hinted, to desist from the vain undertaking, which had cost himself so much blood and treasure; to undo his own favourite work; to resign the claims of his brother to the crown of Spain; and, by restoring the legitimate sovereign to the throne, endeavour to form such an alliance with him as might take Spain out of the list of his enemies, and perhaps add her to that of his friends. Had he had recourse to this expedient in the previous year, Ferdinand's appearance in Spain might have had a very important effect in embroiling the councils of the Cortes. It is well known that the unfortunate distinctions of Royalists and Liberalists, were already broken out among the Spaniards, and from the colours in which his present Majesty of Spain has since shown himself, there is great room to doubt whether he had either temper, wisdom, or virtue sufficient to act as a mediator betwixt the two classes of his subjects, of which both were inclined to carry their opposite opinions into extremes. It is more than probable that a civil war might even then have taken place, between the King, desirous of regaining the plenitude of authority conferred on him by the ancient constitution, and the Cortes, anxious to maintain the liberties which they had recently recovered, and carried, by their new constitution, to the extent of republican license. If such a war had arisen, King Ferdinand would probably have fallen into the snare prepared for him by Buonaparte, and called in his late jailor, in the capacity of his ally, against the Cortes, and perhaps also against the English, who, though not approving of the theoretical extravagances of the system of government, which had divided the patriots into two civil factions, must, nevertheless, have considered that assembly as the representatives of the Spanish people, and the allies with whom the British had formed their league. Talleyrand is said to have recommended the liberation of Ferdinand at a much earlier period. He called the measure an olla podrida for Spain.

But Napoleon's present concession came too late, and was too evidently wrung from him by the most pressing necessity, to permit Ferdinand, however desirous of his liberty, to accept of it on the terms offered. The reader may, indeed, be curious to know in what language Napoleon could address the prince whose person he had seized and imprisoned like a kidnapper, and on whose throne he had so long and so pertinaciously endeavoured to support a usurper. Perhaps, when writing the following letter, Buonaparte was himself sensible that his conduct admitted of no glossing over; he, therefore, came to the point, it will be observed, at once, trusting probably that the hope of being restored to his liberty and kingdom would be so agreeable in itself, that the captive monarch would not be disposed strictly to criticise the circumstances which had occasioned so pleasing an offer, or the expressions in which it was conveyed.

"My Cousin—The state of my empire and of my political situation, lead me to put a final adjustment to the affairs of Spain. The English are exciting anarchy and jacobinism; they endeavour to overthrow the crown and the nobility, in order to establish a republic. I cannot, without being deeply affected, think on the destruction of a nation which interests me, both by its neighbourhood, and its common interest concerning maritime commerce. I wish to re-establish the relations of friendship and good neighbourhood, which have so long been established betwixt France and Spain. You will therefore listen to what the Comte de la Forest will propose in my name," &c.

Considering the terms of this letter, and contrasting them with the manner in which the friendly relations alluded to had been broken off, and that in which the interest taken by Napoleon in the kingdom of Spain had been displayed, the hypocritical professions of the writer were too obviously dictated by necessity, to impose upon the meanest understanding. The answer of Ferdinand was not without dignity. He declined to treat without having an opportunity of consulting with the Regency of Spain, and required permission to hear a deputation of his subjects, who might at once inform him of the actual state of affairs in Spain, and point out a remedy for the evils under which the kingdom suffered.

"If," said the prince, in his reply to Napoleon's proposal, "this liberty is not permitted to me, I prefer remaining at Valençay, where I have now lived four years and a half, and where I am willing to die, if such is God's pleasure." Finding the prince firm upon this score, Napoleon, to whom his freedom might be possibly some advantage, and when his captivity could no longer in any shape benefit him, consented that Ferdinand should be liberated upon a treaty being drawn up between the Duke of St. Carlos, as the representative of Ferdinand, and the Comte de la Forest, as plenipotentiary of Napoleon; but which treaty should not be ratified until it had been approved of by the Regency. The heads were briefly these:—I. Napoleon recognised Ferdinand as King of Spain and the Indies. II.

Ferdinand undertook that the English should evacuate Spain, and particularly Minorca and Ceuta. III. The two governments became engaged to each other, to place their relations on the footing prescribed by the treaty of Dunkirk, and which had been maintained until 1772. Lastly, The new king engaged to pay a suitable revenue to his father, and a jointure to his mother, in case of her survivance; and provision was made for re-establishing the commercial relations betwixt France and Spain.

In this treaty of Valençay, subscribed the 11th of December, 1813, the desire of Buonaparte to embroil Spain with her ally Great Britain, is visible not only in the second article, but in the third. For as Napoleon always contended that his opposition to the rights exercised on the sea by the English, had been grounded on the treaty of Utrecht, his reference to that treaty upon the present occasion, shows that he had not yet lost sight of his Continental System.

The Regency of Spain, when the treaty of Valençay was laid before them, refused to ratify it, both in virtue of a decree of the Cortes, which, as early as January, 1811, declared that there be neither truce nor negotiation with France, until the King should enjoy his entire liberty, and on account of their treaty with England, in which Spain engaged to contract no peace without England's concurrence. Thus obliged to renounce the hopes of fettering Spain, as a nation, with any conditions, Buonaparte at length released Ferdinand from his confinement, and permitted him to return to his kingdom, upon his personal subscription of the treaty, trusting that, in the political alterations which his arrival might occasion in Spain, something might turn up to serve his own views, which could never be advanced by Ferdinand's continuing in confinement. Nothing of the kind, however, took place, nor is it needful either to detain the reader farther with the Spanish affairs, or again to revert to them. Ferdinand is said, by the French, to have received Napoleon's proposals with much satisfaction, and to have written a letter of thanks to the Emperor for his freedom, obtained after nearly six years' most causeless imprisonment. If so, the circumstance must be received as evidence of Ferdinand's singularly grateful disposition, of which we believe there are few other examples to be quoted. The liberated monarch returned to his territories, at the conclusion of all this negotiation, in the end of March 1814. The event is here anticipated, that there may be no occasion to return to it.

Another state-prisoner of importance was liberated about the same time. Nearly at the commencement of the year 1814, proposals had been transmitted, by the agency of Cardinal Maury and the Bishops of Evreux and Plaisance, to Pius VII., still detained at Fontainbleau. His liberation was tendered to him; and, on condition of his ceding a part of the territories of the Church, he was to be restored to the remainder. "The dominions of Saint Peter are not my property," answered the Pontiff; "they belong to the Church, and I cannot consent to their cession."—"To prove the Emperor's good intentions," said the Bishop of Plaisance, "I have orders to announce your Holiness' return to Rome."—"It must, then, be with all my cardinals," said Pius VII.—"Under the present circumstances, that is impossible."—"Well, then, a carriage to transport me is all I desire—I wish to be at Rome, to acquit myself of my duties as Head of the Church."

An escort, termed a guard of honour, attended him, commanded by a colonel, who treated his Holiness with much respect, but seemed disposed to suffer no one to speak with him in private. Pius VII. convoked, however, the cardinals who were at Fontainbleau, to the number of seventeen, and took an affecting farewell. As the Pope was about to depart, he commanded them to wear no decoration received from the French Government; to accept no pension of their bestowing; and to assist at no festival to which they might be invited. On the 24th of January, Pius left Fontainbleau, and returned by slow journeys to Savona, where he remained from the 19th of February to the 19th of March. He reached Fiorenzuola on the 23d, where his French escort was relieved by an Austrian detachment, by whom the Pontiff was received with all the usual honours; and he arrived at Rome on the 18th of May, amid the acclamations of thousands, who thronged to receive his benediction.

With such results terminated an act of despotic authority, one of the most impolitic, as well as unpopular, practised by Buonaparte during his reign. He himself was so much ashamed of it, as to disown his having given any orders for the captivity of the Pontiff, though it was continued under his authority for five years and upwards. It was remarkable, that when the Pope was taken from Rome as a prisoner, Murat was in possession of his dominions, as the connexion and ally of Buonaparte; and now his Holiness found the same Murat and his army at Rome, and received from his hands, in the opposite character of ally of the Emperor of Austria, the re-delivery of the patrimony of Saint Peter's in its full integrity.

EMANCIPATION OF HOLLAND

Thus was restored to its ancient allegiance that celebrated city, which had for a time borne the title of SECOND in the French dominions. The revolution in Holland came also to augment the embarrassments of Napoleon, and dislocate what remained of the immense additions which he had attempted to unite with his empire. That country had been first impoverished by the total destruction of its commerce, under pretence of enforcing the continental system. It was from his inability to succeed in his attempt to avert this pest from the peaceful and industrious Dutchmen, that Louis Buonaparte had relinquished in disgust a sceptre, the authority of which was not permitted to protect the people over whom it was swayed.

The distress which followed, upon the introduction of these unnatural restrictions into a country, the existence of which depended on the freedom of its commerce, was almost incredible. At Amsterdam, the population was reduced from 220,000 to 190,000 souls. In the Hague, Delft, and elsewhere, many houses were pulled down, or suffered to fall to ruin by the proprietors, from inability to pay the taxes. At Haarlem, whole streets were in desolation, and about five hundred houses were entirely dismantled. The preservation of the dikes was greatly neglected for want of funds, and the sea breaking in at the Polders and elsewhere, threatened to resume what human industry had withdrawn from her reign.

The discontent of the people arose to the highest pitch, and their thoughts naturally reverted to the paternal government of the House of Orange, and the blessings which they had enjoyed under it. But with the prudence, which is the distinguishing mark of the national character, the Dutch knew, that until the power of France should be broken, any attempt at insurrection in Holland must be hopeless; they therefore contented themselves with forming secret confederations among the higher order of citizens in the principal towns, who made it their business to prevent all premature disturbances on the part of the lower classes, insinuating themselves, at the same time, so much into their favour, that they were sure of having them at their disposal, when a propitious moment for action should arise. Those intrusted with the secret of the intended insurrection, acted with equal prudence and firmness; and the sagacious, temperate, and reasonable character of the nation was never seen to greater advantage than upon this occasion. The national guards were warmly disposed to act in the cause. The rumours of Buonaparte's retreat from Leipsic—

"for such an host Fled not in silence through the affrighted deep,"

united to prepare the public mind for resistance to the foreign yoke; and the approach of General Bulow towards the banks of the Yssel, became the signal for general insurrection.

On the 14th November, the Orange flag was hoisted at the Hague and at Amsterdam, amid the ancient acclamations of "Orange-boven" (Up with the Orange.) At Rotterdam, a small party of the Dutch patriots, of the better class, waited on the prefect, Le Brun, Duke of Placentia, and, showing the orange cockade which they wore, addressed the French general in these words:—"You may guess from these colours the purpose which has brought us hither, and the events which are about to take place. You, who are now the weakest, know that we are strongest—and we the strongest, know that you are the weakest. You will act wisely to depart from this place in quiet; and the sooner you do so, you are the less likely to expose yourself to insult, and it may be to danger."

A revolution of so important a nature had never certainly been announced to the sinking party, with so little tumult, or in such courteous terms. The reply of General Le Brun was that of a Frenchman, seldom willing to be outdone in politeness:—"I have expected this summons for some time, and am very willing to accede to your proposal, and take my departure immediately." He mounted into his carriage accordingly, and drove through an immense multitude now assembled, without meeting any other insult than being required to join in the universal cry of Orange-boven.

The Dutch were altogether without arms when they took the daring resolution to re-construct their ancient government, and were for some time in great danger. But they were secured by the advance of the Russians to their support, while forces from England were sent over, to the number of 6000 men, under General Graham, now Lord Lynedoch; so that the French troops, who had thrown themselves into two or three forts, were instantly blockaded, and prevented from disturbing the country by excursions.

No event during the war made a more general and deep impression on the mind of the British nation, than the liberation of Holland, which is well entitled by a recent author, "one of the most fortunate events which could at that moment have taken place. The rapidity with which the Dutch, from being obstacles to the invasion of France, became the instruments by which that undertaking was most facilitated, could only have been brought about through the detestable system of government which Buonaparte had pursued with them."[296]

Thus victory, having changed her course, like some powerful spring-tide, had now, in the end of the year 1813, receded at every point from the dominions which its strong and rapid onward course had so totally overwhelmed.

---

[296] See Memoir of the Operations of the Allied Armies in 1813 and 1814, by Major-General Lord Burghersh; second edition, p. 49.

Chapter LXXII

Preparations of Napoleon against the Invasion of France—Terms of Peace offered by the Allies—Congress held at Manheim—Lord Castlereagh—Manifesto of the Allies—Buonaparte's Reply—State of Parties in France—The population of France, in general, wearied of the War, and desirous of the Deposition of Buonaparte—His unsuccessful attempts to arouse the national spirit—Council of State Extraordinary held Nov. 11th, when new taxes are imposed, and a new Conscription of 300,000 men decreed—Gloom of the Council, and violence of Buonaparte—Report of the State of the Nation presented to Napoleon by the Legislative Body—The Legislative Body is prorogued—Unceasing activity of the Emperor—National Guard called out—Napoleon, presenting to them his Empress and Child, takes leave of the People—He leaves Paris for the Armies.

While these scenes were passing in the vicinity of France, the Emperor was using every effort to bring forward, in defence of her territory, a force in some degree corresponding to the ideas which he desired men should entertain of the great nation. He distributed the seventy or eighty thousand men whom he had brought back with him, along the line of the Rhine, unmoved by the opinions of those who deemed them insufficient in number to defend so wide a stretch of frontier. Allowing the truth of their reasoning, he denied its efficacy in the present instance. Policy now demanded, he said, that there should be no voluntary abatement of the lofty pretensions to which France laid claim. The Austrians and Prussians still remembered the campaigns of the Revolution, and dreaded to encounter France once more in the character of an armed nation. This apprehension was to be kept up as long as possible, and almost at all risks. To concentrate his forces would be to acknowledge his weakness, to confess that he was devoid of means to supply the exhausted battalions; and what might be still more imprudent, it was making the nation itself sensible of the same melancholy truth; so that, according to this reasoning, it was necessary to keep up appearances, however ill seconded by realities. The allied sovereigns, on the other hand, were gradually approaching to the right bank of the Rhine their immense masses, which, including the reserves, did not, perhaps, amount to less than half a million of men.

The scruples of the Emperor of Austria, joined to the respect entertained for the courage of the French, and the talents of their leader, by the coalition at large, influenced their councils at this period, and before resuming a train of hostilities which must involve some extreme conclusion, they resolved once more to offer terms of peace to the Emperor of France.

The agent selected on this occasion was the Baron de St. Aignan,[297] a French diplomatist of reputation, residing at one of the German courts, who, falling into the hands of the allies, was set at liberty, with a commission to assure the French Emperor of their willingness to enter into a treaty on equal terms. The English Government also publicly announced their readiness to negotiate for a peace, and that they would make considerable concessions to obtain so great a blessing.[298] Napoleon, therefore, had another opportunity for negotiating, upon such terms as must indeed deprive him of the unjust supremacy among European councils which he had attempted to secure, but would have left him a high and honourable seat among the sovereigns of Europe. But the pertinacity of Napoleon's disposition qualified him ill for a negotiator, unless when he had the full power in his own hand to dictate the terms. His determined firmness of purpose, in many cases a great advantage, proved now the very reverse, as it prevented him from anticipating absolute necessity, by sacrificing, for the sake

---

[297] French Envoy to the Duke of Saxe Weimar.
[298] "M. Metternich told me, that he wished Napoleon to be convinced that the greatest impartiality and moderation prevailed in the councils of the allied powers; but that they felt themselves strong in proportion to their moderation: that none of them entertained designs against the dynasty of the Emperor Napoleon; that England was much more moderate than was supposed; and that there never was a more favourable moment for treating with that power."—*M. de Saint Aignan's Report.* See *Montholon,* tom. ii., Appendix.

of peace, something which it was actually in his power to give or retain. This tenacity was a peculiar feature of his character. He might, indeed, be brought to give up his claims to kingdoms and provinces which were already put beyond his power to recover; but when the question regarded the cession of any thing which was still in his possession, the grasp of the lion itself could scarce be more unrelaxing. Hence, as his misfortunes accumulated, the negotiations between him and the allies came to resemble the bargain driven with the King of Rome, according to ancient history, for the books of the Sibyls. The price of peace, like that of those mysterious volumes, was raised against him upon every renewal of the conferences. This cannot surprise any one who considers, that in proportion to the number of defeats sustained and power diminished, the demands of the party gaining the advantage must naturally be heightened.

This will appear from a retrospect to former negotiations. Before the war with Russia, Napoleon might have made peace upon nearly his own terms, providing they had been accompanied with a disavowal of that species of superior authority, which, by the display of his armies on the frontiers of Poland, he seemed disposed to exercise over an independent and powerful empire. There was nothing left to be disputed between the two Emperors, excepting the point of equality, which it was impossible for Alexander to yield up, in justice to himself and to his subjects.

CONGRESS AT PRAGUE

The Congress at Prague was of a different complexion. The fate of war, or rather the consequence of Napoleon's own rashness, had lost him an immense army, and had delivered from his predominant influence, both Prussia and Austria; and these powers, united in alliance with Russia and England, had a title to demand, as they had the means of enforcing, such a treaty as should secure Prussia from again descending into a state which may be compared to that of Helots or Gibeonites; and Austria from one less directly dependent, but by the continuance of which she was stripped of many fair provinces, and exposed along her frontier to suffer turmoil from all the wars which the too well-known ambition of the

French empire might awaken in Germany. Yet even then the terms proposed by Prince Metternich stipulated only the liberation of Germany from French influence, with the restoration of the Illyrian provinces. The fate of Holland, and that of Spain, were remitted till a general peace, to which England should be a party. But Buonaparte, though Poland and Illyria might be considered as lost, and the line of the Elbe and Oder as indefensible against the assembled armies of the allies, refused to accept these terms, unless clogged with the condition that the Hanse Towns should remain under French influence; and did not even transmit this qualified acquiescence to a treaty, until the truce appointed for the purpose of the congress had expired.[299]

After gaining six battles, and after the allies had redeemed their pledge, that they would not hear of farther negotiation while there was a French soldier in Germany, except as a prisoner, or as belonging to the garrison of a blockaded fortress, it was natural that the demands of the confederated sovereigns should rise; more especially as England, at whose expense the war had been in a great measure carried on, was become a party to the conferences, and her particular objects must now be attended to in their turn.

The terms, therefore, proposed to Napoleon, on which peace and the guarantee of his dynasty might be obtained, had risen in proportion to the success of his enemies.

The Earl of Aberdeen,[300] well known for his literature and talents, attended, on the part of Great Britain, the negotiations held with the Baron St. Aignan. The basis of the treaty proposed by the allies were—That France, divesting herself of all the unnatural additions with which the conquests of Buonaparte had invested her, should return to her natural limits, the Rhine, the Alps, and the Pyrenees, which of course left her in possession of the rich provinces of Belgium. The independence of Italy, Germany, and Holland, were absolutely stipulated. Spain, whom the power of Great Britain, seconded by her own efforts, had nearly freed of the

---

[299] Fouché, tom. ii., p. 150.
[300] George Hamilton Gordon, fourth Earl of Aberdeen K.T., F.R.S., and P.S.A.

French yoke, was to be in like manner restored to independence, under Ferdinand.

Such were the outlines of the terms proposed. But it is generally admitted, that if Buonaparte had shown a candid wish to close with them, the stipulations might have been modified, so as to be more agreeable to him than they sounded in the abstract. There were ministers in the cabinet of the allied sovereigns who advised an acquiescence in Eugene Beauharnois, of whom a very favourable opinion was entertained, being received as King of the upper part of Italy, while Murat retained the southern half of that peninsula. The same counsellors would not have objected to holding Holland as sufficiently independent, if the conscientious Louis Buonaparte were placed at its head. As for Spain, its destinies were now beyond the influence of Napoleon, even in his own opinion, since he was himself treating with his captive at Valençay, for re-establishing him on the throne. A treaty, therefore, might possibly have been achieved by help of skilful management, which, while it affirmed the nominal independence of Italy and Holland, would have left Napoleon in actual possession of all the real influence which so powerful a mind could have exercised over a brother, a step-son, and a brother-in-law, all indebted to him for their rise to the rank they held. His power might have been thus consolidated in the most formidable manner, and his empire placed in such security, that he could fear no aggression on any quarter, and had only to testify pacific intentions towards other nations, to ensure the perfect tranquillity of France, and of the world.

But it did not suit the high-soaring ambition of Napoleon to be contented with such a degree of power as was to be obtained by negotiation. His favourite phrase on such occasions, which indeed he had put into the mouth of Maria Louisa upon a recent occasion,[301] was, that he could not occupy a throne, the glory of which was tarnished. This was a strange abuse of words; for if his glory was at all impaired, as in a military point of view it certainly was, the depreciation arose from his having lost many great battles, and could not be increased by his acquiescing in such concessions as his defeat rendered necessary. The loss of a battle necessarily infers,

---

[301] Speech to the Senate, Oct. 7.

more or less, some censure on the conduct of a defeated general; but it can never dishonour a patriotic prince to make such sacrifices as may save his people from the scourge of a protracted and losing warfare. Yet let us do justice to the memory of a man so distinguished. If a merited confidence in the zeal and bravery of his troops, or in his own transcendent abilities as a general, could justify him in committing a great political error, in neglecting the opportunity of securing peace on honourable terms, the events of the strangely varied campaign of 1814 show sufficiently the ample ground there was for his entertaining such an assurance.

LORD CASTLEREAGH

At this period, Maret, Duke of Bassano, invited the allies to hold a congress at Manheim, for considering the preliminaries of peace; and, on the part of Great Britain, Lord Castlereagh, a cabinet minister, was sent over to represent her on this important occasion. Faction, which in countries where free discussion is permitted, often attaches its censure to the best and worthiest of those to whose political opinions it is opposed, has calumniated this statesman during his life, and even after his death. This is one of the evils at the expense of which freedom is purchased; and it is purchased the more cheaply, that the hour of confutation fails not to come. Now, when his power can attract no flattery, and excite no odium, impartial history must write on the tomb of Castlereagh, that his undaunted courage, manly steadiness, and deep political sagacity, had the principal share in infusing that spirit of continued exertion and unabated perseverance into the councils of the allies, which supported them through many intervals of doubt and indecision, and finally conducted them to the triumphant conclusion of the most eventful contest which Europe ever saw.[302]

In the meanwhile, both parties proclaimed their anxiety for peace, well aware of the advantageous opinion, which the French public in particular could not fail to entertain of that party, which

---

[302] Robert Stewart, Viscount Castlereagh, was born in 1769. In 1821, he succeeded his father, as Marquis of Londonderry, and died in 1822.

seemed most disposed to afford the world the blessings of that state of rest and tranquillity, which was now universally sighed for.

A manifesto was published by the allied monarchs,[303] in which they complain, unreasonably certainly, of the preparations which Buonaparte was making for recruiting his army, which augmentation of the means of resistance, whether Napoleon was to look to peace or war, was equally justifiable when the frontiers of France were surrounded by the allied armies. The rest of this state paper was in a better, because a truer tone. It stated, that victory had brought the allies to the Rhine, but they meant to make no farther use of their advantages than to propose to Napoleon a peace, founded on the independence of France, as well as upon that of every other country. "They desired," as this document stated, "that France should be great, powerful, and happy, because the power of France is one of the fundamental bases of the social system in Europe. They were willing to confirm to her an extent of territory, greater than she enjoyed under her ancient kings; but they desired, at the same time, that Europe should enjoy tranquillity. It was, in short, their object to arrange a pacification on such terms as might, by mutual guarantees, and a well-arranged balance of power, preserve Europe in future from the numberless calamities, which, during twenty years, had distracted the world." This public declaration seemed intended to intimate, that the war of the coalition was not as yet directed against the person of Napoleon, or his dynasty, but only against his system of arbitrary supremacy. The allies further declared, that they would not lay down their arms until the political state of Europe should be finally arranged on unalterable principles, and recognised by the sanctity of treaties.

REPLY TO THE MANIFESTO

The reply of Buonaparte to Maret's proposition, is contained in a letter from Caulaincourt to Metternich, dated 2d December. It declared that Buonaparte acquiesced in the principle which should rest the proposed pacification on the absolute independence of the states of Europe, so that neither one nor another should in future

---

[303] Dated Frankfort, Dec. 1, 1813.

arrogate sovereignty or supremacy in any form whatsoever, either upon land or sea. It was therefore declared, that his Majesty adhered to the general bases and abstracts communicated by M. St. Aignan. "They will involve," the letter added, "great sacrifices on the part of France, but his Majesty would make them without regret, if, by like sacrifices, England would give the means of arriving at a general peace, honourable for all concerned."[304]

The slightest attention to this document shows that Napoleon, in his pretence of being desirous for peace on the terms held out in the proposals of the allies, was totally insincere. His answer was artfully calculated to mix up with the diminution of his own exorbitant power, the question of the maritime law, on which England and all other nations had acted for many centuries, and which gives to those nations that possess powerful fleets, the same advantage, which those that have great armies enjoy by the law martial. The rights arising out of this law maritime, had been maintained by England at the end of the disastrous American war, when the Armed Neutrality was formed for the express purpose of depriving her, in her hour of weakness, of this bulwark of her naval power. It had been defended during the present war against all Europe, with France and Napoleon at her head. It was impossible that Britain should permit any challenge of her maritime rights in the present moment of her prosperity, when not only her ships rode triumphant on every coast, but her own victorious army was quartered on French ground, and the powerful hosts of her allies, brought to the field by her means, were arrayed along the whole frontier of the Rhine. The Emperor of the French might have as well proposed to make the peace which Europe was offering to him, depend upon Great Britain's ceding Ireland or Scotland.

Neither can it be pretended that there was an indirect policy in introducing this discussion as an apple of discord, which might give cause to disunion among the allies. Far from looking on the maritime law, as exercised by Britain, with the eyes of jealousy, with which it might at other times have been regarded, the continental nations remembered the far greater grievances which had been entailed on them by Buonaparte's memorable attempt to put down

---

[304] See the correspondence in Savary's Memoirs, tom. iii., p. 140.

that law by his anti-commercial system, which had made Russia herself buckle on her armour, and was a cause, and a principal one, of the general coalition against France. As Buonaparte, therefore, could have no hope to obtain any advantage, direct or indirect, from mixing up the question of maritime rights with that of the general settlement of the continent, and as mere spleen and hatred to Great Britain would be scarce an adequate motive in a mind so sagacious, we must suppose this inadmissible stipulation to have been thrown in for the purpose of enabling him to break off the negotiation when he pleased, and cast upon the English the unpopularity attending the breach of it. It is very true that England had offered to make sacrifices for obtaining a general peace; but these sacrifices, as was seen by the event, regarded the restoration to France of conquered colonies, not the cession of her own naval rights, which, on no occasion whatsoever, a minister of Britain will, can, or dare, permit to be brought into challenge. Accordingly, the acceptance by Buonaparte of the terms transmitted by St. Aignan, being provided with a slip-knot, as it were, by which he could free himself from the engagement at pleasure, was considered, both by the allies, and by a large proportion of the people of France, as elusory, and indicating no serious purpose of pacification. The treaty therefore languished, and was not fairly set on foot until the chance of war had been again appealed to.[305]

In the meanwhile, the allies were bringing up their reserves as fast as possible, and Buonaparte on his side was doing all he could to recruit his forces. His measures for this purpose had been adopted long before the present emergency. As far back as the 9th October, the Empress Maria Louisa, in the character of Regent, presided in a meeting of the Senate, held for the purpose of calling for fresh recruits to the armies. She was an object of interest and compassion to all, when announcing the war which had broken out betwixt her father and her husband; but the following injudicious censure upon her country was put into the mouth of the young sovereign, without much regard to delicacy. "No one," she said,

---

[305] "The Emperor placed no confidence in the sentiments expressed in the declarations of the allies. He had said long before, 'They have appointed my grave as their place of rendezvous, but none of them will venture to come first.' He now added, 'Their time of rendezvous has arrived. They think the lion dead; and the question is, "Who will give the ass' kick." If France abandon me, I can do nothing.'"—Savary, tom. iii., p. 158.

"can know so well as I what the French will have to dread, if they permit the allies to be conquerors." The closing paragraph was also much criticised, as attaching more importance to the personal feelings of the sovereign, than ought to have been exclusively ascribed to them in so great a public extremity. "Having been acquainted for four years with the inmost thoughts of my husband, I know with what sentiments he would be afflicted if placed on a tarnished throne, and wearing a crown despoiled of glory."[306] The decree of the Senate, passive as usual, appointed a levy of 280,000 conscripts.

When Buonaparte arrived at Saint Cloud, after having brought the remains of his once great army to Mayence, his affairs were even in a worse state than had been anticipated. But before we proceed to detail the measures which he took for redeeming them, it is necessary to take notice of two parties in the state, who, in consequence of the decay of the Imperial power, were growing gradually into importance.

The first were the adherents of the Bourbons, who, reduced to silence by the long-continued successes of Buonaparte, still continued to exist, and now resumed their consequence. They had numerous partisans in the west and south of France, and many of them still maintained correspondence with the exiled family. The old noblesse, amongst whom such as did not attach themselves to the court and person of Napoleon, continued to be stanch royalists, had acquired, or rather regained, a considerable influence in Parisian society. The superior elegance of their manners, the seclusion, and almost mystery of their meetings, their courage and their misfortunes, gave an interest to these relics of the history of France, which was increased by the historical remembrances connected with ancient names and high descent. Buonaparte himself, by the restoration of nobility as a rank, gave a dignity to those who had possessed it for centuries, which his own new creations could not impart. It is true, that in the eye of philosophy, the great man who first merits and wins a distinguished title, is in himself infinitely more valuable and respectable than the obscure individual who inherits his honours at the distance of centuries; but then he is

---

[306] Moniteur, Oct. 10, 1813.

valued for his personal qualities, not for his noblesse. No one thought of paying those marshals, whose names and actions shook the world, a greater degree of respect when Napoleon gave them titles. On the contrary, they will live in history, and be familiar to the imagination, by their own names, rather than those arising from their peerages. But the science of heraldry, when admitted as an arbitrary rule of society, reverses the rule of philosophy, and ranks nobility, like medals, not according to the intrinsic value of the metal, but in proportion to its antiquity. If this was the case with even the heroes who had hewed a soldier's path to honours, it was still more so with the titles granted by Buonaparte, "upon carpet consideration," and the knights whom he dubbed with unhacked rapier. It might be truly said of these that

"Their fire-new stamp of honour scarce was current."[307]

When, therefore, the republican fury died away, and Buonaparte directed the respect of the people at large towards title and nobility, a distinct and superior influence was acquired by those who possessed such honours by hereditary descent. Napoleon knew this, and courted, and in some degree feared, the remainder of the old noblesse, who, unless he could decidedly attach them to his own interest, were exposed to surveillance and imprisonment on circumstances of slight suspicion. They became, however, so circumspect and cautious, that it was impossible to introduce the spies of the police into their *salons* and private parties. Still Napoleon was sensible of the existence of this party, and of the danger which might attend upon it, even while his followers had forgot perhaps that the Bourbons continued to live. "I thought him mad," said Ney (whose head, according to Fouché, could not embrace two political ideas,) "when taking leave of the army at Smorgoni, he used the expression, 'The Bourbons will make their own of this.'"[308]

---

[307] Richard III., act i., scene iii.
[308] *Les Bourbons s'en tireraient.* Memoirs of Fouché, vol. iii., p. 87.—S.

STATE OF PARTIES—THE ROYALISTS

This party began now to be active, and a Royalist confederation organised itself in the centre of France as early as the month of March, 1813. The most distinguished members are said to have been the Dukes of Duras, Trémouille, and Fitzjames; Messrs. de Polignac, Ferrand, Audrien de Montmorency, Sosthène de la Rochefoucault, Sermaison, and La Rochejacquelein. Royalist commanders had been nominated in different quarters—Count Suzannet in the Lower Poitou, Duras in Orleans and Tours, and the Marquis de Rivière in the province of Berry. Bourdeaux was full of Royalists, most of them of the mercantile class, who were ruined by the restrictions of the continental system, and all waited anxiously a signal for action.

Another internal faction, noways desirous of the return of the Bourbons, yet equally inimical to the power of Napoleon, consisted of the old Republican statesmen and leaders, with the more zealous part of their followers. These could not behold with indifference the whole fruits of the Revolution, for which so much misery had been endured, so much blood spilled, so many crimes committed, swept away by the rude hand of a despotic soldier. They saw, with a mixture of shame and mortification, that the issue of all their toils and all their systems had been the monstrous concoction of a military despotism compared with which every other government in Europe might be declared liberal, except perhaps that of Turkey. During the monarchy, so long represented as a system of slavery, public opinion had in the parliaments zealous advocates, and an opportunity of making itself known; but in imperial France all was mute, except the voice of hired functionaries, mere trumpets of the Government, who breathed not a sound but what was suggested to them. A sense of this degraded condition united in secret all those who desired to see a free government in France, and especially such as had been active in the commencement of the Revolution.

This class of politicians could not desire the return of the family in whose exile they had been active, and had therefore cause to fear the re-action with which such an event might be attended; but they wished to get rid of Napoleon, whose government seemed to be alike inconsistent with peace and with liberty. The idea of a regency suggested itself to Fouché and others, as a plausible mode of attaining their purpose.[309] Austria, they thought, might be propitiated by giving Maria Louisa the precedence in the council of regency as guardian of her son, who should succeed to the crown when he came to the age of majority. This expedient, it was thought, would give an opportunity, in the meanwhile, to introduce free principles into the constitution. But, while it does not appear how these theorists intended to dispose of Napoleon, it is certain that nothing but his death, captivity, or perpetual exile, would have prevented such a man from obtaining the full management of a regency, in which his wife was to preside in the name of his son.

GENERAL DISCONTENT—NEW TAXES IMPOSED

A great part of the population of France, without having any distinct views as to its future government, were discontented with that of Buonaparte, which, after having drained the country of men and wealth, seemed about to terminate, by subjecting it to the revenge of incensed Europe. When these were told that Buonaparte could not bear to sit upon a tarnished throne, or wear a crown of which the glory was diminished, they were apt to consider how often it was necessary that the best blood of France should be expended in washing the one and restoring the brilliancy of the other. They saw in Napoleon a bold and obstinate man, conscious of having overcome so many obstacles, that he could not endure to admit the existence of any which might be insurmountable. They beheld him obstinately determined to retain every thing, defend every thing, venture every thing, without making the least sacrifice to circumstances, as if he were in his own person independent of the Laws of Destiny, to which the whole universe is subjected. These men felt the oppression of the new taxes, the terrors of the new

---

[309] Fouché, tom. ii., p. 132. "The conferring of this authority on the Empress Maria Louisa was generally approved. Her good and amiable character was well known; and she was consequently much loved and esteemed. Every one connected with her household had experience of her kindness; and it might with truth be said, that she had won the good-will of the nation, which regarded her with an affectionate respect."—Savary, tom. iii., p. 56.

conscription,[310] and without forming a wish as to the mode in which he was to be succeeded, devoutly desired the Emperor's deposition. But when an end is warmly desired, the means of attaining it soon come to occupy the imagination; and thus many of those who were at first a sort of general malecontents, came to attach themselves to the more decided faction either of the Royalists or Liberalists.

These feelings, varying between absolute hostility to Napoleon, and indifference to his fate, threw a general chillness over the disposition to resist the invasion of the strangers, which Buonaparte had reckoned on as certain to render the war national amongst so high-spirited a people as the French. No effort was spared to dispel this apathy, and excite them to resistance; the presses of the capital and the provinces, all adopted the tone suggested by the Government, and called forth every one to rise in mass for defence of the country. But although, in some places, the peasants were induced to take arms, the nation at large showed a coldness, which can only be accounted for by the general idea which prevailed, that the Emperor had an honourable peace within his power, whenever he should be disposed to accept of it.

In the meantime, new burdens were necessary to pay the expenses of the approaching campaign, and recruit the diminished ranks of the army. Napoleon, indeed, supplied from his own hoards a sum of 30 millions of francs;[311] but, at the same time, the public taxes of the subject were increased by one moiety, without any appeal to, or consultation with the Legislative Body, who, indeed, were not sitting at the time. In a council of state extraordinary, held on the 11th November, two days after his return to Paris, Napoleon

---

[310] It has been given as a sufficient answer to these complaints, that Buonaparte is falsely accused of having drained France of her youth, since, upon the whole, the population is stated to have, on the contrary, increased. This may be the case; but it is no less certain, that the wars of Buonaparte consumed at least a million of conscripts, and it does not occur to us that the population of a country increases under such circumstances, like the growth of a tree subjected to much pruning; still less that the general result would satisfy parents for the slaughter of their children, any more than the sorrow of a mother who had lost her infant would be assuaged by the information that her next-door neighbour had been safely delivered of twins.—S.

[311] "The Emperor possessed a considerable treasure, the fruit of his economy: he transferred thirty millions to the public treasury; but this resource was far from being sufficient to meet the exigencies."—Savary, tom. iii., p. 147.

vindicated the infliction of this heavy augmentation on a discontented and distressed country. "In ordinary times," he said, "the contributions were calculated at one-fifth of the income of the individual; but, according to the urgency of events, there was no reason why it should not rise to a fourth, a third, or a half of the whole income. In fact," he concluded, "the contribution had no bounds; and if there were any laws intimating the contrary, they were ill-considered laws, and undeserving of attention."[312]

REPORT—STATE OF THE NATION

There was then read to the council a decree of the Senate for a new conscription of 300,000 men, to be levied upon those who had escaped the conscription of former years, and who had been considered as exempted from the service. There was a deep and melancholy silence. At length a counsellor spoke, with some hesitation, though it was only to blame the introductory clause of the senatorial decree, which stated the invasion of the frontiers as the cause of this large levy. It was, he suggested, a declaration too much calculated to spread alarm.

"And wherefore," said Napoleon, giving way to his natural vehemence, and indicating more strongly than prudence warranted, the warlike and vindictive purposes which exclusively occupied his breast—"wherefore should not the whole truth be told? Wellington has entered the south; the Russians menace the northern frontier; the Prussians, Austrians, and Bavarians threaten the east. Shame!— Wellington is in France, and we have not risen in mass to drive him back. All my allies have deserted me; the Bavarians have betrayed me—They threw themselves on my rear to cut off my retreat—But they have been slaughtered for their pains. No peace—none till we have burned Munich. A triumvirate is formed in the north, the same which made a partition of Poland. I demand of France 300,000 men—I will form a camp of a 100,000 at Bourdeaux—another at Metz—another at Lyons. With the present levy, and what remains of the last, I will have a million of men. But I must have grown men—not these boy-conscripts, to encumber the hospitals, and die

---

[312] Montgaillard, tom. vii., p. 273.

of fatigue upon the highways—I can reckon on no soldiers now save those of France itself."

"Ah, Sire," said one of the assentators, glad to throw in a suggestion which he supposed would suit the mood of the time, "that ancient France must remain to us inviolate."

"And Holland!" answered Napoleon, fiercely. "Abandon Holland? sooner yield it back to the sea. Counsellors, there must be an impulse given—all must march—You are fathers of families, the heads of the nation; it is for you to set the example. They speak of peace; I hear of nothing but peace, when all around should echo to the cry of war."

This was one of the occasions on which Buonaparte's constitutional vehemence overcame his political prudence. We might almost think we hear the voice of the Scandinavian deity Thor, or the war-god of Mexico, clamorous for his victims, and demanding that they be unblemished, and worthy of his bloody altar. But Buonaparte was unable to inspire others with his own martial zeal; they only foresaw that the nation must, according to the system of its ruler, encounter a most perilous danger, and that, even in case of success, when Napoleon reaped laurels, France would only gather cypress. This feeling was chiefly predominant in the Legislative Assembly; as every representative body which emanates, however remotely, from the people, has a natural aptitude to espouse their cause.

It is true, that the Emperor had by every precaution in his power, endeavoured to deprive this part of the state, the only one which had retained the least shadow of popular representation, of every thing approaching to freedom of debate or right of remonstrance, and by a recent act of despotic innovation, had even robbed them of the power of choosing their own president. He is said also to have exerted his authority over individuals by a practice similar to that adopted by James the Second upon members of parliament, called *closeting*, admitting individuals of the Legislative Body to private interviews, and condescending to use towards them that personal intercession, which, coming from a sovereign, it is so difficult to resist. But these arts proved unsuccessful, and only tended to show to the world that the Legislative Body had independence enough to intimate their desire for peace, while their sovereign was still determined on war. A commission of five of their members, distinguished for wisdom and moderation, were appointed to draw up a report upon the state of the nation, which they did in terms respectful to Napoleon, but such as plainly indicated their conviction that he would act wisely to discontinue his schemes of external ambition, to purchase peace by disclaiming them, and at the same time to restore to the subject some degree of internal liberty. They suggested, that in order to silence the complaints of the allied monarchs, which accused France of aiming at general sovereignty, the Emperor should make a solemn and specific declaration, abjuring all such purposes. They reminded him, that when Louis XIV. desired to restore energy to the nation, he acquainted them with the efforts he had made to obtain peace, and the effect answered his wishes. They recommended the example to Napoleon. It was only necessary, they said, that the nation should be assured, that the war was to be continued for the sole object of the independence of the French people and territory, to reanimate public spirit, and induce all to concur in the general defence. After other arguments tending to enforce the same advice, the report concluded with recommending, that his Majesty should be supplicated to maintain the active and constant execution of the laws, which preserve to Frenchmen the rights of liberty, and security both of person and property, and to the nation the free exercise of its political privileges."[313]

Like the mute prince, who recovered his speech when his father's life was endangered, the extremity of the national distress thus gave the power of remonstrance to a public body which had hitherto been only the passive agents of the will of a despotic sovereign. Yet comparing the nature of the remonstrance with the period of extremity at which it was made, Napoleon must have felt somewhat in the situation of the patriarch of Uz, the friends of whose former prosperity came in the moment of his greatest distresses with reproaches instead of assistance. The Legislative Body had been at least silent and acquiescent during the wonderful

---

[313] Montgaillard, tom. vii., p. 294; Savary, tom. iii., p. 172.

period of Buonaparte's success, and they now chose that of his adversity to give him unpalatable advice, instead of aiding in this emergency to inspire the nation with confidence. A philosophical monarch would nevertheless have regarded the quality of the course recommended more than the irritating circumstances of time and manner in which it was given; and would have endeavoured, by frank confidence and concessions, to reconcile himself with the Legislative Body. An artful and Machiavelian despot would have temporized with the deputies, and yielded for the time, with the purpose of afterwards recovering, at a fitting period, whatever point he might at present be obliged to cede. But Napoleon, too impetuous for either policy or philosophy, gave way to the full vehemence of a resentment, which, though unreasonable and imprudent, was certainly, considering those to whom it was addressed, by no means unnatural. He determined instantly to prorogue the Assembly, which had indicated such symptoms of opposition.[314] Their hall was, therefore, shut against them, and guarded with soldiers, while the deputies, summoned before the throne of the Emperor, received the following singular admonition:—"I have prohibited the printing of your address, because it is seditious. Eleven parts of you are good citizens, but the twelfth consists of rebels, and your commissioners are of the number. Lainé corresponds with the Prince Regent of England; the others are hotheaded fools, desirous of anarchy, like the Girondists, whom such opinions led to the scaffold. Is it when the enemy are on the frontiers that you demand an alteration of the constitution? Rather follow the example of Alsace and Franche Comté, where the inhabitants ask for leaders and arms to drive the invaders back. You are not the representatives of the people—you are only the representatives of the individual departments.... Yet you seek in your address to draw a distinction betwixt the sovereign and the people. I—I am the only real representative of the people. Which of you could support such a burden?—The throne is merely a piece of

---

[314] "'What need have I,' said the Emperor, 'of that assembly, if, instead of giving me the support of its strength, it only throws difficulties in my way? Is this the proper moment, when the national existence is threatened, to speak to me of constitutions and of the rights of the people? In a case analogous to the present state of France, the ancients extended the power of the government instead of restraining it. Here we are losing our time in trifles, whilst the enemy is at our doors. I will adjourn an assembly which is so little disposed to second me.' He immediately signed the decree to that effect, and gave me the order to seize every copy of the Report."—Savary, tom. iii., p. 174.

wood covered with velvet. I—I alone hold the place of the people. If France desires another species of constitution, which does not suit me, I will tell her to seek another monarch. It is at me the enemies aim, more than at France; but are we, therefore, to sacrifice a part of France? Do I not sacrifice my self-love, and my feelings of superiority, to obtain peace? Think you I speak proudly? If I do, I am proud because I have courage, and because France owes her grandeur to me. Yes—your address is unworthy of the Legislative Body, and of me. Begone to your homes. I will cause your address to be published in the *Moniteur*, with such notes as I shall furnish. Even if I had done wrong, you ought not to have reproached me with it thus publicly. People do not wash their dirty linen before the world. To conclude, France has more need of me than I have of France."[315]

LEGISLATIVE BODY PROROGUED

With this philippic, which we have but slightly compressed, he spurned the members of the Legislative Body from his presence.[316] It displays in a remarkable degree his natural vehemence of temper; his view of the constitution as a drama, in which he filled up every part, and performed at once the part of the prince and of the people; his consciousness of his own extraordinary powers, which he boldly weighed in the balance against all France; and the coarse and mean taste of some of his expressions. The suspension of the Legislative Body, the only part, we repeat, of the Imperial constitution which had the least pretence to a popular origin, was

---

[315] "Some deputies replied to certain passages of the Emperor's speech: he listened attentively to them; but did not admit the validity of their excuses, and persisted in the sentiments he had expressed. The audience lasted a full quarter of an hour: it was the last that he ever granted to the Legislative Body."—Savary, tom. iii., p. 178.

[316] "The Emperor having returned to his apartments, sent for the arch-chancellor, M. de Bassano, and myself. In reply to something which fell from M. Cambacérès, he said, 'What would you have had me do with an assembly which only waited for a favourable opportunity to excite a disturbance in the state?—I recollect, besides,' added he, 'that M. Fouché, who was connected with all these men, entertained the same opinion in respect to them. He said, that they only came to Paris for the purpose of asking certain favours, for which they importuned ministers from morning till night, and complained that their wishes were not immediately attended to.' The Emperor added, that this opinion of M. Fouché might be relied upon as sincere, since he had always professed republican principles."—Savary, tom. iii., p. 179.

not qualified to increase the confidence of the public, who now saw want of unity between the Emperor and the popular representatives, added to the other threatening circumstances of the time, and became yet more distracted in their opinions, and unwilling to exert themselves for the common defence.

To give a more favourable impulse to the mind of the nation, Napoleon had recourse to an expedient which, in the time of the Republic, had been attended with universal effect. He sent special commissioners, twenty-seven in number, into the different departments, to arouse the dormant energies of the inhabitants, and induce them to take up arms. But the senators and counsellors, chosen for this purpose, were altogether void of the terrible energies of the Republican proconsuls; and, though endowed like them with the most arbitrary powers, they had neither the furious zeal, nor the contempt of all the prejudices of humanity, which had been displayed by those ferocious demagogues. Their mission, therefore, produced but little effect. The conscription, too, failed to be the ready source of levies which it had so often proved. The lancet had been so often used, that the blood no longer followed it so readily.

HIS UNCEASING EXERTIONS

The unceasing activity of Napoleon laboured to supply these deficiencies. By day he was incessantly engaged in actively reviewing troops, inspecting stores, and all the preparations for a desperate resistance. By night, the lights were seen to glimmer late and long in the windows of his private apartment, in the upper story of the Tuileries.[317] He succeeded in levying twelve fresh regiments, and prepared to augment his veteran force by withdrawing Suchet from Catalonia, and making draughts from Soult's army on the frontiers, which he designed to supply by fresh levies.

---

[317] "His courage and tranquillity of mind remained unshaken. He laboured day and night to create an army capable of defending our territory; but the conscription lists no longer presented disposable men, and the arsenals afforded but meagre resources. His conduct on this trying occasion serves to show what may be effected by genius such as his. Fate seemed to have proportioned the weight of his misfortunes to his power of endurance. Nothing astonished him, or shook his firmness."—Savary, tom. iii., p. 147.

The *Moniteur*, and the other newspapers, magnified the success of the Emperor's exertions, described armies in reserve which had no existence, and dilated upon the *beau desespoir* which was driving all France to arms, while, in fact, most of the provinces waited with apathy the events of the war.

One of the strongest symptoms of Napoleon's own consciousness of approaching danger, was his calling out and arming the national guard of Paris, a force to which he would not have appealed, save in the case of the last necessity, but to which he now felt himself obliged to have recourse. Aware, however, that to mark any want of confidence in the armed citizens at this moment, would be to give occasion to the disaffection which he dreaded, he solemnized his departure to the frontier by convoking a meeting of the officers of the national guard at the Tuileries. He appeared among them with his Empress and his infant child, and in a tone which penetrated every bosom, announced that, being about to place himself at the head of his army, he committed to the faith of the citizens of Paris, the security of his capital, his wife, and his child. Whatever complaints might be justly entertained against Napoleon's political conduct, none were so ungenerous as to remember them at that moment. Many of the officers shared in the emotion which he testified, and some mingled their tears with those of the alarmed and sorrowing Empress.[318]

This scene took place on the 23d of January; on the 25th,[319] Napoleon left that abode of royalty, to which he was doomed not to return until he had undergone strange changes of fortune. His mind was agitated with unusual apprehensions and anticipations of misfortune; feeling also, what was unsuspected by many, that the real danger of his situation arose from the probability of the nation's wishing to recall the Bourbons. He had even, according to his own account, resolved to arrest "the person of a man of great

---

[318] Moniteur, Jan. 26; Savary, tom. iii., p. 203.
[319] "The Emperor's circle that night was composed of persons who enjoyed the favour of private admissions. He withdrew at an early hour, saying to those who were near him, 'Farewell, gentlemen, we shall perhaps meet again.' I had the honour of being in his society that night; and fell a prey to the deepest despondency, when I beheld him taking what to my mind appeared a last farewell. At midnight he set off for Châlons-sur-Marne."—Savary, tom. iii., p. 203.

influence,"[320] whom he supposed most likely to promote this design. His counsellors persuaded him to forbear this arbitrary action at a moment when his power was becoming daily more obnoxious, and reminded him that the suspected person had as much reason to fear the restoration of the Bourbons as he himself had. The Emperor yielded the point, but not without strongly repeating his fears that his advisers and himself would both have to repent of it; and not without charging Cambacérès to make sure of that individual's person in case any crisis should take place in the capital.

Thus, full of melancholy presages, he hastened to the field, where he had but inadequate means to oppose to the accumulated force which was now precipitating itself upon France.

---

[320] Talleyrand is intimated; for Fouché, to whom the description might otherwise have applied, was not at this time in or near Paris.—See Savary, tom. iii., p. 199.

Chapter LXXIII

Declaration of the Allies on entering France—Switzerland—Schwartzenberg crosses the Rhine—Apathy of the French—Junction of Blucher with the Grand Army—Crown Prince of Sweden—Inferiority of Napoleon's numerical Force—Battles of Brienne—and La Rothière—Difficulties of Buonaparte, during which he meditates to resign the Crown—He makes a successful Attack on the Silesian Army at Champ-Aubert—Blucher is compelled to retreat—The Grand Army carries Nogent and Montereau—Buonaparte's violence to his Generals—The Austrians resolve on a general Retreat, as far as Nancy and Langres—Prince Wenceslaus sent to Buonaparte's headquarters—The French enter Troyes—Execution of Goualt, a Royalist—A Decree of Death against all wearing the Bourbon emblems, and all Emigrants who should join the Allies.

It was time that Buonaparte should appear in the field in person, for the eastern frontiers of his empire, assaulted on every point, were yielding an almost unresisted entrance to the invading armies. The allied sovereigns had commenced their operations upon a system, as moderate and prudent in a political point of view, as it was bold and decisive considered under a military aspect.

They had not been too much elated by the successes of the late campaign. These had been bought at a high price, and events had shown, that if Napoleon could be resisted and defeated, it could only be by outnumbering his veteran armies, and accumulating such force against him as even his skill and talents should find irresistible. They recollected also the desperate efforts of which France and Frenchmen were capable, and were prudently desirous to express the moderation of their purpose in such a form as should have no chance of being mistaken.

Their manifestoes disclaimed the intention of dictating to France any particular form of government. They only desired that she should remain within the limits of her ancient territory, a peaceful member of the European commonwealth, allowing to other states, as well as claiming for herself, the full immunities of freedom and independence. The allied sovereigns desired that there should be an end put to the system which decided the fate of kingdoms, not according to the better right, but the longest sword. They wished a total suppression of all domination of the powerful over the weak; of all pretext of usurpation founded on alleged natural boundaries, or, in other words, on the claim of a powerful state to rend from a weak one whatever suited its convenience to possess. In a word, they aimed at the restoration of the balance of power, which had been long the political object of the wisest statesmen in Europe. It is singular, that the three nations who were now united to oppose the aggressions of Buonaparte, had themselves been the first to set the example of violent and unprincipled spoliation in the partition of Poland; and that they had reaped an abundant punishment in the measure of retribution dealt to them by the instrumentality of the very man, whose lawless outrages they, in their turn, were now combined to chastise.

With respect to the nature of the changes which might take place in the internal arrangements of France, in order to bring about the restoration of the balance of power, the allied monarchs professed themselves indifferent. If Napoleon should reconcile himself to the general pacification they proposed, they did not pretend any right to state objections to his remaining in authority. It was the military system of usurpation, not the person of Buonaparte, against which they made war. If, on the other hand, France could not return to a state of peace without a change of her ruler, it was for France herself to consider what that change should be. The allied sovereigns were determined she should no longer work her uncontrolled will upon other states; but they left her at full liberty to adopt what government, and what sovereign she pleased, within her own territories.

THE ALLIES IN SWITZERLAND

At the same time, having limited the purpose of their armament to such a just and moderate object, the allies resolved to put such activity in their measures as to satisfy the French that they had the power of enforcing their demands; and for that purpose they determined to enter the frontier. From Basle to Mentz, from Mentz to the mouth of the Waal, the frontier of France and Belgium is defended by the Rhine, a strong natural boundary in itself, and covered by a triple row of 140 fortresses, some of them of the very first class. Above Basle, where the Rhine divides France from Switzerland, the frontier is more accessible. But then this upper line could not be acted upon without violating the neutrality which Switzerland had asserted, which Buonaparte had admitted as affording protection for the weakest part of the threatened frontier, and which, upon their own principle of respecting the rights of neutrals, the allies were under a sort of necessity of acknowledging. Nevertheless, the extreme facility of entering France on this side, led Austria and Prussia to form the wish to set aside scruples, and disregard the neutrality of Switzerland.

These two powers remembered how little respect Napoleon had shown to neutral rights in the campaign of Ulm, when he marched without hesitation through the Prussian territories of Anspach and Bareuth, in order to accomplish the demolition of the Austrian army; nor did they fail to quote his forcible interference in the affairs of the cantons of Switzerland, at an earlier period of his history. Russia did not for some time acquiesce in this reasoning; but when some plausible grounds were alleged of breach of neutrality on the part of the Swiss, the scruples of Alexander were removed; and it was resolved that the Austrian grand army should traverse the Swiss territory for the purpose of entering France. They halted before Geneva, and took possession of the town, or rather it was yielded to them by the citizens.

The canton of Bern, also, which resented some alterations made by Napoleon to the prejudice of their feudal claims upon the Pays de Vaud, received the Austrians not as intruders but as friends. Buonaparte, in his manifestoes, insisted vehemently upon the injustice of this aggression upon the territories of the Swiss. Undoubtedly the transaction was of a questionable character; but it was inconsistent in Napoleon to declaim against it, since, in the case of the arrest of the Duke d'Enghien, he had laid it down as national law, that the violation of the territory of Baden was an offence pleadable by no other than the sovereign of that territory. On his own doctrine, therefore, it was incompetent in any other nation to resent, on behalf of the Swiss, that which the Swiss did not resent for themselves.

Upon the 21st December, Maréchal Prince Schwartzenberg crossed the Rhine with the Austrian army at four points, and advanced upon Langres, as had been previously agreed. Moving with the extreme slowness and precision which characterise Austrian manœuvres, paying always the same respect to fortresses without garrisons, and passes without guards, as if they had been in a posture of defence, the Austrians, instead of reaching Langres on 27th December, did not arrive till the 17th January, 1814.[321] A serious intention had been for some time manifested to defend the place, and it was even garrisoned by a detachment of Buonaparte's old guard. The approach of the numerous Austrian reinforcements, however, rendered the preparations for defence of the town unavailing, and Langres was evacuated by all the French troops, saving about 300 men, who surrendered to General Giulay on the 17th. A division of the Austrians was immediately advanced to Dijon.

The apathy of the French at this period may be estimated from the following circumstance: Dijon, summoned by a flying party of cavalry, returned for answer, that a town containing 30,000 inhabitants, could not with honour surrender to fifteen hussars, but that if a respectable force appeared before its walls, they were ready to give up the keys of their city.[322] This reasonable request was complied with, and Dijon surrendered on 19th January.[323]

---

[321] Lord Burghersh, *Operations of the Allied Armies*, p. 72.
[322] Lord Burghersh, *Operations*, &c., p. 88.
[323] "On receiving the news of the simultaneous invasion of the French territory at so many different points, Napoleon's firmness of mind did not forsake him. 'I am two months behind-hand,' he said; 'had I that time at command, they should not have crossed the

The city of Lyons, the second in the empire, had itself nearly fallen into the hands of the Austrians; but the inhabitants showed a disposition to defend the town, and being reinforced with troops sent to secure a place of such importance, the Austrian general, Bubna, retired from under its walls. It is allowed, that more activity on the part of the allies might have saved this repulse, which was of considerable importance. It was the only one which they had yet sustained.

While the grand army, under Schwartzenberg, was thus advancing into France, the army of Silesia, which was the name given to that commanded by the veteran Blucher, consisting, as formerly, of Prussians and Russians, had made equal progress, though against greater resistance and more difficulties. His army advanced in four columns, or grand divisions, blockading the strong frontier fortresses of Metz, Sarre-Louis, Thionville, Luxembourg, and others, passing the defiles of the Vosges, and pushing forward to Joinville, Vitry, and Saint Dizier. The army of Silesia was thus placed in communication with the grand army, the advanced divisions of which had penetrated as far into France as Bar-sur-Aube.[324]

BERNADOTTE—HOLLAND

There was yet a third army of the allies, called that of the North of Europe. It was originally commanded by the Prince Royal of Sweden, and consisted of Swedes, Russians, and Germans. But the Crown Prince, whose assistance had been of such material consequence during the campaign of 1813, did not, it appears, take an active share in that of 1814. There may have been two reasons and weighty ones for this inactivity. To assist in driving the French out of Germany, seemed a duty which the Prince of Sweden could

---

Rhine. This may be attended with serious consequences; but I can do nothing single-handed. Unless I am assisted, I must fail in the struggle.'"—Savary, tom. iii., p. 185.

[324] "Marshal Blucher established his army at Nancy in fifteen days from the passage of the Rhine. What would have been the advantages, if, in the same period the great armies had by the end of November advanced to the same position? This question being put to Marshal Ney, he answered, 'Messieurs les alliés auraient pû compter leurs journées d'étapes jusqu'à Paris.'"—Lord Burghersh, *Operations*, p. 80.

not, as such, decline, when the welfare of Sweden demanded it. But an invasion of his native soil might seem to Bernadotte a service unpleasing and unpopular in itself, and in which he could not be so rightfully engaged, at least while the freedom of Germany and the north opened another field of exertions, where his military efforts could be attended with no injury to his personal feelings. Denmark was still in arms, and Davoust still held out at Hamburgh; and the presence of the Swedish army and its leader was necessary to subdue the one, and clear the north from the other. It must also be remembered, that Sweden, a poor kingdom, was not in a condition to sustain a war at a great distance from its frontier, and arising out of causes in which it was more remotely concerned. Her armies could not be recruited with the same ease as those of the greater powers; and Bernadotte, therefore, rather chose to incur the censure of being supposed cold in the cause of his confederates, than the risk of losing the only body of troops which Sweden had been able to fit out, and upon preserving which his throne probably depended. The allied sovereigns, however, directed, that while the Crown Prince remained in the north, a part of the Russian and Prussian corps, who were placed under his command, should be ordered to march towards France, for the purpose of augmenting the force which they already possessed in Holland and Belgium. The Crown Prince having, by a short war with Denmark, compelled that power to yield up her ancient possession of Norway, left Bennigsen to continue the siege of Hamburgh, and advanced in person to Cologne, to assist in the complete liberation of Belgium.[325]

The French troops, which had been drawn together, had been defeated at Merxem by General Bulow, and Sir Thomas Graham; and although the French flag was still flying at Antwerp and Bergen-op-Zoom, Holland might be considered as liberated. General Winzengerode, at the head of the Russian troops, and the Saxons,

---

[325] In a proclamation to the French, issued by Bernadotte from Cologne, Feb. 12, he says, "Once more in sight of the banks of this river, where I have so often fought for you, I feel a desire to communicate to you my thoughts. It has been the constant effort of your Government to debase every thing, that it might despise ever thing: it is time that this system should change. All enlightened men desire the preservation of France; they only require that she shall be no longer the scourge of the earth. The allied sovereigns have not coalesced to make war against nations, but to force your Government to recognise the independence of states: Such are their intentions, and I pledge myself to you for their sincerity."—Meredith's *Memorials of Charles John*, p. 208.

under Thielman, being the corps detached, as above mentioned, from the army of the North of Germany, soon reached the Low Countries, and entered into communication with Bulow. General Sir Thomas Graham, with the English and Saxons, and with such Dutch and Flemish troops as could be collected, was left to blockade Bergen-op-Zoom and Antwerp, whilst Bulow and Winzengerode were at liberty to enter France on the northern frontier: And thus, in the hour of need (which soon afterwards arrived,) they were to act as a reserve to the army of Silesia under Blucher. They pushed on as far as Laon.

PROGRESS OF THE ALLIES

These advances, which carried the armies of the allies so far into the bosom of France, and surrounded with blockades the frontier fortresses of that kingdom, were not made without an honourable though ineffectual opposition, on such points where the French military could make any stand against the preponderating numbers of the invaders. The people of the country in general neither welcomed nor opposed the allies. In some places they were received with acclamation—in a few others some opposition was tendered—they encountered desperate resistance nowhere. The allies did all that discipline could to maintain strict order among their troops; but where there were so many free corps—Huhlans, Croats, and Cossacks—whose only pay is what they can plunder, occasional transgressions necessarily took place. The services of these irregular troops were, however, indispensable. The Cossacks, in particular, might be termed the eyes of the army. Accustomed to act in small parties when necessary, they threaded woods, swam rivers, and often presented themselves unexpectedly in villages many miles distant from the main army to which they belonged, thus impressing the French with an idea of the numbers and activity of the allies far beyond the truth. These Arabs of the North, as Napoleon termed them, always announced their party as the advanced guard of a considerable force, for whom they ordered provisions and quarters to be prepared; and thus awed the inhabitants into acquiescence in their demands. They are not reported to have been cruel, unless when provoked, but were not in general able to resist temptations to plunder. The excursions of these and other light troops were of course distressing to the French territory.

On the other hand, in two or three cases, armed citizens in the towns, summoned by small parties of the allies, fired upon flags of truce, and thus justified severe reprisals. It was said to be by Buonaparte's strict orders, that such actions were committed, the purpose being, if possible, to excite deadly hatred betwixt the French and the allies. Indeed, in the reverse of the circumstances, in which each had formerly stood, Napoleon and the Austrian generals seemed to have exchanged system and sentiments. He now, as the Archduke Charles did in 1809, called out every peasant to arms; while Schwartzenberg, like Napoleon at that earlier period, denounced threats of military execution, without mercy or quarter, to every rustic who should obey the summons. The impartial historian must proclaim, in the one case as in the other, that the duty of resistance in the defence of our native country, does not depend on the character of a man's weapons, or the colour of his coat; and that the armed citizen is entitled, equally with the regular soldier, to the benefit of the laws of war, so long as he does not himself violate them. But from these various causes, it was plain that the present apathy of the French people was only temporary, and that some sudden and unforeseen cause was not unlikely to rouse so sensitive and high-spirited a people into a state of general resistance, by which the allies could not fail to be great sufferers. Rapidity in their movements was the most obvious remedy against such a danger; but this was the military quality least proper to coalitions, where many people must be consulted; and besides, was inconsistent with the well-known habits of the Germans, but especially of the Austrians.

It seems also, that the allies, having safely formed an almost complete military line from Langres to Chalons, found themselves at some loss how to use their advantages. Nothing could be better situated than their present position, for such a daring enterprise as was now termed a *Hourra* upon Paris; and as all the high-roads, departing from various points of the extensive line which they held, converged on the capital as a common centre, while the towns and villages, through which these roads passed, afforded an ample supply of provisions, this march might have been accomplished almost without opposition, but for the tardy movements of the grand army. The real weakness of Napoleon had been disguised by the noisy and exaggerated rumours concerning his preparations; and now when the allies learned that such an opportunity had existed, they learned, at the same time, that it was wellnigh lost, or at least that the road to Paris must first be cleared by a series of bloody actions. In these the allies could not disguise from themselves the possibility of their receiving severe checks; and under this apprehension they began to calculate the consequences of such a defeat, received in the centre of France, as that which they had suffered under the walls of Dresden. There was here no favourable screen of mountains to secure their retreat, no strong positions for checking a pursuing army, as in the case of Vandamme, and turning a defeat into a victory. The frontier which they had passed was penetrated, not subdued—its fortresses, so strong and numerous, were in the greater part masked, not taken—so that their retreat upon the Rhine must be exposed to all the dangers incident to passing in disorder through a country in complete possession of the enemy.

General councils of war seldom agree upon recommending bold measures. In this sense, Solomon says, that in the multitude of counsellors there is safety; meaning that the most cautious, if not the wisest measures, are sure to have the approbation of the majority.

Accordingly, this spirit predominating in the councils of the allies, led to a degree of uncertainty in their movements on this momentous occasion, which, as is usual, endeavoured to disguise itself under the guise of prudence. They resolved that the grand army should halt a short space at Langres, in hopes either that Napoleon, renewing the negotiation, the scene of which was now to be transferred to Chatillon upon the Seine, would avert his present danger, by acquiescing in the terms of the allies; or that the French nation, an event still less likely to happen, would become tired of the military monarch, whose ambition had brought such distress upon the country. In the meanwhile, the allies declined the offers of such royalists as came forward in the name, and for the interest, of the exiled family; uniformly replying, that they would give no weight to any expression of the sentiments of the French people, unless it was made in some quarter of the kingdom where it could not be supposed to be influenced by the presence of the allied army. They trusted chiefly at that moment to the effect of negotiation with the present possessor of the throne.[326]

STATE OF THE ARMIES—BRIENNE

But Napoleon, as firmly determined in his purpose as the allies were doubtful, knowing himself to be the soul of his army, and absolute lord of his own actions, felt all the advantage which a bold, active, and able swordsman has in encountering an opponent whose skill is less distinguished, and whose determination is more flexible than his own. The allies had presented in the grand army a front of 97,000 men, Maréchal Blucher one of 40,000, affording a disposable force of 137,000.[327] To oppose this the French Emperor had only, of old troops, independent of those under Suchet in Catalonia, under Soult near Bayonne, and also of garrisons, about 50,000 men; nor could he hope to add to them more than 70,000 conscripts.[328] Nay, in fact his levies, so far as they could be brought into the field, fell greatly short of this number; for the allies were in possession of a considerable part of the kingdom of France, and, in this moment of general confusion, it was impossible to enforce the law of conscription, which was at all times obnoxious. It was soon proved, that he who so lately had led half a million of men to the Vistula, and 300,000 to the banks of the Elbe, could not now muster, for the protection of the capital of his own empire, a disposable force of more than 70,000 men.

The defensive war had no doubt considerable advantages to one who knew so well how to use them. The highways, by which the allies must advance, formed a half or quarter circle of rays, converging, as already mentioned, on Paris as a centre. A much

---

[326] For the various opinions, as to the military operations to be pursued from Langres, see the memoirs drawn up at the Prussian, Austrian, and Russian headquarters.—*Operations*, &c., pp. 91, 94, and 104.
[327] Lord Burghersh, p. 99.
[328] Jomini, tom. iv., p. 524.

smaller army might, therefore, oppose a large one, because, lying between Paris and the enemy, they must occupy the same roads by a much shorter line of communication than the invaders, who were farther from the centre, where the roads diverged to a greater distance from each other. With this advantage of collocation to balance a great inferiority in numerical force, Buonaparte advanced to play for the most momentous stake ever disputed, with a degree of military skill which has never been matched.

Arrived at Chalons on the 26th January, Buonaparte took the command of such an army as he had been able to assemble, by the concentration of the troops under the Maréchals Victor, Marmont, Macdonald, and Ney, all of whom had retreated from the frontier. So much were the French corps d'armée reduced, that these great and distinguished generals, who, in former times, would have commanded 60,000 or 70,000 men each, had under them all, when concentrated, but a total of 52,000, to which Napoleon was only able to add about 20,000, brought from Paris. But no one ever understood better than Buonaparte, the great military doctrine, that victory does not depend on the comparative result of numerical superiority in general, but on the art of obtaining such a superiority on the field of action itself.

Blucher was, as usual, the foremost in advance, and Napoleon resolved to bestow on this active and inveterate enemy, the terrible honour of his first attack, hoping to surprise the Silesian corps d'armée before it could receive succour from the army of Schwartzenberg. The maréchal was apprised of the Emperor's purpose, and lost no time in concentrating his forces at Brienne, on the Aube, fourteen miles below Bar. This is a small village, seated on the ascent of a hill. The place has but two streets; one of which ascends to the Chateau, occupied formerly as a royal academy for young persons designed for the army; the other conducts to Arcis-sur-Aube. The Chateau is partly surrounded by a park or chase. It was at the military school of Brienne that Napoleon acquired the rudiments of that skill in the military art with which he had almost prostrated the world, and had ended by placing it in array against him; and it was here he came to commence what seemed his last series of efforts for victory;—like some animals of the chase, who, when hard pressed by the hunters, are said to direct their final attempts at escape upon the point from which they have first started.

The alert movements of Napoleon surpassed the anticipation of Blucher. He was at table with his staff in the Chateau. General Alsusieff, a Russian, occupied the town of Brienne, and General Sacken's corps was drawn up in columns, on the road from Brienne to La Rothière. At once a horrible tumult was heard. The Russian cavalry, 2000 in number, were completely driven in by those of Napoleon, and at the same moment Ney attacked the town; while a body of French grenadiers, who, favoured by the wooded and broken character of the ground, had been enabled to get into the park, threatened to make prisoners all who were in the Chateau. Blucher, with his officers, had barely time to reach a postern, where they were under the necessity of leading their horses down a stair, and in that way made their escape with difficulty. The bold resistance of Alsusieff defended the town against Ney, and Sacken advanced to Alsusieff's assistance. The Cossacks also fell on the rear of the French in the park, and Buonaparte's own safety was compromised in the mêlée.[329] Men were killed by his side, and he was obliged to draw his sword in his own defence. At the very moment of attack, his attention was engaged by the sight of a tree, which he recollected to be the same under which, during the hours of recreation at Brienne, he used, when a school-boy, to peruse the Jerusalem Delivered of Tasso. If the curtain of fate had risen before the obscure youth, and discovered to him in the same spot, his own image as Emperor of France, contending against the Scythians of the desert for life and power, how wonderful would have seemed the presage, when the mere concurrence of circumstances strikes the mind of those who look back upon it with awful veneration for the hidden ways of Providence! Lefebvre Desnouettes fell, dangerously wounded, in charging at the head of the guards. The town caught

---

[329] "General Dejean, feeling himself closely pressed, turned about and gave the alarm, by exclaiming, *The Cossacks!* and at the same time attempted to plunge his sabre into the breast of one of the assailants, whom he thought he had secured. But the enemy had escaped; they then darted on the horseman in the grey great-coat who was somewhat in advance. Corbineau instantly rushed forward; Gourgaud made the same movement, and, with a pistol-shot, stretched the Cossack dead at Napoleon's feet."—Baron Fain, *Manuscript de*, 1814.

fire, and was burned to the ground; but it was not until eleven at night that the Silesian army ceased to make efforts for recovering the place, and that Blucher, retreating from Brienne, took up a position in the rear of that town, and upon that of La Rothière.

BATTLE OF LA ROTHIÈRE—TROYES

The result of the battle of Brienne was indecisive, and the more unsatisfactory to Buonaparte, as the part of Blucher's force engaged did not amount to 20,000 men, and the sole advantage gained over them, was that of keeping the field of battle. Napoleon's principal object, which was to divide Blucher from the grand army, had altogether failed. It was necessary, however, to proclaim the engagement as a victory, and much pains was taken to represent it as such. But when it was afterwards discovered to be merely a smart skirmish, without any material results, the temporary deception only served to injure the cause of Napoleon.

On the first of February, Blucher, strongly reinforced from the grand army, prepared in his turn to assume the offensive. It would have been Napoleon's wish to have avoided an engagement; but a retreat across the Aube, by the bridge of Lesmont, which was the only mode of passing that deep and scarce fordable river, would have exposed his rear to destruction. He therefore risked a general action. Blucher attacked the line of the French on three points, assaulting at once the villages of La Rothière, Dienville, and Chaumont. The conflict, in which the Prince Royal of Wirtemberg distinguished himself, was hard fought during the whole day, but in the evening, the French were repulsed on all points, and Buonaparte was compelled to retreat across the Aube, after losing 4000 prisoners, and no less than seventy-three guns. Ney, by the Emperor's orders, destroyed the bridge at Lesmont. The allies were not aware of the amount of their advantage, and suffered the French to retire unmolested.[330]

---

[330] Lord Burghersh, Operations, &c., p. 113; Jomini, tom. iv., p. 527.

A general council of war, held at the castle of Brienne [Feb. 2,] now resolved that the two armies (although having so lately found the advantage of mutual support) should separate from each other, and that Blucher, detaching himself to the northward, and uniting under his command the division of D'Yorck and Kleist, both of whom had occupied St. Dizier and Vitry, should approach Paris by the Marne; while Prince Schwartzenberg and the grand army should descend on the capital by the course of the Seine. The difficulty of finding provisions for such immense armies was doubtless in part the cause of this resolution. But it was likewise recommended by the success of a similar plan of operations at Dresden, and afterwards at Leipsic, where the enemies of Buonaparte approached him from so many different quarters as to render it impossible for him to make head against one army without giving great opportunity of advantage to the others.[331]

Buonaparte reached Troyes, on which he retreated after crossing the Aube, in a disastrous condition; but his junction with his old guard, whose appearance and high state of appointments restored courage to the dejected troops who had been beaten at La Rothière, gave a new impulse to the feelings of his army, and restored the young levies to confidence. He resolved, taking advantage of the division of the two armies of the allies, to march upon that of Blucher. But, in order to disguise his purpose, he first sent a small division upon Bar-sur-Seine, to alarm the Austrians with an attack upon their right wing.[332] Schwartzenberg immediately apprehended that Buonaparte was about to move with his whole force in that direction; a movement which, in fact, would have been most favourable for the allies, since it would have left the road to Paris undefended, and open to the whole. But, terrified by the idea that his left flank might be turned or forced, the Austrian general moved his chief strength in that direction; thus at once suspending his meditated march on the Seine, and increasing the distance betwixt the grand army and that of Silesia. Buonaparte having deceived Schwartzenberg by this successful feint, evacuated Troyes, leaving the Maréchals Victor and Oudinot to oppose the Austrians

---

[331] Lord Burghersh, Operations, &c., p. 121.
[332] We ought to read *left* wing. See Lord Burghersh, Operations, &c., p. 122.—Ed. (1842.)

with very inadequate means, while he directed his own march against Blucher.

Blucher, in the meanwhile, having left Napoleon in front of the grand army, and not doubting that the Austrians would find him sufficient employment, hurried forward to the Marne, forced Macdonald to retreat from Chateau Thierry, and advanced his headquarters to Vertus; while Sacken, who formed his vanguard, pushed his light troops as far as Ferté la Jouarre, and was nearer to Paris than was the Emperor himself. General D'Yorck had advanced as far as Meaux, and Paris was in the last degree of alarm.

Even Buonaparte himself was so much struck by the inextricable situation of his affairs after the defeat of La Rothière, that a thought occurred to him, which posterity, excepting on his own avowal, would hardly give credit to. The plan which suggested itself, was that of sacrificing his own authority to the peace of France, and of abdicating the crown in favour of the Bourbons, while he had yet the means of resistance in his possession. He felt he had reigned and combated long enough for his own glory, and justly thought that the measure of his renown would be filled up by such an act of generous self-denial. But a maxim occurred to him, (suggested, he says, by Mr. Fox,) that restored monarchs could never forgive those who had occupied their place. Probably his thoughts turned also to the murder of the Duke d'Enghien; for there was no other point of personal offence betwixt Buonaparte and the exiled family, which their restoration, if the event took place by his intervention, might not have fully atoned for. If our conjecture be real, it serves to show how such a crime operates in its consequences to obstruct its perpetrator in future attempts to recover the path of virtue and honour. Had Napoleon been really capable of the generous act of self-denial which he meditated, he must have been ranked, in despite of the doubtful points of his character, as one of the greatest men who ever lived.

But the spirit of egotism and suspicion prevailed, and the hopes of accomplishing the discomfiture and defeat of the Silesian army, appeared preferable to meriting, by one act of disinterested devotion, the eternal gratitude of Europe; and the philosopher and friend of humanity relapsed into the warrior and conqueror. There is, no doubt, something meritorious in the conceiving of great and noble resolutions, even although they remain unrealised. But this patriotism of the imagination does not rise to a higher scale of merit, than the sensibility of those who cannot hear a tale of sorrow without weeping, but whose sympathy never assumes the expensive form of actual charity.

ATTACK ON BLUCHER

The army of Napoleon was now to be transferred from the high-road leading from Paris to Troyes, to that leading from Chalons to Paris, on which Blucher was operating, and that by flank marches through an impracticable country; but which, if they could be accomplished, would enable the French Emperor to attack the Silesian army at unawares in flank and rear. The lateral cross-roads, which connect one highway with another through France, are generally scarce passable in winter, even for the purpose of ordinary communication, much less for an army with its carriages and artillery. Buonaparte had to traverse a country intersected with thickets, marshes, drains, ditches, and impediments of every kind; the weather was execrable, and but for the extraordinary exertions of the Mayor of Barbonne, who collected 500 horses to extricate the guns, they must have been abandoned on the road. But by dint of perseverance, Buonaparte accomplished this forced march, on 10th of February, and the flank of the Silesian army was in consequence placed at his mercy.[333] They were moving on without the least suspicion of such an attack. Sacken led the advance, the Russian General Alsusieff followed, and Blucher himself brought up the rear with the main body. All intent upon the advance to Paris, they were

---

[333] "This bold incursion of the enemy roused Napoleon. He resolved, at least, to make the Prussian army pay dearly for their temerity, and formed the design of unexpectedly falling on their flank. The Emperor was poring over his maps, with the compasses in his hand, when the Duke of Bassano presented him with the despatches, which he had prepared for Chatillon! 'Oh! here you are,' said Napoleon, as the duke entered the apartment; 'but I am now thinking of something very different. I am defeating Blucher on the map. He is advancing by the road of Montmirail; I shall set out and beat him to-morrow. I shall beat him again the day after to-morrow. Should this movement prove as successful as I have reason to expect, the state of affairs will be entirely changed, and we shall then see what must be done.'"—Baron Fain.

marching with careless haste, and had suffered such large intervals to take place betwixt their divisions, as to expose them to be attacked in detail.

Buonaparte fell upon the central division of Alsusieff, at Champ-Aubert, surrounded, defeated, and totally dispersed them, taking their artillery, and 2000 prisoners, while the remainder of the division fled into the woods, and attempted to escape individually. The whole force of the Emperor was now interposed between the advanced-guard under Sacken, and the main body under Blucher. It was first directed towards the former, whom Napoleon encountered sooner than he expected, for Sacken, on hearing of the action at Champ-Aubert, instantly countermarched his division to assist Alsusieff, or at least to rejoin Blucher; but he was overwhelmed by the superior force of the French, and having lost one-fourth of his division, about 5000 men, was forced to leave the high-road, upon which Blucher was advancing, and retreat by that on Chateau-Thierry. At this village Sacken was joined by General D'Yorck and Prince William of Prussia; but, still unable to make a stand, they could only secure a retreat by destroying the bridge over the Marne. War began now to show itself in its most hideous forms. The stragglers and fugitives who could not cross the bridge before its destruction, were murdered by the peasantry, while the allied soldiers, in revenge, plundered the village of Chateau-Thierry, and practised every excess of violence. The defeat of Sacken took place on the 12th of February.[334]

Blucher, in the meanwhile, ignorant of the extent of the force by which his vanguard had been attacked, pressed forward to their support, and, in a wide and unenclosed country, suddenly found himself in the front of the whole army of Napoleon, flushed with the double victory which they had already gained, and so numerous as to make a retreat indispensable on the part of the Prussians. Blucher, if surprised, remained undismayed. Having only three regiments of cavalry, he had to trust for safety to the steadiness of his infantry. He formed them into squares, protected by artillery, and thus commenced his retreat by alternate divisions; those battalions which were in motion to the rear, being protected by the

---

[334] Jomini, tom. iv., p. 535; Burghersh, Operations, &c., p. 134.

fire of the others then standing fast, and covering them with theirs while they retired in turn. The French cavalry, though so strong as to operate at once on the flanks and rear, failed in being able to break a single square. After the Prussians had retired several leagues in this manner, fighting every foot of their way, they were nearly intercepted by a huge column of French horse, which, having made a circuit so as to pass them, had drawn up on the causeway to intercept their retreat. Without a moment's hesitation, Blucher instantly attacked them with such a murderous fire of infantry and artillery, as forced them from the high-road, and left the passage free. The Prussians found the village of Etoges, through which they were obliged to pass, also occupied by the enemy; but here also they cleared their way by dint of fighting. This expedition of the Marne, as it is called, is always accounted one of Napoleon's military *chefs-d'œuvre*; for a flank march undertaken through such a difficult country, and so completely successful, is not perhaps recorded in history. On the other hand, if Blucher lost any credit by the too great security of his march, he regained it by the masterly manner in which he executed his retreat. Had the army which he commanded in person shared the fate of his vanguard, it is probable there would have been no campaign of Paris.[335]

The Parisians, in the meantime, saw at length actual proofs that Napoleon had been victorious. Long columns of prisoners moved through their streets, banners were displayed, the cannon thundered, the press replied, and the pulpit joined, in extolling and magnifying the dangers which the citizens had escaped, and the merits of their preserver.[336]

---

[335] Lord Burghersh, p. 136; Jomini, tom. iv., p. 532.
[336] "No sooner had the battle of Champ-Aubert afforded a pretext for exultation, than M. Denon ordered a medal to be executed to designate the state of France at that moment. On the obverse, was the head of Napoleon; on the reverse, an eagle erect; above his head was a star; his claws rested on a thunderbolt; and on one side was the sign Pisces—on the other a flying Victory. This was the only medal record of this memorable campaign."—*Events at Paris*, Feb. 1814, p. 19.

MONTEREAU

In the midst of the joy natural on such an occasion, the Parisians suddenly learned that the town of Fontainbleau was occupied by Hungarian hussars, and that not Cossacks only, but Tartars, Baskirs, and Kalmouks, tribes of a wild and savage aspect, a kind of Asiatic Ogres, to whom popular credulity imputed a taste for the flesh of children, had appeared in the neighbourhood of Nangis. These renewed signs of approaching danger arose from the grand army of the allies having carried, at the point of the bayonet, Nogent and Montereau, and advanced the headquarters of the monarchs to Pont-sur-Seine. This alarm to Paris was accompanied by another. Schwartzenberg, learning the disasters on the Marne, not only pushed forward from three directions on the capital, but despatched forces from his right towards Provins, to threaten Napoleon's rear and communications. Leaving the pursuit of Blucher, the Emperor countermarched on Meaux, and, marching from thence to Guignes, he joined the army of Oudinot and Victor, who were retreating before Schwartzenberg. He here found the reinforcements which he had drawn from Spain, about 20,000 in number, tried and excellent troops. With this army he now fronted that of Schwartzenberg, and upon the 17th February, commenced the offensive at all points, and with success, possessing himself of Nangis, and nearly destroying the corps under Count Pahlen at Mormant. The Prince Royal of Wirtemberg was forced to retreat to Montereau.

So alarmed were the allies at the near approach of their terrible enemy, that a message was sent to Napoleon from the allied sovereigns, by Prince Schwartzenberg's aide-de-camp, Count Par, stating their surprise at his offensive movement, since they had given orders to their plenipotentiaries at Chatillon to sign the preliminaries of peace, on the terms which had been assented to by the French envoy, Caulaincourt.

This letter, of which we shall hereafter give a more full explanation, remained for some days unanswered, during which Napoleon endeavoured to push his advantages. He recovered the bridge at Montereau, after a desperate attack, in which the Crown Prince of Wirtemberg signalized himself by the valour of his defence. In the course of the action Napoleon returned to his old profession of an artilleryman, and pointed several guns himself, to the great delight of the soldiers. They trembled, however, when the fire attracted the attention of the enemy, whose balls began to be aimed at the French battery. "Go, my children," said Buonaparte, ridiculing their apprehensions; "the ball is not cast that is to kill me."

Having taken the place by storm, Buonaparte, dissatisfied with the number of men he had lost, loaded with reproaches some of his best officers. Montbrun was censured for want of energy, and Digeon for the scarcity of ammunition with which the artillery was served; but it was chiefly on Victor, the Duke of Belluno, that his resentment discharged itself. He imputed to him negligence, in not having attacked Montereau on the day before the action, when it was unprovided for resistance; and he ordered him to retire from the service. The marshal endeavoured to obtain a hearing in his own defence, but for some time could not succeed in checking the stream of reproaches. At length they were softened into a charge of broken health, and the love of repose, incident to wounds and infirmities. "The best bed," said the Emperor, "which the quarters afford must now be sought out for the once indefatigable Victor." The marshal felt the charge more severely in proportion as it became moderated within what was probably the bounds of truth; but he would not consent to quit the service. "I have not," he said, "forgot my original trade. I will take a musket. Victor will become a private in the Guard."—Buonaparte could not resist this mark of attachment. He held out his hand.—"Let us be friends," he replied; "I cannot restore to you your corps d'armée, which I have given to Girard; but I will place you at the head of two divisions of the Guard. Go—assume your command, and let there be no more of this matter betwixt us."[337]

It was upon such occasions, when he subdued his excited feelings to a state of kindness and generosity, that Buonaparte's personal conduct seems to have been most amiable.

The allies, in the meantime, remembering perhaps, though somewhat of the latest, the old fable of the bunch of arrows,

---

[337] Baron Fain, Manuscrit de, 1814.

resolved once more to enter into communication with the Silesian army, and, concentrating near Troyes, to accept of battle, if Buonaparte should offer it. The indefatigable Blucher had already recruited his troops, and, being reinforced by a division of the army of the North, under Langeron, moved southward from Chalons, to which he had retreated after his disaster at Montmirail, to Mery, a town situated upon the Seine, to the north-east of Troyes, to which last place the allied monarchs had again removed their headquarters. Here he was attacked with fury by the troops of Buonaparte who made a desperate attempt to carry the bridge and town, and thus prevent the proposed communication between the Silesian army and that of Schwartzenberg. The bridge, which was of wood, was set fire to in the struggle. The sharpshooters fought amid its blazing and cracking beams. The Prussians, however, kept possession of Mery.

RETREAT OF THE AUSTRIANS

A council of war was now held by the allies. Blucher urged the fulfilment of their original purpose of hazarding an action with Napoleon. But the Austrians had again altered their mind, and determined on a general retreat as far as the line between Nancy and Langres; the very position on which the allies had paused when they first entered France. The principal cause alleged for this retrograde movement, by which they must cede half the ground they had gained since their entering France, was, that Augereau, who had hitherto contented himself with his successful defence of Lyons, had been recruited by considerable bodies of troops from the army of Suchet, which had been employed in Catalonia. Thus reinforced, the French marshal was now about to assume the offensive against the Austrian forces at Dijon, act upon their communications with Switzerland, and raise in a mass the warlike peasantry of the departments of the Doubs, the Saonne, and the mountains of the Vosges. To prevent such consequences, Schwartzenberg sent General Bianchi to the rear with a large division of his forces, to support the Austrians at Dijon; and conceived his army too much weakened by this detachment to retain his purpose of risking a general action. It was therefore resolved, that if the headquarters of the grand army were removed to Langres, those of Blucher should be once more established on the Marne,[338] where, strengthened by the arrival of the northern army, which was now approaching from Flanders, he might resume his demonstration upon Paris, in case Buonaparte should engage himself in the pursuit of the grand army of the allies.

This retrograde movement gave much disgust to the Austrian soldiers, who considered it as the preface to a final abandonment of the invasion. Their resentment showed itself not only in murmurs and in tearing out the green boughs with which, as in sign of victory, they usually ornament their helmets and schakos, but also, as is too frequently the case in similar instances, in neglect of discipline, and excesses committed in the country.

To diminish the bad effects arising from this discontent among the troops, Schwartzenberg published an order of the day,[339] commanding the officers to enforce the strictest discipline, and at the same time explain to the army that the present retreat was only temporary, and that on joining with its reserves, which had already crossed the Rhine, the grand army would instantly resume the offensive, while Field-marshal Blucher, at present moving northward, so as to form a junction with Winzengerode and Bulow, should at the same time attack the rear and flank of the enemy. The publishing this plan of the campaign, went far to rouse the dejected confidence of the Austrian army.

On the evening of the 22d February, an answer to the letter of Schwartzenberg was received, but it was addressed exclusively to the Emperor of Austria; and while its expressions of respect are bestowed liberally on that power, the manner in which the other members of the coalition are treated, shows unabated enmity, ill-concealed under an affectation of contempt. The Emperor of France expressed himself willing to treat upon the basis of the Frankfort declaration, but exclaimed against the terms which his own envoy, Caulaincourt, had proposed to the plenipotentiaries of

---

[338] According to Lord Burghersh. (Operations, &c., p. 153,) Schwartzenberg recommended the retreat of the Silesian army to Nancy; but Blucher (*Ibid*, p. 186,) "took upon himself the responsibility of declining to conform," &c.—Ed., (1842.)
[339] Lord Burghersh, p. 168.

the other powers. In short, the whole letter indicated, not that Napoleon desired a general peace with the allies, but that it was his anxious wish to break up the coalition, by making a separate peace with Austria. This counteracted in spirit and letter the purpose of the confederates, distinctly expressed in their communication to Napoleon.

The Emperor Francis and his ministers were resolved not to listen to any proposals which went to separate the Austrian cause from that of their allies. It was therefore at first resolved that no answer should be sent to the letter; but the desire of gaining time for bringing up the reserves of the grand army, who were approaching the Swiss frontier under the direction of the Prince of Hesse-Homberg, as also for the union of the army of the north, under Bulow and Winzengerode, with that of Silesia, determined them to accept the offer of a suspension of hostilities. Under these considerations, Prince Wenceslaus of Lichtenstein was sent to the headquarters of Napoleon, to treat concerning an armistice. The Emperor seemed to be in a state of high hope, and called upon the Austrians not to sacrifice themselves to the selfish views of Russia, and the miserable policy of England. He appointed Count Flahault his commissioner to negotiate for a line of demarcation, and directed him to meet with the envoy from the allies at Lusigny, on 24th February.[340]

On the night of the 23d, the French bombarded Troyes, which the allied troops evacuated according to their latest plan of the campaign. The French entered the town on the 24th, when the sick and wounded, left behind by the allies, were dragged out to grace Napoleon's triumph; and a scene, not less deplorable, but of another description, was performed at the same time.

EXECUTION OF GOUAULT

Amid the high hopes which the entrance of the allies into France had suggested to the enemies of Buonaparte's government,

---

[340] Jomini, tom. iv., p. 529; Lord Burghersh, Observations, &c., p. 143.

five persons, the chief of whom were the Marquis de Vidranges, and the Chevalier de Gouault, had displayed the white cockade, and other emblems of loyalty to the exiled family. They had received little encouragement to take so decided a step either from the Crown Prince of Wirtemberg, or from the Emperor Alexander; both of whom, although approving the principles on which these gentlemen acted, refused to sanction the step they had taken, or to warrant them against the consequences.[341] It does not appear that their declaration had excited any corresponding enthusiasm in the people of Troyes or the neighbourhood; and it would have been wiser in Napoleon to have overlooked such a trifling movement, which he might have represented as arising from the dotage of loyalty, rather than to have, at this critical period, called the public attention to the Bourbons, by denouncing and executing vengeance upon their partisans. Nevertheless, Napoleon had scarce entered Troyes, when the chevalier Gouault (the other Royalists having fortunately escaped) was seized upon, tried by a military commission, condemned, and immediately shot. He died with the utmost firmness, exclaiming, "*Vive le Roi!*"[342] A violent and ill-timed decree promulgated the penalty of death against all who should wear the decorations of the Bourbons, and on all emigrants who should join the allies.[343] The severity of the measure, so contrary to Napoleon's general conduct of late years towards the Bourbons and their followers, whom he had for a long period scarce even alluded to, made the world ascribe his unusual ferocity to an uncommon state of apprehension; and thus it gave farther encouragement to those into whom it was intended to strike terror.

At this period of the retreat of Schwartzenberg from Troyes, and the movement of Blucher towards the Marne, we must leave the armies which were contending in the interior of France, in order to retrace those movements upon the frontiers, which, though

---

[341] The presence of the allies in the ancient capital of Champagne, had reanimated the hopes of the partisans of the Bourbons. The Emperor of Russia could not help observing to them, "that he considered the step they had taken a little premature; that the chances of war were uncertain, and that he should be sorry to see them sacrificed."—Beauchamp, *Hist. de la Champagne de 1814*, tom. i., p. 241.

[342] It has been said that Napoleon had been persuaded to save his life. But the result was similar to the execution, of Clarence.—S.—See Baron Fain, Manuscript de, 1814, p. 156.

[343] Dated Troyes, Feb. 24. Moniteur, March 1.

operating at a distance, tended at once to reinforce the invading armies, and to cripple Napoleon's means of defence.

It is difficult for the inhabitants of a peaceful territory to picture to themselves the miseries sustained by the country which formed the theatre of this sanguinary contest. While Buonaparte, like a tiger hemmed in by hounds and hunters, now menaced one of his foes, now sprung furiously upon another, and while, although his rapid movements disconcerted and dismayed them, he still remained unable to destroy the individuals whom he had assailed, lest, while aiming to do so, he should afford a fatal advantage to those who were disengaged—the scene of this desultory warfare was laid waste in the most merciless manner. The soldiers on both parts, driven to desperation by rapid marches through roads blocked with snow, or trodden into swamps, became reckless and pitiless; and, straggling from their columns in all directions, committed every species of excess upon the inhabitants. These evils are mentioned in the bulletins of Napoleon, as well as in the general orders of Schwartzenberg.

The peasants, with their wives and children, fled to caves, quarries, and woods, where the latter were starved to death by the inclemency of the season, and want of sustenance; and the former, collecting into small bodies, increased the terrors of war, by pillaging the convoys of both armies, attacking small parties of all nations, and cutting off the sick, the wounded, and the stragglers. The repeated advance and retreat of the different contending parties, exasperated these evils. Every fresh band of plunderers which arrived, was savagely eager after spoil, in proportion as the gleanings became scarce. In the words of Scripture, what the locust left was devoured by the palmer-worm—what escaped the Baskirs, and Kirgas, and Croats of the Wolga, and Caspian, and Turkish frontier, was seized by the half-clad, and half-starved conscripts of Napoleon, whom want, hardship, and an embittered spirit, rendered as careless of the ties of country and language, as the others were indifferent to the general claims of humanity. The towns and villages, which were the scenes of actual conflict, were frequently burnt to the ground; and this not only in the course of the actions of importance which we have detailed, but in consequence of innumerable skirmishes fought in different points, which had no influence, indeed, upon the issue of the campaign, but increased incalculably the distress of the invaded country, by extending the terrors of battle, with fire, famine, and slaughter for its accompaniments, into the most remote and sequestered districts. The woods afforded no concealment, the churches no sanctuary; even the grave itself gave no cover to the relics of mortality. The villages were every where burnt, the farms wasted and pillaged, the abodes of man, and all that belongs to peaceful industry and domestic comfort, desolated and destroyed. Wolves, and other savage animals, increased fearfully in the districts which had been laid waste by human hands, with ferocity congenial to their own. Thus were the evils which France had unsparingly inflicted upon Spain, Prussia, Russia, and almost every European nation, terribly retaliated within a few leagues of her own metropolis; and such were the consequences of a system, which assuming military force for its sole principle and law, taught the united nations of Europe to repel its aggressions by means yet more formidable in extent than those which had been used in supporting them.

Chapter LXXIV

Retrospect of Events on the Frontiers—Defection of Murat—Its consequences—Augereau abandons Franche Comté—Carnot intrusted with the command of Antwerp—Attack on Bergen-op-Zoom, by Sir Thomas Graham—The Allies take, and evacuate Soissons—Bulow and Winzengerode unite with Blucher—Wellington forces his way through the Pays des Gaves—Royalists in the West—Discontent of the old Republicans—Views of the different Members of the Alliance as to the Dynasties of Bourbon, and Napoleon—Proceedings of the Dukes of Berri and Angoulême, and Monsieur—Battle of Orthez—Bourdeaux surrendered to Marshal Beresford—Negotiations of Chatillon—Treaty of Chaumont—Napoleon's contre-projet—Congress at Chatillon broken up.

While Napoleon was struggling in the campaign of Paris, for his very existence as a monarch, events were taking place on the frontiers, by all of which his fate was more or less influenced, and in almost all of them unfavourably. Of these events we must give a brief detail, mentioning at the same time, the influence which they individually produced upon the results of the war.

DEFECTION OF MURAT

The defence of Italy had been committed to Prince Eugene Beauharnois, the viceroy of that kingdom. He was entirely worthy of the trust, but was deprived of any means that remained to him of accomplishing his task, by the defection of Murat. We have often had occasion to describe Murat as distinguished on the field of battle—rather an undaunted and high-mettled soldier, than a wise commander. As a sovereign he had little claim to distinction. He was good tempered, but vain, limited in capacity, and totally uninformed. Napoleon had not concealed his contempt of his understanding, and, after the retreat from Russia, had passed an oblique, but most intelligible censure on him, in a public bulletin.[344] In writing to the wife of Murat, and his own sister, Napoleon had mentioned her husband disparagingly, as one who was brave only on the field of battle, but elsewhere, as weak as a monk or a woman.[345] Caroline, in answer, cautioned her brother to treat her husband with more respect. Napoleon, unaccustomed to suppress his sentiments, continued the same line of language and conduct.[346]

Meanwhile, Murat, in his resentment, listened to terms from Austria, in which, by the mediation of that state, which was interested in the recovery of her Italian provinces, England was with difficulty induced to acquiesce. In consequence of a treaty formed with Austria, Murat declared himself in favour of the allies, and marched an army of 30,000 Neapolitans to Rome, for the purpose of assisting in the expulsion of the French from Italy. He speedily occupied Ancona and Florence.[347] There was already in Italy an army of 30,000 Austrians, with whom the viceroy had fought the indecisive battle of Roverbello, after which he retreated to the line of the Adige, on which he made a precarious stand, until the war

---

[344] "The King of Naples, being indisposed, has been obliged to retire from the command of the army, which he has resigned into the hands of the prince viceroy. The latter is more accustomed to the direction of large masses, and possesses the entire confidence of the Emperor."—*Moniteur*, Jan. 27, 1813.

[345] See papers relating to Naples, laid before the British Parliament in 1815, *Parl. Debates*, vol. xxxi., p. 150.

[346] The following letter from Napoleon to Murat, dated Nangis, Feb. 18, 1814, fell into the hands of the allies:—"You are a good soldier in the field of battle; but excepting there, you have no vigour and no character. Take advantage, however, of an act of treachery, which I only attribute to fear, in order to serve me by useful information. I rely upon you, upon your contrition, upon your promises. The title of king has turned your head. If you wish to preserve the former, keep your word."—*Parl. Debates*, vol. xxxi., p. 151.

[347] On the 5th of March, just before the battle of Craonne, Napoleon again wrote to Murat:—"I have communicated to you my opinion of your conduct. Your situation had turned your head. My reverses have finished you. You have surrounded yourself with men who hate France, and who wish to ruin you. What you write to me is at variance with your actions. I shall, however, see by your manner of acting at Ancona, if your heart be still French, and if you yield to necessity alone. Remember that I made you a king solely for the interest of my system. Do not deceive yourself, if you should cease to be a Frenchman, you would be nothing for me."—*Parl. Debates*, vol. xxxi., p. 153.

was concluded. The appearance of Murat's army on the side of Austria, though he confined himself to a war of proclamations, was calculated to end all French influence in Italy. Counter revolutionary movements, in some of the cantons of Switzerland, and in the mountains of Savoy, tended also to close the door through which Buonaparte had so often transferred the war into the Italian peninsula, and from its northern provinces, into the heart of Austria herself.

AUGEREAU

The defection of Murat had the further effect of disconcerting the measures which Napoleon had meditated, for recovery of the south-eastern frontier of France. Augereau had received orders to advance from Lyons, and receive the reinforcements which Eugene was to have despatched from Italy across the Alps. These, it was calculated, would have given the French maréchal a decisive superiority, which might have enabled him to ascend towards the sources of the Saonne, call to arms the hardy peasantry of the Vosgesian mountains, interrupt the communications of the Austrian army, and excite a national and guerilla warfare in the rear of the allies.

To stimulate more highly the energies of his early comrade in arms, Napoleon caused the Empress, Maria Louisa, to wait upon the young Duchess of Castiglione (the maréchal's wife,) to prevail on her to use her influence with her husband, to exert all his talents and audacity in the present crisis.[348] It was a singular feature of the declension of power, when it was thought that the command of the Emperor, imposed upon one of his maréchals, might require being enforced by the interposition of a lady; or rather, it implied that Napoleon was sensible that he was requiring of his officer something which no ordinary exertions could enable him to perform. He wrote, however, to Augereau himself, conjuring him to remember his early victories, and to forget that he was upwards of fifty years old. But exhortations, whether by a sovereign or lady, cannot supply the want of physical force.

---

[348] Manuscript de 1814, p. 139.

Augereau was unable to execute the task imposed upon him, from not receiving the Italian reinforcements, which, as matters stood in Italy, Eugene could not possibly spare. Detachments from Suchet's Spanish veterans did indeed join the maréchal at Lyons, and enabled him to advance on General Bubna, whom he compelled to retreat to Geneva. But the arrival of General Bianchi, with a strong reinforcement, which Schwartzenberg had despatched for that purpose, restored the ascendency of the allied armies on that frontier, especially as the Prince of Hesse-Homberg also approached from Switzerland at the head of the Austrian reserves. The last general had no difficulty in securing the passes of Saonne. Augereau in consequence was compelled to abandon the country of Gex and Franche Comté, and again to return under the walls of Lyons. Napoleon was not more complaisant to his old comrade and tutor,[349] than he had been to the other maréchals in this campaign, who had not accomplished tasks which they had not the means to achieve. Augereau was publicly censured as being inactive and unenterprising.

The north of Germany and Flanders were equally lost to France, and French interest. Hamburgh indeed still held out. But, as we have already said, it was besieged, or rather blockaded, by the allies, under Bennigsen, to whom the Crown Prince of Sweden had left that charge, when he himself, having put an end to the war with Denmark, had advanced towards Cologne, with the purpose of assisting in clearing Belgium of the French, and then entering France from that direction, in support of the Silesian army. The Crown Prince showed no personal willingness to engage in the invasion of France. The causes which might deter him have been already conjectured. The Royalists added another, that he had formed views of placing himself at the head of the government of France, which the allied monarchs declined to gratify. It is certain that, whether from the motives of prudence or estrangement, he was, after his arrival in Flanders, no longer to be considered as an active member of the coalition.

---

[349] "Augereau did not know Napoleon until the latter had become a general-in-chief. Augereau was certainly a good general, but he owed this to the school of Napoleon, and at best he was inferior to Massena, Desaix, Kleber, and Soult."—Louis Buonaparte, p. 92.

In the meantime, Antwerp was bravely and scientifically defended by the veteran republican, Carnot. This celebrated statesman and engineer had always opposed himself to the strides which Napoleon made towards arbitrary power, and had voted against his election to the situation of consul for life, and that of emperor. It does not appear that Napoleon resented this opposition. He had been obliged to Carnot before his unexampled rise, and afterwards, he was so far mindful of him as to cause his debts to be paid at a moment of embarrassment. Carnot, on his part, took the invasion of France as a signal for every Frenchman to use his talents in the public defence, and, offering his services to the Emperor, was intrusted with the command of Antwerp.

Bergen-op-Zoom was also still occupied by the French. This city, one of the most strongly fortified in the world, was nearly taken by a *coup-de-main*, by Sir Thomas Graham. After a night-attack of the boldest description, the British columns were so far successful, that all ordinary obstacles seemed overcome. But their success was followed by a degree of disorder which rendered it unavailing, and many of the troops who had entered the town were killed, or obliged to surrender. Thus an enterprise ably planned and bravely executed, miscarried even in the moment of victory, by accidents for which neither the general nor the officers immediately in command could be justly held responsible.[350] General Graham was, however, reinforced from England, and was still enabled, with the help of the Swedes and Danes, as well as Dutch and Flemish corps, to check any sallies from Bergen or from Antwerp.

The liberation of the Low Countries being so nearly accomplished, Bulow pressed forward on La Fère, and finally occupied Laon. Here, upon the 26th of February, he formed a junction with Winzengerode, who, bequeathing Juliers, Venloo, and Maestricht, to the observation of the Crown Prince, marched through the forest of Ardennes. Soissons offered a show of desperate resistance, but the commandant being killed, the place was delivered up. This was on the 13th February, and the allies ought to have held this important place. But in their haste to join Prince

---

[350] London Gazette Extraordinary, March 14, 1814; Lord Burghersh, Operations of the Allied Armies, p. 281.

Blucher, they evacuated Soissons, which Mortier caused to be presently reoccupied by a strong French garrison. The possession of this town became shortly afterwards a matter of great consequence. In the meantime, Bulow and Winzengerode, with their two additional armies, entered into communication with Blucher, of whom they now formed the rear-guard, and more than restored to him the advantage he had lost by the defeats at Montmirail and Champ-Aubert.

On the south-western frontier the horizon seemed yet darker. The Duke of Wellington having entered Spain, was about to force his way through the strong country, called the *Pays des Gaves*, the land that is, of the ravines formed by rivers and torrents. He maintained such severe discipline, and paid with such regularity for the supplies which he needed from the country, that he was voluntarily furnished with provisions of every kind; while the army of Soult, though stationed in the maréchal's own country, obtained none, save by the scanty and unwilling means of military requisition. In consequence of this strict discipline, the presence of the British troops was far from being distressing to the country; and some efforts made by General Harispe, to raise guerillas among his countrymen, the Basques, to act on the Duke of Wellington's rear, became totally ineffectual. The small seaport town of St. Jean de Luz supplied the English army with provisions and reinforcements. The activity of English commerce speedily sent cargoes of every kind into the harbour, where before were only to be seen a few fishing-boats. The goods were landed under a tariff of duties settled by the Duke of Wellington; and so ended the Continental System.

ROYALISTS OF THE WEST

In the meantime, the state of the west of France was such as held out the highest political results to the British, in case they should be able to overcome the obstacles presented by the strong intrenched camp at Bayonne, on which Soult rested his right flank, extending a line of great length upon the Adour and the neighbouring Gaves.

We have mentioned already the confederacy of Royalists, which was now in full activity, and extended by faithful agents through the whole west of France. They were now at their post, and preparing every thing for an explosion. The police of Buonaparte were neither ignorant of the existence nor purpose of this conspiracy, but they were unable to obtain such precise information as should detect and crush it. The two Messrs. de Polignac were deeply engaged, and, becoming the subjects of suspicion, it was only by a dexterous and speedy flight from Paris that they eluded captivity, or perhaps death. They succeeded in reaching the army of the allies, and were, it is believed, the first who conveyed to the Emperor Alexander an exact state of the royal party in the interior of France, particularly in the capital, which made a powerful impression on the mind of that prince.

Throughout the west of France there started up a thousand agents of a party, which were now to awake from a sleep of twenty years. Bourdeaux, with its loyal mayor, Count Lynch, and the greater part of its citizens, was a central point of the association. A great part of the inhabitants were secretly regimented and embodied, and had arms in their possession, and artillery, gunpowder, and ball, concealed in their warehouses. The celebrated La Rochejacquelein, made immortal by the simple and sublime narrative of his consort, solicited the cause of the Royalists at the English headquarters, and made repeated and perilous journeys from thence to Bourdeaux, and back again. Saintonge and La Vendée were organised for insurrection by a loyal clergyman, the Abbé Jaqualt. The brothers of Roche-Aymon prepared Perigord for a struggle. The Duke of Duras had engaged a thousand gentlemen at Touraine. Lastly, the Chouans had again prepared for a rising under the Count de Vitray, and Tranquille, a celebrated leader, called *Le Capitaine sans peur*. Numerous bands of refractory conscripts, rendered desperate by their state of outlawry, were ready at Angèrs, Nantes, and Orleans, to take arms in the cause of the Bourbons, under the Count de l'Orge, Monsieur d'Airac, Count Charles d'Autichamp, the Count de Suzannet, and Caudoudal, brother of the celebrated Georges, and his equal in courage and resolution. But all desired the previous advance of the *Blue-Flints*, as they called the English, their own being of a different colour. Trammelled by the negotiation at Chatillon, and various other political impediments, and anxious especially not to lead these high-spirited gentlemen into danger, by encouraging a premature rising, the English ministers at home, and the English general in France, were obliged for a time to restrain rather than encourage the forward zeal of the Royalists.

Such caution was the more necessary, as there existed at the same time another conspiracy, also directed against Buonaparte's person, or at least his authority; and it was of importance that neither should explode until some means could be found of preventing their checking and counteracting each other. This second class of malcontents consisted of those, who, like Buonaparte himself, owed their political consequence to the Revolution; and who, without regard to the Bourbons, were desirous to get free of the tyranny of Napoleon. These were the disappointed and degraded Republicans, the deceived Constitutionalists, all who had hoped and expected that the Revolution would have paved the way for a free government, in which the career of preferment should be open to talents of every description—a lottery in which, doubtless, each hoped that his own abilities would gain some important prize. The sceptre of Napoleon had weighed harder upon this class than even upon the Royalists. He had no dislike to the principles of the latter, abstractedly considered; he felt some respect for their birth and titles, and only wished to transfer their affections from the House of Bourbon, and to attach them to that of Napoleon. Accordingly, he distributed employments and honours among such of the old noblesse as could be brought to accept them, and obviously felt pride in drawing to his court names and titles, known in the earlier periods of French history. Besides, until circumstances shook his throne, and enlarged their means of injuring him, he considered the number of the Royalists as small, and their power as despicable. But from those active spirits, who had traded in revolution after revolution for so many years, he had much more both to fear and to dislike, especially as they were now understood to be headed by his ex-minister Talleyrand, with whose talents, both for scheming and executing political changes, he had so much reason to be acquainted.[351] To this class of his enemies he imputed the hardy

---

[351] "I now began to watch M. de Talleyrand narrowly. I considered him as the man who was about to become the leader of a party against the Emperor; though certainly not

attempt which was made, not without prospects of success, to overthrow his government during his absence in Russia. "You have the tail, but not the head," had been the words of the principal conspirator, when about to be executed; and they still rung in the ears of Buonaparte. It was generally supposed, that his long stay in Paris, ere he again took the field against the allies, was dictated by his fear of some similar explosion to that of Mallet's conspiracy. Whether these two separate classes of the enemies of Buonaparte communicated with each other, we have no opportunity of knowing, but they both had intercourse with the allies. That of Talleyrand's faction was, we believe, maintained at the court of London, through means of a near relation of his own, who visited England shortly before the opening of the campaign of which we treat. We have no doubt, that through some similar medium Talleyrand held communication with the Bourbons; and that, in the same manner as the English Restoration was brought about by a union between the Cavaliers and Presbyterians, there was even then upon foot some treaty of accommodation, by which the exiled monarch was, in regaining the crown, to have the assistance of those, whom, for want of another name, we shall call Constitutionalists, it being understood that his government was to be established on the basis of a free model.

It was of the greatest importance that both these factions should be cautious in their movements, until it should appear what course the allied monarchs were about to pursue in the impending negotiation with Buonaparte. The issue of this was the more dubious, as it was generally understood that though the sovereigns were agreed on the great point of destroying, on the one hand, the supremacy of France, and, on the other, in leaving her in possession of her just weight and influence, they entertained a difference of opinion as to the arrangement of her future government.

---

against the dynasty sprung from a revolution in which he had himself acted so conspicuous a part."—Savary, tom. ii., p. 233.

THE BOURBONS

The Prince Regent of England, from the generosity of his own disposition, as well as from a clear and comprehensive view of future possibilities, entertained views favourable to the Bourbons. This illustrious person justly conjectured, that free institutions would be more likely to flourish under the restored family, who would receive back their crown under conditions favourable to freedom, than under any modification of the revolutionary system, which must always, in the case of Buonaparte's being permitted to reign, be felt as implying encroachments on his imperial power. The Bourbons, in the case presumed, might be supposed to count their winnings, in circumstances where the tenacious and resentful mind of Napoleon would brood over his losses; and it might be feared, that with a return of fortune he might struggle to repair them. But there were ministers in the British cabinet who were afraid of incurring the imputation of protracting the war by announcing England's adoption of the cause of the Bourbons, which was now of a date somewhat antiquated, and to which a sort of unhappy fatality had hitherto been annexed. England's interest in the royal cause was, therefore, limited to good wishes.

The Emperor Alexander shared in the inclination which all sovereigns must have felt towards this unhappy family, whose cause was in some degree that of princes in general. It was understood that Moreau's engagement with the Russian monarch had been founded upon an express assurance on the part of Alexander, that the Bourbons were to be restored to the Crown of France under the limitations of a free constitution. Prussia, from her close alliance with Russia, and the personal causes of displeasure which existed betwixt Frederick and Napoleon, was certain to vote for the downfall of the latter.

But the numerous armies of Austria, and her vicinity to the scene of action, rendered her aid indispensable to the allies, while the alliance betwixt her Imperial house and this once fortunate soldier, threw much perplexity into their councils. It was believed that the Emperor of Austria would insist upon Buonaparte's being admitted to treat as sovereign of France, providing the latter gave sufficient evidence that he would renounce his pretensions to general supremacy; or, if he continued unreasonably obstinate, that the Emperor Francis would desire that a regency should be established, with Maria Louisa at its head. Either course, if adopted, would have been a death's-blow to the hopes of the exiled family of Bourbon.

Amid this uncertainty, the princes of the House of Bourbon gallantly determined to risk their own persons in France, and try what their presence might do to awake ancient remembrances at a crisis so interesting.

Although the British Ministry refused to afford any direct countenance to the schemes of the Bourbon family, they could not, in ordinary justice, deny the more active members of that unhappy race the freedom of acting as they themselves might judge most for the interest of their cause and adherents. To their applications for permission to depart for France, they received from the British Ministry the reply, that the princes of the House of Bourbon were the guests, not the prisoners, of Britain; and although the present state of public affairs precluded her from expressly authorising any step which they might think proper to take, yet they were free to quit her territories, and return to them at their pleasure. Under a sanction so general, the Duke d'Angoulême set sail for St. Jean de Luz, to join the army of the Duke of Wellington; the Duke de Berri for Jersey, to correspond with the Royalists of Brittany; and Monsieur for Holland, from which he gained the frontiers of Switzerland, and entered France in the rear of the Austrian armies. The movements of the two last princes produced no effects of consequence.

The Duke de Berri paused in the isle of Jersey, on receiving some unpleasant communications from France respecting the strength of the existing government, and on discovering, it is said, a plot to induce him to land at a point, where he must become the prisoner of Buonaparte.

Monsieur entered France, and was received at Vesoul with great enthusiasm. But this movement was not encouraged by the

Austrian commandants and generals; and Monsieur's proposal to raise corps of Royalists in Alsace and Franche Comté, was treated with coldness, approaching to contempt. The execution of Gouault at Troyes, and the decree of death against the Royalists, struck terror into the party, which was increased by the retrograde movement of the grand army. The enterprise of Monsieur, therefore, had no immediate result, though undoubtedly his presence had a decisive effect, in consequence of ultimate events; and the restoration would hardly have taken place, without that prince having so adventured his person.

The arrival of the Duke d'Angoulême in the army of the Duke of Wellington, had more immediate consequences. His royal highness could only be received as a volunteer, but the effect of his arrival was soon visible. La Rochejacquelein, who had dedicated to the royal cause his days and nights, his fortune and his life, soon appeared in the British camp, urging the general to direct his march on the city of Bourdeaux, which, when delivered from the vicinity of Soult's army, would instantly declare itself for the Bourbons, and be followed by the rising of Guienne, Anjou, and Languedoc. Humanity, as well as policy, induced the Duke of Wellington still to hesitate. He knew how frequently patriotic enthusiasm makes promises beyond its power to fulfil; and he cautioned the zealous envoy to beware of a hasty declaration, since the conferences at Chatillon were still continued, and there was a considerable chance of their ending in a peace between the allies and Napoleon. La Rochejacquelein, undeterred by remonstrances, continued to urge his suit with such intelligence and gallantry, as to receive at last the encouraging answer, "Remain a few days at headquarters, and you shall see us force the Gaves."

THE BATTLE OF ORTHEZ

Here, accordingly, commenced a series of scientific manœuvres, commencing 14th February, by which the Duke of Wellington, pressing step by step on that part of the French army which were on the left side of the Adour, drove them successively beyond the Gave de Mauleon, and the Gave d'Oleron. On the right side of the latter Gave, the French took a position on a very strong ground in front of the town of Orthez, where, joined by Clausel and a strong reinforcement, Soult endeavoured to make a stand. The Duke of Wellington commenced his attack on the enemy's right, storming and taking the village by which it was commanded. The desperate resistance which the enemy made on this point, occasioned one of those critical movements, when a general is called upon, in the heat of battle, to alter all previous arrangements, and, in the moment of doubt, confusion, and anxiety, to substitute new combinations to supersede those which have been planned in the hours of cool premeditation. A left attack upon a chain of heights extending along General Soult's left, was substituted for that to which Wellington had at first trusted for victory.

At the same time, the appearance of General Hill's division, who had forded the river, or Gave, above Orthez, and threatened the enemy's flank and rear, made the defeat complete. For some time Marshal Soult availed himself of the alertness of his troops, by halting and taking new positions, to preserve at least the form of a regular retreat; but at length, forced from one line to another by the manœuvres of the British, sustaining new losses at every halt, and menaced by the rapid approach of General Hill's division, his retreat became a flight, in which the French suffered great loss. Whole battalions of conscripts dispersed entirely, and many left their muskets regularly piled, as if intimating their fixed resolution to retire altogether from the contest.

Another action near Aires, by General Hill, and the passage of the Adour, under Bayonne, by the Honourable Sir John Hope, a manœuvre which might well be compared to a great battle fought, gave fresh influence to the British arms. Bayonne was invested, the road to Bourdeaux laid open, and Soult, left with scarce the semblance of an army, retreated towards Tarbes, to secure a junction with such French corps as might be returning from Spain.

The battle of Orthez, with the brilliant and masterly manœuvres which preceded and followed it, served to establish the superiority of the British forces in points wherein they had till then been deemed most deficient. Since the victories in Spain, it was no longer uncommon to hear a French officer allow, that in the extreme tug of conflict, the English soldier, from physical strength and high energy of character, had perhaps some degree of superiority over his own impetuous but less persevering countrymen. But he uniformly qualified such a stretch of candour, by claiming for the French superior skill in contriving, and promptitude in executing, those previous movements, on which the fate of battles usually depends. The victory of Salamanca, though gained over a general distinguished as a tactician, and in consequence of a previous contest of manœuvres, was not admitted to contradict the opinion with which Frenchmen were generally impressed. Yet, since the commencement of the campaign on the Adour, the French army, though under command of the celebrated Soult (*le Vieux Renard,* as he was familiarly called by his soldiers,) was checked, turned, outmarched, and outflanked, on every occasion; driven from position to position, in a country that affords so many of peculiar strength, without having it in their power to injure their victors by a protracted defence; and repeatedly defeated, not by main force or superiority of number, but by a combination of movements, at once so boldly conceived and so admirably executed, as left throughout the whole contest the palm of science, as well as of enduring energy and physical hardihood, with the British soldier. These victories, besides adding another laurel to the thick-woven chaplet of the English general, had the most decisive effect on the future events of the war, as well as upon the public mind in the south of France.

SURRENDER OF BORDEAUX

Bordeaux being thus left to follow the inclinations of the inhabitants, and encouraged by the approach of an English detachment of 15,000 men, under Field-Marshal Beresford, poured out its multitudes to receive the Duke d'Angoulême. The numbers which thronged out of the city were computed to be at least 10,000 persons. The mayor, Count Lynch, in a short speech, told the English general, that if he approached as a conqueror, he needed not his interposition to possess himself of the keys of Bourdeaux; but if he came as an ally of their lawful sovereign, he was ready to tender them up, with every token of love, honour and affection. Field-Marshal Beresford reiterated his promises of protection, and expressed his confidence in the loyalty of the city of Bourdeaux. The mayor then uttered the long-forgotten signal cry of *Vive le Roi!* and it was echoed a thousand times from the thousands around. Count Lynch then, pulling the three-coloured cockade from his hat, assumed the white cockade of the Bourbons. All imitated his example, and at a concerted signal, the old ensign of loyalty streamed from the steeples and towers of the city, amid general acclamation.[352]

The enthusiasm with which the signals of loyalty were adopted, and the shouts of *Vive le Roi*, repeated on all hands, mingled with blessings upon the heads of the English and their leaders, formed a scene which those who witnessed it will not speedily forget. It was a renewal of early affections and attachments, which seemed long dead and forgotten—a general burst of feelings the more generous and affecting, because they were not only as disinterested as spontaneous, but might eventually be deeply fraught with danger to those who expressed them. Yet they were uttered with a generous enthusiasm, that placed the actors far above the apprehension of personal consequences.

The same lively acclamations hailed the entrance of the Duke d'Angoulême into this fine city. At the prince's entry, the inhabitants crowded round him with enthusiasm. The archbishop and clergy of the diocese recognised him; *Te Deum* was sung in full pomp, while the united banners of France, Britain, Spain, and Portugal, were hoisted on the walls of the town. Lord Dalhousie was left commandant of the British; and if excellent sense, long experience, the most perfect equality of temper, and unshaken steadiness, be necessary qualities in so delicate a trust, the British army had not one more fit for the charge.

Brilliant as these tidings were, they excited in Britain the most cruel apprehensions for the fate which Bourdeaux might incur, if this declaration should unhappily prove to be premature. The treaty at Chatillon seemed to approach a termination, and vessels are said

---

[352] Journal de Bordeaux, No. 1, March 14.

to have been despatched to the Gironde, to favour the escape of such citizens as might be most obnoxious to the vengeance of Buonaparte. Many of those who wished most for British success, were tempted to regret that the victory of Orthez had taken place; so great were their apprehensions for those who had been encouraged by that success, to declare against the government of Napoleon ere his power of injuring them was at an end. That we may see how far those fears were warranted, we shall hastily review the progress of this remarkable negotiation, of which, however, the secret history is not even now entirely known.

The propositions for peace had begun with the communication of the Baron St. Aignan, which had been discussed at Frankfort. The terms then proposed to Napoleon were, that, abandoning all his wider conquests, France should retire within the course of the Rhine and the barrier of the Alps. Napoleon had accepted these conditions as a basis, under a stipulation, however, which afforded a pretext for breaking off the treaty at pleasure, namely, that France was to be admitted to liberty of commerce and navigation; an implied challenge of the maritime law, as exercised by the British. To this, the Earl of Aberdeen, the able and accomplished representative of Britain, replied, that France should enjoy such liberty of commerce and navigation as she had any right to expect.[353] A subject of debate, and a most important one, was thus left open; and perhaps neither of those powers were displeased to possess a means of disturbing the progress of the treaty, according to what should prove the events of the war.

Caulaincourt, Duke of Vicenza, the minister of foreign affairs, was the representative of Napoleon, at Chatillon, upon this most important occasion. His first instructions, dated 4th January, 1814, restricted him to the basis proposed at Frankfort which assigned Belgium to France, thus conceding to the latter what Napoleon now

---

[353] "M. de Metternich said, 'Here is Lord Aberdeen, the English ambassador: our intentions are common, we may, therefore, continue to explain ourselves before him.' When I came to the article about England, Lord Aberdeen observed, that the expressions *liberty of commerce* and *rights of navigation* were very vague. Metternich added, that these words might raise misunderstandings, and that it was better to substitute others. He took the pen, and wrote, that England would make the greatest sacrifices to obtain a *peace on these foundations*," (those previously described.)—*Report of Baron St. Aignan.*

called her natural boundaries, although it certainly did not appear, why, since victory had extended her frontiers by so many additional kingdoms, defeat should not now have the natural effect of retrenching them.[354] But after the inauspicious commencement of the campaign, by the battle of Brienne, in which Napoleon gained little, and that of La Rothière, in which he was defeated, he saw that as peace, like the Books of the Sibyls (to the sale of which the negotiation has been compared,) would rise in price, circumstances might render it necessary, also, that peace should be made by Caulaincourt without communication with Napoleon. Depending upon the events of war, it might be possible that a favourable day, nay, an hour being suffered to elapse, might put the treaty out of his reach. For these reasons, Caulaincourt was intrusted, over and above his instructions, with a definitive and unlimited carte-blanche, in which he was empowered to "bring the negotiation to a happy issue, to save the capital, and prevent the hazards of a battle, on which must rest the last hopes of the nation."[355]

NEGOTIATIONS AT CHATILLON

Caulaincourt reached Chatillon sur Seine, which had been declared neutral for the purpose of the conferences. At this memorable congress, Count Stadion represented Austria, Count Razumowski Russia, Baron Humboldt Prussia, and Great Britain had three commissioners present, namely; Lord Aberdeen, Lord Cathcart, and Sir Charles Stewart. Every politeness was shown on the part of the French, who even offered the English ministers the advantage of corresponding directly with London by the way of Calais; a courtesy which was declined with thanks.

The commissioners of the allies were not long in expressing what Napoleon's fears had anticipated. They declared, that they

---

[354] "You must hear and observe every thing. You must discover the views of the allies, and write to me every day. Italy is yet untouched; before the lapse of a week I shall have collected troops sufficient to fight many battles. If I am seconded by the nation, the enemy are hastening to their destruction. If fortune should betray me, my resolution is taken: I cling not to the throne. I will neither disgrace the nation nor myself by subscribing dishonourable conditions."—Napoleon, *Memoirs*, tom. ii., p. 352; *Manuscript de 1814*, p. 66.
[355] Bassano to Caulaincourt, Troyes, Feb. 5.

would no longer abide by the basis proposed at Frankfort. "To obtain peace, France must be restricted within her ancient limits," which excluded the important acquisition of Belgium. Baron Fain[356] gives us an interesting account of the mode in which Napoleon received this communication. He retired for a time into his own apartment, and sent for Berthier and Maret. They came—he gave them the fatal despatch—they read, and a deep silence ensued. The two faithful ministers flung themselves at their master's feet, and with tears in their eyes implored him to give way to the necessity of the time. "Never," he replied, "will I break the oath by which I swore at my coronation, to maintain the integrity of the territories of the *Republic*, and never will I leave France less in extent than I found her. It would not only be France that would retreat, but Austria and Prussia who would advance. France indeed needs peace, but such a peace is worse than the most inveterate war. What answer would I have to the Republicans, when they should demand from me the barrier of the Rhine? No—write to Caulaincourt that I reject the treaty, and will rather abide the brunt of battle." Shortly after he is said to have exclaimed, "I am yet nearer to Munich than they are to Paris."

His counsellors were not discouraged. In a cooler moment, the ministers who watched his pillow, obtained from him permission that the treaty should proceed. He directed that the articles proposed by the allies should be sent to Paris, and the advice of each privy counsellor taken individually upon the subject. With one exception, that of Count Lacuée de Cessac, all the privy counsellors agreed that the terms proposed at Chatillon ought to be subscribed to. Thus sanctioned, Caulaincourt, on the 9th of February, wrote to the commissioners of the allies, that if an immediate armistice were entered into, he was ready to consent that France should retreat within her ancient limits, according to the basis proposed. He offered, also, that France should cede instantly, on condition of the armistice being granted, some of the strong places, which their acceptance of the terms offered obliged her to

---

[356] Manuscript de 1814—"A narrative which, from the official situation (that of Secretary of the Cabinet of Napoleon) held by its author, is calculated," says Lord Burghersh, "to excite a greater degree of interest, and hereafter to be more relied upon, as an authority, than any other publication which has appeared on the side of the French army."

yield up. But this offer of ceding the fortresses was clogged with secret conditions, to be afterwards explained. The allies declared their readiness to adhere to these preliminaries, and for a day the war might be considered as ended.

But, in the meantime, the successes which Napoleon obtained over Blucher at Montmirail and Champ-Aubert, had elevated him in his own opinion above the necessity in which he stood after the battle of Brienne. From the field of battle at Nangis, he wrote to Caulaincourt to assume an attitude less humiliating among the members of the Congress;[357] and after the defeat of the Prince of Wirtemberg, at the bridge of Montereau, and the retreat of the grand army from Craonne, he seems to have entirely resolved to break off the treaty.

CONGRESS AT CHATILLON

When Schwartzenberg, as we have seen, demanded the meaning of Napoleon's offensive movement, contrary to what had been agreed upon by the congress at Chatillon, he answered, by the letter to the Emperor of Austria, in which he rejected the conditions to which Caulaincourt had agreed, and reprobated them as terms which, if known in Paris, would excite general indignation. "It would realise," he said, "the dream of Burke, who desired to make France disappear from the map of Europe. It was placing England[358] in possession of Antwerp and the Low Countries, neither of which he would ever surrender."[359]

In the same spirit, and at the same time, Napoleon wrote to Caulaincourt, that "when he had given him his carte-blanche, it was for the purpose of saving Paris, and Paris was now saved; it was for

---

[357] "Nangis, Feb. 17.—Providence has blessed our arms. I have made 30 or 40,000 prisoners. I have taken 200 pieces of cannon, a great number of generals, and destroyed several armies, almost without striking a blow: Your attitude ought still to be the same; but my intention is that you should sign nothing without my orders, because I alone know my own situation."

[358] This alluded to the match, then supposed to be on the tapis, betwixt the late Princess Charlotte of Wales and the Prince of Orange.—S.

[359] Lord Burghersh, Observations, p. 156.

avoiding the risk of a battle—that risk was over, and the battle won; he therefore revoked the extraordinary powers with which his ambassador was invested."[360]

We will not stop to inquire into the diplomatic question, whether Caulaincourt had not effectually exercised, on 9th February, those powers which were not recalled until the 17th, six days after; and, consequently, whether his master was not bound, by the act of his envoy, beyond the power of retracting. Enough remains to surprise us in Napoleon's headstrong resolution to continue the war, when, in fact, it was already ended upon terms which had been recommended by all his counsellors, one excepted. His obligation to the Republic of France, to maintain the integrity of its territories, could scarcely remain binding on one, by whom that very Republic had been destroyed; and at any rate, no such engagement can bind a sovereign from acting in extremity as the safety of the community requires. Far less could the terms be said to dishonour France, or strike her out of the map of Europe, unless her honour and existence, which had flourished for twelve centuries, depended upon an acquisition which she had made within twenty years. But the real case was, that Buonaparte always connected the loss of honour with the surrender of whatever he conceived himself to have a chance of being able to retain. Every cession was to be wrung from him; he would part with nothing willingly; and, like a child with its toys, that of which there was any attempt to deprive him, became immediately the most valuable of his possessions. Antwerp, indeed, had a particular right to be considered as inestimable. The sums he had bestowed on its magnificent basins, and almost impregnable fortifications, were immense. He had always the idea that he might make Antwerp the principal station of a large navy. He clung to this vision of a fleet, even at Elba and Saint Helena, repeating often, that he might have saved his crown, if he would have resigned Antwerp at Chatillon; and no idea was more riveted in his mind, than that his refusal was founded on patriotic principles. Yet the chief value of Antwerp lay in the event of another war with Great Britain, for which Buonaparte was thus preparing, while the question was, how the present hostilities were to be closed; and surely the possibility of a navy which had no existence, should not have been placed in

---

[360] Napoleon, Mémoires, tom. ii., p. 389.

competition with the safety of a nation deeply emperilled by the war now waging in the very centre of his kingdom.[361] This he saw in a different light from that of calm reason. "If I am to receive flagellation," he said, "let it be at least under terms of compulsion."[362]

Lastly, the temporary success which he had attained in the field of battle, was of a character which, justly considered, ought not to have encouraged the French Emperor to continue war, but, on the contrary, might have furnished a precious opportunity for making peace, before the very sword's point was at his throat. The conditions which he might have made in this moment of temporary success, would have had the appearance of being gracefully ceded, rather than positively extorted by necessity. And it may be added, that the allies, startled by their losses, would have probably granted him better terms; and certainly, remembering his military talents, would have taken care to observe those which they might fix upon. The reverses, therefore, in the month of February, which obscured the arms of the combined monarchs, resembled the cloud, which, in Byron's tale, is described as passing over the moon to afford an impenitent renegade the last and limited term for repentance.[363] But the heart of Napoleon, like that of Alp, was too proud to profit by the interval of delay thus afforded to him.

The truth seems to be, that Buonaparte never seriously intended to make peace at Chatillon; and while his negotiator, Caulaincourt, was instructed to hold out to the allies a proposal to cede the frontier fortresses, he received from the Duke of Bassano the following private directions:—"The Emperor desires that you would avoid explaining yourself clearly upon every thing which may relate to delivering up the fortresses of Antwerp, Mayence, and Alexandria, if you should be obliged to consent to these cessions; his Majesty intending, even though he should have ratified the treaty, to be guided by the military situation of affairs:—wait till the last moment. The bad faith of the allies in respect to the

---

[361] See Journal, &c., par M. de Las Cases, tom. iv., pp. 47, 53, 60.
[362] Manuscript de 1814, p. 186.
[363] "There is a light cloud by the moon— 'Tis passing, and 'twill pass full soon; If, by the time its vapoury sail Hath ceased her shrouded orb to veil, Thy heart within thee is not changed, Then God and man are both avenged." Byron's *Siege Corinth*.—S.

capitulations of Dresden, Dantzic, and Gorcum, authorises us to endeavour not to be duped. Refer, therefore, these questions to a military arrangement, as was done at Presburg, Vienna, and Tilsit. His Majesty desires that you would not lose sight of the disposition which he will feel, *not to deliver up those three keys of France*, if military events, on which he is willing still to rely, should permit him not to do so, *even if he should have signed the cession of all these provinces*. In a word, his Majesty wishes to be able, after the treaty, to be guided by existing circumstances, to the last moment. He orders you to burn this letter as soon as you have read it."

TREATY OF CHAUMONT

The allies showed, on their side, that the obstinacy of Napoleon had increased, not diminished their determination to carry on the war. A new treaty, called that of Chaumont, was entered into upon the 1st of March, between Austria, Russia, Prussia, and England, by which the high contracting parties bound themselves each to keep up an army of 150,000 men, with an agreement on the part of Great Britain, to advance four millions to carry on the war, which was to be prosecuted without relaxation, until France should be reduced within her ancient limits; and what further indicated the feelings of both parties, the military commissioners, who had met at Lusigny, to settle the terms of an armistice, broke up, on pretence of being unable to agree upon a suitable line of demarcation.[364]

The principal negotiation continued to languish at Chatillon, but without much remaining hope being entertained, by those who were well informed on either side, of the result being favourable.

On the 7th March, Rumigny, a clerk of Buonaparte's cabinet, brought to the Emperor, on the evening of the bloody battle of Craonne, the ultimatum of the allies, insisting that the French envoy should either proceed to treat upon the basis they had offered, namely, that France should be reduced within her ancient limits, or that Caulaincourt should present a *contre-projet*. His plenipotentiary

---

[364] For a copy of the Treaty, see Parl. Debates, vol. xxvii., p. 623.

requested instructions; but it appears that Buonaparte, too able not to see the result of his pertinacity, yet too haughty to recede from it, had resolved, in sportsman's phrase, to die hard. The 10th day of March having passed over, without any answer arriving from Buonaparte to Caulaincourt, the term assigned to him for declaring his ultimatum was extended to five days; the plenipotentiary of France hoping, probably, that some decisive event in the field of battle would either induce his master to consent to the terms of the allies, or give him a right to obtain better.

It is said, that, during this interval, Prince Wenceslaus of Lichtenstein was again despatched by the Emperor Francis, to the headquarters of Napoleon, as a special envoy, for the purpose of conjuring him to accommodate his ultimatum to the articles settled as the basis of the conferences, and informing him that otherwise the Emperor Francis would lay aside those family considerations, which had hitherto prevented him from acceding to the dispositions of the other allied powers in favour of the dynasty of Bourbon. It is added, that Buonaparte seemed at first silenced and astounded by this intimation; but, immediately recovering himself, treated it as a vain threat held out to intimidate him, and said it would be most for the interest of Austria to join in procuring him a peace on his own terms, since otherwise, he might again be forced to cross the Rhine. The Austrian prince retired without reply; and from that moment, it has been supposed, the Emperor resigned his son-in-law, without further effort in his favour, to the consequences of his own ill-timed obstinacy.[365]

Caulaincourt, in the meanwhile, played the part of an able minister and active negotiator. He kept the negotiation as long afloat as possible, and in the meantime, used every argument to induce his master to close with the terms of the allies. At length, however, he was compelled to produce a *contre-projet*, which he hoped might have at least the effect of prolonging the negotiation.

---

[365] In a MS. memorandum, Lord Burghersh denies the whole of this story. He distinctly states that Prince Wenceslaus of Lichtenstein was never sent to Buonaparte after the 23d of February; and that the account in the text misrepresents the feelings and intentions of the Emperor of Russia at the period to which it refers. Compare his "Operations" under the dates.—Ed. (1842.)

CONGRESS DISSOLVED

But the plan he offered was not only too vague to serve the purpose of amusing the allies, but too inconsistent with the articles adopted by all parties as the basis of the conference, to be a moment listened to. He demanded the whole line of the Rhine—he demanded great part of that of the Waal, and the fortress of Nimeguen, which must have rendered the independence of Holland purely nominal—he required Italy, and even Venice, for Eugene Beauharnois, although this important article was not only in absolute contradiction to the basis of the treaty, but peculiarly offensive and injurious to Austria, whom it was so much Buonaparte's interest to conciliate. The possession of Italy embraced, of course, that of Switzerland, either directly or by influence; so that in future wars Austria would lie open to the incursions of France along her whole frontier, and, while concluding a victorious treaty upon French ground, would have been placed in a worse situation than by that which Buonaparte himself dictated to her at Campo Formio! There were stipulations, besides, for indemnities to Jerome, the phantom king of Westphalia; to Louis, Grand Duke of Berg; and to Eugene, in compensation of his alleged rights on the grand duchy of Frankfort. Nay, as if determined to show that nothing which he had ever done, even though undone by himself, should now be considered as null, without exacting compensation at the expense of the rest of Europe, Buonaparte demanded an indemnity for his brother Joseph, not indeed for the crown of Spain, but for that very throne of Naples, from which he had himself displaced him, in order to make room for Murat! The assembled congress received this imperious communication with equal surprise and displeasure.[366] They instantly declared the congress dissolved; and thus terminated the fears of many, who considered Europe as in greater danger from any treaty that could be made with Buonaparte, than from the progress of his arms against the allies.

It was the opinion of such men, and their number was very considerable, that no peace concluded with Napoleon could be

---

[366] Napoleon, Mémoires, tom. ii., pp. 432-468; Manuscript de 1814, p. 296.

permanent, and that any immediate terms of composition could be only an armed truce, to last until the Emperor of France should feel himself able to spend the remainder of his life in winning back again the conquests which he had spent the earlier part of it in gaining. They insisted that this was visible, from his breaking off the treaty on the subject of Antwerp; the chief utility of which, to his empire, must have been in the future wars which he meditated with Britain. It was seeking war through peace, not peace by war. Such reasoners were no doubt in many cases prejudiced against Napoleon's person, and inclined to consider his government as a usurpation. But others allowed that Napoleon, abstractedly considered, was not a worse man than other conquerors, but that a run of success so long uninterrupted, had made war and conquest so familiar to his soul, that to use an expression of the poet, the "earthquake voice of victory" was to him the necessary and indispensable breath of life.[367] This passion for battle, they said, might not make Napoleon hateful as a man, for much, far too much, allowance is made in modern morality for the thirst of military fame; but it must be allowed that it rendered him a most unfit monarch for those with whose blood that thirst was to be stanched. Such reflections are, however, foreign to our present purpose.

It was not the least remarkable contingence in these momentous transactions, that as Caulaincourt left Chatillon, he met the secretary of Buonaparte posting towards him with the full and explicit powers of treating which he had so long vainly solicited.[368] Had Napoleon adopted this final decision of submitting himself to circumstances but one day earlier, the treaty of Chatillon might have proceeded, and he would have continued in possession of the throne of France. But it was too late.

---

[367] "The triumph, and the vanity, The rapture of the strife— The earthquake voice of victory, To thee the breath of life."—Byron.
[368] Baron Fain, p. 213.

APPENDIX

No. I

REFLECTIONS ON THE CONDUCT OF NAPOLEON TOWARDS THE PRINCE-ROYAL OF SWEDEN

(Translated from the original French.)

It was Napoleon himself, who, by his insupportable pretensions, forced Sweden to take a part in opposition to him. From the period of the election of the Prince of Ponte Corvo, the only discussions the Prince had with the Emperor consisted in refusals, on the Prince's part, to enter into engagements hostile to the interests of the nation who had chosen him to be her ruler.

When the first overtures respecting his election in Sweden were made to him by a Swedish nobleman, and by General Count de Wrede, he went immediately to St. Cloud, to inform the Emperor, who said to him:—"I cannot be of any use to you—let things take their course," &c. The Prince went to Plombières. At his return, he paid his respects to the Emperor, who, addressing him in presence of a good many persons, asked if he had lately had any news from Sweden? "Yes, Sire."—"What do they say?" replied the Emperor.—"That your Majesty's *chargé d'affaires* at Stockholm opposes my election, and says publicly that your Majesty prefers the King of Denmark."—The Emperor answered with surprise, "It is not possible;" and changed the subject. It was, however, in consequence of secret instructions given to M. Désaguiers, that he had presented a note in favour of the King of Denmark; but Napoleon, in order not to commit himself in an affair of such delicacy, and in which a check would have been a proof of the decline of his political ascendency, disavowed the conduct of M. Désaguiers. When this agent was recalled a short time afterwards, the Duc de Cadore frankly confessed to M. de Lagerbjelke, the Swedish minister at Paris, *"that they had sacrificed an innocent person."*

The Emperor had expressed himself in the most friendly manner to King Charles XIII., as well as to the Prince of Ponte Corvo, consenting that the Prince should accept the succession to the throne of Sweden. The act of election had been published in the *Moniteur*, and ten days had elapsed without the Emperor's having said any thing about the Prince-Royal's departure. Having finished the preparations for his journey, and seeing that the Emperor still remained silent on the subject, the Prince determined to apply to him for letters-patent, emancipating him (the Prince) from his allegiance. To this formal application, the Emperor replied, that the expediting of these letters had been retarded only by the proposal made by a member of the privy-council, of a preliminary condition.—"What is it?" said the Prince.—"It is that you are to come under an engagement never to bear arms against me." The Prince-Royal, greatly surprised, answered, that his election by the Diet of Sweden, and the consent to it already given by the Emperor, both to himself and to King Charles XIII., had already made him a Swedish subject; and that, in that quality he could not subscribe this engagement.—Here the Emperor frowned, and appeared embarrassed. "Your Majesty tells me," added he, "that this is the proposal of a member of the council. I am very sure it never could have come from yourself, Sire; it must have come from the Arch-Chancellor, or the Grand Judge, who were not aware to what a height this proposal would raise me."—"What do you mean?"—"If you prevent me from accepting a crown, unless I come under an engagement never to fight against you, Sire—is not this, in fact, placing me in your line as a general?" The Emperor, after a moment's reflection, said to him, in a suppressed voice, and with a gesture which betrayed his agitation:—"Well, go;—our destinies are about to be accomplished."—"I beg your pardon, Sire, I did not hear you rightly."—"Go;—our destinies are about to be accomplished," repeated the Emperor, in a more distinct, but equally agitated voice.

When the report first became current that there was an intention in Sweden to elect the Prince of Ponte Corvo Prince-Royal, Mareschal Davoust, thinking to please his master, said, in the Emperor's chamber:—"The Prince of Ponte Corvo suspects nothing." This piece of irony made Napoleon smile. He answered in a low voice,—"He is not yet elected." The Prince, who till then had been very undecided, intimated, that if the King and the States of Sweden fixed their choice on him, he should accept.

During this interval, Napoleon, constantly wishing to prevent him from becoming heir to the throne of Sweden, said to him one day: "You will probably be called to Sweden. I had formed the design of giving you Arragon and Catalonia; for Spain is too great a country for my brother's strength of capacity." The Prince made no reply. For a considerable time back, not wishing to be an object of inquietude to government, he had been considering what means he should use to gain Napoleon's confidence. The greatness of France, the victories gained by her armies, and the eclat which they reflected upon the commander, imposed on the Prince the duty of not endeavouring to emulate the power of the Emperor. In his conversations with Napoleon, he endeavoured to do away the impressions which the Emperor entertained against him. For this purpose he took general views, spoke of the interests of great states—of the fortunes of men who had astonished the world by their successes, of the difficulties and obstacles which these men had had to surmount, and finally, of the public tranquillity and happiness which had been the result of these circumstances, from the moment that secondary interests had been satisfied. The Emperor listened attentively, and seemed almost always to applaud the principles of stability and preservation which the Prince enlarged upon. At times, when the latter reminded the Emperor of the immensity of the means of recompense which he had at his disposal, Napoleon, struck by what he said, held out his hand to him affectionately, when they separated, and seemed, by his manner, to say to him—"Reckon always upon my friendship and support." The Prince used to return from these conversations, thinking himself no longer an object of suspicion to the Emperor. He expressed this belief to the members of Napoleon's family, in order that they, in their turn, might assure the Emperor, that as the Prince went entirely into his system, both from duty and from interest, any mistrust of him should be laid aside.

There were individuals of Napoleon's family, on those occasions, who smiled at the Prince's simplicity, and told him what the Emperor had said the evening before, immediately after the conversation the Prince and he had had together; and all that the Emperor said bore marks of the greatest insincerity, and of an ill-will constantly founded on his ideas of the extravagant ambition of the Prince. This ill-will seemed to be mitigated, when the time came for the Prince's departure for Sweden. One of his friends was in high favour with Napoleon. On the very day the Prince departed, Napoleon, seeing his friend come in, went up to him, and said:—"Well! does not the Prince regret France?"—"Yes, undoubtedly."—"And I, for my part, should have been very glad if he had not accepted the invitation; but there is no help for it——" And then checking himself—"Besides, he does not love me." On its being answered, that Napoleon was mistaken, and that the Prince had chosen his party, and had been frankly and cordially attached to him for a long time past, the Emperor replied—"We have not understood each other: now it is too late: he has his own interests, his own policy, and I have mine." Napoleon had acquiesced in the reasons given him by the Prince, for his refusal to engage not to take arms against him. He saw very well that he ought to have expected such a refusal, and that he ought not to have exposed himself to it. He had even endeavoured to efface any painful impression which his proposal had made on the Prince, by making him the most friendly promises of an indemnity of two millions for the cession of his principality of Ponte Corvo, and his possessions in Poland, and leaving him all the others in property. [The Prince never received more than one million of the two which had been promised him.] He had, besides, permitted him to take with him all his aides-de-camp.

The Prince knew not what was at the bottom of the Emperor's thoughts, but when he left him he was full of confidence in him; and Napoleon had no just motive for imputing to him any designs hostile to his interest, and still less to the interest of France. This illusion, on the part of the Prince, was of short duration. The reception he met with in all the places he passed through, and particularly when he arrived in Sweden—the speeches addressed to him, and the answers he made—all contributed to displease the Emperor. It seemed to him as if the Prince attracted some share of that general attention which should have been fixed on him alone. The patriotic sentiments expressed by the speakers of the four orders, were no more to his taste than those of the Prince in his answers. He and the Swedes were equally the objects of the Emperor's sarcasms, and even of his insults; he treated them as Jacobins, as anarchists; and it was chiefly against the Prince that these attacks were levelled. To show the Prince his displeasure, he annulled all the promises he had made him; and took from him all the lands with which he had endowed him, and which he re-united to his own domains. He recalled all the Prince-Royal's French aides-de-camp. It was in vain that the Prince, in his correspondence, tried to appease him, by writing, among others, the following letter:—

"At the moment when I was going to address my thanks to your Majesty, for your goodness in extending for a year the leave granted to the French officers who have accompanied me to Sweden, I am informed that your Majesty has retracted that favour. This unexpected disappointment, and, indeed, every thing that reaches me from Paris, makes me sensible that your Majesty is not well disposed towards me. What have I done, Sire, to deserve this treatment? I suppose that calumny alone has been the cause of it. In the new situation in which Fortune has placed me, I should doubtless be more exposed to it than ever, were I not fortunate enough to find a defender in your Majesty's own heart. Whatever may be said to you, Sire, I beseech you to believe that I have nothing to reproach myself with, and that I am entirely devoted to your person, not merely through the strength of my old associations, but from a sentiment that is unalterable. If things are not conducted in Sweden entirely according to your Majesty's wish, this is solely owing to the Constitution. To infringe the Constitution is not in the power of the King, and still less in mine. There are still here many particular interests to be melted down in the great national crucible—four orders of the state to be tied up in one bundle—and it is only by means of very prudent and measured conduct that I can hope to sit one day on the throne of Sweden. As M. Gentil de St.

Alphonse, my aide-de-camp, returns to France in conformity to your Majesty's orders, I make him the bearer of this letter. Your Majesty may question him; he has seen every thing; let him tell your Majesty the truth. You will see in what a situation I am placed, and how many measures I have to keep. He will tell your Majesty whether or not I am anxious to please you, and if I am not here in a state of continual torment between the pain of displeasing you, and my new duties. Sire, your Majesty has grieved me by withdrawing from me the officers whom you had granted me for a year. Since you command it, I send them back to France. Perhaps your Majesty will be inclined to alter your decision: in which case, I beg that you yourself will fix the number that you may think proper to send me. I shall receive them from you with gratitude. If, on the contrary, your Majesty retains them in France, I recommend them to your goodness. They have always served with distinction, and have had no share in the rewards which were distributed after the last campaign."

Napoleon's ill-humour against the Prince changed to positive resentment. He repented that he had agreed to his going, and he made no secret of it; for he went the length of saying, before his courtiers—"That he had a mind to make him finish his course of the Swedish language at Vincennes." While the Prince refused to believe the information which he had received from the Tuileries, of such a threat as this, Napoleon was actually thinking of putting it in execution, and of repeating, upon him, the capture of the Duc d'Enghien. The Prince at last was convinced of the truth of what he had heard, by the discovery of a plot formed by Napoleon's agents, for seizing him in the neighbourhood of Haga, and carrying him on board a vessel which they had in readiness. The attempt failed through a mere accident. The conspirators, all foreigners but one, thought themselves discovered; they instantly embarked, and sailed in the night.[369]

---

[369] M. de Salazar, formerly aide-de-camp to the Duke of Ragusa, who had quitted the service, and retired into England, was one of those who gave information respecting a plan formed in France to carry off the Prince-Royal. He made a full communication on this subject to an illustrious personage in England, and to Baron de Rehausen, the Swedish minister at London, who immediately informed Count d'Engestrom of what had been revealed by M. de Salazar, as to the plots which Napoleon was laying against the personal

This conduct, odious as it was, made no change in the disposition of the Prince towards Napoleon. He looked upon it as the effect of intrigues formed by the personal enemies of both, and by enemies of France. He saw nothing in it, besides, but a degree of personal animosity, which might pass away, and which ought to have no influence on the political determinations of Sweden. But Napoleon, listening to nothing but his hatred, knowing that the Prince, being aware of his designs, would now be on his guard, and having no longer any hope of surprising him, desired to place the Prince in open hostility to him. He took the surest method to accomplish this object, by seizing Pomerania, because he thought that this insulting violation of public faith would force the Prince-Royal to revenge the affront put upon Sweden, but at bottom directed against the Prince personally. In order to leave no room for doubt on this subject, the Emperor had given orders that the invasion should take place on the 26th of January, the Prince-Royal's birth-day; but this refinement, so much in character, was thrown away; for the invasion could not be carried into effect till the morning of the 27th.[370]

The news of this invasion did not reach Stockholm till the 11th of February. The Prince immediately wrote the Emperor the following letter:—

"The accounts, which have just arrived, inform me that a division of the army, under the orders of the Prince of Eckmühl, has invaded the territory of Swedish Pomerania, in the night between the 26th and 27th of January; that this division has continued its march, entered the capital of the duchy, and taken possession of the island of Rugen. The King expects that your Majesty will explain the reasons which have led you to act in a manner so diametrically

---

safety of the Prince. In order to facilitate these communications, Baron de Rehausen was instructed to furnish M. de Salazar with money to enable him to go to Sweden. He arrived at Orebro during the diet of 1812, and was admitted to some private audiences, in which he repeated to the Prince the declarations which he had previously made to Baron de Rehausen and Count d'Engestrom.

[370] It was from a similar motive that the Prince-Royal opened the ports of Sweden to all nations on the 15th August, 1812, Napoleon's birth-day, and that the peace with England was signed at the same time.

opposite to the faith of existing treaties. My former connexion with your Majesty authorises me to beseech you to explain your motives without delay, in order that I may be enabled to give the King my opinion as to the future policy which ought to be adopted by Sweden. This gratuitous outrage committed against Sweden is deeply felt by the people, and doubly so, Sire, by me, who am intrusted with the honour of defending them. If I have contributed to the triumphs of France, if I have uniformly wished to see her respected and happy, it never could enter into my thoughts to sacrifice the interests, the honour, and the national independence of the country which has adopted me. Your Majesty, so good a judge of what is right in the case which has happened, has already penetrated my resolution. Though not jealous of the glory and power by which you are surrounded, Sire, I am extremely sensible to the disgrace of being looked upon as a vassal. Your Majesty rules the greater part of Europe; but your dominion does not extend to the country to whose government I have been called. My ambition is limited to her defence; which I look upon as the lot assigned me by Providence. The effect produced on the people by the invasion which I now complain of, may have incalculable consequences; and though I am not a Coriolanus, nor command Volscians, I have a good enough opinion of the Swedes to assure you, Sire, that they are capable of daring and undertaking every thing, to revenge affronts which they have not provoked, and to preserve rights to which they are probably as much attached as to their existence."

When the Emperor received this letter, it was observed that he foamed with rage, and cried, "Submit to your degradation, or die with arms in your hands!" This, indeed, was the only alternative which he wished to leave the Prince; knowing very well what part would be taken by a man whom he himself had called, "A French head, with the heart of a Roman." There was no receding. The Prince declared to the King of England and the Emperor of Russia, that he was at war with Napoleon; and wrote the Emperor Alexander the following letter, dated from Stockholm, the 7th of March, 1812:—

"The occupation of Swedish Pomerania by the French troops, induces the King to despatch Count de Lowenhjelm, his aide-de-camp, to your Imperial Majesty. This officer, who enjoys the entire confidence of his sovereign, has it in charge to acquaint your Majesty with the motives which have served as a pretext for an invasion so diametrically in opposition to the subsisting treaties. The successive annexation of the coasts of the Mediterranean, of Holland, and of the Baltic, and the subjugation of the interior of Germany, must have pointed out, even to the least clear-sighted princes, that the laws of nations being thrown aside, were giving way to a system, which, destroying every kind of equilibrium, would unite a number of nations under the government of a single chief;—the tributary monarchs, terrified at this constantly increasing dominion, are waiting in consternation for the development of this vast plan. In the midst of this universal depression, men's eyes are turned towards your Majesty; they are already raised to you, Sire, with confidence and hope; but suffer me to observe to your Majesty, that in all the successes of life, there is nothing like the magical effect of the first instant;—so long as its influence lasts, every thing depends on him who chooses to act. Minds struck with astonishment are incapable of reflection; and every thing yields to the impulse of the charm which they fear, or by which they are attracted. Be pleased, Sire, to receive with favour the expression of my gratitude for the sentiments which your Majesty has testified towards me. If I have still any wish to form, it is for the continuation of a happiness of which I shall always be worthy, in consequence of the value which I attach to it."

It was not, then, the Emperor of Russia who prevailed upon Sweden to take up arms against Napoleon. It was himself—himself alone—who irresistibly compelled the Prince to throw himself among his enemies. In doing so, the Prince merely did what Napoleon desired; and the latter wished it, because Sweden having given him no motive for directly attacking her, he saw no other way of regaining the mastery of the Prince's fortunes, but by placing him among the number of his enemies, whom he looked upon as already conquered, without suspecting that he was going to force them at last to conquer himself. Meanwhile, still wishing to deceive the Prince, he made proposals to him. The Prince answered them by the following letter, the bearer of which was M. Signeul:—

"Notes have just reached me; and I cannot refrain from expressing myself on the subject of them to your Imperial Majesty, with all the frankness which belongs to my character. When the wishes of the Swedish people called me to succeed to the throne, I hoped, in leaving France, that I should always be able to reconcile my personal affections with the interests of my new country. My heart cherished the hope that it might identify itself with the sentiments of this people, at the same time preserving the remembrance of its first attachments, and never losing sight of the glory of France, nor its sincere attachment to your Majesty—an attachment founded on a brotherhood in arms, which had been distinguished by so many great actions. It was with this hope that I arrived in Sweden. I found a nation generally attached to France; but still more to its own liberty and laws: jealous of your friendship, Sire, but not desirous of ever obtaining it at the expense of its honour and its independence. Your Majesty's minister chose to disregard this national feeling, and ruined every thing by his arrogance: his communications bore no marks of that respect which crowned heads owe each other. While fulfilling, according to the dictates of his own passions, the intentions of your Majesty, Baron Agguier spoke like a Roman proconsul, without recollecting that he was not addressing himself to slaves. This minister, then, was the first cause of the distrust which Sweden began to show as to your Majesty's intentions with regard to her; subsequent events [the invasion of Sweden] were calculated to give it new weight. I had already had the honour, Sire, by my letters of the 19th November and 8th December 1810, to make your Majesty acquainted with the situation of Sweden, and the desire which she felt to find in your Majesty a protector. She could attribute your Majesty's silence to nothing but unmerited indifference; and it became incumbent on her to take precautions against the storm that was ready to burst on the Continent. Sire, mankind has already suffered but too much. For twenty years the earth has been deluged with human blood; and to put a period to these sufferings is the only thing wanting to complete your Majesty's glory. If your Majesty desires that the King should intimate to his Majesty the Emperor Alexander the possibility of an accommodation, I augur enough, from the magnanimity of that monarch, to venture to assure you, that he will give a willing ear to overtures equitable at the same time for your empire and for the North. If an event, so unexpected, and so universally wished for, could take place, with what blessings would the nations of the Continent hail your Majesty! Then gratitude would be increased in proportion to the terror they now feel for the return of a scourge which has already been so heavy upon them, and the ravages of which have left such cruel marks. Sire, one of the happiest moments which I have experienced since leaving France was that in which I became assured that your Majesty had not altogether forgotten me. You have judged rightly as to my feelings. You have been aware how deeply they must have been wounded by the painful prospect of either seeing the interests of Sweden on the eve of being separated from those of France, or of being constrained to sacrifice the interests of a country by which I have been adopted with boundless confidence. Sire, though a Swede by honour, by duty, and by religion, I still identify myself, by my wishes, with that beautiful France in which I was born, and which I have served faithfully ever since my childhood. Every step I take in Sweden, the homage I receive, revives in my mind those bright recollections of glory which were the principal cause of my elevation; nor do I disguise from myself, that Sweden, in choosing me, wished to pay a tribute of esteem to the French people."

Napoleon blames all the world for his reverses. When he has no longer any one to blame, he accuses his destiny. But it is himself only whom he should blame; and the more so, because the very desertion on the part of his allies, which hastened his fall, could have had no other cause but the deep wounds he had inflicted by his despotic pride, and his acts of injustice. He was himself the original author of his misfortunes, by outraging those who had contributed to his elevation. It was his own hands that consummated his ruin; he was, in all the strictness of the term, a political suicide, and so much the more guilty, that he did not dispose of himself alone, but of France at the same time.

No. II

EXTRACT FROM MANUSCRIPT OBSERVATIONS ON NAPOLEON'S RUSSIAN CAMPAIGN, BY AN ENGLISH OFFICER OF RANK

Having examined into the probabilities of Ségur's allegation, that Buonaparte entertained thoughts of taking up his winter-quarters at Witepsk, the military commentator proceeds as follows:—

"The Russian army at Smolensk, seeing the manner in which the French army was dispersed in cantonments between the rivers Dwina and Dneister, moved, on the 7th of August, towards Rudnei, in order to beat up their quarters. They succeeded in surprising those of Sebastiani, and did him a good deal of mischief in an attack upon Jukowo. In the meantime, Barclay de Tolly was alarmed by a movement made by the Viceroy about Souraj, on the Dwina; and he countermanded the original plan of operations, with a view to extend his right flank; and for some days afterwards, the Russian army made various false movements, and was in a considerable degree of confusion. Whether Napoleon's plan was founded upon the march of the Russian army from Smolensk, as supposed by Ségur; or upon their position at Smolensk, in the first days of August, he carried it into execution, notwithstanding that march.

"Accordingly, he broke up his cantonments upon the Dwina on the 10th of August, and marched his army by different columns by corps across the front of the Russian army, from these cantonments to Rassassna, upon the Dnieper. The false movements made by the Russian army from the 7th to the 12th of August, prevented their obtaining early knowledge of this march, and they were not in a situation to be able to take advantage of it. On the other hand, Napoleon could have had no knowledge of the miscalculated movements made by the Russian army.

"Being arrived at Rassassna, where he was joined by Davoust, with three divisions of the first corps, he crossed the Dnieper on the 14th. The corps of Poniatowski and Junot were at the same time moving upon Smolensk direct from Mohilow.

"Napoleon moved forward upon Smolensk.

"The garrison of that place, a division of infantry under General Newerofskoi, had come out as far as Krasnoi, to observe the movements of the French troops on the left of the Dnieper, supposed to be advancing along the Dnieper from Orcha. Murat attacked this body of troops with all his cavalry; but they made good their retreat to Smolensk, although repeatedly charged in their retreat. These charges were of little avail, however; and this operation affords another instance of the security with which good infantry can stand the attack of cavalry. This division of about 6000 infantry had no artificial defence, excepting two rows of trees on each side of the road, of which they certainly availed themselves. But the use made even of this defence shows how small an obstacle will impede and check the operations of the cavalry.

"It would probably have been more advisable if Murat, knowing of the movement of Poniatowski and Junot directed from Mohilow upon Smolensk, had not pushed this body of troops too hard. They must have been induced to delay on their retreat, in order effectually to reconnoitre their enemy. The fort would undoubtedly in that case have fallen into the hands of Poniatowski.

"On the 17th of August, Napoleon assembled the whole of the operating army before Smolensk, on the left of the Dnieper. It consisted as follows:—

The cavalry, under	Murat,	40,000
Guards,		47,000
First Corps,	Davoust,	72,000
Third Corps,	Ney,	39,000
Fourth Corps,	the Viceroy,	45,000
Fifth Corps,	Poniatowski,	36,000

Eighth Corps,	Junot,	18,000
		297,000

"These corps had, about six weeks before, entered the country with the numbers above stated; they had had no military affair to occasion loss; yet Ségur says, they were now reckoned at 185,000. The returns of the 3d August are stated to have given the last numbers only.

"The town had been attacked on the 16th, first, by a battalion—secondly, by a division of the third corps—which troops were repulsed. In the mean time, Bagration moved upon Katani, upon the Dnieper, having heard of Napoleon's movement from the Dwina; and Barclay de Tolly having authorised the resumption of the plan of operations in pursuance of which the Russian army had broken up from Smolensk on the 17th. He moved thence on the 16th, along the right of the Dnieper, back upon Smolensk, and immediately reinforced the garrison. He was followed that night by Barclay de Tolly, who relieved the troops under the command of Bagration, which were in the town: and the whole Russian army was collected at Smolensk, on the right of the Dnieper.

"Bagration moved during the same night with his army on the road to Moscow. Barclay remained in support of the troops in Smolensk.

"Napoleon, after waiting till two o'clock, in expectation that Barclay would cross the Dnieper, and move out of Smolensk, to fight a general battle, attacked the town on the 17th, with his whole army, and was repulsed with loss; and in the evening the Russian troops recovered possession of all the outposts. Barclay, however, withdrew the garrison in the night of the 17th, and destroyed the bridges of communication between the French and the town. The enemy crossed the Dnieper by fords, and obtained for a moment possession of the faubourg called Petersburg, on the right of that river, but were driven back. The Russian army, after remaining all day on the right of the river opposite Smolensk, retired on the night of the 18th; and the French that night repaired the bridges on the Dnieper.

"Before I proceed farther with the narrative, it is necessary to consider a little this movement of Napoleon, which is greatly admired by all the writers on the subject.

"When this movement was undertaken, the communication of the army was necessarily removed altogether from the Dwina. Instead of proceeding from Wilna upon Witepsk, it proceeded from Wilna upon Minsk, where a great magazine was formed, and thence across the Beresina, upon Orcha on the Dnieper, and thence upon Smolensk. The consequences of this alteration will appear presently, when we come to consider of the retreat.

"It is obvious, that the position of the great magazine at Minsk threw the communications of the army necessarily upon the Beresina, and eventually within the influence of the operations of the Russian armies from the southward. Napoleon's objects by the movement might have been three: First, to force the Russians to a general battle; secondly, to obtain possession of Smolensk, without the loss or the delay of a siege; thirdly, to endeavour again to obtain a position in rear of the Russian army, upon their communications with Moscow, and with the southern provinces of the Russian empire. This movement is much admired, and extolled by the Russian as well as the French writers upon this war; yet if it is tried by the only tests of any military movement—its objects compared with its risks and difficulties, and its success compared with the same risks and difficulties, and with the probable hazards and the probably successful result of other movements to attain the same objects—it will be found to have failed completely.

"The risk has been stated to consist, first, in the march of the different corps from their cantonments, on the Dwina, to Rassassna, on the Dnieper, across the front of the Russian army, without the protection of a body of troops formed for that purpose; and, next, in the hazard incurred in removing the communication of the army from Witepsk to Minsk. This will be discussed presently.

"In respect of the first object—that of bringing the Russian army to a general battle—it must be obvious to every body, that the fort of Smolensk and the Dnieper river were between Napoleon and the Russian army when his movement was completed. Although, therefore, the armies were not only in sight, but within musket-shot of each other, it was impossible for Napoleon to bring the enemy to an action on that ground without his consent; and as the ground would not have been advantageous to the Russian army, and an unsuccessful, or even a doubtful result, could not have saved Smolensk, and there was no object sufficiently important to induce the Russian general to incur the risk of an unsuccessful result of a general action, it was not very probable he would move into the trap which Ségur describes as laid for him.

"Neither was it likely that Napoleon would take Smolensk by any assault which this movement might enable him to make upon that place. He had no heavy artillery, and he tried in vain to take the place by storm, first, by a battalion, then, by a division, and lastly, by the whole army. He obtained possession of Smolensk at last, only because the Russian general had made no previous arrangements for occupying the place; and because Barclay knew that, if he left a garrison there unprovided, it must fall into Napoleon's hands a few days sooner or later. The Russian general then thought proper to evacuate the place; and notwithstanding the position of Napoleon on the left of the Dnieper, and his attempts to take the place by storm, the Russian general would have kept the possession, if he could have either maintained the position of his own army in the neighbourhood, or could have supplied the place adequately before he retired from it.

"The possession of the place depended, then, on the position of the Russian army; and what follows will show, that other measures and movements than those adopted were better calculated to dislodge the Russian army from Smolensk.

"There can be no doubt that, upon Napoleon's arrival at Smolensk, he had gained six marches upon his enemy. If Napoleon, when he crossed the Dnieper at Rassassna, had masked Smolensk, and marched direct upon any point of the Dnieper above that place, he could have posted himself with his whole army upon the communications of his enemy with Moscow; and his enemy could scarcely have attempted to pass across his front, to seek the road by

Kalouga. Barclay must have gone to the northward, evacuating or leaving Smolensk to its fate, and Napoleon might have continued his march upon Moscow, keeping his position constantly between his enemy and his communications with that city, and with the southern provinces. The fate of Smolensk could not have been doubtful.

"Here, then, a different mode, even upon the same plan of manœuvring, would have produced two of the three objects which Napoleon is supposed to have had in view by these movements. But these were not the only movements in his power at that time. The Viceroy is stated to have been at Souraj and Velij. If, instead of moving by his right, Napoleon had moved by his left, and brought the first, fifth, and eighth corps from the Dneiper to form the reserve; and had marched from Souraj upon any point of the Upper Dnieper, he would equally have put himself in the rear of his enemy, and in a position to act upon his communications. He would have effected this object with greater certainty, if he had ventured to move the first, and the fifth and eighth corps through the country on the left of the Dnieper. And in this last movement there would have been no great risk—first, because Napoleon's manœuvres upon the Dwina would have attracted all the enemy's attention; secondly, because these corps would have all passed Smolensk, before the Russian generals could have known of their movement, in like manner as Napoleon passed the Dnieper and arrived at Smolensk without their knowledge. By either of these modes of proceeding, Napoleon would have cut off his enemy from their communications, would have obliged them to fight a battle to resign these communications, and in all probability Smolensk would have fallen into his hands without loss, with its buildings entire—an object of the last consequence in the event of the campaign.

"Either of these last modes of effecting the object would have been shorter by two marches than the movement of the whole army upon Rassassna."

END OF VOLUME FOURTH

www.ingramcontent.com/pod-product-compliance
Lightning Source LLC
Chambersburg PA
CBHW060311230426
43663CB00009B/1659